Internet Programming with VBScript and JavaScript

SERGIO GOLDENBERG
sergio@goldenberg.cl

Internet Programming with VBScript and JavaScript

Kathleen Kalata

Oakton Community College

**COURSE
TECHNOLOGY**

™

THOMSON LEARNING　Australia • Canada • Mexico • Singapore • Spain • United Kingdom • United States

Internet Programming with VBScript and JavaScript is published by Course Technology.

Managing Editor	Jennifer Normandin
Senior Product Manager	Jennifer Muroff
Acquisitions Editor	Christine Guivernau
Production Editor	Jennifer Goguen
Development Editor	Lynne Raughley
Associate Product Manager	Tricia Coia
Editorial Assistant	Janet Aras
Composition House	GEX Publishing Services
Text Designer	GEX Publishing Services
Cover Designer	Daniella Chadwick, Black Fish Design
Associate Marketing Manager	Meagan Walsh
Manufacturing Coordinator	Denise Widjeskog

Disclaimer

Course Technology reserves the right to revise this publication and make changes from time to time in its content without notice.

The Web addresses in this book are subject to change from time to time as necessary without notice.

For more information, contact Course Technology, 25 Thomson Place, Boston, MA 02210;
or find us on the World Wide Web at www.course.com.

For permission to use material from this text or product, contact us by

- Web: www.thomsonrights.com
- Phone: 1–800–730–2214
- Fax: 1–800–730–2215

ISBN   0-619-01523-3

Printed in Canada

1 2 3 4 5 WC 05 04 03 02 01

Contents

Certified Internet Webmaster (CIW) EXAMINATION OBJECTIVES
CERTIFICATION   Master CIW Enterprise Developer
EXAMINATION TITLE   Application Developer
EXAMINATION CODE   1D0-430

CIW is administered by Prosoft Training. For more information on this certification program, please visit
http://www.course.com/certification/ciw.

The CIW Program recommends that candidates review the following examination objectives to help prepare for the
certification examination.

Exam Objective ID	Examination Objective Name	Chapter(s)
Section	**CGI Using Perl**	
1.01	Explain Web-based form handling using the Common Gateway Interface (CGI) and HTTP.	
	For objective 1.01, please refer to the Web Warrior title, Database-Driven Web Sites, ISBN 0-619-01556-X	
	For objectives 1.02 through 1.06, please refer to materials at http://www.ciwcertified.com	
1.02	Create a simple Perl script to handle common environment variables.	
1.03	Use Perl statements to create a hit counter.	
1.04	Demonstrate Perl file-handling and data output capabilities using a flat-file database.	
1.05	Integrate databases with Perl using ODBC and SQL.	
1.06	Discuss CGI security issues pertaining to Perl scripts.	
Section	**Dynamic Server Pages**	
	For objectives 2.01 through 2.04, please refer to materials at http://www.ciwcertified.com	
2.01	Install and configure PHP on Web servers.	
2.02	Create basic PHP scripts that demonstrate essential language features.	
2.03	Perform basic database functions using PHP, including file handling, querying, and data modification.	
2.04	Prepare a PHP application for deployment with debugging and error-handling techniques.	
2.05	Install and configure ASP on Web servers.	Chapter 7
2.06	Create basic ASP scripts that demonstrate essential language features.	Chapter 2
2.07	Discuss the object-oriented nature of ASP.	Chapters 3 and 10
2.08	Perform basic database functions using ASP, including file handling, querying, and data modification.	Chapter 12
2.09	Prepare an ASP application for deployment.	Chapter 7
	For objectives 2.10 through 2.11, please refer to materials at http://www.ciwcertified.com	
2.10	Discuss database security issues.	
2.11	Discuss the role of project management in application development.	

TABLE OF

Contents

CHAPTER ELEVEN
The Scripting Library Objects   397

CHAPTER TWELVE
Integrating Databases with ASP Pages   453

Preface

Internet Programming with VBScript and JavaScript will familiarize you with ways to create dynamic Web applications using both client-side and server-side scripting technologies. A well-rounded Internet programmer needs to be able to integrate client-side and server-side scripting technologies to produce Web applications that not only interact with visitors, but also integrate other computer applications.

Web sites today need to use client-side technologies to validate form data, as well as to provide ways of interacting with visitors. In the past, you might have used JavaScript to create client-side scripts. Today, it is important that you understand how to use both JavaScript and VBScript to create client-side scripts. Many industries require their customers and employees to use a standard browser such as Internet Explorer. By using VBScript within Internet Explorer, you will have access to additional programming tools available on the client. Therefore, it is essential that Internet programmers be familiar with both VBScript and JavaScript.

This book will also describe how server-side scripting can be used to enhance your Web applications. Web applications must be able to interact with other computer application systems such as e-mail and databases. Server-side scripts are also known as Active Server Pages (ASP). In this book, you will learn how to use ASP to process form data from the client, and to send out e-mail from a Web page. You will also learn how ASP can be used to interact with other computer applications on the server. You will learn how to use ASP to read and write information to a file on the server, and you will learn how ASP can also be used to build Web applications that interact with a database.

THE INTENDED AUDIENCE

Internet Programming with VBScript and JavaScript is intended for the individual who wants to create dynamic Web applications. You should be familiar with the Windows operating system and know how to use Internet Explorer to view the Web pages. An introduction to the Internet and to HTML is provided. No prior knowledge of programming is required. Background chapters are provided on beginning programming concepts, including object-oriented programming and the Document Object Model. Background chapters will be provided on server-side scripting and the Active Server Page model. No prior knowledge of server programming is required. In the later chapters, the book describes how to create Web pages that interact with an Access database. Background information will be provided which includes relational database concepts, using the Access database environment, and creating SQL queries. No prior knowledge of database programming is required.

The Approach

To facilitate the learning process, this book presents content and theory integrated with sample exercises. Each chapter includes references to additional resources available on the Internet that are relevant to that chapter. Each chapter includes a summary and review questions that highlight and reinforce major concepts that were presented. The summary not only presents a review of the concepts, but also provides samples of the programming code that were presented in the chapter that may be used as a review or as a reference. The Hands-on Projects are guided activities that let you practice and reinforce the techniques presented in the chapter. They also enhance your learning experience by providing additional ways to apply your knowledge in new situations. At the end of each chapter, there are several Case Projects that allow you to use the skills that you have learned in the chapter to solve real-world problems.

The samples provided in each chapter were developed to provide you with the opportunity to practice the skills discussed within the chapter. They are not dependent upon successful completion of the previous chapter. Therefore, you can always move ahead to another chapter, while you are still reviewing content that was presented in a previous chapter.

Overview of This Book

The examples, tutorials, projects, and cases in this book will help you achieve the following objectives:

- Describe the architecture of the World Wide Web
- Create basic Web pages using HTML code
- Use client-side scripts and the Document Object model to create dynamic Web applications
- Validate form data using client-side scripts
- Locate Internet resources that include information on client scripting, server scripting, JavaScript, VBScript, database concepts, and other Internet topics
- Understand how server-side scripts allow Web applications to interact with other server-based applications
- Understand how to integrate your ASP application with ASP Components
- Use server-side scripting to process data, send e-mail from a Web page, read and write to files on the server

- Become familiar with relational database concepts and learn how to create queries using SQL

- Create dynamic Web applications that interact with a database using server-side scripts

In **Chapter 1,** you will learn about the architecture of the World Wide Web. You will learn how to create basic Web pages using HTML. **Chapter 2** describes the differences between client-side and server-side scripts. You will learn to add client-side and server-side scripts to a Web page. You will locate Internet resources about scripting technologies. In **Chapter 3,** you will learn about object-oriented programming and how to create custom objects. You will learn how to use the properties and methods of built-in objects within the Document Object Model to create dynamic Web pages. In **Chapter 4**, you will learn how to store and retrieve data from variables, constants, and arrays. You will learn the difference between local and global variables. **Chapter 5** explains how to use control structures to build complex scripts. You will create expressions using arithmetic, comparison, and logical operators. You will use decision control structures to alter the execution order of a script and looping control structures to repeat blocks of code. You will learn to create nested blocks of code. **Chapter 6** provides an overview of the built-in functions in JavaScript and VBScript. You will also learn how to create and call functions. You will learn to create and call procedures, and to create event procedures in VBScript. **Chapter 7** explains how the server processes ASP code and describes the ASP Object Model. You will learn to create ASP pages and use server-side include files. You will locate Internet resources about ASP. **Chapter 8** describes how to retrieve information from a form using the request object. You will learn how to retrieve the server variables using the request object. You will learn how to send information to the browser using the response object. In **Chapter 9,** you will learn how to maintain state between the client and the server using the Global Application File, application variables, session variables, and cookies. You will learn to read and write cookies using the response object. You will become familiar with the kind of information that should be included in a privacy policy. In **Chapter 10,** you will learn how to integrate your ASP page with ASP Components such as the Browser Capabilities Component, the AdRotator component, and the CDONTS component. In **Chapter 11,** you will learn how to use the Scripting Objects to integrate your Web application with the file system. You will learn how to manage files on the server and to store and retrieve data from a file on the server. You will learn to work with error handling and error messages. In **Chapter 12,** you will learn create a database with a table in Microsoft Access. This chapter describes the ActiveX Data Object Model (ADO) that is used to connect Web pages to a database. You will learn how to store the connection information using connection strings and Data Source Names (DSN). You will learn to display data using the recordset object. You will learn how to create basic queries using SQL and Microsoft Access. Finally, in **Chapter 13,** you will learn to build advanced queries using Access and SQL. You will use ASP, ADO and SQL to insert new records, modify existing records, or delete records from a database. You will learn how to execute advanced queries using the Connection and Command Objects.

FEATURES

- **Chapter Objectives:** Each chapter in this book begins with a list of the important concepts to be mastered within the chapter. This list provides you with a quick reference to the contents of the chapter as well as a useful study aid.

- **Step-By-Step Methodology:** As new concepts are presented in each chapter, tutorials are used to provide step-by-step instructions that allow you to actively apply the concepts you are learning.

- **Modular Approach:** Each chapter contains tutorials, Hands-on Projects, and Case Projects that are self-contained. No chapter depends upon what the user has completed in a previous chapter. This eliminates the need for data disks. All files that you will need will be created as you step through the activities within the chapter.

- **Figures and Tables:** Figures help you visualize Web architecture components and relationships, and other basic concepts. Tables list examples of code components and their variations in a visual and readable format.

- **Tips:** Chapters contain Tips designed to provide you with practical advice and proven strategies related to the concept being discussed. Tips also provide suggestions for resolving problems you might encounter while proceeding through the chapter tutorials.

- **Chapter Summaries:** Each chapter's text is followed by a summary of chapter concepts. These summaries provide a helpful way to recap and revisit the ideas covered in each chapter. They include a list of common sample code techniques that were presented during the chapter that can be used for review or reference while proceeding through the chapter tutorials.

- **Review Questions:** End-of-chapter assessment begins with a set of approximately 20 review questions that reinforce the main ideas introduced in each chapter. These questions ensure that you have mastered the concepts and understand the information you have learned.

Hands-on Projects: Along with conceptual explanations and step-by-step tutorials, each chapter provides Hands-on Projects related to each major topic aimed at providing you with practical experience. Some of the Hands-on Projects provide detailed instructions, while others provide less detailed instructions that require you to apply the materials presented in the current chapter with less guidance. As a result, the Hands-on Projects provide you with practice implementing client-side and server-side scripting in real-world situations.

Case Projects: Approximately four cases are presented at the end of each chapter. These cases are designed to help you apply what you have learned in each chapter to real-world situations. They give you the opportunity to independently synthesize and evaluate information, examine potential solutions, and make recommendations, much as you would in an actual business situation.

TEACHING TOOLS

The following supplemental materials are available when this book is used in a classroom setting. All of the teaching tools available with this book are provided to the instructor on a single CD-ROM.

Electronic Instructor's Manual. The Instructor's Manual that accompanies this textbook includes:

- Additional instructional material to assist in class preparation, including suggestions for lecture topics.
- Solutions to all end-of-chapter materials, including the Review Questions, and, when applicable, Hands-on Projects and Case Projects.

Course Test Manager 1.2. Accompanying this book is a powerful assessment tool known as the Course Test Manager. Designed by Course Technology, this cutting-edge Windows-based testing software helps instructors design and administer tests and pre-tests. In addition to being able to generate tests that can be printed and administered, this full-featured program also has an online testing component that allows students to take tests at the computer and have their exams graded automatically.

PowerPoint presentations. This book comes with Microsoft PowerPoint slides for each chapter. These are included as a teaching aid for classroom presentation, to make available to students on the network for chapter review, or to be printed for classroom distribution. Instructors can add their own slides for additional topics they introduce to the class.

ACKNOWLEDGMENTS

This book has been a team effort from the beginning. A big thanks goes to Lynne Raughley, Development Editor, who has helped me be a better author. A great big thanks goes to Jennifer Muroff, Senior Product Manager, for all her support and guidance. Thank you for taking the time to listen and for bringing me into this project. I would also like to thank Jennifer Normandin, Managing Editor; Christine Guivernau, Acquisitions Editor; Jennifer Goguen, Production Editor; John Freitas, Quality Assurance tester, and the entire team for helping this become a better book.

Thanks to the reviewers who provided invaluable comments and suggestions during the development of this book: David Brownfield, Mt. St. Clare College; Brad Hunt, South Plains College; Dr. Anne Nelson, High Point University; Dennis Robinson, Indian Hills Community College; Joyce Dick, Northeast Iowa Community College; Bret Dickey, Spokane Community College; Laurel Helm, Eastern Washington University and Paula Worthington, Northern Virginia Community College.

Thanks to my students who continually inspire me to continue learning. Thanks to Sandra Wittman, creator of Life Beyond Yahoo, who continues to support and encourage my work. Thanks to my colleagues Kitty Tabers and Soda Parker at Oakton Community College, who allow me be innovative in the classroom and continue to support my work in the World Wide Web. Thanks to Molly Kalata, for taking over the shopping. Thanks to Erin for reminding me to take a break. Thanks to Christy, for being understanding when I couldn't come out to play or watch the Mummy. Thanks to my mother Marijean Shea, who always provided me with inspiration and love. Thanks to Kelly Doherty, Jim Shea, Patrick Shea, and Megan Calto, Roberta and Roger Hughes, and Charlotte Shea for all your support over the years. A big hug goes to my wonderful husband John, for his patience and understanding when I was glued to the computer, out of town at conferences, or when I took the computer with me on vacations. This book could not have been finished without your ongoing support. Finally, I dedicate this book to my father, James Shea, for always being there and who always encouraged me to be my best.

READ THIS BEFORE YOU BEGIN

To the User

You can use your own computer to complete the tutorials, Hands-on Projects, and Case Projects in this book. To use your own computer, you will need the following:

- **Microsoft Windows 95, Windows 98, Windows NT Workstation, or Windows 2000 Professional.** Your computer must be configured so you can connect to the Internet. You must have TCP/IP software loaded on your computer.

- **Microsoft Access 2000** to create the database tables and queries.

- **Microsoft Internet Explorer 5.0** or above. You can download a copy of Internet Explorer for free at the Microsoft Download Center (*http://www.microsoft.com/downloads/search.asp?*).

- **A text editor such as Notepad.** These tutorials and projects can also be created using a variety of Web page editors such as Microsoft FrontPage or Macromedia Dreamweaver. This book does not explain how to use these Web page editors.

- **Data Directories.** You will need a place to store your Web pages. It is recommended that you create a folder on your floppy disk or hard drive for each chapter. (Chapter1, Chapter2, Chapter3, ... Chapter13). Each chapter refers to this directory as your data directory. In each chapter you will be creating many files as you proceed through the tutorials, Hands-On Projects, and Case Projects. It is recommended that you store these files within the data directory for that chapter (Chapter1, Chapter2, Chapter3, Chapter13).

- **An ASP Compatible Web Server such as Microsoft Personal Web Server 4.0 (PWS)** or **Internet Information Server (IIS)**.

Personal Web Server

PWS is the most commonly used local Web server and is available with many programs, including Visual InterDev, FrontPage, Visual Studio, and Windows 98. PWS allows Web programmers to preview their server-side scripts on their desktops without having to connect to the Internet. Internet Information Service 5.0 is not available separately for Windows 95 or Windows 98. PWS running on Windows NT Workstation is referred to as Peer Web Services. PWS is not available for Windows 2000 Professional. You will need to install IE 4.01 or a later version of IE before installing PWS.

You can download the Microsoft Personal Web Server version 4.0 for free from Microsoft at *http://www.microsoft.com/windows/ie/pws/default.htm*. You can also install PWS from the Windows NT Option Pack that comes with Windows NT 4.0. Follow the steps below to download, install, and configure Personal Web Server. Note that these steps will vary depending upon the operating system you are using, your computer network, and where the installation software is located.

To download and install Personal Web Server in Windows 95, 98, and Windows NT Workstation:

1. To download a copy of PWS from the Microsoft Web site, start your browser and go to the page at *http://www.microsoft.com/windows/ie/pws/default.htm*.
2. Click **Download Microsoft Personal Web Server 4.0 for Windows 95**, and then click **Option 1**.
3. Select your operating system from the list box and click **Next**. If you are running Windows 98, select **Windows NT Option Pack Download Wizard for Windows 95.**
4. Click the link **download.exe** to download the software. The File Download dialog box opens.
5. Click **Save this program to disk** and click the **OK** button to download the software and save the file to your hard drive. Although you can download the program and install it directly, you can also perform the installation at a later time.
6. Save the file as **download.exe** to your hard drive. The download.exe program contains the files required to download PWS and is approximately 521 KB in size.
7. After the file has finished downloading, open the folder that contains the download.exe file. Double-click on the file to begin downloading PWS.
8. The end user license agreement will open. Click **Yes** to accept the license agreement.
9. You have two download options to choose from, Install and Download Only. Select **Download Only** and click **Next**. Click **Next** again.
10. There are three types of installations: Typical, Minimum, and Full Installation. Select **Typical Installation** and click **Next**.
11. Specify where to download the files to on your hard drive and click **Next**.

12. Click **Next** to continue.

13. A security warning dialog box appears. Click **Yes** to continue.

14. A dialog box will appear to inform you when the files have been downloaded. (*Note*: The files are approximately 24 MB in size and may take a while to download depending upon the speed of your Internet connection.)

15. Click **OK** to continue.

16. Open the folder that contains the downloaded files.

17. Double-click **setup.exe** to begin installing the files. The Microsoft Windows Personal Web Server Setup dialog box appears.

18. Click **Next** to continue.

19. Read the license agreement, and then click **Accept**. The PWS Server Setup dialog box will open.

20. Select the directory in which you wish to install PWS. By default the directory is C:\InetPub\wwwroot. Choose **typical** installation in the Microsoft Personal Web Server Setup dialog box. (*Note*: Later you can add or remove any of these components using the Add/Remove program located in the Control Panel.)

21. Click **Next**, and then click **Finish**. (*Note*: If you have an error message related to Microsoft Transaction Server (MTS) you should read the support documentation at *http://support.microsoft.com/support/kb/articles/Q246/0/81.ASP*). You will need to restart your machine before your PWS can be started. The PWS icon will then appear on the taskbar.

22. Double click the **PWS icon** on the taskbar to open the Personal Web Manager. Using the Personal Web Manager, you can manage your Web site and virtual directories on your local computer. The Tip of the Day dialog box opens the first time you open Personal Web Manager.

23. Click **Close** to close the Tip of the Day dialog box. The Personal Web Manager is now visible. The Personal Web Manager displays the status of your personal server. If the Web server software was installed correctly, you will see the location of your home page at *http://yourcomputername*, where "yourcomputername" is the name of the computer located in the Identification Tab in the Network Settings window.

24. Click the **Properties** menu and then click **Exit** to close Personal Web Manager. Closing the window does not stop the local Web server. Only clicking Stop in Personal Web Manager will stop the Web service. Likewise, if the Web service has been stopped, you can click Start to start the Web service.

Once you have installed Personal Web Server and started the Web service, you can use the browser to view your Web pages on your local computer. If you are running PWS or IIS, the default directory for your local Web site is `c:\inetpub\wwwroot`. If you saved a file named test.htm to that directory, you can view the Web page by typing *http://yourcomputername/test.htm* in the URL text box in your Web browser.

In order for the Web server to process an ASP page, the page must be given read and script permissions. The system administrator can assign the read and script permissions to the Web site. PWS is set up to assign read and script permissions to all files by default.

 Some programs, such as Visual InterDev, will provide you with FrontPage Extensions. If you are installing Visual InterDev, you should use the extensions that come with the Visual InterDev software. You will then be able to upgrade to Data Access Components 2.0, which will allow you to connect your Web pages to your databases. Microsoft Office 2000 comes with a superset of the FrontPage extensions called Office 2000 extensions. You can still install PWS along with Office 2000.

Internet Information Server

Personal Web Server will not run on Windows NT Server 4.0, Windows 2000 Professional, or Windows 2000 Server. Documentation for Windows 2000 Professional is available at *http://windows.microsoft.com/windows2000/en/professional/help/*. As an alternative to PWS, you can run a Web service called Internet Information Server (IIS). Although Windows 2000 Professional does not install IIS by default, if you have previously installed PWS and then upgrade your system to Windows 2000 Professional, PWS will be upgraded to IIS. IIS on Windows 2000 Professional is limited to 10 connections, one Web server, and one FTP server. You cannot create additional virtual Web or FTP servers with IIS. The complete documentation for IIS 5.0 for Windows 2000 Professional is available at *http://windows.microsoft.com/windows2000/en/professional/iis/*. There are several ways to install IIS. You can install IIS 5.0 when you install Windows 2000, or you can add it later.

To install IIS on a Windows 2000 Professional system:

1. Click **Start**, point to **Settings**, and click **Control Panel.**
2. Click **Add/Remove Programs**.
3. Select **Add/Remove Windows Components**.
4. Select the **Internet Information Services (IIS)**.
5. Click **Next**.
6. Click **Finish**.

On Windows NT Server or Windows 2000 Server, the IIS can be used to host multiple Web sites on the same physical server. When you install Windows NT Server 4.0, you are given the option to install IIS version 2.0. Instead of installing version 2.0, you should install version 4.0, which is available for free from Microsoft. You can download IIS 4.0 from *http://www.microsoft.com/NTWorkstation/downloads/Recommended/ServicePacks/NT4OptPk/*. In IIS 4.0, the tool to manage the Web server is called Internet Server Manager (ISM). After IIS is installed, the Internet Services Manager (ISM) is added to the Windows Administrative

Tools menu. The ISM starts the Microsoft Management Console (MMC) with the Internet Information Services snap-in preloaded. After you install IIS, you can also view the help files at `c:\winnt\Help\iisHelp`. You can find more information on IIS 4.0 at *http://www.microsoft.com/ntserver/web/default.asp/*.

On Windows 2000 Server, you can run Internet Information Server 5.0 (IIS), which is included on the Windows 2000 Professional CD-ROM. IIS 5.0 installed on Windows 2000 Server by default. For Windows NT and Windows 2000, the IIS executable is located at `c:\winnt\system32\Inetsrv`. In IIS 5.0, the tool to manage the Web server is called Internet Information Server snap-in. You can verify that IIS is installed by opening the IIS snap-in. To open the IIS snap-in, click Start, point to Settings, and then click Control Panel. You can double-click the Administrative Tools folder and then double-click Computer Management. Under the Services and Applications mode, you can then expand Internet Information Services. The complete documentation for IIS 5.0 for Windows 2000 Server is available at *http://windows.microsoft.com/windows2000/en/server/iis/*.

Visit Our World Wide Web Site

Additional materials designed especially for you might be available for your course on the World Wide Web. Go to *http://www.course.com*. Periodically search this site for this book title for more details.

1

THE INTERNET AND THE WORLD WIDE WEB

In this chapter you will:

♦ Learn how the Internet evolved from ARPANET
♦ Identify the protocols used to transmit data across the Internet
♦ Identify the TCP/IP utilities that can be used to locate information about a Web site
♦ Use HTML tags to create a Web page
♦ Create a Web page using a text editor

In order to learn Internet programming, you must first understand how your computer interacts with the Internet. This chapter will describe how domain names, IP addresses, domain name servers, Web servers, and various Internet protocols are joined together to form the World Wide Web. You will also learn how to locate and select a Web hosting service provider, and how to create a basic Web page using HTML. Throughout the chapter you will be provided with many links to Internet resources about Internet architecture, HTML, and creating basic Web pages.

THE HISTORY OF THE INTERNET

Today, most people access the Internet using an application called a **Web browser**. The most common Web browsers are Internet Explorer and Netscape Navigator. The browser, which allows you to view Web pages on the Internet, is an example of a **client application**. A client application runs on your local computer, and allows your computer to communicate with other computers on the Internet. Many computers on the Internet are **servers**, which provide programs to clients. Examples of server-based programs include e-mail and Web page publishing. E-mail clients such as Outlook Express allow you to access your e-mail on the e-mail server. Web browsers allow you to access Web pages stored on a Web server. Programming that makes it possible for client applications to communicate with server applications in a network is referred to as **client–server programming**. Today, the Internet is a network of networks, and supports many types of client-server programs. However, the Internet did not always support client-server programming.

The original Internet (then called ARPANET) consisted of a relatively small number of computers that connected government agencies and a handful of participating universities. The Internet was primarily used for science, research, and education. In September 1969, ARPANET consisted of a single network between UCLA, UCSB, Utah, and the Stanford Research Institute, and was primarily a host-to-host network. Each computer was called a **host**. Figure 1-1 shows how the hosts were connected to each other. Each host contained its own set of programs. Individuals needed to log in to the host to access the programs stored on the host. There were no clients in this network scheme. By 1971 ARPANET stretched across the United States through fewer than two dozen universities. In 1976 the Internet was opened to commercial traffic. At this time, the Internet was mainly used for e-mail and Telnet. E-mail programs allow you to send electronic messages to other individuals via the Internet. Telnet programs allow you to remotely access a computer via the Internet, using the Telnet protocol. Telnet allowed students and researchers to remotely log in to the hosts on the network. Students at many of the major universities commonly used Telnet to access the network from local terminals. Later, FTP (File Transfer Protocol) became a commonly used application. An FTP server allows FTP clients to transfer files to and from the server. Files sent across the Internet are converted to usable formats by means of a file translation program. FTP is part of a suite of protocols known as **TCP/IP** (Transmission Control Protocol/Internet Protocol).

By the late 1980s the number of host computers on the Internet had grown to 100,000. TCP/IP became the de facto standard for Internet protocols. TCP/IP consists of a suite of protocols that allowed other programs, such as e-mail, Telnet, and FTP, to provide communication between computers via the Internet. These new Internet programs relied on TCP/IP to route and deliver information. By resolving the issue of how information would be delivered across the Internet, TCP/IP allowed programmers to create more applications. The Internet grew as more **Internet service providers** (**ISPs**), such as CompuServe, provided access to the Internet to greater numbers of people. ISPs provided client software, which provided access to the Internet for individuals who were not students or government

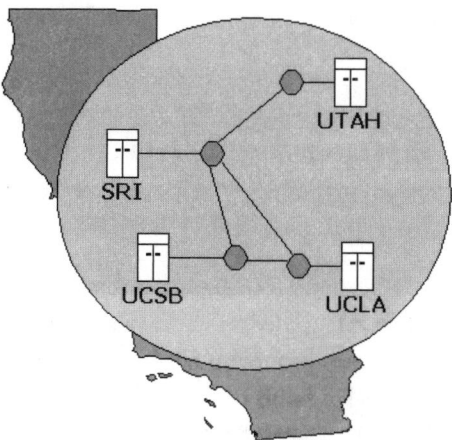

Figure 1-1   ARPANET in 1969

employees. Some ISPs, such as Prodigy and America Online, provided their customers with proprietary client software. The Internet was no longer a small network of computers; it had grown to become the largest network of networks.

But the Internet was just beginning to grow. On June 12, 1991, a new technology provided a means to easily locate and access cross-platform documents over the Internet. These cross-platform documents, called **hypertext documents**, were viewable no matter which computer platform you were using. This technology involved a new language standard, called **Hypertext Markup Language (HTML)**, and a new protocol, called **Hypertext Transfer Protocol (HTTP)**. HTML instructions, called **tags**, instructed a Web browser how to format and process a hypertext document. In 1993, the University of Illinois National Center for Supercomputing Applications (NCSA) released NCSA Mosaic (*http://www.ncsa.uiuc.edu/SDG/Software/WinMosaic/HomePage.html*), the first commercial Web browser.

The two most commonly used browsers are Microsoft Internet Explorer and Netscape Navigator. HTTP is the communications protocol used by the Internet to transfer hypertext documents. Hypertext documents that are shared on the Internet are called **Web pages**, and the location address of these documents is known as a **Uniform Resource Locator (URL)**. Web pages usually contain text, graphics, multimedia, and links to other Web pages. Currently, the WWW Consortium (*http://www.w3c.org*) defines and maintains HTML and HTTP standards, as well as many other Internet standards.

Today the Internet is described as a global information system that uses TCP/IP to provide communications services. Internet applications include more than e-mail and Web publishing services. The Internet is used to send faxes, view movies, and provide real-time messaging services. Some ISPs offer customers the capacity to send voice traffic over the Internet. Many companies are currently developing Internet-based applications to facilitate e-commerce transactions. Business-to-consumer applications include shopping carts, credit card processing, and membership services. Business-to-business applications include order processing and inventory management.

 Business-to-consumer applications are frequently referred to as "B to C." Business-to-business applications are referred to as "B to B" or "B2B."

A graphical view of all Internet traffic is available from Internet Weather (*http://www. internetweather.com*). The Internet Weather Web site helps identify areas where Internet traffic is congested. Companies such as MCI WorldCom and AT&T, which now own large portions of the Internet, are upgrading the Internet infrastructure so that the Internet can handle large increases in traffic.

HOW THE INTERNET WORKS

The Internet is not just a group of homogenous computers communicating with one another. Computers on the Internet use different hardware, software, programs, and operating systems. As you just learned, in order to communicate on the Internet, computers use a suite of protocols known as TCP/IP. TCP/IP includes a variety of other protocols, including TCP, IP, telnet, FTP, HTTP, Simple Mail Transfer Protocol (SMTP), and Network News Transfer Protocol (NNTP). While TCP/IP establishes the basic rules for communication over the Internet, other **network protocols**, such as NetBEUI and IPX/SPX, establish the rules for communication between computers within private networks, called **intranets**. However, these network protocols do not allow computers to communicate over the Internet. All computers that connect to the Internet, both clients and servers, must use the TCP/IP protocol. Because TCP/IP is a scalable network protocol that can be used for local area networks (LANs) and wide area networks (WANs), most operating systems come with the TCP/IP software built in. If you have direct access to the Internet, then your computer has a copy of the TCP/IP software.

Transmission Control Protocol (TCP)

The Transmission Control Protocol (TCP) controls the physical transmission of the Internet data. TCP splits the transmission into small packets, which are sent over the Internet to a destination computer. The TCP software on the destination computer reassembles the packets into the original transmission. En route to the destination computer, each data packet makes several stops, called **hops**, at one or more computers along the way. The computer at each stop is sometimes referred to as the **gateway** computer, because it plots the next leg of the journey and sends the packet on its way. This process is repeated at each gateway computer until the packet reaches its destination.

Internet Protocol (IP)

The Internet Protocol uses an addressing scheme to manage the addressing of each individual packet, to ensure that all packets make it to their final destinations. Gateway computers use the IP address to determine how to plot where the packet should go next. As a result, each packet may take a different route through the Internet, but they all meet up at the same place and are reassembled into the original message. Virtually all Internet traffic travels via this IP routing model.

IP Address

Every computer connected to the Internet, including client computers, has an **IP address** associated with it. The IP address is used by the routing servers on the Internet to determine how to route and deliver Internet packets. Each Web server has a unique computer number, such as 207.252.246.222, which is its IP address. Internet service providers (ISPs) assign a static or dynamic IP address each time a client computer connects to the Internet. A dynamic IP address is an IP address that will change each time the computer connects to the Internet. A static IP address is assigned to a specific computer and does not change. Most large ISPs assign dynamic IP addresses to their clients. A Web server must have a static address so that the routing servers on the Internet will always know the IP address for the Web site. The IP address assigned follows the IP addressing scheme that is defined in the IP protocol version 4.0.

The IP protocol defines an IP address as a 32-bit number that consists of four sets of numbers separated by periods. These four numbers range from 0 to 255. The IP address represents a shorter version of a long binary number. A few IP addresses are reserved for special purposes. For example, the IP address 127.0.0.1 is not assigned to any computer on the Internet; it is known as the **localhost**, and is used to route packets to the local computer. This IP address is often used to test whether TCP/IP is installed correctly, and to test whether the network interface card is working. Internet programmers use the localhost IP address to represent the local Web server during development. Typing *http://127.0.0.1* or *http://localhost* into the browser will direct the user to the Web server located on the local computer. When Web programmers use this address to refer to their local Web server, they are viewing their Web pages locally, not on the Internet.

A static IP address is purchased or leased from a large ISP. Because a finite number of IP addresses are available, the IP protocol is being upgraded to a newer version (version 6.0) that can support many more IP addresses.

HTTP Protocol

The HTTP protocol is used to send HTML documents through the Internet. The HTTP protocol sends the HTML documents in packets, using TCP/IP. With each packet, the HTTP protocol attaches a header, which contains information such as the name and location of the page being requested, the name and IP address of the remote server that contains the Web page, the IP address of the local client, the HTTP version number, and the URL of the referring page. This information is referred to as the server variables. Internet programmers are able to retrieve the values in the header using techniques that will be discussed in later chapters.

It is important to know that HTTP version 1.0 is a **stateless protocol**. This means that when a client requests a document from the Web server, the server will return the Web page to the client and end all communications with the client. If the client requests another page, the Web server normally has no way of knowing that the client has previously visited the Web site. However, by using methods such as cookies, session variables, text files, and databases the server can maintain state—that is, recognize the client over multiple transactions—and thereby remember information from each transaction and link it with the specific client. These techniques will be discussed in later chapters.

In version HTTP 1.1, the Web server and the client can maintain their connection across Web pages. The NT Web server known as Internet Information Server can be configured to support this "keep alive" HTTP 1.1 feature.

TCP/IP Utilities

When you (the client) request a service (for example, that a Web page be sent) from another computer (a server) on the Internet, you are utilizing the client/server model via TCP/IP. There are many TCP/IP utility programs that are used to monitor the network. You can use these utilities to perform some basic diagnostic testing on your Web site. For example, if a customer cannot view your Web site, you can use the ping utility to determine whether the Web server is connected to the Internet. If the Web server is stopped, crashed, or turned off, or if the routing server that routes packets to the Web server is unavailable, then the Web site is no longer connected to the Internet. Two of the more important TCP/IP utilities include ping and tracert.

Ping

The IP address of the Web site can be found using a TCP/IP utility called **ping**. Ping is a utility that is used to test network connectivity (see Figure 1-2). When you ping a site, four packets are sent to the IP address. If the Web site is up, and connected to the Internet, ping will provide its IP address. If the Web site is not connected, then a Request Timed Out message appears. For example, if you ping *www.visualinterdev.org*, you will find that all four packets are returned, and that the IP address is 206.67.49.94, indicating that the Web site is connected to the Internet. To use the ping utility, go to the Command Prompt window by clicking Start on the task bar, then clicking Run. Type Command Prompt in the text box and click OK. The Command window will appear. Type in the command ping, a blank space, and the domain name for the Web site. After you hit the Return button, the ping utility will indicate whether the Web site is connected and provide the IP address for the Web site.

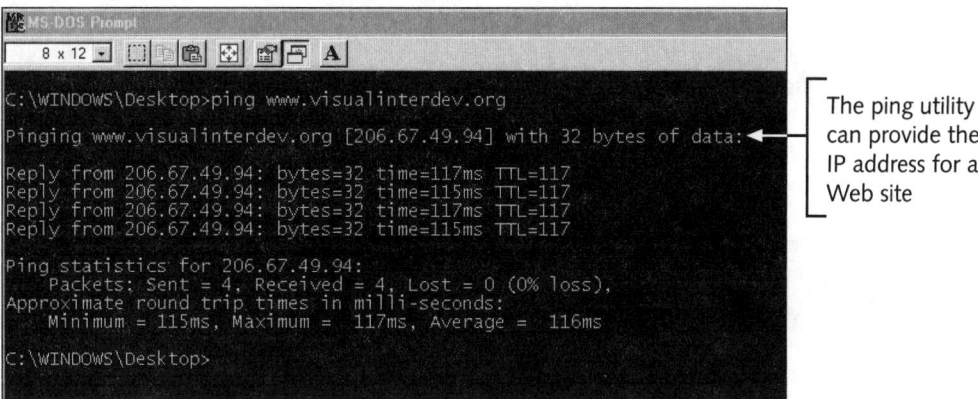

The ping utility can provide the IP address for a Web site

Figure 1-2   The ping utility

Tracert

Another TCP/IP utility used to locate the Web server is a packet-tracing utility known as **tracert**. Tracert provides the path that an Internet packet travels to get from the client to a server (see Figure 1-3). The tracert executable is usually located in your system directory in Windows 98, C:\Windows\tracert.exe, and in Windows NT C:\WINNT\system32\tracert.exe). All Internet communications are sent in small pieces called packets. When the packet stops at a gateway server, the server determines which path the packet should take next. Tracert lists each stop, or hop, that indicates that the packet has been routed to another server (or a router). The last hop on the list indicates the IP address for the Web site. When an asterisk (*) appears on the list, it indicates that the packet has experienced a delay at that server. Therefore, the tracert utility can help you detect latencies, or delays, in routing packets to your Web site. In response, large servers will reroute the packets through other routing servers. If you tracert to *www.visualinterdev.org*, you will find that the IP address is 206.67.49.94. The number of hops will vary. To use the tracert utility, go to the Command Prompt window by clicking the Start button on the task bar, then clicking Run. Type Command Prompt in the text box and click OK. The Command window will appear. Type in the command tracert, a blank space, and the domain name of the Web site. After you press Return, the tracert utility will indicate the IP address for the Web site.

If you do not have access to the DOS command prompt to access ping or tracert, you can use one of the online Web utilities. At *http://www.net.cmu.edu/cgi-bin/netops.cgi* Carnegie Mellon allows you to ping or tracert to hosts on other networks. At *http://networking.cais.net/gateways.html*, CAIS Internet provides tools for the network administrator, including ping and tracert.

In Windows 2000, several of the network utilities have been modified. Instead of tracert and ping, you can use the Path Ping utility (c:\WINNT\ system32\Pathping.exe), which combines the features of tracert and ping. You can learn more about the Windows 2000 network utilities at: *http://www.microsoft.com/windows2000/library/resources/reskit/ samplechapters/pref/pref_tts_omfx.asp*

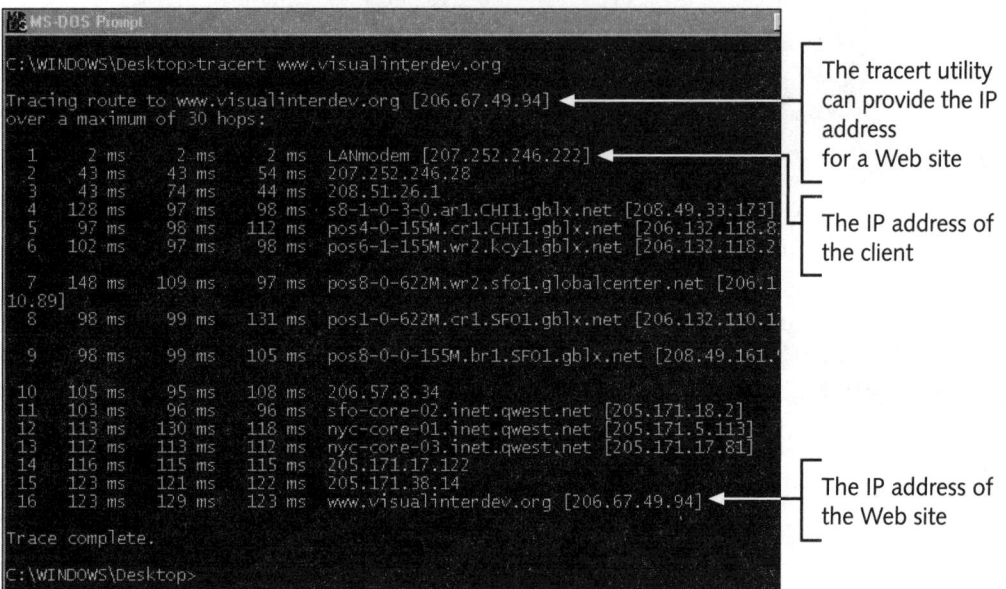

Figure 1-3 The tracert utility

TCP/IP Client Networking Software

In order for your computer to be a client on the Internet, it must have TCP/IP networking client software installed. Client for Microsoft Networks is the networking client software used by Windows-based computers. This software may already be installed on your computer. If it is not installed, you will need to install it in order to complete many of the activities in this book on your local computer.

In Windows 2000 Professional systems, Client for Microsoft Networks is installed and enabled by default, and TCP/IP is installed as the default network protocol if a network interface card is detected.

To verify that Client for Microsoft Networks is installed on your Windows 98 or Windows NT computer:

1. Click **Start**, then point to **Settings**, then click **Control Panel**.

2. Double-click the **Network** icon to open the Network dialog box. This will open to the Configuration tab (see Figure 1-4).

3. The Primary Network Logon list box should contain an entry for Client for Microsoft Networks. If not, click the list arrow and select it. If Client for Microsoft Networks is not on the list, then you need to install it.

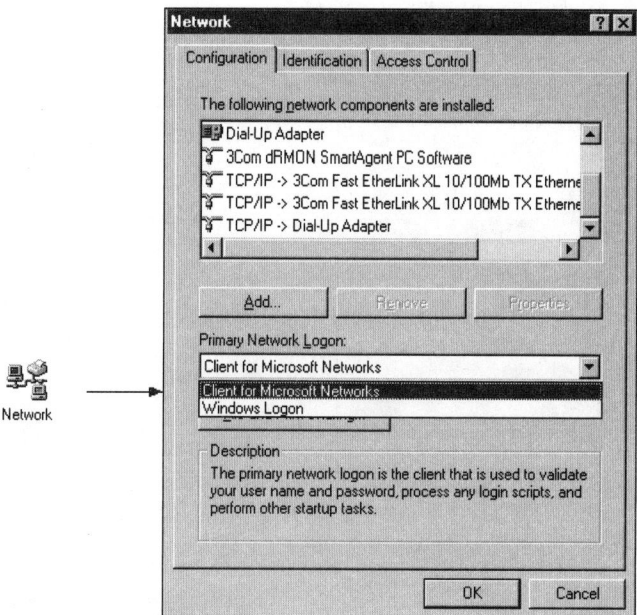

Figure 1-4   The Network dialog box Configuration tab

To install Client for Microsoft Networks on your Windows 98 or Windows NT computer, continue from the previous step.

1. Click the **Add** button on the Configuration tab to open the Select Network Component Type dialog box (see Figure 1-5).

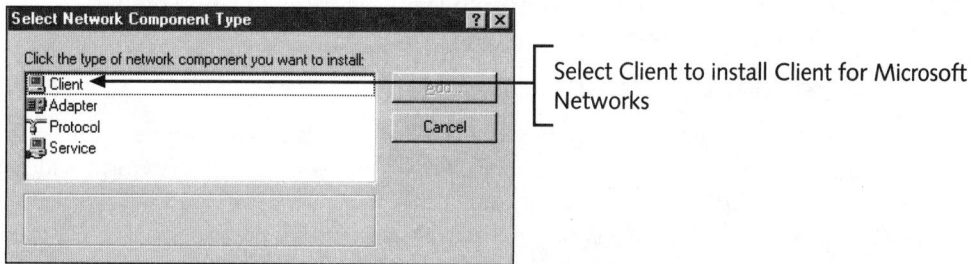

Figure 1-5   The Select Network Component Type dialog box

2. Click **Client** to select the client.

3. Click **Add** to open the Select Network Client dialog box (see Figure 1-6).

4. Click **Microsoft** in the menu of Manufacturers on the left-hand side of the dialog box.

5. Click **Client for Microsoft Networks** in the list in the Network Clients section on the right-hand side of the dialog box.

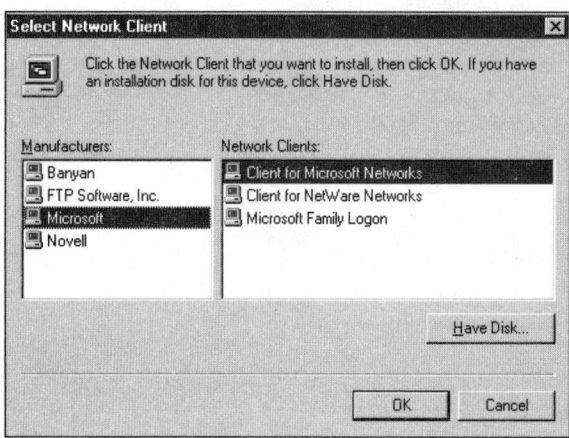

Figure 1-6   The Select Network Client dialog box

6. Click **OK**. You may be required to insert your Windows operating system disks, and to restart the computer after the software is installed.

7. After the computer restarts, click the **Start** menu.

8. Point to **Settings**, and then click **Control Panel**.

9. Double-click the **Network** icon to open the Network dialog box. This will open to the Configuration tab. Verify that Client for Microsoft Networks is installed, as directed above.

10. Click the **Identification** tab to learn the name of your computer. Figure 1-7 shows the name of the computer "Sunshine" in the Identification tab.

IP Configuration Utilities

The TCP/IP settings, such as the IP address of the client, are assigned using the Network program located in the Control Panel. The Windows operating system provides utilities to detect these TCP/IP settings. **Winipcfg** is the utility used for Windows 95 and Windows 98 computers. **Ipconfig** is the utility used for Windows NT computers. Both of these will display the TCP/IP settings for the local computer. To use the Winipcfg utility, click the Start button on the task bar, then click Run. Type winipcfg in the text box and click OK. The IP Configuration window will appear and display the IP address of the local computer. If you

1

click the More Info button, you can obtain additional IP configuration information, which is used to help route packets to and from the local computer. Both of these IP configuration utilities can also be accessed via the command prompt.

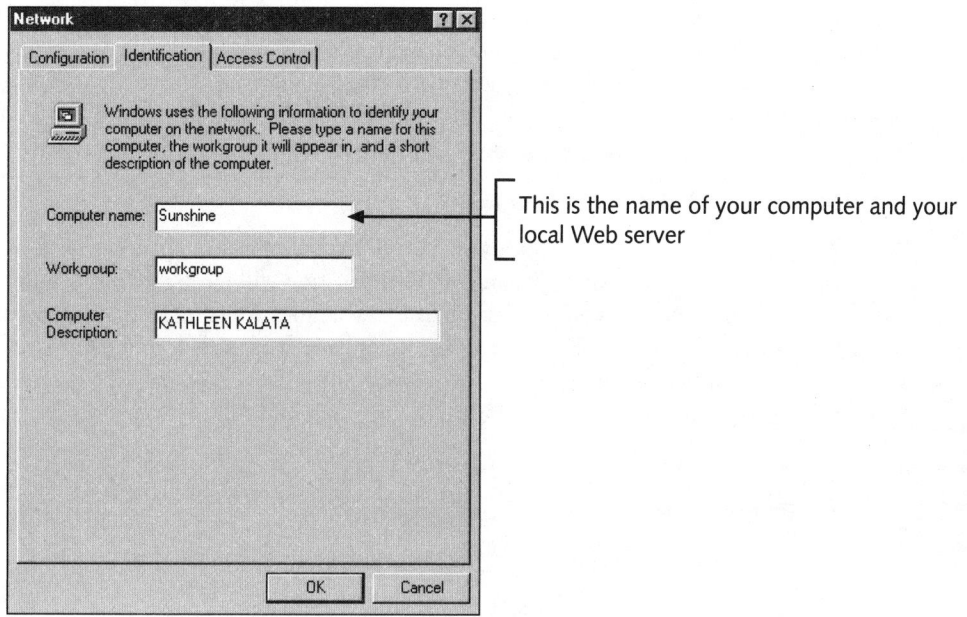

This is the name of your computer and your local Web server

Figure 1-7   The Network dialog box Identification tab

Windows 2000 Professional continues to provide several TCP/IP utilities, including ping and ipconfig. Information about how to use these utilities can be found at the Windows 2000 Professional Documentation Web site (*http://windows.microsoft.com/windows2000/en/professional/help/.*)

Domain Names

A group of related Web pages, files, and directories—called a **Web site**—is stored on the Internet on a **Web server**. A Web server is a computer that contains software that allows you to host Web pages on the Internet. The Web server may host multiple Web sites on the same physical computer. The Web server software is able to differentiate among Web sites by using a different IP address and domain name for each Web site.

A Web site can be identified by its IP address or by its domain name. For example, typing in *http://206.67.49.94* or *http://www.visualinterdev.org* takes you to the same Web site. A **domain name** uniquely identifies a single Web site on the Internet. Examples of domain names are www.visualinterdev.org and www.microsoft.com. Instead of using the IP address, which is not very memorable, users can type in the domain name. All domain names are registered in a global database known as the **registry**. In the early 1990s, Web site sponsors were required to register domain names with **InterNIC** (*http://www.InterNIC.net/*). InterNIC processed all registrations and maintained the registry database. In 1992, InterNIC transferred the domain registration and registry maintenance responsibility to a company called Network Solutions (*http://www.networksolutions.com*). While Network Solutions currently maintains the registry, there are many companies, called **registrars**, which can register the Web site domain name in the registry database. InterNIC provides a list of these registrars at *http://www.InterNIC.net/alpha.html*. Many of these registrars, such as TUCOWS.com (*http://www.tucows.com*) and Tierranet (*hhtp://www.tierranet.com*), allow third-party companies to register second-level domains such as .com, .net, and .org at a nominal cost.

Signing Up for a Domain Name

To sign up for a domain name, access the Web site of one of the registrars, such as Network Solutions at *http://www.networksolutions.com*. The registrar will have a form to query the database to determine whether your domain name is available. After finding a domain name that is available, you will need to fill out a request form to register the domain. Each registrar will have a slightly different form, and the forms may extend over several Web pages. However, all of the forms will require at least the following information:

- Domain name (such as course.com)
- Name, address, and e-mail of the registrant
- Name, address, and e-mail of the administrative contact
- Name, address, and e-mail of the technical contact
- Name, address, and e-mail of the billing contact
- Name and IP address of the primary and secondary DNS servers (the routing servers)
- Billing information for online payment

The **registrant** is the legal owner of the domain. If your Web site is going to provide online e-commerce transactions, changing the domain name registrant (owner of the domain) is a lengthy process. It is essential that the name be entered correctly. To change the owner of the domain, you will have to obtain the domain name transfer forms online, then sign them in front of a notary public. It may take up to six weeks for the domain name to be transferred.

An administrative, technical, or billing contact who has been previously entered into the database will have an **InterNIC handle**. The InterNIC handle, also referred to as a NIC handle, is used to identify an individual or organization within the database. Using the InterNIC handle simplifies the registration process. The first time you register a domain, your name will be assigned an InterNIC handle. During subsequent domain name registrations, you will only need to enter your InterNIC handle. You will not need to reenter your contact information.

Domain Name Service Servers (DNS Servers)

Because a network server can host more than one Web server, the network server needs a means to identify the Web servers on the network. The **Domain Name Service (DNS)** is a network service that translates domain names to IP addresses. Each Web server is assigned an IP address and domain name. When you register your domain, you do not provide the IP address for your Web site. Instead, you provide the name and IP address of a DNS server. The DNS server contains a listing of domain names and their associated IP addresses. The ISP that hosts your Web site will enter your domain name and IP address in their DNS server. When a client requests a Web page, for example by entering a URL, the client's network server locates the relevant DNS server, which then provides the relevant IP address.

The Whois Utility

To locate the DNS servers, InterNIC handle, or registrant information for a Web site, you can use the **whois** utility. The whois utility looks up the information associated with individuals, domain names, and DNS servers in the registry. You can access the whois utility at *http://www.networksolutions.com/cgi-bin/whois/whois.*

To locate the registrant, InterNIC handle, and DNS servers of a Web site using the whois utility:

1. Start your Web browser.

2. In the location bar, type **http://www.networksolutions.com/cgi-bin/whois/whois** to go to the whois utility Web page.

3. Type **visualinterdev.org** in the text box.

4. Click the **Search** button to open a Web page that displays the information about the site.

5. Identify the registrant listed on the Web page. (*Hint:* The registrant is the name found immediately after the word "Registrant.")

6. Identify the InterNIC handle of the administrative contact. (*Hint:* The InterNIC handle is found within parentheses after the name of the administrative contact.)

7. Identify the primary and secondary DNS server names and IP addresses for this site. (*Hint:* The DNS server names and IP addresses are found at the bottom of the page immediately after the statement "Domain servers in listed order:".) Compare your answers to the ones listed in Figure 1-8.

8. Close the browser.

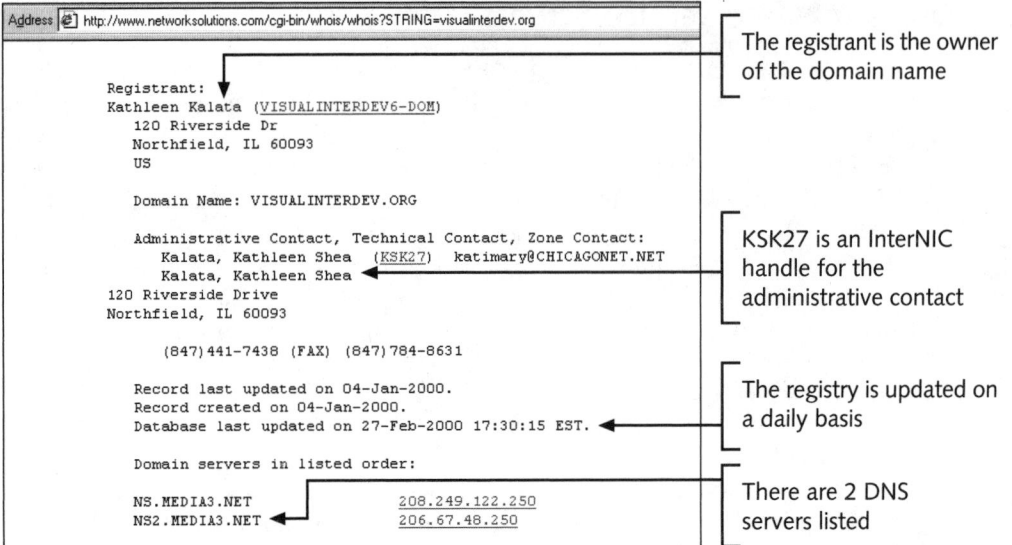

Figure 1-8   The whois utility

 You can also use the InterNIC whois utility at *http://www.internic.net/whois.html* to locate information about the registrar who registered the domain.

The World Wide Web Service

A **network server** is a network software application that provides network-related services such as e-mail, database, messaging, file, and printing services. As you learned earlier, the network software that stores Web pages and processes the requests for Web pages is called the Web server (sometimes also called the **World Wide Web (WWW) Service**). Network administrators can define many Web sites on the same server, and these Web sites are known as **virtual Web servers**. The Web server that hosts your site may reside on your local network, or it may be on the other side of the world. Many companies provide hosting services to host many Web sites on the same computer. Companies that provide hosting services are called **hosting service providers** (HSPs).

 Some HSPs allow you to have **subwebs**. Subwebs are subdirectories of a Web site. The HSP can map a different domain name to the subweb. To the outside world, the subweb domain appears to be a separate domain; in fact, it is physically located within a subdirectory of another domain. Developers often use subwebs to host multiple Web sites at lower rates.

1

The architecture of your Internet application will depend upon the type of application you are developing. Internet programming has been referred to as client/server programming because the client application is communicating with the server application. A browser sends a request from a client machine for an Internet document that exists on a remote Web server. The client communicates with the rest of the Internet via a network server. In many instances, the network server is the ISP's server. The client's network server routes the request packet to the Web server that contains your Web page. The network server routes the packets back to the client's browser. The browser receives and processes the request and **renders** (or displays) the requested Web document. Figure 1-9 illustrates how a browser receives a Web page from the server. Today, this basic model has become more complex because of the number and types of applications on the Internet. Internet applications are no longer limited to a single server. E-commerce Internet applications often communicate with database servers that are not located on the same physical network server as the Web server. So, in addition to client/server programming, servers communicate with other servers.

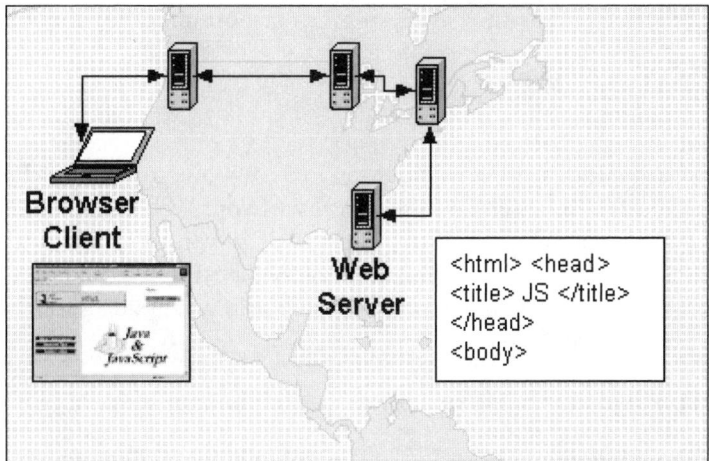

Figure 1-9   Client/server programming using a Web browser and a Web server

Web Servers

Although there are many different types of Web servers, the most common are Apache and Internet Information Server. On the UNIX operating system, Apache is the most common Web server. On Windows NT platforms, Internet Information Server is the most common. When working on desktop Windows computers running Windows 98, developers often use Microsoft Personal Web Server to create a Web environment for testing while they are building their Web sites. There are many other Web server software products on the market. The Netcraft Web site at *http://www.netcraft.co.uk/Survey/whats/* offers a utility that can detect the type of Web server and operating system a Web site is using.

HOSTING SERVICE PROVIDERS

After you have selected a domain name and registered it with one of the InterNIC registrars, you will need a service provider to host your Web site. Internet service providers (ISPs) offer Internet services, which may include dial-up services to connect clients to the Internet, and Web site hosting. Not all ISPs provide high-quality hosting services. Web programmers also need access to additional resources, such as Web programming documentation and support for Web development tools. A hosting service provider (HSP) is an ISP that specializes in Web site hosting. HSPs are also called Web presence providers. Some HSPs specialize in working with Internet programmers, while others provide only general Web hosting services. While many companies have their own Web server, small companies often establish an initial Internet presence using a hosting service provider. Some HSPs offer colocation, whereby they will maintain the equipment connecting the server to the Internet, but the responsibility for maintaining the server software remains with the company. The person who maintains the Web server is called the Webmaster; in small companies where there is no Webmaster, an Internet programmer is often given responsibility for the maintenance of the Web server.

Hosting Criteria

Before searching for an HSP, determine what criteria you will use to evaluate them. Create a list of features that you feel are essential to the success of your Web site. Then, arrange the list in order of priority. Some Web sites on the Internet allow you to search for the features that HSPs often provide. Compiling an evaluation criteria check list will help you find the right HSP for your needs. Some of the questions that will help you evaluate an HSP include:

- Is customer support available 24 hours per day, 7 days a week, 365 days a year?
- Does the HSP have a toll-free number to access customer support?
- Does it have an e-mail address for the customer support team?
- What documentation does it provide? Is the documentation Web-based? Can it be printed for reference?
- Does it provide forums or discussion boards for common customer support questions?
- Is its connection to the Internet reliable?
- Does it have triple redundancy so that if one connection goes down, backups are available?
- Does it back up the Web sites for you?
- Does it provide network-monitoring tools such as raw data log files or third-party Web site tools such as WebTrends (*http://www.webtrends.com/flash.htm*)?
- What operating systems does it use?

- Does it provide free domain name server listings for Web sites?

- Does it provide virtual hosting so that you can use your own domain name? For example, www.mycompany.com or yourcompany.thehspcompany.com?

- Does it provide subwebs?

- Does it provide free domain name registration?

- Does it provide multiple user accounts to access the Web site?

- Does it provide an account control panel or other utility to allow you to change permissions on files and directories?

- Does it provide support for **Secure Socket Layer (SSL)** certificates? (SSL is used to encrypt packets to protect sensitive information, such as credit card numbers, from being read while being transmitted over the Internet.)

- Does it allow server-side includes (SSIs)? (SSIs are files that can be included on multiple Web pages. They are often used to centralize the header and footer information, which can then be reused in multiple pages.)

- Does it allow you to customize your error messages? (For example, a generic error message such as the 404 File Not Found error message can be customized to direct the user to another Web page.)

- Does it provide online file management tools?

- Does it provide access to utilities such as FTP and telnet?

- Does it support publishing with HTML editors such as Dreamweaver or FrontPage?

- Does it support FrontPage 2000 server extensions, which allow you to use the advanced features in FrontPage?

- How many client e-mail accounts (called POP e-mail accounts) does it provide?

- Does it provide a Web e-mail interface as an alternative to using a client e-mail program?

- Does it provide e-mail services such as unlimited aliases, e-mail forwarding, and auto-responders?

- Does it provide mailing list services such as IMail by Ipswitch (*http://www.ipswitch.com*) or List Manager by Lyris (*http://www.lyris.com/*)?

- Which database applications does it support (SQL, Oracle, Access, mySQL, DSNs)?

- Which third-party e-commerce applications does it support? Common e-commerce applications include Miva Merchant by Miva at *http://www.miva.com/* and AbleCommerce at *http://ablecommerce.com*.

- Which e-commerce payment mechanisms does it support? Some common payment mechanisms are CyberCash at *http://www.cybercash.com*, and Authorize.Net at *http://www.authorizenet.com*.

- What partnerships does it have with other software vendors to provide additional services? (For example, bulletin boards and chat room software such as Volano at *http://www.volano.com* or e-Share at *http://www.eshare.com*.)

- Does it provide a reseller or affiliate program?

- How much hard drive disk space does it provide? (The hard disk drive space will determine how many documents, Web pages, and images the Web site will support.)

- How much are the setup fees and monthly costs?

- What support does it provide for Common Gateway Interface (CGI) (such as Perl, cgi-bin directory, free CGI scripts, page counters)?

- Does it support Active Server Pages (ASP)?

- Does it support advanced multimedia such as streaming audio and video, or conferencing?

Locating a Hosting Service Provider

After developing your evaluation criteria, you should compare at least ten different hosting service providers. There are several lists of HSPs on the Internet. Many of these lists provide a ranking of HSPs based on the features they support, or on feedback by their membership. CNET (*http://www.cnet.com*) contains an extensive list of hosting service providers at *http://webhostlist.internetlist.com/*. The following Web sites contain additional lists of hosting service providers.

- *HostIndex* — *http://www.hostindex.com/*

- *TopHosts.Com* — *http://www.tophosts.com/pages/topover.htm*

- *The List* — *http://thelist.internet.com/*

Internet Programming User Groups

Finally, you should ask colleagues for their opinions about your HSP selections. How have other Internet programmers evaluated this HSP? While an HSP may claim to have 24-hour availability, you might in fact find that they have been prone to network slowdowns and outages. If you do not know any Internet programmers, there are many user groups that can help. For example, eGroups (*www.egroups.com*) features several lists that discuss Internet programming. The JavaScript group discusses client-side programming and is available at *http://www.egroups.com/group/javascript*. The beginner ASP group discusses server-side programming using ASP. The ASP Beginner list is available at: *http://www.egroups.com/group/asp-beginer/info.html*. There is also a user group for more advanced ASP programmers at *http://www.egroups.com/group/asp/info.html*.

CREATING A WEB PAGE

Web pages are created using the HTML language that was established by the HTML protocol. The specifications for the most recent version of HTML, 4.01, are available at *http://www.w3.org/TR/html401/*. This book assumes that you have some experience using HTML to create Web pages. The following sections review how to create a basic Web page, and how to use basic HTML tags. Web pages can be created in a simple text editor program such as Notepad, vi, or BBEdit, or in a **Web page editor** such as FrontPage or Dreamweaver. Web editors provide a graphical user interface that allows you to easily manipulate the layout, design, and features within a Web page. The following section lists the most common Web development tools.

Web Development Tools

In the early days of the Internet, companies usually created disconnected static Web pages, often recreations of their advertising and print materials. Companies hired Web developers who used text editors such as Notepad to create these Web pages. Web tools such as HotDog (*http://www.sausage.com/*) and HTMLPro offered programmers a graphical user interface for creating HTML code. However, as Internet technologies evolved, companies wanted to add interactivity to their pages. To create these more complex Web pages, developers started using Web page editors and Web site management tools to create and maintain Web sites. Some of the common Web development tools are:

- Microsoft Visual InterDev (*http://msdn.microsoft.com/vinterdev/* and *http://msdn.microsoft.com/vstudio/*)
- Microsoft FrontPage (*http://www.microsoft.com/frontpage/*)
- Adobe PageMill (*http://www.adobe.com/products/pagemill/main.html*)
- Allaire HomeSite (*http://www.allaire.com/products/homesite/index.cfm*)
- Macromedia Dreamweaver (*http://www.macromedia.com/software/dreamweaver/*)
- Bare Bones BBEdit for Macintosh (*http://www.barebones.com/products/bbedit/bbedit.html*)

Each of these Web editors can be used to develop small or large Web sites. Most of these vendors also provide additional tools that allow the Internet programmer to create more robust Internet applications. For example, Visual InterDev is highly integrated with FrontPage and Visual Studio. Dreamweaver is highly integrated with Macromedia Flash and Fireworks. Allaire has developed a product called Cold Fusion, which allows you to create Web pages that support databases. Today, even Microsoft Office (*http://www.microsoft.com/office/*) allows you to easily create Web pages from within Word, Access, PowerPoint, and Excel. Which Web editor you use will depend upon what type of Web pages you are creating and your experience level.

For the samples and exercises in this book, you can use any text editor, such as Notepad, or a Web editor, such as Visual InterDev 6, FrontPage 2000, or Dreamweaver 3.0. However, this book will not provide you with instructions on how to use the Web editors.

The examples in this book were created using Notepad and FrontPage 2000.

HTML Tags

HTML is a markup language that uses tags to instruct browsers how to format (or render) the Web page. HTML tags are always enclosed within angle brackets (<>). Most require a beginning and a closing tag. The closing tag is differentiated from the beginning tag with the forward slash (/) character. Content to be manipulated by the tags must be between the two tags. All HTML pages begin with the <html> tag—the beginning tag—and end with the </html> tag—the ending tag. There are two parts to a Web page, the **heading section** and the **body section**. The heading section is identified by a pair of head tags (<head> and </head>), while the body section is identified by a pair of body tags (<body> and </body>). A listing of commonly used HTML tags can be found in Appendix A. A complete list of the HTML tags and the syntax is available from the World Wide Web Consortium at *http://www.w3.org/TR/html4/index/elements.html*.

Although the tags are not case sensitive, many programmers prefer to write the tag names in either all uppercase, or all lowercase, to make them easier to identify. In this book, all HTML tags and properties are written in lowercase.

Tags Used in the Heading Section

Many tags can be used in the heading section of the Web page. Table 1-1 lists HTML tags that are commonly used in the heading section of the Web page.

Table 1-1   Common HTML Heading Tags

HTML Tag	Purpose
<head>	Identifies the heading section
<title>	Identifies the page in the title bar, the history list, and the favorites list within the browser application
<meta>	Contains additional information in name/value pairs, such as author and keywords
<link>	Links another document to the Web page, such as a style sheet or JavaScript page
<style>	Contains style information for tags located within the Web document
<script>	Identifies client- and server-side scripts written in a scripting language such as JavaScript or VBScript; may also appear in the body section

The Title Tag The heading section can contain nested HTML tags, such as the title tag. The pair of title tags (<title> and </title>) is used to identify the name of the page. This title is placed in the title bar on the browser, in the history list, and in the favorites list when a user bookmarks a Web page. In the following example, the title of the page is "My Home Page." The entire title name is located between the title beginning and ending tags.

```
<title> My Home Page </title>
```

The Meta Tag The meta tag allows you to provide additional information about the page that is not visible in the browser. User-defined variables are identified with the meta tag's name attribute. The content attribute is used to identify the value for the variable. You can include multiple meta tags within the same Web page. The meta tags are always placed within the heading section of the Web page.

<meta name=" variable" content="value">

The meta tag might be used, for example, to identify the author's name. In the sample code below, the name of the variable is author, and the value is Caitlin Murphy. Today, the meta tag is frequently used to identify keywords that describe the site. One or more keywords can be listed. A comma is used to separate multiple keywords. Search engines use these keywords to catalogue the Web site. Because most search engines will limit the number of keywords to 25, it is important to select keywords that accurately describe the Web site. The following example shows how to use the meta tag to identify the author's name and keywords.

```
<meta name="Author" content="Caitlin Murphy">
<meta name="Keywords" content="Store, Pens">
```

In most browsers, users can reload the page by clicking a button labeled Reload or Refresh. Refresh is often used for pages that change frequently, such as those containing live video or breaking news. The meta tag can be used to force the browser to reload the page. Because the meta tag is defining a system-level variable, the meta attribute used is http-equiv. The meta command used to reload the page is called refresh. Refresh causes the Web page to reload, as if the user had clicked the Reload or Refresh button on the browser.

Refresh can also be used to load a new page into the browser window by adding the URL of the new page. The content attribute identifies the URL of the Web page and the number of seconds that the browser waits before reloading the Web page. A semicolon is used to separate the waiting time and the URL. The process of loading a new page into the browser is referred to as **client-side redirection**. Visitors are aware that they are being redirected to another Web page. The number of seconds can be set to zero to force the Web page to reload quickly.

The following sample code shows how you can use the meta tag to redirect the client to another Web site.

```
<meta http-equiv="refresh"
content="3;url=http://www.visualinterdev.org">
```

Tags Used in the Body Section

The body section is identified with a pair of body tags (<body> and </body>). The body section of a Web page can contain many HTML tags. Some tags are used to format the characters and paragraphs; others are used to insert images, tables, and forms. A list of commonly used HTML tags can be found in Appendix A. Table 1-2 lists tags commonly used within the body section of the Web page.

The heading tag used in the body section is not the same as the head tag used to identify the heading section. The heading tag is used in the body to format a line of text with a predefined format. There are six predefined heading tags, each identified by the letter h and a number (one through six). The heading 1 tag (<h1>) formats the line of text using a large bold font. The heading 6 tag (<h6>) formats the line of text using a smaller font. The bold, italic, underline, and font tags are used to modify the font characteristics.

Table 1-2   Common HTML Body Tags

Tag Name	HTML Tag	Purpose
Body	<body>	Indentifies the body section
Paragraph	<p>	Defines the paragraph
Heading	<h1>, <h2>, <h3>, <h4>,<h5>, <h6>	Predefined formatting styles often used for headings within a Web page
Bold	<b>	Formats text in boldface
Italic	<i>	Italicizes text
Underline	<u>	Underlines text
Font	<font>	Formats the text font style, color, size, type, and other attributes
Center	<center>	Centers the text, images, or other content
Break	 	Inserts a line break
Horizontal Ruler	<hr>	Inserts a horizontal line
Image	<img>	Inserts a graphic
Map	<map>	Identifies coordinates and links on a client-side image map
Blockquote	<blockquote>	Indents the line
Anchor	<a>	Creates a hyperlink to another document or a target within the Web page
Comment	<!-- comment -->	Hides text from the browser window (comments are not hidden from the source view)

HTML Tag Attributes

Within many HTML tags, you can specify additional attributes. These attributes provide a means of altering the tag in some way. For example, the paragraph tag <p> allows you to insert a paragraph. By default, paragraphs are aligned to the left side of the Web page. The align property of the paragraph tag allows you to align the paragraph to left, right, or center, or to justify it. The value is assigned to the attribute using the equal sign (=). You should place quotation marks around the value of the attribute. Some browsers will not recognize the attribute values without the quotation marks. A pair of single or double quotation marks can be used. Some attributes are common to several HTML tags. For example, width is an attribute that identifies the width of an element. The width attribute is available to several tags, including the image tag.

To add an HTML tag, use the following syntax.

<tagname attribute="value">web content</tagname>

For example:

```
<p align="center">Welcome!</p>
```

 When you create simple Web pages, the HTML tags are referred to as tags, and the **attributes** are properties of these tags. However, when you refer to the tag as an entity, it is known as an HTML **element**. The HTML tags are referred to as Web page **elements**, or **Web page objects**, and the attributes are referred to as **properties** of these Web page objects.

Creating a Basic Web Page Using HTML

The following is an example of a basic Web page named storehome.htm, which was created in Notepad. This Web page contains a title in the heading section and a paragraph in the body section. Note the location of the head and body tags, the location of the title, heading, and paragraph tags, and the presence of a beginning and ending tag for each HTML tag. The title tag is nested inside the head tag, while the heading and paragraph tags are nested within the body tags. The bold tags (<b>) are nested within the paragraph tags.

```
<html><head>
<title>Store Home</title>
</head>
<body>
<h1>Home Page</h1>
<p><b>Welcome</b> to our Store!</p>
</body></html>
```

Other HTML Tags

As mentioned previously, the body section can contain many tags. The body tag, which is used to identify the body section, can be modified using several attributes. The image tag is used to insert images. The anchor tag is used to insert hyperlinks to other pages or Web sites. The form tag is used to insert a form. The following sections describe how these tags can be used to enhance your Web pages.

The Body Tag   The body tag is used to alter the format of the entire document. The body tag contains several attributes. Originally, the background of Web pages was gray by default. Today, the body tag contains an attribute called bgColor that allows the programmer to change the color of the background. The color value can be identified by the color name or by the hexadecimal number associated with the color.

For example, the code below changes the color of the background to white. Note that the hexadecimal number associated with the color white is #FFFFFF. Although the value could have been identified using the color name white, some browsers do not support color names as values of an attribute. Therefore, it is better to use the hexadecimal number associated with the color.

```
<body bgcolor="#FFFFFF">
```

 For a list of Web sites that discuss browser-safe colors, background colors, and the use of hexadecimal numbers to identify colors, visit the Web Backgrounds page at Life Beyond Yahoo by selecting Color Page at *http://www.lifebeyondyahoo.com/*.

There are several other attributes commonly used with the body tag. The background property of the body tag can be used to identify a background image for the Web page. Images that are commonly supported by browsers have a .gif or .jpg extension. The text attribute identifies the color of text. The default text color is black. The default colors of the hyperlinks are blue for an unvisited link, purple for a visited link, and red for an active link. These default colors can be changed using the link, vlink, and alink attributes. The link attribute defines the default color for unvisited hyperlinks; the vlink attribute identifies the default color for the visited hyperlinks; the alink attribute identifies the default color for active hyperlinks. Below is the syntax for the common attributes used with the body tag.

<body bgcolor= "color" background = "URL/imagename.gif" link= "color" text= "color" vlink= "color" alink= "color">

List Tags   Lists can be formatted using the unordered list tag, the ordered list tag, or the definitions list tag. Unordered lists use bullets to identify each list item, while ordered lists are identified using alphanumeric characters. You can modify the type of bullet or character used. Both types of list use the list item tag to identify items in the list. The definitions list uses the definition tag to identify the items in the list. The definitions are indented under the definition term. Table 1-3 identifies the commonly used list tags. The following sample code illustrates how you can add an unordered list to a Web page. Note how the list items contain nested italic tags, which are used to format the text within the list item tag.

```
<p>January Products</p>
<ul>
<li><i>Folders</i></li>
<li><i>Notebooks</i></li>
</ul>
```

Table 1-3   List Tags

Tag Name	HTML Tag	Purpose
Unordered List	\<ul\>	Creates a bulleted, or unordered, list
List Item	\<li\>	Identifies items in a list
Ordered List	\<ol\>	Creates a sequential, or ordered, list
Definition List	\<dl\>	Creates a list with no bullets or numbers
Definition Term	\<dt\>	The definition term in a definition list
Definition	\<dd\>	The definition, which is indented below the definition term

The Image Tag   The image tag is used to add a graphic image to the Web page. The image tag contains several attributes. Table 1-4 lists the commonly used attributes for the image tag. It's important to note that the source attribute can be an absolute reference to the complete URL. For example, *http://www.visualinterdev.org/js/bluedisk.gif* will display a graphic image of a blue disk. A relative address would not include the protocol name (http) or domain name (*www.visualinterdev.org*). The relative address includes the location of the image file in relation to the current Web page. For example, if the Web page were named bluedisk.htm and located in the same directory, the relative URL would be "bluedisk.gif". The syntax for the image tag with attributes is shown below.

\<img src = "url/imagename" alt = "n" align= "n" width = "n" height = "n" border = "n" hspace = "n" vspace = "n" usemap= "#mapname"\>

The Anchor Tag   The anchor tag is most often used to create a hyperlink to another document. When the user clicks the content between the anchor tags, the browser opens the page identified by the HREF attribute. The HREF attribute indicates the URL for the hyperlink. The URL can be an absolute or relative address. The following sample code creates a hyperlink to another document.

```
<a href="http://www.visualinterdev.org/">
Visual InterDev
</a>
```

Table 1-4   Attributes of the Image Tag

Tag Name	Sample	Purpose
Source	`src="ship.gif"`	Displays the URL path and name of the image. This URL can be an absolute or relative reference.
Alt	`alt="welcome"`	Displays alternate text if the image is not displayed in the browser or client software. The alt attribute also is displayed in newer browsers when the user places the pointer over the image.
Align	`align="center"`	Alters the alignment of the image with respect to surrounding elements. For example, if the align attribute were set to "left", then the text would wrap around the image on the right site. The align attribute values are top, bottom, middle, left, right, texttop, absmiddle, baseline, and absbottom.
Height and Width	`height="100"` `width="400"`	Determines the dimensions of the image, measured in pixels
Border	`border="2"`	Displays a border around the image. The size of the border is specified in pixels. If the border is "0" then no border is visible.
Horizontal Space and Vertical Space	`hspace="5"` `vspace="5"`	Specifies a runaround space in pixels. The runaround space is like a picture frame around the image, and is used to create space between the text and the image. The hspace is used to identify the space on each side of the image, while the vspace is used to identify the space at the top and bottom of the image.
Usermap	`usemap="#home"`	Identifies the name of the imagemap to use for this image. Imagemaps are images that contain multiple hyperlinks. The coordinates and links for the imagemap are defined by map tag.

You can force the browser to open the Web page in a new window by specifying the target window. The target window can also be identified in the URL. The target window can be identified as _blank, _self, _parent, or _top. The following sample code opens the Web page in a new window, on top of the existing window.

```
<a href="http://www.visualinterdev.org/" target="_top">
Visual InterDev
</a>
```

You can use the anchor tag to create a bookmark within a Web page. Bookmarks are used to specify a location within a Web page. The name attribute is used to identify the name of the bookmark. The following sample code will create a bookmark named test.

```
<a name = "test">
```

You can link to a bookmark within a Web page by using the anchor tag. The URL attribute is appended with a pound sign (#) and the name of the bookmark. To link to a specific target within the same page, the URL can be dropped; you need only use the pound sign and the name of the target. The following sample illustrates how to create a hyperlink to a bookmark named test.

```
<a href="http://www.visualinterdev.org/ip/anchor.htm#test">
Visual InterDev
</a>
```

The Table Tag   The table tag is used to create a table on a Web page. Table 1-5 lists the main tags that are used to create a table. The border property of the table tag is used to create a border around all of the cells in the table. The width property of the table tag can be used to specify the width of the table either in pixels or by percentage of the browser window. The bgcolor property is used to assign a color to the entire table. The table row tag is used to define the beginning and ending of a row. The table cell tag is nested within the table row tags and indicates where cells are placed within the table. The following sample code creates a table with four cells. The syntax and the list of attributes available for the table tag can be found at *http://www.w3.org/TR/html4/struct/tables.html#edef-TABLE*.

```
<table align="center" border="0" width="200"
bgcolor="#C0C0C0" cellspacing="0" cellpadding="5">
<tr>
<td width="50" valign="top">1</td>
<td width="50" valign="top">2</td>
</tr>
<tr>
<td width="50" valign="top">3</td>
<td width="50" valign="top">4</td>
</tr>
</table>
```

Table 1-5   Table Tags

Tag Name	HTML Tag	Purpose
Table	<table>	Inserts a table
Table Row	<tr>	Inserts a new row in a table
Table Cell	<td>	Inserts a new cell inside a table row

The Form Tag   Forms are used to receive information from the user. Forms are commonly used to allow users to register on a Web site, to log in to a Web site, to order a product, and to send feedback. The form tag is used to create the form. Table 1-6 lists some of the tags used to create forms and form fields. The name attribute of the form tag is used to name the form. The name of the form is used in scripting when referring to the form. Forms contain many types of form elements, such as text boxes, radio buttons, check boxes, and drop-down lists. Each form field is assigned a name with the name attribute. Users enter values into the text boxes, or make selections from the radio buttons, check boxes, and drop down lists. The values they enter or select are passed with the name of the form field to the Web server.

The action attribute identifies the program or script that will process the form. Often the action will be the name of a CGI program written in a programming language called Perl, or the name of an ASP page. (In Chapter 7 you will learn how to create ASP pages, and in Chapter 8 you will learn how to use ASP to process the form.) You can specify an absolute or relative URL.

The method attribute of the form tag is used to identify how the form field names and values will be sent to the server. The get method will append the names of the form elements, and their values, to the URL. The post method will send the names and values of the form fields within the TCP/IP packet. Because the post method will not be viewable in the location bar of the browser, it is the preferred method for sending form field results to the Web server. To add a form tag, use the basic syntax below. Values for the method can be get or post.

<form method= "methodName" action= "scriptName" name= "formName">

Table 1-6 Form-related Tags

Tag Name	HTML Tag	Purpose
Form	<form>	Inserts a form, which contains one or more form elements
Input	<input>	Creates form elements such as text and password boxes, hidden fields, radio buttons, check boxes, submit and reset buttons, images, files, and buttons
Select	<select>	Creates elements such as a drop-down list and a list box
Textarea	<textarea>	Creates a multiline text box in a form

The Input Tag Attributes The input tag creates a form element that can retrieve information. The name attribute is used to name the input element. The name of the input element is used in scripting when referring to the input element.

The type attribute identifies the format of the input tag. The possible type attributes are text, password, hidden, checkbox, submit, reset, file, image, and button. The "type text" attribute creates a text box field. The "type hidden" attribute creates a form field that is not visible in the browser. The "type submit" attribute creates a submit button. When the user clicks the submit button, the form is sent to the ASP page or CGI program identified in the action attribute of the form tag.

The value attribute provides a default value for the input tag. This value will be displayed with the form element in the browser. Additional attributes are available with the various types of input elements. The following is an example of several form field elements in a form.

```
<form name="frm" method="post" action="form.asp">
Name <input type="text" name="name" size="20"
 value="Type your name here"><br><br>
Email <input type="text" name="email" size="20"
 value="Type your e-mail here"><br><br>
<input type="checkbox" name="chkYes" value="on">
Yes I want to be on the e-mail list.<br><br>
<input type="submit" value="Send" name="btnSubmit">
<input type="reset" value="Clear" name="btnReset"></p>
</form>
```

Additional Resources

The previous sections cover just a few of the more common HTML elements and their attributes. More HTML elements and their attributes are listed in Appendix A. However, additional Internet resources, which include online tutorials that cover HTML tags and their properties, can be found at Life Beyond Yahoo (*http://www.lifebeyondyahoo.com/*) at *http://www.lifebeyondyahoo.com/life/html.asp*.

Publishing Your Web Pages

Once you have created Web pages using your Web development tool, you must publish them to a Web server to view them. Some Web development tools, including FrontPage, InterDev, and Dreamweaver, allow you to publish Web pages directly to a Web server. However, if you are using a text editor, you will need a program to copy your files to the Web server. You can use FTP software, such as WS_FTP Pro by Ipswitch (*http://www.ipswitch.com*), to transfer your files from your client computer to the Web server. There are many FTP software programs available on the Internet. To locate an FTP program, visit the Tucows Web site at *http://www.tucows.com/*.

CHAPTER SUMMARY

History of the Internet

❐ The early Internet was called ARPANET and was used by the government and universities for research and education. The first browser was created by the University of Illinois National Center for Supercomputing Applications and was called NCSA Mosaic. Hypertext documents are called Web pages. HTML is used to create Web pages. The WWW Consortium defined HTML and HTTP standards.

How the Internet Works

❐ The Internet uses TCP/IP to route and deliver packets from one computer to another. The IP protocol uses the IP addressing scheme to route packets. Every computer on the

Internet has an IP address. The ping utility tests network connectivity. The tracert utility can detect whether a Web site is slow, or disconnected from the Internet. TCP/IP is installed on every computer on the Internet so that the computers can communicate with one another. All domain names are registered in the domain registry. InterNIC allows many registrars to register domains. Network Solutions currently maintains the registry database. The registrant is the legal owner of the site. The InterNIC handle is used to identify individuals, companies, and servers that are listed in the registry. To sign up a domain name, you need to have the IP addresses of the DNS servers that contain the routing information to your Web site. The whois utility can identify information about the Web site owner and DNS servers. The World Wide Web Service is another name for the Web server software that is installed on a network server. Hosting service providers are companies that host multiple Web sites.

Creating Web Pages

❑ You can create Web pages using text editors or Web page editors. HTML documents consist of a heading section and a body section, identified by the head and body tags. A variety of HTML tags is used to format the presentation of the Web page. Personal Web Server (PWS) is available free from Microsoft and allows you to develop and test your Web pages locally. You can also publish your Web pages to the Internet using the publish feature built into Web page editors. There are many resources available online for learning how to create basic Web pages using HTML.

REVIEW QUESTIONS

1. The first browser software was called:
   a. Mosaic
   b. Internet Explorer
   c. Netscape Navigator
   d. FrontPage

2. Which protocol allows you to upload files to a Web server?
   a. HTTP
   b. HTML
   c. FTP
   d. NNTP

3. Which markup language is widely used to create Web pages?
   a. Java
   b. JavaScript
   c. VBScript
   d. HTML

4. The server obtains the IP address of the Web site from:
   a. InterNIC
   b. Network Solutions
   c. a Web server
   d. a domain name server

5. Which IP address represents the local Web server?
   a. 127.0.0.1
   b. 1.0.0.127
   c. 1.27.0.1
   d. 27.0.0.1

6. What is the name of the local Web server?
   a. localserver
   b. mycomputer
   c. localhost
   d. hostname

7. What is the name of the service that displays Web pages?
   a. World Wide Web service
   b. File Transfer Protocol service
   c. Transaction service
   d. Web hosting service

8. What is the required protocol for clients and servers to be able to communicate on the Internet?
   a. TCP/IP
   b. DNS
   c. NetBeui
   d. IPX/SPX

9. Which TCP/IP utility provides the location of the hops that a packet travels across the Internet?
   a. ping
   b. router
   c. tracert
   d. Winipcfg

10. Which organization maintains the list of registrars who can sign up domain names?
    a. InterNIC
    b. Network Solutions
    c. ARPANET
    d. none of the above

11. Which pair of HTML tags is required at the beginning and ending of a Web page?

    a. <html></html>

    b. <head></head>

    c. <title></title>

    d. <http></http>

12. The meta tags are located in _____.

    a. the heading section

    b. the body section

    c. the title tags

    d. the http section

13. Which attribute will change the color of the Web page?

    a. color

    b. bgcolor

    c. background

    d. bkgroundcolor

14. How many heading tags are there?

    a. 1

    b. 3

    c. 6

    d. unlimited number

15. What is another name for an attribute?

    a. tag

    b. element

    c. property

    d. value

16. Which meta tag is used by search engines to catalog a Web site?

    a. title

    b. keywords

    c. refresh

    d. expires

17. Which is an example of an absolute URL?

    a. /images/bluedisk.gif

    b. bluedisk.gif

    c. ../../bluedisk.gif

    d. http://www.visualinterdev.org/images/bluedisk.gif Basic

1

18. Which of the following would correctly insert an image in a Web page?

    a. `<img name= "bluedisk.gif">`

    b. `<img href= "bluedisk.gif">`

    c. `<image = "bluedisk.gif">`

    d. `<img src = "bluedisk.gif">`

19. Which of the following would correctly create a hyperlink to a Web page?

    a. `<a href= "http://www.visualinterdev.org/ "> Click here </a>`

    b. `<a name= "http://www.visualinterdev.org/ "> Click here </a>`

    c. `<a name= "#default"> Click here </a>`

    d. `<a href= "# http://www.visualinterdev.org/ "> Click here </a>`

20. Which is the attribute for the anchor tag used to create a target?

    a. bookmark

    b. target

    c. name

    d. #

21. Which type of program can be used to create a Web page?

    a. Notepad

    b. Visual InterDev

    c. Dreamweaver

    d. all of the above

22. What software do you need to install before installing Personal Web Server?

    a. Client for Microsoft Networks

    b. FrontPage

    c. Visual InterDev

    d. America Online

23. Which of the following tags creates a bulleted list?

    a. `<ul>`

    b. `<li>`

    c. `<ol>`

    d. `<dd>`

24. Which of the following tags indents the section?

    a. `<br>`

    b. `<p>`

    c. `<indent>`

    d. `<blockquote>`

HANDS-ON PROJECTS

Project 1-1

In this project, you will use the ping utility to obtain the IP address of a Web site. Ping sends four packets out to the remote computer, and receives four responses if the remote computer is connected to the network.

1. Click **Start**, and then click **Run**.
2. Type **Command Prompt** in the text box if you are using a Windows 95 or Windows 98 computer. If you are using a Windows NT or Windows 2000 computer, type **cmd**. An MS-DOS window opens.
3. Type **ping** *www.visualinterdev.org*, and press **Enter**. You will see four responses that identify the IP address of the Web server, and the time that it took to receive the response. Read the IP address that is displayed. What is the IP address for the Web site?
4. Try to ping other sites (just once per site).
5. On some sites you will see "Request Timed Out". Write a short statement to explain what this response means.

Project 1-2

In this project, you will use the tracert utility program to trace the route of an Internet packet across hops on the Internet.

1. Click **Start**, and then click **Run**.
2. Type **Command Prompt** in the text box if you are using a Windows 95 or Windows 98 computer. If you are using a Windows NT or Windows 2000 computer, type **cmd**. An MS-DOS window opens.
3. Type **tracert** *www.visualinterdev.org*, and press **Enter**. You will see up to 30 responses that identify the IP address of each hop (or router) that the packet was delivered to and the time that it took to receive the response.
4. Read the IP address that is displayed. What is the IP address for the Web site? (*Hint*: It is the last IP address displayed, because it is the final destination of the packet.)
5. Repeat the above steps for the same Web site from another computer. Is the packet routed the same way? Why, or why not?
6. Try to tracert other sites (just once per site). Repeat the above steps for another Web site. Some hops will display "*". Explain what the asterisk means.

1

Project 1-3

In this project, you will create a basic Web page using basic HTML tags and a text editor. If there are tags or attributes you are unfamiliar with, read the related documentation at *http://www.w3.org/TR/html4/index/elements.html*.

1. Start Notepad. To do this on most systems, click **Start**, point to **Programs**, point to **Accessories**, then click **Notepad**. Your own shortcuts to the Notepad program may vary.

2. Type in the main HTML tags for the page, the heading section and the body section.

3. Type the title in the heading section. The title of the page should be **District 129**.

4. Type the heading on the page in the body section. The heading of the page should be **School Supplies for District 129**, and it should use the H1 heading tag.

5. Add a paragraph telling parents when they will need to purchase supplies. The paragraph should say **Please purchase:**.

6. Add a horizontal rule immediately below the heading on the page.

7. In the body section, type in a bulleted list of school supplies the parents need to purchase. The supply list will include **2 blue pens**, **4 pencils**, **6 notebooks**, **1 pencil case**, and **1 eraser**.

8. Add another horizontal rule immediately below the list on the page.

9. Add a link to an office supply store. The text displayed will be **Click here to visit our office supply store partner.** The link will take you to *http://www.officemax.com*.

10. Save the Web page as **schoolsupplylist.htm**. Be sure to save the filename in quotes. Save the page to your data directory.

11. Copy or FTP the file to your Web server. This can be your local Web server in wwwroot, or a Web server on the Internet.

12. View your Web page in a browser.

Project 1-4

In this project, you will use a text editor to create a Web page that uses tag attributes. If there are tags or attributes you are unfamiliar with, read the related documentation at *http://www.w3.org/TR/html4/index/elements.html*.

1. Open Notepad.

2. Type in the main HTML tags.

3. Type the title in the heading section. The title of the page should be **District 129**.

4. Modify the background property for the page. The new color of the Web page should be **#99FF99**. Change the default text color for the Web page to **#800000**.

5. Type the heading on the page in the body section. The heading of the page should be **School Fees for District 129**. The heading should use the h1 heading tag. Modify the h1 tag to use the align attribute. Change the alignment to **center**.

6. Use the font tag to modify the h1 tag above to use the different color. Change the color to **#000080**.

7. Add a horizontal rule. Modify the horizontal rule tag so that the width is **50%** of the window size. (Use the width attribute.) The thickness of the horizontal rule is **4**. (Use the size attribute.) The color of the horizontal rule is **#800000**. (Use the color attribute.)

8. Add a paragraph that states **Please pay the school fees by October 1st.** Modify the alignment to center with the align attribute.

9. Modify the font with the font tag. Change the color to **#000080**. Change the face of the font to **Verdana** using the face attribute.

10. Create a table with the table tag. Modify the table attributes. The table border should be **0**. Use the border attribute. Spacing between cells should be **0**. Use the cellspacing attribute. Padding between cells and the contents of the cell should be **5**. Use the cellpadding attribute. The width of the table should be **300** pixels. The table should be aligned in the middle of the page. Use the align attribute to center the table. Change the background color to **FFFF99**, using the bgcolor attribute.

11. Create a row using the table row tag. Use both the opening and closing table row tags, **<tr></tr>**.

12. Create a table cell inside the table row pair of tags. Type the fee description between the two cell tags. The fee description is **PTA dues**. Modify the cell using the cell attributes. Change the width to **155** pixels, using the width attribute.

13. Create a second table cell inside the pair of table row tags.

14. Type the amount of the fee, which is **$5.00**, between the two cell tags. Change the width to **93** pixels, using the width attribute. Change the alignment of the text to **right**, using the align attribute.

15. Create a second, third, fourth, and fifth row, using the table row tags.

16. Create two cells in each row. Use **<td></td><td></td>** within each row.

17. Populate each cell according to the following list. The description is placed in the first cell, and the fee in the second cell.

    a. **Book Fee, $75.00**

    b. **Room Supplies, $10.00**

    c. **Field Trip Fee, $10.00**

    d. **Total, $100.00**

18. Modify the first cell in each row. Change the width to **155** pixels, using the width attribute.

19. Modify the second cell in each row. Change the width to **93** pixels, using the width attribute. Change the alignment of the text to **right**, using the align attribute.

20. Add a paragraph that is center-aligned and that says **Click here to visit our school textbook partner.** Link the phrase "textbook partner" to another Web site. Use the HREF attribute of the anchor tag to link to ***http://www.course.com***.

21. Save the Web page as **schoolfees.htm**. Be sure to save the filename in quotes. Save the page to your data directory.

22. Copy or FTP the file to your Web server.

23. View the Web page in a browser.

Project 1-5

In this project, you will visit the InterNIC Web site at *http://www.InterNIC.net* to learn more about registrars and domain name registration.

1. Open your browser and go to the InterNIC home page at *http://www.InterNIC.net*.

2. Click **The Accredited Registrar Directory** link to view the registrar list for the .com, .net, and .org domains.

3. Click **List by Language Supported**.

4. Scroll down the list to view the registrars that support languages other than English.

5. Scroll down the list to view the registrars who support registering domain names in French.

6. Click the **Back** button.

7. Click **Listing by Location of Registrar.** Which registrars are located in Canada? Which registrars are located in the U.S.? Discuss why there are more registrars in the U.S. than in any other country.

8. Click the **Back** button.

9. Click the **Whois** link at the top of the page to use the InterNIC whois utility.

10. Type in **shea-family.com** and click **Submit Query**.

11. What registrar maintains the domain registration for this Web site?

Project 1-6

In this project, you will create a Web page that will redirect the client to another Web site, using the meta tag.

1. Open Notepad and type in the main HTML tags.

2. Type in the title of the page, **Client-Side Redirection Using the Meta Tag**.

3. Add a meta tag in the heading section. Modify the meta tag to use the refresh command. The URL that the page should be redirected to is ***http://www.course.com***. The number of seconds that it should take to redirect the client is **5**.

4. Add a heading to the page. The heading should say **This page is being redirected to the Course Technology Web site**. Use the heading 2 tag to format the heading. Modify the heading 2 tag to center-align with the align attribute.

5. Add a hyperlink below the heading. The hyperlink should say **Click here to go directly to the Course Technology Web site**. The hyperlink should be to *http://www.course.com*.

6. Save the page in your data directory as **courselink.htm**.

7. Copy or FTP your page to your folder.

8. View the Web page in your browser.

CASE PROJECTS

Murphy's Office Supply: Registering Domain Names

You have been hired by Murphy's Office Supply to create their Internet Web site. They have not yet registered their domain name. Visit at least five of the registrars. Prepare a short report for your boss on the process for registering a domain name. The report should include:

- Information about InterNIC and the registrars researched, including the URL to their home pages

- A comparison of the services offered by the various registrars

- A comparison of the cost and duration for which domain names can be registered

- A comparison of the customer support available

- At least five domain names that are not yet reserved

Create your report in a Web page format. Alter the presentation of the Web page using various tags and attributes. Save the Web page in your data directory, using the name registrars.htm. View your Web page in your browser. Print your Web page.

Houston Electronics: Submitting a Web Site to Search Engines

You are responsible for your company Web site at Houston Electronics. Your boss has asked you why the company has not been listed in the major Web search engines. You inform your boss that search engines use keywords to catalogue Web sites. Go to five major search engines. Prepare a report describing how the search engine catalogues your Web site. Your report should include:

- At least three hosting service provider lists

- A list of the five major search engines researched and the URL of their home pages

- Information about how to submit your site to be indexed and catalogued. Which Web page contains the submission forms?

- Information about how often your site can be resubmitted

- Information about how the site is indexed, such as by keywords, title tag, domain name, etc.

- The cost of the index service

- The time that it takes to appear in the index

- A list of 20 keywords that would increase your chance of appearing in the search engines

Prepare your report in a Web page. Alter the presentation of the Web page using various tags and attributes. Save the Web page in your data directory as metakeywords.htm. View the Web page in your browser and then print the page.

Johnson Mills: Selecting a Hosting Service Provider

Your company, Johnson Mills, has decided to host their corporate Web site outside of the company. You are given the assignment of locating a hosting service provider. You research and compare five hosting service providers. In your report, you should provide the following information:

- A list of the five hosting service providers researched and the URL of their home pages

- The cost of Web site hosting at each of the five HSPs

- Features supported at each price level at each HSP

- A list identifying the strengths and weaknesses of each HSP

Select one of the hosting providers. Write a paragraph describing how you made your selection. Prepare your report as a Web page. Alter the presentation of the Web page using various tags and attributes. Save the Web page in your data directory as comparehsp.htm. View the Web page in a browser, and then print the Web page.

Global Media: Internet Resources

You work for a computer training company called Global Media. You have decided to create a Web page that contains links to Web developer resources. Create a Web page using Notepad or a Web page development tool. Create a list of URLs related to the Internet and topics discussed in this chapter. Arrange the URLs by topic. Use a list or table to format the Web page. Provide the name of the Web site, the URL, and a short description of the Web site. Alter the presentation of the Web page using various tags and attributes. Save the Web page in your directory as internetlinks.htm. View the Web page in a browser, and then print the page.

Freebird Hosting: Customer Support

You work for a Web hosting company called Freebird Hosting. Your customers are unfamiliar with many of the Internet terms and phrases that you often use in company brochures and reports. To improve customer support, create a Web page that lists and defines common Internet terms. Use a list or table to format the list of terms. Be sure to provide a definition for each term. Alter the presentation of the Web page using various tags and attributes. Save the Web page in your data directory as internetterms.htm. View the page in a browser, and then print the page.

Freebird Hosting: Troubleshooting

One of your Web hosting customers calls to tell you that your Web site is not working. The domain name is www.visualinterdev.org. You must try to figure out what the problem is. Test your Web site from your desktop and prepare a report for your customer. Include in your report:

- The programs that you will use, and the reasons why you will use them

- Reasons why the customer might not be able to view his Web site from his client

- Reasons why the Web site might not be connected to the Internet

- The primary and secondary DNS servers that are listed in the registry

- The name and InterNIC handle for the technical contact person for the Web site

- The IP address of the Web site

- The IP addresses of the servers that the Web page request must hop across to get to the Web site

Create your report in a Web page. Alter the presentation of the Web page using various tags and attributes. Save your Web page in your data directory as testconnection.htm. View your Web page in your browser, and then print the Web page.

Bike Power: Selecting a Web Page Editor

Your boss at Bike Power has requested that you select a Web page editor with which to create the corporate intranet Web site. Your internal network is running the Windows NT operating system with the Internet Information Server Web server. You need to evaluate the features of at least four Web page editors and prepare a report for the Web team. In your report:

- Include the programs that you researched, including URLs to their Web sites.

- Compare the features that are supported or are not supported across browsers.

- Rank the features according to their importance, with 1 being the highest.

Use one Web page editor to create a Web page that displays your findings. Save the report in your data directory as webtools.htm. Post your Web page to your directory. View the Web page and then print it out.

2

SCRIPT INTEGRATION

In this chapter you will:

♦ Identify the differences between client-side scripts and server-side scripts

♦ Identify the major scripting languages, JavaScript, Jscript, VBScript, and ECMAScript

♦ Add client-side scripts to a Web page

♦ Add server-side scripts to a Web page

♦ Add comments to client-side and server-side scripts

♦ Locate Internet resources about scripting technologies

In Chapter 1, you learned that Web pages are created using a document layout language known as Hypertext Markup Language (HTML). Related Web pages are grouped together and called a Web application. HTML is used to produce static Web pages, which contain fixed content. Today, individuals and businesses require dynamic Web applications. Dynamic Web applications enable users to interact with them. Examples of dynamic Web applications include shopping carts, membership databases, online catalogues, and personalized Web sites. Today, Internet users can plan a trip to Ireland all online, from browsing car rental options to making reservations at hotels, and even making airline reservations. In this chapter you will learn how to create basic scripts, which are the foundation for creating dynamic Web applications.

SCRIPTING TECHNOLOGIES

Technologies such as cascading style sheets (CSS) and scripts allow Web programmers to create dynamic Web pages. A series of commands that belong to a **scripting language**, such as JavaScript and VBScript (also called Visual Basic Scripting Edition), can be assembled into a **script** and embedded within the Web page. Scripting languages use a program called an **interpreter** to translate the script code into an executable format. Scripts can be run on a Web server or in the browser on the client's computer. Scripts that are run on a Web server are called **server-side scripts**. **Client-side scripts** are scripts that run in the browser; they are interpreted when a browser downloads the Web page.

The World Wide Web Consortium (W3C, *http://www.w3c.org*) is responsible for standardizing HTML, CSS, and other Web technologies. The latest version of HTML, HTML 4.01, is the standard used throughout this text. Information on all HTML versions can be found at the W3C site, at *http://www.w3.org/TR/html4/*.

By using scripts, you can add interactivity to Web pages. This interactivity can be simple, for example displaying an alert message when a user enters the Web page, or it can be complex, for example validating and processing a form. By adding scripts to your HTML code, you can establish and store variables that work with data from your page. Most Web sites use some form of scripting to validate any data entered by users, and to communicate with users. For instance, if a page requests numeric data from a user and the user inserts text, a well-executed script will catch the error before a server request is made, thus saving time and computer resources.

CLIENT-SIDE SCRIPTING

When a browser receives a Web page from a Web server, the browser interprets the HTML code and renders the Web page. A pair of script tags separates client-side script from HTML code. The script tag `<script>` identifies the beginning of a script, and `</script>` identifies the end of the script. If a script command is found outside of these script tags, the browser displays an error message, and the Web page is not displayed correctly. A scripting engine built into the browser processes client-side scripts. Figure 2-1 illustrates how client-side scripts are processed. When a Web browser identifies a client-side script, the browser passes the script to the **script engine**, which executes the script as the page is being loaded. After the script is executed, the Web browser continues to interpret HTML code until it encounters another pair of script tags. The Web page can have many scripts interspersed within HTML code, as long as script tags delimit each script.

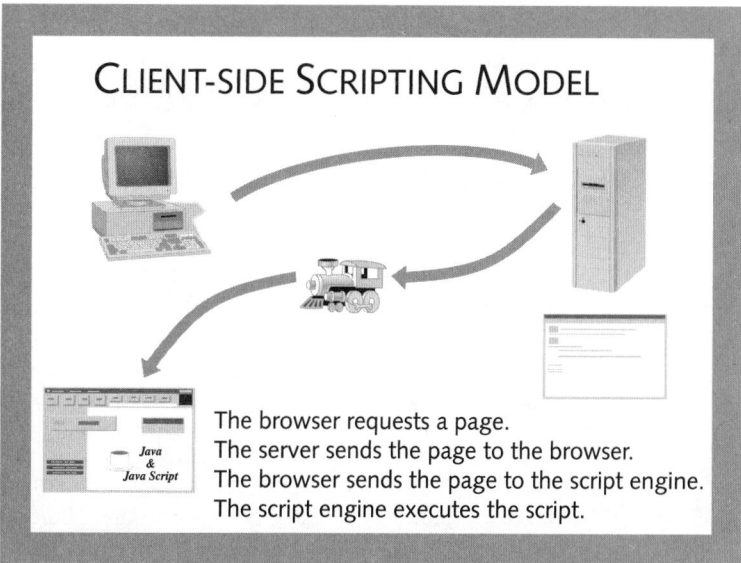

Figure 2-1   The client-side scripting model

Client-side Scripting Languages

Several scripting languages can be used to create client-side scripts. You can identify the script language with the language attribute. If the language attribute is absent , the default client script language is used. The most common client script languages are JavaScript, Jscript, and VBScript. The default client-side script for most browsers is JavaScript. Because the end user can change the default language for client-side scripting, you should always use the language attribute.

The language attribute has the following syntax:

<script language = "languageName">

JavaScript

JavaScript is the most commonly used client-side scripting language because it is supported by most browsers. It was first called LiveScript and later renamed JavaScript. There are several versions of JavaScript. Microsoft modified JavaScript and named their version **JScript**. (Note that neither JScript nor JavaScript is the same as Java. Java is a complete programming language, not a scripting language.) You can specify which version of JavaScript you are using by appending the version number to the language attribute. For example, to specify JScript version 3.0, write `<script language = "JScript3.0">`.

VBScript

VBScript is a scaled-down version of the Microsoft programming language Visual Basic. VBScript was designed to be a fast, portable interpreter for use in Web browsers and applications. To specify VBScript, write `<script language = "VBScript">` or `<script language = "VBS">`.

ECMAScript

All Web browsers do not support all scripting languages. Every scripting language must have its own interpreter to translate its commands. Microsoft Internet Explorer has an interpreter for VBScript and JScript. On the other hand, Netscape Navigator only provides a JavaScript interpreter, and therefore does not natively support VBScript. Cross-browser client-side scripting is difficult, time-consuming, and expensive. You can write scripts that detect which browser the client is using.

These compatibility issues led to the creation of a new scripting standard known as **ECMA-262**. The ECMA-262 standard defines the ECMAScript scripting language, a cross-platform programming language that is supported by both Microsoft and Netscape. ECMAScript was based on early versions of JScript and JavaScript. ECMAScript is only supported for client-side scripting. Currently there is no cross-platform standard for server-side scripting. While both Netscape and Microsoft have agreed to support the standard, it is likely that they will still continue to provide browser-specific features within their individual products.

 The ECMA standards are created by an independent organization called the European Computer Manufacturers Association (ECMA) (*http://www.ecma.ch/*). ECMA is an association that specializes in standardizing information technologies.

Microsoft's implementation of ECMA-262 resulted in JScript. JScript version 3.0 is 100 percent compliant with ECMA-262 and is supported by Internet Explorer version 4. JScript version 5.0 will be compliant with the second edition of ECMA-262. Netscape updated JavaScript to accommodate the new ECMA-262 standard. JavaScript version 1.3 is compatible with Netscape versions 4.06–4.5 and is 100 percent compliant with the ECMA-262 standard. ECMAScript, JScript, and JavaScript all support the ECMA-262 standards.

Inserting a Client-side Script into a Web Page

Scripts can be placed in the head or body sections of the Web page. If you place a script in the head section of the Web page, the script engine interprets that script before it interprets scripts located in the body section. When a script is at the end of the Web page, the Web page loads faster, and users can continue viewing the page while the script engine interprets the script.

In the following sample code, the string "Hello World" is written to the Web page using HTML. This code is saved in a Web page named helloworld.htm. The client-side script also writes "Hello World" and the HTML heading tags onto the Web page, using the **document.write** method. The write method writes the string passed in the parentheses to the browser. The string can contain text and HTML code. The write method belongs to the document object. The document object gives you access to the properties and methods available within the Web page. Both methods will produce the same output on the Web page, as shown in Figure 2-2. The following sample code shows a client-side script that displays a string saying "Hello World".

```
<html>
<head><title>Hello World</title></head>
<body>
<h1>Hello World</h1>
<script language = "JavaScript1.3">
     document.write "<h1>Hello World</h1>";
</script>
</body>
</html>
```

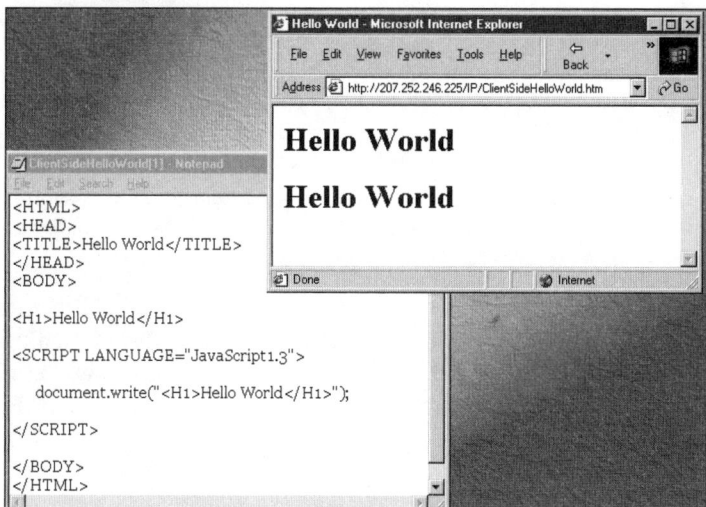

Figure 2-2   Output of the client-side script Hello World example

If a script contains multiple JavaScript statements on the same line, you must use a semicolon after each statement. If there is only one JavaScript statement on a single line, the semicolon is recommended, but not required.

HTML and VBScript are not case sensitive, but JavaScript is. When referring to the document object in your code, do not capitalize the letter d. `Document.Write` is not correct and will produce an error message in the browser. The correct syntax is `document.write`.

External Client-side Scripts

You can place client-side scripts in a document separate from the HTML document. This allows you to reuse scripts across multiple Web pages simply by including a pointer to the script source file.

Creating the Script Source File   You can create the script source file with a simple text editor such as Notepad. In this example, the script source file called `javaSource.js` creates the Web page heading. You will often have to nest quotes within scripts. You can use single quotes around attribute values when they are within double quotes. Note that the script source file extension must end in `.js`. Any valid JavaScript statement can appear within a script source file.

```
document.writeln("<h2 align='center'>");
document.writeln("<font color='#800000'>");
document.writeln("Office Supply Store");
document.writeln("</font>");
document.writeln("<p><font color='#800000'>");
document.writeln("Today is");
d = new Date();
document.writeln(d);
document.writeln("</font></p></h2>");
```

The writeln method performs the same function as the write method, but also appends a carriage return after the line of text. The writeln method is useful when combined with the <PRE> tag to display code in a more legible manner.

Creating the Web Page   The Web page calls the script source file, using the source attribute of the script tag. The location of the script source file can be identified using a relative or absolute address. The following Web page, `javawebpage.htm`, was created with Notepad and includes an external script source file named `javaSource.js`. Figure 2-3 shows how this page looks in a browser.

```
<html>
<head>
<title>Client-side Script Sample</title>
<script language="JavaScript1.3" src="javaSource.js">
</script>
</head>
<body bgColor="#FFCC99">
<p><font color="#800000">
<b>Welcome to our store!</b>
</font></p>
</body>
</html>
```

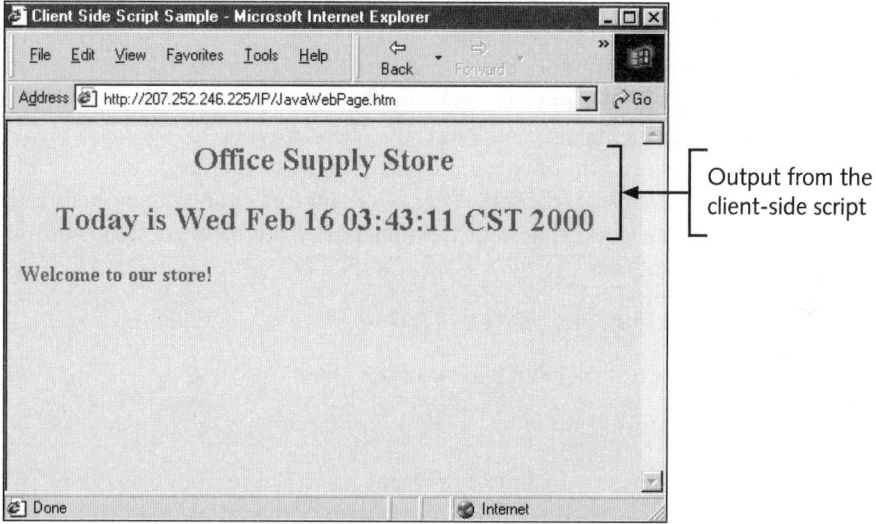

Figure 2-3   Output of a client-side script

 You should always save HTML files using quotation marks around the complete filename, for example "javawebpage.htm". This instructs the program to save the file as a Web page, not a text document.

When you view the Web page in a browser, note that the embedded JavaScript code is not readily displayed in the source code view. However, it is still available; users need only type the script source address in the browser location box to download the script source file. Therefore, external client-side scripts should not be used to hide information from users.

Viewing Client-side Scripts

Visitors can view the client-side script by viewing the Web page source code. To view the client-side script in a Web page using Microsoft Internet Explorer:

1. Log on to the Internet and start your Web browser. (You must be online to view this Web page.)

2. Type *http://www.visualinterdev.org/ip/samples/chapter2/javawebpage.htm* in the location box.

3. Click the **Go** button to the right of the location box, or press **Enter**.

4. Click **View** on the menu bar.

5. Click **Source** to open the source code in Notepad or the default text editor. Note that the client script code is visible.

6. Click **File** on the Notepad menu bar when you are finished viewing the source code.

7. Click **Exit** to close the source code page and exit Notepad.

Inserting Comments into Client-side Scripts

Comments can be used to support older browsers that cannot recognize client-side script. To comment out the entire script code, you can place the code inside a pair of HTML comment tags. Adding comment tags will cause the Web browser to disregard any client-side code within the script tags. The opening comment tag, `<!--`, appears immediately after the opening script tag. The closing comment tag, `-->`, appears immediately before the closing script tag. The following code fragment demonstrates how to encapsulate the script code within HTML comment tags.

```
<script language = "JavaScript1.3">
<!--
document.write "<h1>Hello World</h1>"
//-->
</script>
```

You can also use comments to include important information about the code. Comments often describe the purpose of the code, or explain any unusual methods that are used. The comment symbols for JavaScript and VBScript are different. To add a single-line comment using JavaScript, start the comment line with a double slash, `//`. To add a single-line comment using VBScript, start the comment with a single quote, `'`. The following script fragment illustrates how a single-line client-side comment is used to document a script.

```
<script language = "JavaScript1.3">
document.write "<h1>Hello World</h1>"
// The document.write method is case sensitive
// Do not use Document.Write or Document.write
</script>
```

If you have several lines of comments, you can format the entire comment block using one pair of tags. The beginning of a multiple-line comment in JavaScript begins with `/*` and the last line ends with `*/`.

Multiple-line comments are often used to document long scripts that contain complex code. Using comments not only makes it easier to maintain the code, but also provides other programmers with information about how the code works. The following is a sample of what a programmer might include to document a script.

```
<script language = "JavaScript1.3">
document.write "<h1>Hello World</h1>"
/*
Name:     Login Script
Purpose:  Verifies the user name & password
Author:   Bridie Shea
```

```
Created:   2/1/2001
Modified:  2/27/2001
Platform: Works with IE 5.0 and above
Inputs:    Username, Password from login.htm
Returns:   blnLogin identifies login status
*/
</script>
```

SERVER-SIDE SCRIPTING

Server-side scripts can be used to add interactivity to a Web page, and to allow the Web page or Web application to interact with other programs on the server. Like client-side scripts, server-side scripts are part of the Web document, but they are executed on the server, rather than in the client's browser. A scripting engine installed on the server interprets server-side scripts. Figure 2-4 illustrates how the scripting engine runs the server scripts. After the scripting engine runs the script, the scripting engine sends the output of the script back to the browser. While server- and client-side scripts can coexist in the Web document, only HTML code and client-side script code are sent to the browser. Server-side script source code never appears in the browser.

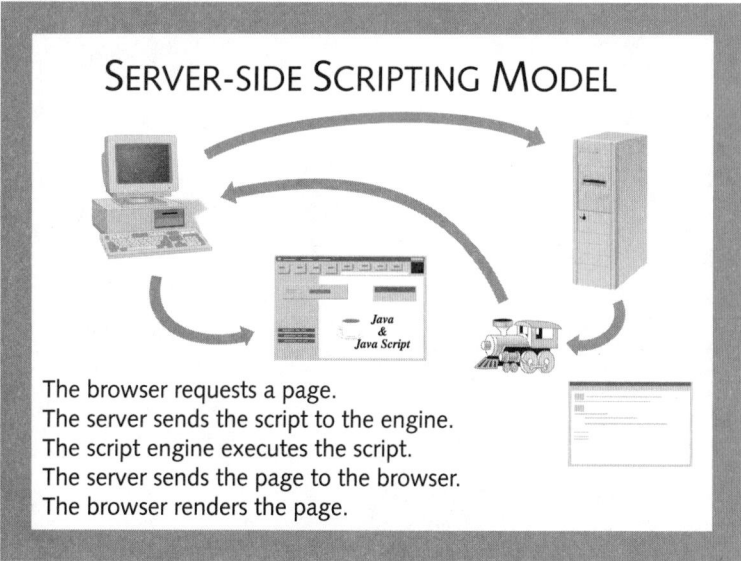

Figure 2-4   The server-side script model

There is no scripting standard available for server-side scripts. Server-side script engines are vendor-specific. Netscape supports JavaScript version 1.4 on the Netscape Enterprise Server. Microsoft supports JScript version 3, and VBScript on Internet Information and Personal

Web Server. Although JavaScript may be used on a Microsoft Web server, VBScript is the default server-side script language. You must view an ASP page on a Web server. The Web server permissions for the Web page must be set to read and script.

Active Server Pages

Microsoft's implementation of server scripting technology is referred to as **Active Server Pages** (**ASP**). All Active Server Pages must have an `.asp` file extension. This differentiates the ASP file from an `.htm` or `.html` file. When the client requests a file with an `.asp` extension, the Web server knows to process the server-side scripts on the Web server and send the results to the client. As illustrated in Figure 2-5, the Web server sends the request to the Active Server Page engine, which parses and processes the server-side scripts. The Active Server Page engine is called `asp.dll` and can be found at `C:\Windows\System\InetSrv`.

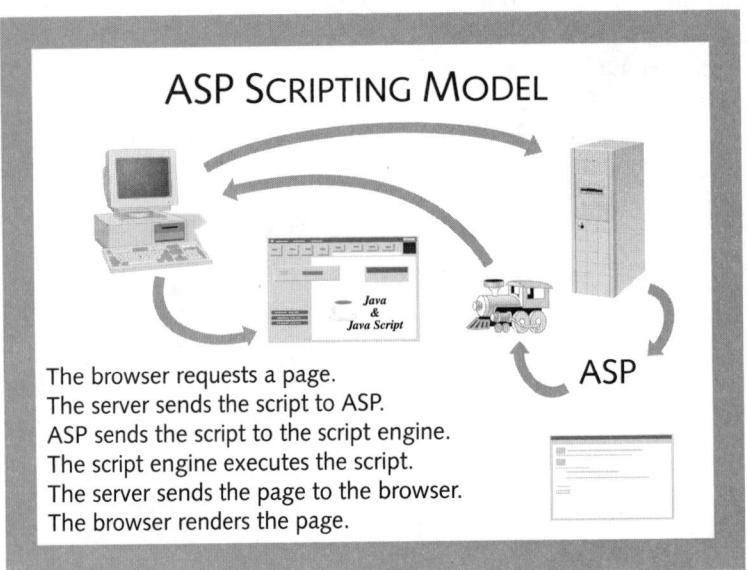

Figure 2-5   The ASP model

The ASP Model

ASP allows you access to all the features of server-side scripting as well as additional built-in objects from the **ASP Object Model**. The six built-in objects within the ASP Object Model are request, response, application, session, server, and objectContext. Built-in objects, such as the request object, allow you to use ASP to obtain the results of a form. The results of the form can be displayed back to the browser using the write method of the response object.

Figure 2-6 lists some of the benefits of ASP. The server object allows the server-side script to communicate with other programs on the server. Therefore, the Web server can do many things, for example interact with databases and send customized e-mail from a Web page. The process of creating new objects on the server is called **instantiation**. For example, the mail server that comes with Internet Information Server contains a mail object that can be used to send e-mail from a Web page. The server-side script can instantiate a mail object on the server. The new mail object can be used to automatically send e-mail from the Web page. Another ASP object called the database access component allows server scripts to communicate with database servers. The database access component can be used to display and modify information stored within a database program such as Access 2000, SQL Server, or Oracle. Because the script is processed on the server, you can hide the business logic and scripting methods used to access the database. Active Server Pages allows you to develop Web pages that are interactive, and that can interact with other programs on the server.

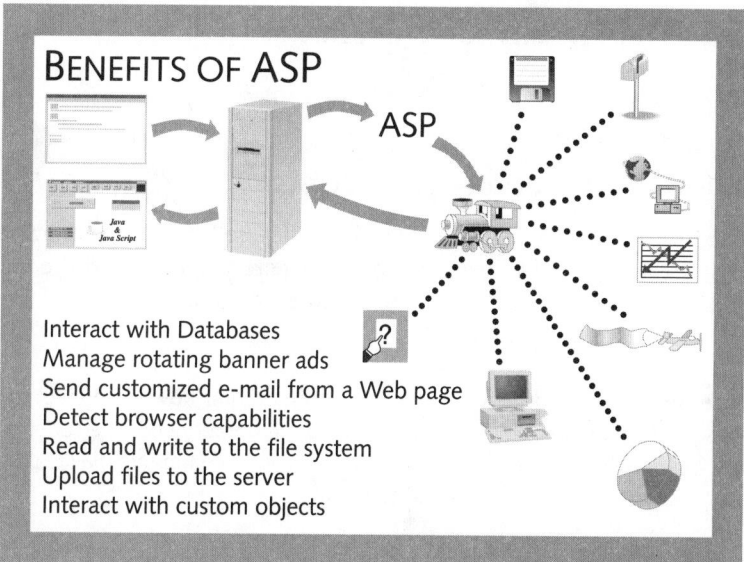

BENEFITS OF ASP

ASP

Interact with Databases
Manage rotating banner ads
Send customized e-mail from a Web page
Detect browser capabilities
Read and write to the file system
Upload files to the server
Interact with custom objects

Figure 2-6   Benefits of ASP

Inserting a Server-side Script into a Web Page

There are two ways to indicate that a script is to be interpreted on the server. The first way is to add the `runat = server` attribute within the beginning `<script>` tag. This technique is known as **block scripting**. All code enclosed within the block script tag is interpreted on the server. The following code fragment illustrates how to create a server-side script that uses the write method to display "Hello World". Note that the response object on the server has a similar function to the document object on the client. Both objects contain a method called write, which writes text, HTML, and client-side script to the browser.

```
<script language = "VBScript" runat = "server>"
response.write "<h1>Hello World/h1>"
</script>
```

The second method you can use to identify server scripts is **inline** scripting. All code enclosed within the inline script tags <% ...%> is interpreted on the server. The inline tags do not have to appear on separate lines from the script code. However, if there are multiple lines of code, you should separate the inline tags from the code, to make the code easier to locate when you are debugging your scripts. If a page contains a mixture of inline VBScript and block scripts, the inline scripts are all processed first, before any of the block scripts. You can place server-side scripts in the head section of the Web page. However, because server-side scripts are executed on the server, you cannot improve performance in the browser by placing server-side scripts at the bottom of the Web page! Scripts can be located anywhere in the page. The code below illustrates how to display the code shown above using the inline script tags.

```
<% response.write "<h1>Hello World/h1>" %>
```

Inserting Comments into Server-side Scripts

Comments inserted into server-side scripts, like the code itself, are not viewable from the browser. All server-side scripts and server-side comments are stripped from the code before the HTML page is sent to the client. Server-side comments are often used to document the server-side script.

Sometimes server-side code that is used repeatedly, such as how to connect to a database, is commented out. Later, when the programmer needs the code, it is simple to remove the comment tag. Using server-side comments makes the server-side code easier to maintain and to modify.

The syntax for VBScript and JavaScript comments is the same regardless of where the script is interpreted. For example, you indicate a single VBScript server-side comment with a single apostrophe before the comment ('), and a single JavaScript server-side comment with a double forward slash (//). The following is a sample of a server-side script that uses inline script tags and server-side comments.

```
<%
response.write "<h1>Hello World</h1>"
' This sample uses response.write for server scripts
' instead of document.write
' which is used for client scripts
%>
```

Server-side Include Files

Sometimes it's convenient to place server scripts in a separate document. External script files on the server are called server-side include (SSI) files. **Server-side include files** allow the programmer to reuse code for multiple Web pages. Web page elements that are often reused include headers, footers, style information, standard logos, and graphics. Server-side include files can contain server-side scripts as well as HTML and client-side scripts. The included file will be included before the ASP engine interprets any other scripts on the page. All statements in the file will be included. Examples of server-side scripts that are often placed in SSI files are database constants and database connection strings. Both of these server-side include files will be described further in Chapter 12. Other common SSI files include headers, footers, and any content that is frequently reused.

Creating the Server-side Include File

The server-side include file can be created with a simple text editor such as Notepad. This file can contain a mixture of scripts, text, and HTML, and is usually saved with an `.inc` or `.asp` file extension and stored in an `/inc`, `/scripts`, or `/asp-bin` directory. The following server-side include file, called `head.inc`, creates a header file, which will be included at the top of the ASP page. The header file identifies the store name using HTML, and the date using inline server-side script.

```
<body bgColor = "#FFCC99">
<h1 align = "center">
<font color = "#800000"><b>
Office Supply Store
</b></font></h1>
<h2 align = "center">
<font color = "#800000"><b>
Today is : <% = Date() %>
</b></font></h2>
```

The date is written using a shortcut for the response.write method. When a single line of code is used, the equal sign (=) can be used to replace the keywords response.write.

Calling the SSI File from the ASP Page

The ASP page calls the server-side include file using the keyword include. The location of the server-side include file is identified by the file attribute or the virtual attribute. The file attribute is used to identify the physical path to the server-side include file. The absolute or relative path may be used. When the physical path is identified, you must use the backward slashes to indicate the path. You can use DOS-based dot notation (such as `..\..\scripts\head.inc`) to identify the relative path to the server-side include file.

The virtual attribute is used to identify the virtual path to the file. The virtual path always starts at the root of the Web. No drive letter is indicated, and forward slashes are used to indicate the path. The first slash represents the directory off the root of the Web site.

In the sample below, the server-side include file and the ASP page are located in the same directory. The Web page is saved as `javawebpage.asp`. The Web page must be saved with an `.asp` file extension.

```
<html>
<head>
<title>Client-side Script Sample</title>
</head>
<!--#include file="head.inc"-->
<p><font color="#800000">
<b>Welcome to our store!</b>
</font></p>
</body>
</html>
```

Line Continuance

You can break a long statement into multiple lines in VBScript to make your code more readable, using the line continuation character, which is a space followed by an underscore. Although VBScript is more commonly used with server-side scripting, you can use this technique for both client- and server-side VBScripts. You cannot put anything else, including comments, after the line continuation character. The following sample code illustrates how line continuance may be used.

```
<%
response.write _
    "<h1>Hello World</h1>"
%>
```

WHICH DO YOU USE? CLIENT- OR SERVER-SIDE SCRIPTS?

A Web application consists of several related Web documents, which may include HTML files, ASP pages, and server-side include files. Today, most Web applications use a combination of client-side script and server-side script. The type of Web browsers the client uses, the type of Web server, and the Web application itself will determine which scripting techniques you should use.

For example, if your Web server requires that you save your Web pages with .htm or .html file extensions, you will have to use client-side scripting. The client's browser will also determine which scripting language to use. If you are building a Web application for a company's intranet, and all employees are required to use Internet Explorer, then you can use VBScript. But if your Web application must be accessible on both browsers, then you must use JavaScript for client-side scripting.

If the Web application will be located on a Microsoft server, you can use server-side script. While the Microsoft Web server supports both JScript and VBScript, you are more likely to use VBScript with Active Server Pages for server-side processing. If you are using a non-Microsoft Web server, you will likely be using server-side JavaScript.

SCRIPTING TOOLS

There is a variety of Web development programs that support client- and server-side script. Although client- and server-side script can be written in Notepad or any text editor, using a Web development tool can help to increase your productivity. Most new versions of Web editors support client-side script and Active Server Pages. Some of the major Web page editors that currently support Active Server Pages include Drumbeat 2000, Dreamweaver 3.0, FrontPage 2000, Visual InterDev 6.0, and the Microsoft Script Editor. You can use Web developer tools such as FrontPage 2000 to create Web pages and manage Web sites. Figure 2-7 shows the FrontPage 2000 Web page editor with a client-side script. FrontPage 2000 allows you to graphically edit your Web pages, or to edit the source code directly.

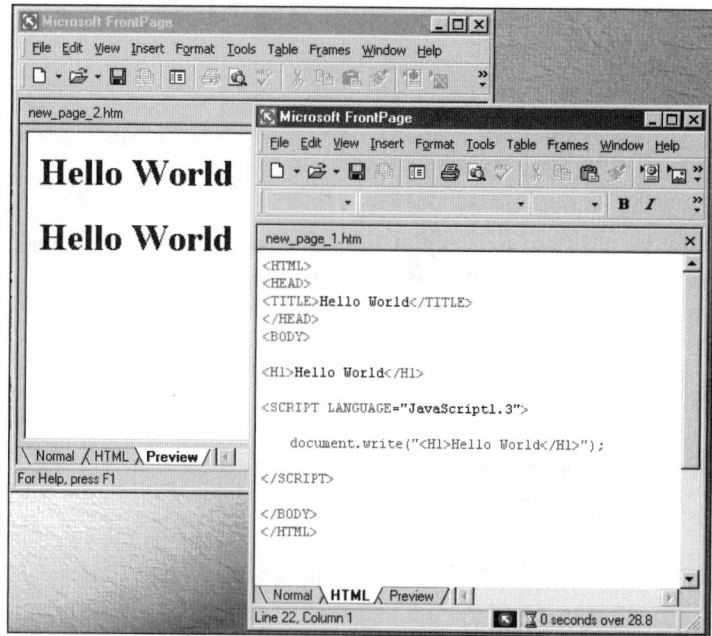

Figure 2-7 The FrontPage 2000 editor with a client-side script

Integrated into FrontPage 2000 is a Script Editor. Figure 2-8 shows the Microsoft Script Editor with a client-side script. The Script Editor is designed exclusively for adding, editing, and debugging scripts, and can be used with JScript, JavaScript, and VBScript. The Script Editor is available with Visual Studio 6.0 and FrontPage 2000. While the Script Editor allows you to create and edit individual files, FrontPage 2000 and Visual InterDev help you create and manage entire Web applications.

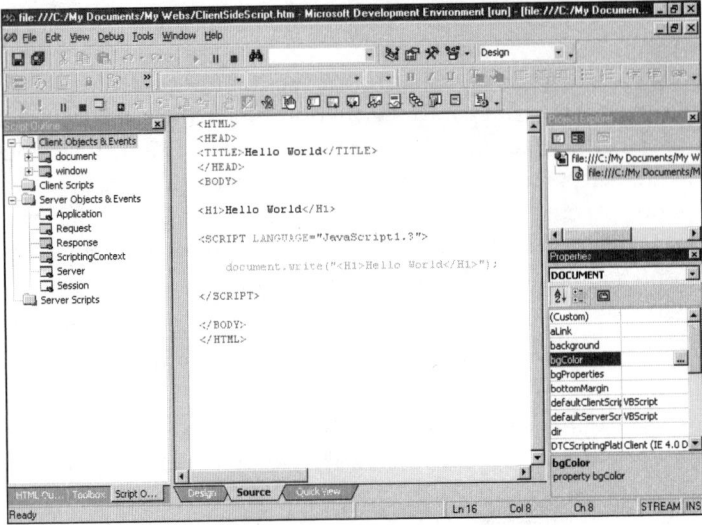

Figure 2-8   The Script Editor with a client-side script

Programming
Tip

The Script Editor, Visual InterDev, and Visual Studio use the **Microsoft Integrated Development Environment**, which provides a common user interface for programmers who are creating and editing Web pages and ASP pages. Figure 2-9 shows the Visual InterDev Editor with a server-side script. You will notice similarities among the Script Editor, Visual Studio, and Visual InterDev, because these programs use the same developing environment.

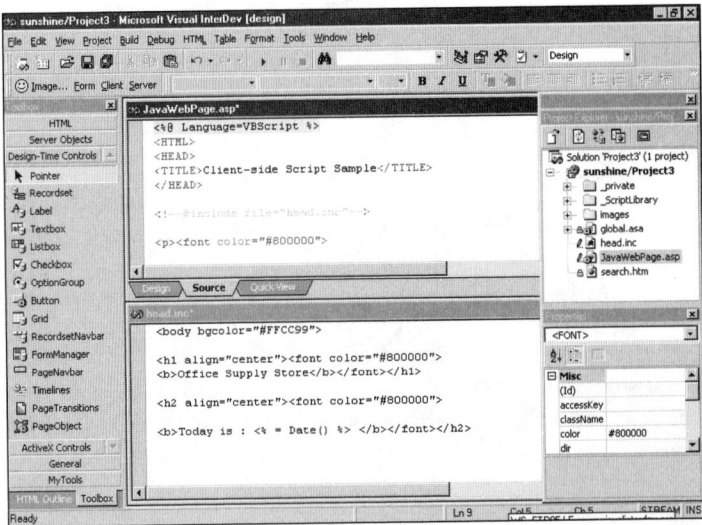

Figure 2-9   The Visual InterDev Editor with a server-side script

INTERNET SCRIPT RESOURCES

There are many resources on the Internet that can help you learn more about scripting languages. Among them are an online reference manual from Netscape describing JavaScript 1.2, located at *http://developer.netscape.com/docs/manuals/communicator/jsref/index.htm*, and a site containing information about JavaScript version 1.4, located at *http://developer.iplanet.com/support/faqs/champions/javascript.html#1-4*.

Microsoft created the Microsoft Developer Network (MSDN) to provide support to developers. The MSDN Library consists of a variety of resources for developers, such as sample code, documentation, technical articles, books, and reference guides. In addition to Visual InterDev, the MSDN Library contains information on many Microsoft products, including FrontPage, Visual InterDev, and Internet Information Server. Figure 2-10 shows the MSDN Online Library, which contains resources for both VBScript and JScript. The entire MSDN Online Library is available at *http://msdn.microsoft.com/library/default.asp*.

To access the MSDN Library on the Internet:

1. Connect to the Internet if you are not already connected, then click the **Start** menu.

2. Point to **Programs**.

3. Click **Internet Explorer** to open the Internet Explorer browser.

4. Type **http://msdn.microsoft.com/library** in the Address text box, and then press **Enter** to go to the MSDN Online Library. On the left is a hierarchical list of topics. When you click a topic on the left, the document will appear on the right side of the window.

5. Click the book icon next to Partial Books to expand the menu.

6. Click the book icon next to Instant JavaScript to expand the menu to view the topics related to JavaScript.

7. Click the book icon next to Language Tour to expand the menu to view the topics related to the JavaScript Language.

8. Click **ECMAScript terminology** to display the document in the right side of the window. Figure 2-10 shows the path to ECMAScript terminology in the MSDN Library. Read the document to learn more about the relationship between ECMAScript and JavaScript.

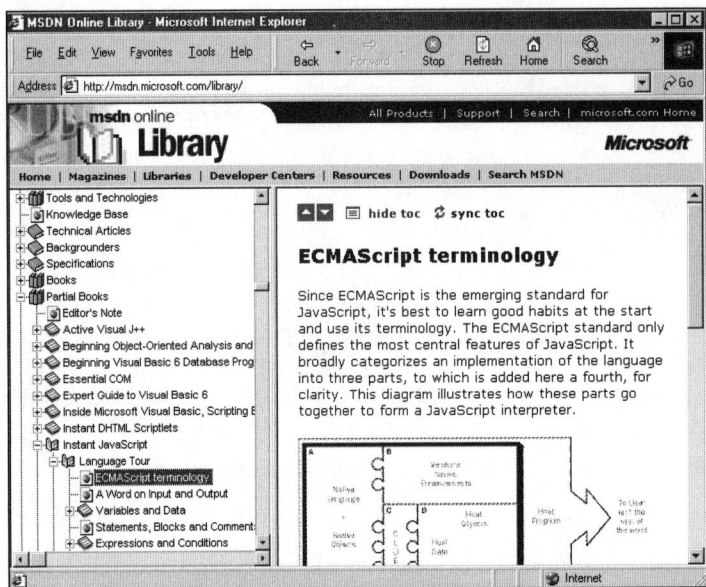

Figure 2-10   The MSDN Online Library

To Search the MSDN Online Library:

1. Click **Search MSDN** to open the MSDN Online Search page.

2. Type **ECMAScript** in the search text box.

3. Click the **Search** button to execute the search. The search returns a list of Web pages that match the search criteria. Figure 2-11 shows the Web page that displays the results from searching the MSDN Library. The name, address, summary, and location of each Web page are provided.

4. Click **ECMAScript terminology**, the name of the first Web page, to open the document. Notice that this is the same page that you viewed earlier.

5. Click the **show toc** button at the top of the page to return to the MSDN Online Library home page.

6. Click **File** on the menu bar.

7. Click **Close** to close the MSDN Online Library browser window.

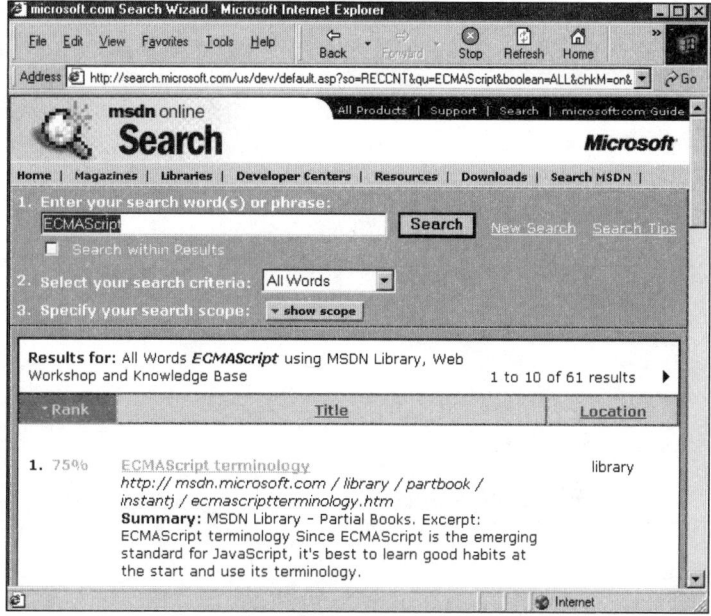

Figure 2-11   Searching MSDN Online Library

There are many more Internet resources on JavaScript, ECMAScript, VBScript, and ASP. Life Beyond Yahoo (*http://www.lifebeyondyahoo.com/life/java.asp*), shown in Figure 2-12, lists dozens of links to JavaScript resources on the Internet.

Figure 2-12   Life Beyond Yahoo: Java and JavaScript

Below is a list of some of the major scripting technology Internet resources. Some of these Web sites, such as the ASP Web Ring, contain links to hundreds of other Web sites.

- ECMA—*http://www.ecma.ch/*

- Netscape JavaScript 1.2—
  http://developer.netscape.com/docs/manuals/communicator/jsref/index.htm

- JavaScript.Com—*http://www.javascript.com/*

- Web Reference JavaScript—*http://www.webreference.com/js/*

- Web Review—*http://webreview.com/wr/pub*

- Yahoo's JavaScript—
  http://dir.yahoo.com/computers_and_internet/programming_languages/javascript/

- The JavaScript Source—*http://javascript.internet.com/*

- Life Beyond Yahoo: Java and JavaScript—
  http://www.lifebeyondyahoo.com/life/java.asp

- ASP Web Ring: List of Web sites—
  http://www.webring.org/cgi-bin/webring?ring=asp101;list

- Microsoft Visual Basic Scripting Web site—*http://www.microsoft.com/scripting/*

- Life Beyond Yahoo: HTML, ASP, XML—
  http://www.lifebeyondyahoo.com/life/html.asp

- Life Beyond Yahoo: The Internet—*http://www.lifebeyondyahoo.com/life/internet.asp*

- The Development Exchange (DevX)—*http://www.devx.com/default.asp*

- Web Builder Magazine—*http://www.webbuildermag.com/*

- Application Developer Training (AppDev)—*http://www.appdev.com/default.htm*

- VBScripts.com—*http://www.vbscripts.com/*

- Archives of InterDev @ listserve.uta.edu—
  http://listserv.uta.edu/archives/InterDev.html

- ASP Developer Visual InterDev Tutorial 1—
  http://www.aspdeveloper.net/VInterDev/page1.asp

- Visual InterDev Online—*http://www.visualinterdev.org*

CHAPTER SUMMARY

Client-side Scripting

❑ The World Wide Web Consortium sets the standards for HTML, CSS, XML, and other Internet technologies. Client- and server-side scripts are used to create dynamic Web applications. Dynamic Web applications enable interactivity between the user and the Web application. Client-side scripts are interpreted and executed by the script engine built within the browser.

❑ VBScript is a scaled-down version of Microsoft Visual Basic. VBScript is a fast, portable interpreter that is used by the Microsoft Internet Explorer browsers and the Microsoft Web servers.

❑ The most recent versions of JScript and JavaScript both comply with the client script standards known as ECMA-262. The ECMA-262 standard defined a standard client-side script language known as ECMAScript.

❑ To create a client-side script, enclose the code in a pair of Script tags: `<script>` ... `</script>`. Specify the script language with the `language` attribute. The entire client-side script can be placed within a pair of HTML comment tags (`<!--...-->`) to support older browsers. To add a single-line comment in VBScript, preface the line with a single apostrophe (`'`). To add a single-line comment in JavaScript, preface the line with two forward slashes (`//`). To add a multiline comment, place the comment between pairs consisting of a forward slash and an asterisk (`/*... */`).

❑ To embed a client-side script, use the same script tag and language attribute, and add the source attribute. `<script language = "JavaScript1.3" src="javasource.js">`. The script file must end with `.js`. HTML, and script commands can be placed in the external script page.

❑ To write output to a Web page using client-side script, use document.write. The document object has methods such as write and writeln. Both display text and literal strings to a Web page, but writeln also adds a carriage return at the end of the statement. The document.write method is case sensitive.

Server-side Scripts

❑ Server-side scripts are interpreted and executed by the script engine on the Web server. Server-side scripts can access and manipulate a Web server's file system, send mail from a Web page, and manage a database application.

❑ To create a server-side script, enclose the code in a pair of script tags (`<script>` `</script>`) or the script inline tags (`<%...%>`). If the block script tags are used, you must specify the `runat = server` attribute.

❑ ASP allows you to combine server-side script and ASP objects to provide access to other third-party objects such as the mail server and database server.

❑ To write output to a Web page using server-side script, use response.write.

❑ To break a long line in VBScript, use a space followed by the underscore character at the end of the line (_).

REVIEW QUESTIONS

1. Client-side scripts are processed by _____.

   a. the script engine built into the browser

   b. the script engine installed on the Web server

   c. the script engine installed in Windows

   d. the HTML script engine

2. Most commercial Web sites use client-side scripting to:

   a. validate data submitted from a form.

   b. communicate with the end user.

   c. send mail from the Web page.

   d. both a & b

3. Which technologies allow the programmer to create dynamic Web sites?

   a. HTML

   b. Cascading Style Sheets

   c. scripting

   d. all of the above

4. Which organization was responsible for developing the client-side script standard?

   a. Microsoft

   b. European Computer Manufacturers Association

   c. Netscape

   d. World Wide Web Consortium

5. What is the name of the Microsoft version of JavaScript?

   a. VBScript

   b. JScript

   c. JavaScript

   d. Java

6. In client-side script, which object is used to output text and literal strings to the browser?

   a. write

   b. response

   c. writeln

   d. document

2

7. JavaScript is a subset of the Java programming language. True or False?

8. Which Microsoft and Netscape products are designed to support the ECMA-262 standard?

   a. ECMAScript and VBScript

   b. JScript and ECMAScript

   c. JavaScript and JScript

   d. VBScript and JScript

9. Where is server-side script interpreted?

   a. in the Web server's scripting engine

   b. in the Web server software

   c. in the server's browser

   d. in the client's scripting engine within the client's browser

10. All client-side scripts must be enclosed in the _____ tags.

   a. `<script open>`...`</script close>`

   b. `<script>`...`</script>`

   c. `<JavaScript>`...`</JavaScript>`

   d. `<ECMAScript>`...`</ECMAScript>`

11. To prevent script code from displaying an error message in browsers that do not support script languages, the _____ must surround the script commands.

   a. HTML comment tags (`!--` ... `-->`)

   b. script tags (`<script></script>`)

   c. HTML tags(`<html></html>`)

   d. BODY tags (`<body></body>`)

12. The single-line comment character for VBScript is the _____.

   a. double slash(`//`)

   b. single quote(`'`)

   c. dollar sign (`$`)

   d. double quote (`" "`)

13. The single-line commenting character for JavaScript is the _____.

   a. double slash (`//`)

   b. single quote (`'`)

   c. dollar sign (`$`)

   d. double quote (`" "`)

14. The multiline commenting character for JavaScript is the _____.
    a. double slash (//   //)
    b. asterisk and slash (*/   */)
    c. dollar sign and slash ($/ $/)
    d. slash and asterisk (/*   */)

15. Active Server Pages process the script block on the server and send the resulting HTML and client-side script to the requesting client. True or False?

16. Active Server Pages require _____ and _____ permission.
    a. read and execute
    b. read and script
    c. script and execute
    d. read and write

17. Server-side comments may be viewed by anyone who can view the Web page. True or False?

18. JavaScript closely resembles the syntax of which programming language?
    a. Java
    b. C/C++
    c. Cobol
    d. Assembly

19. Which attribute is required in the script tag to run a script on the server rather than the client machine?
    a. `runon`
    b. `server`
    c. `atserver`
    d. `runat`

20. The inline script delimiters for server-side script are:
    a. `<%    %>`
    b. `<$    $>`
    c. `<// //>`
    d. `</* */>`

21. The shortcut for the response.write method is:

    a. =

    b. @

    c. /*

    d. $

22. What is the file extension of a server-side include page?

    a. .pl

    b. .inc

    c. .vbs

    d. .cgi

23. What is the name of the Active Server Page engine?

    a. asp.dll

    b. system.ini

    c. asp.ini

    d. windows.asp

24. What is the file extension of an Active Server Page?

    a. .asp

    b. .inc

    c. .js

    d. .html

25. What is the URL for the MSDN Online Library?

    a. *http://msdn.microsoft.com/library*

    b. *http://www.msdn.com*

    c. *http://www.sitebuilder.com*

    d. *http://www.microsoft.com*

26. What object is used by ASP to access database servers?

    a. Database Access Component

    b. ASP Built-in Objects

    c. PWS Objects

    d. script object

HANDS-ON PROJECTS

Project 2-1

In this project, you will create a client-side script that displays text in the browser.

1. Open Notepad or a compatible simple text editor.

Usually there is a shortcut to the Notepad application in the Start Menu. Click the Start menu, point to Programs, point to Accessories, then click Notepad.

2. Type the basic HTML tags required to create a Web page (`html`, `head`, `title`, `body`). The title of the store should be **Office Supply Store**. The background color should be **#FFCC99**.

3. On the Web page, write **Welcome to our Office Supply Store Unlimited**. Format this sentence with heading 2 style. Center the heading using the `align` property.

4. Add a heading style 3 that says **Here is a list of our departments:**

5. Add a client-side script to display a list of departments. Use the beginning client-side script tag `<script>` with `language` attribute set to `JavaScript1.3`.

6. Use the `document.write` method to write the list of departments. For example, `document.write("Pens and Pencils");`. Don't forget to place a semicolon at the end of each JavaScript statement. The departments to list include: Pens and Pencils, Paper, Stationery, School Supplies, Stamps, Notebooks, Markers & Highlighters, Tacks & Paperclips.

7. Use the `document.write` method to write a break tag `<br>` after each department name. For example, type in `document.write("<br>");`.

8. To save the Web page, click **File** on the menu bar, and then click **Save**. In the file-name text box type in "**officedept.htm**". Be sure to use quotation marks around the entire filename to ensure that the file is saved as an HTML file.

9. Open the officedept.htm file in a Web browser to verify that all of the departments are listed.

Project 2-2

In this exercise, you will create a Web page that uses an external client-side script page to display content on a browser. This Web page will display a list of departments for a sports store.

1. Open Notepad or a compatible simple text editor to create the external client-side style sheet.

2

2. Use the `document.write` method to write the list of departments. For example, `document.write("Golf");`. Don't forget to place a semicolon at the end of each JavaScript statement. The departments to list include: Baseball, Tennis, Swimming, Football, Hockey, Gymnastics, and Fishing. Use the `document.write` method to write a break tag `<br>` after each department name. For example, type in `document.write("<br>");`.

3. Your boss informs you that you will be adding two new departments in the next month, named Weight Lifting, and Volleyball. Add these two departments to the list. Comment out these departments so that they do not display in the Web page. You can use JavaScript single-line commenting (`//`) or multiline commenting (`/*  */`).

4. To save the Web page, click **File** on the menu bar, and then click **Save**. Save the embedded script page as "**sportsdept.js**".

5. Open a new file by clicking **File** on the menu bar and clicking **New**.

6. Type the basic HTML tags required to create the Web page (`html`, `head`, `title`, `body`). The title of the store should be **Online Sports Store**. The background color should be **#FFCC99**.

7. On the Web page, write **Welcome to Sports Store Unlimited**. Format this sentence with heading 1 style. Center the heading using the `align = center` property.

8. Add a heading style 3 that says **Here is a list of our main sports departments**:

9. Add a client-side script tag to retrieve the embedded script file. Use the client-side script tag `<script>` with `language` attribute set to `JavaScript1.3`. Specify the SRC attribute path as `sportsdept.js`.

10. To save the Web page, click **File** on the menu bar, and then click **Save**. In the file-name text box type "**sportsstore.htm**". Be sure to use quotation marks around the entire filename to ensure that the file will be saved as an HTML file.

11. Open the **sportsstore.htm** file in a Web browser to verify that all of the departments are listed. View the source code to verify that the department names are not listed in the source code view for the Web page.

Project 2-3

In this exercise, you will create a server-side script that uses the response object to display a list of Web sites.

1. Open Notepad.

2. Type the basic HTML tags required to create the Web page (`html`, `head`, `title`, `body`). The title of the page should be **Online Search Engines**. The background color should be **#CCFF99**.

3. On the Web page, write **Major Search Engines**. Format this sentence with heading 2 style. Center the heading using the `align` property.

4. Add a heading style 3 that says **Here is a list of our recommended search engines**:

5. Add a server-side script to display a list of search engines. Use the beginning server-side script tag `<script>` with `language` attribute set to `"vbscript"`. Specify the `runat` attribute to indicate that this script is to be interpreted and executed on the Web server.

6. Use the `write` method to write the list of five major search engines. For example, `response.write("Alta Vista");`. Do not add a semicolon at the end of the VBScript statement. The additional search engines to list include Excite, GoTo, WebCrawler, and Yahoo.

7. Your boss informs you that she wants the list to be displayed in a bulleted list, with hyperlinks to the search engine Web sites. Modify the `response.write` statement to include the list item tag (`<li>`) for each of the search engine sites listed (see Table 2-1). For example, the AltaVista selection would now appear as:
```
response.write("<li><a href='
http://www.altavista.digital.com/'>AltaVista</a>").
```

8. Note that the entire statement should appear on one line, or use the line continuance character (`_`).

Table 2-1   URLs for the Major Search Engines

AltaVista	*http://www.altavista.digital.com*
Excite	*http://www.excite.com*
GoTo	*http://www.goto.com*
WebCrawler	*http://webcrawler.com*
Yahoo	*http://www.yahoo.com*

9. Include at the top of the list a `response.write` statement to create the unordered list tag (`<ul>`) in order to display the bullets. For example, you can write: `response.write("<ul>")`. Use the `response.write` method to add a closing unordered list tag at the end of the list (`</ul>`).

10. Your boss informs you that you will be adding four new search engines in the next month (see Table 2-2). Add these four search engines at the bottom of the list, the same way you added the previous five search engines. Comment out these search engines so that they are not displayed on the Web page. You can use VBScript single-line commenting (`'`).

Table 2-2   Additional Search Engines

Infoseek	*http://infoseek.go.com*
Lycos	*http://www.lycos.com*
Snap	*http://www.snap.com*
Netscape Search	*http://search.netscape.com*

2

11. To save the Web page, click **File** on the menu bar, and then click **Save**. In the file-name text box type "**searchengines.asp**". Be sure to use quotation marks around the entire filename to ensure that the file will be saved as an ASP file.

12. Copy the file to your data directory. Note that this Web page must reside on a Web site that supports ASP, such as Personal Web Server or IIS.

 Many programmers use an FTP (File Transfer Protocol) application to copy files to a Web server. Many FTP applications are available at TUCOWS at *http://www.tucows.com/*, or one of the TUCOWS mirror sites, such as *http://tucows.tierranet.com/*.

13. View the Web page using a browser.

Project 2-4

In this exercise, you will create a server-side include file that can be reused on multiple ASP pages.

1. Open Notepad.

2. Create the server-side include file. Type in the following code to create the header:

```
<html>
<head>
<meta name="keywords" content="Sports, Golf">
<meta name="Author" content="FirstName LastName">
<title>Sports Store Unlimited</title>
</head>
<body bgColor = "#CCFF99">
<div align = "center">
<h1>Sports Store Unlimited</h1>
<p>Today is:<% = Date()%> </p>
<p>Click <a href = "sportsstore.htm">here
</a> to return to the departments page.</p>
<hr>
</div>
```

3. Save the file as "**sports.inc**". Be sure to use quotation marks around the filename.

4. Open a new page by clicking **File** on the menu bar and clicking **New**.

5. Type in the following code fragment, which creates the link to the server-side include page: `<!--#include file="sports.inc"-->`. Be sure not to have a space between the pound sign (`#`) and the `include` keyword.

6. On the next line, type in the following lines of code to create the rest of the Web page:

```
<div align="center">
<h3>Here is a list of our departments: </h3>
<script language = "JavaScript1.3" src = "sportsdept.js">
</script>
</div>
</body>
</html>
```

7. To save the Web page, click **File** on the menu bar, and then click **Save**. In the file-name text box type in "**sports.asp**". Be sure to use quotation marks around the entire filename to ensure that the file is saved as an ASP file.

8. Copy the file to your directory.

9. View the page in a browser. Again, the Web page must reside on a Web server to display correctly.

CASE PROJECTS

Case Project

Downtown Pediatrics: Developing a Web Site

You are hired as a consultant to develop a very small Web presence for a pediatric group practice. Your task is to design and implement a Web site that contains five pages.

1. Create a header page (headDP.inc) that contains the individual doctors' names, the office address and phone number, and the current date. Add a graphic logo to the page. Add a link to the index page (defaultDP.asp). Display this link on every page, using the server-side include method. Add comments to document the script file.

2. Create the index page (defaultDP.asp), which will include the header page. This page should contain links to each of the three other Web pages. The other three pages are called location.asp, services.asp, and feedback.asp.

3. Create the location page (location.asp). Add the server-side include header file. Type in directions to the office. Add a hyperlink to a map showing where the office is located. In a browser go to *http://maps.yahoo.com/py/maps.py*. Type in the street address of the office (you may use your school address). The map for the school will appear. Highlight the URL in the location text box. Click the Edit menu and click Copy. Go to your Web page and click Paste. Create a hyperlink to this Yahoo Map page.

4. Create the feedback page (feedback.asp). Add the server-side include header file. Add a form. Set the **action** attribute in the form **<form>** tag to *mailto:youremailaddress.com*.

5. Create the services page (services.asp). Add the server-side include header file. Type in a list describing the services that are offered. For example, the doctors may offer services such as: nutrition supplements, physical therapy, preventive medicine, physical examinations, inpatient visits, and home visits.

6. Save your pages and copy them to your directory. Preview your Web pages. Verify that the links work.

Sweet Nothings: Formatting Multiple Web Pages

A candy manufacturing company hires you to create an intranet site.

1. Create a header file (headSN.inc). The file should contain the company name, the logo, and a link to the home page (defaultSN.asp). Add text links to each of the departments in the company: Marketing, Finance, Administration, Training, Human Resources, and Manufacturing. Place the content in a table. The departments should be listed in the same row, but in their own individual cells. Modify the color of the background of the department cells and the color of the department fonts, to reflect the company's official colors (black and gold). Add comments to document the script file.

2. Create an ASP Web page for each department and the home page. Each department page should be named after the department. (Do not use spaces in names. Human Resources should be named HumanResources.asp.) Each page should have a server-side include adding the header file to the page. Add the name of the department to the center of the department page. Add content and graphics to each department page to reflect the purpose of the page.

3. Save your pages and copy them to your directory. Preview your Web pages. Verify that the links work.

The Savvy Shopper: Using Server-side Include Files

You are hired by a retailer to create their online department store. Your job is to create the Web pages so that the upkeep will be minimal. Therefore, you decide to embed some of the department lists. Then, when a change is made, only the department list needs to be updated.

1. Create the header (headSS.inc) file. This file will contain the store logo and name, the date, and a link to the default page (defaultSS.asp). Create a script that will obtain the contents from a JavaScript client-side source file named deptSS.js.

2. Create the JavaScript Source file (deptSS.js), using Notepad. Using client-side script, write out the names of the departments. You can use the **document.write()** method to write out the department names. Each department name should be separated from the next by a (|) character. Currently the departments are:
   Mens | Womens | Childrens | Maternity | Infants | Sport | Electronics | Culinary | Gifts | Jewelry. Each department name should be a link to the department page.

3. Create each department page. Name each department page after the name of the department. For example, the Men's department should be **mens.asp**. Place the name in the center of each page. Add a comment on each page to describe what the page should be used for. The comment should not be displayed in the browser, but should be visible to a visitor in the source view.

4. Save your pages and copy the pages to your directory. Preview your Web pages. Verify that the links work.

Using MSDN Online Library Resources

Your boss at the Savvy Shopper tells you that your Web site must be compliant with both the Microsoft and Netscape browsers. You are told that you can use any script that is compliant with ECMAScript. Find out more information about what JavaScript features you can and cannot use in your site.

Use the MSDN Online Library to locate information about ECMAScript and JavaScript. Visit some of the Web sites listed in the chapter. Describe some of the features that ECMAScript supports. Describe some of the features that Microsoft's JScript supports that are not part of ECMAScript. Describe some of the features that Netscape's JavaScript supports that are not part of ECMAScript. Create a Web page (ECMAScript.asp) that describes your findings.

Using Internet Resources to Locate Information on Scripting

At the Savvy Shopper you are working with a team of beginning Web programmers. All team members are to create their own Web pages, and their own scripts. However, it would be helpful to have a central location for JavaScript references that can be used by everyone.

Visit some of the Web sites listed in the chapter. Locate online tutorials and reference sites about JavaScript. Create a Web page (JavaScript.asp) that lists at least 10 Web sites and provides the related hyperlinks, and that provides a description of what JavaScripts are available. Create a Web page (ASP.asp) that lists at least 10 Web sites, the related hyperlinks, and a description of what ASP or VBScripts are available.

OBJECT-ORIENTED PROGRAMMING

In this chapter you will:

- ◆ Learn about object-oriented programming
- ◆ Create a custom object
- ◆ Learn about the Document Object Model and the Document Object Model hierarchy
- ◆ Use the properties, methods, and event handlers associated with the Document Object Model's objects
- ◆ Create Web pages that read and set object properties
- ◆ Create Web pages that interface with an object's event handler
- ◆ Create Web pages that call the methods of an object

Companies today want Web applications that are easily maintained and that can work with other applications. To accomplish this, you can use object-oriented programming to access the objects, properties, methods, and functions of an object, without having to know about how the objects are created. This chapter will show you how to create custom objects, and how to access the properties and methods of these objects from within a Web page.

OBJECT-ORIENTED PROGRAMMING

In Chapter 2, you learned how to use the write method of the document object to write HTML content and client-side scripts to the Web page. The document object is an example of an object that is built into the browser software. The document object contains a method called write, which you used to write output to the Web page. You passed a string parameter to the write method, which contained the information to be written to the browser. You did not have to know the code that created the document object or the write method; you just needed to know the syntax for using the object. **Object-oriented programming** allows you to use objects that can be accessed by other programs, including Web pages. An **object** is a set of related methods and properties that are compartmentalized. A **method** contains one or more programming statements. You can define a method within a Web page, but if a method is defined within an object, the code can be reused in many Web pages. Objects can have properties, which can be assigned values from your programs. The object property can be assigned different values each time for each object that is created.

The following example demonstrates the process of creating an object and using the object within a Web page. A brick and mortar store, called All We Sell Is Lamp Shades, is located in Illinois. The following sample code creates a banner object, which can be reused in other Web pages.

1. Create a basic Web page named **lampbanner.htm**. Add the basic HTML tags and the opening script tag.

```
<html><head>
<title>Custom Banner</title>
<script language = "javascript">
```

2. Create the object named Lamp using the keyword function. The lamp object is passed one argument, called txtAd, which is the value of the banner ad. Add an opening curly brace.

```
function Lamp(txtAd) {
```

A pair of curly braces {} surrounds all statements within a function.

3. Inside the function, create a property called bannerAd. The txtAd variable is assigned to the bannerAd property.

```
this.bannerAd = txtAd;
```

When using JavaScript, end each statement or command with a semicolon (;).

4. Create a method called show. This method is assigned to another function called display, which is defined later in the script.

```
this.show = display;
```

5. At the end of the function, add a closing curly brace to close the function.

```
}
```

6. Create the display function using the function keyword and the opening curly brace.

```
function display(){
```

7. Add the code that writes out the banner message.

```
document.writeln(this.bannerAd);
```

8. Close the function and the script.

```
}
</script>
```

9. Add the basic HTML code for the beginning body tag and a heading.

```
<body>
<h1>Lamps for Sale</h1>
```

10. Add a beginning script tag.

```
<script>
```

11. Declare a variable named ad, and assign it a text message.

```
var ad = "Sale Today!<br>"
```

 The var keyword is used to declare the variable in JavaScript. You will learn more about variables later in this book.

12. Add a statement that creates a new lamp object using the keyword new. Name the new lamp object theLamp. Pass the variable that contains your message to the new object.

```
theLamp = new Lamp(ad)
```

13. Call the show method of the new object. Notice that the method is referred to using the name of the new object, theLamp, and the name of the method, show. No values are passed because the values were passed when the object was created.

```
theLamp.show()
```

14. Add the code to close the script and the Web page.

```
</script>
</body></html>
```

15. Save the Web page to your directory. View the Web page in a browser.

16. Save the Web page as **lampbanner2.htm**.

17. Change the contents of the ad variable to **All lamps marked 50% off regular price!**.

18. Save the Web page to your data directory. View the Web page in a browser.

Creating a Custom Object

Creating a custom object consists of two separate tasks. The first task is to create the object definition. The **object definition** is the code that contains the methods and properties of the object. The second task is to create a new instance of the object. Then, you can call any of the methods that were defined in the object definition. You can also assign properties that were declared in the object definition. In the example above, the object definition is located in the script, in the head section of the Web page. The newly instantiated object is created in the body section of the Web page. This process is analogous to making chocolate chip cookies. If you have a recipe to make cookies, you know all the ingredients and you know how to combine the ingredients to make the cookie. But, a recipe is not a cookie. When you create the cookie dough, and then bake it, it becomes an edible cookie. In the same way, the object definition contains the directions for creating an object, but just as the cookie must be baked, an object must be instantiated before it exists.

Creating the Object Definition

The object definition, which contains the methods and properties of the object, is created by means of the constructor function. A **function** is a named grouping of one or more programming statements. A **constructor function** is a special type of function that can create new objects. In the example above, to create the lamp object, you created a constructor function using the function keyword. One argument was passed to the constructor function in the parentheses. This argument was used to assign a value to a property of the lamp object.

 To differentiate between constructor functions and regular functions, always capitalize the first letter of the constructor function name.

Adding a Property to the Object Definition   When the lamp object was created, one argument, txtAd, was passed to the new lamp object. The txtAd argument represents the message that is displayed in the banner. Object properties are identified by the name of the object followed by a period, followed by the name of the property. In the example above, you only created the object definition, so you cannot refer to the object by its name. Therefore, the keyword "this" can be used in place of the object name. After you create an instance of the Lamp object, then you can refer to it by the object's name.

To assign a value to a property of an object, use the name of the object and then the property. It is important to note that the syntax always remains the same, regardless of what object property is being set. The following example illustrates the syntax for assigning a value to a property of an object.

objectName.propertyName = value

Adding a Method to the Object Definition

Besides storing data in properties, objects can also perform functions on themselves and other objects. Recall that a function is a named group of one or more programming statements. A method is a function that is called from within an object. For example, a method could be used to manipulate the properties of an object. Some methods simply perform their actions when they are called, while other methods require more information before they can be processed. A method can accept any number of required and optional input arguments.

To add a method to an object, name the method and then assign the method to a function. The code `this.show` refers to the name of the lamp object's method, which will display the banner message. The `this.show` method is assigned to a function called display.

Functions will be covered in detail later in this book.

The syntax for naming a method is similar to the syntax for naming a property. You can pass optional arguments to the method. In JavaScript and VBScript, you access those methods by using the following syntax.

objectName.methodName(arguments)

It is useful to name methods with action words, to reinforce the concept that methods are functions that perform actions.

Using Custom Objects

The lamp object definition was created within the head section of the Web page, and is now available to you. However, an object definition is not an object that you can access directly. Instead, you **instantiate** the object by declaring a new instance of the object. You use the object definition as the template for creating the new object. You can create many objects from the same object definition. The ability to assign different values to each object's properties is called encapsulation. Each object will inherit the properties and methods from the object definition. You can assign additional properties and methods to an object.

Instantiating New Objects

This new lamp object will have all of the same properties and methods of the original lamp object definition. **Instantiation** is the process of declaring and initializing an object. There are two steps to instantiating a new object. First, you must specify the new name for the object. Then, you must assign the new object to the object definition created earlier, using the **new** keyword. Object names must be unique. In the lampbanner.htm sample, the code `theLamp = new Lamp(ad);` created the new instance of an object named theLamp, which was based upon an object definition named Lamp.

A variable called ad, which was assigned a value, was passed as a parameter named txtAd to the new lamp object. The txtAd parameter was used to assign a value to the bannerAd property, using the code `this.bannerAd = txtAd;`. This property was used by the object's show method to display the message.

The methods that were defined within the object's definition are now available to the new lamp object. In the example above, the show method was available to all new lamp objects. The show method called a regular function named display. The display function wrote the message to the browser using the bannerAd property of the theLamp object as an argument to the write method.

Encapsulating Code Within Objects

The above example illustrates how objects are **encapsulated**. Encapsulation means that the inner workings of the object, such as its methods and properties, are maintained within the object. In the real world, you might not have written the object definition, and it would not be located within the same Web page. You would not know how the display function worked. You only need to know how to instantiate the lamp object and how to call the show method. Encapsulation provides an interface by which you can access the methods and properties of an object. You can create multiple objects within the same page based on the same object definition, as long as the names are unique.

To demonstrate encapsulation, this example shows two objects being created using the same object definition. Notice that the name of the new object has been changed, so that the properties will have different values.

1. Open lampbanner2.htm in Notepad or your Web editor. Save the page as **lampbanner3.htm** in your data directory.

2. Add the following code. The code should be placed immediately above the closing body tag.

```
<script language = "javascript">
var ad = "25% Off all lamps!<br>" ;
theLamp2 = new Lamp(ad);
theLamp2.show();
</script>
```

3. Save the page to your data directory. View the page in the browser.

Object Inheritance

When you create a new object with an object definition, the new object maintains the same characteristics as the original object. This characteristic of objects is known as object **inheritance**. Objects inherit the properties and methods of the original object. You are not required to access all of the properties and methods of the original lamp object when you use a new lamp object. Some properties are assigned to the object by default within the object definition. Then, all new objects will inherit the same properties as the original object definition. However, if an object does not assign a value to a property, and a new object is created without assigning a value to the property, the property is assigned the default value, "undefined".

Adding Properties and Methods to an Object

You can extend the new object by adding additional properties and methods to it. In the same lampbanner.htm Web page, you can define another property for the theLamp2 object. Add the code in Step 2 below to the script that defined a new object named theLamp2. This code will create another property called lampColor. Then, you can display the property using the `document.write` method. This property is not available to the first object you created, because this was an additional property that was defined only in the second object.

1. Open lampbanner3.htm in Notepad or your Web editor. Save the page as **lampbanner4.htm** in your folder.

2. Add the following code. The code should be placed immediately above the closing body tag.

```
<script language = "javascript">
theLamp2.lampColor = "Red";
document.write(theLamp2.lampColor);
</script>
```

3. Save the page. View the page in the browser.

Using Custom Objects to Encapsulate

Figure 3-1 shows how objects can be used to separate the presentation of a Web application from its business rules and data. In this example, a shipping object is created to store the formula that calculates the cost of shipping based on the total price of the product. Once the shipping cost is calculated, the shipping object stores the shipping data in a separate customer database. Other in-house programs can access the shipping database. If the formula becomes more complex, it only needs to be changed within the shipping object. The rest of the Web application does not have to be reprogrammed.

Additional objects can also be used to gather data about the item ordered, such as the color, and store it in a user preference table in a database. This information can later be used by the Marketing Department to target customers who prefer that color. You could design the Web site using that color as the background color. Encapsulating objects in your Web applications allows you to separate business logic, data, and presentation, and thus helps you develop Web applications that are easier to maintain and update.

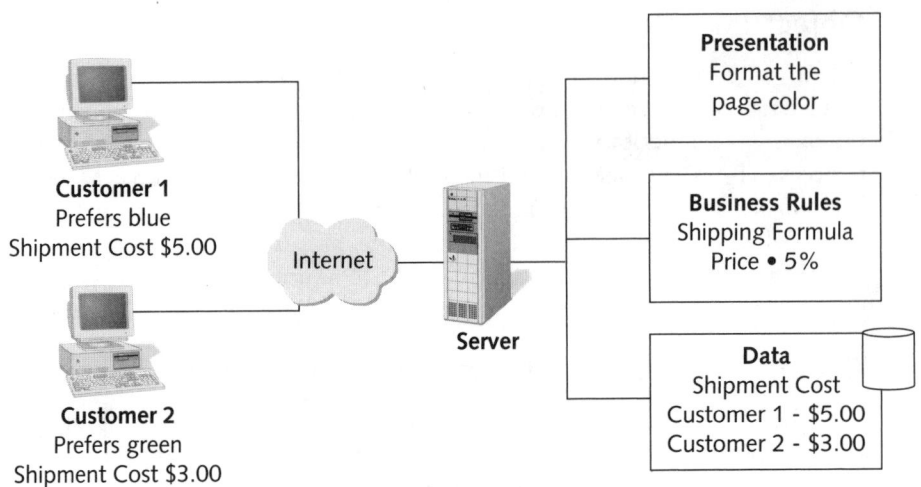

Figure 3-1   How object-oriented programming is used to isolate business logic

USING BUILT-IN OBJECTS

Browser software contains built-in objects. You can access these objects, along with their properties and methods, when building your Web applications. This hierarchical collection of objects follows a standard referred to as the **Document Object Model (DOM)**. The World Wide Web Consortium (*http://www.w3c.org*) is responsible for setting the standards for the DOM. The DOM is built into the browser software. Using client-side scripting, programmers can access all of the objects, properties, and methods within the DOM.

The DOM is sometimes referred to as the Browser Object Model.

Browser Incompatibility

The most common browsers, Microsoft Internet Explorer and Netscape Navigator, have built-in DOMs. Not all browsers meet the current DOM standards. When you include client-side objects, be sure to test them with a variety of browsers, because not all properties and methods are supported across browsers. For example, Netscape Navigator uses the navigator object's language property to display the language used by the Web browser. This property is not supported in Internet Explorer. In Internet Explorer, the navigator object uses the userLanguage and systemLanguage properties. Netscape supports a method called "home," which returns the active window to the default home page. The only way to ensure that a particular browser supports the objects, properties, and methods that you use in your Web applications is to preview the Web pages in that Web browser.

While you can create two separate Web sites for each browser, some Web editing tools, such as FrontPage, Dreamweaver, and Drumbeat 2000, allow you to set up the Web site so that only browser-compatible code is created. These applications allow you to specify which browser versions can access the entire Web site, or a single Web page within the site; but doing so limits your ability to use the additional properties and methods that are included with newer browser versions.

 The navigator object has properties such as userAgent that allow you to detect which browser and version the client is running. This information is also available to the Web administrator in the Web site log files.

Object Hierarchy Within the Document Object Model

All of the objects within the DOM have a position within the DOM hierarchy. When you start the browser software, one or more windows may open. The window object has the topmost position in the object hierarchy. The window can contain many child objects, such as the history object, the location object, the event object, the screen object, the frames object, and the document object. With the exception of the window object, each object within the DOM is contained within a parent object.

Some objects contain one or more child objects. For example, the window object contains the navigator object, the history object, the frames object, the location object, and the document object. The following is a list of objects that are commonly used in client-side programming. Figure 3-2 illustrates the entire collection of objects within the DOM and their hierarchical relationship.

- The window object
- The navigator object
- The location object
- The history object
- The document object
- The forms collection
- The links and anchors collection
- The images collection

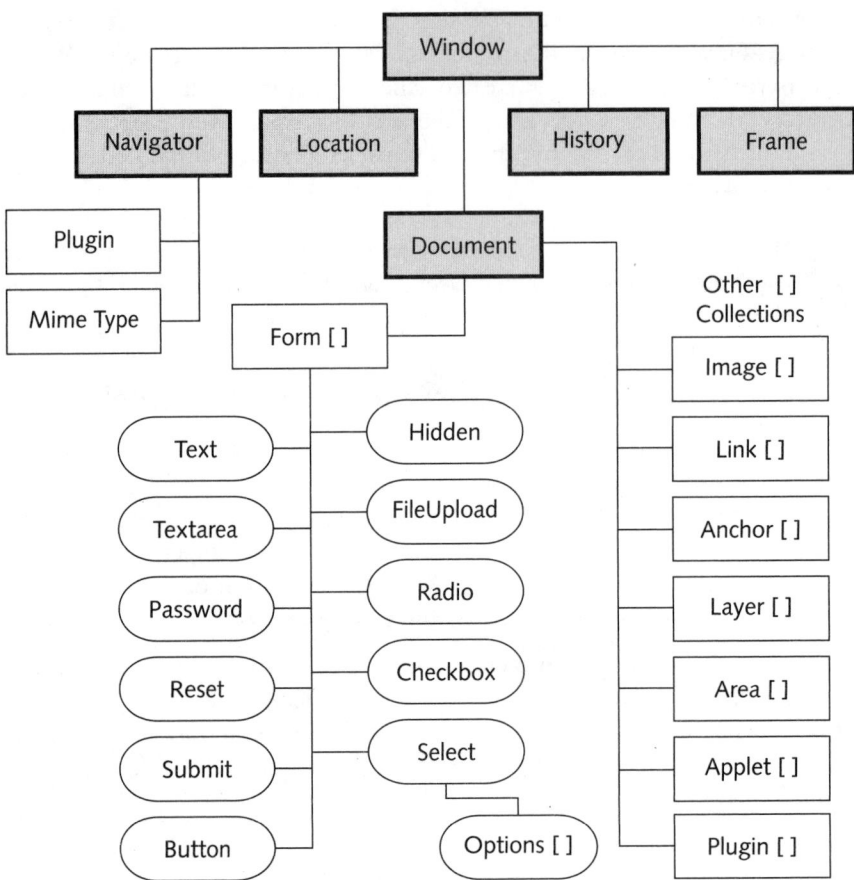

Figure 3-2   The Document Object Model hierarchy

The document object contains its own set of child objects, including the forms collection. A **collection** allows more than one object of the same type to coexist within the same object model hierarchy. In other words, there can be multiple form objects within one document object. The multiple forms are referred to as the **forms collection**. The collection of forms is also known as the forms[] **array**. An **array** is a collection of objects. Each object in the array is numbered according to its sequential position within the array. The objects within the collection are numbered, starting with zero. This number is referred to as the index number and is used to identify each form in the array. Therefore, the first form is the first element of the form array and can be identified as form[0]. If there were four forms on the Web page, the forms would be identified as form[0], form[1], form[2], and form[3].

 More details about creating and using arrays will be covered in later chapters.

The DOM contains several other collections, including the images collection and the form element collection. If there are multiple images on a document, you can refer to each image by its position within the image collection, for example img[0]. Recall that form objects contain different types of form elements, such as text boxes. These form elements make up the form element array. Each element in the form is also numbered sequentially starting with zero. Figure 3-2 shows other collections within the DOM.

This book covers the more commonly used objects, methods, and properties in the DOM. There are additional objects, methods, and properties that are not listed in this book. You can learn more about these by visiting the JavaScript resource Web sites listed in Chapter 2.

Naming Conventions for Objects in the DOM

When you need to refer to an object in a script, you can use the fully qualified name for the object. The fully qualified name includes the name of the object and its hierarchical position within the DOM. For example, a textbox object named lname is in a form called form1 on a Web page. The fully qualified name for this object would be `window.document.form1.lname.` You are not required to identify the name of the window object if you are referring to an object within the current window. Therefore, you can also refer to the text box object as `document.form1.lname.`

To refer to the property of an object, use the name of the object followed by a period and the name of the property. For example, to refer to the contents of the text box named lname, use the value property. You can specify the fully qualified name, `window.document.form1.lname.value,` or if the object exists within the current window, use `document.form1.lname.value.` Because the name property of an object is used to refer to the object within scripts, you should assign each object a unique name.

Properties, Methods, and Events

Each object and collection contains its own set of properties, methods, and events. Some of these properties, methods, and events are common among objects, like the name property. You can assign values to some properties, for example document.title. Some properties are read-only, which means you cannot change their values. To retrieve a value of a property of an object, use the complete name of the object. For example, to retrieve the value of a text box called name, which is on a form named form1, and assign its value to a variable called txtName, you could use `document.form1.name.value = txtName.` To assign a value to an object, you would also use the complete name of the object. For example, to change the label value on a button named btnSubmit, which is on a form named form1, you could use the code `btnSubmit.value = "Submit Me".`

Objects within the DOM have built-in methods that can be called form scripts. Calling a method is very similar to setting or obtaining a property value. To call a method, use the complete name of the object followed by a period and the name of the method. For example, to close a window using the close method, you could use window.close().

Arguments can be passed to the method. In Chapter 2, you passed a string as the argument to the write method of the document object. You could call the write method with `window.document.write("Welcome")` or `document.write("Welcome")`. Before you call a method, you should ask yourself whether it requires any inputs or returns any outputs.

Some built-in methods return a value to the script that called them. If a method has a return value, then it will pass this value back to the script that called it. A method may return a value indicating that the processing occurred correctly, or it may return a value obtained from the processing. You may or may not need to use the return value in your application. If the information contained in the return is valuable, then invoking the method as part of a larger statement can capture it. If it is not needed, then the return value can be ignored. In the following example, in statustest.htm, when the user places the mouse pointer over the first hyperlink, the window status will change to the new string. When the user places the mouse pointer over the second hyperlink, the status message will not be altered; instead, the filename will appear. The `return false` statement will stop the browser from displaying an error message. The `return true` statement catches the error and continues to process the script.

```
<a href = "product1.htm"
    onMouseOver =
        "window.status='Claddagh Ring';
    return true">
    New Ring</a>
<br>
<a href = "product2.htm"
    onMouseOver =
            "window.status='Claddagh Earrings';
return false">
New Earrings</a>
```

Do not break strings into multiple lines. The strings in this book are broken up to make the string readable. Breaking a string into multiple lines will generate an error message.

In Chapter 2, you learned that scripting could be used to increase interactivity between the user and the Web page. Events allow the object to interact with the programmer, and allow objects to interact with the program itself. Users interact with the Web page by performing actions called **events**, such as clicking, scrolling, and entering information in a text box. The command statements that respond to an event are called the **event handler**. This event handler can contain code that is executed when the event occurs. You can create a group of programming statements that responds to an event. For example, when the user clicks an object, an event called **onClick** is generated for that object. The following code in customer.htm will catch the click event using three different techniques. When the click event is detected, an alert box containing a message appears. The first method uses the onClick event handler for the button object.

```
<body>
<h1>Call Customer Support</h1>
<form name="form1">
<input type = "button" name = "btnCall1"
    value = "Click Here for Help"
    onClick = window.alert("1-800-555-5555");>
</form>
```

The second method in customer.htm demonstrates how you can use a function to handle an event. The following sample code uses a function named callUs, which is used when the click event is detected.

```
<form name="form2">
<input type = "button" name = "btnCall2"
    value = "Click Here for Help"
    onClick = "callUs()";>
</form>
<script language="javascript">
function callUs(){
    window.alert("1-800-555-5555")
}
</script>
```

The third method in customer.htm demonstrates how you can access these events in the DOM directly. You can force the click event to occur. To accomplish this, you can create a function that will be assigned the event handler. In VBScript, you can use a procedure that is called when the event is detected. In the following sample code, the same click event is detected, and an alert message is displayed. You can then directly call the event handler by calling the procedure from a script, or the procedure will be automatically called when the user clicks the button. Notice how the name of the procedure is a combination of the name of the object, an underscore, and the name of the event.

```
<form name="form3">
<input type = "button" name = "btnCall3"
value = "Click Here for Help">
</form>
<script language="vbscript">
sub btnCall3_onClick()
    window.alert("1-800-555-5555")
end sub
</script>
```

Graphical editors, such as FrontPage 2000 and Visual InterDev, expose the properties, methods, and events related to any object on a Web page. The property value can be set using the property window in Visual InterDev. If you are using FrontPage 2000, you can use the property dialog boxes in the Microsoft Script Editor to assign values to the properties of objects. The Microsoft Script Editor is a scripting tool that can be installed when you install FrontPage 2000. It provides a graphical interface to the properties, methods, and events related to any object on the Web page.

More details on creating and using functions and procedures can be found later in this book.

The Window Object

The window object is the highest level of an object that can exist in the DOM; it is a representation of the physical space that holds your HTML document. The window object provides a direct link to many of the capabilities of the actual browser. Since the window object represents the browser window, the properties and methods associated with it are handled through the window object. The window object contains child objects, properties, methods, and events, and is the parent to several child objects, including documents, frames, location, and navigator.

Although Microsoft and Netscape have slightly different versions of the DOM, both versions utilize the window object as the top object in the browser model hierarchy.

The Window Object Properties

The most often used window properties include the **self**, **name**, **default status**, and **status** properties. There can be multiple windows open at the same time. The self property is a reference to the current window. The name property allows you to refer to a specific window within the program code, such as `window.self.` The default status property allows you to set the default string that is displayed at the bottom of the browser window in the **status message bar**. The status property can be used to temporarily set the contents of the status message bar. For example, you could set the default status property using `window.defaultStatus = "Sale starts Monday".`

The Status Property of the Window Object   The following snippet of code illustrates how you might modify the message in the status message bar by altering the status message property of the window object. Like the defaultStatus property, the status property displays a string at the bottom of the browser window in the status message bar. The following sample code illustrates how to change the default status message in the status message bar.

```
window.status = "Course Technologies"
```

3

Normally, if you have not assigned a value to the defaultStatus property, the status message bar will not display anything unless you place the mouse pointer over a link, and then it displays the URL for the link. In the real world, the status message can be altered to bring attention to some content, such as a new product offering, or how to contact customer support. In this sample code, in statusMessage.htm, the default string in the status message bar will be the name of the company, Office Store Unlimited.

```html
<html><head>
<script language = "javascript">
window.defaultStatus = "Office Store"
</script>
<title>Changing the Status Message</title>
</head>
<body>
<h2>Change the Status Message</h2>
```

The sample continues below. The two hyperlinks below will temporarily change the status message when the user places the mouse pointer over the hyperlink. When the user moves the mouse pointer off the link, the status message changes back to the default message. The property changes as the result of a mouseover event.

```html
<a href="Claddagh.htm"
    onMouseOver = "window.status='Claddagh';
    return true">
New Product
</a>
</body>
</html>
```

The property can be set to a string, such as "Office Supply Store", or an empty string " ". A null value will not display any string on the status message bar.

The Window Object Methods

The window object contains several methods that can be accessed from a script. Multiple windows can be opened at the same time. The open and close methods are used to open and close windows within the browser. The scroll method scrolls down the window to a specific coordinate within the window. When multiple windows are opened, only one window may be active at a time. The window that is active has the focus. Blur and focus are methods used to change the focus. Focus will make the window the active window, and blur removes the focus. Focus and blur are examples of methods used with other objects, such as text boxes, that are covered later in this chapter.

Opening and Closing Windows   The open window method allows you to open a new browser window on the fly. Using the open method, you can create a new window by specifying an existing page, or create a new page. The open method has several arguments that can be used to modify the layout of the window: URL, window name, window features, and replace. The URL argument is the location of the file to open. The URL can include an absolute or relative path to the file. The window name is the name assigned to the window. The window name is used to refer to that window in scripts. The keyword null or " " can be used instead of a window name. Using the replace argument allows you to load the page within the current window. The window features are a string of options and their values that allow you to modify the layout of the window. The windows features consist of the window dimensions and a string of various options and their values. The height and width properties, which are measured in pixels, are used to specify the size of the window. The height and width of the window are identified in pixels, and are also contained within the quotes.

Within quotes, each option is listed using its name and value, delimited by commas. Window options that can be turned off or on include the location, menubar, toolbar, directories, status, and scrollbars. The directories toolbar is also known as the links toolbar and contains special links buttons. Top and left are two properties available in Internet Explorer that allow you to specify the topmost and left position of the window in pixels. You can then also control the location where windows open. You can turn off the menus and toolbars by setting the menu value to no or 0. To force the menu or toolbar to be displayed, set the toolbar value to yes or 1. The resizable option can be used to prevent the user from resizing the window. Figure 3-3 illustrates the browser window with the menu bar, toolbar, and scroll bar removed. Below is the syntax for opening a new window in a browser. The URL, windowName, and the option list are all enclosed within quotation marks.

window.open ("URL", "windowName", "options=value, width=xxx, height=yyy");

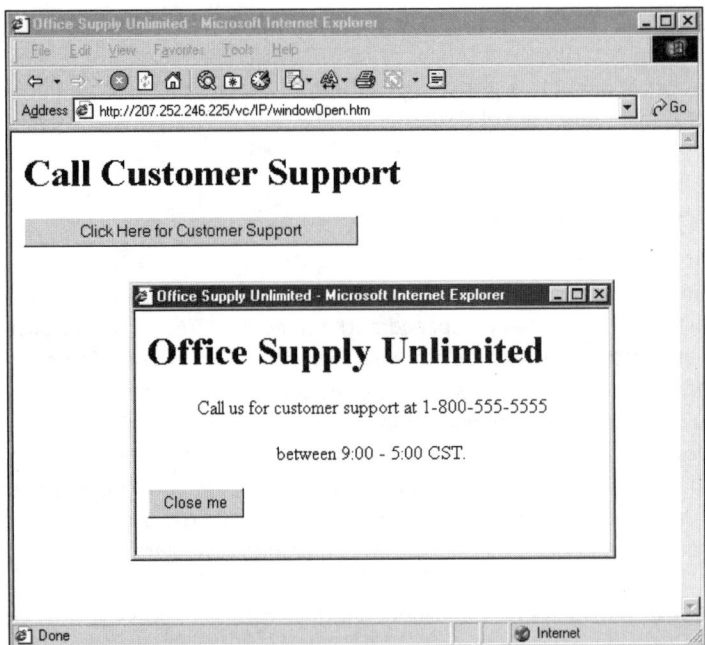

Figure 3-3   Modifying the appearance of a window

The sample code below illustrates how to open a new window named newWin that contains a document named office.htm. The dimensions of the window are 400 pixels wide by 200 pixels high. The status message bar, toolbar, menu bar, and location bar are all turned off. The scroll bar is not turned off, and the user can resize the window.

```
window.open("office.htm","newWin","height=200,width=400,
     status=no,toolbar=no,menubar=no,location=no")
```

 Removing the menus and toolbars is not a secure way to hide information. Even with the menus removed, it is possible for a user to obtain the source code for the Web page.

The close method closes the current window. To close a specific window, pass the name of the window that is to be closed to the window method. If a specific window is not identified, the window that contains the close method will be closed. To close the current window, you can pass the name of the current window, or pass no argument. Depending on the browser security settings, a dialog box may appear that asks you if you are sure you want to close the window. In this example, the close method is used to close the current window.

```
<script language = "javascript">
document.close()
</script>
```

In the following example, the window object open and close methods are combined to increase the user's involvement in the Web page. The user opens a Web page named windowOpen.htm. When the user clicks a button, the program detects that an OnClick event has occurred. When the onClick event occurs, the OpenContactWindow function is called. The openContactWindow function creates a new window, and then writes HTML and text to the Web page, using the **document.write** method.

1. Create a Web page named **windowOpen.htm**, using Notepad or your Web page editor. Add the basic HTML tags.

```
<html><head>
<title>Office Supply Unlimited</title>
</head>
```

2. In the heading of the Web page, add the code to open a new window and create a new Web page within the window. The openWin function creates a new instance of a window object named newWin. The name of the new Web page loaded into the new window is office.htm. The Web page will have dimensions of 200 pixels high by 400 pixels wide. The status message bar, toolbar, menu bar, and location bar will all be off.

```
<script language = "javascript">
function openWin(){
var newW = window.open("office.htm",
     "newWin","height = 200,width = 400,
     status = no, toolbar = no,
     menubar = no, location = no");
```

Because the options list is passed as a string, you need to write the entire string on one line of code within your Web page. The code is split across multiple lines here to increase readability. If you split the string into multiple lines, your page will generate an error message.

3. Create a variable to hold the string that will be written to the new window. You can concatenate strings in JavaScript using the plus (+) sign, and in VBScript using the ampersand (&). In this example, the variable named strH holds the entire string, which will be written to the new window.

You can concatenate strings, HTML tags, and variables. Because the entire argument can become very long, programmers often break up their string, and use a variable named strH to hold the value of the string.

```
var strH ;
strH = "<html><head><title>";
strH = strH "Office Supply Unlimited</title>";
strH = strH + "<h1>";
strH = strH + "Office Supply Unlimited";
strH = strH + "</h1>";
strH = strH + "<center>";
strH = strH + "Call us for customer support ";
strH = strH + "at 1-800-555-5555 ";
strH = strH + "<BR>";
strH = strH + "<BR>between 9:00 - 5:00 CST. ";
strH = strH + "</center>";
```

4. Once the window is open, you can access all the properties and methods of the new window and document. Because this is a Web page, you can use the `document.write` method to write HTML tags and text to the Web page. However, there are two windows currently open. To write to the new window, you must identify it by name. The last section of the string will contain a form with a button. When the button is clicked, it will close the new window, using the close method. Make sure there is a space immediately after the closing single quote after the word button.

```
strH = strH + "<form><input type = 'button' ";
strH = strH + "value ='Close me'
     onClick = 'window.close()'>";
strH = strH + "</form>";
newW.document.write(strH);
}
</script>
```

3

5. Create the button in the Web page that the user will click to open the new window. When the user clicks the button, the click event is detected by the button object and handled by the onClick event handler. The openWin function is the function that is assigned to handle the click event. So, when the user clicks on the button, the openWin function will open a new window.

```
<body>
<form><h1>Call Customer Support</h1>
<input type = "button"
        value = "Click Here for Customer Support"
            onClick = "openWin()">
```

6. Close the tags to the form and the Web page.

```
</form></body></html>
```

7. Save the Web page to your data directory. View the Web page in a browser.

Creating Window Dialog Boxes   Dialog boxes are used to obtain information from the user, or to provide the user with information. The three window methods that create dialog boxes are the alert, confirm, and prompt methods. Figure 3-4 shows how the three types of dialog boxes look in a browser. The syntax and an example of each method are listed in Table 3-1.

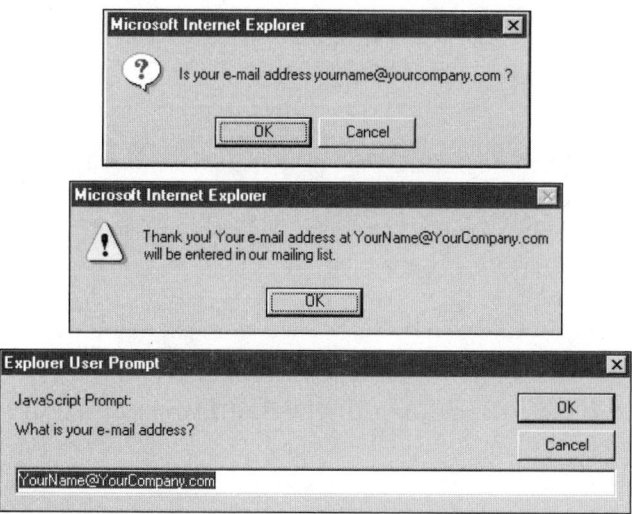

Figure 3-4   Dialog boxes created using the window object

The alert method creates an alert dialog box, which is often used on a form to provide a simple message to the user, such as "You forgot to enter your name." The alert box creates a small window that contains a single message and an OK button. This method is often used to warn users, for example that they have failed to fill out a form correctly. The alert dialog box has a single string input.

The confirm method is often used to require the user to accept or reject some condition. The confirm dialog box contains the message, an OK button, and a Cancel button. For example, a confirmation box might appear when a user attempts to send an e-mail message without a subject. You can create a script that captures the value returned when the user clicks a button. The user could click the Cancel button, which would return false, and then the script would stop submitting the e-mail, and return to the form so that the user can enter a subject. Clicking the OK button would return true, and the e-mail would be sent without a subject.

The prompt method creates the prompt dialog box, which is used to obtain information from the user. The prompt dialog box uses a string, which can be used to indicate to the user what type of information to enter. The information the user enters in the prompt dialog box can then be retrieved. For example, the user might be prompted to enter an e-mail address. The prompt dialog box contains the prompt message, a default string to be placed inside the text box, an OK button, and a Cancel button.

Table 3-1   Window Method Syntax and Examples

Method	Syntax	Example
Alert	window.alert("String")	`window.alert("Please enter your name in the form.")`
Confirm	window.confirm("String")	`window.confirm("Do you want to leave the message line blank?")`
Prompt	window.prompt("Prompt", "Default String")	`window.prompt("Enter your e-mail address","YourName@YourCompany.com")`

In the following sample code, the body of the Web page named windowDialogue.htm creates a form with a button. When the user clicks the button, the onClick event is triggered. The onClick event triggers the EmailPrompt function. This script can be used to prompt the user for information, or to perform error checking, as well as to provide feedback about errors made by the visitor. Note that the variable yourEmail was included in the message sent back to the user. Once this information is obtained from the user, it can be accessed throughout the Web page.

1. Create a new Web page named **windowDialog.htm** with Notepad or your Web page editor.

2. Add the basic HTML tags.

```
<html><head>
```

3. Add a script tag. Create a function named emailPrompt. The emailPrompt function is a script located in the header section of the Web page.

```
<script language = "javascript">
function emailPrompt() {
```

4. The script creates a variable called yourEmail, which will hold the string that the user enters in the text box.

```
var yourEmail = new String() ;
```

5. Then the prompt method is called, and the result returned to the browser is the string. The string is assigned to the variable named yourEmail.

```
yourEmail = window.prompt("What is your e-mail address?",
"YourName@YourCompany.com");
```

6. If the value of the variable returned is null, then the user did not enter any text, and an alert message is displayed; if the user entered an e-mail address, then an alert message informs the user that the sign-up for the e-mail list was successful. The function does not verify that the e-mail address is valid.

```
if (yourEmail == ""){
    alert("You didn't enter an e-mail address yet.") ;
}
else{
    alert("Thank you! Your e-mail address at " +
        yourEmail +
        " will be entered in our mailing list.") ;
}
}
</script>
```

The double equal signs (= =) are used to compare two statements in JavaScript. They are used to check whether one expression is equal to another expression. You must enclose the comparison statement within parentheses. You will learn more about comparing expressions later in this book.

7. Add the code to create the rest of the Web page. Add code to create a button named btnEmail. When the user clicks the button, the onClick event will call the emailPrompt function.

```
<title>E-mail List Sign-up</title>
</head>
<body>
<form name = "form1">
<h1>Click the button to sign up
on our e-mail list.</h1>
<input type = "button" value = "Sign Me Up!"
    name = "btnEmail"
    onClick = "emailPrompt()">
</form></body></html>
```

8. Save the Web page to your data directory, and view it in a Web browser.

There are additional window object properties, methods, and event handlers. Some of these are not well documented, and may not be cross-browser compatible. For example, the navigate method of the window object will change the URL. To use the navigate method, you could use window.navigate("http://www.course.com/");.

Window Event Handlers

The window object, like other objects, is able to respond to events. Two events that a window object responds to are onLoad and onUnload. The onLoad event handler is a block of code that executes immediately after the Web page is loaded. The onUnload event handler is a block of code that executes just before the page is closed. This event is triggered when the user leaves the page for another page. This event handler is very similar in syntax to the onLoad event handler in that it does not require any input, and you can code the response. Because the event is associated with the page, the events are often programmed along with the HTML body tag. Below is a sample of code from windowLoad.htm, which displays alert windows when the page opens and closes.

```
<body onLoad = "alert('Welcome to this page')"
      onUnload = "alert('Goodbye!')">
```

You can indicate a function to be executed, which allows you to execute a group of JavaScript statements. `<body onLoad = "startCode()">`

Recall that the Web page is a document object within a window object. Therefore, you can access the event handlers through the document object using `document.load` and `document.unload`.

The Navigator Object

The navigator object is a child object of the window object. The navigator object provides information about the browser application. For years, the two main browsers, Internet Explorer and Netscape Navigator, have supported HTML standards and JavaScript in their own ways. In spite of ECMAScript and the ECMA-262 standards, these browsers continue to use their own proprietary objects, methods, and properties. Because the different browsers support different features, you can use the navigator object to detect which browser the client is using, and then, if necessary, redirect the user to a Web page that is configured for the correct browser.

There are two main ways to identify the client's browser. With client-side script, the navigator object can provide the browser name and version. The navigator object only allows you to read the properties of the navigator object. However, with server-side script, an object called the browser component can be used to identify not only the browser name and version, but also the objects, properties, and methods supported in that particular browser. The browser component will be covered in detail in a later chapter.

The Navigator Object Properties

The appName property of the navigator object identifies the name of the browser application. The appVersion property identifies the version. The userAgent, which identifies the user agent, is often captured in the Web site log files to determine which browser and operating system platform the visiting client is using. The syntax for reading a navigator object property is navigator.propertyname.

For example, in a Web page named browserVer.htm you could write a short script to detect the browser version, using the appName property. In this example, the known values of the browser names are compared to the appName property. Once the browser version is detected, the browser name and the appName values are written out to the window. You could add an additional statement to redirect the user to a browser-specific page, as shown below.

1. Create a Web page named **browserVer.htm** in Notepad or using your Web page editor.

2. Enter the following HTML and JavaScript statements.

```
<html><head>
<script language = "javascript">
if(navigator.appName == "Netscape"){
    document.write("appName is " + navigator.appName);
}
if (navigator.appName == "Microsoft Internet Explorer") {
    document.write("appName is " + navigator.appName);
}
</script>
<title>Detecting Browser Versions</title>
</head>
<body>
</body></html>
```

3. Save the Web page to your data directory. View the Web page in your browser. If you can, view the Web page in a different browser.

The Location Object

The location object is another child object of the window object. Every window contains a location object. The location object provides information about the URL of the current document, but it only allows you to read the location object properties. The methods associated with the location object are used to redirect the browser window to another URL. You can retrieve the location object from the document object using the location property of the document object, `document.location`.

The Location Object Properties

There are several properties associated with the location object. The HREF property identifies the full URL address for the Web page, for example *http://www.visualinterdev.org/ip/locationobject.htm*. The HREF property returns the same information retrieved from `document.location`. Recall from Chapter 1 that the URL is a combination of the TCP/IP protocol, the domain name, and the path and filename. The protocol is the version of the TCP/IP protocol that is being accessed from the Web page. The usual protocol accessed from a Web page is HTTP, the Hypertext Transport Protocol. In this instance, the TCP/IP protocol is http. Another name for the domain name is the host name. The hostname property identifies the domain name, or host name. For example, the host name for the above URL is *www.visualinterdev.org*. The host property is a combination of the host name and the port number property. Recall from Chapter 1 that the default port for a Web server is 80. Most Web sites do not specify a port number because they use the default port number. If the port number is not specified in the URL, the host of the above URL will be *www.visualinterdev.org*. The pathname property is the path to the file, and includes the filename. The pathname property in the above URL would return `/vc/ip/locationobject.htm`. If there is a bookmark appended to the URL, you can retrieve that information using the hash property. For example, if the URL is *http://www.visualinterdev.org/ip/hash.htm#top*, then the hash property will return #top.

The syntax for reading a location object property is location.propertyName. To display the properties of the location object, you can use the document.write method to write out the name of the location property and the value. The following sample, called location.htm, illustrates how to display some of the common location object properties.

The syntax for the location object can be fully qualified using `document.location.propertyName` or `document.location.method`. However, you do not need to specify the document object. If you are referring to the current document, then you can simply write `location.propertyName` or `location.method`.

1. Create a Web page named **location.htm** in Notepad or using your Web page editor.

2. Enter the following HTML and JavaScript statements.

```
<html><head>
<title>Location Properties</title>
</head>
<body>
<script language = "javascript">
var b = "<BR>";
document.write("document.location = ");
document.write(document.location + b);
document.write("href = ");
document.write(location.href + b);
document.write("protocol = ");
document.write(location.protocol + b);
document.write("host = ");
document.write(location.host + b);
document.write("hostname = ");
document.write(location.hostname + b);
document.write("port = ");
```

```
document.write(location.port + b);
document.write("pathname = ");
document.write(location.pathname + b);
</script>
</body></html>
```

3. Save your Web page as locationProp.htm in your data directory. View the Web page in your browser. If you can, view the Web page in a different browser.

The Location Object Methods

The HTML meta tag allows you to redirect the browser to another Web page. This tag only allows you to configure the number of seconds that lapse before this redirection is initiated. The redirection process cannot be stopped unless the visitor presses the Escape key or clicks the Stop button on the browser. However, you can redirect the browser to another Web page by altering the `location.href` property. This method allows you to redirect the user from within scripts. Therefore, you have more control over when and under what conditions the redirection should take place.

The syntax for redirecting the user with the HREF property is `location.href = "URL"`. The URL can be an absolute or relative address. For example, you can write a script with the statement `location.href="http://www.course.com/"`. This is equivalent to typing in the URL in the address text box on the location bar. Because you are going to this Web page, the page will be included in the history list.

You can use the location methods to change the Web page based upon a condition. The following is a basic Web page named locationCourse.htm that would redirect the user to another Web page. The username variable is compared to a string. If the two strings match, then the browser is redirected to one Web site. If the strings do not match, then the user is redirected to an alternate Web site.

1. Create a Web page named **locationCourse.htm** in Notepad or using your Web page editor.

2. Enter the following HTML and JavaScript statements.

```
<html><head>
<title>Client Redirection</title>
</head>
<body>
<script language = "javascript">
username = "admin";
if (username == "admin"){
     location.href="http://www.course.com/";
}
else {
     location.href="http://www.visualinterdev.org";
}
</script></body></html>
```

3. Save the Web page to your data directory. View the Web page in your browser. If you can, view the Web page in a different browser.

You could have redirected the browser to separate pages within the same Web site by specifying each page's URL.

The reload method, with no arguments passed or with the true argument passed, forces the browser to reload the current Web page in the current window. Arguments can be null, true, or false. The reload method with the false argument passed will cause the browser to reload only if the contents of the Web page have changed. The reload method is equivalent to clicking the Reload button on the browser. The following sample code in reload.htm would create a button that will reload the page.

```
<input type="button" name="reload"
value="Reload the page"
onClick='location.reload()'>
```

The replace method will replace the current URL with a new URL. The replace method replaces the current document entry in the browser's history list. The following sample code would create a button that will replace the current page with a new Web site.

```
<input type="button" name="replace"
value="Replace the page"
onClick='location.replace("http://www.course.com/")'>
```

The History Object

The history object is another child object of the window object. Every window contains a history object. The history object provides information about the URLs that were recently visited. The list of the URLs recently visited is stored in the history list. The history object only allows you to read the history list that was generated during the current browser session. Therefore, you cannot access a previous user's history list. The methods associated with the history object are often used to redirect the user to another URL.

The History Object Properties

The length property identifies the number of entries in the history list. Other properties, such as next and previous, are not enabled, in order to protect the visitor's privacy. To view the number of entries on the list, simply use the **document.write** method to write out the value of the length property, as demonstrated in the sample code below from historyLength.htm.

```
document.write("The length of the ");
document.write("current history list is ");
document.write(window.history.length);
```

The History Object Methods

You can use the history methods next, back, and go to navigate to other pages in the history list. Figure 3-5 illustrates the location of the history list in the browser. Because of security, the history object will not provide the names of the items in the list, so that Web site developers, programmers, and companies cannot obtain the URLs of visitors' history lists. However, these methods do allow you to call a method that accesses the list, and change the current page to the one specified when the method is called.

The syntax for the history object can be fully qualified using `window.history.propertyName` or `window.history.method`. However, you do not need to specify the window object. You can simply write `history.propertyName` or `history.method`.

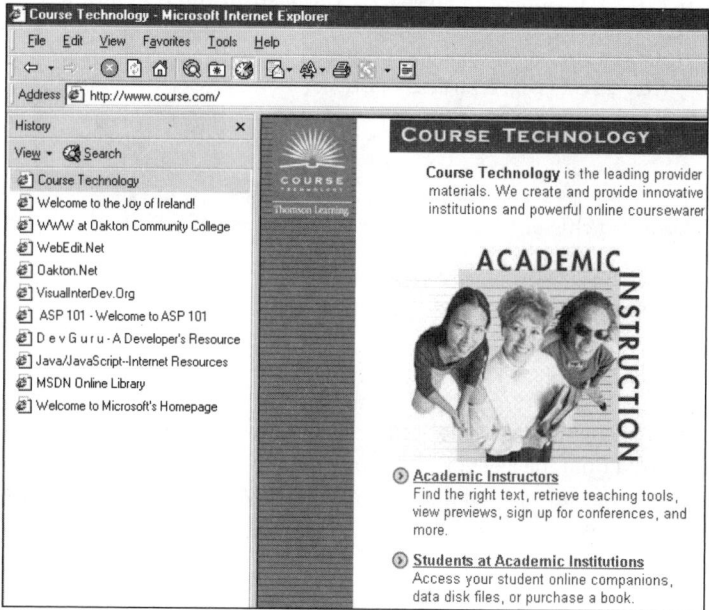

Figure 3-5   The Internet Explorer history list

The back method causes the browser to return to the previous URL in the history list, and the forward method causes the browser to navigate to the next URL in the history list. The following sample code, from historyMethods.htm, creates two buttons that send the browser to the next or the previous listing in the history list.

```
<form>
<input type="button" name="back"
     value="<-  Go Back"
     onClick='history.back()'>
<input type="button" name="forward"
     value="Go Next  ->"
     onClick='history.forward()'>
</form>
```

You can use an image as the link instead of the button. To create an image link to go to a previous page, create a back arrow graphic in a graphics program. Name the back arrow image back.gif. Use the following snippet of code to create the anchor and the image tag. Note that the anchor HREF property retrieves the URL from the previous entry in the history list by using the back method.

```
<a href = "javascript:history.back()">
<img src = "back.gif"></a>
```

Another way to accomplish this task is to use the onClick event for the anchor hyperlink.

```
<a href = "http://www.course.com/"
    onClick='javascript:history.back()';>
<img src = "back.gif">
</a>
```

You can use the keyword javascript to direct the browser to run a script. The script is separated from the keyword by a colon. This is a useful technique when you want to run a JavaScript statement within an HTML object without having to use the script tags.

The go method allows you to specify a URL in the history list based on its sequential number, and then go to that page. The go method can take a positive or negative number as an argument. A negative number causes the browser to move backwards in the history list, and a positive number causes it to move forward. The go method can also take a string as an argument; in the sample below, it searches the history list and goes to the page that best matches the search criteria. Buttons, images, and other objects can use the go method. The following sample code illustrates how to create buttons that will go to a specific listing in the history list.

```
<form>
<input type="button" name="back"
    value="Go Back 1"
    onClick='history.go(-1)'>
<input type="button" name="forward"
    value="Go Forward 1"
    onClick='history.go(1)'>
</form>
```

3

The Document Object

The document object is a child object of the window object. Every window contains a document object. The document object allows direct access to the current Web page. While the window object represents the actual browser window, the document object represents the actual Web page within the window.

The syntax for the document object can be fully qualified using `window.document.propertyName` or `window.document.method`. However, you do not need to specify the window object when referring to the current window. You can simply write `document.propertyName` or `document.method`.

The document object contains many child objects. Because the document object can contain multiple child objects of the same type, these objects are stored in collections, which are also called arrays. These child objects include: the all collection (which contains all of the HTML tags), hyperlinks called anchors, applets, classes for style sheet classes, embeds for embedded objects, forms, ids for style sheet IDs, images, layers for layered objects, text areas, links, plug-ins, and tags for style sheet tags. Later in this chapter, you will learn more about the forms and images collection.

Document Object Properties

HTML tags, such as title and body, can be used to alter the appearance of a Web page. You can also use the document object to control the appearance of a Web page, with the advantage that it allows you to modify its properties, and therefore the appearance of the Web page, on the fly. Table 3–2 lists some of the properties of the document object.

Table 3-2   Document Properties Table

Property	Description
alinkColor	The color of the active hyperlinks on the Web page. Default is red. An active hyperlink is clicked but not yet visited.
background	Identifies a background image to use
bgColor	The background color. If you have an image in the background, then this property will not override the image.
cookie	The document's cookie
defaultClientScript	The default client scripting language—usually JavaScript
defaultServerScript	The default server-side scripting language—usually VBScript
domain	The domain name of the Web server that provided the Web page
fgColor	The foreground color, used for text and headings
lastModified	The date the Web page was last modified or changed
linkColor	The color of the hyperlinks on the Web page. Default is blue.
referrer	The URL of the referring page
text	The default text color
title	The text string that will be displayed in the caption bar
url	The URL of the current page
vlinkColor	The color of the visited hyperlinks on the Web page. Default is purple.

The syntax for retrieving the value of the property is `document.property`. The syntax for setting the document object properties is `document.property = value`. The following sample code, in documentProperties.htm, sets the title and page color properties of the document object and then displays the current properties.

```
<script language = "javascript">
document.title = "Chapter 3 Exercise";
document.bgColor = "silver";
document.fgColor = "maroon";
document.writeln("bgColor is " + document.bgColor + "<br>");
document.writeln("fgColor is " + document.fgColor + "<br>");
document.writeln("alinkColor is " + document.alinkColor +
"<br>");
document.writeln("vlinkColor is " + document.vlinkColor +
"<br>");
document.writeln("linkColor is " + document.linkColor +
"<br>");
</script>
```

You can use the name of the color or the hexadecimal value for the color. For more information about Web page colors and background images, visit *http://www.lifebeyondyahoo.com/life/color.asp*. The document object will display the color values using the hexadecimal value.

3

The following sample code, from documentColor.htm, creates a button that will change the background color of the Web page. You can also set the background color in a script without using a button or hyperlink.

```
<input type="button" name="Silver"
    value="Silver"
    onClick='document.bgColor="silver"'>
```

The following sample code, from documentColor.htm, creates a hyperlink that will change the background color of the Web page. Note that the keyword javascript is used here in combination with the keyword void(0). Void prevents the selected event from occurring. In this case, it stops the hyperlink from going to another URL. Therefore the change in the background color will occur within the current page.

```
<a href="javascript:void(0)"
    onClick='document.bgColor="silver"'>
Silver</a>
```

The referrer is a useful property that allows the script to detect which page provided the link to the current document. The syntax to retrieve the referring URL is `document.referrer`. You can write the information out to the Web page, using `document.writeln(document.referrer)` or you can store the information in a variable using `varlink = document.referrer`. Once you have the information, you can easily write it to a file on the Web server or store it in a database (you will learn more about files and database storage later in this book).

The cookie property allows you to store and read cookies that are associated with the document. A cookie consists of a cookie name and a value, separated by an equal sign. For example, you can create a cookie named CookieState with the value IL by writing `document.cookie = "CookieState=IL";` You can also assign the cookie an expiration date. (You will learn more about cookies and server-side cookie management later in this book.) The following code from documentCookie.htm sets a cookie named userID with a value of John1234 and an expiration date, and reads the cookie into a variable named ReadCookie.

```
document.cookie = "userID=John1234;
    expires=Monday, 01-Jan-02 12:00:00 GMT";
readCookie = document.cookie;
```

The Document Object Methods

The document object has several methods, among them captureEvent, write, and writeln. The captureEvent method, which is only available in Netscape Navigator, is used to capture events that need to be handled. As you have already learned, the write and writeln methods of the document object allow you to write HTML code to your page. The syntax for using the write method is `document.write("string")`. Although both methods have one input, which can consist of text, HTML tags, expressions, and variables, in any combination, the output is a single string. Therefore the text, HTML, expressions, and variables must resolve to a single string.

Combining text, HTML tags, expressions, and variables within the same string is accomplished by means of a process called **concatenation**. A concatenation operator is used to glue the items together as one unified string. Text and HTML tags are always within quotes. The concatenation operator for JavaScript is the plus sign (+). The writeln method differs from the write method, in that it appends a carriage return to the end of the string. This is useful when used in conjunction with the <PRE> tag to create a fixed presentation of the output from the method. The following example, from concat.htm, shows how to use the concatenation operator to concatenate a string and an expression.

```
<script language = "javascript">
document.write("Today is " + Date());
</script>
```

The date method is used to retrieve the current date.

Additional methods that are available to the document object include open and close. The open method is like a whiteboard—it removes the old content from the current document so that it's ready for new content to be written. After it removes the content, it opens a stream to the document, and allows new content to be written. The stream is the connection to the file that allows information to be placed within the document. The close method will close the stream, stopping any further output to the document. The following method, found in concat.htm, illustrates the open and close methods.

```
<script language = "javascript">
document.open();
document.write("Today is " + Date());
document.close();
</script>
```

Another method that is available to the document object is getSelection. This method retrieves the selection that a user has highlighted. However, this is one example of many properties and methods that are not cross-browser compatible. The getSelection method is only available in Netscape Navigator.

Document Object Event Handlers

The document object, like all objects, responds to events. Just as the window object responds to events with event handlers, the document object responds with document handlers. When the user clicks on the page, the onClick event is triggered. Table 3-3 lists descriptions of events that can occur, and the event handler that is triggered.

Table 3-3   Common Document Object Event Handlers

Event Handler	Description
onClick	Action performed when the user clicks a button
onDblClick	Action performed when the user clicks a button twice
onKeyDown	Action performed when the user presses a key
onKeyPress	Used with onKeyDown; action performed while the user holds a key
onKeyUp	Action performed when the user releases a key
onMouseDown	Action performed when the user presses the mouse button
onMouseUp	Action performed when the user releases the mouse button

3

The Forms Collection

The forms collection is a collection of form objects within the document object. The document object is the parent object for the forms collection. While there may be multiple forms within the same document, it is recommended that you assign each form a unique name, using the name property, to make it easier to identify a particular form during the processing of the script. A collection of forms is also known as a forms array. An array is a collection of objects. Each object is numbered according to its sequential position within the array.

There are several form elements, including input, select, and fileupload. The fileupload box contains a type attribute value of file. The fileupload object is used to browse your system for a file location to be uploaded to the server. More details on the fileupload object will be discussed in a later chapter.

Form Properties

The forms collection contains several properties. To refer to a specific form within a script, use the array name or the form name. You must also identify the parent of the form. There are several correct ways to retrieve a form property. If you are retrieving a property that applies to the entire form, you can specify the name of the form or the index number and the property name.

document.form[indexNumber].property
document.form[formName].property

For example, the length property identifies the total number of elements on a form. To retrieve the number of elements on a form, use **document.form.length**.

The first form is the first element of the form array and can be identified as **form[0]**. Each form is identified in the array by its index number. For example, the last form on a page with four forms would be in position 3, and would therefore be identified as **form[3]**. Likewise, each element within the form belongs to an element array. The first text box can be identified as **textbox[0]**. The type of element and the index number identify each element. If you are retrieving a property that applies to a specific element within the form, you can specify the name of the form or the index number, the name of the element or the element type with its index number, and the property name.

document.form[formName].elementName.property
document.form[indexNumber].elementType[indexNumber].property

The name property returns the name of the form field element. Therefore, the complete name for the first text box on the first form on the page would be `document.form[0].textbox[0].name`.

The following script will write out the length property and the other properties of a form. First, create a Web page named formproperties.htm that contains a form. This sample will display the name, method, action, and length of elements in the forms element array.

1. Create a new page named **formproperties.htm** using Notepad or your Web editor.

2. Add the following HTML code to create the page and a form.

```
<html><head>
<title>Form Properties</title>
</head>
<body>
<form name = "login" id = "login"
      method = "post" action = "javascript:void(0)">
<h3>Login Form</h3>
<font face = "Verdana">Username
<input type = "text" name = "username"
      size = "20"><br> Password  
<input type = "text" name = "password"
      size = "20"><br>
<input type = "submit" value = "Submit"
      name = "btnSubmit">
</form><hr>
```

3. Then, add a script following the form to display the properties.

```
<script>
document.write("<b>Login Form Properties </b>");
document.write("<br>");
document.write("<b>Name Property: </b>");
document.write(document.login.name);
document.write("<br>");
document.write("<b>Action Property: </b>");
document.write(document.login.action);
document.write("<br>");
document.write("<b>Method Property: </b>");
document.write(document.login.method);
document.write("<br>");
document.write("<b>Length Property: </b>");
document.write(document.login.length);
</script></body></html>
```

Because the script is referring to the form objects, it must follow the form in sequential order. Placing this script in the heading will cause an error.

4. Save the page to your data directory. View the page in your browser.

Form Methods

The two methods of the forms object are the submit method and reset method. These methods are used when the script submits or resets the form without requiring the user to click the Submit or Reset button. The script can then submit the form when the user types in a username, instead of waiting until the user clicks the Submit button. The submit method can be called explicitly from within a script. In the following sample code, submitForm.htm, when the user types in an e-mail address and presses Enter, the form is submitted using the submit method, the submit event is called, and the onChange event handler calls the alert method.

```
<form name = "email" method = "get"
      action = "formmethods.asp"
      onSubmit = "alert('Thanks for registering!')">
<h3>Sign in with Your E-mail Address</h3>
<input type = "text" name = "email"
      size = "20" onChange = "submit()">
</form>
```

Form Event Handlers

The form object can respond to events such as submit. The onSubmit handler will execute when the submit method is called by the form, or by a script. The onSubmit handler is executed when the submit method is called by a script, or when the user clicks on the Submit button on a form. The onReset handler is executed when the reset method is called by a script, or when the user clicks the Reset button on a form.

Form Elements Event Handlers

Forms can contain a variety of child objects, including text boxes, radio buttons, check boxes, select drop-down list boxes, text areas, and buttons. Each form element has its own set of properties, methods, and events. The following are some examples of how these objects are used to develop interactive Web pages. Form elements can respond to a variety of events, such as click, and have event handlers to respond to these events, such as onClick. Table 3-4 lists several of the event handlers that apply to several types of form elements.

Radio buttons are also called option buttons.

Table 3-4   Form Field Event Handlers

Event Handler	Description
onAbort	Action performed when the user clicks the Stop button in the browser
onBlur	Action performed when an object loses focus
onChange	Action performed when the user changes a value and moves off the object
onClick	Action performed when the user clicks a button
onDragDrop	Action performed when the user drags and drops an object into the window object
onError	Action performed when an error occurs in the script
onFocus	Action performed when an object has the attention
onKeyDown	Action performed when the user presses a key
onKeyPress	Used with onKeyDown; action performed while user holds a key
onKeyUp	Action performed when the user releases a key
onLoad	Action performed when a document object is loaded
onMouseDown	Action performed when the user presses the mouse button
onMouseMove	Action performed when the user moves the mouse
onMouseOut	Action performed when the mouse moves off an object
onMouseOver	Action performed when the user moves the mouse over an object
onMouseUp	Action performed when the user releases the mouse button
onReset	Action performed when the user clicks the Reset button
onResize	Action performed when a window is resized
onSelect	Action performed when the user highlights text
onSubmit	Action performed when the user clicks the Submit button
onUnload	Action performed when a document object is unloaded

The Input Object   The input object is used to create a text box and other form elements. When the type property is set to text, a text box is created, and can be used to retrieve data from the user, or to display information. The textbox object can be used to display information entered by the user at run time. A text box must be declared in the HTML section of code before it can be manipulated by the script code. Properties of the text box object include value, defaultValue, form, name, and type. The value of the text box may be assigned by default, using the value property. You can capture the contents of the text box by accessing this property. Additional properties are available with the input object, such as maxLength, SRC, size, type, and align. Some properties, such as the readOnly property, are only available in Internet Explorer. In the example below, when the user clicks the button, a prompt window opens. The script retrieves the value entered by the user and enters the string into the text box by assigning the string to the value property of the text box.

1. Create a Web page named **inputObject.htm** using Notepad or your Web page editor.

2. Add the following HTML to create a form.

```
<html><head>
<title>Enter Your Name</title>
</head>
<body>
<form name = "form1">
<h1>Click the button to sign in.</h1>
<input type = "text" value = ""
    name = "txtName">
<input type = "button" value = "Click Me"
    onClick = "Prompter()"><br>
</form>
```

3. Add the function, which is called when the user clicks on the button.

```
<script language = "javaScript">
function Prompter() {
var strName = new String()
strName = window.prompt("What is your name?",
    "FirstName");
if (strName == "")
    alert("You need to enter your name. Try again.");
else
    document.form1.txtName.value=strName;
}
</script> </body></html>
```

4. Save the page to your data directory. View the Web page in your browser.

You can use the readOnly property to prevent users from editing text box contents. This allows users to view the text in the text box but not make any changes, as demonstrated below in readonly.htm.

```
<form name = "form1">
<input type = "text" value = "Read Only"
    name = "txtName">
</form>
<script language = "javascript">
document.form1.txtName.readOnly = "True";
</script>
```

The three methods that apply to the textbox object are the blur method, the focus method, and the select method. The blur and focus methods work the same way as they did for the window object. The purpose of the focus method is to make the object the active object. Making a text box active means that the cursor will be placed inside the text box. The focus method is used so that the user can type directly into the text box, without having to click in the text box first, which saves the user a step. The focus method can help you direct the user to the form fields to be completed first. To call the focus method to an object called txtName, the code `txtName.focus()` is used. No parameters are passed to the focus method. To use the focus method in a form, you can call the focus method using code such as `document.form1.user.focus();`.

The select method makes the text box active, just as the focus method does, but it also selects any text in the text box. The selected text is highlighted, as if the user had selected it. This allows the user to easily change the text, by simply typing over it. For example, you can add the select method to the body tag to select a form field when the page loads. The code would look something like `<body onload='document.form1.userName.select()'>`. You can also call the select method in a form using code such as `document.form1.txtName.select();`.

The type property of the input element can be set to text, hidden, password, checkbox, or radio button. Many of the properties, methods, and event handlers are the same for the various input elements. However, the checkbox element has an additional property called checked that indicates whether the object is currently checked. DefaultChecked is the property that is used to make the object checked by default when the user loads the page. Checked and defaultChecked are Boolean properties, and therefore the possible values are either true or false. To change the checked property of a check box named chkbox on a form named form1, so as to indicate that the check box has been checked, you would write `document.form1.chkbox.checked = true`.

The click method and the onClick event handler apply to both the radio button and the checkbox form input elements. The onClick event handler can be used to detect the click event. When the user clicks the object, the onClick event handler is called. The programmer can write commands that execute when the onClick event is detected. The following sample, called onClickColor.htm, illustrates how the radio button onClick event handler is called.

```
<html><head>
<title>onClick Event Handler</title>
</head>
<body>
<input type = "radio" name = "rdbtn1"
    onClick = "return rdbtn1_onclick()">
Click here to change your background color.
<script language = "javascript">
function rdbtn1_onclick() {
    document.write("This is your color.");
    document.fgColor = "Maroon";
    document.bgColor = "Silver";
}
</script></html>
```

The Select Object The list box and drop-down list box are both select form objects created with the select html tag. A select object must be declared in the HTML section of code before it can be manipulated by the script code. A list box displays all items in the list. A drop-down box is configured to occupy less screen space, and that fact alone can make it preferable to the list box. The drop-down box allows the users to select one or more items in a predefined list. If the number of items in a drop-down box exceeds the available screen space, then scroll bars appear automatically.

Again, the select object contains methods such as blur and focus, and event handlers such as onBlur, onChange, and onFocus. The properties for the select object include name, form, and type. Type returns `select-multiple` or `select-one` to indicate which type of select object was used. Additional properties include length, options, selectedIndex, and text. Length is an integer that identifies the number of options in the list. The length property retrieved as `document.select.length` is not the same thing as the size property. Size is the select attribute that allows you to specify how many options are visible without scrolling. A size of more than one will create a basic list. A size of one creates a drop-down list box. The size property is retrieved with `document.select.size`. The name is the string of the name of the selection list.

Each item in the list is called an option. The options are all members of an array, and are referred to by their position in the array. The position is known as the index number. The first item has an index number of zero and is called `option[0]`. The selectedIndex property is an integer that contains the index number of the currently selected option. To retrieve the selectedIndex integer you could write `document.form1.select.selected Index`. The value property of the list box allows you to obtain the value of the selected option during run time. The value property only works if the value attribute of the list box is set in HTML. To find the value property for the select object in the following example, you would use the following code: `document.form1.select.options[0].value`. The following sample creates a drop-down list box using the select html tag.

1. Create a page named **selectList.htm** using Notepad or your Web editor.

2. Enter the HTML below to create the form.

```
<html><head>
<title>Select List</title>
</head>
<body>
<form name = "form1">
<select size = "1" name = "product" onChange = "cp()">
<option value = "Pencils">Pencils</option>
<option value = "Pens">Pens</option>
<option value = "Paper">Paper</option>
</select></form>
```

3. Enter the script that will display the properties of the select object. The variable named b is used to store a line break tag.

```
<script language = "javascript">
var b = "<BR>";
document.write(b + "Length: ");
document.write(document.form1.product.length);
document.write(b + "Size: ");
document.write(document.form1.product.size);
document.write(b + "Choices:");
document.write(b + document.form1.product[0].value);
document.write(b + document.form1.product[1].value);
document.write(b + document.form1.product[2].value);
</script>
```

4. Enter the script that will display the value of the selected item, after it is selected. The cp function is called when the user selects an item in the list.

```
<script language = "javascript">
function cp(){
     document.write("You selected item: " +
     document.form1.product.value);
}
</script></body></html>
```

5. Save the page to your data directory. View the page in your browser.

 The value attribute must be set to effectively use the drop-down box.

The Button Object   The button object is used to allow the user to start a sequence of events. When it is clicked, the custom code that is written in its event procedure can be executed. A button must be declared in the HTML code before a script can manipulate it. When the button is clicked, the click event is detected and the onClick event handler code is executed. The following sample, from buttonProperty.htm, will change the text displayed on the push button, using the value property.

```
<html><head>
<title>Button Property</title>
</head>
<body>
<form name = "form1">
<input type="button" value="Click Here!"
     name="btn1" onClick="tryagain()">
</form>
<script language = "javascript">
function tryagain(){
document.form1.btn1.value = "Great!";
}
</script></body></html>
```

The push button only needs to be clicked once to trigger its events. If the user double-clicks the button, then the event procedure will be invoked twice. When you click a push button, you also trigger a mouse up and a mouse down event. Errors often occur when conflicting code is written for these three events.

3

The Image Object   The images collection is a collection of image objects within the document. The document is the parent object for the images collection. Images can be referred to by their name, or by their index number in the images array. The image object contains many properties, including border, height, width, hspace, vspace, lowsrc, and name. The three event handlers of the image object are onAbort, onError, and onLoad.

The most common use of the image object is the mouseover, or image swap. An image swap will change the image source property of an image when an event occurs. This event is often a mouseOver event for an anchor object, a mouseOver event for the image object, or a click event for a button object. The sample below creates an image swap based on the mouseOver event of the anchor object. A more detailed example of an image swap is found in a later chapter.

1. Visit Life Beyond Yahoo at *http://www.lifebeyondyahoo.com/life/graphics.asp* to locate two graphics. Save the two images to your data directory. (*Hint*: To save the images, right-click the mouse over the image and click Save Picture As.) Alternately, you can create your own images in a desktop publishing or art program. You can also retrieve two graphics from *http://www.visualinterdev.org/ip/samples/chapter3/one.gif* or *http://www.visualinterdev.org/ip/samples/chapter3/two.gif*.

2. Create a page named **imageswap.htm** with Notepad or your Web editor.

3. Add the basic HTML code, an image, and a hyperlink. Make sure to name the image. The height and width properties of your object may vary. Add a button and an onClick event handler for the button. When the user clicks on the button, the changeImage function will be called.

```
<html><head>
<title>Image Swapping</title>
</head>
<body><center>
<form name = "form1">
<img name ="myImg" src = "one.gif"><br>
<input type = "button" value = "Change Image"
     onClick = "changeImage()">
</form></center>
```

You can rename the first image one.gif and rename the second image two.gif, or modify the code to reflect the filenames of the images you selected.

4. Place the changeImage function after the HTML code to ensure that the objects are created before the code is executed. Change the source property of the image to a new URL. The source property can be indicated using `document.form1.myImg.src`. You can specify the absolute or relative path to the new image.

```
<script language = "javascript">
function changeImage(){
document.form1.myImg.src = "two.gif";
}
</script></body></html>
```

5. Save the page to your data directory. View the page in your browser.

CHAPTER SUMMARY

Object-oriented Programming

❑ Object-oriented programming allows you to access built-in and custom objects. Objects contain collections of methods and properties. Methods are also known as functions. Functions are a group of programming commands. Properties are characteristics of the object that are assigned a name and value. You can use objects to store methods and properties that can be reused across applications. You can also use objects to separate business logic rules from the presentation of the application. Browsers contain built-in objects that can be accessed using client-side scripting. You can also create custom objects using client-side scripting. The server software contains built-in objects that can be accessed using server-side scripting.

❑ Object methods and properties are encapsulated within the object definition. The object definition is created with a constructor function. New objects are instantiated. Instantiation is the process of creating new objects, based upon an existing object. You use the Web application to interface with the newly instantiated object.

Browser Object Model

❑ The Browser Object Model contains many built-in objects that exist in a hierarchical structure. These objects contain their own sets of methods, properties, and event handlers. Event handlers are functions that are executed when the program detects an event, or change in the system. The window object is the highest object in the hierarchy.

❑ The object name refers to the object name and its complete ancestry.

ObjectName.Property
ObjectName.Method()

3

To alter the status message bar

```
window.status="This is the status message"
```

To create dialog boxes

```
window.alert("This is the alert message")
window.confirm("This is the confirm message")
window.prompt("This is the prompt message",
"This is the default string in the text box")
```

To open a new window and alter its appearance

```
window.open("MyPage.htm", "windowName",
"height = 200, width = 400,
status = no, toolbar = no,
menubar = no, location = no")
```

To close a window

```
window.close()
```

To display the browser name

```
navigator.appName
```

To display the browser version

```
navigator.appVersion
```

To display the user agent

```
navigator.userAgent
```

To display the complete URL of the current document

```
location.href
```

To display a portion of the URL, such as the hostname

```
location.hostname
```

To redirect the window to a new document

```
location.href = ("http://www.course.com/")
```

To display the number of entries in the history list

```
window.history.length
```

To move to the previous window in the history list

```
window.history.back()
```

To move to the next window in the history list

```
window.history.next()
```

To move to a specific entry in the history list

```
window.history.go(2)
```

To write to the document in the current window, or in a specific window

```
document.write("StringAndHTML" + Variables)

windowName.document.write("StringAndHTML" + Variables)
```

To display the document properties, such as the document title, referring page, and last modified date

```
document.title
document.referrer
document.lastModified
```

To change the document properties, such as the background and foreground colors

```
document.bgColor = "green"
document.fgColor = "white"
```

To handle events such as when the document loads or closes

```
<body onLoad="alert('Welcome to this page')"
onUnload="alert('Goodbye!')">
```

To display the form properties, such as the name of the form

```
window.document.loginform.name
```

To submit the form without the user's intervention

```
submit()
```

To handle events such as when the form is submitted

```
<form name = "email" method = "get"
action = "formmethods.asp"
onsubmit = "alert('Thanks!')">
```

3

To display the object properties, such as the name

```
document.form1.txtName.name
```

To display the object properties, such as the value

```
document.form1.txtName.value
```

To change the contents of a property, such as the value property readOnly

```
document.form1.txtName.value = "Pencils"
document.form1.txtName.readOnly = "True"
```

To change the focus to the object or remove the focus

```
document.form1.txtName.focus()
document.form1.txtName.blur()
```

To change the focus to the object and highlight the contents of the object

```
document.form1.txtName.select()
```

To handle events such as when the object is clicked (onClick)

```
<input type = "button" name = "btn1"
value = "Change Image"
onClick = "ChangeImage()">
```

To change the contents of a property, such as the src property

```
window.document.myImg.src = "img.gif";
```

REVIEW QUESTIONS

1. Client-side scripting will be rendered the same way in all browsers. True or False?
2. VBScript and JavaScript contain all the same objects, methods, properties, and event handlers. True or False?
3. A radio button must be created in HTML before it can be modified by any script code. True or False?
4. An object definition is used to instantiate the object. True or False?

5. To set an object's property, use the _____ syntax.

   a. property.object = value

   b. object.value = property

   c. object.property = value

   d. either a or b

6. You created a button named btnNextPage. Which of the following would change the text that appears on the button to the word "Next"?

   a. `NextPage.value = "Next"`

   b. `name.btnNextPage = "Next"`

   c. `btnNextPage.value = "Next"`

   d. `btnNextPage.name = "Next"`

7. What type of function is used to create a new custom object definition?

   a. constructor function

   b. regular function

   c. new function

   d. ObjectCreator function

8. Which of the following is an example of a method?

   a. `document.form1`

   b. `window.document.image.src = "one.gif"`

   c. `close()`

   d. `height`

9. Which of the following is the topmost object in the Browser Object Model?

   a. window

   b. document

   c. navigator

   d. browser

10. Which of the following is the parent to the forms collection of objects?

   a. window

   b. document

   c. navigator

   d. browser

11. Which term describes the process used to create a new object?

    a. encapsulation

    b. instantiation

    c. new()

    d. newObject()

12. An object can perform functions by calling its _____.

    a. properties

    b. methods

    c. events

    d. none of the above

13. Which property distinguishes a drop-down box from a list box?

    a. number

    b. value

    c. option

    d. size

14. Which event handler will be executed when the user clicks on a link?

    a. onMouseUp

    b. onMouseOut

    c. onClick

    d. onMouseOver

15. What is the scripting language supported by both Netscape Navigator and Microsoft Internet Explorer browsers?

    a. JScript

    b. JavaScript

    c. VBScript

    d. Visual Basic

16. Actions such as clicking, double-clicking, and scrolling are called _____.

    a. functions

    b. methods

    c. events

    d. procedures

17. The contents of a text box displayed in the browser are stored in its
_____ property.

a. text

b. value

c. length

d. name

18. Which method is used to make a text box active, but not highlight the contents of the text box?

a. focus

b. change

c. select

d. blur

19. You have a variable named FirstName, which contains the user's name. You want to greet the user personally. Which of the following statements would be displayed correctly in the browser?

a. `document.write("Welcome FirstName to SSI")`

b. `document.write("Welcome" FirstName "to SSI")`

c. `document.write("Welcome" + FirstName + "to SSI")`

d. `document.write(Welcome FirstName to SSI)`

20. To create a dialog box to retrieve e-mail addresses, which method should you use?

a. alert

b. prompt

c. confirm

d. window

HANDS-ON PROJECTS

Project 3-1

In this project, you will create a custom object that will display the customer's e-mail address.

1. Open Notepad or your Web editor to create a new page named **emailObject.htm**.

2. Add the basic HTML tags (html, head, title, body).

3. In the heading, add a client-side script tag. Make sure to specify the language attribute as JavaScript and add the closing script tag.

4. Between the script tags, create a constructor function. The name of the object should be CustomerEmail. The function will contain one property, named CEMail, which will be retrieved when the object is created. Pass the first name of the customer to the

constructor function when the object is created, using the variable name email. There is one method defined in the constructor function. Name the method getCustomerEmail. The getCustomerEmail method will call the function getEmail. Use the following code as a guide.

```
function CustomerEmail(email) {
this.CEMail= email;
this.getCustomerEmail = getEmail;
}
```

5. Create the getEmail function in the same script, to display the customer e-mail address.

```
function getEmail(){
document.write("Your email address is: "
     +  this.CEMail);
}
```

6. In the body of the Web page, add the client-side script tag. Make sure to include the language attribute and the closing script tag. Replace the e-mail address below with your e-mail address.

```
newEmail = new
CustomerEmail("yourname@youraddress.com");
```

7. Call the object method that will display the e-mail address.

```
newEmail.getCustomerEmail();
```

8. Save the Web page to your data directory. View the Web page in a browser.

Project 3-2

In this project, you will create a Web page that changes the status message.

1. Open your Web page editor, or use Notepad to create a page named **statusMsg.htm**.

2. Add the basic HTML tags (html, head, title, body).

3. In the heading, add a client-side script tag. Make sure to specify the language attribute as JavaScript and add the closing script tag.

4. Between the script tags, change the status message to your school name.

5. Save the page to your data directory. View the page in your browser.

Project 3-3

In this project, you will create a Web page named windowCreate.htm that will open a new instance of a window object.

1. Open your Web page editor, or use Notepad and create a page named **windowCreate.htm**.

2. Add the basic HTML tags (html, head, title, body).

3. Create a button that will open a window at the Course Technology Web site. In the input tag, call a function named NewWindow() when the user clicks the button.

```
<input type = "button"
value = "Visit Course Technology Web site"
onClick = "NewWindow();">
```

4. In the heading, add a client-side script tag. Make sure to specify the language attribute as JavaScript and add the closing script tag.

5. Between the script tags, add a function named NewWindow.

6. In the newly created function, create a new window, and open the Course Technology Web site. Turn off all of the toolbar, status, location, and menu bars. The window should be 300 pixels wide by 400 pixels high. Don't forget to keep the statements all on one line of code.

```
function NewWindow(){
window.open("http://www.course.com","",
    "height=400,width=300,status=no,
    toolbar=no,menubar=no,location=no");
}
```

7. Save your page in your data directory. View the page in the browser. Test the button.

Project 3-4

In this project, you will create a group of Web pages that allow the user to move back and forth through the history list by clicking a button.

1. Open your Web page editor, or use Notepad.

2. Create five pages, named **first.htm, second.htm, third.htm, fourth.htm, and fifth.htm**.

3. On each page you create, add the basic HTML tags (html, head, title, body).

4. Add a heading that identifies the name of the Web page. (*Hint*: <h1> First </h1>)

5. Create a table of contents named **toc.htm** that will display the list of pages you just created.

6. Create a link to each of the pages.

```
<p><a href = "first.htm">first.htm</a></p>
<p><a href = "second.htm">second.htm</a></p>
<p><a href = "third.htm">third.htm</a></p>
<p><a href = "fourth.htm">fourth.htm</a></p>
<p><a href = "fifth.htm">fifth.htm</a></p>
```

7. On the bottom of the page, create two buttons that, when clicked, move the user back to the previous page in the history list.

```
<form>
<input type = "submit" value = "<- Go Back"
    onClick= "window.history.back();">
```

```
<input type = "submit" value = "Go Next ->"
    onClick= "window.history.forward();">
</form>
```

8. In between the two buttons, add a third button that will move the user to the table of contents page when the user clicks it.

```
<input type = "submit" value = "Table of Contents"
onClick = "location.href='toc.htm'">
```

9. Copy and paste the code for the hyperlinks and the three buttons on the bottom of each of the five pages.

10. Save all of the pages in your data directory.

11. View the index page in the browser. Click on all of the links to test them.

Project 3-5

In this project, you will create a Web page that obtains information from the user, using dialog boxes.

1. Open your Web page editor, or use Notepad and create a page named **prompter.htm**.

2. Add the basic HTML tags (html, head, title, body).

3. In the body tag, include an event handler called onLoad that calls a function named prompter. When the page loads in the browser, the onLoad event will be handled by the onLoad event handler, and the prompter function will be executed. The prompter function will create the dialog boxes.

```
<body onLoad = "prompter()">
```

4. In the heading, add a client-side script tag. Make sure to specify the language attribute as JavaScript and add the closing script tag.

5. Between the script tags, create a function called prompter. Don't forget the curly braces!

```
function prompter(){
}
```

6. In the prompter function, create two variables named strName and strEmail that will hold the user's name and e-mail address.

```
var strEmail, strname
```

7. Use the `window.prompt` method to create a dialog box that will get the user's name.

```
strName = window.prompt("What is your name?",
"FirstNameOnly");
```

8. Use the `window.prompt()` method to create a dialog box that will get the user's e-mail address.

```
strEmail = window.prompt("What is your E-mail Address?",
"yourname@yourcompany.com") ;
```

9. Use the `document.write` method to write out the user's name and e-mail address.

```
document.write("Welcome " + strName)
document.write("<BR>")
document.write("Your e-mail address is listed as : " +
strEmail)
```

10. Save the page to your data directory. View the page in your browser.

CASE PROJECTS

Online Consulting, Inc.: Human Resources

You have been hired as a consultant to create a Web site that maintains employee data. You would like to store this information in a custom object named employee, so that the information and methods can be used anywhere in your Web page.

a. Create a Web page named **caseCustom.htm**, using Notepad or your Web page editor. Create a custom object using the constructor function that will display the user's name, address, e-mail address, phone number, and department.

b. Create the properties of the object within the constructor function. The names of the properties should be: first, last, street, city, state, zipcode, emailaddress, phone, department. Don't forget that these properties will retrieve their values when the object is created. Therefore, you will have to pass the values in an argument in the constructor function.

c. Create a method named getEmp within the constructor function that will call on another function named getEmployee.

d. Create the getEmployee function that will display the employee information. The output from the function should appear as in the following example:

Moira Coughlin

555 Main Street

Yorktown, IL, US 60099

mailto:Moira@visualinterdev.org

312-555-5555

e. Within the Web page, instantiate a new employee object.

f. Change the properties of the employee object when you create the object. You should pass the values when you instantiate the object.

g. Call the object method to display the information.

h. Save the Web page to your data directory. View the Web page in your browser.

Online Consulting, Inc.: Internet Programming Resources

You are responsible for creating a Web site for your fellow consultants that contains an online dictionary of Internet programming terms.

a. Using your Web page editor, create five Web pages. Each Web page will list the name and definition of one of the new terms mentioned in this chapter. Save the page with the name of the term. Do not use spaces in the file name.

b. Create a Web page named **caseterm.htm** that lists the five terms.

c. Create a hyperlink from each term to the corresponding definition page.

d. Create a button on the page that closes the window when clicked.

e. Save all the pages to your data directory. View the pages in the browser, and test the links.

f. Open caseterm.htm in your editor.

g. Modify the links, so that when the user clicks on a link, a new window will open with the corresponding definition page. The toolbar, menu bar, location, and status bar should not be visible. The scroll bars may be left on. Alter the width and height property to a size appropriate to your content.

Online Consulting, Inc.: Product Display

You have been hired to help develop a Web site that will display the company's products. To do this, you will create a Web page that contains buttons. When the user clicks a button, the product image will appear on the page.

a. Search the Internet for five pictures of products that you plan to offer at your store. The pictures should be equal in size (width and height). If they are not the same height, use a Web graphics editor to crop them to the same dimensions. Make sure that you only select freeware graphics. Freeware graphics are graphics that you have a legal right to display on your site without permission from the owner. If you have a graphics program, you can create your own graphics.

b. Using your Web page editor, create one Web page named **caseProducts.htm**.

c. Add one of the graphics to your Web page. This will be your default graphic image. Name the image switcher. Below is an example.

```
<img name = "switcher" border = 0"
src = "pencilsFan.gif"
width = "256" height = "192">
```

d. Create four buttons on the Web page. Don't forget to add the form tag, and to name the form!

e. Name each button with the name of the product it will display.

f. Add an onClick event handler to the button tag.

g. The onClick event handler should change the source of the switcher image to the new image. Below is an example. Make sure to put the name of the image in single quotes!

```
<input type = "button" name = "yellowpad"
value = "Large notepads"
onClick = "window.document.form1.switcher.src =
yellownotepad.jpg';">
```

h. Repeat this for the other three buttons.

i. Save your page to your data directory. View the page in the browser. Test the buttons by clicking on each one. The new image should appear where the original image was located.

Online Consulting, Inc: Browser Identification

You have been asked to help a company that is having problems with their Web site, as a result of browser incompatibility. To solve the problem, you will create a page that can redirect the user to another page, depending upon the browser the client is using.

a. Using your Web page editor, create a page named **caseBrowser.htm**.

b. Create two pages, named **IE.htm** and **NN.htm**. On the IE.htm page, include a heading that states **This is the IE page**. On the NN.htm page, include a heading that states, **This is the NN Page**.

c. In the heading of the caseBrowser.htm page, create a function named check-browser().

d. In the function, write a script that will retrieve the browser name from the navigator object. Create a variable named bn that will hold the browser name.

e. Assign the bn value to the browser name. You can get the browser name from the navigator object's appname property.

```
bn = navigator.appName
```

f. Test the bn variable to see if it is "Netscape".

```
if(bn== "Netscape")
```

g. If it is, then redirect the user to the NN.htm page.

```
location.href = "NN.htm"
```

h. If it is not, then redirect the user to the IE.htm page.

```
location.href = "IE.htm"
```

i. Save your page to your data directory. View the page with both browsers. Try to test the page in different versions of Internet Explorer and Navigator.

4

DATA STORAGE

In this chapter you will:

- Learn what variables are, and how to declare and name them
- Use variables to store and retrieve data
- Learn about the variable data types
- Create local variables and global variables
- Create custom constants
- Create and declare arrays

In the previous chapter you learned how to create basic objects, and how to implement the Document Object Model. You used object-oriented programming to manipulate objects and their properties, methods, and event handlers. In this chapter you will use JavaScript and VBScript to implement variables, constants, and arrays. These data structures are used widely in Web applications, for example to store application-wide variables that do not change, or to store data that varies from user to user.

VARIABLES

Variables are used to store data that can be retrieved at a later time. For example, a variable might be used to store a value that is to be used in a calculation that occurs later in a script. If you need to calculate several values, compare values, or perform multiple operations on a value, then it is worthwhile to use a variable to store the value in lieu of using the value itself. The code can then refer to the variable instead of the value.

A variable consists of two parts: a **variable name** and a **data type**. While it is obvious that the name refers to the variable name, it is less obvious that the name also refers to a section of memory on the computer. This section of memory defines the location where the variable is stored while the program executes. The exact location of the variable in the computer's memory is unimportant because the programmer can refer to the location by using the name of the variable. Although JavaScript and VBScript follow the generic programming naming conventions, each has different rules for naming and declaring variables.

The data type identifies what kind of data the variable can store. For example, a variable might be an **integer** used in a calculation, or it might be a **string** of characters that will be used to store the name of a company. JavaScript and VBScript support different data types.

Variable Declaration

Some programming languages require you to declare a variable before you can use it in a script or program. **Declaring** a variable is the process of reserving the memory space for the variable before it is used. Although neither JavaScript nor VBScript requires you to declare variables, declaring variables is a good programming practice. If a variable is not declared, the memory to store it will be allocated when the variable is first used. Variables are declared within the **scope** in which they are being used. Some variables are used within a local function. Some variables, called **application** or **global variables**, are used across the Web site. The value of a variable can be assigned when it is declared, or later in the script.

In JavaScript, a variable is declared with the keyword `var` and the name of the variable. In VBScript, a variable is declared with the keyword `dim` and the name of the variable. Variables declared with the dim (VBScript) or var (JavaScript) keyword exist as long as the procedure in which they are declared exists. There are several common naming conventions used for variables. Naming conventions are used to make it easier to identify the type of data stored in the variable. For example, `str` is used as the prefix in the variable name if it stores a string. The name of the variable does not require you to store a particular type of data, nor does it affect how the memory space is reserved for the variable. Although you can name your variable without using any naming convention, following the naming convention makes it easier for you to identify the variable data type. The syntax for declaring a variable using JavaScript is **var variableName**. The syntax for declaring a variable using VBScript is **dim variableName**.

If you have multiple variables to declare, you can declare each one on a separate line, or use a single line. To declare several variables on a single line, use the declaration keyword once, followed by the list of variables separated by commas.

The following sample code shows how to declare a variable using JavaScript.

```
var strProduct, intQuantity, intPrice, intCost, strName,
strEmail;
```

Recall that in JavaScript each statement ends in a semicolon (;).

The following sample code shows how to declare a variable using VBScript.

```
dim strProduct, intQuantity, intPrice, intCost, strName,
strEmail
```

You can force a program written in VBScript to declare all variables before the variables can be used. Although you are not required to force the declaration of variables before they are used, doing so will make it easier to debug your code. For example, it will help you catch spelling and syntax errors. If you type in the wrong name for a variable, the program will not run until you declare the variable with the correct name. Use the term Option Explicit to force all variables to be declared before they can be used. This statement must be placed at the top of the Web page, before any other HTML or scripts. When this code is executed on the Web server, the inline script tag must be used to indicate that this rule is to be applied to the server-side script. The code to force variable declaration with server-side VBScript is `<% option explicit %>`.

Data Storage and Retrieval

Both JavaScript and VBScript allow you to store values in variables using the assignment operator. In both VBScript and JavaScript, the assignment operator is the equal sign (=). To assign a value to a variable, enter the name of the variable on the left side of the assignment operator, and enter the new value of the variable on the right side of the assignment operator.

Note that the equal sign is an assignment operator, not an arithmetic operator.

In Figure 4-1, a Web page named vassign.htm displays the total cost of an oatmeal cookie order. The code assigns values to several variables. Assigning a variable a value is the same in JavaScript and VBScript. The variable strP holds the product name. The variables intQ, intP, and intC hold the integer numbers for the quantity, price, and total cost of a product. The variables strN and strE hold the user's name and e-mail address. After the variables are defined, a calculation is performed using two variables, intP and intQ. The result of this formula is stored in another variable, intC. The intC variable is a calculated variable.

If the variable has not been assigned a value before it is retrieved, then the value "undefined" is assigned to it. If you write an unassigned variable to a Web page, the word "undefined" is displayed.

The example below, which creates the Web page illustrated in Figure 4-1, demonstrates how to declare and assign values using both JavaScript and VBScript. It also demonstrates how to retrieve data from a value, and how to use the value in an expression. The main difference between using JavaScript and VBScript in these two examples is the use of the keyword var or dim, and the addition of the semicolon at the end of each JavaScript statement.

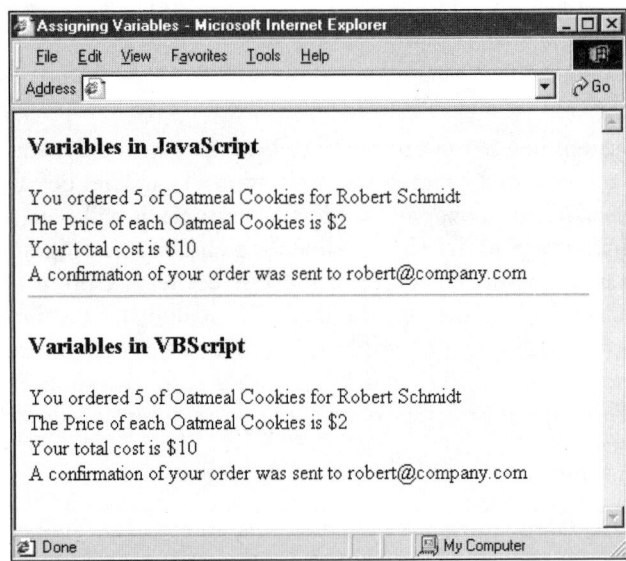

Figure 4-1   Declaring and assigning a value in JavaScript and VBScript

1. Use Notepad or a Web development tool to create a new Web page named **vassign.htm**.

2. Add the basic HTML tags to create the Web page.

```
<html><head><title>Assigning Variables</title></head>
<body bgcolor = "#FFFF99">
<h3>Variables in JavaScript</h3>
<hr>
<h3>Variables in VBScript</h3>
</body></html>
```

3. Immediately below the first heading, add a script to declare variables in JavaScript and assign them values. After a variable is assigned a value, the value can be used within the scope of the variable.

```
<script language = "javascript">
var strP, intQ, intP, intC, strN, strE, b;
b = "<br>";
intQ = 5;
intP = 2;
strN = "Robert Schmidt";
strE = "robert@company.com";
strP = "Oatmeal Cookies";
```

4. The intC variable is assigned to the product of product (intP) multiplied by the quantity (intQ). To assign a calculated value to a variable, enter the name of the variable on the left side of the assignment operator, and enter the formula that will calculate the new value on the right side of the assignment operator.

```
intC = (intP * intQ);
```

5. The variables are displayed in the Web browser using the **document.write** method. Note that the variables can be written to the Web page alongside the text and HTML tags.

```
document.write("You ordered " + intQ + " of ");
document.write(strP + " for " + strN + b);
document.write("The Price of each " + strP);
document.write("is   $" + intP + b);
document.write("Your total cost is $" + intC + b);
document.write("A confirmation of your order ");
document.write("was sent to " + strE);
</script>
```

Recall that when you use the **document.write** method in JavaScript, you must use parentheses to enclose the arguments.

6. Below the second heading, add a script to declare variables in VBScript and assign them values.

```
<script language = "vbscript">
dim strP, intQ, intP, intC, strN, strE, b
b = "<br>"
intQ = 5
intP = 2
strN = "Robert Schmidt"
strE = "robert@company.com"
strP = "Oatmeal Cookies"
```

7. Add the code to calculate the value of the cost of the product.

```
intC = (intP * intQ)
```

4

8. The variables are again displayed in the Web browser using the `document.write` method. Notice that the concatenation operator in VBScript is an ampersand (&).

```
document.write("You ordered " & intQ & " of ")
document.write(strP & " for " & strN & b)
document.write("The Price of each " & strP)
document.write("is  $" & intP & b)
document.write("Your total cost is $" & intC & b)
document.write("A confirmation of your order ")
document.write("was sent to " & strE)
</script>
```

9. Save the page to your data directory. View the Web page in your browser.

Calculating Values Based on User Input from a Form

Variables contain values, which can be used in other parts of the script. In the oatmeal cookie example above, modifying the quantity of the item would require reprogramming the Web page. In the previous chapter you learned how to access objects, properties, and events using the Document Object Model. The example below illustrates how the value of the variable can be used to store information that is obtained from the user. The user enters the information, such as the quantity, into a form. When the user submits the form, the script calculates the cost based on the quantity ordered. The following example, illustrated in Figure 4–2, demonstrates how to retrieve values from a form using both JavaScript and VBScript. The Web page will assign a value to a variable based upon the value entered on a form.

1. Use Notepad or a Web editor to create a new Web page named **vorder.htm**.

2. Add the basic HTML tags to create the Web page.

```
<html><head><title>Assigning Variables</title></head>
<body bgcolor = "#FFFF99">
<h3>Variables in JavaScript</h3>
<hr>
<h3>Variables in VBScript</h3>
</body></html>
```

3. Immediately below the first heading, add the code to create a form with three text boxes, as shown below. Note that the name of the form is "formJS". The form must have a name to distinguish it from the second form in the Web page. The value attribute of the input tag is used to assign a default value for the txtQ and txtP fields.

```
<form name = "formJS" method = "post">
<input type="text" value="0" name="txtQ" size="7">
Quantity <br><br>
<input type="text" value="0" name="txtP" size="7">
Price <br><br>
<input type="text" name="txtC" size="7">
Total Cost <br><br>
```

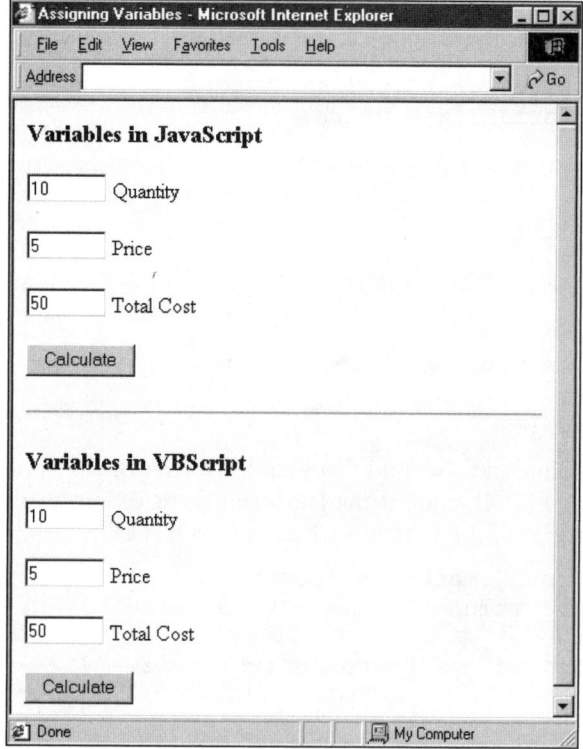

Figure 4-2   Using variables to calculate values based on input from a form

4. Add a Submit button. The function that is called when the Submit button is clicked is called calcJS.

```
<input type="button" value="Calculate" name="btnSubmit"
    onClick="calcJS()">
</form>
```

5. Create the calcJS function to declare the variables, calculate the new value for the cost, and then display the new cost in the txtC text box. To define the function, use the keyword function, the name of the function, a pair of parentheses (), and the open curly brace.

```
<script language = "javascript">
function calcJS(){
```

6. Declare the three variables on a single line, using the var keyword.

```
var intQ, intP, intC;
```

7. Assign the value of the txtQ text box to a variable named intQ text box. Note that you must name the txtQ text box using the full ancestry and form field name, as you learned in the previous chapter. This means that you must include the name of the form, formJS. The value in the txtQ text box is retrieved from

the form field using the value property. Assign the value of the txtP text box to the intP variable, using the value property.

```
intQ = document.formJS.txtQ.value;
intP = document.formJS.txtP.value;
```

8. The cost variable is calculated using the product of the two variables intQ and intP.

```
intC = (intP * intQ);
```

9. Assign the value of the txtC field to the intC variable. End the function with the closing curly brace.

```
document.formJS.txtC.value = intC;
}
</script>
```

10. Below the second heading, add a second form named formVB, as shown below. The form has the same HTML code as the JavaScript form, except that the name of the form, and the name of the function when the form is called, is calcVB.

```
<form name = "formVB" method = "post">
<input type="text" value="0" name="txtQ" size="7">
Quantity <br><br>
<input type="text" value="0" name="txtP" size="7">
Price <br><br>
<input type="text" name="txtC" size="7">
Total Cost <br><br>
```

11. Add a Submit button. The function that is called when the Submit button is clicked is called calcVB.

```
<input type="button" value="Calculate"
name="btnSubmit" onClick="calcVB()">
</form>
```

12. Create the VBScript function to declare the variables, calculate the new value for the cost, and then display the new cost in the txtC text box, as shown below. In VBScript, you create a function using the keyword function, the name of the function, and a pair of parentheses (). You do not use curly braces in VBScript functions. When the function is ended, you use the end function term.

```
<script language="vbscript">
function calcVB()
```

13. Declare the three variables on a single line, using the dim keyword.

```
dim intQ, intP, intC
```

14. Assign the value of the txtQ text box to a quantity variable named intQ text box. You must name the txtQ text box using the full ancestry and form field name, as you learned in the previous chapter. You must include the name of the

form, formVB. The value in the txtQ text box is retrieved from the form field using the value property. Assign the value of the txtP text box to the intP variable, using the value property.

```
intQ = document.formVB.txtQ.value
intP = document.formVB.txtP.value
```

15. The cost variable is calculated using the product of the two variables intQuantity and intPrice.

```
intC = (intP * intQ)
```

16. Assign the value of the txtC field to the intC variable. Again, refer to the form field using its full ancestry and name, which includes the form name, formVB. End the script with the end function term.

```
document.formVB.txtC.value = intC
end function
</script>
```

17. Save the Web page to your data directory, and then view it in a browser.

18. Change the values for the price and quantity fields in the JavaScript section. Click the **Calculate** button. What is the total?

19. Change the values for the price and quantity fields in the VBScript section. Click the **Calculate** button. What is the total? What happens if you enter a value such as 5.99 in the price field? *Note:* You will learn how to use built-in functions to round numbers in a later chapter.

Naming Variables

When naming your variables, your options are almost infinite, but there are certain naming conventions in JavaScript and VBScript that must be adhered to. Violations of these conventions will result in errors in your programs. One important convention is case sensitivity. VBScript commands and variables are case insensitive. For example, VBScript will interpret intPrice and INTPRICE and intprice the same way. JavaScript is case sensitive, and would assume that INTPRICE and intPrice are different variables.

Variables are more useful if they are named using a standardized naming convention. This makes them easier to identify, and also makes spelling and syntax errors less likely. It is also useful to name your variables with a descriptive name, one that has some meaning or association with the contents or purpose of the variable. For example, the variable that holds the price of a product may be named intPrice.

VBScript and JavaScript have some rules that must be followed when naming variables. In JavaScript, variable names must begin with a letter, an underscore (_), or a dollar sign, and they cannot be a **reserved word**. Reserved words are words that in JavaScript have a predefined meaning that cannot be changed by programmers. The reserved words in JavaScript are:

■ abstract	■ default	■ goto	■ null	■ this
■ boolean	■ do	■ if	■ package	■ throw
■ Boolean	■ double	■ implements	■ private	■ transient
■ break	■ else	■ import	■ protected	■ true
■ byte	■ extends	■ in	■ public	■ try
■ case	■ false	■ instanceof	■ return	■ var
■ catch	■ final	■ int	■ short	■ void
■ char	■ finally	■ interface	■ static	■ while
■ class	■ float	■ long	■ super	■ with
■ const	■ for	■ native	■ switch	
■ continue	■ function	■ new	■ synchronized	

VBScript variable names must begin with a letter, may not contain a period, cannot be longer than 255 characters, and must be unique within their scope.

Data Types and Naming Conventions

A variable's data type determines how its value is stored. When a variable is initialized with its first value, the type of data that will be stored in the memory location must be specified. The data type will then act like a filter. Once stated, the data type property will perform a check to make sure that the variables only store values of that matching data type.

It is a standard convention to begin your variable name with a three-character prefix to identify its data type. If you are creating a variable that will contain an integer, you can begin the variable name with the prefix int, for example, intVariableName. This way, other programmers reading your code will be able to determine that the variable is an integer. Using the data type prefix and a descriptive variable name will make your code much more readable. Table 4-1 below provides commonly used variable prefixes for various data types.

Table 4-1   Recommended Prefixes for Variable Names

Variable Subtype	Prefix	Example
Boolean	bln	blnYes
Byte	byt	bytZero
Date or Time	dtm	dtmToday
Double	dbl	dblPrecision
Error	err	errMessage
Integer	int	intPrice
Long	lng	lngNumber
Object	obj	objShipping
Single	sng	sngAverage
String	str	strProduct
Real Number (used in Javascript)	flt	fltWeight

VBScript Data Types

VBScript has only one data type, called a **variant**. A variant data type contains a collection of data types called **subtypes**. Since variant is the only data type used in VBScript, the data type does not have to be identified when a variable is declared. The variant data type means that you must identify the data type by examining the contents of the variable, which requires additional processing steps within the program. To distinguish between numbers and text, you can use quotes around values to store them as variant variable with a text subtype. If the value is a number and is not in quotes, then it is stored as a variant variable with a number subtype. The advantage of using a variant data type is that you can place any type of data in the variable, and the variable will behave according to the type of data it stores.

 All functions, whether predefined in VBScript or created by you, will return variables as a variant data type. If you want them to be a different data type, you will need to convert the value, using a data type conversion function.

The most commonly used data subtypes are numeric and string, but there are many others. The date subtype is used for variables that store dates. Variables that store Boolean values use the **Boolean** subtype. A Boolean value only has two possible values. Usually the values are on/off, yes/no, true/false, or 0/1, but they can be any set of exactly two values. Check boxes and radio buttons use Boolean values to determine whether the form element is checked or not checked. Variables that store monetary values have a subtype called **currency**. Variables can also contain objects. These variables use the object subtype. The object subtype allows the programmer to access all of the object's properties and methods using the variable. The object subtype is commonly used during server-side programming with VBScript. Table 4-2 lists the commonly used variant subtypes and a description of the values they can contain.

Table 4-2 Data Subtypes for Variant Variables in VBScript

Subtype	Description
Empty	Uninitialized
Null	Contains no valid data (" ")
Boolean	A logical value of either True or False
Byte	Contains integers from 0 to 255
Integer	Contains integers from −32,768 to 32,767
Currency	−922,337,203,685,477.5808 to 922,337,203,685,477.5807
Long	Contains integers from range −2,147,483,648 to 2,147,483,647
Single	Contains a single-precision, floating-point number in the range −3.402823E38 to −1.401298E-45 for negative values; 1.401298E-45 to 3.402823E38 for positive values
Double	Contains a double-precision, floating-point number in the range −1.79769313486232E308 to −4.94065645841247E-324 for negative values; 4.94065645841247E-324 to 1.79769313486232E308 for positive values
Date (Time)	Contains a number that represents a date between January 1, 100 to December 31, 9999
String	Contains a variable-length string that can be up to approximately 2 billion characters in length
Object	Contains an object
Error	Contains an error number

JavaScript Data Types

Unlike VBScript, JavaScript has several data types. The data types in JavaScript are string, integer number, **floating-point number**, Boolean, object, null, and undefined. Dates are handled as objects, not numbers. JavaScript also uses the same type of naming conventions as VBScript for the data types that JavaScript supports. The typeof method, which takes one argument, the name of the variable, will return the data type of the variable. The syntax for obtaining the data type of a variable in JavaScript is **typeof(VariableName)**. When the typeof method evaluates a variable that contains a string, it will return "string". The variable that contains an empty string returns a string data type. Table 4–3 lists the values that are returned by the typeof method. The following sample code in typeof.htm illustrates how the typeof method can be used to return the data type of a variable that contains a string, an empty string, a number, an object, boolean, null, and undefined.

```
<html><head><title>Data Subtypes</title></head>
<body bgcolor = "#FFFF99">
<h1>Data Type</h1>
<script language = "javascript">
var dT1, dT2, dT3, dT4, dT5, dT6, dT7, b;
b = "<br>";
dT1 = "The total cost was $5.00.";
```

```
dT2 = 5.00;
dT3 = new Date();
dT4 = true;
dT5 = null;
dT6 = "";
document.write("dT1: ");
document.write(typeof(dT1) + b);
document.write("dT2: ");
document.write(typeof(dT2) + b);
document.write("dT3: ");
document.write(typeof(dT3) + b);
document.write("dT4: ");
document.write(typeof(dT4) + b);
document.write("dT5: ");
document.write(typeof(dT5) + b);
document.write("dT6: ");
document.write(typeof(dT6) + b);
document.write("dT7: ");
document.write(typeof(dT7) + b);
</script></body></html>
```

Table 4-3   Data Types Returned by the typeof Method in JavaScript

Value Assigned to the Variable	Data Type	Data Type Returned from typeof
dT = "Total cost was $5.50.";	String	String
dT = "5.50";	String	String
dT = 5.50;	Floating-point Number	Number
dT = "5";	String	String
dT = 5;	Integer Number	Number
dT = "True";	String	String
dT = true;	Boolean	Boolean
dT = "0";	String	String
dT = "";	String	String
dT = " ";	String	String
dT = "null";	String	String
dT = null;	Null	Object
No value specified	Undefined	Undefined
dT = new Date()	Object	Object

The string is a value that is enclosed in double quotation marks. If the value in the variable contains a quotation mark, the value must use a single quotation mark. If the programmer needs to include a double quotation mark within a string, then a pair of single quotation marks must surround the double quotation mark.

A string can contain an empty value. In this case, the value is considered a zero-length or empty string and has a value of " ". An empty string is not the same thing as a null or undefined value.

Escape Characters in JavaScript

Strings can contain values other than alphanumeric characters, such as a carriage return. In JavaScript, these nonalphanumeric characters have an assigned **escape character** that identifies that special character. For example, the escape character for a carriage return is the letter r. To add these nonalphanumeric values to the string, you must use the **escape sequence**. The escape sequence is a backslash followed by the escape character. So, the escape sequence for a carriage return would be \r. Table 4-4 provides the escape characters, the escape sequences, and examples for some of the special characters commonly used in Web pages.

Table 4-4   Escape Characters in JavaScript

Special character	Escape Character	Escape Sequence	Example
Carriage return	r	\r	window.alert "Welcome " & strName & "\r" & "to our Web site"
Backslash	\	\\	document.write("Your Web page is located at: " & "C:\\InetPub\\wwwroot\\home.htm")
New line	n	\n	window.alert "Welcome " & strName & "\n" & "to our Web site"
Tab space	t	\t	document.write("\t" & "Your total cost is $4.50. ")
Backspace	b	\b	"document.write("Click to continue.\b?")
Single quotation mark	'	\'	window.alert "Welcome \'" & strName & "\'"
Double quotation mark	"	\"	window.alert "Welcome \"" & strName & "\""
Form feed	f	\f	"wdocument.write("Click to continue.\f")

 Table 4-4 uses the `window.alert` method to illustrate how JavaScript escape characters can be used in a Web page. In VBScript, you can also use a message box (**MsgBox**) or input box (**InputBox**) to display messages to the user and to receive input from the user. You can customize the prompts, the buttons, the icons, the messages, and the default buttons. However, the MsgBox and the InputBox are only available with the Internet Explorer browser.

The JavaScript numeric data type supports integers and **real numbers**. An integer is a whole number that can be negative, positive, or 0. An integer can be represented in decimal, **octal**, or hexadecimal format. An octal number can only contain digits zero through seven, for example 7654123. If an eight or a nine is present, then the value is treated as a decimal number, not an octal number. A real number includes numbers in decimal format, such as 3.2352, or in scientific notation. A real number is referred to in JavaScript as a floating-point number. Both integers and real numbers return "string" if they are enclosed within quotation marks. The quotation marks determine whether a number is treated as a string or as a number. Both integers and real numbers without quotation marks will return "number".

As in VBScript, the JavaScript Boolean data type contains only two values. However, in JavaScript the Boolean data type stores the values true or false. The Boolean value "true" in quotation marks returns the data type "string". Boolean values must be entered without quotes and are case sensitive. Only the values true and false may be used as Boolean values.

Typically, in binary math, one represents true, and zero represents false. However, when a Boolean value is used within a mathematical expression, the value of the Boolean variable is converted to a number. In JavaScript, false is converted to the value of zero, and true is converted to the value of one.

The object data type will be returned for variables that contain objects. A variable assigned to a date object will return the object data type. A variable assigned to null will return an object data type because null is an object. The variable that is defined as null has no value assigned. A null variable is not the same thing as an empty string. The null variable returns the data type "object", not "string". Older browsers will return the data type null when evaluating a variable that has not yet been defined. In browsers that support JavaScript 1.3 or Jscript, a variable that has not yet been defined will return the data type undefined.

Scope

Recall that a variable is defined within a **scope**. The scope is the location in which the variable can be used. Variables that can only be used by a portion of the program are referred to as **local variables**, while variables that can be used throughout an application are **global variables**. Up to now, all of the examples in this chapter showed variables that were declared and used within the same function. These are examples of local variables. If a variable is declared outside of a procedure or function, then it is a global variable, and may be modified by any part of the application. In client-side programming, global variables defined in the heading of the Web page can be used within the same Web page. In server-side programming, you can define global variables that can be used across Web pages and across users. You will learn more about variables in server-side programming in a later chapter. JavaScript and VBScript handle the scope of variables differently in client-side scripts.

Variable Scope in JavaScript

Recall that a variable is a place in the computer's memory that is used to store values. When the variable is local, the memory of that variable is freed when the function ends. Therefore, the variable itself only exists when the function is running, and other functions cannot use that local variable. If you need to use a variable across functions, then you need to declare and use a global variable. In the following example two global variables are defined in the first script, which is located in the heading. Only the global variables can be called from the second script within the body. Figure 4-3 shows the Web page, along with the alert dialog box.

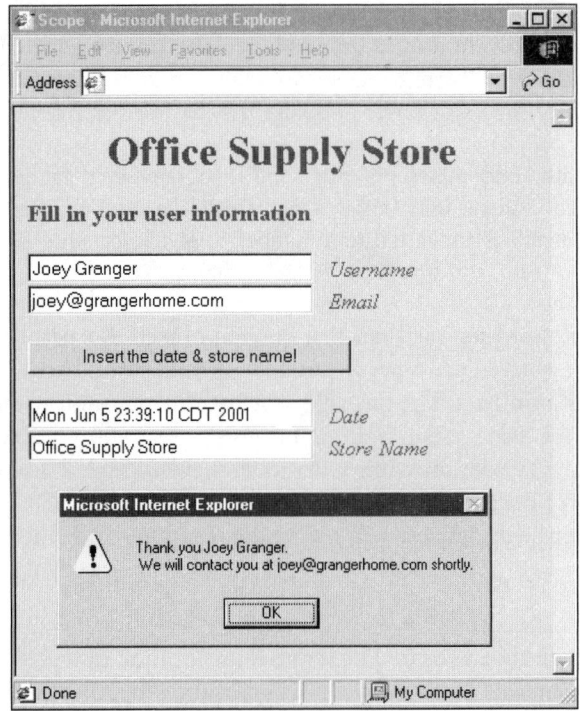

Figure 4-3   Local and global variables

1. Open Notepad or a Web editor to create a Web page named **scopeJS.htm**.

2. Create the basic HTML tags.

```
<html><head><title>Scope</title></head>
<body bgcolor="#FFCC99" text="#800000">
</body></html>
```

3. In the heading, create the script shown below. This script declares two variables, gSN and gD. The global variable gD gets the current date and time. The global variable gSN is assigned the value "Office Supply Store". Write the value of the gSN variable to the browser.

```
<script language = "javascript">
var gD, gSN;
gD = new Date();
gSN = "Office Supply Store";
document.write("<h1 align='center'>" + gSN + "</h1>");
```

4. Add a function named getM that contains a local variable named sSA. This variable is not available within the rest of the script. If the getM function were called, it would refresh the page and write out the store address.

```
function getM(){
     var sSA;
     sSA ="555 Main Street";
     document.write(sSA);
}
</script>
```

5. Create the form and the body section of the Web page, as shown below. Note that the form name frm has been specified, and that the text box names have the prefix txt. Text boxes and other form elements are also named with prefixes to distinguish between the form element and the variable that contains the value of the form element. For example, the variable txtN has a value that will be assigned to the variable strN. The prefix helps distinguish form elements from variables. The form contains a button that, when clicked, calls the handler onClick. The onClick handler in turns calls the getD function.

```
<form name = "frm">
<h3>Fill in your user information</h3>
<input type="text" name="txtN" size="30">
<i>  Username</i><br>
<input type="text" name="txtE" size="30">
<i>  Email</i><br><br>
<input type="button"
     value="Insert the date & store name!"
     name = "btnSubmit" onClick = "getD()";>
<br><br>
<input type="text" name="txtD" size="30">
<i>  Date</i><br>
<input type="text" name="txtSN" size="30">
<i>  Store Name</i><br>
</form>
```

6. Create the getD function, as shown below. This function declares and uses the local variables strN and strE. The script uses the local variables to create an alert dialog box. The alert box concatenates the local variables and text. (Note how the

4

escape character \n is used to create a new line in the dialog box.) The global variables are entered into the two remaining text boxes. If you attempt to use the variables in the getM function, you will generate an error that the variable is undefined.

```
<script language = "javascript">
function getD(){
    var strN, strE;
    strN = document.frm.txtN.value;
    strE = document.frm.txtE.value;
    window.alert("Thank you " + strN +
        ". \n We will contact you at " +
        strE + " shortly.");
    document.frm.txtD.value = gD;
    document.frm.txtSN.value = gSN;
}
</script>
```

7. Save the Web page to your data directory. View your Web page in a browser.

 Because local variables cannot be shared across functions, variable names can be reused across functions. A local variable and a global variable can have the same name. However, when the local function is executed, only the local variable is used. Because of this potential conflict, you should not assign global variables the same name as local variables. You can avoid this conflict by prefixing the name of global variables with gbl or g, to distinguish the global and variable names. For example, strName would be used as the local variable, gblstrName would be used as the global variable.

Variable Scope in VBScript

As in JavaScript, a variable's scope in VBScript is determined by where the variable is declared. A variable declared within a function or procedure is considered a local variable. Only the code within the local procedure or function may access or manipulate the local variable. Variables created within a local scope are said to exist at the procedure level. Global variables are defined outside a function or procedure, and can be accessed by all of the procedures in your script. The variable defined outside of a procedure or a function exists at the script level and has a global scope.

In VBScript, variables declared in a local procedure, event handler, or subprocedure are called procedure-level variables, and can only be seen by the function that declared the variable. Variables created in the heading section within event handlers and subprocedures are still local variables. Global variables must be declared inside a script located in the heading section, but not within a function, procedure, or event handler. These global variables are available to outside functions, procedures, and event handlers. Therefore, you can use a script in the heading to declare global variables, which will allow the variable to be accessible to all of the scripts on the Web page.

The following example is similar to the above JavaScript example. However, there are some differences. In addition to the lack of a semicolon and curly braces, VBScript uses the dim keyword instead of var. Recall that VBScript uses the "end function" statement to identify the end of the function instead of using the curly braces, and the statement that retrieves the current date does not use the keyword new in VBScript. The form in both examples is identical.

1. Open Notepad or a Web editor to create a Web page named **scopeVB.htm**.

2. Add the basic HTML tags and the form on the Web page.

```
<html><head><title>Scope</title></head>
<body bgcolor="#FFCC99" text="#800000">
</body></html>
```

3. In the heading, declare the variables, assign the current date to gD, assign the string to gSN, and write out the value of the gSN variable in a heading. Note that the keyword new is not used with the built-in function date to retrieve the current date. JavaScript and VBScript handle date functions differently.

```
<script language = "vbscript">
dim gD, gSN
gD = Date()
gSN = "Office Supply Store"
document.write("<h1 align='center'>" & gSN & "</h1>")
```

4. Add the getM function, which declares and assigns the local variables.

```
function getM()
    dim sSA
    sSA ="555 Main Street, Chicago, IL 60066"
    document.write(sSA)
end function
</script>
```

5. Add the code for the form.

```
<form name = "frm">
<h3>Fill in your user information</h3>
<input type="text" name="txtN" size="30">
<i>  Username</i><br>
<input type="text" name="txtE" size="30">
<i>  Email</i><br><br>
<input type="button"
value="Insert the date & store name!"
name = "btnSubmit" onClick = "getD()">
<br><br>
<input type="text" name="txtD" size="30">
<i>  Date</i><br>
<input type="text" name="txtSN" size="30">
<i>  Store Name</i><br>
</form>
```

6. In the body section, but after the closing form tag, add the getD function, as shown below. When the user clicks the btnSubmit button, the onClick event is called. The onClick event handler calls the getD function.

```
<script language = "vbscript">
function getD ()
```

7. Declare two variables to hold the values from the form. Assign the values from the form fields to the variables.

```
dim strN, strE
strN = document.frm.txtN.value
strE = document.frm.txtE.value
```

8. Display the form field values in an alert window. The getD function also displays the user name in an alert dialog box.

```
window.alert("Thank you " & strN & "." & chr(10) & _
        "We will contact you at " & strE & " shortly.")
document.frm.txtD.value=gD
document.frm.txtSN.value=gSN
end function
</script>
```

9. Add a script that writes out the global variable gSN. Call the getM function which writes out the value of a local variable. Format the output with a heading 3 tag.

```
<h3 align="center">
<script language = "vbscript">
document.write gSN & "<br>"
getM()
</script>
</h3>
```

10. Save the Web page to your data directory. View your Web page in your browser.

Special Characters in VBScript

Instead of the escape characters used in JavaScript, VBScript has built in functions to obtain special characters. The chr function will return the special character. The chr function takes one argument, the number of the ANSI character code. ANSI character 10 will insert a line feed. Therefore, in the example above, chr(10) is used instead of the \r escape sequence. Other commonly used special characters are listed in Table 4-5. You can use the following sample code from ansi.htm to loop through all of the 254 special characters in VBScript.

```
<html><head><title>Special Characters</title></head>
<script language = "vbscript">
for i = 1 to 254
document.write("chr(" & i & ") = "  & chr(i) & "<br>")
next
</script>
</body></html>
```

Table 4-5 Special Characters in VBScript

Special Character	Character	ANSI Code
Backspace		8
Tab space		9
New line		10
Carriage return		11
Space		32
Double quote	"	34
Pound sign	#	35
Dollar sign	$	36
Ampersand	&	38
Single quote	'	39
Forward slash	/	47
At symbol	@	64
Back slash	\	92
Copyright	©	169
Trademark	™	153
Registered	®	174

CONSTANTS IN VBSCRIPT

A **constant** is similar to a variable; it stores a value that can be retrieved at a later time. However, a constant is a specific, unchanging value. The value can be a string or a number. For example, pi is a common constant that represents the number 3.14159265358979323846264338832795. You can avoid having to remember and enter this long number by using the constant pi to refer to it. Constants are declared using the **const** keyword. Constants are usually created as global entities. They are often stored in an external file sometimes referred to as a library or server-side include, and can be reused across Web pages and Web projects. Some constants are intrinsic, that is, built into the VBScript scripting language. You can declare and create your own custom constants. Figure 4-4 shows a Web page named constantVB.htm that uses custom constants to store and display data.

Figure 4-4   Using constants in VBScript

You can create constants by using the const keyword followed by the name of the constant. To distinguish between constants and variables in your code, it is strongly recommended that you prefix all constant names with con, const, or c. Then, you assign a value to the constant. Assigning a value to a constant is similar to assigning a value to a variable, except that the constant value is assigned in the same statement as the constant declaration. Of course, the most important distinction is that the value of a constant does not change within the program.

Constants in VBScript are like variables; they both have the variant data type. VBScript will extrapolate the data type for you based on the value of the constant. Later, you can refer to the value of the constant by using the constant's name. When declaring numeric constants, the use of any special character is prohibited. To declare a constant that will contain date and time values, include the pound sign before and after the date. The syntax for declaring a constant for a string, number, and date in VBScript is as follows.

Syntax Example

Const conConstantName = "Value"
Const conConstantName = Number
Const conFallSemesterStart = #MM-DD-YY#

The example below shows you how to create a Web page that declares and uses constants. The benefit of using the constants in this example is that the constants can change. If the price or the sales price changes, then the change only has to be modified in one location, where the constant value was declared. Because this is a constant, you can be assured that the other parts of the code will not change the value of the constant.

1. Use Notepad or a Web editor to create a Web page and save it as **constantVB.htm.**

2. Add the basic HTML tags and the form on the Web page, as follows:

```
<html><head><title></title></head>
<body bgcolor="#FFCC99" text="#800000">
</body></html>
```

3. The heading section, above the title tags, add the constants as follows:

```
<script language = "vbscript">
const conName = "Office Store"
const conTitle = "Store Web Site"
const conURL = "www.store.com"
const conDate = #09-28-36#
const conTime = 20
const cone = "help@store.com"
const conCurConversion = 0.8
const conPrice1 = 4.50
const conPrice2 = 1.25
const conName1 = "Pens"
const conName2 = "Pencils"
const conSale = 0.15
const cH = "<h3 align='center'>"
const cH2 = "</h3>"
</script>
```

4. Note that the title tag is empty. To enter a title using a constant, change the title property of the document object to the constant value. After the closing title tag, enter the following code:

```
<script language = "vbscript">
document.title = conTitle
</script>
```

5. In the body, add the following code to retrieve and display the constants:

```
<script language = "vbscript">
document.write cH & conName & cH2
document.write cH & "Please visit us at " _
     & conURL & cH2
document.write cH & "Our e-mail address is " _
     & conE & cH2
</script>
```

4

6. Add a horizontal rule and line breaks.

```
<br><hr width="75%" size="4" color="#800000"><br>
```

7. Create a new script that will display the constants.

```
<script language = "vbscript">
document.write cH & "Our " & conName1 & _
    " usually cost $" & conPrice1 & cH2
document.write cH & "Our " & conName2 & _
    " usually cost $" & conPrice2 & cH2
```

8. Change the conSale constant to a percentage by multiplying it by 100, and then display the results.

```
document.write (cH & "Everything is off " _
    & (conSale * 100) & " %" & cH2)
</script>
```

9. Add a horizontal rule and line breaks

```
<br><hr width="75%" size="4" color="#800000"><br>
```

10. Create a new script that will calculate and then display the sales price for each product, using the constants. Declare two local variables. Assign the discounted price for each product to the new variables.

```
<script language = "vbscript">
dim newPrice1, newPrice2
newPrice1 = (conPrice1-(conPrice1 * conSale))
newPrice2 = (conPrice2-(conPrice2 * conSale))
```

11. Format the new price using the built-in formatCurrency method. The formatCurrency method will round the number to the nearest cent, and add a dollar sign.

```
newPrice1 = formatCurrency(newPrice1)
newPrice2 = formatCurrency(newPrice2)
```

12. Display the new price for each product, using the local variables.

```
document.write (cH & "Our " & conName1 & _
    " nowcost " & newPrice1 & cH2)
document.write (cH & "Our " & conName2 & _
    " now cost " & newPrice2 & cH2)
</script>
```

13. Save the Web page to your data directory. View your Web page.

Server-side Includes

In server-side scripting, the constants are often defined in an external file, which is called a **server-side include**. Often it is useful to create a Web page that contains only constants. The page is saved as an include page, with an .inc file extension. Then, within the main Web page, you add a statement that directs the Web server to literally include the entire file inside this main Web page. This has essentially the same effect as typing the code into the page. If the value of one of the constants ever changes, you need only modify the value once, in the include page. Include pages are included before any server-side JavaScript or VBScript is executed. The Web page on the server must be named with an .asp extension if it is on an NT Web server. One commonly used include file is ADOVBS.INC. This file declares constants that are used when connecting a Web page to a database. You will learn more about server-side includes in a later chapter.

4

ARRAYS

Up until now you have declared, assigned, and manipulated variables that store single values. Every value has been stored in a particular memory location and has been referred to as a variable. Every variable has been given a unique variable name. Using this method, if you have five variables, then five variable names must be declared. If there were hundreds of variables to declare and assign values to, the process would be very lengthy, and prone to design-time errors. Also, the processing of so many variables could slow the performance of the application. An alternative is to treat all of the input values as an **array**. Arrays can have a single dimension or multiple dimensions. A collection of variables is called a **one-dimensional array**. One-dimensional arrays are primarily used to hold lists. An array is like an egg carton; both are containers. You can refer to the carton as a whole, or to an individual egg in that carton. In an array, you can refer to the array as a whole, or refer to an individual element within the array.

To create an array, you must assign a unique name to identify the collection of values. When you declare the array you must reserve a memory storage area large enough to hold the entire set of values. A single value in the one-dimensional array, called an **element**, is referred to by its relative position within the array.

Declaring Arrays

A single array variable is used to replace a long list of variables of the same type. When you declare an array you must identify the name of the array and the type of data the array will store. In VBScript, declaring an array is similar to declaring a variable. The dim keyword is used, followed by the name of the array and then parentheses that contain the number of elements that the array will store. Identifying the number of elements allows the computer to reserve sufficient memory space to hold all of the values that could be stored within the array. Declaring an array in JavaScript is similar, but the keyword new is used instead of the usual var. The new keyword is used because the array is an object, and the new keyword instantiates a new array object. The keyword Array is used to indicate that the object is an array.

 Because JavaScript is case sensitive, make sure to use the word Array and not array.

In VBScript, the syntax for declaring an array is **dim arrayName (numberofElements)**. For example, to declare an array called Products that has 11 items, you would write **dim Products(10)**. In JavaScript, the syntax for declaring an array is **var arrayName = new Array (numberofElements)**. For example, to declare an array called Products that has 11 items, you would write **var Products = new Array(10);**. In these two examples, the array declaration instructs the computer to reserve eleven blocks of memory. Each block of memory will be able to hold a single value from the Products array. Each value is assigned to a position within the array, called an index. You can use the index number to refer to individual elements in the array. The index of the array always begins at zero and ends with the number that was indicated when the array was declared. So, each value in the Products array is assigned an index number from 0 to 10. You cannot have more elements than the number that you declared when you created the array.

Arrays in both VBScript and JavaScript are zero-based. Unless otherwise explicitly stated, array indexes begin with zero. An array declared with a size of 10 actually has 11 elements or values.

Populating Arrays

As with all variables, the value of each element within the array is undefined until you assign the element a value. Assigning values to elements in an array is called **populating the array**. You can populate the array, or you can obtain values from the user with which to populate the array. To populate the array, specify the index number, and then specify the value for each element. Elements are not required to have an assigned value when the array is created. The values within the array can be modified at a later time. You populate an element in the array by setting the arrayName(indexNumber) equal to the value of the element. In VBScript, the syntax for populating an array is **arrayName(indexNumber) = Value**. In JavaScript, the syntax for populating an array is **arrayName[indexNumber] = Value;**. Note that the syntax is the same, except for the semicolon at the end of each JavaScript statement. Also, JavaScript uses brackets instead of parentheses when assigning values to elements in the array. Any value that can be stored in a variable can be stored in an element in an array. Although array elements are often used to store strings or numbers, they can be used to store any valid data type.

The following sample code illustrates how to populate an array that contains six elements, using VBScript and JavaScript. In this example, there are six product names listed. The name of the array is Products. The index is 6, which means that the index numbers range from 0 through five, for a total of six elements in the array. The first element in the array will always have an index number 0.

```
dim Products(6)
Products(0) = "Pencils"
Products(1) = "Pens"
Products(2) = "Paper"
Products(3) = "Markers"
```

```
Products(4) = "Notepads"
Products(5) = "Scissors"
```

```
Var New Products(6);
Products[0] = "Pencils";
Products[1] = "Pens";
Products[2] = "Paper";
Products[3] = "Markers";
Products[4] = "Notepads";
Products[5] = "Scissors";
```

Note that in JavaScript the index number of the element is enclosed within square brackets, and in VBScript the index number of the element is enclosed within parentheses.

Using Array Elements

After the array is populated, the program can retrieve the value of any element in the array. To retrieve the value of an array element, use the array name and the index number of the element. The value from the array is then available to be used in an expression, displayed in a Web page, or placed into a variable. When the array element is used in an expression or assigned to a variable, the array element should appear on the right side of the assignment operator (=). If you write the array element to a Web page using the **document.write** method, make sure that you use the parentheses if you are using JavaScript. To write out the first element of an array to the Web page using VBScript, you can write **document.write Products(0)**. To write out the first element of an array to the Web page using JavaScript, you can write **document.write(Products[0]);**.

Array elements can be directly manipulated, or the values of the array elements can be assigned to a variable, and the variable can be manipulated. In the following sample code, the first array element is written to the Web page. Instead of directly manipulating the array element, you assign the value of the array element to the variable called productName. Then, the variable productName is written out to the Web page using the **document.write** method.

```
dim productName
productName = Products(0)
document.write productName
```

```
var productName;
productName=Products[0];
document.write(productName);
```

Referencing an Array Object and Array Elements Using JavaScript

In JavaScript, when you declare a new array, you are declaring a new object that has the data type array. The array object provides support for the creation of arrays of any data type. So, array elements can hold values that are of any valid data type. In JavaScript, there are two main methods used to reference the elements of an array. The previous sample used the name of the array and the index number of the element to refer to an element in the array. You could instead use an integer variable in place of the actual index value for the element. In the sample code below, the array that is defined contains three elements (0, 1, 2). A variable, ProductIndex, is declared that will hold the value of the index number of the element. The array is populated with a value. The value of the element is retrieved using the array name (Products) and the value of the variable storing the index number (ProductIndex).

```
var Products = new Array(2);
var ProductIndex = 1;
Products[1]= "Pencils";
document.write(Products[ProductIndex]);
```

Because an array is an object, it has methods and properties. Any of the members of an object can be referred to by their name. The array object has several methods, including concat, join, reverse, slice, sort, toString, and valueOf. An array also has several properties, including constructor, prototype, and length. Previously you learned the dot notation naming convention to refer to the object. The object.property naming convention also applies to arrays. Therefore, to refer to the length of the array in the previous example, you would specify `document.write(Products.length);` in your script.

CHAPTER SUMMARY

Variables

◻ Variables are used to store data that can be retrieved at a later time. When you declare variables, the computer reserves memory to store the variables.

◻ Local variables are declared within a function, and are not available to other functions. Global variables are available to other functions. Use the keyword var to declare the variable in JavaScript, and use dim in VBScript.

◻ JavaScript and VBScript have naming rules and standards for variables. JavaScript has a list of reserved words that cannot be used to name variables.

◻ A variable that has not been assigned a value is "undefined".

◻ JavaScript variables are case sensitive, while VBScript variables are case insensitive.

Data Types

◻ A variable's data type determines how its data is stored in the memory of the computer. All VBScript variables have the variant data type. These variant variables have subtypes, such as integer and string, which are assigned to the variable when the values are assigned to the variable.

❐ JavaScript data types are string, integer number, floating-point number, Boolean, object, null, and undefined. The typeof method returns the data type of a variable. Boolean in JavaScript is either true or false. True returns one, and false returns zero.

❐ You can include special characters in your Web pages. For example, the escape character for a carriage return in JavaScript is "\r", and the backslash is "\\". In VBScript the new line character is chr(10), and the backslash is chr(92).

Constants

❐ Constants are variables whose values do not change within the application. The constant is declared using the const keyword. At the time the variable is declared, the constant is assigned a value. In the script, the programmer uses the constant to refer to the value. The constant value can only be changed where the constant was declared.

Arrays

❐ An array is a collection of elements. A one-dimensional array is often used for storing a list. An array must specify the number of elements in the array when the array is declared.

❐ VBScript uses () and JavaScript uses [] to refer to elements in the array. JavaScript arrays are actually new array objects instantiated with the keyword new.

❐ An array element is referenced by its index number within the array.

To declare a variable

```
var strProduct, intQuantity, intCost;
```

```
dim strProduct, intQuantity, intCost
```

To assign a value to a variable

```
intQuantity = 5;
myDataType = "5.50";
myDataType = true;
```

```
intQuantity = 5
myDataType = "5.50"
myDataType = true
```

To assign a variable to the value of a form element

```
document.frm.txtName.value = gblstrName;
```

```
document.frm.txtName.value = gblstrName
```

To write out a variable to a Web page

```
document.write("Your cost is $" + intCost);
```

```
document.write("Your cost is $" & intCost)
```

To force the Web page to declare all variables

```
% option explicit %
```

To create a function

```
function calculateJS(){
}
```

```
function calculateVB()
end function
```

To retrieve the data type of a variable in JavaScript

```
var myDataType;
myDataType = "Your order is $5.00.";
document.write("Data Type is: ");
document.write(typeof(myDataType));
```

To add a new line in a window dialog box

```
window.alert "Welcome" & "\n" & strName;
```

```
window.alert "Welcome" & chr(10) & strName
```

4

To create a constant in VBScript

```
const conName = "Office Store"
const conDate = #09-28-36#
const conTimeOut = 20
```

To assign a constant to a form field element or write it out to the Web page

```
document.write "<H1>" & conName & "</H1>"
document.title = conTitle
```

To declare and populate a one-dimensional array

```
var Products = new Array(1);
Products[0] = "Pencils";
Products[1] = "Pens";
```

```
Dim Products(1)
Products(0) = "Pencils"
Products(1) = "Pens"
```

To write an array element value to a Web page

```
document.write(Products[0]);
```

```
document.write Products(0)
```

REVIEW QUESTIONS

1. When you declare a variable, you inform the program about it in advance so that memory space can be assigned to the variable to store the values. True or False?

2. The dim keyword is used by VBScript to declare a variable. True or False?

3. The data type for a JavaScript variable is variant. True or False?

4. The chr function is used by JavaScript to identify special characters. True or False?

5. You can assign a string to a variable without placing the string in quotation marks, if the string is less than twenty characters. True or False?

6. A null value is the same thing as an empty string. True or False?

7. When assigning a date value to a constant, you must enclose the data value in a pair of pound signs. True or False?

8. The names of all constants must start with const. True or False?

9. The names of all arrays must start with obj. True or False?

10. The first element in an array defined in JavaScript as Products is identified as products[0]. True or False?

11. A _____ is a section of memory that is created by the programmer.

    a. variable

    b. value

    c. scope

    d. var

12. The assignment operator in VBScript and JavaScript is:

    a. =

    b. /

    c. +

    d. &

13. Which is the concatenation operator in VBScript?

    a. =

    b. /

    c. +

    d. &

14. Which of the following is a valid variable name in JavaScript?

    a. strCust.New

    b. 21Cust

    c. strCustomer

    d. New Customer

15. Which of the following is a value that can be assigned to a JavaScript Boolean variable?

    a. false

    b. True

    c. "true"

    d. 0

16. Which of the following is the correct way to declare a variable in VBScript?

    a. `var strCustomer`

    b. `dim strCustomer`

    c. `new strCustomer`

    d. `dim strCustomer;`

17. What is the term used to force VBScripts to declare all variables before they are used within a script?

    a. `option explicit`

    b. `var explicit`

    c. `dim varExplicit`

    d. `dim noOption`

18. Which of the following is the correct way to declare multiple variables on one line in JavaScript?

    a. `var strCustomer, var strProducts, varStrCompanyName`

    b. `var strCustomer, strProducts, StrCompanyName:`

    c. `var strCustomer, strProducts, StrCompanyName;`

    d. It's not possible to declare multiple variables on one line in JavaScript.

19. What is the correct way to refer to a value of a text box named txtCustomer on a form named frmEmail?

    a. `document.txtCustomer.frmEmail.value`

    b. `document.txtCustomer.value(frmEmail)`

    c. `document.frmEmail.txtCustomer.value`

    d. `var document.txtCustomer.value`

20. Which variable data type does VBScript support?

    a. variable

    b. string

    c. numbers

    d. variant

4

21. Which VBScript data subtype represents 3.145?

    a. constant

    b. integer

    c. byte

    d. single

22. Which JavaScript data type represents 3.145?

    a. constant

    b. integer

    c. floating-point

    d. undefined

23. Which JavaScript method returns the data type of a variable?

    a. datatype

    b. typeof

    c. getType

    d. none of the above

24. What does null mean?

    a. "   "

    b. empty string

    c. string of length 0

    d. no value

25. What is the escape sequence for a carriage return in JavaScript?

    a. \r

    b. \n

    c. \\

    d. \t

26. What is the special character for a new line in VBScript?

    a. Chr(64)

    b. Chr(10)

    c. Chr(8)

    d. Chr(47)

27. A variable defined in the script located in the heading is called a _____ variable.

    a. local

    b. constant

    c. global

    d. array

28. VBScript variables declared within a script within a function are known as
    _____ variables.

    a. local

    b. global

    c. constant

    d. array

29. Which keyword is used to declare a constant in VBScript?

    a. const

    b. con

    c. dim

    d. const(2)

30. Individual pieces of data in an array are called _____.

    a. collections

    b. elements

    c. variables

    d. variants

31. Which method declares an array in JavaScript?

    a. `Dim Products(5);`

    b. `var Products = new Array(2);`

    c. `var Products = new array(i);`

    d. `Dim Products = new Array(2);`

32. Which method populates an array in VBScript?

    a. `Products(0) = "Pencils"`

    b. `Products[0] = "Pencils"`

    c. `Products[0] = "Pencils";`

    d. `Products(0) = "Pencils";`

33. Which method writes out the first element to the Web page using JavaScript?

    a. `document.write (Products[0]);`

    b. `document.write Products(0)`

    c. `document.write Products[0];`

    d. none of the above

4

HANDS-ON PROJECTS

Project 4-1

In this project, you will create a customer feedback form for a hardware store. The feedback form will get the values from the form, and write the results out to the Web page, as illustrated in Figure 4-5. You will create this form using JavaScript.

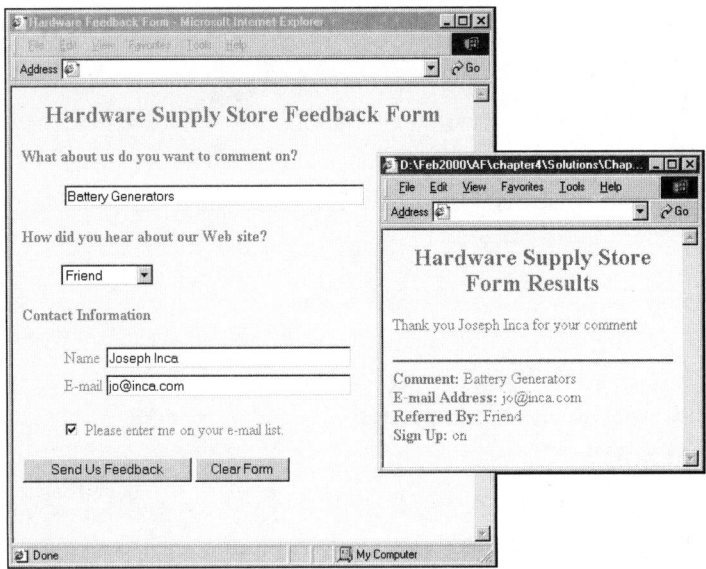

Figure 4-5   Using variables to process a form

1. Open your Web page editor, or use Notepad. Create a Web page named **hwFeedbackJS.htm**.

2. Add the basic HTML tags:

   ❑ The title of the page is **Hardware Feedback Form**.

   ❑ The background color is #FFFF99.

   ❑ The default text color is #993333.

   ❑ Add a heading 2 aligned in the center that says: **Hardware Supply Store Feedback Form**.

3. Add a form named frmHardware.

4. Add the following fields to the form:

❏ Text box named txtComment to get the user comments

❏ Drop-down list named lstSource to store information on how the user heard about the Web site. The options should be: Yahoo, Commercial, Magazine, E-mail, Friend, (Other)

❏ Text box named txtName to store the customer name

❏ Text box named txtEmail to store the customer e-mail address

❏ Check box named chkEList to determine whether the user wants to join the e-mail list

5. Add a Submit button that says **Send Us Feedback** and a Reset button that says **Clear Form**.

6. Add a JavaScript handler to the form that calls the displayJS function when the Submit button is clicked.

7. Create a JavaScript function named displayJS that will:

❏ Declare variables: strComment, strSource, strName, strEmail, strEList

❏ Assign the values from the form field to the variables above

❏ Use the `document.writeln` method to write out the response page:

- Add the basic HTML tags.

- Add the body tag with the background color of #FFFF99 and default text color #993333.

- Add a heading number 2 that is aligned in the center and says: **Hardware Supply Store Form Results**.

- Write out a thank-you message to the customer, and include the customer's name in the message. Add a break line after the welcome message and a horizontal rule whose thickness is 2 pixels and color is #800000.

- List, on a separate line, the title and the value for each form field. Use the following titles for the fields: Comments, E-mail Address, Referred By, Sign Up. Retrieve the value from the corresponding variable.

8. Save your Web page to your data directory. Print your source code.

9. View the Web page. Print out the feedback form and the response form.

4

Project 4-2

In this project, you will complete the previous exercise using VBScript instead of JavaScript.

1. Save the hwFeedbackJS.htm Web page as **hwFeedbackVB.htm**.
2. Modify the Web page to support VBScript. Change the name of the function from displayJS to displayVB.
3. Save the Web page to your data directory. Print your source code.
4. View the Web page. Print out the feedback form and the response form.

Project 4-3

Your manager at the hardware store would like a welcome message on the home page to welcome the user by name when the page opens. In this project, you will use JavaScript to create a window that retrieves the user's name and e-mail address, and then displays it in the alert window.

1. Open your Web page editor, or use Notepad. Create a Web page named **hwWelcomeJS.htm**.
2. Add the basic HTML tags. The title of the page should be **Customer Welcome Page**.
3. When the document loads, call the getCustomerName function.

   ```
   <body onLoad = "getCustomerName()";>
   ```
4. Create a function in the heading section that creates a new string object. Assign the new string object to a variable called yourName.
5. Create a window that will prompt the user for input. The prompt should say: **What is your name?** The input text box should say: **Enter your first name here**.
6. Assign the yourName variable to the response received from the user.

   ```
   YourName = window.prompt("What is your name?", "Enter your first name here");
   ```
7. Create a dialog box that displays "Welcome," the user's name, and an OK button. The user's name should be on the second line in the dialog box.

   ```
   window.alert("Welcome\r" + yourName);
   ```
8. Save the Web page to your data directory. Print your source code. View the Web page.

Project 4-4

In this project, you will complete the previous exercise using VBScript instead of JavaScript.

1. Save the hwWelcomeJS.htm Web page as **hwWelcomeVB.htm**.
2. Modify the Web page to support VBScript.
3. Save the Web page to your data directory. View the Web page. Print your source code.

Project 4-5

In this project, you will create a Web page that tells customers the total cost of their order, including tax. The customer will enter the total amount of the product in a text box, as illustrated in Figure 4-6. The current tax rate is 8.5%. The sales tax will be automatically calculated by the Web page. Your boss would like to be able to modify the sales tax.

4

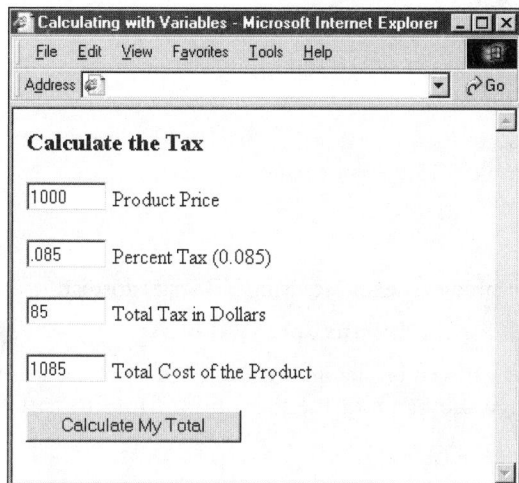

Figure 4-6 Using variables in mathematical expressions

1. Create a Web page, and save it as **hwTaxFormJS.htm**.

2. Add the basic HTML tags. The title of the page should be **Calculating with Variables**. The background color should be #FFFF99. Add a heading 3 that says: **Calculate the Tax**.

3. Add a form named frmJS. Add text boxes named txtPrice, txtTax, txtTotalTax, and txtTotalCost. The labels to these text boxes are Product Price, Percent Tax (0.085), Total Tax in Dollars, and Total Cost of the Product. The text boxes should have a maximum size of 7. The Submit button, named btnSubmit, should say: **Calculate My Total**. When the Submit button is clicked, a function named calculateJS should be called.

4. Add a script using JavaScript with a function called calculateJS to calculate the tax.

   ❑ Create four variables: intPrice, intTax, intTotalTax, and intTotalCost.

   ❑ Assign the value to intPrice from the form field txtPrice. Assign the value to intTax value from the form field txtTax.

   ❑ Calculate the total tax from the product of intPrice and intTax, and place the results within the intTotalTax variable. Use the intTotalTax variable to set the value to the txtTotalTax form field in the form.

    ❑ Calculate the total cost from the sum of the intPrice and intTotalTax, and place the results within the intTotalCost variable. Use the intTotalCost variable to set the value to the txtTotalCost form field in the form. (*Hint*: If you use the plus sign, (+), this will not work. JavaScript interprets the field as a string, not a number. To force JavaScript to deal with the variables as a number, use another mathematical operator in the equation. In this case, you can multiply the product by 1. For example, 1 * intPrice + intTotalTax would produce a numerical result. In a later chapter you will learn how to use conversion formulas to change the data type from a string to a number.)

5. Save the Web page to your data directory.

6. View the Web page. Print your source code. Enter the price 1000 and the tax .0085, then click on the Submit button. Print the results page.

Project 4-6

In this project, you will complete the previous exercise using VBScript instead of JavaScript.

1. Save the hwTaxFormJS.htm Web page as **hwTaxFormVB.htm**.

2. Modify the Web page to support VBScript. Change the name of the function from calculateJS to calculateVB. Change the name of the form from frmJS to frmVB.

3. Save the Web page to your data directory.

4. View the Web page. Print your source code. Enter the price 1000 and the tax .0085, then click on the Submit button. Print the results page.

Project 4-7

In this project, you will use VBScript to create a generic shopping cart for a Web development company. Rather than customizing each cart, you have decided to use global variables and constants to define their user settings in their home page.

1. Create a Web page, and save it as **hwGlobalVB.htm**.

2. Add the basic HTML tags.

3. Create a script using VBScript in the heading section that will create global variables and constants.

    ❑ Create global variables gblDate, gblBgColor, gblTxtColor as follows: gblDate should contain the current date, gblBgColor should contain #FFCC99, and gblTxtColor should contain #800000.

    ❑ Create the following constants: conDate, containing the date 09-28-36 (make sure to use the date format); conStoreName containing the text **Hardware Store**; conEmail containing the e-mail address support@hardware.com.

4. After the title tag, add a script to do the following:

❏ Change the title of the document to the conStoreName value, and change the body color and default text color to gblTxtColor and gblBgColor. (*Hint:* The document method to change the text color is fgColor, not text.)

❏ Write three headings that are all center-aligned. The first should use heading 1, which should display the conStoreName. The second should use heading 2, and should display conEmail. The last should use heading 3, and should display the conDate constant.

5. Save the Web page to your data directory.

6. View the Web page. Print your source code. Print the Web page.

Project 4-8

In this project, you will complete the previous exercise using JavaScript instead of VBScript.

1. Save the hwGlobalVB.htm Web page as **hwGlobalJS.htm**.

2. Modify the Web page to support JavaScript. (*Hint:* Because JavaScript does not support constants, you will have to use variables to store the values. To retrieve the date, you could use the code `var conDate = new Date(1936, 8, 28);` You will have to use the plus sign (+) instead of the ampersand (&) to concatenate the variables.)

3. Save the Web page to your data directory.

4. View the Web page. Print your source code. Print the Web page.

CASE PROJECTS

Applebee Bookstore Customer Feedback Form

You are hired to work for Applebee Bookstore as their Web programmer. They have decided to add a Web page to allow customers to send feedback to their Sales Department. Your role is to get the results from the customer feedback form, and place them into variables. You are also instructed to display a similar looking page to the user to let the user know what values were submitted. You must name your form fields and values according to programming standards. You must include at least 10 fields on the form, and a Submit button. Evaluate at least five other feedback forms from other stores on the Internet. The form fields must include a variety of text boxes, drop-down list boxes, and check boxes. You must format the page to look professional. Modify the appearance of the page to enhance the presentation of the form. Choose background colors, fonts, and images to make your form more appealing to the customer. When you are finished, save your Web page as applebeeBooks.htm in your data directory. Print the source code. View the form. Print the form. Enter values and submit the form. Print out the response page.

Applebee Bookstore Customer Feedback Form

Your manager at Applebee Bookstore would like a Web page that shows customers how much they would save on a book by buying online and not paying sales tax. When the customer enters the total cost of the book in a text box, the sales tax will be automatically calculated by the Web page. Your boss does not want the customer to be able to modify the sales tax. (*Hint:* You can use a hidden field, a global variable, or a constant for the sales tax.) The sales tax rate he wants entered is 8.5%. Write the price of the product, the sales tax rate, and the sales tax to the Web page. Modify the appearance of the page to enhance the presentation of the form. When you are finished, save your Web page as applebeeTax.htm in your data directory. Print the source code. View the form. Enter values and submit the form. Print out the response page.

Applebee Bookstore Summer Sales

The manager of Applebee Bookstore has decided to add another page to the store Web site. The manager is planning the "Summer Art Book Festival" that they have each year. This year, the manager would like a page that will display in a table a list of ten books, their regular prices, the amount saved during the sale, and the final price of the book. At the top of the page, display the name of the bookstore, the name of the sale, the current date, and the discount rate. Create a list of titles and product ID numbers for 10 books. The manager plans to start by discounting the cost of the books by 25%. (*Hint:* Create a text field that contains the discount rate, so that the manager can test to see what would happen at different discount levels.) After you have finished testing the page, you can change this property to read-only or to hidden, to prevent the customer from changing the discount rate.

Each book should be given a regular sale price in a variable, a hidden field, or visible read-only text field. Create a variable for each book that contains the price of the book retrieved from the price text field. Calculate the discounted price for each book, and place the results in a new variable for each book. Calculate the difference between the original price and the discounted price. Display the discounted price and the difference, next to the price of the book. After you have completed filling out the table, calculate the total costs of all ten books, and the total amount customers could save if they purchased all ten books, then write the results to the bottom of the Web page. Use tables to format the page. Modify the appearance of the page using images, fonts, and colors. When you are finished, save your Web page as applebeeSummer.htm in your data directory. Print the source code. View the form. Print out the page.

Applebee Bookstore Employee Rolodex

The Applebee Bookstore manager has decided to create a list of all the employees. Because the staff changes so frequently, you decide to use JavaScript to create an array Employees that must hold at least 20 employee names. Add at least ten names in the array. Use the array to generate a list of employees on a Web page. Modify the appearance of the page using images, fonts, and color. When you are finished, save your Web page as applebeeRolodex.htm in your data directory. Print the source code. View the page. Print out the page.

Red River Boats—Play it Again!

You have been hired by Red River Boats to maintain their Web site. You decide that you want to reuse some of the projects that you previously created. Select one of the cases above. Modify the Web page using another scripting language. Your solution should be essentially the same as that of the previous project. Make sure to save the original file with a new name, so that you do not overwrite your previous work. Modify the appearance of the page using images, fonts, and color to reflect the new company. Save the Web page as redRiverBoats.htm to your data directory. Print out the source code and the Web page.

4

Red River Boats—Registration Page

Your manager at Red River Boats has requested a customer registration page. Add forms to collect the visitor's e-mail address, username, password, first name, last name, street address, city, state, zip code, country, phone number, and favorite type of boat. When the Submit button is pressed, a function is called that will retrieve the values from the form, and assign the values to an array. Then, write out the values in the array to the Web page. (*Hint*: Instead of assigning a variable to an array element, you can assign the value from a form field to the array element.) Modify the appearance of the page using images, fonts, and color. Save the Web page as redRiverBoatsRegistration.htm to your data directory. Print out the source code and the Web page.

5

PROGRAMMING WITH CONTROL STRUCTURES

In this chapter you will:

♦ Create scripts that use arithmetic, comparison, and logical operators
♦ Create conditional expressions
♦ Use If Then, Select Case, and Switch Case decision control structures to alter the execution order of a script
♦ Use Do While, While Do, and For Next looping control structures to repeat blocks of code
♦ Create nested blocks of code

In previous chapters you collected data from a form, stored the data, and then used the data in basic scripts. You also created scripts containing action statements that execute when an event occurs, or when they are called by an event handler. In this chapter you will learn how to create decision control structures, which allow you to conditionally change the order in which a program is executed. For example, you might wish to write code that displays a registration form when a user visits a Web site, if it is the user's first visit to the site, and a welcome message if the user has visited the site before. You will also learn how to create looping control structures, to repeat sections of code—useful for looping through all the elements in an array, for example—and nested control structures, which make your code easier to write and maintain. Because VBScript and JavaScript both support control structures, examples from both scripting languages are included in this chapter.

OPERATORS

Both VBScript and JavaScript support assignment, concatenation, arithmetic, comparison, and unary operators. As you learned earlier in this book, assignment operators are used to assign a value or an object to a variable. The assignment operator in both JavaScript and VBScript is the equal sign (=). JavaScript has additional assignment and arithmetic operators that are not supported in VBScript. As you learned earlier in this book, the concatenation operator is used to append expressions, such as a string and a variable. The concatenation operator in JavaScript is the plus sign (+), while the concatenation operator in VBScript is the ampersand (&). The comparison and unary operators will be described later in this chapter.

Arithmetic Operators

Arithmetic operators allow you to perform mathematical calculations on values and variables. Table 5-1 lists the arithmetic operators supported by both JavaScript and VBScript. Because in JavaScript the addition operator is the same key as the assignment operator, you need to be careful that you do not append a string to the number. The number 1 and the string "1" are differentiated by quotation marks. If you append a string to a number, for example 1 + a, the result will be the string "1a".

Table 5-1   Arithmetic Operators

VBScript	JavaScript	Description	Example
+	+	Addition	x + y
−	−	Subtraction	x − y
*	*	Multiplication	x * y
/	/	Division	x / y

When constructing complex or lengthy calculations, it is important that you use parentheses to indicate the order in which you want the calculations to occur. The expressions within the parentheses will be calculated first. In the following sample code from order.htm, the parentheses change the order of execution. While the same numbers and operators are used, all three expressions evaluate to different values. The total1 variable evaluates to 2575, total2 to 2500.9615384615385, and total3 to 3800.

```
<script language = "javascript">
var total1, total2, total3;
total1 = 100 * 25 + 50 / 2 + 50;
total2 = (100 * 25) + 50 / (2 + 50);
total3 = 100 * (25 + 50) / 2 + 50;
document.write(total1);
document.write("<br>");
document.write(total2);
document.write("<br>");
document.write(total3);
</script>
```

CONTROL STRUCTURES

There are two types of programming statements in VBScript and JavaScript: action statements and control statements. Action statements, which you learned to write in previous chapters, consist of code that carries out a task, such as displaying text on a Web page, and are executed in the order in which they are written (this is known as linear programming). You can control the execution order of a script using a control structure. **Control structures** use **control statements** to control the execution order of scripts and action statements. Control statements allow you to conditionally determine both whether and how an action statement is executed, and the order in which action statements are executed. The benefits of using control structures include: clearer and more readable Internet programming; less time spent debugging, testing, and modifying the script; increased productivity; and improved script quality, reliability, and efficiency.

To make it easier to identify control statements within their code, programmers often indent the action statements within a control structure.

The two types of control structures are decision control structures and loop structures. Decision control structures allow you to alter the execution order of action statements on the basis of conditional expressions. A conditional expression is an expression that is evaluated by the scripting engine as true or false. Loop structures allow you to repeat action statements on the basis of conditional expressions.

Both types of control structures use control statements to alter the order in which action statements are executed. There are three types of control statements: looping statements, branching statements, and jumping statements. **Looping statements** allow you to conditionally repeat a block of code. **Branching statements** allow the program to decide which of two or more blocks of code to run, basing its decision on some identified criteria in the control statement. **Jumping statements** allow you to conditionally exit a code block and jump to another section of code within your program. Both JavaScript and VBScript support looping statements, branching statements, and jumping statements. These three types of control statements can be used in both client-side and server-side scripting.

Algorithms and flowcharts make visually clear the sequence in which a script is executed. You should plan the order in which you want the script to be able to execute before writing the code.

Decision Control Structures

Decision control structures allow the program to select which statements to execute. The **If Then** statement is the most frequently used decision control structure. This statement is supported in both VBScript and JavaScript. The If Then statement allows only two options for altering the order in which statements are executed. Another decision control structure is the **Select Case** statement. This statement provides more than two options for altering the order in which statements are executed, but is only supported by VBScript. Therefore, this type of decision control structure is most often used in server-side scripts. JavaScript uses a **Switch Case** statement to provide the same functionality. Because JavaScript is supported in both browsers, this statement can be used for both client and server programming.

If Then Statements

The If Then statement allows a script to alter the order in which statements are executed, on the basis of a conditional expression. The conditional expression tests whether a certain condition is true or false, and therefore is often known as a **Boolean expression**, because Boolean variables can only be resolved to true or false. In JavaScript a pair of parentheses encloses the conditional expression.

 George Boole developed a branch of mathematics related to outcomes of true or false.

If the condition in the conditional expression is met, then the expression is evaluated as true, and the script immediately following the conditional expression is executed. In VBScript, the keyword "then" is used to identify the block of code to execute if the condition is true. In JavaScript, curly braces are used to identify two blocks of code. Also, a semicolon is used to identify the end of each action statement. When the condition is not met, the conditional expression is evaluated as false, and the program skips the first block of code and moves to the next block of code. The keyword `else` identifies where the next block of code begins. In VBScript, the keywords `end if` are used to identify that the decisional control structure has ended. In JavaScript, the keywords `end if` are not required because the closing curly brace identifies the end of the block of code.

The syntax for the If Then statement in VBScript is:

```
if (conditional expression) then
     action statements
else
     action statements
end if
```

The syntax for the If Then statement in JavaScript is:

```
if (conditional expression) {
     action statements;
}
else {
     action statements;
}
```

The end of an action statement in JavaScript can be indicated by a semicolon. This optional semicolon is also called a terminator. However, because control statements are not action statements, a semicolon is not used at the end of the control statement. Therefore, there is no semicolon after "if ", "else", or "end if " statements.

Conditional Expressions   Conditional expressions often consist of two expressions and a **comparison operator**. A comparison operator is used to compare two or more expressions. The expression can be a value, such as a number or string, or a variable, or even another expression! Both of the expressions must be the same data type. You cannot compare an expression that contains a string to an expression that contains a number. For example, you cannot compare the word "customer" and the number "25". Table 5-2 lists the comparison operators in JavaScript and VBScript. JavaScript and VBScript use different comparison operators for evaluating equality and inequality. When you are comparing a string to a value, the case must match exactly, in both JavaScript and VBScript. For example, if the value is "password" and the variable contains the value "Password", the conditional expression will evaluate to false. The syntax for the conditional expression is:

expression1 <comparison operator> expression2

Table 5-2   Comparison Operators Used in Conditional Expressions

Condition Being Tested	JavaScript Operator	JavaScript Example	VBScript Operator	VBScript Example
Equal to	= =	var1 = = var2	=	Var1 = var2
Not equal	!=	var1 != var2	<>	Var1 <> var2
Less than	<	var1 < var2	<	Var1 < var2
Greater than	>	var1 < var2	>	Var1 > var2
Less than or equal to	<=	var1 <= var2	<=	Var1 <= var2
Greater than or equal to	>=	var1 >= var2	>=	Var1 >= var2

The equality operator in JavaScript is a pair of equal signs. Placing a space between the two equal signs will give you an error when the script is run.

The example below illustrates a basic If Then statement. In this example, a Web page named emaillist.htm contains a form that allows visitors to indicate whether they would like to sign up for the e-mail list. Normally, the method attribute for the form tag is used to identify the script that will process the form when the form is submitted. If you call a different script when the Submit button is clicked, an error message will occur because the form has detected a submit event. To prevent this, the form called frm uses the JavaScript void method as the action for the form. The JavaScript void method will prevent errors from occurring if the form is submitted and there is no form handler identified. When the Submit button is clicked, the onClick event handler calls a JavaScript function named signup. The signup function contains an If Then statement that uses the checked property of a radio button on the form to determine whether to add the user to the e-mail list. Figure 5-1 shows a Web page named emaillist.htm that uses an If Then control statement to obtain information from the user and then display a dynamic response in an alert message.

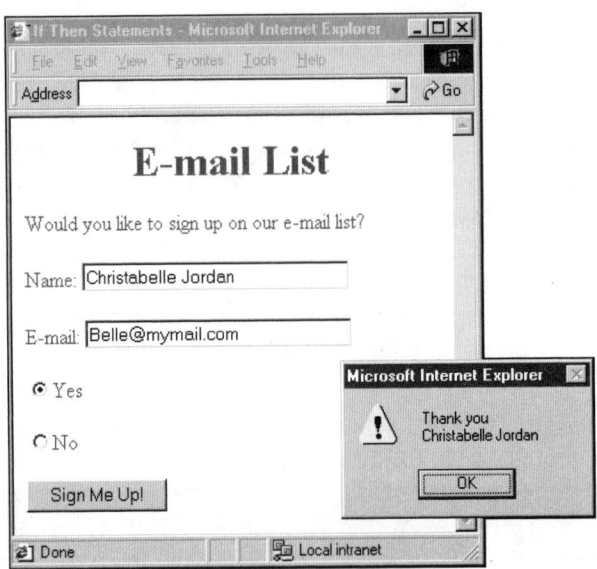

Figure 5-1   Using an If Then control statement to process a form

To use JavaScript to create a Web page that uses an If Then control statement to process a form:

1. Create a Web page named **emaillist.htm** with a form named frm, as shown below.

```
<html><head>
<title>If Then Statements</title></head>
<body text="#800000" bgcolor="#FFFFCC">
<h1 align="center">E-mail List</h1>
<p>Would you like to sign up on our e-mail list?</p>
<form method="post" name="frm" action="javascript:void(0)">
<p>Name:
<input type="text" name="name" size="28"></p>
<p>E-mail:
<input type="text" name="address" size="28"></p>
<p><input type="radio" checked name="email">Yes</p>
<p><input type="radio" name="email">No</p>
<p><input type="submit" value="Sign Me Up!"
      name = "btnSignUp" onClick = "signup()";></p>
</form>
```

JavaScript has a special operator called **void** that does nothing. It is used to pre-vent errors from occurring in code that is expecting an action to occur. Void will cause nothing to occur, which prevents the error from occurring.

2. Add a JavaScript function called signup that will test the value of the radio button, as shown below. If the radio button labeled Yes is checked, then the checked property is true. The conditional expression tests if the checked property for the radio button is equal to true. The word true is not in quotes because it represents the state of the button being checked, not a string.

 The default value for a radio button or check box that is checked is the string "on". If the radio button or check box is not checked, then no value is submitted. The value property can be assigned another value. If the radio button or check box is checked, then the new value is submitted.

```
<script language="javascript">
function signup(){
var strName;
strName = window.document.frm.name.value;
if (document.frm.email[0].checked==true){
    window.alert("Thank you\n" + strName);
}
else {
    window.alert("You may sign up later");
}
}
</script>
```

3. Add the code to close the script and the Web page.

```
</body></html>
```

4. After saving the page to your data directory, view the Web page in a browser. Enter your name and e-mail address, and click **Yes**. Then click the submit button labeled Sign me up!, and an alert dialog box will appear with the name you entered in the name field.

 You must refer to any element in a script by its name or index number. The name property assigned for the radio button is the name for the group of buttons, not the individual button. Therefore, the radio button must be referred to by its index number. As you learned in the previous chapter, an array is a group of elements, which can be variables, values, or objects. In this case, the array is a group of radio buttons. The radio button labeled Yes is the first button in the array, so refer to it by the name of the radio button group and the index number 0.

5

The example below from emaillistVB.htm illustrates how to process the same form using VBScript. Note that while the syntax is different, the programming principles are the same. The radio button is identified by the index number, using parentheses instead of square brackets. The keywords **then** and **end if** are used instead of curly braces. The keywords **end function** are used to identify the end of the signup function.

```vbscript
<script language="vbscript">
function signup()
dim strName
strName = window.document.frm.name.value
if (document.frm.email(0).checked=true) then
  window.alert("Thank you" & chr(10) & strName)
else
  window.alert("You may sign up later")
end if
end function
</script>
```

It is not necessary to have a second condition. You can drop the else statement if you are only testing for one condition. The following is the same example, testing for one condition.

```vbscript
<script language="vbscript">
function signup()
dim strName
strName = window.document.frm.name.value
if (window.document.frm.email(0).checked=true) then
  window.alert("Thank you")
end if
end function
</script>
```

Logical Operators   You can combine two conditional expressions and test them at the same time. A **logical operator** is used to compare two or more conditional expressions. Recall that a conditional expression is the same thing as a Boolean expression. The conditional expression will evaluate to true or false. Therefore, the program can evaluate two expressions, and compare the two results. Table 5-3 lists the logical operators used in JavaScript and VBScript. Although the operators are different, the meaning is the same in both languages.

Each conditional expression must be enclosed in parentheses, and a group of conditional expressions and logical operators must be enclosed within parentheses.

Table 5-3   Logical Operators in JavaScript and VBScript

JavaScript	Example	VBScript	Example	Meaning
&&	if ((a = = 1) && (b = = 2))	AND	if ((a = 1) and (b = 2))	If both expressions are true, the result is true. If either expression is false, the result is false.
||	if ((a = = 1) || (b = = 2))	OR	if ((a = 1) or (b = 2))	If either expression is true, or both are true, the result is true. If both are false, the result is false.
!	if (! (a = = 1))	NOT	if (not (a = 1))	Used to negate a single expression. If the expression is true, the result is false. If the expression is false, the result is true. The "not" operator takes a single Boolean expression and reverses its value.

It is possible to compare multiple conditional expressions. However, it is important to enclose each set of expressions within parentheses.

The following sample code from logical.htm illustrates how the logical operator can be used to evaluate and compare two conditional expressions. Because both expressions evaluate to true, the `if` statement evaluates to true.

```
<script language="javascript">
var a, b;
a = 1;
b = 2;
if ((a == 1) && (b == 2)){
  document.write("true");
}
else{
  document.write("false");
}
</script>
```

In the form you created previously, you did not check to see whether the visitor left the name text box empty. To verify that the visitor did not leave the text box empty, you can test the condition. You do not have to add a new script; you can combine multiple expressions using logical operators. Simply add the condition and a logical operator to the original conditional expression. Add a pair of parentheses around the entire expression. The following sample code from testblankJS.htm returns false if the user has left the name text box blank.

```javascript
if ((document.frm.name.value != "")&&
(document.frm.email[0].checked==true)){
```

The following sample code from testblankVB.htm shows that you can also combine multiple expressions using logical operators in VBScript. However, VBScript uses different logical operators. The logical operator **and** is used instead of **&&**.

```vbscript
if ((document.frm.name.value <> "") and
(document.frm.email(0).checked=true)) then
```

Nested If Then Statements   When a condition is met, the block of script that is executed may contain action statements and/or control statements. In the previous examples, action statements were executed when the condition was met. In the following example, an If Then control statement is executed. This is an example of a nested statement. You can nest one If Then statement within another If Then statement. The process of nesting can be repeated indefinitely. Nested statements provide more flexibility than multiple conditional expressions. Both of the following examples produce the same output as the multiple conditional expressions shown above. The sample below is the previous VBScript example modified to use nested statements and saved as a new Web page named testnestedVB.htm.

```vbscript
<script language="vbscript">
function signup()
if (document.frm.name.value <> "") then
        if (window.document.frm.email(0).checked = true) then
                window.alert("Thank you")
        else
                window.alert("You may sign up later")
        end if
else
        window.alert("You may sign up later")
end if
end function
</script>
```

The sample below is the previous JavaScript example modified to use nested statements and saved as a new Web page named testnestedJS.htm.

```javascript
<script language="javascript">
function signup(){
var strName;
strName=window.document.frm.name.value;
if (document.frm.name.value != ""){
        if (document.frm.email[0].checked==true){
                window.alert("Thank you");
        }
```

```
        else{
             window.alert("You may sign up later");
        }
   }
   else {
        window.alert("You may sign up later");
   }
   }
   </script>
```

Select Case Statements

The second type of decision control structure is called the **Select Case** statement. This statement, an extension of the If Then statement, is used to include more than two conditions in the conditional expression. A Select Case statement could be broken into many nested If Then statements, but if you use a Select Case statement, your code will be shorter, and also easier to follow. Because the Select Case statement is only supported by VBScript, it is most often used with server-side scripts.

In the Select Case statement, an expression is evaluated using the keyword **case**. The expression may be a variable, for example, which is compared to a value. If the condition is met, then the action statement associated with that condition is executed. If not, then the next condition is evaluated. This process continues until a condition is met. If no condition is met, then an alternate block of code may be executed. (That is why the Select Case statement is also known as the Case Select statement.) An optional **case else** statement is used to assign an action statement if no criteria have been met. The case statement ends with the keywords **end select**. The syntax below illustrates how the Select Case statement is used.

```
select case variableName
case value1
      action statement
case value2
      action statement
case value_n
      action statement
case else
      action statement
end select
```

Below is sample code from caseselectVB.htm, which illustrates how to use the Select Case statement to display the price of an item.

```
<script language="vbscript">
dim strP
strP = 1
select case strP
case 1
      window.alert ("The cost is $" & strP)
```

```
case 2
    window.alert ("The cost is $" & strP)
case else
    window.alert ("The cost is $" & strP)
end select
</script>
```

Just as you can nest If Then statements, you can nest other control structures. Any control statement can be nested within another control statement. The example below, from giftfinderVB.htm, illustrates how to nest a Select Case statement within an If Then statement. Figure 5-2 shows how this giftfinderVB.htm Web page looks in the browser. A form named frm contains two drop-down list elements named gender and price. The user may select any combination from both lists. The form includes a button called btnSubmit, which triggers an event handler when the user clicks it. Because the button is not a Submit button, it does not trigger the submit method. This onClick event handler will call a function named getGift.

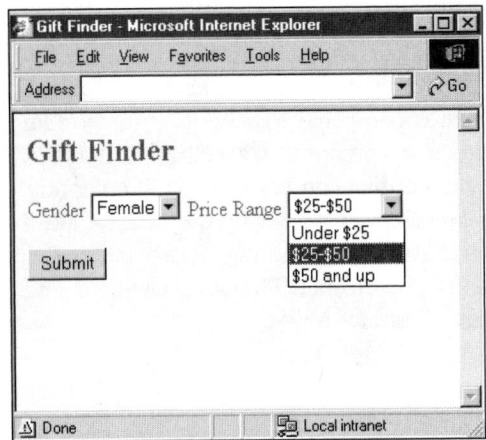

Figure 5-2 Using a Select Case control statement to process a form

To create a Web page that uses a Select Case statement to process a form:

1. Create a Web page named **giftfinderVB.htm** that contains a form and two drop-down lists, using the following code.

```
<html><head><title>Gift Finder</title></head>
<body bgcolor="#FFFF99" text="#800000">
<h2>Gift Finder</h2>
<form method="post" name="frm"
    action="javascript:void(0)">
<p>Gender
<select size="1" name="txtGender">
    <option value="M">Male</option>
    <option value="F">Female</option>
</select>
Price Range
```

```
<select size="1" name="txtPrice">
     <option value="1">Under $25</option>
     <option value="2">$25-$50 </option>
     <option value="3">$50 and up</option>
</select></p>
<p>
<input type="button" value="Submit"
     name="btnSubmit" onClick="getGift()";>
</p>
</form>
```

2. Create the script to process the form, using the code below. Remember to use VBScript instead of JavaScript, since JavaScript does not support the Select Case statement. The values from the form are assigned to the variables strP and strG. A variable named strGP is used to store the name of a Web page that contains the related products. The name of the Web page is obtained from concatenating the gender, price, and the .asp file extension.

VBScript

```
<script language="vbscript">
function getGift()
dim strP, strG, strGP
strP = document.frm.txtPrice.value
strG = document.frm.txtGender.value
strGP = strG & StrP & ".asp"
```

3. Add the If Then statement to determine which txtGender value was detected.

```
if (strG = "M") then
```

4. Nest the Select Case statement within the If Then statement.

```
     select case strP
     case 1
          window.alert("Go to " & strGP & " ?")
     case 2
          window.alert("Go to " & strGP & " ?")
     case else
          window.alert("Go to " & strGP & " ?")
          end select
else
     select case strP
     case 1
          window.alert("Go to " & strGP & " ?")
     case 2
          window.alert("Go to " & strGP & " ?")
     case else
          window.alert("Go to " & strGP & " ?")
     end select
end if
end function
</script>
</body></html>
```

5. Save the page to your data directory and view the page in your browser. When you select any combination from the two lists, a custom alert message will appear.

In the above example, the getGift function obtains the value of the gender and price form fields and assigns them to variables named strG and strP. The If Then statement determines whether the user selected Male or Female by comparing the value of the strG variable to a known value. Then, the getGift function uses the Select Case statement to determine which action to execute. The Select Case statement is used to iterate through multiple conditional statements. The Select Case statement is nested to determine which price is selected. The action statement causes a custom alert message identifying the name of a Web page to appear.

The action statements in this example can be customized to display the price or the gender, or to perform another action. The action statement could easily be changed to redirect the browser to a new page, on the basis of the user's selections. You could replace the alert method with the `location.href` method to redirect the browser to another page. The name of the Web page is obtained by concatenating the gender, price, and the .asp file extension. However, you could have replaced the variable with any valid URL. To modify this script so that the user is redirected to the page, change the action statement to the following:

```
window.location.href = strGP
```

You can include any number of action statements, as well as call other functions, within a control statement. The following sample code illustrates how to include additional action statements and functions within the case statement. The getUserName function is called, the `document.write` method writes content to the Web page, an alert message is displayed, and the browser is redirected to another Web page. All of these actions occur within a single case statement.

```
case 2
    getUserName()
    document.write("Welcome " & username)
    document.write("<br>")
    document.write("You are going to be ")
    document.write("redirected to another page.")
    window.alert("Go to " & strGP & " ?")
    window.location.href = strGP
```

Switch Case Statements

JavaScript contains a Switch Case statement that is similar to the VBScript Select Case statement. Both allow you to evaluate multiple statements. JavaScript uses the keyword **switch** to identify the beginning of the statement. The entire statement is enclosed within curly braces ({ }). Therefore, no ending statement is required. Each condition is identified with the **case** keyword. If no condition is met, the single keyword **default** can be used to identify a default action statement. The program will read through each case statement, and if a condition is met, the action statement will be executed. The program continues through the rest of the case statements to evaluate other conditions. This process repeats until the end of the case statement is reached, or until a break statement, indicated by the keyword **break**, occurs. A **break statement** is used to exit control structures such as the Switch Case statement. The break statement is an example of a jump control, because it allows you to jump out of the script block being executed. If you want to stop a script inside a loop structure and start over, you can use the **continue** statement. Below is the syntax for the Switch Case statement.

```
switch (variableName){
case var1:
    action statement;
    break;
case var2:
    action statement;
    break;
case var_n:
    action statement;
    break;
default:
    action statement;
    break;
}
```

The code below demonstrates how the Switch Case statement can be used instead of the VBScript Select Case statement to code the above giftfinderVB.htm example. The name of this Web page is giftfinderJS.htm. Both Web pages use the same form, but process the script differently. Both scripts produce the same result, although here the break statement is added after each action statement to force the program to jump out of the control structure if a condition is met.

```
<script language="javascript">
function getGift(){
var strP;
var strG;
var strGP;
strP = document.frm.txtPrice.value;
strG = document.frm.txtGender.value;
strGP = strG + strP + ".asp";
if (strG = "M") {
    switch (strP){
    case 1:
        window.alert ("Go to " + strGP + " ?");
        break;
    case 2:
        window.alert ("Go to " + strGP + " ?");
        break;
    default:
```

```
                    window.alert ("Go to " + strGP + " ?");
                    break;
            }
    }
    else {
        switch (strP){
        case 1:
            window.alert ("Go to " + strGP + " ?");
            break;
        case 2:
            window.alert ("Go to " + strGP + " ?");
            break;
        default:
            window.alert ("Go to " + strGP + " ?");
            break;
        }
    }
}
</script>
```

Loop Structures

Sometimes, you want a program to execute the same action statements more than once. For example, you might want to list all the elements in an array. You could list each element individually, and if the array had 100 elements, you would create 100 statements to write out the name of each element. However, using a **loop structure**, you can repeat action statements or control statements any number of times. To list all 100 elements in the array would require approximately seven lines of code, using a looping structure. If the number of elements in the array increases, the number of lines of code will remain the same.

The statements contained in the loop are called the **body** of the loop, and may consist of a single statement or several statements. Each repetition of a loop is called an **iteration**. The number of iterations can be explicitly stated or stored in a variable. A variable that keeps track of the number of iterations is referred to as a **loop index variable**. It is very common for the letter "i" or the word "count" to represent the loop index variable. An **update statement** is used to determine how to change the loop index variable. If you do not include an update statement, the program will continue to run until the browser program is exited, or the computer is turned off. When the loop continues without a natural ending, it is called an **infinite loop**. It is important to prevent your code from going into an infinite loop.

 You can use the loop index number to keep track of the number of times that the loop has been repeated. You can start the loop at a predetermined number, such as 0 or 1, and increment the loop index number by one after each iteration. When the loop has ended, the loop index number provides the total number of iterations.

The loop uses a conditional expression to determine when to stop—the loop stops when the conditional expression is true. The conditional expression often tests to see whether the loop index variable equals a number, or another variable. Usually, the conditional expression tests to see whether a variable is equal to a predetermined number. As the program runs, the update statement within the script block alters the loop index number. If the conditional expression never returns false, then the loop becomes an infinite loop. You can reverse this situation by modifying the conditional expression and using different comparison operators.

 Because it is easy to create an infinite loop, you should first diagram your programming logic using a flow chart. Then, walk through your flow chart with sample values to determine if the loop structure executes in the intended order.

The two main looping structures are While Do loops and For Next loops. The Do While loop is an alternate version of the While Do loop. The For In loop is a modified version of the For Next loop. These looping structures vary in their syntax and looping methods. However, all of them allow you to repeat blocks of code within your scripts.

While Do Loops

The **While Do** loop will repeat a block of code for as long as a conditional expression is evaluated as true. The While Do loop is supported in VBScript and JavaScript. The conditional expression is identified by the keyword `while`. Variables used within the conditional expression should be declared before the keyword while is used. The update statement will alter one of the variables within the conditional expression. If the update statement does not alter one of the variables within the conditional expression, the code will create an infinite loop. After the iteration is completed, the conditional expression is evaluated again. If the conditional expression is evaluated as true, the script stops processing the While Do loop. The following is the syntax for a While Do loop in JavaScript.

```
while (conditional expression){
    action statements;
    update statement;
}
```

In the following example, an array stores the names of five departments. The variable varD array holds the values of the department names. The While Do statement writes out the department name for each department, according to the number in the array. The loop index number, represented by the variable i, is used to keep track of the number of iterations, and to identify which element in the array to display. The numMax variable is used in the conditional expression to identify when the looping should stop. When the loop index number reaches the numMax variable, the loop will stop. The numMax variable can also act as the counter, and provide the total number of departments. Figure 5-3 shows the whileDoJS.htm Web page in a Web browser.

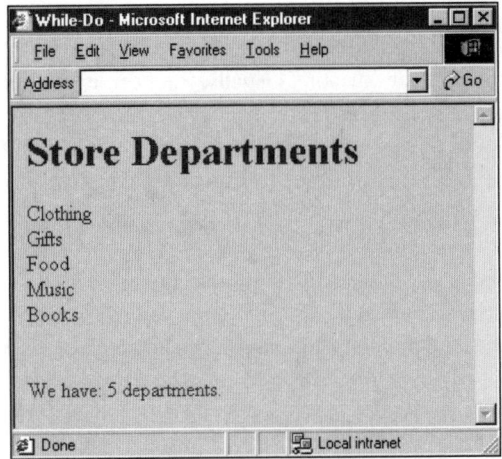

Figure 5-3 Using a While Do control statement to process a form

```
<html><head><title>While-Do </title></head>
<body bgcolor="#B1B6DE" text="#000080">
<script language = "javascript">
document.write("<h1>Store Departments</h1>");
var varD = new Array();
varD [0]="Clothing";
varD [1]="Gifts";
varD [2]="Food";
varD [3]="Music";
varD [4]="Books";
var numMax = 5;
var i = 0;
while(i != numMax ){
  strName= i;
  document.write((varD[i]) + "<br>");
  i++;
}
document.write("<br><br>");
document.write("We have: " +  i + " departments.");
</script>
</body></html>
```

In this example, the number of iterations was predetermined. The numMax variable was explicitly assigned a value, 5. You could have retrieved the value from a form field or a property, such as the length property of the array object. In both cases, the numMax value was predetermined before the script began. The following sample code illustrates how to retrieve the value from a form element or the length property of the array object.

```
var numMax = 5;
var numMax = document.frm.txtNumber.value;
var numMax = document.write(Products.length);
```

Unary Operators   In the previous example, a unary operator, increment, was used to modify the loop index number in the conditional expression. Unary operators are used to alter a value of a variable. Table 5-4 lists the unary operators that are supported in JavaScript and VBScript. The increment operator increases the value of a variable by one. For example, if the variable named Count was equal to 5, and the unary operator ++Count was applied, then the value of Count would change to 6. Likewise, the decrement operator decreases the value of a variable by 1. The negation operator is used to change the value of the variable. If the variable is positive, the negation operator will change the sign to negative. If the variable is a negative number such as −5, the negation operator will change the number to a positive number, 5. Unary operators apply to both VBScript and JavaScript. They are most often used to increment values such as the loop index number in a looping statement.

Table 5-4   Unary Operators Supported in JavaScript and VBScript

Operator	Purpose	Example	Result if Count = 5
++	Increments a counter by 1	Count = ++Count;	Count = 6
--	Decrements a counter by 1	Count = --Count;	Count = 4
−	Negation: changes the sign to the inverse sign	−Count	Count = −5

Do While Loops

The **Do While** loop structure is similar to the While Do structure. Both While Do and Do While loop structures cause the loop to end when the conditional statement is evaluated as false. However, in a Do While loop, the script is executed once before the conditional statement is evaluated. Therefore, there will be at least one iteration before the loop stops. In a While Do loop, the conditional statement is evaluated first. If the condition is evaluated as false, the code does not process any code within the loop body. There is another less commonly used loop structure called a **Do Until** loop that is similar to the Do While loop. The Do Until loop continues until a condition is met. Below is the syntax for a Do While loop in JavaScript.

```
do {
    action statements;
    update statement;
}
while (conditional expression);
```

The following example, from doWhileJS.htm, illustrates how to implement the Do While loop using JavaScript. In this example, the conditional expression does not test for equality, but for inequality. The conditional expression will still be evaluated as true or false. This example also demonstrates how to use the unary operator (++) to increment a variable. When this page is viewed in a browser, the alert message will appear five times, because the condition will be met after the completion of the fifth loop. At that time, the variable i will equal 5, which will cause the conditional statement to be evaluated as true. Then, the loop will stop executing.

```
<script language="javascript">
var aNumber = 5;
var i = 0;
do{
     window.alert(i);
     i++;
}
while(i != aNumber);
</script>
```

The syntax for the Do While statement is slightly different in VBScript. The following sample code, from doWhileVB.htm, illustrates how to implement a Do While loop using VBScript. In VBScript, the conditional expression is placed immediately after the keyword do, and the end of the loop is identified by the keyword loop. Notice that you do not need to use the parentheses around the conditional expression. The update statement in this example just adds the number five to the index number. In both JavaScript and VBScript, you are not required to use a unary operator in an update statement. When this page is viewed in a browser, the body of the loop will be executed twice before the condition is met.

```
<script language="vbscript">
dim aNumber
aNumber = 5
dim i
i = 0
do while i <= aNumber
     window.alert(i)
     i = i + 5
loop
</script>
```

For Next Loops

The For Next loop, like the Do While loop, repeats action statements for a fixed number of times. However, the syntax of the For Next statement is very different from that of the Do While statement. The For Next loop identifies not only the conditional expression but also the loop index number and the update statement as parameters in the "for" statement. In both VBScript and JavaScript, the loop index number and other variables are declared before the loop begins. Also, the loop index number can be explicitly stated or identified using a variable. The update statement updates the loop index number.

However, in VBScript the loop body begins with the keyword for. In the syntax sample below, startExpression is the value that is assigned to the loop index variable when the loop begins. The startExpression and endNumber variables are known as **loop counters**. Therefore, the startExpression and endNumber variables must be integers. When the loop starts the first loop, the loop index number is modified by the update statement. The update statement is identified by the keyword step and the stepNumber. The stepNumber is an expression that identifies how to change the loop index number. Very often the stepNumber is an expression that will increment the loop index number by 1. If there is no update stepNumber, then the loop index number is incremented by 1. Each time the loop begins, the program evaluates the loop index number. If the loop index number is equal to the endNumber variable, then the loop ends.

For LoopIndex = startExpression to endNumber step stepNumber
   Action statements

Next

The two examples below show how the startExpression, endNumber, and stepNumber variables can be variables or explicit values. The following example, from forNextVB.htm, illustrates how to implement a For Next loop in VBScript. Notice that the values for the startExpression, endNumber, and stepNumber variables are explicitly stated in the for statement. The value of the startExpression variable is 1; the EndNumber is 5; and the stepNumber is 1. This example writes out the numbers 1 through 5 on individual lines.

```
<script language="vbscript">
document.write("How many books do you want?<br>")
for varCount = 1 to 5 step 1
    document.write(varCount & "<br>")
next
</script>
```

The following example, from forNextVB2.htm, illustrates how to implement in VBScript a For Next loop, using variables for the startNumber, endNumber, and stepNumber values. The values for the variables are declared and assigned values before the loop begins.

```
<script language="vbscript">
dim startNum, endNum, stepNum, i
startNum = 0
endNum = 5
stepNum = 2
for i = startNum to endNum step stepNum
    window.alert(i)
next
</script>
```

JavaScript also supports the For Next loop, and also identifies the startNumber, the endNumber, and the stepNumber in the "for" statement. However, the JavaScript syntax for the For Next loop is slightly different. In JavaScript you must use a semicolon to separate each statement from the next. The keyword loop is not required because JavaScript uses curly braces to identify the beginning and ending of the loop body. The startExpression variable is used not only to identify the startNumber, but also to assign that value to the loop index number. The variable can be declared with the keyword **var** within the startExpression, instead of before the loop begins. In the syntax example below, the conditional expression compares the loop index number to the endNumber. The stepNumber is an expression that is used to modify the loop index number each time the loop is repeated. Semicolons separate the startExpression, conditional expression, and stepNumber.

```
for (startExpression; conditional expression; stepNumber) {
    action statements;
}
```

In the following sample code, from forNextJS.htm, the loop index number is represented by the variable "i", which is declared and assigned a value in the "for" statement. The conditional expression (i <= 5) means that the loop will continue until the value of the loop index number is less than or equal to 5. Each time the loop is repeated, starting with the first iteration, the loop index number will be increased by 1. The value of the loop index number can be written out incrementally, as it is in this example. The loop index number could be written out to the Web page at the end as a loop counter indicating the number of iterations that have passed through the loop.

```
<script language = "javascript">
for(var i = 0; i <= 5; i=i+1){
    document.writeln("Your number is " +  i + ".<br>");
}
</script>
```

For In Loops

The For In loop is similar to the For Next loop in that they both allow you to repeat action statements. However, the For In loop is most often used to retrieve the properties of objects. You will recall that some of the objects within the Document Object Model include collections of similar objects. For example, a document can contain multiple forms. Each form object is part of a collection that belongs to the document object. The For In loop retrieves information about the properties of an object and the **collections** of the object.

The number of iterations is not based on a loop index number, but on the number of properties or elements within the object. Therefore, the "for" statement must contain the name of the variable that will hold the name of the element, the keyword **in**, and the name of the object. The beginning and ending of the body of the loop are delimited with curly braces. Any number of action statements can exist within the body of the loop. The action statement can be used to display the names and values of the properties that belong to the object. Below is the syntax for implementing the For In Loop using JavaScript.

```
for (variable in object){
    action statements;
}
```

To create a Web page that uses a For In loop to list the properties of an object:

1. Create a Web page named **forInJS.htm** in your Web page editor, using the code below. In this code, the body tag is altered to change the properties of the document. The properties that are modified include the background color, foreground color, link colors, and title.

```
<html><head><title>For In</title></head>
<body  bgColor="#FFFF99" text="#800000"
    topmargin="5" leftmargin="5"
    link="#008000" vlink="#808000"
    alink="#0000FF">
<h1>Properties of the Document Object</h1>
```

2. Add the For In loop using JavaScript, as shown below. The eachKey variable contains the properties of objects defined within the document object. Notice that as the loop continues, the value of eachKey is displayed. Because the list of properties and objects constitutes an array for the document object, each element can be referred to by its index value in the array. The document([eachKey]) statement retrieves the value for that element in the document array.

These properties and collections are part of an array that belongs to the object. You previously learned that in JavaScript the syntax for retrieving the array element is square brackets. Therefore, you can refer to the property by using the position within the array (document[eachKey]) or the name of the property (document.title).

```
<script language = "javascript">
for(var eachKey in document){
    document.write(eachKey);
    document.write(" = ");
    document.write(document[eachKey]);
    document.write("<br>");
}
</script>
```

3. Add the closing tags and save the page in your data directory.

```
</body></html>
```

4. View the Web page. Figure 5-4 shows the page displayed in a browser. Notice how the properties and the objects are listed. All of the document's subordinate objects are listed with their name and the value "[object]" after their name. Properties and methods that are undefined are listed as "null". You must view this page on a Web server, such as Personal Web Server, or you will receive an error message. The properties shown include information passed from the Web server.

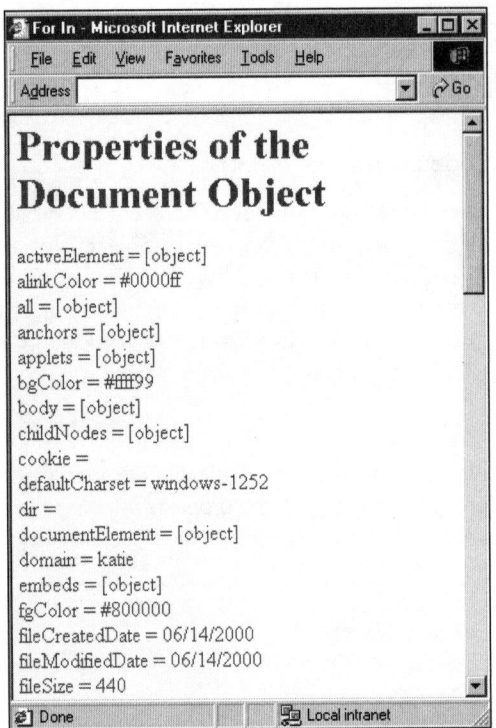

Figure 5-4   Using the For In control statement to list the properties of an object

The syntax for VBScript For In loops is slightly different. In VBScript you use parentheses to retrieve the array element. Instead of using the keyword **for**, VBScript uses the keywords **for each**. The action statement can be used to display the names and values of the properties that belong to the object. The keywords **exit for**, which are optional, cause the program to exit out of the loop, and are often used in combination with another control structure, such as an If Then statement. The end of the body of the loop is identified by the keyword **next** with the eachElement variable name. If this statement is not included, the loop will end the body of the loop as if it were included. Below is the syntax for creating a For In loop in VBScript.

```
for each (eachElement in object)
    action statements
    exit for
next eachElement
```

As you learned above, the For In loop is often used for displaying properties and elements within objects and arrays. In the previous chapter, you learned how to create and populate an array called Products. To retrieve the contents of the array, you need to specify the index number for the array element. A variable named i is created to store the index number for the individual array elements within the loop. Then, the value of the array element can be retrieved using the name of the array and the index number of the element. In the sample code below, from forInVB.htm, the For In loop is used to display the elements within the array.

```
<script language = "vbscript">
dim Products(5)
Products(0) = "Pencils"
Products(1) = "Pens"
Products(2) = "Paper"
Products(3) = "Markers"
Products(4) = "Notepads"
Products(5) = "Scissors"
dim i
i = 0
for each eachElement in Products
    document.write(Products(i) & "<br>")
    i = i+1
next
</script>
```

CHAPTER SUMMARY

Control Structures

❑ Control structures allow you to determine the conditions under which an action statement is executed and the order in which the action statements are executed. Two types of control structures are decision control structures and looping structures.

❑ Decision control structures allow you to control which block of action statements is executed, on the basis of certain criteria. Looping structures allow you to repeat a block of action statements. Examples of decision control structures are: If Then, Select Case, and Switch Case. Examples of looping structures are: While Do, Do While, For Next, and For In. The syntax of many of the control structures will vary between JavaScript and VBScript.

Operators

❑ Assignment operators are used to assign a value or an object to a variable. The assignment operator is the equal sign (=) for both VBScript and JavaScript. The concatenation operator in JavaScript is the plus sign (+), while the concatenation operator in VBScript is the ampersand (&). Arithmetic operators allow you to perform calculations on values and variables. Comparison operators allow you to compare two expressions. Comparison operators are different in JavaScript and VBScript. A conditional expression is a Boolean expression that evaluates to true or false. Unary operators allow you to evaluate multiple expressions by combining them into one statement. Unary operators are different in JavaScript and VBScript.

To create an If Then statement

```javascript
if (a = 1) {
    window.alert("a");
}
else{
    window.alert("not a");
}
```

```vbscript
if (a = 1) then
    window.alert("a")
else
    window.alert("not a")
end if
```

To create a Select Case statement

```vbscript
select case aNumber
case 1
    window.alert("1")
case 2
    window.alert("2")
case else
    window.alert("other")
end select
```

To create a Switch Case statement

```javascript
switch (aNumber){
case 1:
    window.alert("1");
    break;
case 2:
    window.alert("2");
    break;
default:
    window.alert("other");
    break;
}
```

To create a While Do statement

```javascript
var aNumber;
aNumber = 5;
var i;
i = 0;
while (i != aNumber){
    window.alert(i);
    i++;
}
```

```vbscript
dim aNumber
aNumber = 5
dim i
i = 0
while (i != aNumber){
    window.alert(i)
    i++
}
```

To create a Do While statement

```javascript
var aNumber = 5;
var i = 0;
do{
    window.alert(i);
    i++;
}
while(i != aNumber);
```

```vbscript
dim aNumber
aNumber = 5
dim i
i = 0
do while i <= aNumber
    window.alert(i)
    i = i + 5
loop
```

5

To create a For Next Loop statement

```javascript
var aNumber;
aNumber = 5;
var i;
i = 0;
while (i != aNumber){
     window.alert(i);
     i++;
}
```

```vbscript
for varCount = 1 to 5
     document.write(varCount & "<br>")
next
```

To create a For In Loop statement

```javascript
for(var eachElement in document){
     document.write(eachElement + " = ");
     document.writeln(document[eachElement]);
     document.writeln("<br>");
}
```

```vbscript
for each eachElement in Products
     document.write(Products(i) & "<br>")
     i = i+1
next
```

REVIEW QUESTIONS

1. The If Then statement is the only control structure that can contain nested control statements. True or False?

2. An unnested If Then statement allows you to select a maximum of two choices. True or False?

3. An unnested Select Case statement allows you to select a maximum of two choices. True or False?

4. A Boolean expression can only have the value true or false. True or False?

5. The logical operator that represents "and" in VBScript is "&&". True or False?

6. The logical operator that represents "or" in JavaScript is "||". True or False?

7. JavaScript does not support concatenation. True or False?

8. The concatenation operator in VBScript is "&". True or False?

9. A loop that continues without a natural ending is called an infinite loop. True or False?

10. A semicolon appears after all control statements in JavaScript. True or False?

11. A _____ construct allows you to repeat blocks of code.

    a. decision control structure

    b. looping control structure

    c. repeating control structure

    d. variable control structure

12. The logical "and" operator in JavaScript is:

    a. ||

    b. &&

    c. +

    d. &

13. Which is the concatenation operator in JavaScript?

    a. =

    b. /

    c. +

    d. &

14. _____ are used to specify the order of precedence of an arithmetic expression.

    a. Variables

    b. Constants

    c. Parentheses

    d. Terminators

15. What is the comparison operator in JavaScript that means "equal to"?

    a. =

    b. ==

    c. ||

    d. &&

16. What is the comparison operator in VBScript that means "not equal to"?

    a. not equal to

    b. !=

    c. <>

    d. !<>

5

17. What should be added to the form tag to prevent an error message when the onSubmit event handler is called by the Submit button in a script?

    a. `method = "vbscript:void(0)"`

    b. `method = "javascript:void()"`

    c. `method = "void()"`

    d. `method = "javascript:void(0)"`

18. In addition to the `if` keyword and the "conditional expression," what other keyword must be included in the "if" statement line in VBScript?

    a. {

    b. next

    c. then

    d. end if

19. What keyword is used to exit out of the Switch Case control structure?

    a. end case

    b. case end

    c. break

    d. case

20. If count = 10, and the statement says "++count" what is the value of count?

    a. 9

    b. 10

    c. −10

    d. 11

21. An example of a unary operator is _____.

    a. ++

    b. &&

    c. ||

    d. = =

22. What is used to identify the end of the For Next loop in JavaScript?

    a. {

    b. }

    c. end

    d. loop

23. Which control structure can be used to list the properties of an object?

a. Do While

b. While Do

c. For Next

d. For In

HANDS-ON PROJECTS

5

Project 5-1

In this project, you will create a Web page that uses arithmetic operators to calculate the total cost of a product based on the user's selections. Use VBScript to complete this exercise. Figure 5-5 shows the productOrderVB.htm Web page, which uses arithmetic operators to calculate a value based on the values selected in a form.

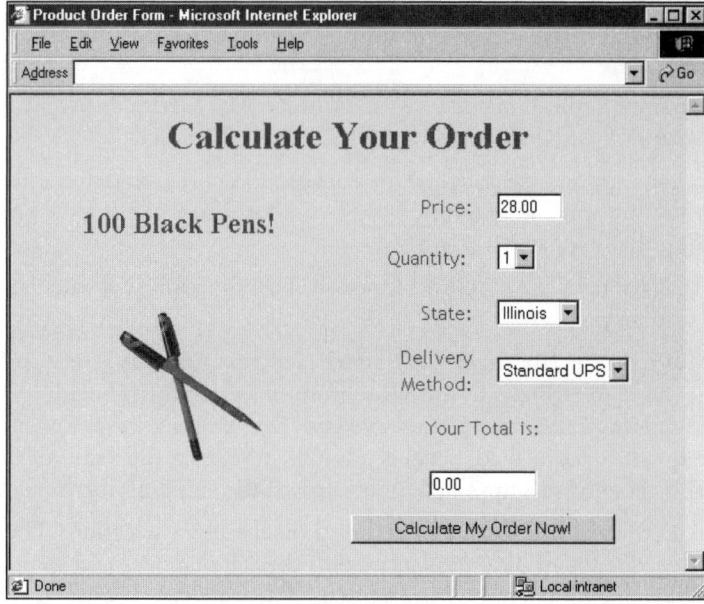

Figure 5-5   Using arithmetic operators to calculate values from a form

1. Using a Web page editor or Notepad, create a Web page named **productOrderVB.htm**.

a. The title of the page should be **Product Order Form**.

b. Add a heading formatted as heading 1 and centered that says **Calculate Your Order**.

2. Add a form named **frmProd**. Don't forget to add the action property and call the void method. (*Hint:* the syntax is `action="javascript:void(0)"`.) Modify the form tag: Use the void() method in the form action property so that users will not be redirected to a new page when they submit the form. The form method should be post.

3. Add the following fields to the form.

   a. A text box named **price** with a default value of 28.00. The label should read **Price**.

   b. A text box named **total** with a default value of 0.00. The label should read **Your Total is:**.

   c. A drop-down list named **quantity** with size of 1. The label should read **Quantity**. The possible options are **1, 2,** and **3** and have corresponding values of 1, 2, and 3. 1 should be selected by default.

   d. A drop-down list named **state** with size of 1. The label should read **State**. The possible options are **Illinois, Indiana,** and **Other**, and have corresponding values of 0.085, 0.7, and 0. Illinois should be selected by default.

   e. A drop-down list named **shipping** with size of 1. The label should read **Delivery Method**. The possible options are **Standard UPS, Overnight,** and **Pickup,** and have corresponding values of 0.02, 0.05, and 0. Standard UPS should be selected by default.

4. Create a button named btnSubmit that says **Calculate My Order Now!** When the user clicks the button, a function named calcProd should be called.

5. Modify the Web page appearance. Change the background color, modify the text format using your favorite font, and add graphics. Modify the form to make it look presentable. Use a table to align the fields and labels.

6. Create a script that contains the calcProd function. This function will calculate the value of the total form field.

7. In the calProd function, declare the variables **strPrice, strQuantity, strState,** and **strTotal**. Set the value of strPrice to the value from the price form field: `strPrice=document.frmProd.price.value`. Set the value of strQuantity to the value of the quantity form field. Set the value of strState to the value of the state form field. Set the value of strShipping to the value of the shipping form field.

8. Create the formula to assign strTotal, a value based on the user's selections. The formula should be the price multiplied by the quantity, plus the state tax fees and shipping fees. The state field holds the sales tax rate for each state. The state tax is equal to cost times the state field. The shipping field holds the percentage that is used to calculate the shipping cost for each shipping method. The shipping cost is equal to the cost multiplied by the shipping field.

9. Assign the value of the total field on the frmProd form to the new value in the total variable. (*Hint:* Use the complete name for the total field (`document.frmProd.total.value=strTotal`).)

You can round numbers in VBScript with the built-in round function. Built-in functions such as round will be covered in the next chapter.

10. Save the Web page to your data directory. View the Web page. Print your source code. Print the Web page.

Project 5-2

In this project, you will complete the previous project (productOrderVB.htm) using JavaScript instead of VBScript.

1. Save the productOrderVB.htm Web page as **productOrderJS.htm**.

2. Modify the Web page to support JavaScript instead of VBScript.

3. Save the Web page to your data directory. View the Web page. Print your source code. Print the Web page.

Project 5-3

In this project, you will create a login form that verifies a user. Use VBScript to complete this exercise. Figure 5-6 shows a Web page that uses nested control structures to process a form. The form uses the If Then and Select Case control structures to validate the user.

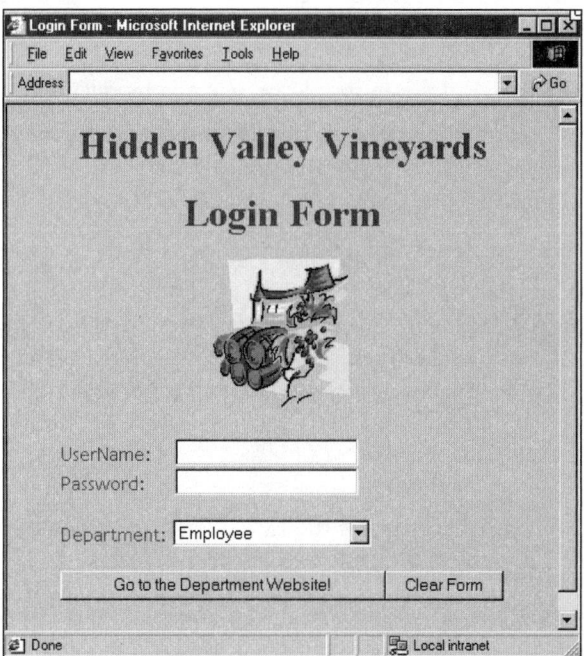

Figure 5-6 Using nested control structures to process a form

1. Create ten Web pages, one for each department.

   a. Name the pages **administration.htm**, **customer.htm**, **employee.htm**, **finance.htm**, **hr.htm**, **it.htm**, **management.htm**, **manufacturing.htm**, **marketing.htm**, and **webmaster.htm**.

   b. Add a heading 1 with the name of the department on each of the pages. For example, the Administration page, administration.htm, should say **Administration**. The Information Technology Web page should say **Information Technology**, but the name of the page should be "it.htm". The Human Resources Web page should say **Human Resources**, but the name of the page would be "hr.htm".

2. Create a Web page named **loginFormVB.htm**, entitled **Login Form**.

3. Add a heading, formatted as heading 1 and centered, that says **Login Form**.

4. Create the form named **frmLogin**. The form method should be post. Add the void method to the action property so that users will not be redirected to a new page when they submit the form.

5. Add the following fields to the form.

   a. A text box named **txtUserName**. The label should read **UserName**.

   b. A text box named **txtPassword**. The label should read **Password**.

   c. A drop-down list named **lstDepartment** with size of 1. The label should read **Department**. The possible options are **Administration**, **Customer**, **Employee**, **Finance**, **Human Resources**, **Information Technology**, **Management**, **Manufacturing**, **Marketing**, and **Webmaster**, and they have corresponding values of administration, customer, employee, finance, hr, it, management, manufacturing, marketing, and Webmaster. Employee should be selected by default.

6. Create a button named btnLogin that says **Go to the Department Website!** When the user clicks the button, a function named login should be called.

7. Create a reset button named btnClear that says **Clear Form**.

8. Modify the Web page background color, add graphics, and change the text format, using your favorite font.

9. Create a script that contains the login function. The login function will verify whether or not the user is a valid user, and redirect the user to the department home page. Declare the variables **strUserName**, **strPassword**, **strDepartment**. Set the value of strUserName to the value of the txtUserName form field. Set the value of strPassword to the value of the txtPassword form field. Set the value of strDepartment to the value of the lstDepartment form field.

10. Test to see if the strUserName variable matches the first UserName, using the Select Case control structure that follows. Use the table below for valid users.

```
select case strUserName
case  "KFoster"
```

UserName	Password
KFoster	MST3K
CSchwab	OKC802
FHelms	Telcom52
KShea	Ghost716

5

11. If the user is valid, then check to see if the password matches the user's password. Use a nested If Then statement to see if the password is correct. (*Hint*: Use the statement `if strPassword = "MST3K" then`.)

12. If the user is a valid user and the password matches, redirect the user to the department Web page. (*Hint*: Use the `location.href` property to redirect the user to the appropriate Web page.) Redirect the user by using the strDepartment variable and appending the **.htm** extension, using the concatenation operator. (*Hint*: The concatenation operator in VBScript is the ampersand (&).) Don't forget to use quotation marks for the extension because it is a string! The strDepartment variable does not use quotation marks! So the code looks like `location.href = strDepartment & ".htm"`.

13. If the user is not a valid user, redirect the user to the loginFormVB.htm page. Apply client-side redirection using the `location.href` property. Use the keyword `else` and then `location.href="loginFormVB.htm"`. Don't forget to end the If Then statement with the **end if** keywords.

14. Repeat Steps 10 through 13 for the other three valid users listed in the table in Step 10.

15. Add the **End Select** keywords to end the Select Case control structure.

16. Save the Web page to your data directory.

17. View the Web page. Print your source code. Print the Web page.

Project 5-4

In this project, you will do the previous exercise using JavaScript instead of VBScript.

1. Save the loginFormVB.htm Web page as **loginFormJS.htm**.

2. Modify the Web page to support JavaScript instead of VBScript. You will need to change the Select Case statement to a Switch Case statement. (*Hint*: Don't forget that JavaScript requires you to use curly braces instead of some keywords, and remember to use parentheses around conditional expressions.)

3. Save the Web page to your data directory. View the Web page. Print your source code. Print the Web page.

Project 5-5

In this project, you will use JavaScript to validate a username and redirect the browser to the department home page. Each employee will have a different username, but all use a common password. You will create a multiple conditional expression to test to see if the name entered in the form matches one of the valid usernames. You will then create a nested If Then statement to see if the password matches the group password.

1. Create a new Web page named **company.htm**, which is the employee home page for company employees.

   a. Add a heading that says **Michigan Wildlife Deer Folundation**.

   b. Format the page using color, text, and images of your choice.

   c. Save the Web page to your data directory. Close the Web page.

2. Create another Web page that will allow users to log in. After they log in they will be redirected to the company home page. Create a Web page named **loginJS.htm**, and entitled **Login Form**. Figure 5–7 shows a group login form in a browser window.

Figure 5-7   Using nested control structures to validate users

3. Add the same headings and graphics as you did in company.htm. Add a heading, formatted as heading 1 and centered, that says **Group Login Form**.

4. Add a form named **frmLogin**. Don't forget to add the action property and assign the void method to the action property. The form method should be post.

5. The Web form contains two fields. Add a text box named **txtUserName** labeled **Username**. Add a text box named **txtPassword** labeled **Password**.

6. Create a button named btnLogin and labeled **Go to the Department Website!** When the user clicks the button, a function called login should be called.

7. Create a reset button named btnClear. Label the button **Clear Form**.

8. Modify the Web page appearance to match the employee.htm page.

5

9. Create a script that contains the login function. This function will determine whether the user is a valid user and redirect the user to the department home page.

10. Declare the variables **strUserName** and **strPassword**. Set the value of strUserName to the value of the txtUserName form field. Set the value of strPassword to the value of the txtPassword form field.

11. Use a single If Then statement to test to see whether the strUserName variable matches a username. To determine whether the user is a valid user, use the If Then statement. The names of the four users who should be able to sign in to the site include KFoster, CSchwab, FHelms, and KShea. (*Hint:* The "||" statement is used for JavaScript. For example, here is the script to validate the strUsername for two users:
`if (strUserName=="KFoster" || strUserName=="CSchwab"){`.)

12. Use a nested If Then statement to see if the password is valid. The password this month is **MST3K**.

    a. If the login name is that of a valid user, and the password matches, use the window alert method to welcome the user. The message should say **Welcome!** Then use the `location.href` property to redirect the user to a new Web page.

       `location.href="company.htm"`

    b. If the password does not match, use the window alert method to inform the user. The message should say **You entered the wrong password. Try again.** Then use the reset method to clear the form. (*Hint:* To call the reset method, you need to specify the form name, not the reset button name! For example, here is the script to reset a form named frmLogin: `document.frmLogin.reset();`.)

13. If the user did not enter a valid username, use the alert method to display the message **You are not listed in our membership. Try again.** Then use the reset method to clear the form.

14. Save the Web page to your data directory. View the Web page. Print your source code. Print the Web page.

Project 5-6

In this project, you will complete the previous exercise using VBScript instead of JavaScript.

1. Save the loginJS.htm Web page as **loginVB.htm**.

2. Modify the Web page to support VBScript instead of JavaScript. (*Hint:* You will need to change the logical operators from | | to **OR**. For example, here is the script to validate the strUsername for two users:
   ```
   if strUsername = "KFoster" OR strUsername = "CSchwab".)
   ```

3. Save the Web page to your data directory. View the Web page. Print your source code. Print the Web page.

Project 5-7

In this project, you will use a looping statement to look up members in an array. Use JavaScript to complete this project.

1. Create a Web page named **memberJS.htm** and entitled **Membership Directory**.

2. Add a heading, formatted as heading 1 and centered, that says **Search the Membership Directory**.

3. Add a form named **frmSearch**. Don't forget to add the action property and call the void method.

4. Add one field to the Web form, a text box named **txtUserName**.

5. Add a button named btnSearch that displays the message **Search for a Member!** This is a regular button. When the button is clicked, the function searchMember is called.

6. Add a button named btnClear that displays **Clear Form**. This is a reset button.

7. Add a script named **searchMember**. Declare a variable named strUserName to hold the value from the UserName field on the form. Assign the value from the UserName field to the strUserName variable, using the following sample code:
   ```
   strUserName = window.document.frmSearch.txtUserName.value;.
   ```

8. Create an array named varMembers, using the following code:
   ```
   var varMembers = new Array();.
   ```
   Add four items to the array: **KFoster**, **CSchwab**, **FHelms**, and **KShea**. For example, to add KFoster to the array you would write `varMembers[0]="KFoster";`. Create a new variable named numMax to hold the number of items in the array. Assign the length property of the array to the numMax variable, using the following sample code:
   ```
   var numMax = varMembers.length;.
   ```

9. Create a For statement that will loop through each element in the array until it reaches a match to the UserName field. The first parameter in the for statement will declare a variable named "i", and assign 0 to "i". The "i" variable will be used as an index loop counter. The second parameter is the conditional statement. The conditional statement should determine if "i" is less than the numMax variable. The third parameter indicates that the loop index number, "i", should be incremented by 1 each time the loop is repeated. When these three parameters are added to the For statement, the code should look like this: `for (var i = 0; i < numMax ; ++ i){.`

10. Create an If Then statement that will detect whether the value of the current array element is equal to the variable that holds the value from the UserName field. If they are equal, then redirect the user to the company.htm page, using the HREF method. (*Hint:* When you compare the array element and the variable, use two equal signs. Also, use the keyword continue to cause the loop to restart the loop if there is no match. This way, the loop will continue until it reaches a match. Don't forget to close the For loop with a closing curly brace.)

```
if (varMembers[i] == strUserName)
location.href="company.htm";
continue;
}
```

5

11. Add a statement that will assign an empty string to the UserName field by using the code `window.document.frmSearch.txtUserName.value = ""`. This statement is included so that if the user did not fill in the correct answer, it will clear the field for the user to try again.

12. Save the Web page to your data directory. View the Web page. Print your source code. Print the Web page.

CASE PROJECTS

Harvey's Hardware Outlet Store

You are hired as the Webmaster for Harvey's Hardware Outlet Store, which allows members to purchase commercial hardware products at discount prices. Your employer wants you to create some Web pages that will only be available to members. The Web site currently has 10 members. Assign each member a username and password. You decide to create a login page named hardwareLogin.htm where members can sign in with their username and password. Use decision control structures to determine whether the username and password matches that of a member. You can use JavaScript or VBScript. If the member does not sign in to the site correctly, the user should be redirected to the login page. If the username and password are correct, then redirect the user to a welcome page named hardwareMember.htm. Modify the layout using a table, color, and graphics to make the Web page look professional. Save your Web pages to your data directory.

Night Crawlers IT Department

You have decided that you want to create a restricted-access administration page on the store Web site. Using an If Then control structure, create a login script that allows users to log in to the administration page using their username and password. The administrator's username is admin, and the password is pass. If the user does not log in correctly, the user should be redirected to the login page. You also need to allow the store manager access to the administration page. Add the manager's username to the If Then control structure, using a logical operator. The manager's username is manager, and the password is pwd. Modify the layout using a table, color, and graphics to make the Web page look professional. Save your Web page to your data directory as adminlogin.htm.

Markers! Markers! Markers!

You are creating an online store. Create a Web page with one product. Include a form with the product name and other options, such as color, size, style, and so on. The form fields should also include the cost of the item, the state tax, shipping charges, a total field, and a button. When the user clicks the button, the tax is calculated and displayed in the tax field, the shipping charge is calculated and placed in the shipping field, and the total is calculated and displayed in the total field. You have brick and mortar stores in six states: Illinois, Indiana, Florida, Texas, New York, and California, which are listed in a drop-down list box. Tax rates in these states are 0.085, 0.07, 0.07, 0.05, 0.09, and 0.65 respectively.

Current law requires that an online store charge sales tax only for customers who live in the state where the brick and mortar store is physically located. A brick and mortar store in Illinois would not charge sales tax for a customer who lives in Wisconsin. The sales tax laws are likely to change in the future. You need to be familiar with your state laws when designing online shopping applications.

Offer at least five delivery options: Standard UPS, Overnight, Next Day Air, Book Rate, and Pickup. Each delivery option should have a different cost associated with it. Calculate the total by adding the total amount for shipping, tax, and cost. Modify the layout using a table, color, and graphics to make the Web page look professional. Save your Web page to your data directory as product.htm. You can use JavaScript or VBScript. You do not need to round the total amount. Rounding and other built-in functions will be discussed in the next chapter.

Krannert School of Web Design

You are hired as a liaison between the IT department and the faculty. You have been asked to create an online quiz for an instructor who teaches a Web design course. The instructor tells you that you are to create a pre-quiz that can be used to test the students on the first day of class. There should be at least five questions. Each question has the option of a, b, c, or d. Use a form to retrieve the answer. You can use a text box or drop-down list to indicate the answer. (*Hint*: If you use a radio button or check box, you will have to do significantly more programming with arrays for the form elements in order to detect which element was selected.) Modify the layout using a table, color, and graphics to make the Web page look professional.

At the top of the Web page there should be a text box that displays the total number of correct answers after the user has submitted the quiz. Create a script that uses If Then, Select Case, or Switch Case statements to check the users' answers. Display the number of correct answers in the correct answer text box. If the user answers all five questions correctly, display an alert message that says A perfect score!. Save your Web page to your data directory as selectQuiz.htm. You can use JavaScript or VBScript.

Karen's Boutique—The Gift Finder

You have been hired at Karen's Boutique to enhance their Web site. After talking to Karen's customers, you learn that she provides customized gift advice. Customers will ask for a list of recommended products for a particular gender, in a particular price range. To enhance the Web site, you decide to apply her knowledge in a new page called The Gift Finder. The Gift Finder will allow customers to search for items based on gender, price, and age group. The gender group consists of male and female, and the age group consists of child and adult. The price group consists of products under $50 and products over $50. Create a Web page that contains three drop-down list boxes, one for each group. Use decision control structures and looping structures to determine which selections were made. Send users to a page specific to their selections. (*Hint:* You can use the values from their selections, append them together, and append the `.htm` file extension to create the filename.) Then, create a page for each possible combination. Modify the layout, using a table, color, and graphics to make the Web page look professional. Save your Web page to your data directory as selectLists.htm. You can use JavaScript or VBScript.

5

6

FUNCTIONS AND PROCEDURES

In this chapter you will:

♦ Use built-in functions in JavaScript and VBScript
♦ Create functions in JavaScript and VBScript
♦ Call functions in JavaScript and VBScript
♦ Create and call procedures in VBScript
♦ Create event procedures in VBScript

In the previous chapter you learned how to use control statements to change the order in which action statements are executed. In this chapter you will learn how to use the functions that are built into JavaScript and VBScript to perform common programming tasks. You will also learn how to create and call custom functions and procedures that can be reused within your Web application. Programmers refer to this process as "write once, use many." This common saying refers to the productivity gained by using functions and procedures to perform tasks that recur within a Web page or throughout an entire Web application. Because functions are used in client- and server-side scripting, you will learn to create custom functions and call them from your scripts, using both JavaScript and VBScript. You will also learn how to create and call procedures using VBScript.

BUILT-IN FUNCTIONS AND METHODS

Both JavaScript and VBScript support several built-in objects and **built-in functions**. Recall that when an object contains a built-in function it is referred to as a **method**. Built-in functions include mathematical, date and time, string, and formatting functions, among others. Some built-in functions are common to both JavaScript and VBScript. Each also includes additional built-in functions, which will be described separately.

JavaScript Math Object Methods

The JavaScript language includes a built-in math object, which exposes many mathematical methods. Because the math object is built in, you do not have to declare the object before accessing its methods. You learned previously that a method is a function that is defined within an object. To access these methods on some platforms, you will need to specify the fully qualified name of the object. For example, the **abs** method would be written as **Math.abs()**. These mathematical methods are useful when you work with numbers. For example, in JavaScript, the **floor** method will round a number to the next lowest integer. Table 6-1 identifies a few of the common mathematical methods that JavaScript supports. A complete list of mathematical methods can be found in Appendices B and C. The sample code below uses the **random** method of the math object to select a random number between 0 and 1.

```
<script language = "javascript">
var randNum = Math.random()
document.write(randNum)
</script>
```

Table 6-1   Common Methods of the Math Object

Method	Description	Example	Result
Abs	Returns the absolute value of a number	`Math.abs(-5)`	5
Floor	Rounds the number to the next lowest integer	`Math.floor(5.05)`	5
Ceil	Rounds the number to the next highest integer	`Math.ceil(5.05)`	6
Random	Returns a random number between 0 and 1	`Math.random()`	varies
Round	Rounds the number to the nearest integer	`Math.round(5.5)`	6
Min	Returns the lower of 2 numbers	`Math.min(1,10)`	1
Max	Returns the higher of 2 numbers	`Math.max(1,10)`	10

JavaScript String Object Methods

In previous chapters you created a string object by assigning a string to a variable, for example **varName = "George"**. You could also explicitly define a string object with the keywords new String, as in **varName = new String("George")**. The string object exposes several built-in properties and methods. The length property returns the number of characters in the string. The toLowerCase method converts the string to all lowercase. The following example demonstrates how the toLowerCase method can be used to convert a string to all lowercase characters. In this sample code, the string is not passed as an argument, but it is the object that is invoking the method. Therefore, the syntax is the name of the object, followed by a dot, followed by the method name and a set of empty parentheses. You could have combined this into a single step such as

```
document.write("PassWord".toLowerCase());.
```

```
<script language = "javascript">
var myPWD = "PassWord";
var myNewPWD = myPWD.toLowerCase();
document.write(myNewPWD);
</script>
```

Table 6-2 identifies a few of the common string methods. Some of these string methods could be replaced with basic HTML tags. For example, the anchor tag usually defines a hyperlink. However, you could use the link method to accomplish the same task. The sample code below shows how to create a hyperlink using the link method. This will create a hyperlink that displays a hyperlink called Home Page. The hyperlink would take you to the *http://www.course.com* Web site. The destination URL is a parameter to the method. The string here is the name of the hyperlink that is displayed in the Web page. Again, you could combine this into a single step, for example

```
document.write("Home Page".link("http://www.course.com"));.
```

```
<script language = "javascript">
var myURL = "http://www.course.com";
var myLinkName = "My Home Page";
var myNewURL = myLinkName.link(myURL);
document.write(myNewURL);
</script>
```

Table 6-2 Common Methods of the String Object

Method	Description	Example
bold	Displays the string in a bold style	`var vs = "Click Here"; vs.bold();`
anchor	Creates an anchor (also referred to as a bookmark); same as the HTML code: `<a name="click">Click Here</a>`	`var vs = "Click Here"; vs.anchor ("click");`
fontcolor	Displays the string in the specified color. The name or hexadecimal value for the color may be used.	`var vs = "Click Here"; vs.fontcolor ("990000");`
fontsize	Displays the string in the specified size. The size ranges from 1 to 7.	`var vs = "Click Here"; vs.fontsize(4);`

6

Table 6-2   Common Methods of the String Object (continued)

Method	Description	Example
link	Creates a hyperlink	`var vs = "Click Here"; var vl vl = "http://www.go.com"; vs.link(vl);`
toLowerCase	Converts the string to all lowercase	`var vs = "Click Here"; vs.toLowerCase();`
toUpperCase	Converts the string to all uppercase	`var vs = "Click Here"; vs.toUpperCase();`
charAt	Returns 1 single character from a string at the position indicated. Start counting the first character as 0.	`var vs = "Click Here"; vs.charAt(4);`
indexOf	Searches for a specified string within a string object. You can specify which position to begin the search. Returns -1 if no match is found, or the index number of the first character of the string found.	`var vs = "Click Here"; vs.indexOf ("H", 0);`
lastIndexof	Searches for a specified string, starting from the end of the string	`var vs = "Click Here"; vs.lastIndexOf ("H", 0);`
substring	Returns a subset of a string. The first number indicates the starting position. The second number indicates the position of the last character to be returned.	`var vs = "Click Here"; vs.substring (0, 4);`
split	Splits the string into an array of smaller strings. A separator character is used to determine where to split the string.	`var vs = "one, two, three"; var nAR = vs.split(","); document.write(nAR [2]);`

The toString Method

The toString method belongs to several objects, including the string, number, and math objects. The toString method of the number object converts a number to a string. The toString method of the math object is used to convert a math object to a string. The toString method of the string object will return the string. The following sample code shows how to use the toString method to convert a number, math, and string object to a string object.

```
<script language="javascript">
var aNum = Number(4);
document.write(aNum.toString());
document.write("<br>");
```

```
var aNum = Math.round(5.5).toString();
document.write(aNum);
document.write("<br>");
var vs = new String("Hello");
document.write(vs.toString());
</script>
```

The toString function can also be used to convert a function to a string. The following sample code illustrates how the toString function converts the entire function to a string. Unlike the toString method, this function returns the entire contents of the function, including the keyword function.

```
<script language="javascript">
function doit(){
    document.write("Hello");
}
var newString = doit.toString();
document.write(newString);
</script>
```

JavaScript Global Functions

When a value is passed from a form, the value is passed as a string. You cannot perform mathematical calculations on strings. Whether you are working in JavaScript or VBScript, you will need to convert string variables and strings to numbers. In JavaScript, there is a global object that contains functions that are not associated with other JavaScript objects. The functions within the global object can be accessed without creating an instance of the global object. These functions include eval, isNaN, parseInt, and parseFloat.

The Eval Function

The eval function of the global object will evaluate a string of JavaScript statements that can consist of expressions, variables, functions, and objects. The eval function can do more than just convert a string to a number. It evaluates the statement and returns the result. If the argument passed to the eval function is a number, then the results will be returned as a number.

The eval function is useful when you receive a number as a string object from a form, and need to convert it back to a number. The following sample code from evalJS.htm will illustrate how the eval function can be used to convert the form field values to a number. The form contains a text box named txtQ that is used to obtain the quantity of items purchased. When the user clicks the Submit button, the form calls the calcTotal function.

```
<form method="post" name="form" action="javascript:void(0);">
<input type="text" name="txtQ" size="20">
<input type="submit" value="Submit"
    name="btnSubmit" onClick="calcTotal();">
</form>
```

The calcTotal function retrieves the quantity purchased from the text box in the form. The calcTotal function uses the eval function to return the value of the form field as a number, which can then be used in a calculation. The number is multiplied by the cost of the item, to obtain the total cost. If the number entered in the text box is 4, then the result displayed will be 9.00. However, if the eval function were not used, the plus sign would be interpreted as a concatenation operator. Then the result displayed would be 45.00, which is not the total cost of the items.

```javascript
<script language="javascript">
function calcTotal(){
var strQ;
var strT;
strQ = document.form.txtQ.value;
strT = eval(strQ);
document.write("Your total cost is : $ ");
document.write(strT + 5.00);
}
</script>
```

The isNaN Function

If you attempt to use a nonnumeric value in a mathematical equation, the script will cause an error. How do you know if the value in the variable is a number or a string? In JavaScript, the isNaN function, known as the "is not a number" function, can determine whether the value is something other than a number. The importance of the isNaN function is the ability to help you avoid these errors by determining whether a value is a number before the value is used in a mathematical equation. The isNaN function returns false if the value is a number, or true if the value is not a number. In the following code sample, the isNaN function evaluates whether the strQuantity value is a number or not. The result of the isNaN function, which is true or false, is placed in the strNumber variable. You can use conditional statements to execute action statements based on the value of the strNumber. For example, if a user entered a non-number in a quantity field, you could write an action statement to display an error message to the user.

```javascript
<script language="javascript">
var strQuantity = 3;
var strNumber = isNaN(strQuantity);
if (strNumber = true) {
    document.write("Number");
}
else{
    document.write("Not Number");
}
</script>
```

The ParseInt and ParseFloat Functions

There are additional built-in functions that allow you to convert strings to numbers. The parseFloat function converts a string into a floating-point number. The parseInt function converts a string into a number. The parseInt function takes two parameters, the string and the **radix**. The radix identifies which base numbering system you want to use when converting the string to a number. For example, a radix of 2 will use the binary numbering system, while a radix of 16 will use the hexadecimal numbering system. The default radix is 10, which represents the decimal numbering system. In the example below, the quantity string, strQuantity, is returned as a number using the decimal system. Then, the quantity is used in a mathematical calculation to calculate the total cost of the item, strTotal. Because the value uses the decimal numbering system, the radix does not have to be explicitly stated.

```javascript
strQ = parseInt(strQuantity);
strTotal = strQ * 5.00;
document.write(strTotal);
```

You do not need to convert a string in JavaScript if it contains only numbers with or without leading or trailing blank spaces, for example if strWidth = " 100 " and strAvg = strWidth/2. When you write out the value of strAvg using document.write(strAvg), the result displayed is 50.

VBScript Built-in Functions

VBScript supports a wide range of built-in functions that can be called from any script. While some of the mathematical methods, such as abs and round, are supported in both VBScript and JavaScript, these functions are not associated with any particular object in VBScript. Although some functions are unique to each scripting language, some functions have different names but perform similar tasks. For example, in VBScript the isNumeric function is used to determine if the value of a variable is numeric or not. If the value is a number, the result is true, and if the value is not a number, the result is false.

```vbscript
<script language = "vbscript">
dim strQuantity
strQuantity = 3
strNumber = isNumeric(strQuantity)
if (strNumber = true) then
    document.write("Number")
else
    document.write("Not Number")
end if
</script>
```

VBScript supports additional built-in data conversion functions such as cInt, which converts a string to an integer. VBScript also supports several built-in formatting functions. For example, the formatCurrency function formats a number as currency. This would include adding the currency symbol, which is usually the dollar sign, and limiting the digits to two places after the decimal. VBScript contains several built-in date and time functions that are used to retrieve information about a specific date, and functions that can manipulate a string. For example, the len function returns the number of characters in a string. Table 6-3 identifies a few of the common built-in functions that VBScript supports. A complete listing of built-in VBScript functions is available at the Microsoft Windows Script Technologies Web site at *http://msdn.microsoft.com/scripting/default.htm?/scripting/vbscript/doc/vbstoc.htm*.

Table 6-3 Common VBScript Built-in Functions

Method	Description	Example
cDate	Converts the expression to a date subtype	`cdate(date)`
chr	Returns the character associated with the ANSI character code	`chr(number)`
cInt	Converts the expression to an integer subtype	`cInt(expression)`
cLng	Converts the expression to a long integer subtype	`cLng(expression)`
cStr	Converts the expression to a string subtype	`cStr(expression)`
date	Returns the current date	`date()`
eval	Evaluates an expression and returns the result	`eval(strNumber)`
formatCurrency	Formats the value as currency	`formatCurrency(Number)`
int	Returns the integer portion of a number	`int(number)`
lCase	Returns the string in all lowercase characters	`lcase(string)`
len	Returns the number of characters in a string	`len(expression)`
rnd	Returns a random number	`rnd()`
round	Returns a number rounded to a specified number of decimal places	`round(strNumber, 2)`
strReverse	Returns the string in reverse order	`strReverse(string)`
ucase	Returns the string in all uppercase characters	`ucase(string)`

VBScript includes two built-in functions that display information within a browser. The InputBox function is similar to a prompt window. You can capture what the user enters in the text box. You can learn more about the syntax for the InputBox function at *http://msdn.microsoft.com/scripting/default.htm?/scripting/vbscript/doc/vsfctInputBox.htm*. The MsgBox function is similar to the alert window. The MsgBox function displays a message and one or more buttons. The button labels and values can be customized. The function returns a value indicating which button was clicked. You can learn more about the syntax for the MsgBox function at *http://msdn.microsoft.com/scripting/default.htm?/scripting/vbscript/doc/vsfctMsgBox.htm*.

It is important to recall that Netscape Navigator does not support VBScript. Therefore, to create compatible scripts, you will need to use JavaScript built-in functions. However, if you are writing server-side scripts, you can use any of these built-in functions, since the functions are executed on the server, and not on the client's browser. Built-in functions are very useful and easy to implement on the server, although some of them, such as the message box function, are not usually used on the server because they require user interaction from the client via the browser.

USING FUNCTIONS

A function is a block of code that is grouped into a named unit. The function is identified by a unique name. JavaScript and VBScript have different methods for creating functions. JavaScript and VBScript both use the keyword `function` to identify the start of a function. A pair of parentheses follows the name of the function. The parentheses are used to pass zero or more arguments, also known as parameters, to the function when the function is called. If no argument is passed, an empty pair of parentheses is used. If multiple arguments are used, a comma separates each argument from the next. The function can be called several times, passing different arguments each time. Both functions and procedures can accept several arguments. Functions in VBScript can be public or private. **Public functions** are visible to all other functions in the script. **Private functions** are only available within the script in which they were declared. The keyword `public` is optional; if a function is not declared public or private, it is public by default. Therefore, many programmers do not use the keyword `public` to explicitly declare the function public. The public or private status is identified before the `function` keyword.

In JavaScript, the block of code is enclosed in a pair of curly braces. The closing curly brace identifies the end of the function. In VBScript, curly braces are not used. Therefore, the end of the function is identified with the keywords `end function`. The block of code can contain any number of action statements or control statements. In JavaScript, a semicolon is used to identify the end of each statement.

A function can return a value to the script that called it, but it is not required to return a value. If a function does return a value, it can only return one value. If no return value is explicitly identified by the function, the last value in memory will be the return value. In VBScript the keywords `exit function` are used to exit a function. Exit function is an example of a jumping control that allows you to temporarily halt the execution of a code block, and move to another section of code. Unlike the end function statement that appears at the end of a function, the keywords exit function can appear as an action statement in the middle of the function code. The syntax for creating functions in JavaScript and VBScript is as follows.

```
function nameFunction(argument1, argument2, ...argumentN){
        action and control statements;
        return returnValue;
}
```

```
[Public | Private] function nameFunction(argument1, argument2, ...argumentN)
        action and control statements
        nameFunction = returnValue
end function
```

The function is called by another part of the script, which then executes the statements within the function. You must create the function before calling it, and therefore functions are often defined in the heading section of a Web page. Functions are similar to procedures in that they both can make calls to themselves. The syntax below indicates how to call a function in JavaScript.

nameFunction(argument1, argument2, …argumentN);

In VBScript a script can use the keyword `call` to call a function. The `call` keyword is optional, but if it is used, then the arguments passed to the function must be enclosed in parentheses. If no arguments are passed, you do not have to use parentheses. When you use the keyword `call` to call a user-defined function, the return value of the function is discarded. The syntax below indicates how to call a function in VBScript.

[Call] nameFunction(argument1, argument2, …argumentN)

Calling a Function from an Event Handler

Functions are often called when an event occurs. Event handlers can be used to intercept an event and to cause the program to call a user-defined function. In the following example, you will create a form that obtains the quantity of items purchased, as shown in Figure 6-1. A function will calculate the total cost of all of the items purchased. When the user clicks the Submit button, the click event is detected. The onClick event handler is triggered to handle the click event. The onClick event handler calls a function named calcTotal. The calcTotal function is a user-defined function that calculates the total cost of the user's shopping cart.

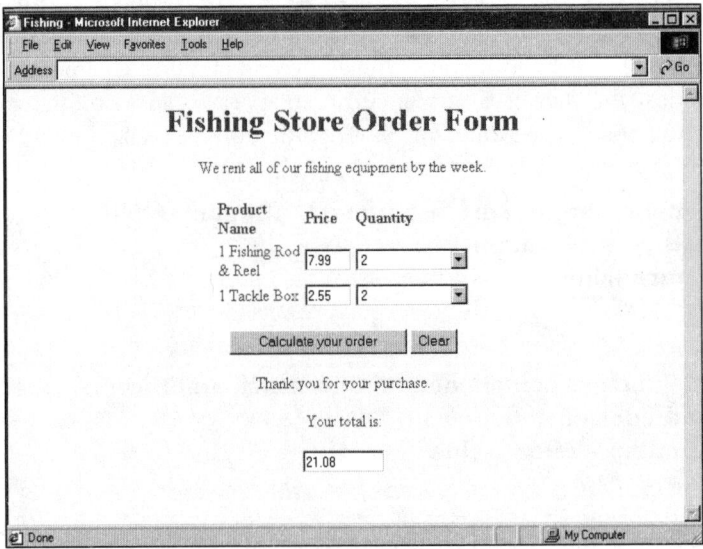

Figure 6-1   A Web page that uses a function to process a form

To create a Web page that uses a function to process a form:

1. Create a Web page called **fishing.htm**, which contains an order form, using the code shown below. The title of the page should be **Fishing**. Add a heading that says **Fishing Store Order Form**.

```
<html><head><title>Fishing</title></head>
<body bgcolor="#FFFF99" text="#800000">
<h1 align="center">Fishing Store Order Form</h1>
<p align="center">We rent all of our fishing
        equipment by the week.</p>
```

2. Create a form using the code shown below. Note that the action property uses the JavaScript void method to prevent the form from being submitted.

```
<form method="post" name="form"
     action="javascript:void(0)">
```

3. In the form, add two fields to store the quantity of items and two fields that display the cost of the items. This form uses a table to align the form fields. Tables are an effective way to align fields on a form.

```
<table border="0" width="39%" align="center">
<tr>
<td width="48%"><b>Product Name</b></td>
<td width="10%"><b>Price</b></td>
<td width="43%"><b>Quantity</b></td>
</tr><tr>
<td width="48%">1 Fishing Rod &amp; Reel</td>
<td width="10%">
<input type="text" name="txtRod" size="5"
        value="7.99"></td>
<td width="43%"><select size="1" name="qRod">
<option selected value="0">
        Select Quantity</option>
<option value="1">1</option>
<option value="2">2</option>
<option value="3">3</option>
</select></td></tr><tr>
<td width="48%">1 Tackle Box</td>
<td width="10%">
<input type="text" name="txtBox" size="5"
        value="2.55"></td>
<td width="43%"><select size="1" name="qBox">
<option selected value="0">
        Select Quantity</option>
<option value="1">1</option>
<option value="2">2</option>
<option value="3">3</option>
</select></td></tr></table>
```

4. Add a Submit button that says **Calculate your order**. When the user clicks the Submit button, the form calls the JavaScript function named calcTotal.

```
<p align="center">
<input type="submit" value="Calculate your order"
    name="btnSubmit" onClick="calcTotal()">
<input type="reset" value="Clear" name="btnClear">
<p align="center">Thank you for your purchase.</p>
<p align="center">Your total is:</p>
<p align="center">
<input type="text" name="txtTotal" size="10"
    value="0.00"></p>
</form>
```

5. Create the calcTotal function, as shown below. The function can be placed in the heading section or the body section of the page. Within this function, create two variables that store the quantity of each product. Values are assigned to these variables based on the values in the quantity field that the customer selected. Create two variables to store the price of each product.

```
<script language="javascript">
function calcTotal(){
    var strRod, strBox, prRod, prBox, strTotal;
    strRod=document.form.qRod.value;
    strBox=document.form.qBox.value;
    prRod=document.form.txtRod.value;
    prBox=document.form.txtBox.value;
```

6. The cost of each item is calculated on the basis of the price of the product multiplied by the quantity. The total cost is the sum of the cost of each item. The strTotal variable holds the total cost. The value of the txtTotal form field is assigned the total cost value stored in the strTotal variable.

```
    strRod=parseInt(strRod)* prRod;
    strBox=parseInt(strBox)* prBox;
    strTotal=(strRod + strBox);
    document.form.txtTotal.value=strTotal;
}
</script></body></html>
```

7. Save the Web page as **fishing.htm** to your data directory. View the Web page.

Passing an Argument to a Function

In the example above, no arguments were passed to the function. In this next example, you can see how events, methods, and functions can be combined to create an interactive Web page. The user can change the color of the background of the Web page (see Figure 6-2). When the user clicks a button, the onClick event handler will call a function, and pass an argument to the function. Each event handler will call the same function, but will pass a different argument. In this case, the argument is the color of the background. The result of the function will be different each time, because the argument that is passed will be different each time.

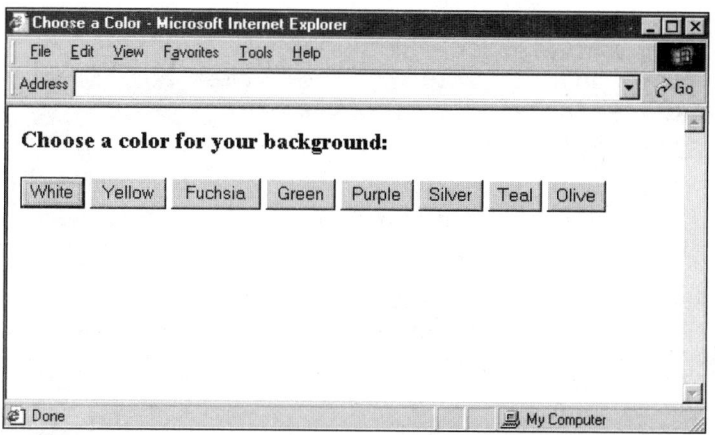

Figure 6-2   A Web page that uses an argument to pass a value to a function

To create a Web page that uses an argument to pass a value to a function:

1. Create a Web page named **chooseColor.htm**. Add a title and heading, as indicated below.

```
<html><head><title>Choose a Color</title>
</head>
<body>
<h3>Choose a color for your background:</h3>
```

2. Create a form with eight buttons, as shown below. Each button will have a different value. The onClick event handler should call the selectColor function and pass the name of a color as a parameter. Because the color is a string within another string, is it enclosed within single quotes. Then, each time a button is clicked, the selectColor function is called, and a different argument will be passed to the function.

```
<form name="frmColor" action="javascript:void(0);">
<input type="submit" value="White" name="bW"
    onClick="selectColor('White')">
<input type="submit" value="Yellow" name="bY"
    onClick="selectColor('Yellow')">
<input type="submit" value="Fuchsia" name="bF"
    onClick="selectColor('Fuchsia')">
<input type="submit" value="Green" name="bG"
    onClick="selectColor('Green')">
<input type="submit" value="Purple" name="bP"
    onClick="selectColor('Purple')">
<input type="submit" value="Silver" name="bS"
    onClick="selectColor('Silver')">
```

```
<input type="submit" value="Teal" name="bT"
     onClick="selectColor('Teal')">
<input type="submit" value="Olive" name="bO"
     onClick="selectColor('Olive')">
</form></body></html>
```

3. Create the function named selectColor within the heading section of the page. This function will use the argument to change the background color property for the Web page.

```
<script language="javascript">
function selectColor(selectColor){
     document.bgColor=selectColor;
}
</script>
```

4. Save the page as **chooseColor.htm** in your data directory. View the Web page.

In previous chapters you learned how to explicitly change the status message, using the window.status property or the window.defaultStatus property. The following sample code is used to change the default status message in the status bar.

```
<script language="javascript">
window.defaultStatus="Welcome to Fish Cove!";
</script>
```

As you learned previously, to change the status message you use the status property. In the following example, the onMouseOver event handler changes the status property. You passed the string to display in the status message bar to the status property of the window object.

```
<a href="supplies.htm" onMouseOver="window.status='Fishing
Supplies';return true";>Fishing Supplies</a>
```

But it is not necessary to code this for each hyperlink. Instead, you can create a function that changes the status message property using an argument that is passed to it. In the following example, when the user places the pointer over a hyperlink, a function is called, and an argument indicating what the status message should be will be passed (see Figure 6-3). The function then uses the argument to change the status message.

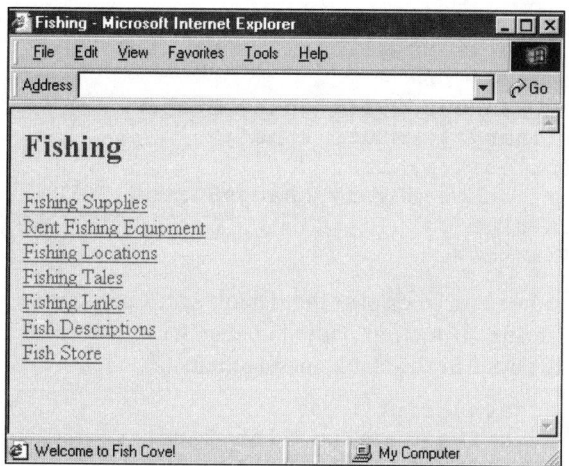

Figure 6-3 A Web page that uses a function to change the status message

To create a Web page that uses a function to change the status message:

1. Create a basic Web page named **fishingLink.htm**, using the code below.

```
<html><head><title>Fishing</title>
</head>
<body bgcolor="#99FF66" text="#003300">
<h2>Fishing</h2>
</body></html>
```

2. Create the hyperlinks in the body section of the Web page, as shown below. The onMouseOver event handler should call the changeStatus function and pass a string as a parameter. Be sure to include the `return true` statement. The string must be in single quotes because it is located within a pair of double quotes. The last hyperlink does not display any message. To prevent a message from being displayed, the last hyperlink passes an empty string, which is identified by a pair of single quotes, separated by a blank space: ' '.

```
<a href="supplies.htm" onMouseOver="changeStatus
    ('Fishing Supplies');return true";>
    Fishing Supplies</a><br>
<a href="rent.htm" onMouseOver="changeStatus
    ('We rent supplies daily!');return true";>
    Rent Fishing Equipment</a><br>
<a href="location.htm" onMouseOver="changeStatus
    ('Maps to nearby lakes!');return true";>
    Fishing Locations</a><br>
<a href="tales.htm" onMouseOver="changeStatus
    ('Share your fishing tales!');return true";>
    Fishing Tales</a><br>
```

```
<a href="links.htm" onMouseOver="changeStatus
    ('Links to other fish sites');return true";>
    Fishing Links</a><br>
<a href="fish.htm" onMouseOver="changeStatus
    ('Fish Dictionary');return true";>
    Fish Descriptions</a><br>
<a href="fish.htm" onMouseOver="changeStatus
    (' ');return true";>
    Fish Store</a><br>
```

3. Create the script in the heading to display the default status message, as shown below. The script also creates a function named changeStatus that takes one argument, a string that is displayed in the status message bar.

```
<script language="javascript">
window.defaultStatus="Welcome to Fish Cove!";
function changeStatus(statusMessage){
    window.status=statusMessage;
}
</script>
```

4. Save your Web page as **fishingLink.htm** in your data directory. View the Web page.

Returning a Value from a Function

The previous examples all used JavaScript, but VBScript also supports user-defined functions. The following example uses VBScript to create and call a user-defined function, and also demonstrates how the function can return a value to the script that called it (see Figure 6-4). There are some differences between VBScript and JavaScript functions. JavaScript functions return a value using the keyword `return`, and the value. VBScript functions assign the value to the function.

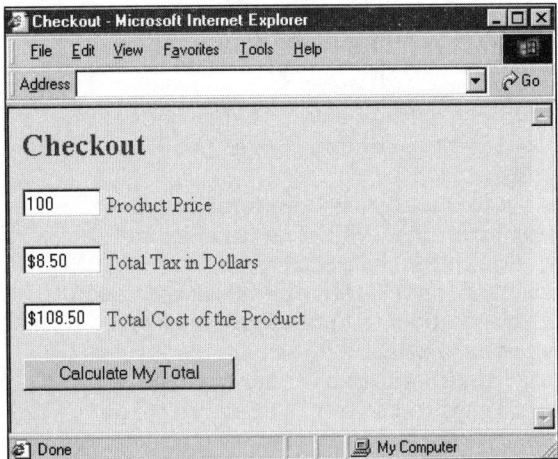

Figure 6-4   A Web page that uses a function to return a value

To create a Web page that uses a function to return a value:

1. Create a Web page named **checkout.htm**.

```
<html><head><title>Checkout</title>
</head>
<body bgcolor="#99FF66" text="#003300">
<h2>Checkout</h2>
```

2. Using the code below, create the form that contains the fields required to calculate the total cost of a product.

```
<form name="form" method="post"
      action="javascript:void(0);">
<input type="text" value="0" name="txtP" size="7">
Product Price <br><br>
<input type="text" name="txtT" size="7">
Total Tax in Dollars <br><br>
<input type="text" name="txtC" size="7">
Total Cost of the Product <br><br>
```

3. Add a Submit button that will call the calcVB function when the onClick event
handler is called. No arguments are passed.

```
<input type="button" value="Calculate My Total"
       name="btnSubmit" onClick="calcVB()">
</form></body></html>
```

4. Create the script in the heading section that will calculate the total cost, as shown
below. Declare variables to hold the price of the product, tax rate, total tax, and
product cost. Assign the price variable to the value entered in the price form field
named txtP.

```
<script language = "vbscript">
function calcVB()
      dim price, tax, total, cost
      price = document.form.txtP.value
```

5. Write the statement to retrieve the tax rate and assign it to the tax variable.
Notice that the variable tax does not get the value from a form field. Rather, it is
assigned the value of the result from another function called getTaxVB. This is an
example of the way function can be used in an expression. Note that subprocedures cannot be used as part of an expression.

```
tax = getTaxVB()
```

6. Use the tax and price variables to calculate the total, and the total cost. Assign the
values from the total and cost variables to the tax and cost form fields. Notice that
the formatCurrency function is applied to the variables to format the number as
currency.

```
total = (price * tax)
document.form.txtT.value = formatCurrency(total)
```

6

```
        cost = price + total
        document.form.txtC.value = formatCurrency(cost)
end function
</script>
```

7. Create the getTaxVB function in the heading section, which sets the value of the tax to a variable. The function returns the value of this variable to the previous function.

```
<script language = "vbscript">
function getTaxVB()
    taxRate = 0.085
    getTaxVB = taxRate
end function
</script>
```

8. Save your page as **checkout.htm** in your data directory. View the Web page.

USING PROCEDURES

Using functions in JavaScript and VBScript, you can create a named block of code and call it from another location. In VBScript you can also create another kind of code block, called a procedure. A **procedure** is similar to a function, in that it is a block of code that can be called from other locations. This allows you to create blocks of code that can be reused within your Web application. Adding a procedure call is synonymous with typing the procedure into the code itself. However, instead of writing the same code over and over again, you only need the procedure call to reference the code.

Like a function, a procedure can accept zero or more arguments. Variables declared within the procedure are local and only available to the procedure. When the procedure is created, it is declared public or private. Public procedures are available to all other procedures in all the scripts, while private procedures are only available to other procedures in the script in which they are declared. If a procedure is not declared public or private, it is made public by default. Therefore, many programmers do not use the keyword `public` to explicitly declare a procedure public.

The main differences between functions and procedures are that procedures do not return values, and they cannot be used in an expression. Programmers refer to procedures as **subprocedures** because they are declared using the keyword `sub`. You can use the statement `exit sub` to exit the procedure. Procedures are often used to respond to an event such as a user clicking a button. The syntax for a subprocedure is shown below. The keyword `sub` indicates that the procedure is being created. The name of the procedure and the arguments are identified in the sub statement. The procedure can issue action and control statements. The end of the procedure is identified with the keywords `end sub`. The sub statement is referred to as a **procedure call**. Procedure calls look and act like regular VBScript statements—they allow you to create new statements that can then be included as part of the language. It is important to note that the order in which procedures are declared does not affect the order of their execution. Procedures always execute in the order in which they are called, not the order in which they are created. The syntax for creating a procedure in VBScript is as follows.

Sub ProcedureName (arguments)
      Action and Control Statements
End Sub

Procedure calls can be used more than once and anywhere within your application, including within other procedures, functions, or control structures. Once your procedure has been declared, it is executed by specifying the name of the procedure. The keyword `call` can be used to call a function or procedure, and it is optional. If the keyword `call` is used, then the arguments passed to the procedure must be enclosed in parentheses. Multiple arguments are passed in a comma-delimited list. The syntax for calling a procedure in VBScript is as follows.

[call] procedureName (arguments)

The following exercise demonstrates how to create and call a procedure from another function. The form contains a Submit button, which will call a function when the button is clicked. The function in the following example will call two procedures. Functions cannot define other functions, but they can call other functions. You can call multiple procedures in the same function. This allows for a program to be segmented. Segments can be reused in other scripts, which can help you produce more efficient code. The procedures are executed in the order in which they are called. In this example, the first procedure will calculate the total cost, and the second will display the results. Each step can be called separately from the script. One benefit of using multiple procedures is that if one of the steps changes, then only that step needs to be modified. By using multiple procedures instead of combining them into one, you can reuse each procedure without having to rewrite entire sections of code. If multiple variables are to be used across functions and procedures, they need to be global to the application and defined before the functions and procedures that reference them.

You previously learned that procedures do not return values. But there are ways to access values from a procedure. In this example, because the procedure will not return a value, the procedure assigns the value to the value property of the form fields. This way, the values can be made available to both procedures.

Figure 6-5 shows a Web page that uses a function to call two procedures named getCost and showCost. The getCost procedure will retrieve the price and quantity values from the form and calculate the cost of the product. Because procedures cannot return a result, the getCost procedure will assign the cost of the product directly to the value property of a form field named txtT. The showCost procedure will use the value from the form field to display an alert message with the total cost to the user.

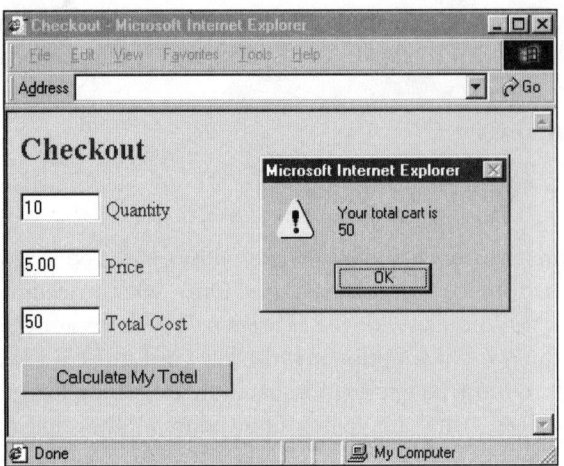

Figure 6-5   A Web page that uses a procedure to calculate the total cost of a product

To create a Web page that uses procedures to calculate the total cost of a product and display the results to the user:

1. Create a Web page named **checkoutPro.htm**.

```
<html><head><title>Checkout</title>
</head>
<body bgcolor="#99FF66" text="#003300">
<h2>Checkout</h2>
```

2. Create a form that contains three form fields for the price, quantity, and total cost. Add a Submit button named btnSubmit. Add the code to call the calcVB function when the Submit button is clicked.

```
<form name="form" action="javascript:void(0);">
<input type="text" value="0" name="txtQ"
     size="7">Quantity <br><br>
<input type="text" name="txtP" size="7">
Price <br><br>
<input type="text" name="txtT" size="7">
Total Cost <br><br>
<input type="button" value="Calculate My Total"
     name="btnSubmit" onClick="calcVB()">
</form></body></html>
```

3. Create a script in the heading section that will contain the calcVB function and two procedures. Create the calcVB function, which will call the two other procedures, getCost and showCost. No arguments are passed to the procedures.

```
<script language="vbscript">
function calcVB()
     call getCost()
     call showCost()
end function
```

4. Create the getCost procedure. The procedure will retrieve the values from the form fields, assign them to variables, calculate the total cost, and assign the total cost to the total form field. Note that no arguments are required because the price and quantity are retrieved directly from the value property of the form field.

```
sub getCost()
    dim quantity, price, total
    price = document.form.txtP.value
    quantity = document.form.txtQ.value
    total = price * quantity
    document.form.txtT.value=total
end sub
```

5. Create the showCost procedure, which retrieves the value from the total cost form field and displays the value in an alert window. Note that this procedure must be called after the getCost procedure because it uses the form field values that were defined in the getCost procedure.

```
sub showCost()
    dim cost
    cost = document.form.txtT.value
    window.alert("Your total cart is " & _
    chr(10) & cost)
end sub
```

6. Save the Web page as **checkoutPro.htm** to your data directory. View the Web page.

Event Procedures

Previously, you have called event handlers from within the HTML tag. The event handler was identified with the prefix "on" and the event name. Events such as click and load would be intercepted by event handlers such as onClick and onLoad. This method is supported in both JavaScript and VBScript. However, VBScript also allows you to intercept the event using an **event procedure**. An event procedure is a type of procedure that is attached to an object. Therefore, an event procedure does not return a value. When an object recognizes an event, it will immediately call the event procedure. The event procedure provides a connection between the object and the code. An event procedure will not be executed until an event triggers the event procedure.

Event procedures are named according to the name of the object and the event name. An underscore (_) is used to separate the object name and the event name. For example, if you decide to create a button named btnExit to call an event procedure when the button is clicked, you would name the event procedure btnExit_onClick. You must assign the name of the object in the HTML code before you define an event procedure. If you change the name of your object after defining an event procedure for that object, you must change the name of the procedure to match the new name of the object. Because no arguments are being passed, parentheses are not required. Note that the event procedure is not called, but rather is triggered when the event occurs for that specific object. The object will call the event procedure when it detects that the event has occurred. Below is the syntax for creating event procedures.

sub objectName_eventHandler
        action and control statements
end sub

To create a Web page that uses an event procedure to call another procedure:

1. Save the checkoutPro.htm Web page you created in the previous exercise as **eventPro.htm**.

2. Remove the onClick event handler from the Submit button in the form. The HTML code used to create the Submit button should look like the code below.

   ```
   <input type="button" value="Calculate My Total"
           name="btnSubmit">
   ```

3. Change the calcVB function into a procedure by replacing the keywords `function` and `end function` with **sub** and **end sub**, as shown below. Change the name of the function from calcVB to **btnSubmit_onClick**. Notice that the action statements within the procedure are the same as in the previous example.

   ```
   sub btnSubmit_onClick()
           call getCost()
           call showCost()
   end sub
   ```

4. Save your Web page as **eventPro.htm** in your data directory. View your Web page.

CHAPTER SUMMARY

Functions

❐ Both VBScript and JavaScript support built-in functions. While some built-in functions overlap, each scripting language supports additional built-in functions. Built-in functions are called by calling the name of the function and passing the required parameters.

❐ You can create functions, which are blocks of code that can be reused. The blocks of code are assigned a name. To execute the block of code, the script calls the function, using this name. Optional arguments can be passed to the function. The block of code in JavaScript must be enclosed in curly braces. The end of the block of code in VBScript is identified with the keywords **end function**. In both scripting languages, you can exit the function using the keyword **exit**.

❐ A function can be used in an expression because it can return a value to the script that called it, using the keyword return. If a return value is not specified, the last value in memory in the function will be used as the return value.

Procedures

❑ Procedures are only supported in VBScript. Procedures are similar to functions in that they represent a named block of code. However, procedures cannot be used in an expression, nor can they pass a value back to the script. Procedures are created using the keyword **sub**. The end of the procedure is identified with the keywords **end sub**. Optional arguments can be passed to the procedure.

❑ Event procedures are used to define a procedure that is executed when an event occurs. The event procedure is specific to a single event and a single object. The name of the event procedure is a combination of the name of the object and the event. If event procedures are used, the event handler is not used in the object tag. However, the object must be assigned a name.

❑ Multiple procedures and functions can be called from a single script. This allows for a program to be segmented. Segments can be reused in other scripts, which can help you produce more efficient code.

To call a built-in function

```
Math.ceil(5.05);
```

```
lcase("MyPassWord")
```

To change a "number" string into a number

```
strQ = parseInt(strQuantity);
strQ = parseFloat(strQuantity);
strQ = eval(strQuantity);
```

```
strQ = int(strQuantity)
strQ = cLng(strQuantity)
```

To detect if the value of a variable is not a number

```
strNumber = isNaN(strQuantity);
document.write(strNumber);
```

To detect if the value of a variable is a number

```
strNumber = isNumeric(strQuantity)
document.write(strNumber)
```

To create a function

```
function calcTotal(){
    var strRod;
    strRod = document.form.qRod.value;
    strRod = parseInt(strRod) * 7.99;
}
```

```
function calcTotal()
    dim strRod
    strRod = document.form.qRod.value
    strRod = parseInt(strRod) * 7.99
end function
```

To call a function

```
calcTotal();
```

```
call calcTotal()
calcTotal()
```

To create an event procedure

```
sub btnSubmit_onClick
    document.write("Welcome")
end sub
```

To call multiple procedures from an event handler

```
sub btnSubmit_onClick()
    call getPrice()
    call getTaxRate()
    call calcTax()
    call getTotal()
end sub
```

REVIEW QUESTIONS

1. A _____ is a named block of code that returns a value.

   a. procedure

   b. function

   c. control statement

   d. subprocedure

2. The keyword _____ is used to create a procedure in VBScript.

   a. sub

   b. dim

   c. var

   d. create

3. The keywords _____ are used to indicate the end of a procedure in VBScript.

   a. sub end

   b. end function

   c. end sub

   d. sub function

4. A _____ is used separate arguments passed to a function.

   a. comma

   b. semicolon

   c. colon

   d. parenthesis

5. _____ are used to enclose the block of code in JavaScript.

   a. Curly braces

   b. Parentheses

   c. Commas

   d. Square brackets

6. Which built-in JavaScript function will change a string to a number?

   a. evaluate

   b. changeNum

   c. parseInteger

   d. parseInt

6

7. Which built-in function in VBScript will detect whether or not a variable is a number?

   a. isNumeric

   b. isNaN

   c. isN

   d. isNumber

8. Which built-in function in JavaScript will detect whether or not a variable is a number?

   a. isNum

   b. isNaN

   c. isN

   d. isNumber

9. Which built-in function in JavaScript will round a number to the next highest integer?

   a. round

   b. floor

   c. ceil

   d. abs

10. Which of the following is used to identify the end of a function in JavaScript?

   a.]

   b.)

   c. }

   d. end function

11. A button is named btnGo. What is the name of the event procedure that would be called if the user clicked the button?

   a. btnGo_click

   b. btnGo_click

   c. btnGo_onClick

   d. onClick_btnGo

12. Which keywords are used to exit a function in VBScript before the function ends?

   a. exit function

   b. end function

   c. break function

   d. end sub

13. Which keywords are used to exit a procedure?

    a. exit sub

    b. break

    c. end sub

    d. end procedure

14. Exiting a function early is called a _____ control statement.

    a. forward

    b. looping

    c. jumping

    d. leaping

15. Where should a variable be declared if it is to be used by multiple procedures?

    a. in the first procedure

    b. in a separate script tag

    c. before all of the procedures

    d. at the end of the first procedure

16. The keyword _____ is used to call a procedure in VBScript.

    a. call

    b. get

    c. return

    d. dim

17. A function can return a value to a script. True or False?

18. A procedure can return a value to a script. True or False?

19. An event procedure can return a value to a script. True or False?

20. Event procedures can be created using JavaScript or VBScript. True or False?

6

HANDS-ON PROJECTS

Project 6-1

In this project, you will create a Web page that uses built-in function operators to calculate the total cost of the product. The total cost should be rounded to the nearest dollar. Use VBScript to complete this exercise. Figure 6-6 shows the Web page roundVB.htm, which uses the round function to round the total cost to the nearest dollar.

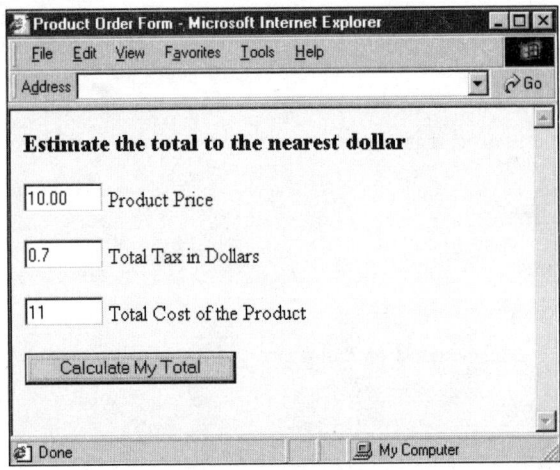

Figure 6-6   Using the built-in round function to round a value

1. Create a Web page named **roundVB.htm** and entitled **Product Order Form**.
2. Add a heading formatted as heading 3 that says **Estimate the total to the nearest dollar**.
3. Add a form named **form**. Don't forget to add the action property that calls the void method. The form method should be post.
4. Add the following fields to the form.
   a. A text box named **txtPrice**. The size should be 7 and the default value should be 0. The label should read **Product Price**.
   b. A text box named **txtTax**. The size should be 7. The label should read **Total Tax in Dollars**.
   c. A text box named **txtCost**. The size should be 7. The label should read **Total Cost of the Product**.

5. Create a button named btnSubmit. This is just a plain button. The button should say **Calculate My Total**. When the user clicks the button, a function named getTotal function should be called.

6. Modify the Web page background color, add graphics, and change the text format using your favorite font.

7. Create a script using VBScript that contains the getTotal function. This function will calculate the value of the total form field. In the function, declare the variables **price**, **taxRate**, **tax**, **total**, and **cost**.

8. Set the value of price to the value from the price form field.

```
price = document.form.txtPrice.value
```

9. Set the value of the taxRate variable to 0.07.

10. Calculate the tax and place the value in the tax variable. The tax is equal to the price times the taxRate variable. Place the tax amount in the txtTax form field.

11. Calculate the cost based on the total of the tax and price variables. Use the built-in round function to round the value to the nearest integer. Place the cost in the txtCost form field.

12. Save the Web page to your data directory. View the Web page. Print your source code. Print the Web page.

6

Project 6-2

In this project, you will complete the previous project (roundVB.htm) using JavaScript instead of VBScript.

1. Save the roundVB.htm Web page as **roundJS.htm**.

2. Modify the Web page to support JavaScript. (*Hint:* You will have to change several steps in addition to the syntax. When you retrieve the value from the price field, you should use the parseFloat function to change the string to a number. Because there is no formatCurrency method in JavaScript, you will have to round the tax field differently. Multiply the price times the taxRate times 100. This will move the decimal place to the right two places. Then, apply the round function to round off the decimals. Finally, divide the tax by 100 to move the decimal place to the left two places.)

```
tax = Math.round(price * taxRate * 100);
tax = tax/100;
```

3. After calculating the cost of the product, you should round the results and display the value in the txtCost form field.

4. Save the Web page to your data directory. View the Web page. Print your source code. Print the Web page.

Project 6-3

In this project, you will create a Web page that allows the user to input a value into a form field (see Figure 6-7). You will create a script that will retrieve the value and determine if the value is a number or a string. If the value is a number, then you will alert the user that the value is a number. If the value is a string, then you will alert the user that the value entered was a string.

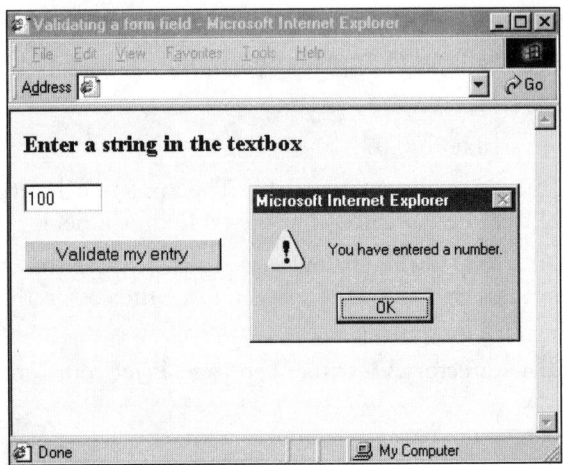

Figure 6-7   Validating a form field using the isNumeric function

1. Create a Web page named **checkNumberVB.htm**. The title of the page should be **Validating a form field**.
2. Add a heading, formatted as heading 3, that says **Enter a string in the textbox**.
3. Create a form called **form**. The form method should be post. Use the void() method in the form action property so that users will not be redirected to a new page when they submit the form.
4. Add one field to the form named **txtString**. The size should be 7.
5. Create a button named btnSubmit. This is just a plain button. The button should say **Validate my entry**. When the user clicks on the button, a function named validate should be called.
6. Modify the Web page background color, add graphics, and change the text format using your favorite font.
7. In the body section of the page, below the closing form tag, create a script that contains the validate function. This function will validate whether the user entered a number or a string.
8. Declare the variable named **strString**, which will contain the value that the user entered in the text box. Set the value of strString to the value of the txtString form field.

9. Test to see whether the value of strString is a string or a number, using the isNumeric function. If strString is a number, then create an alert message box that says **You have entered a number**. Otherwise, if strString is a string, then create an alert message box that says **You have entered a string**. (*Hint:* You can use an If Then control statement or other control statements to determine which alert message box to display.)

10. Save the Web page to your data directory. View the Web page. Print your source code. Print the Web page.

Project 6-4

In this project, you will complete the previous project (checkNumberVB.htm) using JavaScript instead of VBScript.

1. Save the checkNumberVB.htm Web page as **checkNumberJS.htm**.

2. Modify the Web page to support JavaScript. You will need to change the isNumeric function to the isNaN function. (*Hint:* You will also have to modify your control statement to reflect the opposite values that are returned from the isNaN function. Because you are using the isNaN function, if the user enters a blank space or no value, the response returned will be a string, because the value of a form field is a string by default.)

3. Save the Web page to your data directory. View the Web page. Print your source code. Print the Web page.

Project 6-5

In this project, you will create an event procedure so that when a user types a color in a text box and clicks a button, the color of the background changes to that color (see Figure 6-8).

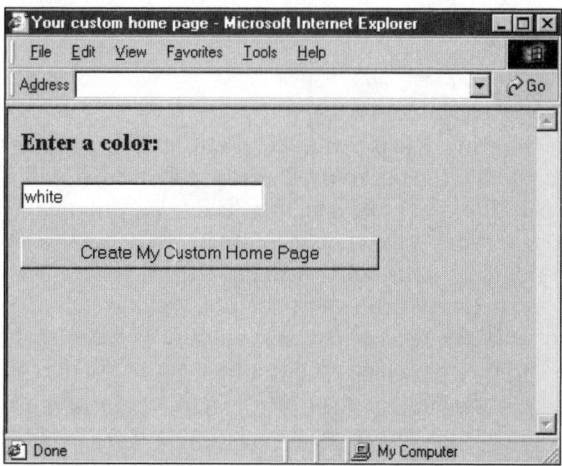

Figure 6-8   Using an event procedure to customize a Web page

1. In your Web page editor, create a Web page named **eventVB.htm**. The title of the page should be **Your custom home page**. Modify the body tag to create a silver background. Add a heading 3 that says **Enter a color:**.

2. Create a form named **form**. Add a text box named **txtColor**. The size should be 25. The default value should be white. Add a button named btnMyPage. The button should say **Create My Custom Home Page**.

3. Create an event procedure that will execute when the user clicks the btnMyPage button. The event procedure will change the color of the background to the color that the user entered. (*Hint*: Retrieve the value from the form field, then assign that value to the bgColor property for the Web page.)

4. Save the Web page to your data directory. View the Web page. Print your source code. Print the Web page.

CASE PROJECTS

Gemini Electronics

You are hired to be the Webmaster at Gemini Electronics. Your employer wants you to create a Web page that displays four buttons and an image named imgLogo. When the user clicks a button, the imgLogo will change to a different image. The four buttons represent the four departments in the store: computers, televisions, accessories, and calculators. Create five images, one for each department, and one for the store logo. The store logo is the default image that will appear if the user has not clicked a button. The buttons should be named according to the name of each department. You can use JavaScript or VBScript. Modify the layout using a table, color, and graphics to make the Web page look professional. Save your Web page as departments.htm to your data directory. View the Web page. Print out the Web page and the source code.

Stepan Accounting Corporation

You are hired by the Stepan Accounting Corporation to create a Web page to help their employees calculate their net income after taxes. You will create a form that will retrieve the user's income, then you will display the user's tax rate, total taxes, and income. You can use JavaScript or VBScript. Create a form with a form field to obtain your income level. Create form fields to display the tax rate, total taxes, and total net income. Create a script that retrieves the user's income level and calculates the user's tax rate, total taxes, and net income. You are told that the formula to calculate the tax rate and amount is based on the income level. If you make less than $34,550, then you have to pay a base tax of $0, plus 15% of your income. If you make more than $34,550 and less than $89,149, then you have to pay a base tax of $5,182.50, plus 28% for any income you make over $34,550. If you make more than $89,150 and less than $144,400, then you have to pay a base tax of $20,470.50, plus 31% for any income you make over $89,150. (*Hint*: Use an If Then statement to determine which group the income level belongs to. Then, for each group, assign the base taxes, the tax rate, and the level at which additional income will be taxed. The formula to calculate your total taxes is equal to (base + ((income-level)* rate)). The total net income is equal to income minus taxes paid.) Write the total tax, the tax rate, and the total net income to the form fields. If you are using VBScript, use the formatCurrency method to format these amounts as currency. If you are using JavaScript, round these amounts to 2 decimal places. Modify the layout using a table, color, and graphics to make the Web page look professional. Save your Web page as taxes.htm to your data directory. View the Web page. Print out the Web page and the source code.

Northfield Children's Zoo

You work as a beginning Web programmer at the Northfield Children's Zoo. Your boss would like you to add interactivity to the Web site. You decide to add a fun facts page where you will display four questions. Next to each question is the zoo's logo. When the user places the mouse pointer over the logo, a graphic will be displayed that will provide the user with the correct answer. For example, a question could be, "What is the name for the building where the corn grain is stored?" When the user places the mouse icon over the zoo logo next to that question, a picture of a farm with a grain silo will appear. When the user places the mouse icon out of the image, the zoo logo will reappear. You decide to create this using the onMouseOver and onMouseOut event handlers. Both event handlers call a function and pass two arguments. The first argument is the index number for that image. The second argument is the name of the graphic that will be displayed. Then, create a function that receives two arguments. The function changes the source property, using the name of the image passed to the function. Use the index number passed to the function to determine which image to change. You can refer to the image by its index number within the images collection. Recall that the first image is in position 0. If you put a logo at the top of the page, that image will be counted in the image array too. Create the five images, one for the zoo logo, and one for each question. You can use JavaScript or VBScript. Modify the layout using a table, color, and graphics to make the Web page look professional. Save your Web page as zoo.htm to your data directory. View the Web page. Print out the Web page and the source code.

Growlite Marketing

You are hired as a Web site designer by a marketing firm called Growlite Marketing. The company is trying to attract new customers. They have decided to display custom pages to their customers. Your job is to collect the user preferences, and to display a Web page based on their preferences. User preferences can include page elements such as the page background color, font color, and topics of interest. The preferences should be retrieved from a form that users fill out when they register in the Web site. Use a function or procedure to create a Web page that retrieves their preferences, and formats the page using their preferences. You can use JavaScript or VBScript. Modify the layout using a table, color, and graphics to make the Web page look professional. Save your Web page as memberPrefs.htm to your data directory. View the Web page. Print out the Web page and the source code.

Frye Web Design

You are hired by Frye Web Design to help them reprogram their Web site. Currently, they use VBScript for client scripting because the company has only supported Internet Explorer. Because they are moving some of their Web pages onto the Internet, they need to support Netscape Navigator. Your boss would like you to convert all of the VBScript scripts to JavaScript. Your first step is to document a list of the built-in functions, mathematical functions, scripting functions, string and number conversions, date functions, and formatting functions. Create a Web page named builtin.htm. List the name of the function, a description of what the function is used for, and the syntax for using the function. Select functions from both VBScript and JavaScript. Use an asterisk (*) to indicate the functions that are supported by both JavaScript and VBScript. Separate the JavaScript from VBScript functions. Modify the layout using a table, color, and graphics to make the Web page look professional. Save your Web page as builtin.htm to your data directory. View the Web page. Print out the Web page and the source code.

7

INTRODUCTION TO SERVER-SIDE SCRIPTING: ACTIVE SERVER PAGES (ASP)

In this chapter you will:

♦ Learn how an ASP page is processed by a Web server

♦ Identify the differences between client-side scripts and server-side scripts

♦ Learn about the built-in objects in the ASP Object Model

♦ Create Active Server Pages

♦ Create server-side include files

♦ Locate Internet resources about Active Server Pages

In previous chapters, you created client-side scripts using JavaScript and VBScript. Client-side scripts are interpreted by a scripting engine that is built into the browser, and their source code is accessible to anyone who visits the Web site. Client-side scripts can use the objects built into the browser's Document Object Model to create more interactive Web pages. In this chapter you will begin to learn how to create server-side applications using **Active Server Pages** (ASP). Because the server-side script is processed on the server, the source code is never accessible to the visitor. Therefore, ASP can be used to implement security rules within a Web site. Because server-side scripts are not executed within a browser, they cannot access the browser's Document Object Model. However, they can access the ASP Model, which includes many built-in objects that allow you to create more dynamic and interactive Web pages.

 To use this chapter effectively, you should have access to a Web server that supports ASP, such as Personal Web Server (PWS) or Internet Information Server (IIS). Both of these Web servers are available free from Microsoft. Information on how to download and install PWS is provided in the Before You Begin section of this book.

INTRODUCTION TO ASP

As you learned earlier in this book, HTML is a markup language. Internet browsers interpret HTML tags. The script tag is used to designate client-side scripts, and the browser contains a scripting engine that executes them. An Active Server Page (ASP) is a Web page that contains server-side script. ASP pages may also contain HTML and client-side scripts, but only the server-side scripts are executed on the server. When the server has completed the server-side script, it sends the HTML and client-side script to the browser to be interpreted on the client. Figure 7-1 illustrates the processes that occur when an ASP page is requested by a browser.

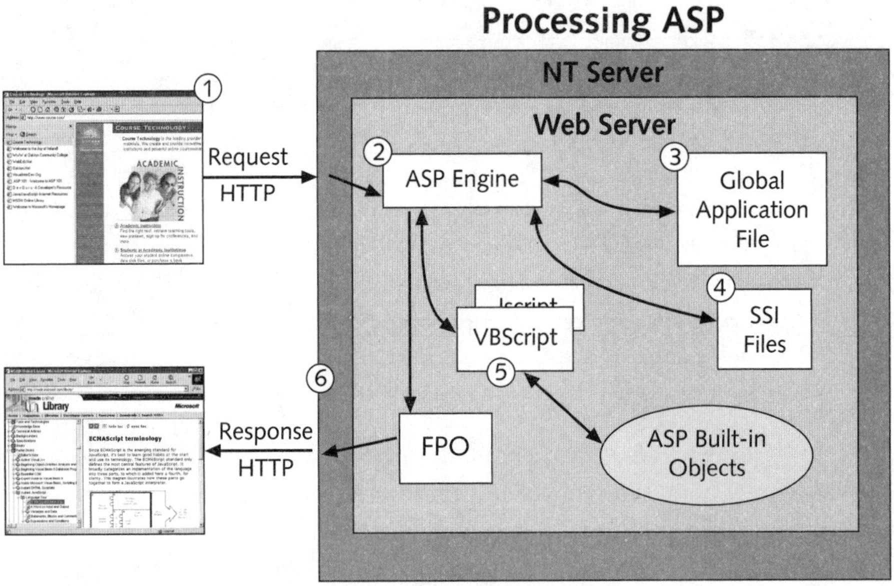

Processing ASP

NT Server

Web Server

Request HTTP → ② ASP Engine → ③ Global Application File

①

VBScript ⑤

④ SSI Files

Response HTTP ← FPO ⑥ ← ASP Built-in Objects

Figure 7-1   How the Web server processes an ASP page

The term ASP is used as a catchall phrase. It is used to refer to Web pages that contain server-side scripts, but it is also used to refer to the server-side scripting technology as a whole. An **ASP application** is a collection of more than one ASP pages. An ASP application includes a global application file called the global.asa that allows you to tie the pages together so that information can be shared across the pages.

First, using the HTTP protocol, a browser requests from a server a Web page containing server-side scripts. ASP pages carry the file extension .asp, as opposed to .htm or .html. When the Web server recognizes the .asp file extension, it sends the request to the ASP engine. The ASP engine (also known as the ASP interpreter) is actually a **dynamic-link library** called asp.dll, which is installed on the Web server. A dynamic-link library is a collection of common code. With ASP 3.0, you can assign all HTML pages an .asp file extension without sacrificing performance.

Programming Tip If you have Personal Web Server installed on your machine, the asp.dll file can be found in the directory C:\Windows\System\InetSrv.

After the request has been passed to the ASP engine, the ASP engine executes scripts in the Global Application File. The Global Application File is a text file containing scripts that are executed when the Web application starts and ends, and scripts that are executed when a browser session starts and ends. The Global Application File is always named global.asa, and is always located in the root directory of the Web application.

After the ASP engine executes scripts in the Global Application File, the ASP will include any server-side include (SSI) files indicated in the ASP page. The code within the include files is not executed by the ASP engine. Server-side include files are used to split code into two or more Web pages, and they can contain HTML, client-side script, or server-side script. Although SSI files can contain something as simple as the title of the Web application, often they will consist of functions, variables, and constants that are used by many ASP pages. The ASP page indicates where the SSI file is to be placed within the Web page; it can be located anywhere within a Web page. An ASP page may contain any number of server-side include files. The ASP engine assembles the SSI files and the original ASP page into one single page. The ASP engine is like a piece of tape that binds pages together.

After the ASP engine assembles the SSI files and the ASP page, the ASP engine sends the scripts to a scripting engine to be processed. The scripting engine is responsible for interpreting the server-side script. Server-side scripts are interpreted, not compiled like C or Visual Basic. Server-side scripts are designated by a block script tag or an inline script tag. The language property for the block script tag and the inline script tag can be set to VBScript or JavaScript. The ASP script engine will execute JavaScript block statements first, then inline script statements, and finally VBScript block statements. Although server-side scripts are most often written using VBScript or JScript, the ASP architecture can support PerlScript and several other scripting languages if the associated scripting engine is installed on the Web server. The scripting engine processes the instructions from the scripts and sends the results back to the ASP engine. The default server script language can be set within the Web server configuration files. For performance reasons, it is better not to mix scripting languages within the same Web page.

The Web server uses HTTP to send the file back to the browser. Because the Web server is using HTTP, it sends HTML along with client-side scripts. The browser interprets the HTML and client-side script and displays the output. Browser compatibility problems occur because not all browsers support all HTML tags and properties, and problems can arise with any HTML or client-side script. However, server-side script is browser-independent because server-side scripts are never sent to the browser; they are always executed on the Web server. JavaScript is the preferred client-side language, since it is recognized by both of the major browsers, Microsoft Internet Explorer and Netscape Navigator. VBScript is the language of choice for server-side scripts.

Built-in Objects in the ASP Object Model

The ASP process on the Web server uses a scripting engine to execute JavaScript or VBScript statements. As you learned in previous chapters, scripting languages support object-oriented programming, and you can integrate your client-side scripts with objects built into the browser's Document Object Model. Similarly, you can integrate your server-side scripts with built-in objects from the ASP Object Model. The built-in ASP objects are:

- Request—Used to access information that is passed from the client's browser to the Web server. For example, the Request object is used to retrieve information that a user entered in a form.

- Response—Used to send information from the Web server to the client's browser. For example, the Response object is used to redirect the user to another Web page.

- Session—Used to share information between a single client and the Web server. The session object is used to store data during the course of a session. The session begins when the brower makes its first request for an ASP page. For example, the name of the visitor can be shared as a session variable. When the user closes the browser, the session ends, and the session variable no longer exists. The session can also end when the default session timeout is reached.

- Application—Allows developers to treat a sequence of Web pages as a single application, which means that information, such as the name of the application or the total number of visitors on the Web site, can be shared among all the users of an ASP application. When it first began, the World Wide Web was stateless, which meant that every Web page was independent, and information could not be shared among Web pages. The capacity to treat a collection of pages as a single application greatly broadened the possibilities for application development. The application object is created when the first ASP page is requested.

- Server—Used to access the Web server's properties and methods. For example, the CreateObject method instantiates new COM objects on the server. COM objects are objects that are installed on the server and conform to the Component Object Model. The ScriptTimeout property will set the timeout value for scripts running on the server.

- ASPError—Used to retrieve information about the last error that occurred. The GetLastError method of the server object provides access to the ASPError object.

The server scripts can access the properties and methods of these built-in objects. Figure 7-2 shows the built-in objects and the relationships among them. In the next few chapters, you will learn more about how to use these ASP objects.

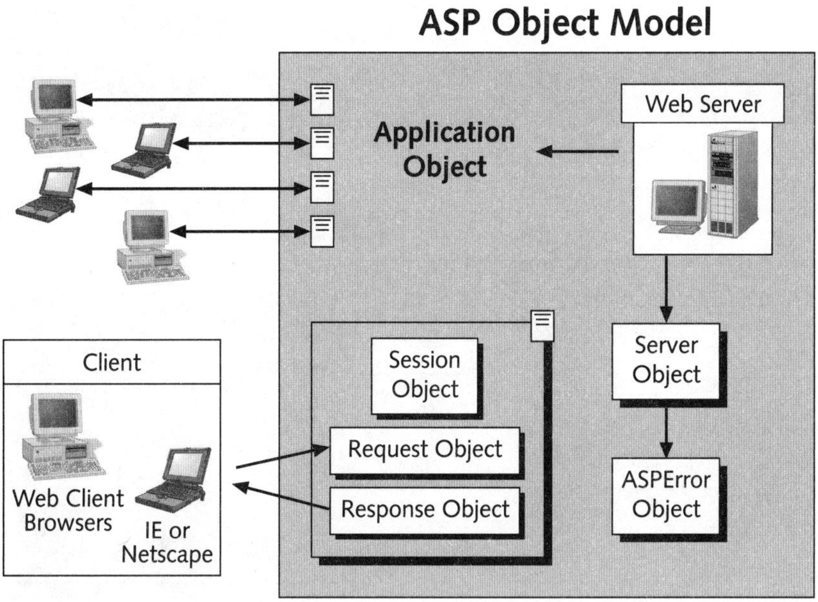

ASP Object Model

Figure 7-2   The ASP Object Model

Third-Party and Custom Objects

As your Web programming needs grow, you will want to use additional objects to perform unique tasks. For example, you might want to configure your Web page to send an e-mail message when a user fills out a form. You can use the request object to retrieve information from the form, but there is no built-in object to send e-mail. However, the server object has a method, called CreateObject, which can instantiate third-party objects. By using the CreateObject method, you can interact with many other objects and their properties and methods. For example, an object called SendMail is built into the SMTP Mail Server. The server object can instantiate a SendMail object, which allows you to send e-mail from an ASP page, using the SendMail object's Send method.

Interaction with other third-party objects allows you to create ASP Web applications that can send e-mail, connect to a database, upload files to the Web server, and write files on the Web server. There are many companies developing third-party objects that can be accessed from your ASP code. You can also create your own objects with a high-level programming language such as Visual Basic. These objects must be installed and registered on the Web server. Figure 7-3 illustrates how the ASP Object Model interacts with third-party ASP objects. The browser requests an ASP page from the Web server. The ASP engine passes the script to the VBScript engine. The VBScript uses the CreateObject method of the server object to instantiate a third-party object. The ASP engine passes any returned data back to the Web server, which will deliver the Web page to the browser.

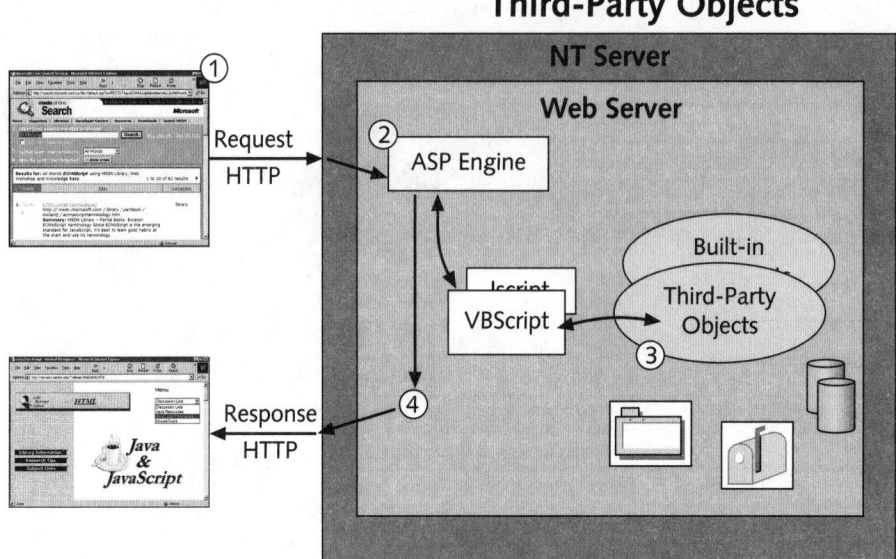

Figure 7-3   Using third-party ASP objects

CREATING BASIC ACTIVE SERVER PAGES

A simple text editor such as Notepad can be used to build your ASP pages. Visual editors such as FrontPage, Visual Studio, and Microsoft Script Editor all support ASP technology. These editors offer additional features such as error checking or color-coded keywords. FrontPage is often used for Web page layout and design and Web site management. Visual Studio is often used to create a customized development environment. Visual Studio also provides a graphical user interface and programming tools for many ASP built-in objects. Third-party companies such as Hunt Interactive (*http://www.huntinteractive.com*) provide Visual Studio plug-ins for ASP objects.

To view an ASP page, you must view the page via a Web server that supports ASP, such as Personal Web Server (PWS) or Internet Information Server (IIS). Both of these Web servers can be downloaded free from Microsoft at *http://www.microsoft.com*. The Web server must be ISAPI-compliant and must support ODBC. ASP is an Internet Server Application Programming Interface (ISAPI) application, so as long as your Web server is ISAPI-compliant and has the ASP and script engines installed, then Active Server Pages should work just fine. Information on how to obtain and set up PWS is found in the Before You Begin section of this book.

Block Scripts

Server-side scripts are written inside block script tags or inline script tags. Block script tags use the same script tag as client-side script. The block script tag is not case sensitive. The scripting language is identified using the language attribute. However, to distinguish a client-side script from a server-side script, you must use the runat attribute. To identify a server-side script, assign the runat attribute to "server." Because the default value is "client," if the runat attribute is not specified, the script will be processed on the client. The server script can contain action and control statements. Like the client-side script, the server-side script must contain a closing script tag. Below is the syntax for adding a server-side script to an ASP page.

<script language = "vbscript" runat = "server">
action and control statements
</script>

Inline Scripts

Inline script tags are used to delimit inline scripts. Remember that if you use both block and inline script tags in the same Web page, the code within the inline script tags will be executed first. The inline script tags <%   %> are used to indicate inline script. If there is only one line of code, often both script tags will appear on the same line. However, if there are multiple lines of code, you can place the tags on separate lines to make the code more readable.

<%
action and control statements
%>

The default language for inline script is VBScript. Therefore, you do not need to specify a language when you use the inline script tags. However, you can use another language, such as JScript, by specifying the language at the top of the Web page, using the @language attribute. The scripting engine for that language must be installed on the Web server in order for the scripts to be processed.

<% @language = "jscript" %>

The Response.Write Method

In previous chapters you learned how to use client-side scripts and the document object write method to write the output to the browser. In server-side scripts, the response object is used to send output from the Web server to the browser. The response object contains a method called write, which sends the output to the browser. This expression can be a simple string, the results of an expression, the contents of a variable, HTML, or even client-side scripts! Although the parentheses are not always required, it is recommended that you use them to clearly identify what is to be written to the browser. Below is the syntax for using the write method.

<% response.write(expression) %>

All of the VBScript techniques that you have learned in this book can be applied in your server scripts. The following script demonstrates how the write method can be used to display the value of a variable in a browser. In this example, the heading 1 HTML tag is used to format the output from the inline server script.

```
<% @language = "vbscript" %>
<html><head><title>Hello World!</title></head>
<body><h1>
<% dim strHello = "Hello World! "
response.write strHello
%>
</h1>
</body></html>
```

You can use the write method to send HTML tags and client script to the browser. The following example uses the write method to display output in the browser, along with the HTML tags. The entire string must be enclosed with double quotation marks. If the string contains a quotation mark, you can use a single quotation mark instead.

In ASP 3.0, by default, the server will keep all the content in a buffer area on the server until the server scripts have completed processing. No output will be seen in the browser until all of the server scripts have finished processing.

```
<% @language = "vbscript" %>
<html><head><title>Hello World!</title></head>
<body>
<% response.write "<h1 align='center'>Hello World!</h1>" %>
</body></html>
```

The equal sign (=) is a shortcut key that can be used instead of typing out response.write. However, you can only use the shortcut key for one statement. If the script contains more than one statement, you cannot use the shortcut key. The following example shows how this script could have been written using the shortcut key.

```
<% @language = "vbscript" %>
<html>
<% dim strHello = "Hello World!"
%>
<head><title>Hello World!</title></head>
<body><H1 align = "center">
<% = strHello %></H1>
</body></html>
```

The same ASP page could be written using block script tags. However, the placement of the text would be different because of the order in which the Web server executes the script. Therefore, programmers often prefer to use inline script tags when they are mixing HTML and server-side script. Below is an example of how you can use the block script tags to display the same output.

```
<html><head><title>Hello World!</title></head>
<body>
<script language = "vbscript" runat = "server">
response.write "<H1 align='center'>Hello World!</H1>"
</script>
</body></html>
```

Server-side Programming

Server-side scripting is similar to client-side scripting. You can use any valid VBScript or JavaScript statement within a server-side script delimiter. You can create action statements as well as control statements. You can declare and use variables, constants, expressions, and concatenate expressions using the concatenation operator. In VBScript the concatenation operator is the ampersand (&). You can use built-in objects and methods such as date, time, and now. You can use methods such as Int and Rnd. You can perform arithmetic calculations and data type conversions. In other words, all of the script tools available to you on the client are also available to you on the server.

Although many functions are available on both the client and Web server, there are some differences you should be aware of. For example, on the client, the MsgBox function is used to display messages to the user. On the server, the MsgBox is not useful because there is no "person" sitting at the Web server console to view the message. Another commonly used function in client- and server-side scripting is the date function. Remember that the date function retrieves the current date. The date and time displayed are the date and time on the Web server, not on the client. There are additional functions that can be used in conjunction with the date function. For example, the Weekday function is used to obtain the index number of the day of the week. The WeekdayName function is used to convert the index number to the name. The Month function is used to obtain the index number of the month. The MonthName function is used to convert the index number to a name. The Day function retrieves the day of the month. The year is obtained using the Now function instead of the Date function because when the Year function is applied to the Date function, it returns the number "1899" when the actual year is "2000." Applying the Year function to the results of the Now function will retrieve the correct year.

The following sample code uses server-side script to display the current weekday name, month name, day, and year. Because this code spans multiple lines, the shortcut key for the write method cannot be used. In between the day, month, date, and year, commas and blank spaces can be included. You can use a blank space within quotes to represent a single blank space. If you include more than one blank space, you should use the HTML code that represents a blank space: . The results from the function and the strings are concatenated into one string. The underscore character is used so that the statement can extend over multiple lines to increase readability. The string could have been split into multiple strings using multiple response.write statements.

```
<% response.write WeekdayName(Weekday(Date)) & ", " & _
    MonthName(Month(Date)) & " " & _
    Day(Date) & ", " & _
    Year(Now())
%>
</p>
```

If you have a long VBScript statement, you can separate the lines using the underscore character (_). However, you cannot use the underscore within a string.

The following example illustrates how to use the programming techniques you have already learned to develop server-side scripts. This exercise demonstrates how to use basic VBScripting techniques in a server-side script.

1. Create a Web page named **cartTotal.asp** using Notepad or an ASP-compatible editor. Save the Web page to your data directory. Make sure that when you save the file you use the .asp file extension. You should also use quotation marks around the entire filename so that the file will be saved as an ASP page and not a TXT document.

2. In the heading, identify the server-side script with the runat attribute identified within the block script tag, as shown below. Three constants are declared. The constants cName and cEmail are strings that display the company name and the company e-mail address. The benefit of having the constant is that the information can be placed in a central location. Then if the e-mail address changes, it only has to be changed in one location. The shipFee is a number that is used in arithmetic calculations later in the ASP page.

```
<html><head><title>Shopping Cart Total</title>
<script language = "vbscript" runat = "server">
const cName = "Indian River Garden Store"
const cEmail = "info@IRGS.com"
const shipFee = 2.00
</script>
</head>
```

3. Add the headings on the Web page. Note that the company name is obtained from the constant cName that was defined in the heading script. The company name was written using the shortcut key to the write method.

```
<body bgcolor = "#CCFFCC" text = "#008000">
<div align = "center"><h1><% = cName %><br></h1>
<h2><% = cEmail %></h2>
<h3>Your Shopping Cart</h3>
You purchased your products on <br><br>
```

4. The next section of code, shown below, writes out the current day of the week and the date, using the write method.

```
<% response.write WeekdayName(Weekday(Date)) & ", " & _
    MonthName(Month(Date)) & " " & _
    Day(Date) & ", " & _
    Year(Now())
%>
<br><br>
```

5. The next section of code, shown below, declares four variables named Cost, Tax, Total, and State. Because the page uses VBScript, the dim keyword is used to declare variables instead of var. The Cost variable is assigned the number **40.00**.

The State variable is assigned the string **IL**. Then, a control statement is used which determines whether the state variable is equal to a specific value. If the State variable is IL, then the visitor pays a higher tax. Notice how the Cost and Tax variables are numbers, and therefore are not enclosed within quotation marks. The Total variable is assigned a value based on the sum of the Cost and Tax variables, and the shipFee constant. Notice that the shipFee constant is called by simply stating the name of the constant.

```
<%
Dim Cost, Tax, Total, State
Cost = 40.00
State = "IL"
If State = "IL" then
     Tax = 3.00
else
     Tax = 2.00
end if
Total = Cost + Tax + shipFee
%>
```

6. The code below illustrates how you can use a control statement on the Web server to specify which HTML is sent to the browser. In this case, if the Total cost is not equal to zero, then the visitor has placed something in his or her shopping cart. Therefore, the code displays the values of the Cost and Tax variables, the shipFee constant, and the calculated Total variable. Notice how the formatCurrency method is used to format the number as currency. The HTML tags can be used to format the script output, or you can use the write method to write out HTML formatting tags.

```
<% if Total <> 0 then %>
    <table align = "center"  width = "150" >
    <tr><td>Cost</td><td align="right">
    <% = formatCurrency(Cost) %>
    </td></tr>
    <tr><td>Shipping</td><td align="right">
    <% = formatCurrency(shipFee) %>
    </td></tr>
    <tr><td>Tax</td><td align="right">
    <u><% = formatCurrency(Tax) %></u>
    </td></tr>
    <tr><td>Total</td><td align="right">
    <% = "<B>" & formatCurrency(Total) & "</B>" %>
    </td></tr>
    </table>
```

7

7. If the Total cost is equal to zero, then the visitor's shopping cart has nothing in it, and an alternate block of HTML code is displayed. Notice how this control statement is split around the HTML tags. It is not necessary to keep the entire control statement within the same script tags.

```
<% else %>
     You have nothing in your shopping cart!
<% end if %>
</div>
</body></html>
```

8. Save your Web page to your data directory on the Web server. View the Web page in the browser.

9. View and print the source code in the browser. It is very important to look at the source code of each ASP page that you create, in order to understand what the Web server is sending to the browser. ASP code is never sent to the browser. Only HTML tags, along with client-side scripts, are sent to the browser. Many errors are related to the syntax of the HTML being sent to the browser, such as a missing closing tag, or a missing quotation mark. By viewing the source code in the browser, you can more quickly locate the HTML syntax errors.

Make sure that you are using the HTTP protocol to view the ASP pages in the browser *(http://yourservername/yourdatadirectory/cartTotal.asp)*. Because previously you were using client-side script, you were not required to run the scripts on a Web server. However, ASP pages contain server scripts, which are interpreted on the Web server. The ASP pages will not be displayed correctly without a Web server.

PROGRAMMING WITH ASP BUILT-IN OBJECTS

In addition to all of the scripting language objects, properties, and methods, server-side scripts have access to all of the built-in ASP objects, properties and methods. You can access built-in ASP objects in much the same way that you access objects in the Document Object Model. Objects and their methods and properties are referred to using dot notation. The object name is followed by a "." which is then followed by the property or method being called. In the example above, cartTotal.asp, you used the write method, which belongs to the response object. The next two examples will show you how to use some of the other ASP built-in objects and methods. You will learn about these built-in ASP objects, custom objects, and third-party objects in more detail in later chapters.

The example below uses the request object and the response object. This example demonstrates how to combine basic scripting techniques with ASP built-in objects. The request object is used to obtain information from the client's browser, from the form. The form collection is a member of the request object. The Form collection contains all of the fields on the form. In this case, there is a form field named txtName and txtPass. Notice that this script is similar to the login form that you created earlier in this book using client-side scripting. The user can only log in by using the correct name and password. More details on using the request object to process forms will be discussed in the next chapter.

1. Create a Web page named **builtinObjects.asp** using Notepad or another ASP-compatible editor. Save the Web page to your data directory.

2. Insert the heading section of the Web page and the body tag, using the code below.

```
<html><head><title>Built-In ASP Objects</title></head>
<body bgcolor = "#CCFFCC" text = "#008000">
```

3. A control statement, shown below, determines which content is displayed in the remainder of the Web page. If the user fills out a form correctly, then a welcome message will be displayed. If the user does not fill out the form correctly, then the form will be redisplayed. The If Then statement is used to test the information that the user typed in the form. (*Hint:* To require that the user complete both fields correctly or to combine the two conditional statements, use the keyword.)

```
<%

if request.form("txtName") <> "admin" or _

    request.form("txtPass") <> "pass" then %>
```

4. It the user does not log in correctly, then the form is redisplayed. The code below creates the form. Forms can be processed on the same page, or on a different ASP page. Notice that the action is builtinObjects.asp, which will call the same page to process the form. The form method is post. In order to use the Form collection to retrieve the value of a field on a form, you must use the post method as opposed to the get method.

Because the get method appends the name and value of the form fields to the URL, and submits the results in the QueryString, the form information is readily accessible in the location bar and the history menu. Therefore, you should not use the get method to send sensitive information such as credit card, login, personal, or financial information.

```
<h1 align="center">Login Form</h1>
<form method="post" action="builtinObjects.asp">
<input type="text" name="txtName" size="20"> Name
<br><br>
<input type="password" name="txtPass" size="20"> Password
<br><br>
<input type="submit" value="Login" name="btnSubmit">
<input type="reset" value="Clear" name="btnClear">
</form>
```

5. If the user has logged in correctly, then a welcome message is displayed.

```
<% else %>
    <h3 align="center">Welcome Back!</h3>
<% end if %>
```

6. The last section of code includes the ending tags to the Web page. Although Internet Explorer will display the page without the closing tags, many browsers will display error messages unless all of the required HTML tags are present. Therefore, it is important to include the closing HTML tags on each Web page.

```
</body></html>
```

7. After you have completed the previous steps, save your Web page to your data directory on your Web server. View your Web page in a browser and view the source code.

The following sample shows how to use the request object along with another built-in ASP object called the session object. In addition to the forms collection, the request object contains a collection of server variables that are passed with the file in the header. The header includes information that is needed to identify how to send the file and where to send the file. These server variables can be retrieved using the ServerVariables method of the request object. The server variables are always referred to using all uppercase characters. The PATH_INFO server variable will retrieve the virtual path to the file. The virtual path is the relative path from the root of the Web site. The server object contains several methods, including the MapPath, which is used to convert the virtual path to the absolute path. You can pass a virtual path that is returned from the PATH_INFO server variable to the MapPath method of the server object to retrieve the complete physical path to a file.

The session object has a property called timeout, which is used to set the time limit for the session between the browser and the Web server. When the timeout limit is reached, the session will end, and all session-related information will be lost. The default timeout is set to 20 minutes. However, sometimes visitors spend more time on a Web site. To keep the session alive longer, you can modify the timeout property. Session variables are variables that apply to the individual session between a specific client and the Web server. The session object can contain many session variables. The session variables are stored in the Contents collection of the session object. The session variable name is placed in quotation marks when the session variable is defined. Session variables can contain strings, numbers, expressions, and objects.

The SessionID property of the session object is one way to identify the client to the Web server. The Web server is able to distinguish clients using the SessionID property. You cannot assign a value to the SessionID. In general, the SessionID is a unique number because it is created using a combination of numbers, including the IP addresses of the client and server, and the date and time. You can retrieve the SessionID by using the SessionID property of the session object.

1. Create a Web page named **builtinObjects2.asp**, using Notepad or another ASP-compatible editor. Save the Web page to your data directory.

2. Set the timeout property of the session object to 30 minutes.

```
<%
Session.Timeout = 30
```

3. The next statement defines a session variable. In this example, the session variable is named **sStart** and is assigned the value of an expression. The Now expression will return the date and time, which will then be assigned to the session variable.

```
Session.Contents("sStart") = Now()
```

4. The next section of code obtains the physical and virtual paths to this file and stores them in two variables named strPathInfo and strPhysicalPath. The virtual path returned from the PATH_INFO server variable is assigned to the strPathInfo variable. The MapPath method is applied to the virtual path stored in the strPathInfo variable to retrieve the physical path to this file.

```
dim strPathInfo, strPhysicalPath
strPathInfo = Request.ServerVariables("PATH_INFO")
strPhysicalPath  = Server.MapPath(strPathInfo)
%>
```

5. Insert the heading section of the Web page and the body tag, using the code below.

```
<html>
<head><title>More Built-In Objects</title></head>
<body bgcolor = "#CCFFCC" text = "#008000">
```

6. The div tag can be used to center-align the content displayed on the page. Add two headings.

```
<div align="center">
<h1>Built-In Objects</h1>
<h3>Path Information</h3>
```

7. The next section of code simply displays the strPathInfo and strPhysicalPath variables, which display the virtual and physical paths to the file. The Response.write shortcut key is used to write the values of these two variables to the Web page.

```
The virtual path to this file is: <br>
<b><% = strPathInfo %></b>
<br><br>
The physical path to this file is: <br>
<b><% = strPhysicalPath %></b>
<br><br><br><br>
```

8. Add another heading and display the timeout property of the session object. The new value for the timeout property is displayed. The Response.write shortcut key is used to write the value of the timeout property to the Web page.

```
<h3>Session Information</h3>
The session timeout has been set to: <br>
<b><% = session.timeout %> minutes</b>
<br><br>
```

7

9. Use the Response.write shortcut to write the value of the session variable sStart to the Web page. The full name of the variable is identified by Session.Contents("sStart"). However, the contents collection keyword is optional.

```
Your session started at: <b><br>
<% = Session.Contents("sStart") %></b>
<br><br>
```

10. Use the Response.write shortcut key to write the value of the SessionID property to the Web page.

```
Your session ID is: <br>
<b><% = Session.SessionID %></b>
</div></body></html>
```

11. After you have completed the previous steps, save your Web page to your data directory on your Web server. View your Web page in a browser and view the source code.

SERVER-SIDE INCLUDE FILES

Many languages contain a method to include the contents of one file in another file. In Java, for example, you can use an import statement to include code from one file in another. Server-side include files (also referred to as SSI files or include files) are often used to insert code that can be reused for other Web pages, for example headers and footers. The server-side include file may contain header or footer information, style information, logos and images, constants, other expressions, formulas, or meta tag information. This content may be composed of HTML tags, text, or client- or server-side scripts. A server-side include file containing information that is displayed on the top of the Web page is often named "head.inc" or "header.inc". The naming convention will vary with individual programmers. The ASP page can contain multiple statements to retrieve multiple server-side include files. Sometimes, the heading section of a Web page is broken up into smaller pieces. For example, there might be an include page for the title tags called title.inc, and one for the meta tags called meta.inc.

 The SSI file will be included before the ASP engine interprets the page. Therefore, you cannot use ASP code to decide which server-side include file to include within a Web page. Furthermore, all statements in the server-side include file will be included.

Creating the SSI File

Server-side include files can contain text, HTML, and client- and server-side scripts. Server-side include files are saved with the file extension .inc or .asp, because Web servers are by default configured to support include files with the .inc or .asp file extensions. The server-side include page can be created using a text editor such as Notepad, or a Web management tool such as FrontPage 2000 or Visual Studio. Usually it is recommended that you store server-side include files in a separate directory. This directory is often named /inc or /Scripts to indicate that the directory is storing included files. The sample include file below will write out a title to the Web page, and the date.

'While it is common to use the .inc file extension for server-side include files, it is important to note that there are differences between .inc and .asp files. A file with the extension .inc can be easily viewed via a browser. A file that ends in .asp will execute the server-side scripts before the page is sent to the browser. Therefore, if your server-side include file contains any sensitive information, you should name it using the .asp file extension.

1. Using Notepad or your Web development tool, create a file named **garden.inc**. You might have to save the file using double quotes to ensure that the file is saved as an include file and not a .txt file. Add the following code to create a heading that displays the name of the store and the address.

```
<div align="center">
<h2>Garden Supply Store</font></h2>
<i>555 Main Street<br>
Chicago, IL 60011</i>
<br><br>
<font face="Verdana" size="2">
```

2. Add the following code to display the current date and time. Notice that the VBScript Now method is used to display the date and time. Server-side script can be included in the server-side include file. Finish the Web page by adding the closing font, paragraph tags and a horizontal ruler.

```
Today is <% = now() %>
<br><br>
<HR width="75%" size="4" color="#008000">
</div>
```

3. Save the server-side include page to your data directory on the Web server.

Including SSI Files in an ASP Page

The syntax for including a server-side include file is straightforward. To instruct the Web server to include a server-side include file, use an include statement. The include statement uses the keyword `include`. The pound sign (#) precedes the include keyword to indicate that the include keyword is a command to include another file. There are no spaces between the pound sign and the include keyword. The path and the filename are identified in the include statement. There are two ways to identify the path to the server-side include file. You can use the virtual path or the physical path. The entire include statement is enclosed in a pair of HTML comment tags. The Web page must be saved with the .asp extension in order to use a server-side include file. Below is the syntax for including a server-side include file in an ASP page.

<!--#include = path & filename -->

Physical Paths

Physical paths are identified using the keyword file. The path can be an absolute path, which identifies the drive letter, path, and filename, or a relative path, which identifies the relative path and filename. Recall that in DOS-based and Windows-based systems, the directories and filenames are separated with backward slashes (\). If you do not know the physical path to your directories and files, you can use the MapPath method of the server object to obtain the physical path. Below are the syntax and sample code for including a server-side include file using a physical path.

<!--#include file = "driveLetter:\AbsolutePath\FileName.inc" -->

```
<!--#include file = "c:\Web\garden.inc" -->
```

You can refer to the physical location of the file using an absolute or relative path to the file. To refer to the relative path, use the forward slash (/) and not the drive letters. The relative location of the server-side include file is expressed in its relationship to the location of the ASP page. As shown in the sample code below, if no path is identified, it is assumed that the server-side include file is in the same physical directory as the Web page. If the folder is in a directory above, you can use the DOS dot notation naming convention, like this: "../scripts/filename.inc" or "../../scripts/filename.inc". Below are the syntax and sample code for including a server-side include file using a relative path.

<!--#include file = "RelativePath/FileName.inc" -->

```
<!--#include file = "garden.inc" -->
```

Virtual Path

If you do not know the physical path, you can use a virtual path. The virtual path identifies the location of the include file starting from the root of the Web directory. To use a virtual path you must use the keyword **virtual**. The first slash is used to indicate that the path to the file starts from the root of the Web directory. Below are the syntax and sample code for including a server-side include file using a virtual path. Before ASP 3.0, if you used the virtual path, the ASP engine did not verify the user's file security settings. You could bypass these security settings and view the include file. In ASP 3.0, ASP will verify the security settings for the include file, whether the virtual or absolute path is used.

<!--#include virtual = "/VirtualPath/FileName.inc" -->

```
<!--#include virtual = "/garden.inc" -->
```

Creating the Include Statement in the ASP Page

In the example below, the ASP page gardenInclude.asp is located in the same directory as the server-side include file, garden.inc. The garden.inc page contains information that can be used as a header for the ASP page.

1. Create a Web page called **gardenInclude.asp**, using Notepad or your Web development tool.

2. Add the basic HTML tags to the Web page, as follows.

```
<html><head><title>Garden Supply Store</title></head>
<body bgcolor = "#99FF99" text = "#008000">
```

3. Add the include statement, as shown below. The include statement refers to the server-side include file named garden.inc. The include statement uses the physical relative path to the server-side include file. Don't forget to add the ending tags to the Web page.

```
<!--#include file = "garden.inc"-->
</body></html>
```

4. Save the Web page to your data directory on the Web server. View the gardenInclude.asp page in the browser. View the source code. Notice that there is no indication that the Web page was assembled from two distinct files.

Other Methods for Including Data

Server-side includes are not the only way to reference external information in ASP 3.0. Instead of using SSI, you can run an external script file directly from the script tag by specifying the source property. Below is the syntax that you would use to include an external script file using the script tag. The pathname can be identified using the virtual or physical path.

<script language = "language" runat = "server" src = "path/filename" > </script>

Another reason to use SSI files is to include constants. Some of these constants are available directly from a library of code called a type library. Rather than using an SSI, in ASP 3.0 you can now reference the type library of a component using the metadata tag. The metadata tag is placed within HTML comment tags in the heading section of the ASP page. Below is the syntax for using the metadata tag.

<!-- metadata type = "typelib" file = "path/filename" -->

INTERNET RESOURCES

There are a vast number of Internet sites devoted to programming, JavaScript, VBScript, and ASP. In Chapter 2, you learned about some of these sites and visited the MSDN Online Library. Table 7-1 lists many ASP sites that contain free support for ASP developers. The MSDN Online Library, located at *http://msdn.microsoft.com*, is an excellent resource for information about ASP and VBScript. Microsoft has added an additional Web site for scripting support for developers, at *http://msdn.microsoft.com/scripting/*. And because members of the ASP development community have supported each other from the start, you will find on the Internet many samples, tutorials, discussion forums, e-mail lists, magazines, and conferences devoted to developing ASP applications. One of the best links to ASP resources is the ASP Web Ring at *http://www.webring.org/cgibin/webring?ring=asp101;list*. They provide links to other ASP Web sites, as well as to companies that provide ASP programming and ASP third-party software.

Table 7-1 Links to ASP-related Internet Resources

Description	URL
15 Seconds	http://www.15seconds.com/
4GuysFromRolla	http://www.4guysfromrolla.com/
Active Server Corner	http://www.kamath.com
Active Server Developer's Journal	http://www.zdjournals.com/asp/
Application Developer's Training Company (AppDev)	http://www.appdev.com/
ASP 101	http://www.asp101.com/
ASP Alliance	http://www.aspalliance.com/
ASP DevCon Conference	http://www.aspdevcon.com/
Asp Developer Network	http://www.aspdeveloper.net/
ASP Developer Visual InterDev Tutorial 1	http://www.aspdeveloper.net/VInterDev/page1.asp
ASP Guild International	http://www.aspguild.org/
ASP Island	http://www.aspisland.com
ASPLists	http://www.asplists.com/asplists/
ASP News	http://www.aspnews.com
ASPPages	http://www.asppages.com/
ASP Resource Index	http://www.aspin.com/
ASP Resources	http://www.asp-dev.com/
ASP Sites	http://www.aspsites.com/
ASP Today	http://www.asptoday.com/
ASP Toolbox	http://www.tcp-ip.com/
ASP WebRing	http://www.webring.org/cgi-bin/ webring?ring=asp101;list
ASPWire	http://www.aspwire.com/
aspZone	http://www.aspzone.com/
AspEncrypt	http://www.aspencrypt.com/
ASPFree.com	http://www.aspfree.com/default.asp
ASP-Help.com	http://www.asp-help.com
ASPUpload	http://www.aspupload.com/
DevGuru	http://www.devguru.com/
GetScripts.com	http://www.scripts.com
Halcyon Software iASP	http://www.halcyonsoft.com/products/iasp.asp
Hunt Interactive	http://www.huntinteractive.com/
IIS Development	http://www.alphasierrapapa.com/IisDev/3WSites.asp
Internet.com	http://www.internet.com/

Table 7-1   Links to ASP-related Internet Resources (continued)

Description	URL
LearnASP	http://www.learnasp.com/
Microsoft Active Server Support	http://support.microsoft.com/support/default.asp?PR=asp&FR=0&SD=GN&LN=EN-US
Microsoft Windows Script Technologies	http://msdn.microsoft.com/scripting/
MSDN Online Library	http://www.msdn.microsoft.com/library/default.asp
Persits Software, Inc.	http://www.persits.com/
ServerObjects	http://www.serverobjects.com/
Software Artisans: ASPstudio	http://www.aspstudio.com/
The Development Exchange (DevX)	http://www.devx.com/
VBScripts.com	http://www.vbscripts.com/
VisualInterDev.org	http://www.visualinterdev.org
WebReference.com	http://www.webreference.com/
Web Review	http://webreview.com/
Yahoo's Programming Languages	http://dir.yahoo.com/computers_and_internet/programming_languages/

7

CHAPTER SUMMARY

ASP Overview

❏ The Web server recognizes Active Server Pages by the .asp file extension. The Web server passes the file to the Active Server Pages engine, asp.dll. The ASP engine processes the scripts located in the Global Application File, global.asa.

❏ The ASP engine includes any server-side include files within the Web page. The scripting engine then executes the server-side scripts, interpreting inline VBScript statements before block VBScript statements. Server block script is identified using the runat attribute. Inline script is identified using inline script tags <% %>.

❏ Active Server Pages are written with scripts and are interpreted, not compiled like C or Visual Basic. ASP pages can be written using a text editor such as Notepad. Because the script is interpreted on the server, it is never accessible to the client. Only the HTML and client-side scripts are sent to the browser. Therefore, server scripting is browser-independent. ASP pages must be viewed on a Web server that supports the ASP engine.

ASP Built-in Objects

❏ The ASP Object Model consists of several built-in objects, including application object, request object, response object, server object, session object, and ASPError object.

❏ The request object is used to receive information from the browser, and the response object is used to send information to the browser. The application object is used to maintain information for the entire application, while the session object is used to maintain information about a single user session. The server object is used to access resources on the server, including instantiating other third-party objects. The ASPError object is used to retrieve information about the last error.

Server-side Include Files

❏ Server-side include files allow you to include the entire contents of one file in another file. The SSI file must have an.asp or .inc file extension. The SSI file can contain HTML, client-side script, or server-side script. The ASP page uses the include keyword to include a file. The virtual path is the path of a file in relationship to the root of the Web site. The physical path is the DOS-compatible path to the file, and can be the absolute path or relative path.

To create a server-side block script

```
<script language = "vbscript" runat = "server">
response.write("Hello World")
</script>
```

To write content using Response.Write

```
<% response.write("Hello World") %>
<% response.write(strUserName) %>
<% = strUserName %>
<% = "Hello World" %>
<% response.write("Hello" & strUserName) %>
```

To write out the date

```
<% = WeekdayName(Weekday(Date))%>
<% = MonthName(Month(Date))%>
<% = Day(Date)%>
<% = Year(Now())%>
```

To format the value as currency

```
<% = formatCurrency(Cost) %>
<% = formatCurrency(129.52) %>
```

To identify the default scripting language

```
<%@language = "vbscript" %>
```

To retrieve the value of a form field using request.form

```
<% request.form("txtName")%>
<form method = "post" action = "process.asp">
```

To display a server variable using the ServerVariables collection

```
<% = Request.ServerVariables("PATH_INFO")%>
```

To display the absolute path to a file using the MapPath method

```
<% = Server.MapPath(strPathInfo)%>
```

To change the timeout property and write it to the Web page

```
<% Session.Timeout = 30 %>
<% = Session.Timeout%>
```

To create a session variable and write it to the Web page

```
<% Session.Contents("sStart") = Now() %>
<% = Session.Contents("sStart") %>
```

To retrieve the SessionID and write it to the Web page

```
<% = Session.SessionID %>
<% strSessionID = Session.SessionID %>
```

To insert a server-side include file

```
<!--#include file = "C:\Web\garden.inc" -->
<!--#include file = "garden.inc" -->
<!--#include virtual ="/garden.inc" -->
```

REVIEW QUESTIONS

1. The ASP script code is compiled. True or False?

2. ASP can easily run on Netscape and Internet Explorer browsers. True or False?

3. Server-side script is not accessible from the source code view in a Web page. True or False?

4. Session variables are created within the Web page. True or False?

5. The ASP engine is contained in the _____ file.

   a. global.asa

   b. global.exe

   c. asp.dll

   d. asp.asa

6. The first file to be called when a user attempts to start a new session is
   _____ .

   a. global.asa

   b. global.dll

   c. asp.asa

   d. session.asa

7. Which one of the following languages is supported by ASP?

   a. PerlScript

   b. VBScript

   c. JavaScript

   d. all of the above

8. Which of the following is a valid ASP page?

   a. mypage.html

   b. mypage.asp

   c. mypage.asa

   d. mypage.htm

9. What product must be installed before you can view ASP pages in a Web browser?

   a. Visual Basic

   b. Personal Web Server

   c. FrontPage

   d. Notepad

10. Which of the following can be used to create .asp applications?

    a. Notepad

    b. FrontPage

    c. Microsoft Script Editor

    d. all of the above

11. Which kinds of scripts are processed first?

    a. local scripts

    b. block script

    c. inline scripts

    d. client scripts

12. Which property identifies the server script using the block script tag?

    a. runat = server

    b. run = server

    c. server.runat

    d. @run=server

13. The default server script language for inline scripting is:

    a. VBScript

    b. JavaScript

    c. Perl

    d. Visual Basic

14. Which keyword is used to indicate the absolute DOS path to a server-side include file?

    a. include

    b. #include

    c. virtual

    d. file

15. Which of the following is not a built-in ASP object?

    a. workstation

    b. response

    c. request

    d. session

16. The _____ object allows you to share information between a single browser and the Web server.

    a. application

    b. response

    c. request

    d. session

17. The _____ object allows you to receive information from the browser.

    a. application

    b. response

    c. request

    d. session

7

18. The _____ object allows you to send information to the browser.

    a. application

    b. response

    c. request

    d. session

19. Which is the correct syntax to retrieve a server variable?

    a. `request.servervariables("PATH_INFO")`

    b. `request.servervariables(path_info)`

    c. `request.servervariables("path_info")`

    d. `servervariables. request (Path_Info)`

20. Which property will retrieve the SessionID?

    a. ServerVariable

    b. SessionID

    c. ServerID

    d. Path_ID

HANDS-ON PROJECTS

Project 7-1

In this project, you will create a Web page that calculates an arithmetic expression using server-side script.

1. Create a Web page named **aspbooks.asp**, using your text editor or Web development tool.

2. Add an inline server script that defines two constants: bkName is assigned the value **Chancy's Bookstore**; bkEmail is assigned the value **info@chancybooks.com**.

3. In the same inline script, create four variables, one for each book, and one for the total for the shopping cart. The variables should be named **bk1**, **bk2**, **bk3**, and **total**. Also declare a variable named **today** that will be used to hold the current date.

4. Assign values to each of the variables: bk1 costs **$1.99**; bk2 costs **$2.99**; bk3 costs **$3.99**. Assign the value of the total variable to the total of all of the book variables.

5. Assign the today variable the current date. Use the format "Monday, November 5, 2001". (*Hint:* You have already learned to format the date and write the output to the browser. Instead of using the write method, assign the expression to the today variable. You can refer to the sample code below.)

```
today = WeekdayName(Weekday(Date)) & ", " & _
MonthName(Month(Date)) & " " & _
Day(Date) & ", " & Year(Now())%>
```

6. Add the basic HTML tags. The title of the page should be **Shopping Cart**. The background color of the page should be **#CCCCFF**, and the color of the default text should be **#000080**. Add a div tag to center-align the contents of the Web page.

7. Add a heading formatted as heading 2 that displays the bookstore name stored in the bkName constant. Add a heading formatted as heading 3 that displays the bookstore e-mail address stored in the bkEmail constant. Add a heading 3 that states **Your Shopping Cart**.

```
<h2><% = bkName %></h2>
<h3><% = bkEmail %></h3>
<h3>Your Shopping Cart</h3>
```

8. Add a sentence that says **You purchased your products on:**. Add two line-break tags. Add the current day of the week, using the **today** variable. (*Hint:* You can use the write method to write the today variable to the Web page. Use inline script tags.) Add two more line-break tags.

9. If the Total is not 0, then write out the values of each of the Books and the Total; otherwise, write out an expression that says **You have nothing in your shopping cart!**. (*Hint:* You can use an If Then statement to test the value of the Total variable.)

10. Use a table to display the book titles and their values. In each row, write out the name of each book (**Book1, Book2, Book3**) and the cost of each book. (*Hint:* The cost of each book is stored in the variables **bk1, bk2**, and **bk3**.) Format the cost of the book as currency. Right-align the three cells that contain the costs of each book. Underline the expression that contains bk3.

11. In the fourth row in the table, write out **Total** and the value of the Total variable. Format the Total variable as currency, make it boldface, and right-align the cell.

12. Add the closing HTML tags. Modify the Web page appearance.

13. Save the Web page to your data directory. View the Web page. Print your source code. Print the Web page.

Project 7-2

In this project, you will create a Web page that uses server script to process a login form. Once the user has correctly filled out the form, a welcome back message will be displayed; otherwise, the form will be displayed.

1. Create a Web page named **aspLoginForm.asp**, using your text editor or Web development tool.

2. Add an inline server script that declares two variables (**name** and **pass**) to hold the values from the form. Assign the values from the form fields to the variables. (*Hint:* You can use the request object to retrieve the values from the form, for example `name = request.form("txtName").`)

3. Add the basic HTML tags. The title of the page should be **Login Form**. The background color of the page should be **#CCCCFF**, and the color of the default text should be **#000080**.

4. Use the code below to add a control statement to determine if the user has filled out the login form correctly. The control statement should detect whether the name variable has the value **Admin** and the pass variable has the value **Pass**. If they have not, then a login form is displayed.

```
<% if name <> "Admin" or _
      pass <> "                          Pass" then %>
```

5. Create a login form. Add a heading above the form that is center-aligned, formatted as heading 2, and says **Login Form**. The form name should be **form**, and the method should be **post**. The action should be **aspLoginForm.asp**. Create two form fields. The first should be a text box that is named **txtName** and has a size of **20**. Write **Name** following the textbox. The second form field should be a password text box named **txtPass** and should be size **20**. Write **Password** following the password text box. Place two line breaks after each form field. Add a Submit button that is named **btnSubmit** and has a value of **Login**.

6. Add the welcome message that is displayed if the user completes the form correctly. The welcome message should say **Welcome Back!** and should be formatted with heading 2 and center-aligned.

7. Add the closing HTML tags. Modify the Web page appearance.

8. Save the Web page to your data directory. View the Web page. Print your source code. Print the Web page.

Project 7-3

In this project, you will create a Web page that uses server variables and server methods to determine the physical and relative paths to a file.

1. Create a Web page named **pathfinder.asp**, using your text editor or Web development tool.

2. Add an inline script. Declare two variables, **strPathInfo** and **strPhysicalPath**. Assign the value of the server variable named PATH_INFO to the strPathInfo variable.

3. Use the MapPath method of the server object to retrieve the physical path to the file. Pass the strPathInfo as the argument to the MapPath method. Assign the value to the strPhysicalPath variable.

4. Add the basic HTML tags. The title of the page should be **Path Finder**. The background color of the page should be **#CCCCFF**, and the color of the default text should be **#000080**. Add a heading 2 that is center-aligned and says **Path information for this Web page**.

5. Add the text **The virtual path to this file is:** and a line break. Add the value of the strPathInfo variable and two line breaks.

6. Add the text **The Physical Path to this file is:** and a line break. Add the value of the strPhysicalPath variable.

7. Add the closing HTML tags. Modify the Web page appearance.

8. Save the Web page to your data directory. View the Web page. Print your source code. Print the Web page.

Project 7-4

In this project, you will create a Web page that uses session variables to store user information from a form.

1. Create a Web page named **sessionform.asp**, using your text editor or Web development tool.

2. Add the opening HTML tags. The title of the page should be **Session Variables**. Add a heading 1 that is center-aligned and says **Session Login Form**.

3. Create a login form named **form**. The method should be **post**. The action should be **sessionvariables.asp**. Create two form fields. The first should be a text box that is named **txtName** and has a size of **20**. Write **Name** following the text box. The second form field should be a password text box named **txtPass** and should be size **20**. Write **Password** following the password text box. Place two line breaks after each form field. Add a Submit button that is named **btnSubmit** and has a value of **Login**.

4. Add the closing HTML tags. Modify the Web page appearance. Save the Web page to your data directory.

5. Create another page named **sessionvariables.asp** that will display the form results and the session variables.

6. Create a session variable named **sStart**, using the Session.Contents collection. Assign the current date to the sStart session variable, using the Now method.

7. Create two session variables named **sUser** and **sPass**, using the Session.Contents collection.

8. Retrieve the values from the form, using the Request.Form method, and assign the values to the session variables.

```
Session.Contents("sUser") = request.form("txtName")
Session.Contents("sPass") = request.form("txtPass")
```

9. Add the basic HTML tags. The title of the page should be **Session Variables**. The background color of the page should be **#CCCCFF**, and the color of the default text should be **#000080**. Add a Heading 3 statement that says **Session Parameters:**.

10. Write out **Your SessionID to track your session is:** and write out the SessionID, using the SessionID property of the session object. Add a line break after the statement.

11. Write out **Your session started at:** and write out the value of the sStart session variable. Add a line break after the statement.

12. Write out **Your user name is:** and write out the value of the sUser session variable. Add a line break after the statement.

13. Write out **Your password is:** and write out the value of the sPass session variable. Add a line break after the statement.

14. Add the closing HTML tags. Modify the Web page appearance.

15. Save the Web page to your data directory. View the Web page. Print your source code. Print the Web page.

CASE PROJECTS

Pets and More!

You are hired by a company named Pets and More! to create a Web page named asppetsform.asp that will allow users to log in to a membership area on the Web site. The form should contain at least five fields. Create a page named asppets.asp that will process the form. After the user completes the form, the asppets.asp page will assign the values from the form to session variables and display the session variables to the user. Modify the layout using color and graphics to make the Web page look professional. Save your Web page to your data directory. View the Web page. Print out the Web page and the source code.

Grapes Off the Vine

You are hired by a company named Grapes Off the Vine to create a Web page that will allow users to log in to a membership area on the Web site. Create a membership login form on a Web page named grapes.asp. The form should contain at least three fields: the username, the password, and the e-mail address. Use server-side script to test whether the user is a member. Create at least two valid users who can log in to the Web site. If a valid user logs in, welcome the user by name. If the user is not a valid member, display the form. (*Hint:* Assign the values from the form fields to variables. Use an If Then statement to test the contents of the variables. Don't forget to place parentheses around the entire condition, and around each expression within the conditional statement. You can test if the user matches, then display the message or the form.) Modify the layout using a table, color, and graphics to make the Web page look professional. Save your Web page as grapes.asp to your data directory. View the Web page. Print out the Web page and the source code.

Potato Crops

You are hired by a company named Potato Crops. They want you to develop a header and footer that will appear on every page in their Web site. Create a heading file named phead.inc and a footer file named pfoot.inc. In the heading, add the company name and a graphic. In the footer, add the company name, e-mail address, mailing address, current date, and Web page address. Create a test Web page named potato.asp that will include the header and the footer files. Modify the layout using a table, color, horizontal rulers, and graphics to make the Web page look professional. Save your Web page to your data directory. View the potato.asp Web page. Print out the potato.asp Web page and the source code for the page.

Webrings

Visit the ASP Webring at *http://www.webring.org/cgi-bin/webring?ring=asp101;list*. Create a Web page named webring.asp. Add links to at least ten sites within the Webring. Add a short explanation of why the site is valuable to Web programmers. Add a link to the Webring at the top of the page. Save your Web page to your data directory. View the Web page. Print out the Web page and the source code.

Web Links

Visit ten of the links listed in Table 7-1. Create a Web page named asplinks.asp. Add links to at least ten of the listed sites. Add a short explanation of why the site is valuable to ASP Web programmers. Save your Web page to your data directory. View the Web page. Print out the Web page and the source code.

ASP Discussion Lists

Join a discussion group (e-mail list) that discusses ASP. You can find several ASP groups at Egroups at *http://www.egroups.com* or from Web sites listed in Table 7-1. After joining the list, read the e-mails that appear over a week. Create a Web page named aspemails.asp that lists the name of the group, the home page of the e-mail group, the directions for signing up and signing off the list. Add at least three issues that came up in the e-mail list. Write a short paragraph explaining what the discussion was about. If possible, identify how many members are in the list. Add a short explanation of why the e-mail list is valuable (or not) to ASP Web programmers. Save your Web page as aspemails.asp to your data directory. View the Web page. Print out the Web page and the source code.

7

8

USING THE REQUEST AND RESPONSE OBJECTS

In this chapter you will:

♦ Retrieve information from a form using the Form and QueryString Collections

♦ Retrieve server variables using the request object

♦ Redirect users to another page using the response object

♦ Control output that is sent to the browser using the response object

♦ Control the caching of content on a Web page using the response object

---

In the previous chapter, you learned that there are several objects within the ASP model, each with its own properties and methods that you can access from your scripts. In this chapter, you will learn how to use two of these objects, the request object and the response object, to process a form, retrieve the server variables, write content to the browser, redirect the user to another page, and modify the caching of the Web page. In the next chapter, you will learn how to use the request and response objects to read and write cookies to a user's file system.

THE REQUEST AND RESPONSE OBJECTS

As you learned in the previous chapter, the request and response objects are built into the ASP Object Model. When a browser sends a request to a Web server, the request object can be used to retrieve information about that request. For example, the browser request will include the date and time, the type of request (get or post), the page requested, and the HTTP version. Additional information includes the default language, the referring page, the host IP (the IP address for the client), the cookie associated with that domain, and the user agent. This information helps to identify the client. If there is a form, the form name and value pairs are sent. If the form method was get, then the form was sent appended to the URL. If the form method was post, it was sent as part of the HTTP request body. If the client has a certificate, the values from the certificate are sent with the request. The request object allows you to retrieve this information. The cookies are retrieved using the cookies collection, and the client certificate fields are retrieved using the ClientCertificate collection. The form and QueryString collections allow you to collect information sent from a form. Any information that is sent with the request in the HTTP header can be retrieved using the server variables collection.

The response object is used to send information to the browser. Some of this information identifies the server. For example, the IP address of the server, the name of the operating system, and the Web server software versions are sent to the client. The cookies collection is used to send a cookie to the browser. A status code is sent, to indicate that the request was successful or encountered an error. In addition to appending information to content that is written to the browser, the response object allows you to redirect the browser to another page, and to hold the contents of a page in a buffer until you send the page. The methods and properties of the response object allow you to control the caching of content from the ASP page. The response object allows you to append information to the Web server log, and add custom information to the HTTP header.

RETRIEVING INFORMATION FROM A FORM

As you learned in the previous chapter, a form passes name and value pairs to the Web server. The name and value are separated by an equal sign (=). Each name and value pair is separated from the next by an ampersand (&). The two methods that pass the form field information are the get method and the post method. The get method appends the name and value pairs to the URL with a question mark (?). The information sent using the get method is readily accessible in the location bar and the history menu, so you should not use it to send sensitive information. The post method sends the name and value pairs as part of the HTTP request body. The method used to send the data is identified in the HTML form tag.

The request object is used to retrieve form information that has been submitted to the server. The request object contains a forms collection and a QueryString collection. If the form is sent using the get method, then the QueryString collection is used to retrieve the name and value pairs. If the form is sent using the post method, then the form collection is used to retrieve the name and value pairs.

The name and value pairs are sent URL-encoded, which means that spaces are replaced with plus signs (+), and special characters are replaced with the percent sign (%) and the hexadecimal value for the character. In order to retrieve the name and value pairs as they were sent, you would have to split the name and value pairs, parse the name and values, then replace the plus signs and hexadecimal values with blank spaces and the special characters. The request object allows you to retrieve the name and values without having to perform these tasks. The sample code below demonstrates how the name and value pairs are sent URL-encoded using the get method.

```
http://www.company.com/rq.asp?name=Jim&dept=Human+Resources
```

The Form Collection

The form collection allows you to retrieve the names and values of fields from a submitted form. The form collection can retrieve the entire form collection, or a single field. To retrieve the entire form collection, specify the request object name and form. Retrieving the form collection will retrieve all form fields that have a name and value. If the form field does not have a form field name specified in the form field tag, the value will not be sent. Most form fields with a name will be received in the form collection, including the Submit button. However, the Form Field button and the Reset button will never send a value. The Form Field button is usually used to call a function or submit a form. If a Submit button has a name but does not have a value, then the value will be assigned "Submit Query". But if the Submit button does not have a name, the value will not be sent. Below is the syntax for retrieving the entire form collection.

request.form

You can detect if a user has completed a form by determining whether the form collection is empty. If the form collection is empty, then the user has not completed the form. The following sample code could be used to detect if the form collection is empty. This sample code could also be used to determine whether the QueryString collection is empty.

```
<% if request.form = "" then %>
    <h1>The Form Collection is empty</h1>
<% else %>
    <h1>The Form Collection is: </h1>
    <% = request.form %>
<% end if %>
```

To retrieve a single field from the form collection, specify the request object name, the form object, and the name of the field, inside quotation marks. Below is the syntax for retrieving a single field from the form collection.

request.form("formFieldName")

8

You can also determine if a user has completed a particular form field. In the following sample code, the user must have entered a value, or selected an option from each of the form fields listed. You could create additional code to redisplay the form if the form is incomplete.

```
<% if request.form("txt1") = "" or _
request.form("txt2") = "" or _
request.form("chk3") = "" or _
request.form("chk4") = "" or _
request.form("sel5") = "" or _
request.form("rad6") = "" then %>
```

The following example demonstrates how to retrieve the values from a form using the form collection of the request object. A form named frmC is used to submit the customer information. The Web page called post.asp, shown in Figure 8-1, also includes a script to detect whether users have completed the form with the correct information. If they have, they are welcomed by name. Otherwise, the form is redisplayed.

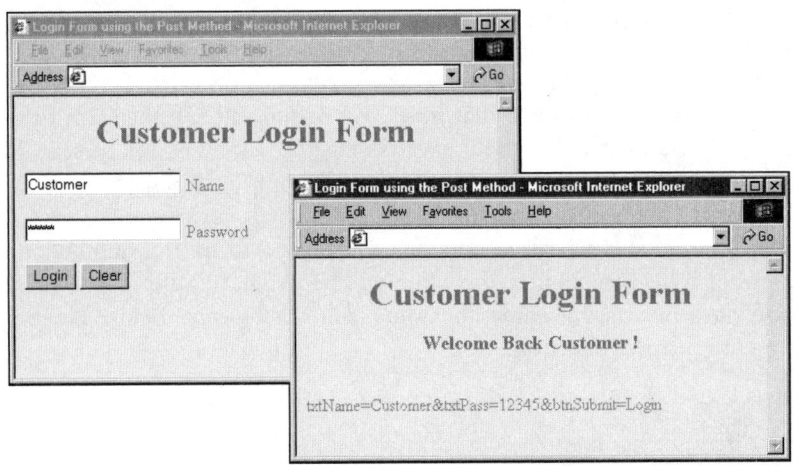

Figure 8-1   Using the form collection in the request object to display the results of a form

1. Create a Web page named **post.asp**, using Notepad or an ASP-compatible editor. Save the Web page to your data directory.

2. Add the basic ASP tags as indicated below. The option explicit statement will require you to declare all variables before they are used in the page. The response.buffer statement will hold the results from the server scripts at the Web server until all scripts are executed. In ASP 3.0, the buffer is set to true by default. If you are using ASP 2.0, you should set the buffer to true.

```
<% option explicit %><% response.buffer = "true" %>
```

3. Add the basic HTML tags, and a heading 1 that is center-aligned and says **Customer Login Form**.

```
<html><head><title>Customer Login Form</title></head>
<body bgcolor = "#CCFFCC" text = "#008000">
<h1 align = "center">Customer Login Form</h1>
```

4. Add the HTML form tags required to create the form as indicated below. The action is set to the same page because this page will collect and process the form information.

```
<form method="post" name="frmC" action="post.asp">
<input type="text" name="txtName" size="20"> Name
<br><br>
<input type="password" name="txtPass" size="20"> Password
<br><br>
<input type="submit" value="Login" name="btnSubmit">
<input type="reset" value="Clear" name="btnClear">
</form>
```

5. Add the code to validate the customer. If the customer typed in the username "Customer" and the password "12345," then display the results; otherwise, display the form. The following code can be used to validate the user. Remember that this code must be placed before the form. You can place this code immediately before the beginning form tag. Notice that the request object is used to retrieve the values of the form fields named **txtName** and **txtPass**. The keyword **or** is used to create a multiple conditional statement. Therefore, the user must fill out the correct name and password. Because this code extends over more than one line, you need to use the line continuation character (_).

```
<% if request.form("txtName") <> "Customer" or _
request.form("txtPass") <> "12345" then %>
```

6. After the closing form tag, add the code below. This code will display the form results if the user is validated. Declare three variables named **strName**, **strPass**, and **strForm**. The strName and strPass variables are used to hold the values from the fields on the form. The strForm variable is used to hold the form collection, which includes the name and values of all of the form fields. This code uses the variables to write the values to the Web page with the Response.write shortcut key (=). The code also writes the form collection to the Web page. HTML tags such as the heading 3 tag (<h3>) and the line break tag (<br>) are used to format the output. Because you used an If Then control statement to test the values the user entered, the **else** and **end if** statements must be used. Don't forget to include the closing HTML tags at the bottom of the page.

```
<% else %>
    <% dim strName, strPass, strForm
    strName = request.form("txtName")
    strPass = request.form("txtPass")
    strForm = request.form %>
    <h3 align="center">Welcome Back <% = strName %>
!</h3>
    <br><% = strForm %>
<% end if %>
</body></html>
```

8

7. After you have completed the previous steps, save the Web page to your data directory on your Web server. View your Web page. Try to log in with the username **Customer** and the password **12345**. Look at the output from the form collection. While the greeting says "Welcome Back Customer", the form collection displays "txtName=Customer&txtPass=12345&btnSubmit=Login". The form collection is still encoded with the ampersands and equal signs. The benefit of calling the individual fields is that you do not have to decode the special characters in the form collection. View the source code to see the information that was passed to the client. The code that performs the authentication is not available to the client.

The QueryString Collection

The QueryString collection allows you to retrieve the name and values of fields from a submitted form. The QueryString collection can retrieve the entire QueryString collection or an individual field. To retrieve the entire QueryString collection, specify the request object name and QueryString. Retrieving the QueryString will retrieve all form fields that have a name and value. If the form field does not have a form field name specified in the form field tag, the value will not be sent. All form fields with a name will be received in the QueryString collection, including the Submit button. Below is the syntax for retrieving the entire QueryString collection.

request.querystring

It is important to understand that the QueryString is also accessible through the server variables collection The following sample code shows how to retrieve the Querystring using the request object and the server variables collection.

```
<% = request.querystring %>
<% = request.servervariables("QUERY_STRING") %>
```

To retrieve a single field from the QueryString collection, specify the request object name, the QueryString object, and the name of the field, inside quotation marks. Below is the syntax for retrieving a single field from the QueryString collection.

request.querystring("formFieldName")

The following example demonstrates how to retrieve the values from a form using the QueryString collection of the request object. This example is identical to the previous example, except that here the method used to send the form is get. Therefore, the request object uses the QueryString collection to retrieve the values from the form.

1. Save the page you created in the previous example, post.asp, as **get.asp**, using Notepad or another ASP-compatible editor. Make sure that you have saved the Web page to your data directory.

2. Change the method property in the form tag from post to **get**.

3. Change the action property in the form tag from post.asp to **get.asp**.

4. Change all of the references to request.form to **request.querystring**.

5. Save your changes.

6. View the Web page in a browser. Try to log in with the username **Customer** and the password **12345**. Notice that the page is identical to the previous page. The QueryString returns the name and value pairs as "txtName=Customer&txtPass=12345&btnSubmit=Login". The name field is also returned. Look in the location text box in the browser. The main difference between these two examples is that the entire QueryString is viewable in the location text box in the browser.

Displaying the Form and QueryString Collections Without the Form Field Names

To create a Web page that displays the names and values of fields without knowing the names of the fields, you have to use a For Each statement. Recall from previous chapters that you can list the properties and objects that are in a parent object. The QueryString and form collections are child objects of the request object. You can use the For Each statement to loop through each of the form field objects in the collection, and retrieve the name of the form field and the value. This process can be used for both the form collection and the QueryString collection. The following example uses the QueryString collection to display the form field results. This exercise could also be modified to use the form collection to display the form field results.

1. Open the page named get.asp, which you created in the previous exercise. You can use Notepad or another ASP-compatible editor. Save the page as **getall.asp**. Make sure that you have saved the Web page to your data directory.

2. Change the action in the form to **getall.asp**.

3. Under the line where you previously wrote out the QueryString using `<% = strForm %> !</h3>`, add two line breaks. (*Hint:* You can use two break tags: `<br><br>`)

4. Add the following code to write out each of the form fields and their values. First, declare a new variable called **formField** to hold a temporary form field name. The For Each control statement will loop through each object in the QueryString collection.

```
<% dim formField
for each formField in request.querystring
```

5. Then, use the write method to write out the name of the field, temporarily known as formField. Write out an equal sign to separate the name of the field from the value. Place a blank space before and after the equal sign. Note that if you want to add more than a single blank space, you must use the HTML value for a blank space ( ).

```
response.write formField
response.write " = "
```

6. Use the Response.write method to write out the value of the form field, which is retrieved using request.querystring(formField). No quotation marks are used here because formField is a variable that temporarily holds the name of the form field.

```
response.write request.querystring(formField)
```

7. Write out a line break tag to separate the name and value pair on a separate line.

```
response.write "<br>"
```

8. Use the following command to cause the loop to start over. Close the server script with a closing inline script tag.

```
next %>
```

9. Save your changes.

10. View the Web page in a browser. The distinction from the previous exercise is that all the form field names and their values are listed on individual lines on the Web page.

Other Types of Form Fields

Text boxes are not the only type of field that forms can contain. Some of the other types of form fields include drop-down lists, radio buttons, and check boxes. Retrieving the values of these form fields is similar to retrieving the value of a text box. You can use the Form or QueryString collection to retrieve the values from these form elements.

Drop-down List Boxes

Drop-down list boxes are used to provide a specific list of choices, called options. In a form, the select tag <select> identifies a drop-down list box. The drop-down list box can be configured to display one option at a time, or the entire list, by using the "size" property in the select tag. When the size property is set to "1", then only one option is shown at a time. The drop-down list box can be configured to allow users to select multiple options, or to limit them to one selection by using the multiple property in the select tag. The text displayed and the values can be specified for each option. Below is the syntax for a drop-down list.

```
<select size = "1" name = "selName" multiple>
<option selected value = "option1value"> Option1 Display Text </option>
<option value = "option2value"> Option2 Display Text </option>
<option value = "optionnvalue"> Optionn Display Text </option>
</select>
```

There is no difference between the code used to display a text box and the code used to display the selection from a drop-down list box. Use the form or QueryString collection to retrieve the value by specifying the name of the field. The syntax below illustrates how to retrieve the drop-down list box value using the form and QueryString collections.

```
<%
request.form("formFieldName")
request.querystring("formFieldName")
%>
```

The only difference between a text box and a drop-down list box is that the user can select more than one item from a drop-down list box if you specify the multiple property in the select tag. If the user selects additional options by holding down the Shift key and clicking on the additional selections, then multiple values are sent to the server. When the script retrieves the values from the form field, all of the values from the form field will appear in a comma-delimited list. The only way to retrieve the individual values from a multiple selection list is by referring to the options by their index number and the name of the form field. Unlike most arrays, the index number for a drop-down list box begins with one. The following example creates a page named select.asp with a drop-down list called selProducts.

1. Create a Web page named **select.asp**. You can use Notepad or another ASP-compatible editor. Make sure that you have saved the Web page to your data directory. Add the beginning HTML tags and the title tag, as shown below.

```
<html><head><title>Drop Down List Form Field</title></head>
<body>
<h3>Select two departments</h3>
```

2. Create the form using the form tag, as shown below. The method should be **post**, because you are using the form collection to retrieve the value of the form field. The action should be **select.asp** because you are processing the form in the same page. The select tag is used to create the drop-down list box. The size property is set to **6**, so that all of the options are displayed at the same time. The multiple property is set to allow the user to select multiple options. The values are displayed in quotes, and between the option tags is the text that appears in the drop-down list box.

```
<form name="frm" method="post" action="select.asp">
<select size="6" name="selDepartments" multiple>
<option value="admin">Administration</option>
<option value="mark">Marketing</option>
<option value="fin">Finance</option>
<option value="hr">Human Resources</option>
<option value="op">Operations</option>
<option value="tech">Technology</option>
</select>
<input type="submit" value="Submit" name="btnSubmit">
</form>
```

3. Add code to detect whether the form collection is empty. If the collection is empty, and you try to retrieve a field from the collection, an error message will result. Below the form, add the code below.

```
<% if request.form <> "" then %>
```

8

4. Add the following code to display the values of the entire form collection. For each option selected, the form collection will return the name of the field, and the value. In this example, the form collection will return the name of the drop-down list box and the value, for each option selected. It does not return the name for the option. All of the values for the selected options are returned with the name of the drop-down list box, selDepartments. In this example, if you selected Marketing and Operations, the form collection that would be returned is "selDepartments=mark&selDepartments=op&btnSubmit=Submit".

```
<% = request.form%>
```

5. Two break tags are used to create two line breaks, to make it easier to read the displayed results.

```
<br><br>
```

6. The next line of code retrieves the values of all of the options selected without the name of the form field. The values are returned in a comma-separated list. This does not display a single value. In this example, if you selected Marketing and Operations, the form collection that would be returned is "mark, op". Two more break tags are used to create two line breaks, to make it easier to read the displayed results.

```
<% = request.form("selDepartments")%>
<br><br>
```

7. To display a single value from the drop-down list, add the following code. Each element in the drop-down list box is referred to by its index number. The index number is enclosed in a pair of parentheses and follows the form name. This code will display the first and second options selected. In this example, if the user selects fewer than two options, an error message will result. A pair of line break tags separates the two selected options.

```
<% = request.form("selDepartments")(1)%>
<br><br>
<% = request.form("selDepartments")(2)%>
<% else %>
<% end if %>
</body></html>
```

8. Save your changes.

9. View the Web page in a browser. Select two items and click on the Submit button. In Internet Explorer you must hold down the Control key to select multiple items. Note that the results page differs from that of the previous exercise because when you select multiple items, the form collection displays the entire list with form field names and values. If you use the form collection and specify the form field name, you receive the values of the form field in a comma-separated list. However, if you specify the index number and the form field name, you receive

the value of just one of the options selected. If you select only one item in the list, you get an error saying, "An array index is out of range." This is because your script was told to write out two selections, and you only selected one. You can use client-side or server-side form field validation to ensure that the user has selected two items.

Check Boxes and Radio Buttons

Check boxes and radio buttons are used to provide lists of choices, similar to a drop-down list box. Like text boxes, check boxes and radio buttons use the input tag. The type property is used to identify the form field. To specify a text, password, or hidden field, the type property is set to text, password, or hidden. To specify a check box, the type property is set to checkbox. Usually, the user is able to select multiple check boxes. You can specify a different name for each check box, which will make it easier to retrieve the individual check box. Below is the syntax for placing a check box in a form.

```
<input type="checkbox" name="chkName1" value="Yes" checked>Click here for Yes
<input type="checkbox" name="chkName2" value="No">Click here for No
```

To specify a radio button form field, the type property is set to radio. The radio button is also known as an option group because the user can only select one option from the group of radio buttons. Unlike check boxes, radio buttons do not allow the user to select more than one choice. If you want to allow the user to select more than one radio button, you must specify a different name for each radio button, effectively making each button its own option group. Below is the syntax for placing a radio button in a form.

```
<input type="radio" name="radName1" value="Yes" checked>Click here for Yes
<input type="radio" name="radName1" value="No">Click here for No
```

For both check boxes and radio buttons, you need to include text to identify each option for the user. Values can be specified for each check box or radio button. If a value is not specified, the value that is sent when the user submits the form is "on". It's important to know that check boxes and radio buttons will not send a value to the server if none of the options is selected. To avoid this problem, you can ensure that one of the options is checked with the checked property.

There is no difference between the code that displays a check box and the code that displays the results from a text box. This is because each check box and text box is identified by a unique name. Use the form or QueryString collection to retrieve the value, by specifying the name of the field. The syntax shown below illustrates how to retrieve the check box value using the form and QueryString collections.

```
<%
request.form("formFieldName")
request.querystring("formFieldName")
%>
```

8

If you assign the same name to multiple check boxes, such as chk1, the entire form collection will display the name and value for each check box selected. If you specify the field name, the values of the check boxes will appear in a comma-separated list. As you did with the drop-down list, you can specify the index number to display the value of one of the check box results. The following code displays the form collection, the list of values, and the first two selected values. Note that the code is similar to the previous example, which displayed multiple values selected from a drop-down list box.

```
<% = request.form%><br><br>
<% = request.form("chk1")%><br><br>
<% = request.form("chk1")(1)%><br><br>
<% = request.form("chk1")(2)%>
```

You can specify the number of values in a form field by using the keyword count. The keyword count can be applied to form fields that are retrieved from the form collection and the QueryString collection. Below is the syntax for retrieving the number of values returned from a form using the count property.

request.querystring("formFieldName").count
request.form("formFieldName").count

The following sample code displays the number of values that a user has selected from the check boxes listed on a form. The check boxes are all named chk1, but each has a different value. The form is saved on a Web page named count.asp. It is important that the form method used is post when retrieving the values from a form with the form collection. An If Then control statement is used to determine whether to display the form or the number of values returned by the form. This method can be used with the form collection or the QueryString collection.

```
<html><head><title></title></head>
<body>
<% if request.form("chk1") = "" then %>
    <form method="post" action="count.asp">
    <h2>Select one or more colors</h2>
    <input type="checkbox" name="chk1" value="1">red<br>
    <input type="checkbox" name="chk1" value="2">blue<br>
    <input type="checkbox" name="chk1" value="3">green<br>
    <input type="checkbox" name="chk1" value="4">black<br>
    <br>
    <input type="submit" value="Submit" name="btnSubmit">
    </form>
<% else %>
    <h2>The number of colors you selected was: </h2>
    <% = request.form("chk1").count%>
<% end if %>
</body></html>
```

In the example above, you could also use the form collection to retrieve and display all of the values selected from the form. To display only those check boxes with a value, use a For Next control statement to loop through the results. The total number of values displayed in the results page is the number identified by the count property. The same example can be reworked to use the QueryString collection instead of the form collection.

```
<h2>You selected:</h2>
<% dim i, results
for i = 1 to request.form("chk1").count
     results = request.form("chk1")(i)
     response.write i & " " & results
     %>
     <br><br>
<% next %>
```

For a group of radio buttons, you need only specify the field name of the radio button. You can only select one option from a group of radio buttons. The following code illustrates how you might retrieve the form collection and the value of a group of radio buttons named rad1. The form collection will only display a single value for the group of radio buttons.

```
<% = request.form%>
<br><br>
<% = request.form("rad1")%>
```

The example below creates a page named checkbox.asp. The first section on the form contains a group of individually named check boxes. The second section on the form contains a group of radio buttons with the same name. A table is used to enhance the layout of the form. In order to avoid an error message, an If Then control statement determines whether the form fields are empty. If all of the fields are empty, then the user did not fill out the form, and the form is displayed. If the user did fill out the form, the results are displayed. This same example can be reworked to use the QueryString collection instead of the form collection.

1. Create a Web page named **checkbox.asp**. You can use Notepad or another ASP-compatible editor. Make sure that you save the Web page to your data directory. Add the beginning HTML tags and a heading, as shown below.

```
<html><head><title>Select a Department</title></head>
<body>
<h2 align = "center">Select a Department</h2>
```

2. Below the body tag, write an If Then control statement to test whether the user has filled out the form. The form fields are named men1, men2, men3, and radW. If the values of all of the form fields are empty, as indicated by an empty string, then the user has not filled out the form, and the form should be displayed. Because the statement extends over several lines, the line continuation character (_) is used.

```
<% if request.form("men1") = "" and _
request.form("men2") = "" and _
request.form("men3") = "" and _
request.form("radW") = "" then
%>
```

3. Create the form, using the form tag. The method should be **post**, because you are going to use the form collection to retrieve the value of the form field. The action should be **checkbox.asp** because you will be processing the form in the same page.

```
<form method="post" action="checkbox.asp">
```

4. Add the form as shown below. The check boxes are named with different names and have different values. Notice that all of the radio buttons have the same name, "radW", but they have different values. A table is used to enhance the layout of the form fields. A break tag is used to add a line break after each option.

```
<table width = "500" align = "center">
<tr>
<td><b>Clothing for Men</h2></b>
<td><b>Clothing for Women</h2></b>
</tr>
<tr><td>
<input type="checkbox" name="men1" value="1">Coats<br>
<input type="checkbox" name="men2" value="2">Ties<br>
<input type="checkbox" name="men3" value="3">Shirts<br>
</td>
<td>
<input type="radio" name="radW" value="1">Shirts<br>
<input type="radio" name="radW" value="2">Dresses<br>
<input type="radio" name="radW" value="3">Finance<br>
</td></tr>
<tr>
<td><input type="submit" value="Submit"><td>
<td></td></tr>
</table></form>
```

5. Add the section of code that will be displayed if the form has been filled out. This section begins with the else statement.

```
<% else %>
```

6. Add the following code to display the entire form collection, the results from the check box form fields, and the results from the radio buttons. Notice that you only have to use one line of code to display the value from the radio buttons, because only one value is returned for the entire group. You cannot select more than one value from an option group.

```
<table width = "500" align = "center">
<tr><td><h3>The Form collection is: </h3></td>
<td><% = request.form %></td></tr>
```

```
<tr><td><h3>Display the check box results</h3></td>
<td>
men1 has a value of <% = request.form("men1")%><br>
men2 has a value of <% = request.form("men2")%><br>
men3 has a value of <% = request.form("men3")%><br>
</td></tr>
<tr><td><h3>Display the radio button results</h3></td>
<td>radW has a value of <% = request.form("radW")%><br>
</td></tr>
</table>
```

7. The "end if" statement is used to close the If Then control statement. The closing body and HTML tags must be included at the bottom of the page.

```
<% end if %>
</body></html>
```

8. Save your changes and view the Web page in a browser. Notice that the form only appears if there is no choice selected in any of the check boxes or radio buttons. It is better to perform form field validation to detect whether the form field is empty before writing the code to process the form.

8

RETRIEVING THE SERVER VARIABLES

The server variables are a collection within the request object. When a browser sends a request for a page to a Web server, it also sends information in the HTTP headers. This information, which includes the name of the page requested, the IP address of the destination Web server, and the IP address of the client, is used to process the request. Therefore you can use the request object to retrieve the names of the HTTP header fields and their values. To retrieve the value of a header, you can specify the name of the server variable. The name of the server variable is enclosed within double quotes and is always written in all caps. Table 8-1 lists several of the commonly used server variables. Below is the syntax for retrieving the value of a specific server variable.

request.servervariables("SERVER_VARIABLE_NAME")

The code below demonstrates how to display the server variables on a Web page. In the first script, the value of the server name is written directly to the browser. In the second script, the server variable is also written directly to the browser, using the write method. In the third script, a variable is used to store the value of the server name, and the value of the variable is written to the Web page. Each of these statements achieves the same results—that is, writing the server name to the Web page.

```
<% = Request.ServerVariables("SERVER_NAME") %>
<% response.write Request.ServerVariables("SERVER_NAME") %>
<% dim strServerName
strServerName = Request.ServerVariables("SERVER_NAME")
response.write strServerName
%>
```

Table 8-1   Server Variables

Variable Name	Description	Example
SERVER_NAME	The name of the Web server	www.domainname.com
SERVER_SOFTWARE	The operating system of the server and the Web server software	Microsoft-IIS/4.0
SERVER_PORT	The number of the requested server port The default is 80	80
LOCAL_ADDR	The local IP address of the server's computer	208.249.124.77
SERVER_PROTOCOL	The protocol being used to deliver the request (HTTP 1.0 or HTTP 1.1)	HTTP/1.1
HTTP_REFERER	The current page the client is requesting the new page from	http://www.domainname.com/index.asp
HTTP_USER_AGENT	The name of the user agent that can be used to determine the browser name and version used on the client	Mozilla/4.0 (compatible; MSIE 5.0; Windows 98; DigExt)
REMOTE_ADDR	The remote IP address of the client's computer	207.252.246.222
URL	The URL of the file being requested	/ip/FormCheckbox.asp
PATH_INFO	The virtual path to the file being requested	/ip/FormCheckbox.asp
PATH_TRANSLATED	The virtual path translated into the physical path (similar results to using the MapPath method of the server object)	C:\InetPub\wwwroot\ip\FormCheckbox.asp
REQUEST_METHOD	The method that a form is using to send information—either post or get	POST
HTTP_CONTENT_LENGTH	The length of the file attached to the header, which may include the results from a form that uses the post method This value is 0 if the get method is used	61
QUERY_STRING	The querystring generated from the name and value pairs from a form that used the get method	chk2=mark&chk5=op&rad1=fin&btnSubmit=Submit
HTTP_COOKIE	Name and value of a cookie, if the client has one written from the same server	CookieColor=Green

Remember that the request object allows you to retrieve information that was sent by the browser. This information includes the server variables. For example, the server variables can identify how much information is being sent to the server in the HTTP_ CONTENT_LENGTH server variable. You can also access this same information using the totalbytes property of the request object. The totalbytes property identifies the total number of bytes that the client sends to the server. Therefore, there is more than one way to access information being sent from the client to the server. The sample code to retrieve the total bytes sent, using both methods, is shown below.

```
<% = request.totalbytes %>
<% = request.servervariables("HTTP_CONTENT_LENGTH") %>
```

You can display individual server variable values, or display the entire collection of server variables. The following sample code lists all of the names and values of several commonly used server variables. To display the entire ServerVariable collection, loop through the collection using a For Each control statement as you did with the form and QueryString collection. The following sample code lists all of the names and values of the server variables. This sample declares a variable named strSV, which will hold the temporary value of the server variable. The code loops through each server variable in the ServerVariable collection, and displays the name and value of each server variable. Figure 8-2 shows how the server variables look when they are written to the Web page.

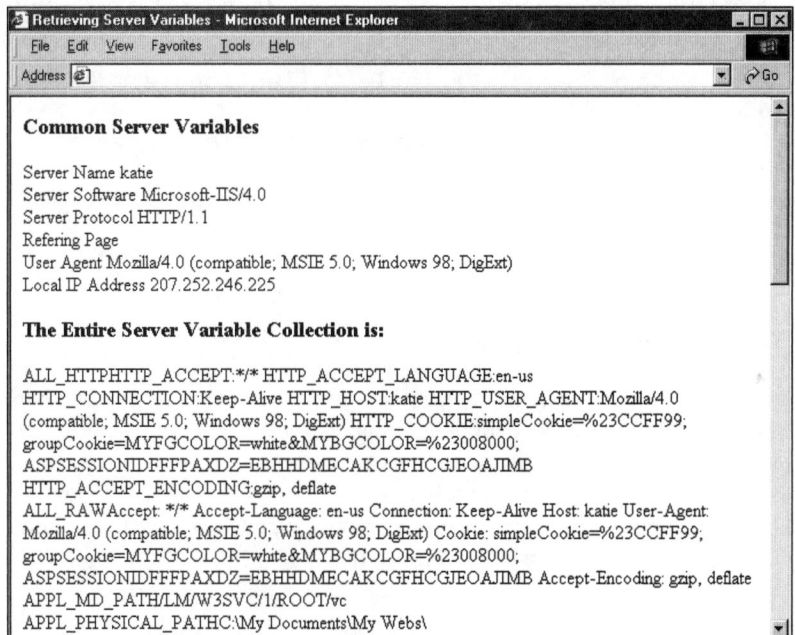

8

Figure 8-2 Displaying the server variables

1. Create a Web page named **sv.asp**. You can use Notepad or another ASP-compatible editor. Make sure that you save the Web page to your data directory. Add the beginning HTML tags and a heading as shown below.

```
<html><head><title>Server Variables</title></head>
<body>
<h3>Common Server Variables</h3>
```

2. Add the code to display the server name, server software, server protocol, URL for the referring page, user agent for the client, and IP address for the server.

```
Server Name
<% = Request.ServerVariables("SERVER_NAME") %>
<br>Server Software
<% = Request.ServerVariables("SERVER_SOFTWARE")%>
<br>Server Protocol
<% = Request.ServerVariables("SERVER_PROTOCOL") %>
<br>Referring Page
<% = Request.ServerVariables("HTTP_REFERER") %>
<br>User Agent
<% = Request.ServerVariables("HTTP_USER_AGENT") %>
<br>Local IP Address
<% = Request.ServerVariables("LOCAL_ADDR") %>
```

3. Add the code to loop through the servervariable collection and display each name and value. Use an equal sign (=) to separate the variable name from the value. Use a break tag to separate each name and value pair from the next.

```
<h3>The Entire Server Variable Collection is:</h3>
<% dim strSV %>
<% for each strSV in Request.ServerVariables %>
<% = strSV %>
<% Response.Write Request.ServerVariables(strSV) %>
<br>
<% next %>
</body></html>
```

4. Save your changes and view the Web page in a browser.

Although HTTP_USER_AGENT sounds like a great way to detect the browser version, it is often more useful to detect what features a browser supports. For example, does the browser support frames? The server variable will not provide this information. However, another server object called the Browser Component will tell you which features a browser supports. You will learn how to use the Browser Component in Chapter 10.

REDIRECTING THE REQUEST TO ANOTHER PAGE

As you learned earlier in this book, in client-side scripting you can redirect a user to another Web page by changing the HREF property of the location object. You can also use the refresh command in the META tag to redirect the user, as shown in the sample code below. When you use the refresh command, you specify the URL and the number of seconds to wait before redirecting the user to a new page. Both of these methods are executed on the client, which can create certain problems. For example, some older browsers do not support client-side redirection. Furthermore, the client is able to see the change in the location bar, and can stop it by hitting the Escape key or by clicking the Stop button.

```
<meta http-equiv="refresh" content="0;
URL=http:/ /www.course.com/">
```

When you use server-side redirection, the client cannot stop the redirection from occurring. The redirect method sends an HTTP header to the browser that says "HTTP/1.1 302 Object Moved" and "Location /newpath/newwebpage.asp". After reading the new header, the browser retrieves the new page. Although this is similar to using the meta tag, it is not the same. If you set the time to refresh the location object to 0 with the meta tag, the user could stop the redirection. When you use the redirect method, users will not even be aware that they have been redirected, and therefore they cannot stop the redirection.

To redirect the user, simply call the redirect method of the response object. The redirect method takes one parameter, the destination URL. The URL can be the absolute URL or the relative URL. The URL should be placed inside double quotation marks; within parentheses is optional. Below is the syntax for server-side redirection using the response object. The parentheses and quotation marks are not required.

response.redirect("URL")

The following sample code shows how to redirect a user with server-side redirection. You can assign the URL directly, or pass the value using a variable. You can redirect users to a specific Web page or a directory. You can specify an absolute or relative path.

```
<% response.redirect("http://www.course.com") %>
<%
dim strGo
strGo = "http://www.course.com"
response.redirect(strGo)
%>
```

You can combine the redirect method with other methods. For example, many companies have purchased multiple domains for marketing reasons. You might be assigned the task of redirecting these domains to specific directories or Web pages on your Web server. In this sample code, the name of the domain is stored in the SN variable. You can compare the value of the SN variable to the value retrieved from the SERVER_NAME server variable. If they match, then redirect the browser to the new directory, Web page, or Web site.

```
<% dim SN
SN = "www.domain1.com"
if request.servervariables("SERVER_NAME")= SN then
response.redirect "http://www.company.com/"
else
end if
%>
```

The sample code below shows how a script can determine which option is selected by a user. A Web page named redirectform.asp contains a form field named selectpage. The form field is a drop-down list box that contains several options. The script will redirect the user to a new page, based on the option that the user selected.

8

1. Create a Web page named **redirectform.asp**. You can use Notepad or another ASP-compatible editor. Make sure that you save the Web page to your data directory.

2. Add the beginning HTML tags, heading, and form, as shown below.

```
<html><head><title>Redirect Form</title></head>
<body>
<h3>Choose a Web site</h3>
<form method = "post" action = "redirect.asp">
<select size = "1" name = "selectpage">
<option value = "1">Course Technology</option>
<option value = "2">Microsoft</option>
<option value = "3">MSDN Online</option>
</select>
<input type = "submit" value = "submit">
</form>
</body></html>
```

3. Save the changes.

4. Create a Web page named **redirect.asp**. You can use Notepad or another ASP-compatible editor. Make sure that you save the Web page to your data directory.

5. Add the beginning HTML tags, heading, and form, as shown below. You need to set the buffer property to **true** so that the content is held at the server until all of the scripts on the page are processed. Otherwise, the Web server will send the HTTP header information. When the script tries to send more HTTP header file information, an error message will result.

```
<% response.buffer = "true" %>
<html><head><title>Redirect</title></head>
<body>
```

6. Add the code that will determine which form field was selected, and then redirect the browser. Notice that the default redirection is to the server variable page that you created in the previous exercise.

```
<%
select case request.form("selectpage")
        case 1
                response.redirect "http://www.course.com"
        case 2
                response.redirect "http://www.microsoft.com"
        case 3
                response.redirect "http://msdn.microsoft.com"
        case else
                response.redirect "sv.asp"
end select
%>
</body></html>
```

7. Save your changes and view the redirectform.asp Web page in a browser.

 If you attempt to redirect the user to another page, after you have written any content to the browser you will receive an error stating, "The HTTP headers are already written to the client browser. Any HTTP header modifications must be made before writing page content." To correct this error, you must include `<% response.buffer = "true" %>` on the top line of your Web page. If you are using ASP 3.0, the buffer property is set to true by default.

CONTROLLING THE OUTPUT TO THE BROWSER

You have already learned how to use the response object to send output to the browser. In this section, you will learn to control how the output is sent to the browser. Information that is sent to the browser is sent in the HTML output stream, which is called the **buffer**. Before ASP 3.0, the buffer property was set to false by default, which meant that the output from the ASP scripts and HTML was sent directly to the Web page as the server processed it. But as shown in the previous exercise, sometimes you need to control when the information is sent to the browser. For example, the redirect method needs to send information in the HTTP header. If the HTTP header content had already been sent to the browser, an error would occur. Therefore, you needed to temporarily hold the content in the buffer by setting the buffer property to true.

When the buffer property is set to true, you can write ASP and HTML statements that are held in the buffer until you direct the buffer to release the output stream to the browser. The response object has a method called flush that releases the output stream to the browser, and another method called clear that erases the contents of the buffer without releasing it to the browser. The response object also has a method called end, which stops any HTML and ASP code from being released to the browser, including any closing body and HTML tags.

The following example, bufferQuiz.asp, demonstrates how to use the buffer and response methods and how to detect whether the user selected a correct answer. In this example, the buffer property is set to true to indicate that the code will control the output to the browser. If the value of the form field radHTTP is empty, then the user has not filled out the form, and the form is displayed. Otherwise, a congratulations message is sent to the buffer. If the user selects the wrong answer, the buffer is cleared and a new message is written to the browser and flushed to the browser. If the user selects the right answer, then the message in the buffer is flushed to the browser using the flush method.

1. Create a Web page named **bufferQuiz.htm**. You can use Notepad or another ASP-compatible editor. Make sure that you save the Web page to your data directory.

2. Add the beginning HTML tags, heading, and form, as shown below. Set the buffer property to **true**.

8

```
<% response.buffer = "true" %>
<html><head><title>HTTP Quiz</title></head>
<body>
```

3. Write a heading that says **HTTP Quiz**. Since the heading is to be displayed at all times, use the flush method to send the content to the browser.

```
<h2>HTTP Quiz</h2>
<% response.flush %>
```

4. Add the code to detect whether the form was completed. If there is no form field value passed, then the form was not completed, and the form is displayed.

```
<% if request.form("radHTTP") = "" then %>
    <form method="post" action="bufferQuiz.asp">
    What is the latest version of the HTTP protocol?<br>
    <input type="radio" value="0" name="radHTTP">1.0<br>
    <input type="radio" value="1" name="radHTTP">1.1<br>
    <input type="radio" value="4" name="radHTTP">4.0<br>
    <input type="radio" value="6" name="radHTTP">6.0<br>
    <input type="submit" value="Correct" name="btnSubmit">
    <br>
    </form>
```

5. Use the write method to write out **Congratulations, you are correct!**. Because the buffer property was set to true, the content will be held in the buffer and not yet displayed in the browser.

```
<% else %>
    <% response.write "Congratulations, you are correct!"
```

6. Use an If Then statement to detect whether the answer was incorrect. If the value of the form field was not "1", then answer was incorrect. Therefore, the code empties the buffer using the clear method. Then, write out a new message to the buffer that says **Sorry, you were wrong!**. Then, use the flush method to send the content in the buffer to the browser.

```
if request.form("radHTTP") <> "1" then
        response.clear
        response.write "Sorry, you were wrong!"
        response.flush
```

7. If the answer is correct, then the code writes the message, which is in the buffer, to the browser, using the flush method. The ending "End If" statements are applied.

```
else
        response.flush
    end if
    %>
<% end if %>
```

8. The end method is applied no matter which answer the user selects. The end method stops the closing tags from being sent to the browser. The end method does not erase content that has already been sent to the browser. If the buffer is cleared and no content has been sent to the browser, a default HTTP header is sent with default HTML tags.

```
<% response.end %>
</body>
</html>
```

9. Save your changes and view the Web page in a browser. View the source code of the Web page. You will see that the closing body and HTML tags are missing. These tags were never sent from the server because the end method was called from the server-side script.

CACHING WEB PAGES

You can use the meta tag to control how the browser will cache a Web page. When you cache a Web page, you instruct the browser to store a local copy of the Web page and all of its contents in a temporary directory on the client. In a default setup in Windows98, the temporary directory is located at `C:\WINDOWS\Temporary Internet Files`. By using a local copy of the Web page, the browser is able to deliver the content more quickly. Because most ASP content is dynamic, it is sometimes preferable not to cache a local copy of a Web page. The response object contains several properties that control when the Web page expires.

It is important to note that today many corporate networks use **proxy servers** that provide security functions. For example, proxy servers are used to hide the client's IP address from the Internet. Proxy servers are also used to decrease network traffic to the Internet by caching Web pages. You can set a property called CacheControl, which prevents the proxy server from caching the page. However, some proxy servers can override this property and cache the pages anyway. Below is the syntax for setting the CacheControl. The CacheControl property is set to Private by default. Private allows the proxy server to cache the Web page. To prevent caching, set the property to Public. You must set the CacheControl property before the HTML tag.

response.cachecontrol = "Public"
response.cachecontrol = "Private"

The expires property of the response object is used to specify the number of minutes after which the cached version of a Web page should expire. Once the cached Web page expires, the browser must retrieve the Web page from the Web site. The ExpiresAbsolute property of the response object also allows you to specify when a cached page should expire, but it sets a specific date and time on which the page expires. The date and time is entered using pound signs before and after the date and time. If you set the expires property to 0, or set the ExpiresAbsolute property to a date in the past, the browser will not be able to cache the Web page. However, some browsers do not allow you to override the cache settings that are set in the browser. Below is the syntax for using the expires and ExpiresAbsolute properties of the response object.

response.expires = minutes
response.expiresabsolute = #datetime#

To cache this page locally for 5 minutes, you could change the expires property to 5. After you change the expires property and view the Web page, a copy of the file is located in the temporary directory. Below is a sample of how to set the cache to expire in 5 minutes and on a specific date and time.

```
<% response.expires = 5 %>
<% response.expiresabsolute = #Dec 1,2001 12:00:00# %>
```

CHAPTER SUMMARY

Processing a Form

❑ Forms pass names and values to the Web server. The name and value are separated in the QueryString by an equal sign. Each name and value pair is separated from other name and value pairs by an ampersand. A question mark is used to append the QueryString to the URL.

❑ The get method sends the name and value pairs appended to the URL. The name and value pairs are then retrieved with the QueryString collection of the response object.

❑ The post method sends the name and value pairs as part of the HTTP request body. The names and values are retrieved with the form collection of the request object.

❑ The names of the fields must be specified in the form if you want to be able to retrieve the values using the request object. A user may select more than one check box, even if they have the same name. Therefore, more than one value is returned from a group of check boxes. A user may select only one radio button from a group of radio buttons with the same name. Therefore, only one value is returned. If no value is specified for check boxes and radio buttons, then a checked form field will send the value "on". If no value is specified and the value is not checked, then no value is sent.

The Request Object and the Response Object

❑ The request object is used to retrieve information from the browser. The request object receives the form field name and value pairs using the QueryString and form collections. The request object can retrieve the server variables that are sent in the HTTP header using the ServerVariables collection.

❑ The response object is used to send information to the browser. The redirect method will redirect the user to another Web page. The response object uses the write method to send output to the Web page. The output to the Web page can be controlled using the buffer property. The clear method clears the buffer, while the flush property sends the contents of the buffer to the browser. The end method stops the page from sending any further content to the browser. The response object is also able to configure the Web page to expire at an identified date and time. The CacheControl property is used to prevent proxy servers from caching Web pages. The expires property is assigned a relative value in minutes. The ExpiresAbsolute property is assigned an absolute date and time, which is surrounded by pound signs.

To retrieve the value from a form field that uses the get method

```
<%request.querystring("txtName")%>
```

To retrieve the entire QueryString collection which includes the name and value pairs

```
<%request.querystring%>
```

To retrieve the entire QueryString collection of name and value pairs

```
<%for each formfield in request.querystring
response.write formfield & " = "
response.write(request.querystring(formfield) & "<BR>")
next%>
```

To retrieve the entire form collection which includes the name and value pairs

```
<%request.form%>
```

To retrieve the value from a form field named txtName that uses the post method

```
<%request.form("txtName")%>
```

To retrieve the size of the total bytes sent using the post method

```
<%response.request(totalbytes)%>
```

To retrieve the first value returned from several selected form fields with the same name

```
<%request.form("txtName")(1)
<%request.querystring ("txtName")(1)%>
```

8

To retrieve a comma-separated list of values from several form fields with the same name

```
<%request.form("txtName")%>
<%request.querystring("txtName")%>
```

To retrieve the number of values returned from several form fields with the same name

```
<%request.form("txtName").count%>
<%request.querystring("txtName").count%>
```

To retrieve a specific server variable value

```
<%request.servervariables("SERVER_NAME").count%>
```

To write out all the server variables

```
<%for each strServervariables in request.servervariables
response.write strServervariables & " = "
response.write(request.servervariables(strServervariables))
next%>
```

To redirect the user to another Web page

```
<%response.redirect "http://www.course.com"%>
<%response.redirect "default.htm"%>
```

To control the output to the browser

```
<%response.buffer = "true"%>
```

To erase the contents of the buffer

```
<%response.clear%>
```

To send the contents of the buffer to the browser

```
<%response.flush%>
```

To stop sending content to the browser

```
<%response.end%>
```

To control caching the Web page

```
<%response.cachecontrol = "Public"%>
<%response.expires = 5 minutes%>
<%response.expiresabsolute = #Jun 10,2001#%>
```

REVIEW QUESTIONS

1. A(n) _____ control statement allows you to retrieve child objects of a parent object.

   a. For Next

   b. For Each

   c. If Then

   d. Do While

2. The character that is used to append the QueryString to the URL is:

   a. ?

   b. &

   c. +

   d. @

3. The character that is used to separate name and value pairs is:

   a. =

   b. ?

   c. /

   d. &

4. The _____ method is used to send the name and value pairs with the URL.

   a. QueryString

   b. form

   c. get

   d. post

5. Which statement correctly retrieves a field named txtName from a form that uses the post method?

   a. request.form("txtname")

   b. request.form(txtname)

   c. request.querystring("post")

   d. request.querystring("txtname")

6. Which statement correctly retrieves a field named txtName from a form that uses the get method?

   a. request.querystring("txtname")

   b. request.querystring(txtname)

   c. request.form("post")

   d. request.form("txtname")

8

7. How is the information sent from a form using the post method?
   a. appended to the URL
   b. in the QueryString
   c. in the location text box
   d. in the body attached to the HTTP header

8. Which property sets the value of an option in a drop-down list box?
   a. option
   b. value
   c. name
   d. form

9. Which property allows the user to select multiple options in a drop-down list box?
   a. option
   b. value
   c. multiple
   d. selected

10. Which property sends a value in case the user does not choose a value?
   a. option
   b. value
   c. multiple
   d. selected

11. Which of the following retrieves the entire form collection?
   a. request.form("txtname")
   b. request.form(txtname)
   c. request.form
   d. request.querystring

12. Which of the following retrieves the number of values for a group of check boxes with the same name?
   a. multiple
   b. selected
   c. count
   d. totalbytes

13. Which of the following allows you to refer to the second value from a group of values that were returned from check boxes all named chkBox1?

    a. request.form("chkBox1")(1)

    b. request.form("chkBox1")(2)

    c. request.form("chkBox1").2

    d. request.form(chkBox1).1

14. Which of the following gives you the size of the form collection being sent from the form?

    a. multiple

    b. selected

    c. count

    d. totalbytes

15. Which of the following displays the server operating system?

    a. request.servervariables(OS)

    b. request.servervariables(USER_AGENT)

    c. request.servervariables(SERVER_SOFTWARE)

    d. request.servervariables(HTTP_VERSION)

16. Which of the following displays the IP address of the client's computer?

    a. request.servervariables(LOCAL_ADDR)

    b. request.servervariables(REMOTE_ADDR)

    c. request.servervariables(LOCAL_IP)

    d. request.servervariables(REMOTE_IP)

17. What are the possible values for the server variable named REQUEST_METHOD?

    a. true, false

    b. on, off

    c. get, post

    d. 0, 1

18. Which server variable is used to store the value of the cookie?

    a. request.servervariables(COOKIE)

    b. request.servervariables(SERVER_COOKIE)

    c. request.servervariables(ALL_COOKIES)

    d. request.servervariables(HTTP_COOKIE)

8

19. Which of the following displays the physical path to a file on the computer?

    a. request.servervariables(PATH_INFO)

    b. request.servervariables(PATH_TRANSLATED)

    c. request.servervariables(URL)

    d. request.servervariables(HTTP_REFERER)

20. Which of the following redirects the user to the Microsoft MSDN Online Library Web site?

    a. response.redirect("http://msdn.microsoft.com/library")

    b. redirect.goto "http://msdn.microsoft.com/library"

    c. request.redirect "http://msdn.microsoft.com/library"

    d. request.goto "http://msdn.microsoft.com/library"

21. Your browser displays an error message about sending HTTP headers. Which of the following would you add to the top line of your Web page to correct the problem?

    a. response.flush

    b. response.buffer = "true"

    c. response.end

    d. response.clear

22. Which of the following sends the content in the buffer to the browser?

    a. response.flush

    b. request.buffer

    c. response.end

    d. response.clear

23. Which of the following configures a cached Web page to expire after 60 minutes?

    a. response.cache = 60

    b. request.buffer = 60

    c. response.absolute = #60#

    d. response.expires = 60

HANDS-ON PROJECTS

Project 8-1

In this project, you will create a Web page that displays the names and values of fields using a For Each statement, since you don't know the names of the fields. Recall from previous chapters that you can list the properties and objects that are in a parent object. The QueryString and forms collections are children objects to the request object. Modify the post.asp Web page to display the form field names and values without specifying the field names.

1. Create a Web page named **registration.asp**. Save the Web page to your data directory. Add the basic HTML tags and a heading, as shown below.

```
<html><head><title>Red River Boats</title></head>
<body bgColor="#99FF66" text="#006600">
<div align="center">
<h1>Red River Boats</h1>
<h2>Customer Registration Form</h2>
<hr color="#008000" width="350">
</div>
```

2. Add a registration form, using the code below. A table is used to format the layout of the form fields on the Web page. Note that the form fields consist of text fields, a hidden field, and a password field.

```
<form method="post" action="register.asp">
<input name="hiddenID" type="hidden" value="1234">
<table align="center" width="350">
<tr><td>E-Mail</td>
<td><input type="text" size="25" name="tEmail"></td></tr>
<tr><td>Username</td>
<td><input type="text" size="25" name="tUser"></td></tr>
<tr><td>Password</td>
<td><input type="password" size="25" name="tPass"></td></tr>
<tr><td>First</td>
<td><input type="text" size="25" name="tFN"></td></tr>
<tr><td>Last</td>
<td><input type="text" size="25" name="tLN"></td></tr>
<tr><td>Address</td>
<td><input type="text" size="25" name="tStreet"></td></tr>
<tr><td>City</td>
<td><input type="text" size="25" name="tCity"></td></tr>
<tr><td>State</td>
<td><input type="text" size="25" name="tState"></td></tr>
<tr><td>Zip Code</td>
<td><input type="text" size="25" name="tZipCode"></td></tr>
<tr><td>Country</td>
<td><input type="text" size="25" name="tCountry"></td></tr>
<tr><td>Phone</td>
<td><input type="text" size="25" name="tPhone"></td></tr>
<tr><td></td><td><input type="submit" value="Register">
<input type="reset" value="Clear Form"></td></tr>
</table></form></body></html>
```

3. Save your changes.

4. Create a new page named **register.asp** that will be used to process the form. Save the Web page to your data directory. Add the basic HTML tags and add the headings shown below.

```
<html><head><title>Red River Boats</title></head>
<body bgcolor="#99FF66" text="#006600">
<div align="center">
<h1>Red River Boats</h1>
<h2>Customer Registration Form</h2>
<hr color="#008000" width="350">
```

5. Declare a new variable called **strForm** to hold a temporary form field name. Use the For Each control statement to loop through each object in the form collection. Use the write method to write out the name of the field, temporarily known as strFormField. Separate the name of the field from the value using blank spaces and an equal sign. Use the write method to write out the value of the strFormField, which is retrieved using request.form(strFormField). Write out a line break tag to separate the name and value pair on a separate line. Use the Next command to cause the loop to start over.

```
<% dim strFormField
for each strFormField in request.form
    response.write strFormField
    response.write " = "
    response.write request.form(strFormField)
    response.write "<br>"
next
%>
</body></html>
```

6. Modify the Web page appearance. Modify the background color and modify the text format using your favorite font.

7. Save the changes. View the registration.asp Web page in a browser. Print your source code. Print the Web page.

Project 8-2

In this project, you will create an ASP page that processes a form that uses different types of form fields. Use an If Then statement to determine whether the user has filled out the form. If so, display the form results; otherwise, display the form. Use the form collection to retrieve the values from the form.

1. Create a Web page named **feedbackform.asp**. Save the Web page to your data directory.

2. The title of the page should be **Feedback Form**.

3. Add a heading formatted as heading 1 and centered that says **Feedback Form**.

4. Create the form named **frmLogin**. Modify the form tag so that the action is **feedback.asp** and the method is **post**.

5. Modify the Web page appearance. Modify the background color and modify the text format using your favorite font.

6. Add the form fields. Add additional properties as desired. Add a text box named **name** with a label that says **Name** and has a size of **25**. Add a text box named **email** with a label that says **E-mail** and has a size of **25**. Add a check box named **Mail** that has a label that says **Do you want to receive e-mail from us?** The value for the check box should be **Yes**, and the check box should be checked by default.

7. Add the text **When is the best time to reach you?**

8. Add a group of two radio buttons named **time**. The labels of the radio buttons should say **Morning** and **Evening**. The values of the radio buttons should be **am** and **pm**. The radio button labeled Morning should be selected by default.

9. Add the text **What is your area of interest?**

10. Add a drop-down list box named **area**. The first option in the list, **Web Design**, has a value of **wd** and is selected by default. The second option is **Web Programming** and has a value of **wp**. The third option is **Web Marketing** and has the value of **wm**. The fourth option is **Web Administration** and has the value of **wa**. Only one item in the list should be viewable at one time. The user should have to scroll to see the other items. The user should only be able to select one option.

11. The Submit button, named **btnSubmit**, should say **Submit**.

12. Use a table to format the layout of the form.

13. Save the changes to your Web page.

14. Create a new page named **feedback.asp**. Save the Web page to your data directory. Display the form results using the form collection. You can use any of the methods covered in the chapter. Use a table to format the results.

15. Modify the results page using different fonts, colors, and images.

16. Save the changes to your Web page. View the feedbackform.asp Web page. Print your source code. Print the Web page.

Project 8-3

In this project, you will create an ASP page that displays the server variables using the request object.

1. Create a Web page named **mysv.asp**. Save the Web page to your data directory.

2. The title of the page should be **Server Variables**.

3. Add a heading formatted as heading 1 and centered that says **Server Variables**.

4. Modify the Web page appearance. Modify the background color and modify the text format using your favorite font.

5. Display the following server variables from the HTTP headers:

   a. the server name

b. the server IP address

c. the client IP address

d. the URL of the page being requested

e. the URL of the referring page

f. the browser version of the client

g. the server software version of the server

h. the virtual path to the file

i. the physical path to the file

j. the HTTP protocol being used

k. the port number being used

6. Create a table that lists all of the server variables. You can use the For Each control statement as shown in this chapter to loop through the list of server variable names and values. (*Hint:* The beginning table and ending table tags should not appear in the For Each loop. Create the loop first, test it, then go back and add the table row and table cell tags.) Modify the table tag to include a border that is one pixel.

7. Save the changes to your Web page. You can modify the appearance of the page using line breaks, images, headings, and fonts.

8. View the Web page. Print your source code. Print the Web page.

Hands-on Project

Project 8-4

In this project, you will create a form named go.asp that redirects users to a page of their choosing.

1. Create a Web page named **go.asp**. Save the Web page to your data directory.

2. The title of the page should be **Redirect Method**.

3. Add a heading formatted as heading 1 and centered that says **Redirect Method**.

4. Modify the Web page appearance. Modify the background color and modify the text format using your favorite font.

5. Create a form that uses the **post** method to send data to a Web page named go.asp.

6. Display a set of radio buttons named **radGo**. Each button redirects the user to one of the following URLs. Display the text label listed. Place a line break after each label.

a. *http://www.course.com*, Course Technology

b. *http://www.microsoft.com*, Microsoft

c. *http://msdn.microsoft.com*, MDSN Online Library

d. *http://www.lifebeyondyahoo.com*, Life Beyond Yahoo!

e. go.asp, Return to this page

7. Add two line breaks and a Submit button that says **Go**.

8. Write an **If Then** statement to detect which option has been selected. If no option was selected, then display the form. Otherwise, redirect the user to the new page. You will have to set the buffer property of the response object to **true** on the first line in the Web page.

9. Save the changes to your Web page.

10. View the Web page. Print your source code. Print the Web page.

CASE PROJECTS

The Walter Library—Intranet Web Site

You have been hired by the local library to enhance its Web site. You are asked to build an intranet Web site that cannot be viewed by individuals outside of your intranet. Create an Intranet home page called walterintranet.htm, and an Internet homepage named walterinternet.htm. Modify the appearance of the two home pages using fonts, colors, headings, and images. You must develop a Web page named walterheader.asp that will detect if the users computer is within the intranet. To test your scripts, use the IP address of your local computer to represent the library's Intranet IP address. If the IP of the visitor's computer matches the IP of the library's Intranet, then the visitor is redirected to the library Intranet home page. If the IP address of the client does not match, the visitor is redirected to the Internet home page. Save the Web pages to your data directory. View the walterheader.asp page in the browser. Print out the Web page and the source code.

ASP Help—Server-side Redirection

You have been asked to create a page that directs a visitor to a site that discusses ASP topics. Create a form on a Web page named asphelpform.asp with a drop-down list box. The options in the drop-down list box should be names of at least ten Web sites that discuss ASP-related topics. Name the form field aspresources. The value should be the domain name and path to the Web site (such as *<http://www.asplearn.com*). Use the Get method to send the information to the server. Create a second page named asphelp.asp that will be used to redirect the user to the new site. Use the QueryString collection to retrieve the value from the form field. You should append "http://" to the value retrieved from the form field. Then, redirect the browser to the new Web site using the URL. Modify the appearance of the Web page by changing the background and font colors and styles. Save the Web page to your data directory. View the Web page in a browser. Print out the Web page and the source code.

The Walter Library—Visitor Profiles

The librarian has asked you to find out who has been visiting the library's Web site. You respond by creating a Web page that displays some of the information that can easily be retrieved when a user visits the Web site. Create a Web page named waltervp.asp. Select at least five server variables that would relate to the client's system and software. Display the

8

results in a table. Modify the appearance of the Web page by changing the background and font colors, styles, and images. Save the Web page to your data directory. View the Web page in a browser. Print out the Web page and the source code.

The Walter Library—Registration Form

The librarian would like to create a registration form so that visitors can apply for a library card online. Create a user registration form on a Web page named walterregistration.asp. Create a form with seven text boxes to collect the first name, last name, street address, city, state, zip code, and phone number. Add two radio buttons that are labeled "Over 21" and "Under 21". The user can only select one of these options. Add a drop-down list box with the following categories of books: Fiction, Non-Fiction, Mystery, Autobiographical, Historical, and Children's. Display the results to the user in the same Web page. Use an If Then control statement to determine whether the user completes the form. If the form collection is empty, then the user did not complete the form. If the user did not complete the form, then redisplay the form. Otherwise, display the results from the form. Modify the appearance of the Web page by changing the background and font colors and styles. Save the Web page to your data directory. View the Web page in a browser. Print out the Web page and the source code.

The Walter Library—Security

The librarian is concerned about the security of the information in the registration form, since the information is sent across the Internet to the Web server. She has asked you to explain how to protect the information from being read by other individuals on the Internet. Using the Internet, find out how to submit a form using a security protocol called SSL. SSL is used to encrypt information as it is being delivered across the Internet. You can look on the Microsoft site, as well as on Verisign at <http://www.verisign.com/http://www.verisign.com and Equifax at <http://www.equifax.com/http://www.equifax.com. Create a page named walterssl.asp.

In this page, write a short description of what the SSL security protocol is and how to submit a form using the SSL security protocol. Give an example of how the form tag is configured to support the SSL protocol. Modify the appearance of the Web page by changing the background and font colors and styles. Save the Web page as walterss/.asp/ in your data directory. View the Web page in a browser. Print out the Web page.

9

MAINTAINING STATE BETWEEN THE CLIENT AND SERVER

In this chapter you will:

♦ Become familiar with the subroutines within the Global Application File

♦ Create application variables using the application object

♦ Create session variables using the session object

♦ Write cookies using the response object

♦ Read cookies using the request object

♦ Become familiar with the kind of information that should be included in a privacy policy

In the past, Web pages were stateless, and therefore could not send or receive information. On the World Wide Web today many, if not most, Web applications frequently send and receive data; e-commerce, for example, entirely depends upon this capacity. In previous chapters of this book, you learned how to use the request and response objects to process forms. In this chapter, you will learn how to create application- and session-level variables that allow you to maintain form information and other data throughout an individual user's session, across the entire application, or across several sessions. You will also learn how to use cookies to maintain information across user sessions.

What Is a Web Application?

Web applications are defined by the Web server software; Personal Web Server, for example, can define a single Web application, while Internet Information Server (IIS) has the capacity to define multiple Web applications on the same computer. A **Web application** is a group of files and folders (including virtual folders) located under the Web application's root directory. In IIS, the root directory may be configured as a virtual Web, or virtual directory. With a Web application, you can create scripts that run when the Web application starts and stops. These scripts are stored within a Global Application File. You can create instances of server objects, such as database access components, within the Global Application File, and then these objects are available to the entire Web application. You can also create application-level and session-level variables that are available to any page within the Web application.

Defining a group of Web pages as a Web application has many other benefits. For example, with IIS you can run your Web application in its own memory space to prevent an error in one Web application from bringing down the rest of the Web applications on your server. This memory space is referred to as an **isolated process**, and is separate from the process that contains the IIS Web server. You can learn more about this at *http://msdn.microsoft.com/library/periodic/period97/IIs40.htm*.

Remember that the Web application executes the subroutines within the Global Application File before executing server-side includes or ASP scripts. A Web application can have only one **Global Application File**. The Global Application File is a text file called global.asa, which must reside in the root directory of the Web application.

The Global Application File contains only server-side script. It does not contain any HTML or client-side scripts. The Global Application File defines four subroutines, which run when the application starts and ends, and when the session starts and ends. Because the Global Application File uses VBScript, the subroutines begin with the keyword "sub" and end with the keywords "end sub". The four subroutines that are available in the Global Application File are:

- Application_OnStart
- Application_OnEnd
- Session_OnStart
- Session_OnEnd

 It is useful to keep all four subroutines listed in the Global Application File, even ones that are not used, since you might want to add code to the subroutines later.

The application and session objects are part of the ASP built-in object model. One of the biggest challenges in creating interactive Web pages is maintaining the state of the user. When you visit a Web site, the site maintains information about you, such as who you are, which pages you clicked and when, when you visited the site, what browser you are using, and what your preferences are. Any information can be tracked across user sessions and across the entire application. Some of this information is retrieved from the HTTP headers, using the ServerVariables collection. Some of this information is retrieved from the properties of the session object, such as the SessionID. Some of this information is retrieved when the user submits form information.

 It is important to consider the privacy needs of the user when you are designing your Web site. If you collect information on a user, you should inform the user. A **privacy policy** is often used to inform the user about the type of information that is being collected, and to inform the user what is being done with that information. You will learn more about privacy policies later in this chapter.

The application object allows you to maintain application state. You can maintain information across the entire Web application with the application object. The application object stores the application variables in the server's memory; the application variables can then be accessed from any page within the Web site. The session object is used to maintain session state. The session state maintains information across a single session. The session variables are also stored in the server's memory. However, the session variables can only be accessed within the session that declared and assigned the session variables. When the session ends, the session variables are released from memory. The application variables are only released from memory when the Web application is stopped, when the Web server is stopped, when the server is stopped, or when the script calls the Remove or RemoveAll methods.

In order to use ASP to maintain state within an application, the client must support **per-session cookies**. A per-session cookie is used to allow the server to identify the client. The per-session cookie is temporary, and is deleted when the session ends. The per-session cookie can be identified in the HTTP headers and the server variables. As shown in Figure 9-1, Internet Explorer 5.0 can be set to allow per-session cookies, but not cookies that are stored on the user's hard drive. To access these settings, start Internet Explorer 5.0, click Tools, and then click Internet Options. Click the Security tab, and then click the Custom Level button. Scroll down the Settings area until you see the settings for Cookies. Click the Cancel button twice to close the Internet Options dialog box.

9

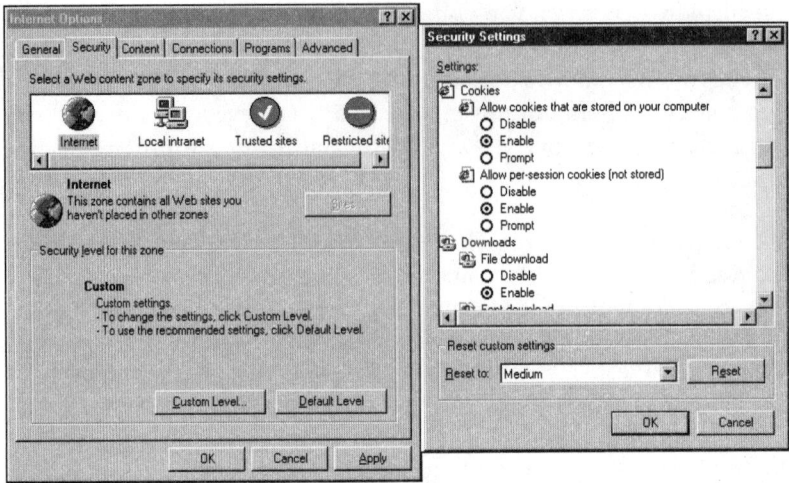

Figure 9-1 Accepting per-session cookies in Internet Explorer

To perform some of the activities in this chapter, you must have access to a Web application. There are many ways that Web applications can be set up on a server. If you are running Personal Web Server, then by default your Web application is located in C:\Inetpub\wwwroot. You can store your Global Application File in C:\Inetpub\wwwroot. If you are running IIS, your default Web application is also located at C:\Inetpub\wwwroot. You can copy your Web application files into this directory. If you are running IIS in a multiuser environment, you can create multiple Web applications using virtual Webs or virtual directories. Installing and configuring IIS is beyond the scope of this book. You can learn more about IIS at *http://www.microsoft.com/ntserver/Web/default.asp* and *http://msdn.microsoft.com/workshop/server/default.asp*. The Help files that are installed when you install IIS will also provide information about configuring virtual Webs and directories. The Help files are located on IIS at C:\WINNT\help\ iis\default.htm. You can also access the Help files through the default Web site at *http://www.yourdomain.com/iishelp/*.

THE APPLICATION OBJECT

The application starts when the first user accesses a page with the .asp file extension. When the application starts, the Application_OnStart subroutine is executed. This subroutine can be used to initialize application variables. Application-level variables can keep track of information across multiple users within the same application. For example, application variables can include the name of the Web application. The application variables are maintained in the application contents collection. Application variables do not change from user to user. Functions and subroutines that are defined within the Global Application File are considered local; they are not available to other Web pages. However, variables that are defined within the

Global Application File are considered global, and are available to all Web pages in the Web application. Previously, when you created Web pages with global variables, these variables were only available to scripts within the same Web page. Because these global application variables are available to any Web page in the Web application, sometimes they are called "super global" variables. You can learn more about the application object at *http://msdn.microsoft.com/library/psdk/iisref/vbob8zw4.htm*.

 You can learn more about the ASP built-in objects and Web applications at *http://msdn.microsoft.com/library/psdk/iisref/iiwauslw.htm*. A quick reference card for all the built-in ASP objects is at *http://msdn.microsoft.com/library/psdk/iisref/iiwaref.htm*.

Application Variables

The application variables are stored within the application object's contents collection as an array of name and value pairs. To create an application variable, identify the application object, the name of the variable inside a pair of quotation marks, the assignment operator (=), and the value. You can identify the variable as part of the application contents collection, but this is optional. If the value of the application variable is numeric, do not use quotation marks. It is useful to add a prefix such as "app" or "a" to the application variable to make a distinction between application- and session-level variables and local variables. Below is the syntax for declaring an application variable and assigning the variable a numeric value. Because the keyword Contents and the Item property are optional, all three samples will produce the same results.

Application.Contents.Item("ApplicationVariableName") = NumericExpression
Application.Contents("ApplicationVariableName") = NumericExpression
Application("ApplicationVariableName") = NumericExpression

Below is the syntax for declaring an application variable and assigning the variable a string value. The string can be an expression that resolves to a single string. All three samples will produce the same results.

Application.Contents.Item("ApplicationVariableName") = "String Expression"
Application.Contents("ApplicationVariableName") = "String Expression"
Application("ApplicationVariableName") = "String Expression"

 Whenever you use application or session variables, you are using system resources, including memory, to store the values for the variables. Therefore you should only use application and session variables when necessary. For example, if a session variable is only used to welcome the user on the home page, then use a local variable instead of a session variable.

Unlike the form collection and QueryString collection, the contents collection of the session object requires you to directly retrieve the values from all session variables. Because the application variables are stored within a collection array, you must specify which variable you want to retrieve by using its name or its index position within the collection array. The first application variable in the collection is identified by the number 1. The following sample code illustrates how to retrieve the first application variable.

```
<% = Application.Contents(1) %>
<% = Application.Contents.Item(1) %>
```

After you have assigned a value to the application variable in the Global Application File, you can retrieve this value in any Web page within the Web application. To retrieve the application variable, specify the application object and the name of the variable. Once you retrieve it, you can do many things with the application variable. For example, you can use the write method of the response object to write out the value of the application variable to the Web page. You can also put the value into a local variable. The sample of code below shows you how to retrieve an application variable named appName, write it to the Web page, and store the value of the application variable in a local variable.

```
<%= application("appName")
dim strAppName
strAppName = application("appName")%>
```

Once the application variable is retrieved, it can be displayed on a page, written to a file, added to a database, and used in functions, procedures, forms, and calculations. If the server is stopped, the memory used to store the application variables is released. Therefore, it is recommended that you assign the static application variables in the Application_OnStart subroutine. These values will be reassigned when the server is restarted. If the values are dynamic, then you should write them to a file or database, retrieve them in the Application_OnStart subroutine, and reassign them to application variables. You will learn how to read and write to the file system and to a database later in this book.

The count property, as shown in the sample code below, will return the number of items in the application contents collection. The count property can also be used to iterate through the entire contents collection. In the sample code below, the script will display the count value, then display each value within the application contents collection. Notice that the iteration must start with 1 because the contents array starts with 1. The code makes use of the count property to determine how many times to iterate through the contents list.

```
The total number of application variables is:
<% = Application.Contents.Count %>
<br><br>
Here is a list of the application variables
in the contents collection: <br><br>
<% dim i
For i = 1 to Application.Contents.Count
     Response.Write(Application.Contents(i) & "<br>")
     i = i+1
next %>
```

The ever-present programming challenge is the various methods that can be used to accomplish the same task. The sample code below uses the element name instead of its index position to retrieve the value.

```
<%
for each eachElement in Application.Contents
     response.write(Application.Contents(eachElement) & "<br>")
next %>
```

Because the contents collection of the application object is an array, it can store strings, numbers, objects, and even other arrays. The following sample code assigns an array named Courses to an application variable named appcourse. Within the global.asa, the code declares a variable named appcourse.

```
Sub Application_OnStart
Application.Contents("appcourse")= 0
End Sub
```

The code below creates the array named Courses, and assigns the contents of the array to the application variable.

```
Dim Courses(3)
Courses(0) = "Internet Basics"
Courses(1) = "Introduction to HTML"
Courses(2) = "JavaScript"
Courses(3) = "ASP"
Application.Contents("appName") = Courses
```

Then, you can easily retrieve the array within any ASP page in the Web application by assigning the array to the application variable. You can then do things like display the individual elements of the array. The sample code below creates the array named Courses, and then retrieves the elements in the array from the application variable appcourse. Then, the code displays the contents of the array using a For Next loop. When you learned to create loops in Chapter 4 they were client-side loops; notice here that the loop is being interpreted on the server, so the response.write method is used instead of document.write.

```
Dim Courses(3)
Courses = Application("appcourse")
Response.write "The list of courses we offer is:"
Response.write "<br><br>"
dim i
i = 0
for each eachElement in Courses
     response.write(Courses(i) & "<br>")
     i = i+1
next
%>
```

You can remove an application variable individually, or remove all of the variables within the contents collection. The remove method allows you to remove a single variable. The sample below would remove an application variable named appcourse. You can use the name or the index number to identify which variable to remove.

```
<% Application.Lock
Application.Contents.Remove "appcourse"
Application.UnLock
%>
```

When the application ends, all of the application variables are removed automatically. The RemoveAll method allows you to remove the entire array of variables. The sample code below releases all the application variables and is usually placed in the Application_OnEnd subroutine in the Global Application File.

```
<% Application.Lock
Application.Contents.RemoveAll
Application.UnLock
%>
```

Creating an Application Variable

Follow the steps below to create the Global Application File, define an application variable, and retrieve an application variable. Your data directory must be defined as a Web application for this activity to work.

1. Open Notepad or your Web page editor.

2. Add the code to create the four subroutines, as shown below. You must specify the runat property to identify that the script is to be processed on the server.

```
<script language = "vbscript" runat = "server">
Sub Application_OnStart
End Sub
Sub Application_OnEnd
End Sub
Sub Session_OnStart
End Sub
Sub Session_OnEnd
End Sub
</script>
```

3. In the Application_OnStart subroutine, declare three application variables.

```
Application("AppName") = "Tech World"
Application("AppEmail") = "info@techworld.com"
Application("AppCounter") = 0
```

4. Save the page as **global.asa** in the root of your data directory. Your data directory must be defined as a Web application for this activity to work.

5. Using Notepad or your Web editor, create a Web page to retrieve the global variables.

```
<html><head>
</head>
<body>
</body>
</html>
```

6. Add the title tags. In the title tags, add the code to display the application name from the application variable AppName.

```
<title><% = Application("AppName") %></title>
```

7. In the body, add a heading that writes out the application name from the application variable AppName.

```
<h2>Welcome to the <% = Application("AppName")%> Web
site</h2>
```

8. Write out the value of the AppEmail application variable, as a parameter to the anchor tag. This allows the user to click the link and send e-mail to the e-mail address that is listed in the AppEmail application variable.

```
<h3>E-mail us at:
<a href="mailto:<% = Application("AppEmail")%>">
<% = Application("AppEmail")%></a></h3>
```

9. Write out the number of visitors from the AppCounter application variable.

```
<h3>There have been <% = Application("AppCounter")%>
visitors to this Web site.</h3>
```

10. Save the page as **globalVariable.asp** to your data directory. View the Web page in your browser.

Notice that in the previous exercise, the information from the application variables was written out to the Web page. However, the number of visitors was always displayed as "0". In order to change the application variable, you must create a script within the Global Application File. Since all users have access to the Global Application File subroutines, it is important that the value of the application variable be locked, so that only one user can change the value at one time. When the user has finished changing the application variable, the variable is unlocked so other users can access it. Changing the application variable does not occur in the Application_onStart subroutine. Because an individual user is modifying the application variable, you need to use the Session_OnStart subroutine to modify the application variable. Follow the steps below to create a Web site counter using application variables.

1. Rename the previous global.asa file as **global1.asa**. You will create a new Global Application File. There can be only one Global Application File in a Web application.

2. Open Notepad or your Web editor.

3. Add the code to create the four subroutines.

```
<script language = "vbscript" runat = "server">
Sub Application_OnStart
End Sub
Sub Application_OnEnd
End Sub
Sub Session_OnStart
End Sub
Sub Session_OnEnd
End Sub
</script>
```

4. In the Application_OnStart subroutine, declare a single application variable called **AppNumUsers**, which will store the total number of users who have visited your site.

```
Application("AppNumUsers") = 0
```

5. In the Session_OnStart subroutine, add a script that increments the AppNumUsers variable by one. You must lock the variable before modifying it, and unlock the variable after modifying it.

```
Application.Lock
Application("AppNumUsers") = Application("AppNumUsers") + 1
Application.Unlock
```

6. Save the page as **global.asa** in the root of your data directory. Your data directory must be defined as a Web application for this activity to work.

7. Open Notepad or your Web editor to create a Web page that will display the number of previous visitors to the Web site. Add the appropriate HTML tags and title the page **Number of Visitors**.

```
<html><head><title>Number of Visitors</title></head>
<body>
</body></html>
```

8. Add a heading 2 tag that identifies the number of users in the site using the AppNumUsers application variable.

```
<h2>There have been <% = Application("AppNumUsers")%>
visitors to this Web site.</h2>
```

9. Save the page as **myCounter.asp** to your data directory. View the Web page in your browser.

The StaticObjects Collection

A **component** is an executable code that is encapsulated within a dynamic-link library (.dll) or in an executable (.exe) file. After you install a component on the server or client, you can use the objects, properties, methods, and event handlers built within the component. The component must be installed and registered using the RegSvr32 utility on the Web server.

A component can contain a collection of objects, and is therefore sometimes referred to as an object. You can read more about components at the MSDN Online Library (*http://msdn.microsoft.com/library/*) and at *http://msdn.microsoft.com/ workshop/components/*.

Before you can use the properties and methods of these objects, you must instantiate the component. You can install components on the server or client. Because installing an untrusted object could compromise security on the client, many users will not allow you to install a component on their computer. The components discussed in this section are server components. The ASP built-in server object has a method called CreateObject that allows you to instantiate an object on the server. When the CreateObject method creates the object, it will immediately begin to use system resources. To conserve system resources, it is important to release objects created with the CreateObject method as soon as they are no longer needed.

An alternative to the CreateObject method is the StaticObjects collection. The StaticObjects collection contains objects added by means of the <object> tag. The application and session object both contain a StaticObjects collection. Session objects created with the object tag are only available to the individual session. Application objects created with the object tag are available to all sessions. If you use the object tag, the server object is not created until it is called from the code. Therefore, use of the object tag does not consume any system resources.

To call a server object with the object tag, the component must be installed on the server. You need to identify the component by the component's registered name (PROGID) or its registered number (CLSID). Below is a sample of code that creates an ad rotator object using the object tag, using both naming conventions.

```
<object runat = "server" ID = "WebAds"
classid = "Clsid:1621F7C0-60AC-11CF-9427-444553540000">
</object>
<object runat = "server" ID = "WebAds"
progid = "MSWC.AdRotator">
</object>
```

The object tag also allows you to insert objects such as ActiveX controls in the client browser. The browser would install the object on the client. For more information on building ActiveX controls using Visual Basic visit *http://msdn.microsoft.com/ library/devprods/vs6/vbasic/vbcon98/vbconcreatingolecomponents.htm*.

Application and session objects can be easily misused. If you store many or large objects within the application or session objects, they will consume large amounts of the server's memory resources, which will negatively affect performance on the server. Another common misuse occurs when you store database objects, such as the connection object, within a session object. The connection object allows you to create and open a connection to a database. Databases limit the number of concurrent connections. If you create a connection object, open the connection, and store the connection in the session object, you will negatively impact the performance on your server. If you store the open connection in a session object, the connections will remain open as long as the session object is open. There could be a large number of sessions that contain a database connection, but are not actively using the connection. This will decrease the available number of database connections for your Web site.

THE SESSION OBJECT

A session begins when a user requests an ASP page from a Web application. This first ASP page request directs the Global Application File to start the Session_OnStart subroutine. When the session ends is not as clearly defined as when the session starts. The session remains open as long as the user remains active on the server. The session ends when the user closes the browser application or when the timeout period has been reached, or when the session is abandoned with the abandon method. When the session ends, the Session_OnEnd subroutine is called.

Within the session object is a contents collection, which contains all of the session variables. Session-level variables track information across a single user's session. Therefore, the values stored in the session variables can vary from user to user. While application variables must be declared in the Global Application File, session variables can be created within any ASP page in the Web application. The session object includes several properties, such as timeout, that help you configure the session. The session object contains several read-only properties, including the SessionID, that allow you to identify an individual user's session. Using the session variables, it is possible to track a variety of information about the user. You can save this information in a file, cookie, or database. This information can be retrieved later when the user opens a new session. Therefore, it is possible to track this information across user sessions. Privacy.Net provides an analysis Web page that lists information that can be monitored on a per-user basis. The Web site only needs one unique piece of information, such as your IP address or your e-mail address, to track your information across user sessions. When you log back into the Web site, the server can retrieve all of the information about you from the file, cookie, or database. You can learn more about the session object at *http://msdn.microsoft.com/library/psdk/iisref/iiapsess.htm.*

In a multiuser environment, a Web application can only have one Global Application File. If each user's directory were located within the default Web site, the directory would be within the default Web application. The default Global Application File would be shared among users. Because session variables do not have to be defined within the Global Application File, you can use session variables without editing the Global Application File. The default Global Application File that is shared among users does not need to be modified. Developers can create their own session variables within their Web pages without conflicting with other developers.

Session Variables

To create a session variable, identify the session object, the name of the session variable in quotation marks, the assignment operator (=), and the value. You can identify the variable as part of the contents collection, but this is optional. If the value of the session variable is numeric, do not use quotation marks. It is useful to add a prefix such as "sess" or "s" to the session variable to distinguish application- and session-level variables from local variables. Below is the syntax for declaring a session variable and assigning a value.

Session.Contents("SessionVariableName")= NumericValue
Session("SessionVariableName")= NumericValue
Session("SessionVariableName")= "StringValue"

After you have assigned a value to the session variable, you can retrieve that value in any ASP page in the Web site. To retrieve the session variable, specify the session object and the name of the variable. Like application variables, session variables can be used to do many things, such as displaying the value in the Web page and assigning the value to a variable. Below is sample code that shows how to retrieve a session variable, write it to the Web page, and store the value of the session variable in a local variable.

```
<%= Session.Contents("SessionVariableName")%>
<%= Session("SessionVariableName")%>
<%dim strSessVarName
strSessVarName = Session ("SessionVariableName")%>
```

Session variables, like application variables, are stored within a collection. You cannot retrieve the variables from all session variables directly, as you can from the form and QueryString collections. You must specify which variable you want to retrieve by its name, or by its index position within the collection. The first session variable in the collection is identified by the number 1. The following sample code shows how you would retrieve the first session variable and write it to the browser.

```
<% = session.contents(1) %>
```

The session object contents collection, like the application object contents collection, is an array. The remove and RemoveAll methods apply to the session object contents collection. You can use the count property to identify the number of elements in the collection. You can also assign an array to a session variable, as you did with the application object.

Using Session Variables

In the exercise below, you will create a page named create.asp that will statically assign the session variables. You will then create a page named member.asp that will retrieve the session variables. If the user is a member, then the Web page displays the session variables that apply to the member. If the user is not a member, he or she will be redirected to a nonmember Web page named nonmember.asp. The nonmember Web page displays the session variables that apply to the nonmember.

Follow the steps below to define and retrieve session variables.

1. Create a Web page using Notepad or another ASP-compatible editor.

2. Create a script to define five session variables, as shown below. The sessMemberName variable will hold the visitor's Name. The sessMemberFee and sessNonMemberFee variables hold the fee that is charged to the visitor's account. The sessMember variable is used to identify if the user is a registered member of the site. Because this page does not need to display any content to the user, you do not need to add any HTML tags.

```
<%
session.contents("sessMemberName")= "Maria Murphy"
session.contents("sessMemberFee")= 35.00
session.contents("sessNonMemberFee")= 50.00
session.contents("sessMember")= "No"
session("sessLastTimeVisited") = now()
%>
```

3. Save the page as **create.asp** to your data directory.

4. Create a second Web page using Notepad or another ASP-compatible editor. This page will display the session variables for nonmembers.

5. Add the basic HTML tags and a heading 2 that says **Nonmembers**.

```
<html><head>
<title>Nonmembers</title></head>
<body>
<h2>Nonmembers</h2>
```

6. In the body, add a script to display the sessMemberName, sessNonMemberFee, and sessLastTimeVisited session variables.

```
Welcome
<% = session.contents("sessMemberName") %><br>
You were last here on
<% = session.contents("sessLastTimeVisited") %><br>
<hr>
The cost of your purchase is
$<% = session("sessNonMemberFee") %><br>
```

7. Use the session variables in a calculation. Calculate the difference between the nonmember fee and the member fee. Format the output as currency with the formatCurrency method, and write the output to the page using the write method.

```
<% dim sv
sv = session("sessNonMemberFee")-session("sessMemberFee")
%>
You would have saved
<% = formatCurrency(sv) %>
if you were a member
</body></html>
```

8. Save the page as **nonmember.asp** to your data directory.

9. Create a third ASP page in Notepad or another ASP-compatible editor. This will be the page that is displayed for members.

10. Add the basic HTML tags and set the buffer property of the response object to true.

```
<% response.buffer = "true" %>
<html><head>
<title>Members</title>
</head>
<body>
```

11. Add a script in the body that checks whether the user is a member. If not, then redirect the user to the page nonmember.asp. If the visitor is a member, then display a personalized statement, which indicates the amount the visitor saved by being a member.

```
<% if session("sessMember")="No" then
    response.redirect("nonmember.asp")
else %>
    <h2>Members Only</h2>
    Welcome
    <% = session.contents("sessMemberName") %>
    <br>
    You were last here on
    <% = session.contents("sessLastTimeVisited") %>
    <hr>
    The cost of your purchase is
    $<% = session("sessMemberFee") %>
    <br>
    <% dim sv
    sv = session("sessNonMemberFee")-session("sessMemberFee")
    %>
    You saved <% = formatCurrency(sv) %>
    because you are a member
<% end if %>
</body></html>
```

9

12. Save the page as **member.asp** to your student directory.

13. View the create.asp page in your browser. This page creates the session variables. You will see a blank Web page. The source code in the browser will show the default HTML tags that are sent to the browser when no content is specified.

14. View the member.asp page in your browser. Because you set the sessMember session variable to "No", the nonmember is redirected to the nonmember.asp page.

15. Go back and change the sessMember session variable in create.asp to **Yes**. Save your changes.

16. View the create.asp page to reset the values of the session variables.

17. View the member.asp page in your browser. Because you set the sessMember session variable to "Yes", the visitor is welcomed to the site, and the amount the visitor saved by being a member is displayed.

In the above exercise, you statically assigned the session variables. In this next exercise, you will create a form that will allow users to enter their name and select their membership status (see Figure 9-2). Then, you will create a page that will retrieve the values and assign them to session variables. The user will be redirected to the same member.asp page that you created in the previous exercise. Instead of assigning the session variables with a static value, this method allows the user to enter his or her name and membership status.

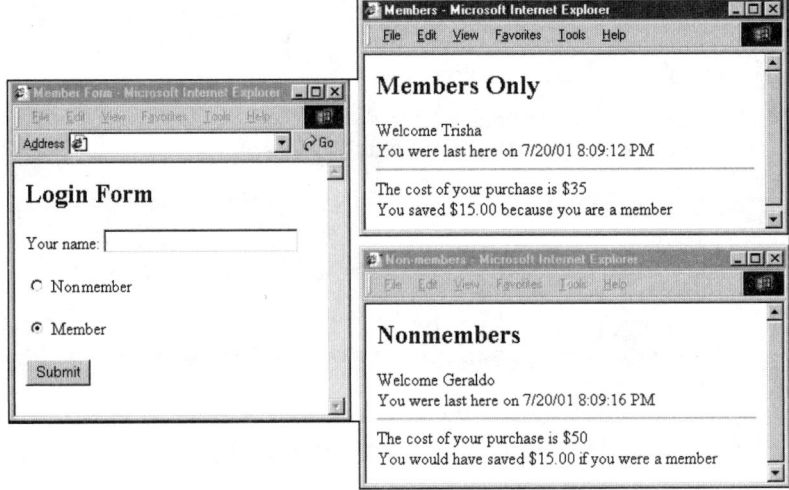

Figure 9-2   Using session variables to store data

1. Using Notepad or your Web page editor, create a page that will contain a form that retrieves the user's information and assigns it to the session variables.

2. Add the basic HTML tags and form tags. The form is going to be sent using the post method and processed by a page called checkmember.asp.

```
<html>
<head><title>Member Form</title></head>
<body>
<h2>Login Form</h2>
<form method="post" action="checkmember.asp">
Your name:
<input type="text" name="txtName" size="25">
<br><br>
<input type="radio" value="No" name="member">
Nonmember <br><br>
```

```
<input type="radio" value="Yes" name="member" checked>
Member <br><br>
<input type="submit" value="Submit" name="btnSubmit">
</form>
</body></html>
```

3. Save the page as **memberform.asp** to your data directory.

4. Open create.asp in Notepad and save the page as **checkmember.asp**. Modify the code as shown below to retrieve the form values, and assign them to the session variables. Notice that some of the session values are static and some are assigned dynamically from the form fields.

```
<%
session.contents("sessMemberName") = request.form("txtname")
session.contents("sessMemberFee") = 35.00
session.contents("sessNonMemberFee")= 50.00
session.contents("sessMember") = request.form("member")
session("sessLastTimeVisited") = now()
%>
```

5. View the memberform.asp page in the browser. Enter your name and select the Member radio button. Click the Submit button to go to the member.asp page. The member information is displayed. Go back to the checkform.asp page and select the Nonmember radio button. Click the Submit button to go to the member.asp page. The nonmember information is displayed.

6. Modify the checkmember.asp page so that when the user completes the form, the browser is redirected to the member.asp page immediately. (*Hint:*You can add the code shown below after the session variables are defined. Make sure the code is inserted before the closing inline script tag.)

```
response.redirect "member.asp"
```

7. Save the checkform.asp page to your data directory.View the checkform.asp page in the browser. Enter your name, select the Member radio button, and click the Submit button. Go back to the checkform.asp page and select the Nonmember radio button. Click the Submit button.

The Timeout Property

The session object contains several properties and methods that can be accessed from ASP pages. One of these, the timeout property, identifies the amount of time that a session is allowed to remain open while the user is inactive. In other words, if a user visits a page, then goes to dinner for an hour and returns, the session will have expired.When the user clicks a new ASP page, a new session is started. Although the user does not notice any change, the session variables are not saved between sessions.You need to assign the session variables to cookies, a text file, or a database in order to save the values of the session variables.You can then retrieve the values and reassign them to the session variables when the user returns to the site. This value is inherited by all user sessions, not just the active user session. The amount of time is measured in minutes, and the default timeout is 20 minutes. If you change the timeout property, do not place quotes around the timeout value. Below is the syntax for retrieving the timeout property of the session object.

Session. Timeout

The timeout property only applies to the session object. The application object does not have a timeout property. The application object is available while the Web application is running. Even if a user's session ends, the contents within the application variables will still be available in the user's next session. Below is the syntax for changing the timeout property of the session object.

Session. Timeout = timeoutInMinutes

The SessionID Property

A unique identifier called the SessionID identifies each session. The SessionID can be obtained via the SessionID property of the session object. This number is determined by several factors, such as the current date and the IP addresses of the client and server. You cannot change the value of the SessionID property, which uses a special session cookie to maintain the session information. When the session ends, the cookie is discarded, including the SessionID number. If the user opens a new session, a new SessionID is issued. Therefore, a SessionID can be used to track a user across a single session, but not across multiple sessions. To track a user across multiple sessions, other information and techniques can be used in combination with the SessionID. For example, cookies and databases are used to store information about the identity of an individual. The SessionID is not a recommended method for identifying an individual in an e-commerce application, because it is possible that duplicate SessionIDs may be issued if the server is shut down or crashes, or if you are using multiple Web servers to host the Web application. Below is the syntax for retrieving the SessionID property of the session object.

Session.SessionID

You can assign the value of the SessionID to a variable or to a field in the database, or you can write the value to a cookie. The SessionID can also be passed as a parameter in a form, as a hidden field, or an input field. The sample code below shows how to display the SessionID property in a text box and a hidden form field (see Figure 9-3).

```
<input type = "text" name = "txtSID"
    value = "<% = Session.SessionID %>">
<input type = "hidden" name = "hiddenSID"
    value = "<% = Session.SessionID %>">
```

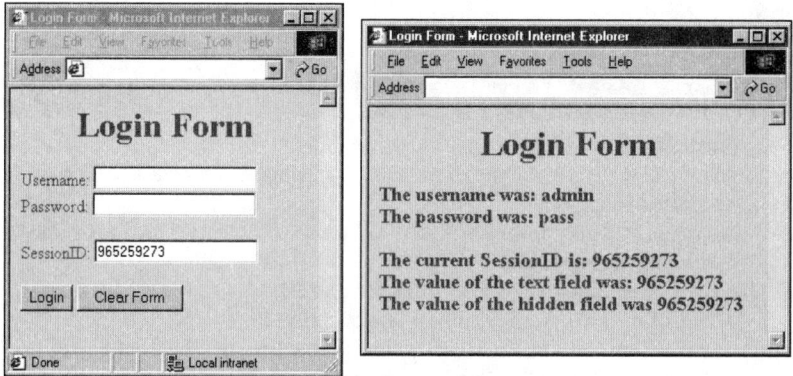

Figure 9-3   Passing the SessionID in a form field

Follow the steps below to pass the SessionID using a form.

1. Create a Web page using Notepad or another ASP-compatible editor.

2. Add the basic HTML tags and a heading, and set the buffer property to true.

```
<% response.buffer = "true" %>
<html><head><title>Login Form</title></head>
<body bgcolor="#FFCC99" text="#800000">
<h1 align="center">Login Form</h1>
```

3. Add the code to validate the user. The username is admin, and the password is pass.

```
<% if request.form("txtName")= "admin" _
     and request.form("txtPass")= "pass" then %>
```

4. Add the code that displays the form field values and the SessionID if the user is the admin account.

```
<h3>
The username was: <% = request.form("txtName") %>
<br>
The password was: <% = request.form("txtPass") %>
<br><br>
The current SessionID is: <% = session.sessionID %>
<br>
The value of the text field was:
<% = request.form("txtSID") %>
<br>
The value of the hidden field was
<% = request.form("hiddenSID") %>
</h3>
```

5. Add the code that displays the form if the user is not the admin account.

```
<% else %>
    <form name="form" method="post"
        action="loginSession.asp">
    Username:
    <input type="text" name="txtName" size="20">
    <br>Password:
    <input type="password" name="txtPass" size="20">
    <br><br>SessionID:
    <input type="text" name="txtSID"
    value = "<% = Session.SessionID %>">
    <input type="hidden" name="hiddenSID"
    value = "<% = Session.SessionID %>">
    <br><br>
    <input type="submit" value="Login" name="btnLogin">
    <input type="reset" value="Clear Form" name="btnClear">
    </form>
```

6. Add the closing tags.

```
<% end if %>
</body></html>
```

7. Save the Web page as **loginSession.asp** to your data directory.

8. View the Web page in your browser. Fill out the form, using the username **admin** and the password **pass**. Click the **Login** button. The value of the current SessionID should be the same for the hidden and text box form fields.

9. Close the browser, which will end the session. View the Web page again in your browser. The value of the SessionID should be different.

The Abandon Method

The session stops when the session timeout is reached, the user closes the browser, or the session is abandoned. Some browsers keep the session open, even if the user is visiting another Web site. Most browsers end the session when the browser application is closed. You can force the session to be abandoned by calling the abandon method of the session object. The abandon method stops the session gracefully; the ASP engine executes the Session_OnEnd subroutine before ending the session. However, because all browsers don't treat sessions the same way, sometimes the sessions remain open, even if the abandon method is called, until the user closes the browser. Some Web sites will include a Logout button that will execute scripts to close the session gracefully for the user. You could call the abandon method when the logout script is called. Below is the syntax for abandoning the session with the abandon method.

Session.Abandon

The abandon method can be used to log a user out of a protected site. You can use the redirect method or create a Logout button or hyperlink that will direct the user to a logout page.

CodePage and LCID Properties

Today many Web applications are being used internationally. For international Web sites, other useful session properties include the CodePage and LCID. These properties are used when developing Web sites that will be used outside of the U.S. The CodePage identifies the type of characters, digits, and punctuation symbols that are specific to a location, which is referred to as the **locale**. The CodePage is assigned a numeric value that must match the same character set that is installed on the server. If you are running PWS on a computer that has the default settings, the LCID will return 0. If you are running IIS on a server with the default settings, the LCID will return 1252, which represents the Western Language (the U.S. English language). Whether you are running PWS or IIS, the default LCID setting is 2048, which represents the U.S. English locale ID. Below is the code used to display the CodePage settings.

```
<% = Session.CodePage %>
```

The LCID is used to format the local settings for date, time, and currency. Below is sample code that displays the default LCID settings and formats an integer with the default setting. Then the code sets the LCID property to another value, and formats the integer with the new currency setting. The LCID value 2057 represents British English. Once you change the LCID, any page within the session will use those settings. To return to the default settings, the user must close the browser to end the session, or the user can call the abandon method from the script to end the session.

```
<% dim i
i = 2420.35 %>
The default LCID is <% = Session.LCID %><BR>
Today is : <% = date() %> <BR>
The cost was: <% = formatcurrency(i) %><BR><BR>
<% Session.LCID = 2057 %>
The new LCID is <% = Session.LCID %><BR>
Today is : <% = date() %> <BR>
The cost was: <% = formatcurrency(i) %>
```

COOKIES

Cookies are used to maintain information about an individual user across sessions. Recall from earlier chapters that a cookie is a small piece of information that is stored on a client's local computer. If you are using Netscape Navigator, all cookies are stored as a single text file named cookies.txt, which usually resides in the root directory of the Netscape application. All Web servers have the ability to write to this cookie file. If you are using Internet Explorer on Windows 98 or 95, then the cookies are usually located in a directory called

Cookies, under the system root directory, where you store your temporary Internet files. In Windows 2000, they are usually in the directory in which you store your temporary Internet files. Each Web server writes a separate cookie file in this directory.

Because clients can delete their cookies at any time, your Web application should not be dependent upon the existence of a cookie. Always provide an alternate method for users who elect not to accept cookies, or who delete their cookies. Customers often misunderstand the purpose, value, structure, and security of cookies. It's recommended that you create a Web page on your site that informs the user of the site's privacy and security policies. On this page, you should provide a definition of cookies, inform the user whether the site uses cookies, explain what information is stored in the cookies, and describe what the cookies are used for. You should also inform the user that only the server that writes the cookie can read the cookie. TRUSTe (*www.etrust.com*) provides samples of what you might want to include in your privacy and security policy Web page. Below is a list of Web pages that contain more information about cookies, privacy issues, and links to more Web sites that discuss cookies.

Life Beyond Yahoo Web sites:

- *http://www.lifebeyondyahoo.com/life/cookies.asp*

Microsoft Web sites:

- *http://www.microsoft.com/info/cookies.htm?RLD=291*

- *http://msdn.microsoft.com/library/wcedoc/wcecomm/wininet_18.htm*

- *http://msdn.microsoft.com/library/default.asp?URL=/library/wcedoc/wcecomm/wininet_16.htm*

- *http://msdn.microsoft.com/workshop/server/toolbox/cookie.asp*

Most users do not have a thorough understanding of what a cookie is all about. The cookie file stores the name of the cookie, the value, and the name of the server that wrote the cookie. Figure 9-4 shows the contents of a cookie. The information stored in a cookie could easily be stored on the server. Storing the cookies on the client provides a means of automating activities such as the login process or filling out a form. It's very useful to provide a sample of what a cookie looks like, on the security and privacy page. Cookies are limited to four KB of data. Most cookies are about 100–200 bytes in size. The maximum number of cookies allowed is currently 300. If the limit is reached, the oldest cookies are deleted. The maximum disk space for cookies is 1.2 MB, which is about the size of a floppy disk. Today, hard disk drives are available that can hold gigabytes of data. Therefore, cookies do not "eat up" a client's hard drive space. Most of the time, the culprit is the browser cache file that contains all of the graphics and Web pages that the client has visited.

Figure 9-4 A cookie written by Internet Explorer

Writing a Cookie

ASP provides a simple method to write and read cookies. Cookies are written using the response object, and read using the request object. To create a cookie, you name the cookie and give it a value. You must also identify when the cookie expires. The browser deletes cookies when they reach their expiration date. Some browsers automatically delete cookies with no expiration date when they close. Therefore, it is important to set the expiration date for a cookie each time the cookie is written. The date can be an absolute reference to a month, day, and year, or a relative date. Below is the syntax for writing a simple cookie using an absolute expiration date.

```
<% Response.Cookies("myCookie") = "value" %>
<% Response.Cookies("myCookie").Expires = "MM DD,YYYY" %>
```

You will often wish to use relative dates when defining expiration dates, because if you use an absolute date, then the page must be edited each time the date is reached. A relative date requires no additional maintenance, because the date is relative to the current date. Remember that the date object returns the current date. You can specify the number of days (n) from the current date that you want the cookie to expire. If your visitors visit daily, then you can set the cookie to expire in "Date + 1" days. If your visitors visit monthly, you can set the cookie to expire in "Date + 30" days. Below is the syntax for writing a simple cookie using a relative date.

```
<% Response.Cookies("myCookie") = "value" %>
<% Response.Cookies("myCookie").Expires = "Date + n" %>
```

The following sample code creates a cookie named memberstatus with a value of active. The expiration date is set to 30 days from the current date.

```
<% Response.Cookies("memberstatus") = "active" %>
<% Response.Cookies("memberstatus").Expires = "Date + 30" %>
```

If you want the browser to delete the cookie, you can specify a date in the past, such as "Date − 1" or "July 4, 1776". The browser will then delete the cookie because the cookie has expired. You should offer users the option to remove their cookie, or to view their cookie in the browser. This will help reassure them, and educate them about the kinds of information that cookies actually store. Below is the syntax for deleting a cookie using a relative date.

```
<% Response.Cookies("myCookie") = "value" %>
<% Response.Cookies("myCookie").Expires = "Date - n" %>
```

The value assigned to the cookie can be hard-coded in the script, or soft coded. Hard-coded means that the value is written in the code and will not change unless the script is rewritten. The value can be specified directly or come from a variable. Soft-coded means that the value may change. The value is often obtained from a form, or the script. The following sample code shows how to retrieve the value from a form, and assign the value to a cookie.

```
dim username
username = Request.Form("txtUserName")
<% Response.Cookies("myCookie") = username %>
<% Response.Cookies("myCookie").Expires = "Date + 30" %>
```

You might want to store more than one value in a cookie. For example, you might store the user preferences or contact information in a cookie. You can create a cookie with multiple names and values. This type of cookie file is really a **named group of cookies**. To create the cookie, name the group of cookies with the same name, and then name the individual cookies along with their values.

The named group of cookies is also referred to as a **dictionary cookie**, and the individual cookies within it are sometimes referred to as cookie **keys**.

All cookies within the named group of cookies share the same expiration date. When you write a cookie that contains multiple cookies, you must write them all at the same time. Only the cookies specified when the cookie is written are created. If a cookie has already been written with the same name, and you are changing the cookie or changing the expiration date, the cookie is actually overwritten. Therefore if you intend to make a cookie persist by rewriting the cookie each time the visitor comes to your site, be sure to write all of the cookies and their values at that time. The syntax for writing the cookie requires that you specify the name of the group of cookies.

Notice that the response object will write the cookie. The write method is not used to write the cookie. The write method is used to write the value of a string to the Web page. The Response.Cookies object actually sends the cookie to the browser that writes the cookie to the client's file system.

Below is the syntax for writing a group of cookies.

<% Response.Cookies("GroupCookieName")("CookieName_1")="value" %>
<% Response.Cookies("GroupCookieName")("CookieName_2")="value" %>
<% Response.Cookies("GroupCookieName")("CookieName_n")="value" %>
<% Response.Cookies("GroupCookieName").Expires = "Date [+/-] n" %>

The following sample code creates a named group of cookies, called login. The expiration date is set to 30 days from the current date.

```
<% Response.Cookies("login")("username") = "admin" %>
<% Response.Cookies("login")("password") = "pass" %>
<% Response.Cookies("login")("email") = "me@company.com" %>
<% Response.Cookies("login").Expires = "Date + 30" %>
```

Reading a Cookie

You can retrieve a cookie's value—whether from a simple cookie or from a group of cookies—using the request object. To retrieve a simple cookie with one value, specify the name of the cookie. One of the benefits of using ASP rather than client-side scripting is that the request object parses out the cookie names and values for you. It is easy to retrieve the value of a cookie with one line of code. Below is the syntax for retrieving a simple cookie with one value.

<% Request.Cookies("CookieName") %>

To retrieve the value of a single cookie from a group of cookies, you must identify the name of the cookie group as well as the name of the individual cookie. Below is the syntax for retrieving a single cookie from a group of cookies.

<% Request.Cookies("GroupCookieName")("CookieName_n") %>

The cookie is passed from the client to the server in the HTTP header. You can retrieve the entire cookie from the header by using the request object. The variables collection includes all of the HTTP variables, including the HTTP_COOKIE variable, which contains the cookie. You can use this server variable to write the entire cookie to the Web page. This is an effective way to demonstrate to the client what the cookie looks like, without having to explain where the cookies are located or how to open the cookie files. Below is the syntax for retrieving a cookie from the HTTP header using the server variable HTTP_COOKIE. You can look at the list of server variables available at *http://msdn.microsoft.com/library/psdk/ iisref/vbob5vsj.htm.*

<% Request.Servervariables("HTTP_COOKIE") %>

There is a property called "hasKeys" that identifies whether a cookie contains multiple cookies. It is useful to test a cookie to see if it contains multiple values in order to avoid accidentally writing over a cookie (remember that when you rewrite a cookie that has multiple cookies, you must write the values of all of the cookies contained in the group). If you leave one of the values out, that individual cookie will be deleted from the group. The hasKeys property returns a Boolean value—true or false. If the cookie contains multiple cookies, then the hasKeys property returns a "true" value. Below is the syntax for identifying if a cookie has multiple cookies.

<% Request.Cookies("GroupCookieName").HasKeys %>

Creating Web Pages That Use Cookies

Cookies can be written and retrieved from the same Web page, or from different Web pages. Follow these steps to hard-code a single cookie using a variable. The value of the cookie is used to change the background color by assigning the value of the cookie to the bgColor property.

1. Create a Web page using Notepad or another ASP-compatible editor.

2. At the top of the page, add a script to write a cookie named **simpleCookie**. Using the code below, get the value of the cookie from a variable named myBgColor. The value of myBgColor is hard-coded as **#CCFF99**. Set the expiration date for the cookie to **30** days from today.

```
<%
dim myBgColor
myBgColor= "#CCFF99"
Response.Cookies("simpleCookie")= myBgColor
Response.Cookies("simpleCookie").Expires = Date + 30
%>
```

3. Add the basic HTML tags and a title that says **Simple Cookie**.

```
<html><head><title>Simple Cookie</title></head>
```

4. Retrieve the value of the cookie using the request object. The value of the cookie is used as the parameter for the bgColor property for the body tag.

```
<body bgColor = "<% = Request.Cookies("simpleCookie") %>">
```

5. Add a heading formatted as heading 1, center-aligned, that says **Simple Cookie**.

```
<h1 align="center">Simple Cookie</h1>
```

6. Write the value of the cookie to the Web browser, using the write method.

```
<h2>The value of your cookie was:
<% = request.cookies("simpleCookie") %></h2>
</body></html>
```

7. Save the page as **simplecookie.asp** to your data directory. View the Web page in your browser. The Web page should have a colored background.

Cookies can also be soft-coded, and can obtain their values from users. In the example below, shown in Figure 9-5, the user enters information onto a form, and the values from the form are used to write a group of cookies. The values from the cookies could be used to perform various tasks, such as logging the user into the network, or modifying the user's profile. In this example, the values of the cookies will be displayed in the browser.

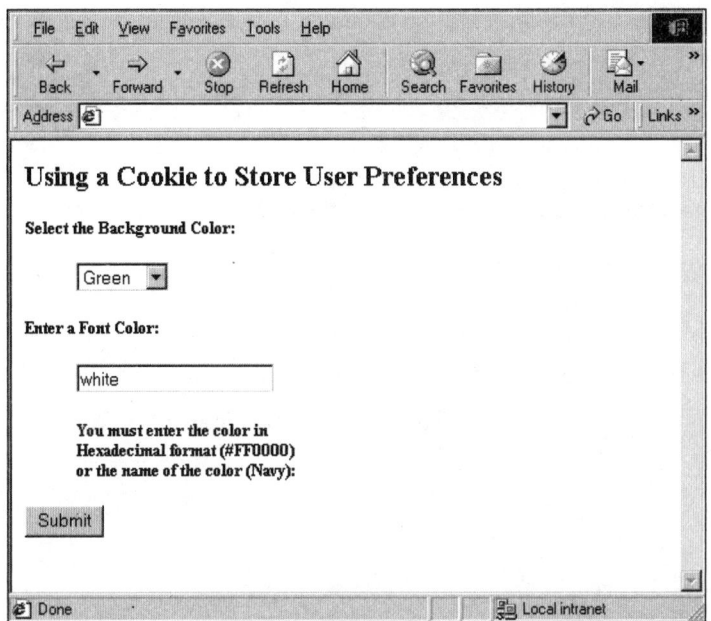

Figure 9-5   Writing the values from a form to a cookie

1. Create a Web page using Notepad or another ASP-compatible editor.

2. Add the HTML tags and a heading to the page.

```
<html><head><title>Choose Cookie</title></head>
<body><h1>Using a Cookie to Store User Preferences</h1>
```

3. Add the form. The form will have one drop-down list box that lists seven colors. The color chosen will be used to format the background of the Web page.

```
<form method="post" action="groupcookies.asp">
<h3>Select the Background Color:</h3>
<blockquote><p><select size="1" name="bc">
<option value="#008000">Green</option>
<option value="#800000">Maroon</option>
<option value="#800080">Purple</option>
<option value="#000080">Navy</option>
<option value="#FF0000">Red</option>
<option value="#000000">Black</option>
<option value="#FFFFFF">White</option>
</select></p></blockquote>
```

9

4. Add a text form field to allow the user to type in a selection for the font color.

```
<h3>Enter a Font Color:</h3>
<blockquote><p>
<input type="text" name="fc" size="20"></p>
<h3>You must enter the color in <br>
Hexadecimal format (#FF0000) <br>
or the name of the color (Navy):</h3></blockquote>
<p>
<input type="submit" value="Submit" name="btnSubmit">
</p>
</form></body></html>
```

5. Save the Web page as **bgcolorform.asp** to your data directory.

6. Create a Web page using Notepad or another ASP-compatible editor. Add a script at the top of the page that retrieves the values for the text and background colors from the form.

```
<%
dim bc, fc
bc = request.form("bc")
fc = request.form("fc")
```

7. Add code to write the group of cookies. The name of the group of cookies is "gc", and the names of the individual cookies are "bc" and "fc". Set the cookie to expire in 30 days.

```
Response.Cookies("gc")("bc") = bc
Response.Cookies("gc")("fc") = fc
Response.Cookies("gc").Expires = Date + 30
%>
```

8. Add the basic HTML tags, including the title tag.

```
<html><head><title>Simple Cookie</title></head>
```

9. Retrieve the values of the cookies, using the request object. Use the values as the parameters for the bgColor and text properties for the body tag.

```
<body bgColor = "<% = request.cookies("gc")("bc") %>"
   text = "<% = request.cookies("gc")("fc") %>">
```

10. Add the code to write a heading and the values of the cookies to the Web page.

```
<h1 align = "center">
Using a Cookie to Retrieve User Preferences</h1>
<h2>The name of the cookie group was gc</h2>
<h2>The value of your cookie named bc was:
<% = request.cookies("gc")("bc") %></h2>
<h2>The value of your cookie named fc was:
<% = request.cookies("gc")("fc") %></h2>
</body></html>
```

11. Save the Web page as **groupcookies.asp** to your data directory.

12. View the bgcolorform.asp page using your browser. Select a color from the drop-down list box, and type a valid color in the text box. When you click on the Submit button, the page that appears will use the colors you selected to alter the background and font colors for the Web page.

Creating Pages Without Cookies

You can create applications that can maintain information without using cookies. One of the choices is to carry the information across pages using a hidden text field. This option would require you to use a form within each page of your Web application. Another method is to use a hard-coded hyperlink. When users log in, you would assign each a unique user identifier. You can create a hyperlink that uses this identifier to identify the user. All hyperlinks would need to be encoded with this identifier. You would append the identifier to the URL. Because you are essentially creating a QueryString, you could use the request object to retrieve the value of the identifier. A third option would be to use the session identifier (SessionID) to identify the client. The sample code below shows how a hyperlink could be hard-coded with an identifier. The first sample hard-codes the identifier. The second sample retrieves the value from a form field. The third sample retrieves the value from a session variable. The fourth sample uses the SessionID as the identifier.

```
<a href = "cart.asp?ID=123456">
Click here to see your cart</a>
<a href = "cart.asp?ID=<% = Request.QueryString("userid")
%>">
Click here to see your cart</a>
<a href = "cart.asp?ID=<% = Session("userid") %>">
Click here to see your cart</a>
<a href = "cart.asp?ID=<% = Session.SessionID %>">
Click here to see your cart</a>
```

If the user turns off cookies, only the first method can be used, because using ASP requires cookies. To avoid having to hard-code the identifier, you could use client-side scripting to retrieve the value from the form when the user enters a user ID. You could use the Document Object Model to set the HREF property for that anchor object. However, that would only help create the hyperlink on the fly for that page. There would be no way to use client-side scripting to retrieve information from a previously visited page. Therefore, many Web sites do require users to have session cookies turned on. Then, they can use the application and session variables. You can educate the user on the differences between client-side cookies and session cookies. Information from the session can then be sent to a file or database to connect a user across multiple sessions. Whatever method is chosen, it is important to be able to maintain state for the duration of the user's session.

9

Privacy Policies

Today many users do not want to allow Web sites to keep information about them. Privacy is an issue that all Web sites must address, whether they use cookies or not. Below are some Web sites that discuss privacy issues and privacy policies.

- TRUSTe *(http://www.truste.org/)*

- Electronic Frontier Foundation *(http://www.eff.org/)*

- Life Beyond Yahoo *(http://www.lifebeyondyahoo.com/life/privacy.asp)*

- Privacy.net *(http://www.privacy.net/)*

- CDT – Center for Democracy & Technology *(http://www.cdt.org/)*

- ACP – Americans for Computer Privacy *(http://www.computerprivacy.org/)*

- Watchdog *(http://watchdog.cdt.org/)*

CHAPTER SUMMARY

Web Applications

- A Web application is a group of files and folders configured by Web server software. The Global Application File is used to maintain information that is used across the Web application. The Global Application File is called global.asa and must reside in the root directory of the Web application. The Global Application File contains four subroutines that are executed when the application starts and stops, and when the user session starts and stops.

The Application Object

- The application object can be used to create application variables that will apply to all users. The application variable must be defined in the Global Application File. If you change an application variable, you need to lock the variable before changing the value, and then unlock the variable afterward. This prevents multiple users from changing the values at the same time.

The Session Object

- The session object can be used to create session variables that apply to a specific user and a specific session. Session variables can be created in any Web page, and retrieved by any Web page within the Web application.

- The session object contains other useful properties, such as timeout. The timeout property will limit the length of the user session. The default timeout property is set to 20 minutes.

❏ The SessionID property is assigned by the server, and provides a way to identify the client during the user session.

❏ The abandon method can be used to stop the individual user session. The user can also stop the session by closing the browser application.

Cookies

❏ A cookie can be used to maintain information across multiple sessions for a specific user. The cookie is a text file that is stored on the client's computer. Web customers should be educated on what the cookie is used for, and how the cookie affects their computer system. The cookie is passed in the header with the other HTTP server variables.

❏ A simple cookie can be written to store a single value, or multiple cookies can be stored in a named group of cookies. The cookie is written using the response object, and retrieved using the request object.

To create an application variable in the Global Application File

```
Application("AppName") = "Tech World"
Application.Contents("AppName") = "Tech World"
```

To retrieve an application variable from a Web page and assign it to a variable

```
<%dim strAppName
strAppName = Application("AppName")%>
```

To change the value of an application variable in the Global Application File

```
Application.Lock
Application("AppNumUsers") = Application("AppNumUsers") + 1
Application.Unlock
```

To create a session variable in an ASP page

```
<%Session("sessMember") = "Maria Murphy"%>
<%Session.Contents("sessMember") = "Maria Murphy"%>
```

To retrieve a session variable from a Web page and assign it to a variable

```
<%dim strSessMember
strSessMember = Sess("sessMember")%>
```

9

To write the timeout property of the session object to the Web page

```
<%= Session.Timeout%>
```

To change the timeout property of the session object

```
<%Session.Timeout = 30%>
```

To call the abandon method of the session object

```
<%Session.Abandon%>
```

To retrieve the SessionID property of the session object

```
<%Session.SessionID%>
```

To create a simple cookie

```
<%Response.Cookies("simpleCookie")= "red"%>
```

To read a simple cookie and write it to the Web page

```
<%= Request.Cookies("simpleCookie")%>
```

To create a named group of cookies

```
<%Response.Cookies("gc")("bc")= "red"%>
<%Response.Cookies("gc")("fc")= "white"%>
<%Response.Cookies("gc").Expires = Date + 30%>
```

To read a cookie from a group of cookies and write it to the Web page

```
<%= Request.Cookies("gc")("bc")%>
<%= Request.Cookies("gc")("fc")%>
```

To read an entire cookie from the server variable and write it to the Web page

```
<%= Request.Servervariables("HTTP_COOKIE")%>
```

To determine if the cookie contains a group of cookies

```
<%Request.Cookies("gc").HasKeys%>
```

Review Questions

1. The Global Application File is located in:

   a. the root directory

   b. the include directory

   c. the cgi-bin directory

   d. the scripts directory

2. The name of the Global Application File is:

   a. global.inc

   b. global.gbl

   c. global.asp

   d. global.asa

3. Which of the following would create an application variable named "appName"?

   a. Request.Application(appName)

   b. Application.Response(appName)

   c. Contents.Application("appName")

   d. Application("appName")

4. Which of the following would create a session variable named "sessName"?

   a. Request.Session(sessName)

   b. Session.Response(sessName)

   c. Contents.Session ("sessName")

   d. Session("sessName")

5. Session variables must be defined in the Global Application File. True or False?

6. Which of the following subroutines is not contained in the Global Application File?

   a. Session_OnStart

   b. Session_OnAbandon

   c. Application_OnStart

   d. Application_OnEnd

7. Which session property is used to change the amount of time that a session is open?

   a. Session.Time

   b. Timeout.Session

   c. Session.Close

   d. Session.Timeout

8. Which of the following sets the user timeout property to half an hour?

    a. Session.Time(0.5)

    b. Timeout.Session = 0.5

    c. Session.Timeout = 30

    d. Session.Timeout(30)

9. Which session property retrieves the identification number for the session?

    a. Session.ID()

    b. Session.SessionID

    c. SessionId.Session

    d. Session.SID

10. Which method forces the end to the session?

    a. Session.End()

    b. Session.Abandon

    c. Abandon.Session

    d. Abandon.Session()

11. Which method stops users from changing an application variable?

    a. Application.Lock

    b. Session.Lock

    c. Application.Unlock

    d. Session.Open

12. If you want to track a variable across all users, which of the following should you use?

    a. local variable

    b. application variable

    c. session variable

    d. cookie

13. If you want to track a variable across a specific user in a single session, which of the following should you use?

    a. local variable

    b. application variable

    c. session variable

    d. cookie

14. If you want to track a variable across a specific user over several sessions, which of the following should you use?

   a. local variable

   b. application variable

   c. session variable

   d. cookie

15. Which method is used to write a cookie named "mycookie" to the user's file system?

   a. Request.MyCookie("mycookie")

   b. Response.Form(mycookie)

   c. Response.Cookies(mycookie)

   d. Response.MyCookie(mycookie)

16. Which method is used to write a cookie named "mycookie" to the browser?

   a. = Request.Cookies("mycookie")

   b. Response.Cookies(mycookie)

   c. = Response.Cookies(mycookie)

   d. Response.Write(mycookie)

17. Which of the following is not true about cookies?

   a. Cookies are binary files.

   b. Cookies can be deleted by the user.

   c. Only the server that wrote the cookie can read the cookie.

   d. Netscape writes all the cookies in a text file named cookie.txt.

18. Which of the following properties determines whether the cookie contains multiple cookies?

   a. keys

   b. cookie.keys

   c. hasKeys

   d. dictionary.keys

19. Which of the following assigns an expiration date 30 days from today to a cookie named "myCookie"?

   a. Response.Cookies("myCookie").Expires = Date + 30

   b. Response.MyCookie.Expires = Date + 30

   c. Response("myCookie").Expires = (Date + 30)

   d. Response.Cookies("myCookie")("Expires") = Today + 30

9

20. Which server variable is used to store the value of the cookie?

   a. Request.ServerVariables(COOKIE)

   b. Request.ServerVariables(SERVER_COOKIE)

   c. Request.ServerVariables(ALL_COOKIES)

   d. Request.ServerVariables(HTTP_COOKIE)

HANDS-ON PROJECTS

Project 9-1

In this project, you will use the Global Application File to keep track of the number of active users on a Web site. Your data directory must be set up as a Web application for this activity to work correctly.

1. If you currently have a global.asa file, save the file as **globalbackup.asa**.

2. Using Notepad, create a new Global Application File named **global.asa**. Save this file to the root of your Web application in your data directory.

3. Create an application variable named **appcounter** that will keep track of the number of active users. (*Hint*: Create the variable in the Application_OnStart subroutine.)

4. Modify the variable so that when the user session begins, the appcounter variable is incremented by one. (*Hint*: When the session starts, add one to the appcounter variable.)

5. When the session ends, decrement the appcounter variable by one. (*Hint*: When the session ends, subtract one from the appcounter variable.)

6. Save your changes to the Global Application File.

7. Using Notepad, create a Web page to display the Web counter.

8. Add a script that will display the application variable **appcounter** in the Web page. (*Hint*: You can assign the number to a variable named strCount and then use response.write to display the value.)

9. Modify the Web page with your favorite fonts and colors and text.

10. Save your Web page as **counter.asp** in your data directory.

11. View the Web page in the browser.

12. Have a friend or colleague view the Web page in the browser. The page should display two users.

13. Print your source code for the Global Application File and the counter.asp page. Print out the Web page that displays the Web counter showing two active users.

Project 9-2

In this project, you will use session variables to store user information. The user will complete a form. You will create a page that retrieves the form field values and stores them in session variables. Then, you will create a page that will display the session variables to the user.

1. Create a Web page using Notepad or another ASP-compliant editor.

2. The form should use the **post** method, and the action should be **set.asp**.

3. Add a heading 2 that is center-aligned and says **Feedback Form**.

4. Add the following code to create the form fields and the labels.

```
How did you hear about our Web site?<br><br>
<select name="source" size="1">
<option value="yahoo">Yahoo</option>
<option value="commercial">Commercial</option>
<option value="magazine">Magazine</option>
<option value="email">E-mail</option>
<option value="friend">Friend</option>
<option selected value="Other">(Other)</option>
</select><br><br>
What is your comment?<br><br>
<input name="txtName" size="54">
<br><br>How would you like us to contact you?<br><br>
<input name="contact" type="checkbox" value="email">
E-mail
<input name="contact" type="checkbox" value="phone">
Phone
<input name="contact" type="checkbox" value="mail"
Mail <br><br>
Would you like to subscribe to our mailing list?
<br><br>
<input type="radio" value="Yes" name="email"> Yes
<input type="radio" value="No" name="email" checked> No
<br><br>Where can we contact you? <br><br>
<input name="name" size="20"> Name <br>
<input name="email" size="20"> E-mail address <br>
<input name="street" size="20"> Address <br>
<input name="city" size="20"> City, State, Zip Code <br>
<input name="phone" size="20"> Phone<br><br>
<input name="btnSubmit" type="submit" value="Send">
<input name="btnClear" type="reset" value="Clear Form">
```

5. Modify the Web page appearance using your favorite fonts, colors, and images.

6. Save the Web page as **myform.asp** to your data directory.

7. Using Notepad, create a Web page named set.asp to retrieve the values from the form and assign the values to session variables.

8. Create and declare session variables to hold each of the values returned from the form. Get the values from the form using the request.form method, and assign the

values to the variables. (*Hint*: Use the sample code below to retrieve the first form field and assign it to a session variable. Do not add any HTML tags to this page.)

```
<% Session("source") = Request.Form("source")
```

9. Add a statement that will redirect the user to another page named get.asp.

```
Response.Redirect "get.asp" %>
```

10. Save your page as **set.asp** in your data directory.

11. Using Notepad or a Web editor, create a page to display the session variables.

12. Add the basic HTML tags and a heading.

```
<html><head><title></title></head>
<body bgcolor="#CCFF66" text="#800000">
<h2 align="center">Feedback Form</h2>
```

13. Write a personalized message to the user.

```
Thank you <% = session("name") %> for your comment
about <% = session("name") %>. <br><br>
We will contact you shortly. <br>
Here is a copy of what you submitted. <br>
You may print this out for your records. <br><br>
```

14. Write out the values of the session variables to the Web page. Add a description of what the variable contains. (*Hint*: Follow the sample code below to display the value from the source session variable.)

```
Referred by: <% = Session("source") %> <br><br>
```

15. Use line breaks, lists, or a table to format output from the session variables.

16. Modify the Web page appearance with your favorite fonts, colors, and images.

17. Save the Web page as **get.asp** to your data directory.

18. View the myform.asp Web page. Submit the form. Print your source code for each page. Print out each Web page.

Project 9-3

In this project, you will create a privacy policy and a page that educates the user about cookies.

1. Open Notepad or your editor and create a Web page.

2. Add the basic HTML tags. The title of the page should be **Cookies**.

3. Add a heading formatted as heading 2, centered-aligned, that says **What You Should Know About Cookies**.

4. Research the Internet to learn more about cookies. Visit five Web pages that discuss cookies. Here are a few Web pages from Life Beyond Yahoo and the Microsoft Web sites that contain information about cookies.

   a. *http://www.lifebeyondyahoo.com/life/cookies.asp*

b. *http://www.microsoft.com/info/cookies.htm?RLD=291*

c. *http://msdn.microsoft.com/library/wcedoc/wcecomm/wininet_18.htm*

d. *http://msdn.microsoft.com/library/default.asp?URL=/library/wcedoc/wcecomm/wininet_16.htm*

e. *http://msdn.microsoft.com/workshop/server/toolbox/cookie.asp*

5. Write a paragraph that explains what a cookie is, what a cookie is used for, and what you will do with the information contained in the cookie. Describe the security information that relates to reading and writing cookies.

6. Add a heading formatted as heading 2, centered-aligned, that says **Cookie Resources**. Then, create a list of links to five Web pages on the Internet that discuss cookies. Format the list as a bulleted list.

7. Add a heading formatted as heading 2, centered-aligned, that says **Your Cookie**.

8. Display the cookies that have been written from your domain to the client's computer using the HTTP_COOKIE server variable. The ASP session cookie will be displayed to the user along with any other cookies that have been created by your domain.

```
Here is the cookie that has been written
to your computer from this domain: <br><br>
<% = Request.Servervariables("HTTP_COOKIE") %>
```

9. Modify the Web page appearance with your favorite fonts, colors, and images. You can also modify the layout using a table, line breaks, blockquotes, or other HTML tags.

10. Save the Web page as **cookies.asp** to your data directory.

11. Using Notepad, create a page that will contain your company privacy policy.

12. Add the basic HTML tags. Add a heading formatted as heading 2, centered-aligned, that says **Sample Privacy Policies**.

13. Visit the privacy policies at four different Web sites. List these four sites and create links to them.

14. Visit the TRUSTe Web site (*http://www.etrust.com*). Then, go to the Privacy Central Page at *http://www.truste.org/webpublishers/pub_privacy.html* and read about privacy policies. Read the sample content that they recommend that you include in your privacy policy at *http://www.truste.org/webpublishers/pub_modelprivacystatement.html*. You can also locate Web sites that discuss privacy from Life Beyond Yahoo at *http://www.lifebeyondyahoo.com/life/privacy.asp*.

15. Add a heading formatted as heading 2, centered-aligned, that says **Our Privacy Policy**.

16. Add at least one paragraph describing your Web site's privacy policy.

17. Modify the Web page appearance with your favorite fonts, colors, and images. Use blockquote tags, line breaks, tables, or other HTML tags to format the layout of the page.

18. Save the Web page as **privacy.asp** to your data directory.

19. View the Web pages. Print out both Web pages.

Project 9-4

In this project, you will create a page with a registration form. The page that processes the form assigns the form field values to a cookie. The browser will be redirected to a page that will retrieve the cookie values, assign them to session variables, and display the session variables.

1. Open Notepad or your editor and create a Web page that will contain the registration form.

2. Add the basic HTML tags. The title of the page should be **Registration Form**.

3. Add a heading formatted as heading 2, center-aligned, that says **Registration Form**.

4. Add two text box form fields with labels named **user** and **pass**.

5. Add a hidden field named **sid**. The value of the field is the SessionID.

```
<input type="hidden" name="sid"
     value="<% = Session.SessionID%>">
```

6. Save the page as **register.asp** in your data directory.

7. Open Notepad or your editor and create the page that will be used to retrieve the form values.

8. Retrieve the form fields and write their values to cookies. The cookie group name should be **sc**. Assign the current date to a cookie named **date**. Assign the server variables HTTP_REFERER and REMOTE_ADDR to cookies named **referer** and **ip**.

```
<%
Response.Cookies("sc")("name") = Request.Form("name")
Response.Cookies("sc")("pass") = Request.Form("pass")
Response.Cookies("sc")("sid") = Request.Form("sid")
Response.Cookies("sc")("date") = Date
Response.Cookies("sc")("referer") = _
     Request.Servervariables("HTTP_REFERER")
Response.Cookies("sc")("ip") = _
     Request.Servervariables("REMOTE_ADDR")
```

9. Redirect the user to a page named **display.asp**.

10. Save your page as **session.asp** in your data directory.

11. Open Notepad or your editor and create a Web page.

12. Set the buffer property to **true**.

13. Retrieve all the values from the cookies and assign them to session variables with the same name. (*Hint:* The sample code to assign the name cookie value to a name session variable is shown below.)

```
Session("name") = Request.Cookies("sc")("name")
```

14. Add the basic HTML tags and heading.

```
<html><head>
<title>Session Variables & Cookies</title>
</head>
<body>
<h2 align="center">Session Variables</h2>
```

15. Display all the session variables in the browser. Use line breaks, blockquotes, tables, or other HTML tags to format the page layout. (*Hint:* The sample code to display the name session variable is shown below.)

```
Name: <% = Session("name") %><br>
```

16. Display the cookie using the HTTP_COOKIE server variable.

```
Here is the cookie that has been written
to your computer from this domain: <br><br>
<% = Request.Servervariables("HTTP_COOKIE") %>
```

17. Add the closing HTML tags. Modify the Web page appearance using your favorite fonts, colors, and images.

18. Save the Web page as **display.asp** to your data directory.

19. View the register.asp Web page. Print your source code for each page. Print out the Web page.

Project 9-5

In this project, you will practice reading and writing cookies. You will create a Web page that will collect the user's name and password. The form field values will be saved as a cookie. When the user returns to the same Web page, the cookie will be used to automatically log the user into the Web page.

1. Open Notepad and create a Web page.

2. Add the code to determine whether the user filled out the form.

```
<% response.buffer = "true" %>
<% if (request.form("name") <> "") and _
(request.form("pass") <> "") then
```

3. If the user filled out the form, then retrieve the values from the form fields and assign them to the cookies. Name the group cookie **lc** and the cookies **name** and **pass**. The cookie should expire in 7 days from the current date.

```
Response.Cookies("lc")("name") = request.form("name")
Response.Cookies("lc")("pass") = request.form("pass")
Response.Cookies("lc").expires = Date + 7
else
end if
%>
```

9

4. Add the basic HTML tags.

```
<html><head><title>Login Cookie</title></head>
<body>
```

5. Add a script to detect whether a cookie is present. The cookie must have both a name and password stored in the cookie.

```
<% if (request.cookies("lc")("name") <> "")
     and (request.cookies("lc")("pass") <> "") then %>
```

6. If there is a cookie, add a heading 2 that says **You were logged in with your cookie.** Retrieve the values from the cookie and display them in the browser.

```
<h2 align="center">
You were logged in with your cookie. </h2>
Name = <% = Request.Cookies("lc")("name")%> <br>
Password = <% = Request.Cookies("lc")("pass")%>
```

7. If there is no cookie, add a heading 2 that says **Login Form**. Display a form for the user to enter a name and password. The form method should be **post**, and the action should be the **logincookie.asp** page.

```
<% else %>
    <h1 align="center">Login Form</h1>
    <form method="post" action="logincookie.asp">
    <input type="text" name="name" size="20">
    Name<br><br>
    <input type="password" name="pass" size="20">
    Password<br><br>
    <input type="submit" value="Login" name="btnSubmit">
    <input type="reset" value="Clear" name="btnClear">
    </form>
<% end if %>
</body></html>
```

8. Modify the Web page appearance using your favorite fonts, colors, and images.

9. Save the Web page as **logincookie.asp** to your data directory.

10. View the Web page. Print your source code. Print out the Web page.

Project 9-6

In this project, you will practice reading and writing cookies. You will create a Web page that will collect the user's name and password. The form field values will be saved as a cookie. When the user returns to the same Web page, the cookie will be used to fill in the values in the form.

1. Open Notepad and create a Web page.

2. Add the code to determine if the user filled out the form. If the user filled out the form, then retrieve the values from the form fields and assign them to the cookies.

Name the group cookie **nc** and the cookies **name** and **pass**. The cookie should expire in 7 days from the current date.

```
<% response.buffer = "true" %>
<% if (request.form("name") <> "") and _
    (request.form("pass") <> "") then
      Response.Cookies("nc")("name") = request.form("name")
      Response.Cookies("nc")("pass") = request.form("pass")
      Response.Cookies("nc").expires = Date + 7
else
end if
%>
```

3. Add the basic HTML tags and a heading, as shown below.

```
<html><head><title>Login Cookie</title></head>
<body>
<h2 align="center">Login Form</h2>
```

4. Add a script to detect whether a cookie is present. The cookie must have both a name and password stored in the cookie.

```
<% if (request.cookies("nc")("name") <> "") _
      and (request.cookies("nc")("pass") <> "") then %>
```

5. If there is a cookie, display the form. Retrieve the values from the cookie and display them in the form fields. (*Hint*: Assign the cookie values to the value property of the form field.) Make sure to assign the action to the redisplay.asp page and use the post method.

```
<form method="post" action="redisplay.asp">
<input type="text" name="name" size="20"
     value="<% = Request.Cookies("nc")("name")%>">
Name<br><br>
<input type="password" name="pass" size="20"
     value="<% = Request.Cookies("nc")("pass")%>">
Password<br><br>
<input type="submit" value="Login" name="btnSubmit">
<input type="reset" value="Clear" name="btnClear">
</form>
```

6. If there is no cookie, display a form for the user to enter a name and password. The form method should be **post**, and the action should be the **redisplay.asp** page. No values are assigned to the form fields. Add the closing HTML tags.

```
<% else %>
     <form method="post" action="redisplay.asp">
     <input type="text" name="name" size="20">
     Name<br><br>
     <input type="password" name="pass" size="20">
     Password<br><br>
     <input type="submit" value="Login" name="btnSubmit">
```

9

```
            <input type="reset" value="Clear" name="btnClear">
            </form>
      <% end if %>
      </body></html>
```

7. Modify the Web page appearance using your favorite fonts, colors, and images.

8. Save the Web page as **redisplay.asp** to your data directory.

9. View the Web page. Click the **Login** button. Notice that the form is displayed with empty form fields because there is no cookie.

10. Fill out and submit the form. Enter **admin** for the name field and **pass** for the password field. Click the **Login** button. Notice that the form is displayed with the values in the form fields. To make sure that it was the cookie that set the values for the variables, close the browser. Open the browser. View the Web page. The form is displayed with the values in the form fields.

11. Print your source code. Print out the Web page.

CASE PROJECTS

Global Metrics—Privacy Policy

Your manager has asked you to research privacy policies. Create a Web page named globalprivacy.asp. Add a heading that says "Global Metrics Privacy Policy Resources". On the Internet locate four public Web sites that contain privacy policies. Provide a link to privacy policies for each of the Web sites. Write a summary of the key points that were common in all of the policies. List the sites that use cookies. Describe what type of information each stores in its cookies (if known). Write a short summary of the key points that varied among the sites, or were unique. Modify the appearance of the Web page by changing the background and font colors and styles. Save the Web page to your data directory. View the Web page in a browser. Print out the Web page.

Global Metrics—Maintaining State with the Application Object

You are hired by Global Metrics to maintain their Web sites. The Internet site and the intranet site both use application variables to maintain global information about the Web site. Your job is to create a new Global Application File that will be used to maintain global information about the Web site. Save the old Global Application File as globalbak.asa. Create a new Global Application File named global.asa in the root of your data directory. Add the four default subroutines. Within the Application_OnStart subroutine, create five application variables in the Global Application File. The application variables should include the name of the Web site, the e-mail address of the Webmaster, the URL of the company's Web site, the color for the background, and the color for the default font. Assign each of the application variables a value. The name of the Web site is "Global Metrics Web Site". The e-mail address for contacting the Webmaster, webmaster@company.com, should be stored in an application variable named "email". The URL for the Web site is *http://www.company.com*.

The background color should be #CCFF66, and the text color should be #800000. Create a Web page named globalmetrics.asp to display your application variables. Use the application name variable to display the title of the Web page, and the application variables to change the color of the default font and background. Add a heading 2 that is center-aligned and displays the company name, using the name application variable. Create a hyperlink using the URL application variable. Create a hyperlink that will be used to e-mail the Webmaster, using the email application variable. Modify the appearance of the Web page using images, color, and different fonts. Save the Web page as globalmetrics.asp in your data directory. (*Note:* The Global Application File can only exist in the root directory of a Web application. Therefore, you must have your data directory set up as the root directory for your Web server. If you are running Personal Web Server, you can change the default directory for the Web server in the Advanced tab in the Personal Web Manager. For more information about using Personal Web Server, refer to the Before You Begin section of this book.) View the Web page in a browser. Print out the Web page and the source code for the Global Application File and your Web page.

Global Metrics—Protecting the Intranet Site

Global Metrics wants you to create a way to prevent users from visiting their intranet pages. Outside visitors should only be allowed to see the Internet pages (see Figure 9-6). Your boss tells you that the employees access the Internet through a proxy server. Therefore, all of the computers are using one IP address. You decide that you will protect the intranet site by maintaining state with the session object. To do this, you will first create a home page named internet.asp for the Global Metrics Internet Web site. Save the page in your data directory. The title should say Global Metrics, and a heading should say Internet Web page. On the page, put a link to the intranet Web page named intranet.asp.

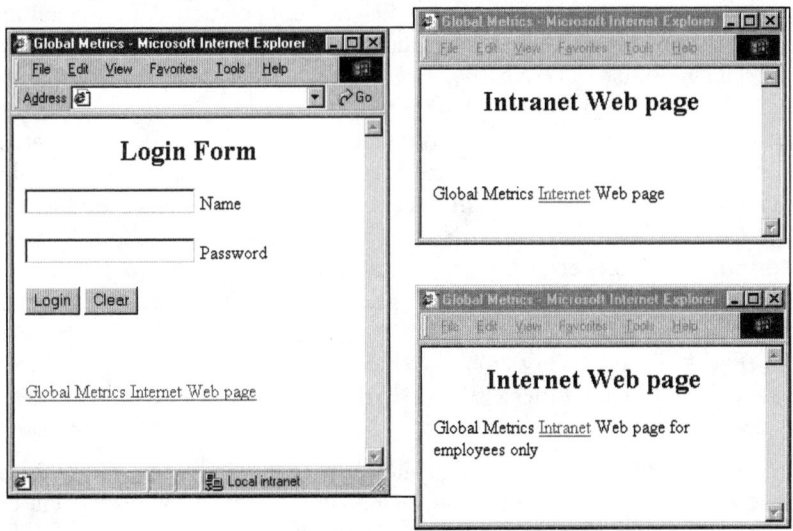

Figure 9-6   Using server variables to detect IP addresses

Next, create the Global Metrics intranet Web page named intranet.asp. Save the page in your data directory. The title should say Global Metrics, and a heading should say Intranet Web page. On the page, put a link to the Internet Web page (internet.asp). In the heading of the intranet.asp page, write a script that detects whether a session variable named flagIP is false or empty. (*Hint*: Use a pair of quotation marks to represent an empty string.) If either of these conditions occurs, redirect the user to the globallogin.asp page. Otherwise, let the user view the intranet.asp page. Next, create a page named globallogin.asp and save it in your data directory. The page will contain a login form with two text boxes named "name" and "pass". Add a hidden field named "ip". Assign the value of the "ip" field that contains the user's IP address. Put a hyperlink on the page to the company's Internet home page at internet.asp. The same page will be used to process the form. Each form field should be assigned to a session variable. Create a session variable named flagIP. If the user's IP address matches the company IP address, then set the flagIP session variable to true; otherwise set the variable to false. For testing purposes, use your workstation's IP address to represent the company's IP address. Modify the appearance of the Web pages using images, color, and different fonts. Save the changes to your Web pages. View the intranet.asp Web page in a browser. It should take you to the globallogin.asp page. Fill out and submit the form. You should be taken to the intranet page. Click Refresh. You should be able to view the intranet page without having to log in again. Print out the Web pages and the source code.

Global Metrics—Editing the Customer Profile Using Cookies

Your manager wants you to create a page to collect customers' personal profiles and store the information on the customers' computers in a cookie. You point out that the Web site should allow the customers to edit their profiles. Figure 9-7 shows the customer profile registration form, and the form the customers can use to edit their profiles. Create a customer registration form named globalprofile.asp that will collect the user information. Add a heading that says Create Your Customer Profile. Create a form that will be used to collect the user's username, password, e-mail address, first and last name, street address, city, state, zip code, and phone number. Create a hidden form field named date that will be used to store the current date. You can use the server-side Date function to assign the date to the value of the date form field. The globalprofile.asp page should also process the form. In the heading of the globalprofile.asp page, create a script that will save the form field values as a cookie when the form is submitted. (*Hint*: The following sample code would save the username form field as a cookie named username: `Response.Cookies("gm")("user") = Request.Form("user")`.) The name of the group of cookies should be "gm". The cookie should expire 30 days from today. (*Hint*: You can determine whether the form has been submitted by testing if the form collection is empty.) If the collection is not empty, then create the cookies and then redirect the user to a page named globaledit.asp; otherwise, display the Web page with the form. Save the page to your data directory.

Create a page named globaledit.asp that will allow the user to edit her or his customer profile. Add a heading that says Edit Your Customer Profile. Create a form that will be used to display the user's username, password, e-mail address, first and last name, street address, city, state, zip code, and phone number. Create a hidden form field named date that will be used to store the current date. (*Hint:*You can copy the same form from the globalprofile.asp page.) For each of the visible form fields, get the value of the form field from the cookie. (*Hint:* In the value property you can use server script to write out the value of the cookie. For example, the code to retrieve the cookie value for the username might look like this: `<input type="text" name="user" size="20" value = "<% = Request.Cookies ("gm")("user") %>">` Username`<br>`.) You can use the server-side Date function to assign the current date to the value of the date form field. The globalprofile.asp page should also process this form. Save the page to your data directory. Modify the appearance of each Web page by changing the background and font colors and styles. View the globalprofile.asp page in a browser. The form fields are blank. Complete the form and submit it. You should be redirected to the globaledit.asp page, which will display what you entered in the form fields. Print out each Web page and the source code for each page.

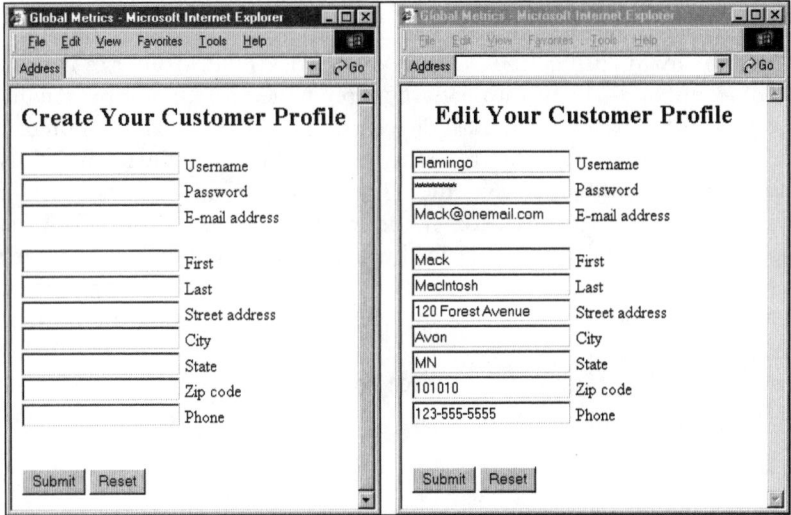

Figure 9-7   Writing cookie values into form fields

Global Metrics—Who is visiting our Web site?

Your manager wants to know what information you can retrieve about the visitors on the Web site. You create a Web page to display the information that you can collect about a visitor without having the visitor's consent, and without using cookies. You plan to use the session object to store the information temporarily, until you can create a script to store it in a database. Create a Web page named visitors.asp and save the page in your data directory. Add a heading that says What we know about our visitors. Retrieve the values of at least four server variables and store them in four session variables. Store the current date in a session variable named date. Display the SessionID and session variables in the same page.

Global Metrics—Detecting Screen Resolution

Your manager wants to know if you can retrieve information that is not in the HTTP headers from the client's system. You decide to demonstrate that you cannot only retrieve client-side information, such as the screen resolution, but also store it in the session variables—without any user intervention. Using Notepad or your Web editor, create a page named clientdata.asp. Add a form named form that is processed by a page named moredata.asp. Add four hidden form fields named resol, color, ht, and wt. After the closing form tag, add a client-side script that calls a function named "go". At the top of the page, create a client-side function named "go" that will assign values to the form fields. (*Hint*: To assign the resolution to the "resol" form field, you can use the code: `document.form.resol.value=screen.width + 'x' + screen.height;`. To assign the color depth to the "color" form field, you can use the code: `document.form.color.value=screen.colorDepth;`. Follow the same pattern to assign the values to the "ht" and "wt" form fields. The properties for the available screen height and width are screen.availHeight and screen.availWidth.) After assigning values to the form fields, submit the form using the submit method. (*Hint*: You can use the code `document.form.submit();` to automatically submit a form.) Do not put any headings or text on this page. Save the page to your data directory. Create a page named moredata.asp. Add a server script that uses the request object to retrieve the values from the form and assign them to session variables. (*Hint*: To retrieve the "resol" form field you can use the code: `Session("resol") = Request.form("resol")`.) Add the basic HTML tags, and a heading. Display all the session variables in the browser. (*Hint*: You can use this code to display the screen resolution: `<b>Screen resolution:</b> <% = Session("resol") %> pixels<br>`.) Modify the appearance of the Web page by changing the background and font colors and styles. Save the Web page to your data directory. View the Web page in a browser. Print out the Web page and the source code.

10

ASP COMPONENTS

In this chapter you will:

♦ Learn how the Component Object Model is used within a Web application

♦ Use the server object to integrate your ASP page with ASP components

♦ Detect support for specific browser features using the Browser Capabilities component

♦ Create a Web page that rotates banner ads using the AdRotator component

♦ Send e-mail via an ASP page using the CDONTS object

♦ Locate other third-party ASP components on the Internet

In the last several chapters you learned how to use built-in objects to perform activities such as writing to the Web browser and processing a form. In this chapter, you will learn how to integrate other third-party components within your Web application, using the server object. These third-party components help you to incorporate more advanced features and functions into your Web application. The three components that will be covered in detail in this chapter are the Browser Capabilities component, which is used to detect which features are supported by the current browser, the AdRotator component, which is used to manage rotating banner ads, and the CDONTS component, which is used to send e-mail from a Web page. There are many more third-party components available, some provided by Microsoft, and others by a variety of companies. You will learn to locate Internet resources that will help you build and implement third-party components.

ASP COMPONENTS

In previous chapters you learned how to create an object using a constructor function, and how to call the object's methods from a script. A **component** is a piece of software code that defines objects, properties, and methods, and encapsulates the entire code within itself. You learned that when objects are encapsulated, the programmer does not need to know or understand the code used to create the object. Reusable code is one of the benefits of object-oriented programming.

Components that conform to the **Component Object Model (COM)** are known as **COM objects**. The Component Object Model is a standard that allows independent components to communicate with each other. The COM defines how COM objects interact with other COM objects. COM objects are compiled programs often written in programming languages such as Visual Basic, C, C++, and even Java. COM objects are packaged as executable programs (.exe) or dynamic-link libraries (.dll). In general, executables provide better security, while dynamic-link libraries provide better performance.

COM objects can be installed on a client's computer or on the server. Client-side COM objects are often referred to as ActiveX controls. Initially, only Internet Explorer supported ActiveX controls by using an <object> tag to add an ActiveX control to a Web page. Netscape can support some ActiveX controls using a plug-in supplied by NCompass Labs (*http://www.ncompasslabs.com*). However, NCompass Labs will no longer support or distribute the plug-in. Therefore, at this time only Internet Explorer fully supports ActiveX controls. Server-side COM objects are often referred to as **server components**, **active server components**, or **ASP components**. ASP components are simply COM objects installed on the server that are used within Web applications.

When you install the Internet Information Server, the ASP built-in objects are also installed. If you would like to perform activities that are beyond the scope of the ASP built-in objects, you can use ASP components that other developers have written. Microsoft provides several additional ASP components, including the **Browser Capabilities component**, the **AdRotator component**, the **Database Access component,** and the **CDONTS component**. The Browser Capabilities component identifies the browser software and determines which features it supports. The AdRotator component allows you to create rotating banner ads on a Web page. The Data Access component (which is covered in a later chapter of this book) allows you to create Web pages that interact with your database. Third-party software such as the Microsoft **SMTP Server** contains ASP components that can be used to interface with their software. The SMTP Server uses the **CDONTS component** to interface with the SMTP Server. You can use CDONTS to send e-mail from an ASP page. You can also create your own ASP components and implement them in your Web application.

Figure 10-1 shows how ASP Web applications can interface with COM objects. Because COM objects communicate with each other by means of the COM standards, the programmer only needs to interface to the COM object. For example, the programmer only needs to integrate the ASP pages with the Data Access component (DAC). The database server does not have to reside on the same physical server as the Web server.

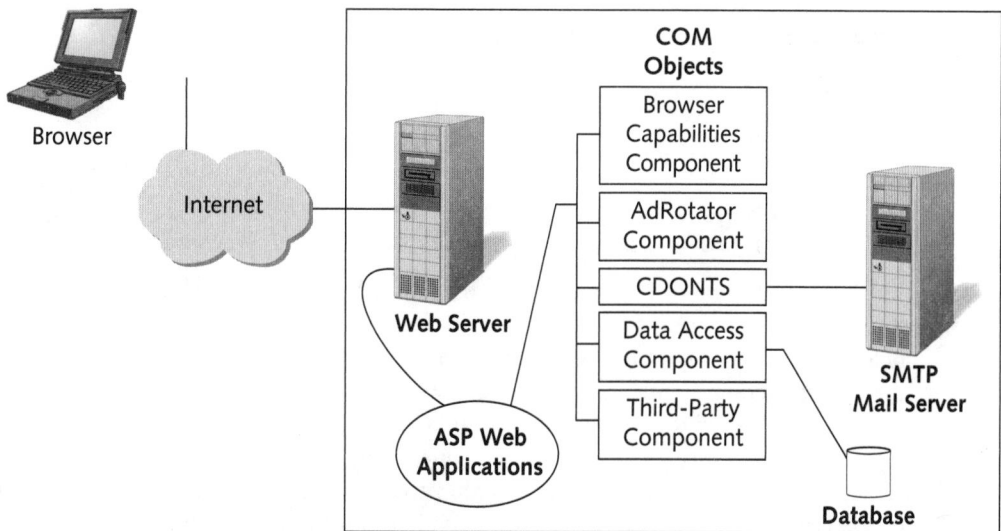

Figure 10-1   How ASAP applications communicate with server components

Integrating ASP Components into ASP Pages

Because ASP components are COM components, they can contain predefined objects, properties, and methods. After the ASP components are installed, your Web pages can access their objects, properties, and methods. Like built-in objects, the ASP component objects are not accessed directly. The COM object can be instantiated using the server object's createobject method, or the <object> tag.

The term COM object is often used as a synonym for COM component.

The ASP built-in server object contains a method called createobject that allows you to create an instance of an object from any ASP page. The component name is used to identify the type of object to instantiate. The actual component name will vary with the type of component installed. For example, the component name for the Browser Capabilities component is "MSWC.BrowserType". The new instance of the object is assigned to a variable. You can then refer to the variable to call methods and set the properties of the object. Use the syntax below to create an instance of an ASP component.

dim objVariableName
set objVariableName = server.createobject("ComponentName")

It is useful to add the prefix "obj" or "o" to a variable name for an object.

Use the sample code below to create a Browser Capabilities component.

```
dim objBC
set objBC = server.createobject("MSWC.BrowserType")
```

The object can also be created on the server using the <object> tag in the Global Application File. The <object> tag is an HTML tag. Notice that in the syntax example below, the object tag is located outside the script tags in the Global Application File. This method is used to create an object within the scope of the application or session. The runat property is assigned the Server value to indicate that the object is to be created on the server. The scope property is assigned the value "Application" or "Session", which identifies whether the object is to be created within the scope of the entire Web application, or is to be session-based. The PROGID property identifies the type of object to create by specifying the component name. The id property allows you to assign a name to the object, which you can use when referring to the object in your scripts. The COM object is not created until the object is referred to from within the ASP script.

<object runat = "server" Scope = "Application" PROGID = "ComponentName" id = "objName"></object>

Then, you can use the following syntax to call an object and set its properties within the scope of the application. If the value is a string, you must enclose the string within quotation marks.

<% Application("objName").Property = value %>

Although page-level objects are easily scalable, creating objects and storing them in session or application variables is generally not recommended. You can learn more about how to use application and session objects and how to increase performance in your Web applications from LearnASP (*http://www.learnasp.com/learn/*).

Assigning Properties and Calling Methods

Once you have created the instance of the object using the component, you can access its properties and methods by referring to the name of the variable and the name of the property or method. You can retrieve the property and write the value to the Web page, or store the value in another variable. The syntax below illustrates how to retrieve the property value of an object, store it in a variable, and write it to the Web page.

<% varProperty = objName.PropertyName %>
<% = varProperty %>

To modify the value of the property, you must identify the name of the object, the property name, and the new value. If the expression is a string, you must enclose the string in quotation marks. If the value is a number, then do not use quotation marks. The following syntax illustrates how to assign a value to a property of an object.

objName.PropertyName = expression

In the following sample code, the name of the object is objMail, and the name of the property is name. You could have assigned the string to a variable, and then assigned the value of the property to the variable.

```
objMail.name = "Matthew"
```

The new value can be the result of an expression. In the sample code below, the value assigned to the property was received from a form. The property is assigned the value from a form field named firstname.

```
objMail.name = request.form("firstname")
```

When you call the method of an object, you can pass arguments (also called parameters) to the method. If you want to call the method as a function, don't forget to enclose the arguments in parentheses, and to assign the results to a variable. The syntax below illustrates how to call a method of an object.

objName.MethodName Arg1, Arg2,…,ArgN

The following syntax illustrates how to call a method of an object as a function that will return a value.

returnValue = objName.MethodName(Arg1, Arg2,…,ArgN)

When you assign an object to a variable, you are assigning a memory location to the object. If you assign a memory location, that space is unavailable to the system. After you have finished using the variable, it is highly recommended that you release the variable from memory. Assigning the variable to the VBScript Nothing constant will free the memory used by the variable.

Set objName = Nothing

It is very important to close objects and set them to Nothing after they are no longer required. Do not trust the server to close a connection to an object or release the object from memory. Database connection objects that are left open continue to remain open until they are closed. (You will learn how to close database connection objects in a later chapter.) Not only will you be wasting memory, but you will also have a connection that is not being used, which can affect performance.

THE BROWSER CAPABILITIES COMPONENT

In a previous chapter, you learned that the HTTP_USER_AGENT server variable, which is passed in the HTTP header, contains information about the client's Web browser. To use this information, you must parse the returned string. The Browser Capabilities component parses the HTTP_USER_AGENT server variable to provide you with information about the client's browser, including its type and the version number. It also provides information about which features that particular browser supports. The Browser Capabilities component is a program named Browsercap.dll, which is installed on the Web server. The Browser Capabilities component refers to an external text file on the server known as the **Browser Capabilities Detection File**, which contains information about most of the browser software programs.

 The location of the Browser Capability Detection File is usually `c:\windows\system\inetsrv\browscap.ini` on a Windows 98 computer, and `c:\winnt\system32\inetserv\browscap.ini` on a Windows NT Server or Windows 2000 Professional computer. You will only be able to locate the browscap.ini file if PWS or IIS is installed.

Figure 10-2 shows a portion of the contents of a default Browser Capabilities Detection File. Notice that the Browser Capabilities Detection File contains a date at the top of the file to identify when the file was last updated. The file needs to be updated frequently to keep up to date with the newer browsers. You can obtain the latest versions of the Browser Capabilities Detection File from third-party developers such as cyScape (*www.cyscape.com*). Microsoft has a Web page that describes how to locate the Browser Capabilities Detection File (*www.microsoft.com/ISN/faq/latest_browscapini_file.asp*). Once you have downloaded and unzipped the files, simply copy the Browser Capabilities Detection File over the old version.

The Browser Capabilities Detection File lists each browser with its version number and a list of features it supports. At the top of each entry, the HTTP_USER_AGENT string is identified. The Browser Capabilities Detection File provides information that is specific not only to the browser version, but also to the client's platform. A parent is identified, which indicates that the browser can inherit properties from another browser version. Some of the browser information is "inherited" from the browser parent listed. Parent information is provided because, although the browser may be at version 4.0, the 4.0 versions might differ slightly, depending on which platform they are running. If no browser version matches the version identified in the HTTP_USER_AGENT string, then the default browser settings are used. If the feature is supported, the value is True; otherwise the value is False. The semicolon can be used to add comments in the file.

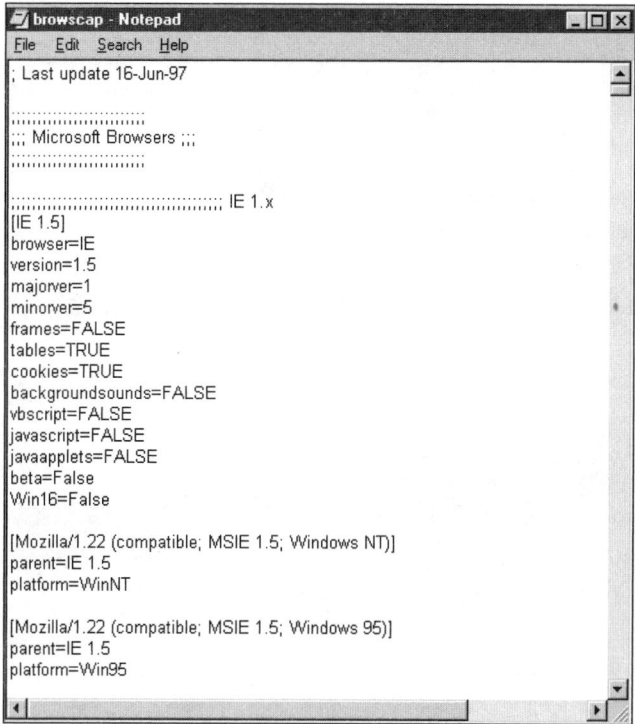

Figure 10-2   The Browser Capabilities Detection File

While Browscap.ini contains many of the features supported by browsers, it does not contain all of them. There are other third party components such as BrowserHawk from cyScape (*www.cyscape.com*) that can detect more features for a wider selection of browsers. Microsoft is currently developing the next version of ASP+, which will greatly extend the capabilities of the Browser Capabilities component. A summary of the features of the BrowserHawk component is listed at *http://www.browscap.com/products/bhawk/compare.asp*. The complete documentation for the installation and use of the BrowserHawk component may be found at *http://www.cyscape.com/products/bhawk/getstarted.asp*.

You can find all the properties and learn more about the Browser Capabilities component from *http://msdn.microsoft.com/library/psdk/iisref/comp3xx0.htm* or *http://msdn.microsoft.com/training/free/chapters/mwd64/mwd9800347.htm*.

To detect the browser features using the Browser Capabilities component:

    1. Open Notepad or your editor and create a new ASP page.

2. Add the basic HTML tags, as shown below.

```
<html><head><title>Browser Detection</title></head>
<body>
<h2>Browser Detection</h2>
```

3. Below the body tag, add a server-side script that declares the variable to hold the Browser Capabilities component. Create the object using the createobject method of the server object.

```
<% dim bc
Set bc = server.createobject("MSWC.BrowserType")
%>
```

4. Add the following code that will display the HTTP_USER_AGENT server variable.

```
Here is the value of the <br>
HTTP_USER_AGENT server variable: <br><br>
<% = request.servervariables("HTTP_USER_AGENT") %>
```

5. Add the following code, which will display the browser name, the version, and the operating system that is being used on the client.

```
<br><br>
Here is the information from the <br>
Browser Capabilities component: <br><br>
Browser Name: <% = bc.browser %><br>
Version: <% = bc.version %><br>
Platform: <% = bc.platform %><br>
```

6. Add a script that detects whether the browser supports VBScript. If the browser supports VBScript, then write a custom message to the user; otherwise, tell the user that the browser does not support VBScript.

```
<% if bc.vbscript = TRUE then %>
    Welcome! You support VBScript.
<% else %>
    This site uses VBScript. <br>
    You do not support VBScript. <br>
<% end if %>
</body></html>
```

7. Save the page to your data directory as **mybc.asp**.

8. View the mybc.asp Web page. Print your source code. Print out the Web page.

THE ADROTATOR COMPONENT

Many Web sites earn revenue from banner advertisements. You can use the AdRotator component to create and maintain banner advertisements on ASP pages. Although there are third-party server objects that provide more advanced management features, such as target-based marketing, the AdRotator component provides a free, simple, easy-to-use tool for managing your basic banner ads. The AdRotator component, called Adrot.dll, contains a method that you can use not only to display the ad, but also to manage the frequency with which the banner ad is displayed. The information used to manage the ad is located in a single text file called the **Rotator Schedule File**, which means that you can change the ad across several Web pages simply by editing this one file.

When a user visits an ASP page that has a banner ad, an instance of the AdRotator object is created. The ASP page uses the Rotator Schedule File to determine which ad to display. When users click the ad, they are redirected to a new Web page by a **Redirection File**. The Redirection File receives the request from the image link, and redirects the user to the new page.

 You can learn more about the AdRotator component at *http://msdn.microsoft.com/library/psdk/iisref/asps4v5e.htm* and *http://msdn.microsoft.com/library/psdk/iisref/comp59f8.htm*.

Creating the Rotator Schedule File

The Rotator Schedule File, which you create using a text editor such as Notepad, is a text file that contains information about the ads to be displayed on an ASP page. It is divided into two sections; the first section defines the general parameters for all ads, and the second section contains the parameters for specific ads. A single line with an asterisk (*) divides the two sections. This file is often named Adrot.txt or AdSchedule.txt.

The top line of the first section contains a statement that redirects the user to an ASP page that contains a redirection script. The first section also contains information that applies to all banner ad images. The information is used to construct an image tag and its properties. The border, height, and width parameters, by default measured in pixels, are used to construct the border, height, and width properties of the image object. While many banners have a height of 50 and width of 400, there are no required dimensions for the banner ad images. Banner ads can display images of varying sizes, such as a 50 by 50 pixel image. If you do not specify a parameter, the component will insert the default parameters. The default width is 440, height is 60, and border is 1. A default URL can be added to redirect users when they click an ad that does not specify a URL. Below is the syntax for the first section of the Rotator Schedule File.

redirect redirectpage.asp
border n
height n
width n
http://www.yourdomain.com/path/filename
*****

The second section of the Rotator Schedule File identifies four specific parameters for each ad as it rotates into the Web page. Do not leave any of the four parameters blank. The first parameter identifies the name of the graphic file to be displayed. You can use the absolute or relative URL to locate the file. This information is used to construct the value for the SRC property of the image tag. The second parameter identifies the URL to redirect users when they click the image. This can be a relative or absolute URL. This value identifies the HREF property in the anchor tag. You do not need to specify the http:// prefix. In addition, you can use the mailto: prefix to create a link to an e-mail address. If no link is provided, you must use a hyphen (-).

Often the URL for the banner ad is the home page of the advertiser. It can be a specific page or a directory. The AdRotator is a simple component that can be used to set up and manage banner ads. Banner ads are a major source of revenue for many Web sites today. You can even set up the component to refresh to an intermediate page where you could keep track of the number of hits for each ad. Each property of the AdRotator can be changed on the fly, by modifying the Rotator Schedule File. In the next chapter you will learn how to use the TextStream object of the File Access component to modify text pages. You can use this component to change the text content in the Rotator Schedule File on the fly.

The third parameter provides a text description of the ad for browsers without graphics capabilities. This value is used to identify the alternate text property (alt) in the image tag. The last parameter is the weighted relative frequency with which the ad is displayed. The relative frequency number is an integer that can range from 0 to 4,294,967,295. However, it is recommended that you use numbers for which the total of all the weighted frequencies is a multiple of 10, 100, 1000, or 10,000. For example, three ads have relative frequencies of 20, 30, and 50. The total of the relative frequencies is 100. Therefore, it is easy to see that the first ad is viewed 20% of the time, the second ad is shown 30% of the time, and the third ad is shown 50% of the time. Below is the syntax for the second section of the Rotator Schedule File.

imageURL/imageName.gif
http://www.yourdomain.com/path/filename
Your default text goes here
N

Creating the Redirection File

The Redirection File is an ASP page that can be created in Notepad. The name of the Redirection File must match the page identified in the first line of the Rotator Schedule File. When users click the image in the ASP page, they are redirected to the Redirection File. The Redirection File retrieves the URL for the link from the QueryString. Then the Redirection File uses server-side redirection to redirect users to the specified URL. The contents of the Redirection File can simply redirect the user to the new page. Below is a sample of code that could be placed in the Redirection File.

```
<% Response.Redirect(Request.QueryString("url")) %>
```

You can modify the Redirection File to determine whether there is a value for the URL before redirecting the user to the new URL. As shown in the sample code below, if no URL is specified, the user is not redirected to another page.

```
<% If Request.QueryString("url") <> "" Then
        Response.Redirect(Request.QueryString("url"))
    End If %>
```

Creating the ASP Page to Display the Banner Ads

The banner ad is displayed in an ASP page. In the sample code below, a variable named objAd stores the new AdRotator object. An instance of the AdRotator component is created using the createobject method of the server object. The name of the AdRotator component is "MSWC.AdRotator".

 MSWC is the Microsoft Windows Component.

```
<% Dim objAd
    Set objAd = Server.CreateObject("MSWC.AdRotator")%>
```

Then, in the sample code below, a variable named varAd will hold the information that will be used to create the image and anchor tags. The GetAdvertisement method uses the Rotator Schedule File to determine which parameters to send to the browser. The absolute or relative path to the Rotator Schedule File is placed inside quotation marks.

```
<% Dim varAd
    varAd = objAd.GetAdvertisement("AdSchedule.txt")%>
```

Within the ASP page, the write method is used to write out the information returned from the GetAdvertisement method. Use the write method in the body of the page where you want to display the banner ad. The AdRotator component can be located anywhere on the Web page, not just at the top! The AdRotator component will write out an anchor tag and an image tag with the properties determined by the Rotator Schedule File.

```
<% Response.Write varAd  %>
```

The GetAdvertisement method of the AdRotator component writes out the anchor and image tags for the banner ad. The following code is created by the GetAdvertisement method, and can be viewed in the browser.

```
<a href="ad_redirect.asp?url=http://www.course.com&image=
banner1.gif">
<img src="banner1.gif" alt="This is the first image"
width=400 height=50 border=2>
</a>
```

10

The other properties of the AdRotator component include border, which allows you to override the border settings in the Rotator Schedule File; clickable, which allows you to specify whether you want the image to contain active hyperlinks, and which is set to true by default; and TargetFrame, which indicates into which frame the image is loaded. By default the TargetFrame property is set to "No Frame", which indicates that the image will be loaded into the current frame. This TargetFrame property can also be one of the special frame keywords such as _TOP, _NEW, _CHILD, _SELF, _PARENT, or _BLANK. Below is an example that demonstrates how to implement some of the additional properties of the banner object. Notice that the write method writes the content returned from the GetAdvertisement directly, without first assigning it to a variable.

```
<%
dim objAd
Set objAd = Server.CreateObject("MSWC.AdRotator")
objAd.TargetFrame = _TOP
objAd.Clickable = FALSE
objAd.border = 4
Response.write(objAd.GetAdvertisement("adschedule.txt"))
%>
```

Banner Ad Graphics

You can create your own banner ads, using a graphics program. There are many commercial graphics programs available, including Paint Shop Pro from Jasc (*www.jasc.com*) and Photoshop from Adobe (*www.adobe.com*). Life Beyond Yahoo (*http://www.lifebeyondyahoo.com/life/graphics.asp*) contains links to many Web sites that contain free graphics, banners, icons, buttons, and animated graphics. For example, a site called Coder.com   (*http://www.coder.com/creations/banner/banner-form.pl.cgi*) contains a useful banner generator to create text-only banners.

 Tucows (*www.tucows.com*) mirror sites offer several freeware and shareware graphics-editing programs.

Creating a Banner Ad

To create a Web page that displays a banner ad:

1. Open your browser and go to the Coder.com Web site at *http://www.coder.com/creations/banner/banner-form.pl.cgi*. Use their banner generator to create three banners.

2. To create the first banner:

   a. In the Banner Text field enter **Course Technology**.

   b. In the Font Size text box type **46**.

   c. In the Border text boxes enter **15** and **15**.

    d. Select the radio button named **Longhand Fonts**. From the Longhand Fonts drop-down list, select **DomCasual-Thin-Normal**.

    e. In the Foreground Color drop-down list box select **white**.

    f. In the Background Color drop-down list box select **red**.

    g. In the Advanced Algorithms section, in the first drop-down list box, select **Swirl 20%**.

    h. Click on the **Submit Banner** button. A page will load that will display your banner.

    i. Right-click over the image to display the shortcut menu and select **Save Picture As**. Save the picture as **banner1** in your data directory.

3. To create the second banner, click the **Back** button in the browser to return to the banner generator page. Change the Background Color drop-down list box selection to **blue**. Click on the **Submit Banner** button. A page will load that will display your banner. Right-click over the image to display the shortcut menu and select **Save Picture As**. Save the picture as **banner2** in your data directory.

4. To create the third banner, click the **Back** button in the browser to return to the banner generator page. Click **rgb** in the Background Color list box. Change the value in the rgb (color-list) field to **#551A8B**. Click the **Submit Banner** button. A page will load that will display your banner. Right-click over the image to display the shortcut menu and select **Save Picture As**. Save the picture as **banner3** in your data directory.

5. To create the fourth banner, click the **Back** button in the browser to return to the banner generator page. Change the value in the rgb (color-list) field to **#006400**. Click on the **Submit Banner** button. A page will load that will display your banner. Right-click over the image to display the shortcut menu and select **Save Picture As**. Save the picture as **banner4** in your data directory.

6. Open Notepad and create a text file that will contain the Rotator Schedule File. Add the **redirect** command. The Redirection File is named **adredirect.asp** and is located in the same directory as your graphics. Set the height parameter to **67** and the width parameter to **277**. Set the border parameter to **0**. Add the asterisk (*) to divide the two sections in the Rotator Schedule File.

7. Create the second section of the Rotator Schedule File, using the following parameters for the individual banner ads. Add the code below, which contains the parameters for the first banner ad.

```
banner1.gif
http://www.course.com/
Course Technology
40
```

10

8. Add the parameters for the last three banner ads, using the values in the table below.

Image Name	Alternate Text	Hyperlink URL	Relative Weight
banner2.gif	Student Learning	http://www.course.com/sl/default.cfm	30
banner3.gif	Web Warrior Series	http://www.course.com/webwarrior/	20
banner4.gif	Academic Instructors	http://www.course.com/at/default.cfm	10

9. Save the Rotator Schedule File as **adschedule.txt** in your data directory.

10. Using Notepad, create a new page that will contain the server-side redirection.

11. Add the following code to redirect the user to the URL retrieved from the hyperlink.

```
<% Response.Redirect(Request.QueryString("url")) %>
```

12. Save the Redirection File as **adredirect.asp** in your data directory.

13. Create the ASP Page using Notepad. Add the basic HTML tags.

```
<html><head><title>Banner Ads</title></head>
<body>
```

14. Add the following code to create the AdRotator component, call the GetAdvertisement method, and write the banner ad to the Web page. Add the ending HTML tags.

```
<% Dim objAd, varAd
Set objAd = Server.CreateObject("MSWC.AdRotator")
varAd = objAd.GetAdvertisement("AdSchedule.txt")
response.write varAd
%>
</body></html>
```

15. Modify the Web page appearance by changing the background, font, and colors, and adding content.

16. Save the file as **myadpage.asp** in your data directory.

17. View your Web page in the browser. Print out the Web page and the source code. Refresh the page until the other two ads appear. View the code that creates the banner ad on each page. Print out the Web page and the source code for each ad displayed.

18. Print out the source code for the Rotator Schedule File, the Redirection File, and the ASP page.

THE CDONTS COMPONENT

The CDONTS component is an example of a third-party component. The CDONTS component is a scaled-down version of a collection of objects known as **Collaborative Data Objects (CDO)**. CDO is typically used to integrate your applications with active messaging systems such as Microsoft Outlook and Microsoft Exchange Services. CDONTS is a collection of objects, properties, and methods that connect the SMTP Service with the Web application.

CDONTS is located in a server component called cdonts.dll, which is located in `c:\winnt\system32\` and is made available when you install the Microsoft SMTP Server. The SMTP Server is included in the NT Option Pack. The **Simple Mail Transfer Protocol (SMTP)** is a protocol, or set of rules, used to transfer mail between servers. SMTP Server provides an easy way to transmit Internet mail.

CDONTS is only available with NT Server. It is not available with Personal Web Server or NT Workstation because SMTP will only work with NT Server. You must have access to a directory on an NT server with SMTP Server running and with CDONTS installed in order to complete the activities in this section. CDONTS is also available with Windows 2000 Professional using IIS.

10

SMTP Server contains several default folders, including Pickup, Queue, Badmail, Drop, and SortTemp. These folders are located by default in `C:\Inetpub\MailRoot\`. The Pickup folder is used to store outgoing mail messages. These messages will be sent from SMTP Server to other servers. The default port for SMTP Server is 25. Mail messages can be placed in this directory by hand or by other programs such as cdonts.dll. The CDONTS component will place your message in the Pickup folder.

You can find additional information on how to use CDONTS at *http://msdn.microsoft.com/library/periodic/period99/email.htm* and *http://msdn.microsoft.com/library/periodic/period99/asp9951.htm*.

Some hosting service providers do not use the SMTP mail server. You need to contact your HSP to determine what components interface with their mail server. Some hosting service providers may use SMTP Server, but require you to use a different mail component. For example, ServerObjects Inc. (*http://www.serverobjects.com/*) provides two mail components named AspMail and AspQMail (*http://www.serverobjects.com/products.htm*) that are commonly used to enable an ASP page to send e-mail. Although the syntax is slightly different, the programming methods between CDONTS and AspMail are very similar. You can view the documentation on AspMail 3.X at *http://www.serverobjects.com/comp/Aspmail3.htm* and AspQMail 2.x at *http://www.serverobjects.com/comp/AspQmail.htm*.

Creating Web Pages That Send E-mail

The CDONTS component contains an object named newmail, and newmail contains a method called send, which is used to create the e-mail message and send it to the Pickup folder. From there SMTP Server will retrieve and send the message.

The syntax below shows how to create a new instance of the newmail object. First declare a variable to store the newmail object. Then use the createobject method of the server object to instantiate a new newmail object. The name of the CDONTS component is CDONTS.NewMail.

Dim objMail
Set objMail = CreateObject("CDONTS.Newmail")

The newmail object has several properties that must be set before the message can be sent. These properties include the recipient, the sender, the subject, and the message body. You can explicitly set the properties for the newmail object individually.

objMail.From = "sender@senderaddress.com"
objMail.To = "recipient@recipient.com"
objMail.Subject = "Subject"
objMail.Body = "Message Body"

The send method of the newmail object will create the message in the required format and write it to the Pickup folder. SMTP Server will then deliver the message. Below is the syntax for using the send method of the newmail object. After the message has been sent, you should set the object to the keyword Nothing to release the object from memory.

objMail.Send
Set objMail = Nothing

You can pass the properties as parameters of the send method instead of defining each property individually. The from property is placed first, followed by the to property, the subject, and the message. The following code illustrates how an e-mail message can be sent in as little as three lines of code!

```
Set objMail = CreateObject("CDONTS.Newmail")
objMail.Send("sender@sender.com", "recipient@recipient.com",
"Subject", "Message")
Set objMail = Nothing
```

Additional Properties of the Newmail Object

The from property is used to identify the sender. Although it is possible to send anonymous e-mail by omitting the from property entirely, it is not recommended. You should specify a complete e-mail address for the sender. Some e-mail programs will not accept e-mail when the sender's address is not valid. It is useful to change the from property on the basis of the message. For example, if the e-mail is being generated to customers, you might set the from property to "help@mydomain.com". That way, your customer would recognize who is sending the e-mail. You cannot specify more than one address when using the from property.

On the other hand, you can specify multiple recipients by using the to property. You can separate multiple recipient addressees with semicolons (;). You can specify a "carbon copy" (CC) to be sent to another recipient by using the CC property. You can also specify a blind carbon copy (BCC) to be sent to another recipient by using the BCC property. Blind carbon copies are used when you do not want the recipients to know that other individuals have been sent the same message. For example, you could send your customer an e-mail message and send a blind carbon copy to your manager. Customers would not know that you have sent a copy to your manager; they also would not know your manager's e-mail address.

You can use the importance property to indicate to the e-mail application the importance of the message. Some e-mail applications provide indicators, such as an exclamation point, to indicate that a message has been given a certain priority level. The importance property will not send mail faster. The three importance property levels that you can set with the newmail object are 2 (cdohigh), 1 (cdoNormal), and 0 (cdoLow). You can use the CDONTS constants or the numbers. If you use the constants, you must add the server-side include file that contains the constants. More information on defining a page that contains constants for CDONTS is available at *http://support.microsoft.com/support/kb/articles/Q218/6/07.ASP.* Below is the syntax for setting these parameters.

objMail.To = "recipient1@yourdomain.com; recipient2@yourdomain.com"
obj.Mail.CC = "copyEmail@yourdomain.com"
obj.Mail.BCC = "blindCopyEmail@yourdomain.com"
objMail.Importance = ImportanceLevel

Sending E-mail from a Web page

To create a Web page that sends a static message to a single recipient:

1. Open Notepad and create a new ASP page.

2. Add the code to create the newmail object.

```
<% Dim objMail
Set objMail = CreateObject("CDONTS.Newmail")
```

3. Modify the properties to send the e-mail message to your e-mail address. Assign the to and the from properties to your e-mail address. Assign the message the highest level of importance. The subject should say **CDONTS Exercise**. The message should say, **I have completed the CDONTS exercise**.

```
objMail.From = "youraddress@yourdomain.com"
objMail.To = "youraddress@yourdomain.com"
objMail.Importance = 2
objMail.Subject = "CDONTS Exercise"
objMail.Body = "I have completed the CDONTS exercise"
ObjMail.Send
Set objMail = Nothing
%>
```

4. Save the file as **sendit.asp** in your data directory.

10

5. View your Web page in the browser.

6. Print out the Web page and the source code for the page.

7. Open your e-mail application. Print out the e-mail message.

It is important to understand that the mail server and network configuration affect how you can send outbound e-mail from your ASP pages. If you have a firewall, or special routing, you will have to modify your code. For example, in some networks, if your e-mail address were john@yourschool.edu, you might have to explicitly state the domain of the mail server. If the mail server's name were darkstar, the e-mail address would be john@darkstar.yourschool.edu.

Sending E-mail with HTML

The newmail object allows you to send the body of your message using different formats, such as basic text and HTML. The format for the message body is basic text by default. The constant for text is CdoBodyFormatText or the number 1. The constant for HTML is cdoBodyFormatHTML or the number 0. To change the format to HTML, you must change the BodyFormat property of the newmail object to CdoBodyFormatHTML. Then, you can specify HTML content in the body of the message. It is useful to specify the HTML message in a variable, and then assign the body property to the HTML variable. The sample code below shows how you would change the default BodyFormat and body properties to support HTML.

```
Dim sHTML
sHTML = "<B>This message is in bold </B>"
sHTML = sHTML + "because the message supports HTML"
objMail.BodyFormat = 0
objMail.Body = sHTML
```

Sending E-mail with Attachments

The newmail object has a method called AttachFile, which allows you to attach files to your e-mail messages. These attached files are often called **attachments**. The AttachFile method has three parameters. The location property identifies the absolute location of the attached file. The Caption property is a default caption. The third property is the type of encoding. If you use the default encoding, the encoding property is optional. Default attachments are encoded with the UUEncode parameter. You can specify the use of UUEncode encoding format with the cdoEncodingUUEncode parameter. Again, you can use the constant cdoEncodingUUEncode or the number 0. You can change the encoding parameter to support attachments that must be sent using binary encoding, with the cdoEncodingBase64 parameter. The constant cdoEncodingUUEncode can be used, or the number 1. The sample code below shows how you can use the AttachFile method to send a graphic as an attachment. The graphic must be located on the same server as the SMTP server that is sending the message.

```
objMail.AttachFile("c:\images\disk.gif", "Disk Image")
objMail.AttachFile("c:\images\disk.gif", "Disk Image",
cdoEncodingBase64)
```

LOCATING OTHER THIRD-PARTY SOFTWARE COMPONENTS ON THE INTERNET

As previously stated, several of the additional ASP components that Microsoft initially provided have been modified and improved by third-party companies. CyScape (*www.cyscape.com*) has created the BrowserHawk 2000 to provide additional features beyond those provided by the Browser Capabilities component. ServerObjects (*www.serverobjects.com*) provides several ASP components, including ASPQMail and ASPMail, which are similar to CDONTS and are frequently used by Internet service providers to integrate ASP pages with the SMTP Server.

While Microsoft provides a basic FileUpload component, Software Artisans (*www.aspstudio.com*) provides the SA-FileUp component to upload files from ASP pages to the Web server. More information on the other components that Microsoft provides can be found in the MSDN Online Library at *http://msdn.microsoft.com/library/psdk/iisref/comp275c.htm*. IISDev (*www.alphasierrapapa.com/IisDev/Components*) provides several free components that work with IIS. Hunt Interactive (*www.huntinteractive.com*) provides ASP components to make it easier to create ASP scripts within Visual InterDev. You can find other companies that provide third-party components at the ASP WebRing (*www.webring.org/cgi-bin/webring?ring=asp101;list*). You will also find support documentation for building your own ASP components on the Microsoft Web site (*www.microsoft.com*). ASP components can be written in a variety of languages, including Visual Basic and C++.

10

Installing ASP Components

ASP components, like other software, are registered in the Windows System Registry when the program is installed. Built-in components are installed automatically when you install Internet Information Server. Microsoft provides some documentation on registering server components at *http://msdn.microsoft.com/library/devprods/vs6/visualj/vjcore/vjctlregisteringcontrol.htm*. Server components must be listed in the Registry of the computer that will run the component. The Registry contains information that is required for the program to communicate with other COM objects installed on the computer. You must have administrative rights and access to the server to install and register a COM component.

You can use the Registry Installation Wizard to install the component or use the command line program called Windows Regsvr32. The Windows Regsvr32 program is used to register COM components on a computer. In Windows NT, the Regsvr32.exe program is usually located in `c:\windows\system32\`. The program is run from the Command window. To open the Command window, click Start, then click Run, then type in Command Prompt and press Enter. Specify the name of the Regsvr32 executable (Regsvr32.exe) and the name of the component, as shown below. Because the component is likely to be in a different directory, you should specify the path to the component.

Regsvr32.exe Path/componentName

Many issues come up when you are working with COM objects. If you are hosting your own Web applications on your own Web server, you will have administrative rights to the Web server. You will be able to install COM objects. However, if a hosting service provider is hosting your Web application, you will have to contact them to determine if they will install and register your COM object.

 ASP is evolving into a newer technology called ASP+. ASP+ will be backward-compatible and support ASP 3.0. One of the benefits of ASP+ is that the COM objects do not have to be registered. Therefore, it will be easier for you to install your COM objects on a Web server hosted by a hosting service provider. Visit the Microsoft MSDN Web site (*http://msdn.microsoft.com/default.asp*) to see updates on ASP+ as they become available.

CHAPTER SUMMARY

ASP components

❏ ASP components are COM objects or ActiveX controls that are used with ASP pages. The COM model allows you to work with the COM object without knowing how the COM object was created. Therefore, programs can interact without knowing how the individual programs were written.

The Browser Capabilities component

❏ The Browser Capabilities component uses information from the server variable HTTP_USER_AGENT and the Browscap.ini file to determine which browser is being used, and which features the browser supports. Because browsers are constantly being updated, the browscap.ini file needs to be updated frequently.

❏ Third party components such as BrowserHawk from cyScape are similar to the Browser Capabilities component, but maintain a more thorough list of features supported by the various browsers.

The AdRotator component

❏ The AdRotator component allows you to create and manage rotating banner ads on ASP Web applications.

❏ The Rotator Schedule File maintains the default settings for all of the banner ads, and the individual settings for each banner ad.

❏ The Rotator Schedule File contains the name of the Redirection File. The Redirection File maintains hyperlinks for the banner ads, so that when users click on an ad, they are redirected to another Web page.

❏ The method used to write the banner ad to the ASP is GetAdvertisement. The GetAdvertisement method takes the name of the Rotator Schedule File as a parameter.

The CDONTS component

❑ The CDONTS component is only available if the SMTP mail server is installed.

❑ The name of the CDONTS object used to send e-mail from a Web page is CDONTS.Newmail. The properties of the newmail object include To, From, Subject, Message, CC, BCC, and Importance.

❑ CDONTS can be used to send e-mail in different formats, including HTML, by altering the BodyFormat property.

❑ The AttachFile method is used to send e-mail with attachments.

❑ Third-party components such as ASPQMail and ASPMail are often used by hosting service providers to send e-mail from an ASP page.

Third-Party ASP components

❑ Third-party components are programs that are not installed when you install your Web server. Microsoft offers several additional components, for example CDONTS, which allows you to send outbound e-mail from a Web page, and the Posting Acceptor, which allows you to upload files to the server from a Web page.

❑ You can purchase components from other companies, or write your own ASP components. ASP components can be written in a variety of software languages, including C++ and Visual Basic. If you install a third-party component on the server, it must be registered using the Windows Regsvr32 program.

To create an application scope object in the Global Application File

```
<object runat = "Server" Scope = "Application"
PROGID = "ComponentName"  id = "objName">
</object>
```

To assign a value to a property of an application object

```
<% Application("objName").Property = value %>
```

To retrieve the HTTP_USER_AGENT server variable

```
<%request.servervariables("HTTP_USER_AGENT")%>
```

To create a Browser Capabilities component object

```
<%dim bc
Set bc = server.createobject("MSWC.BrowserType")%>
```

To retrieve the support status of a feature of the browser

```
<%bc.frames%>
```

10

To create the first section of the Rotator Scheduler File

```
Redirect RedirectPage.asp
border 4
height 50
width 400
http://www.course.com/
*
```

To create the second section of the Rotator Scheduler File

```
images/imageName.gif
http://www.course.com/
Course Technology
50
```

To create the Redirection File

```
<%Response.Redirect(Request.QueryString("url"))%>
```

To create the AdRotator component in the ASP page

```
<%dim objAd
Set objAd = Server.CreateObject("MSWC.AdRotator")%>
```

To call the GetAdvertisement method to write the banner ad in the ASP page

```
<%varAd = objAd.GetAdvertisement("AdSchedule.txt")
response.write varAd%>
```

To create the newmail object from the CDONTS component

```
<%dim objMail
Set objMail = CreateObject("CDONTS.Newmail")%>
```

To set properties of the newmail object

```
<%objMail.From = "sender@senderaddress.com"
objMail.To = "recipient@recipient.com;
recipient2@yourdomain.com"
objMail.CC = "recipient@recipient.com"
objMail.BCC = "recipient@recipient.com"
objMail.Subject = "Subject"
objMail.Importance = cdoHigh
objMail.Body = "Message Body"%>
```

To call the send method of the newmail object

```
<%objMail.Send
Set objMail = Nothing%>
```

To send HTML instead of text in the message body

```
<%dim sHTML
sHTML = "<B>This message is in bold </B>"
objMail.BodyFormat = cdoBodyFormatHTML
objMail.Body = sHTML%>
```

REVIEW QUESTIONS

1. A COM object can have which of the following file extensions?

   a. .asp

   b. .ini

   c. .dll

   d. .txt

2. Which tag is used to place a client-side ActiveX control on the Web page?

   a. <com>

   b. <object>

   c. <uid>

   d. <obj>

3. Which ASP component is used to display a rotating banner ad?

   a. Browser Capabilities component

   b. AdRotator component

   c. CDONTS component

   d. Posting Acceptor component

4. In the Global Application File, which tag is used to create an object?

   a. <com>

   b. <obj>

   c. <uic>

   d. <object>

5. COM objects created in the Global Application File can have a(n) _____ or _____ scope.

   a. application, server

   b. application, session

   c. server, session

   d. runat, state

10

6. Which of the following is the correct way to set the value of a property named "count" that has an application-level scope and has been defined in the Global Application File?

   a. Application("objName").value = 3

   b. Session("objName").count = 5

   c. Application("objName").count = 3

   d. Application("SessionName").count = 5

7. Which built-in ASP object is used to instantiate other COM objects?

   a. session

   b. server

   c. application

   d. response

8. Which method is used to instantiate a new COM object?

   a. scriptTimout

   b. createobject

   c. createobj

   d. newobject

9. Which of the following statements would return a value to the function that called the method?

   a. objName.MN "Jim", 6, "555 Main St"

   b. varName = objName.MN "Jim", 6, "555 Main St"

   c. varName = objName.MN("Jim", 6, "555 Main St")

   d. objName.MN = "Jim", 6, "555 Main St"

10. Which method releases the object from the system's memory?

    a. Set objName = " "

    b. Set objName = Abandon

    c. Set objName = None

    d. Set objName = Nothing

11. Which server variable is used to retrieve information about the user's browser version?

    a. HTTP_USER_AGENT

    b. http://USER_AGENT

    c. HTTP_user_agent

    d. HTTP_OS

12. What is the filename of the Browser Capabilities component?

    a. MSWc.BrowserHawk

    b. Browscap.ini

    c. Browscap.dll

    d. BrowserHawk

13. What is the name of the Browser Capabilities Detection File?

    a. MSWc.BrowserHawk

    b. Browscap.ini

    c. Browscap.dll

    d. BrowserHawk

14. Which company provides the most current versions of the Browser Capabilities Detection File for free?

    a. cyScape

    b. Yahoo

    c. Netscape

    d. Internet Explorer

15. What is the name of the AdRotator component?

    a. adrot.dll

    b. ad.dll

    c. adrotator.dll

    d. adrot.ext

16. Which file contains the default settings for all the banner ads?

    a. Rotator Schedule File

    b. Redirection File

    c. Browser Capabilities Detection File

    d. Ad Manager File

17. What character separates the two sections in the Rotator Schedule File?

    a. *

    b. /

    c. #

    d. $

10

18. The border, height, and width parameters are used to set properties for which HTML tag?

    a. <a>

    b. <img>

    c. <p>

    d. <ul>

19. It is possible to modify the height and width properties for individual banner ads by changing the default height and width properties in the Rotator Schedule File. True or False?

20. Which method is used to write the banner ad to the Web page?

    a. GetAdvertisement

    b. GetBannerAd

    c. DisplayBanner

    d. CreateObject

21. What software is required by the CDONTS component?

    a. SMTP Server

    b. Microsoft Exchange Server

    c. Telnet Server

    d. FTP Server

22. What object from the CDONTS component is used to send e-mail from a Web page?

    a. SMTP

    b. Newmail

    c. Send

    d. CDONTS

23. Which property sends a blind copy to another recipient?

    a. to

    b. from

    c. cc

    d. bcc

24. Which character is used to separate addresses when you are sending e-mail to multiple recipients?

    a. ;

    b. #

    c. −

    d. ,

25. Which folder on SMTP Server is used to store outbound e-mail waiting for delivery?

   a. BadMail

   b. Outbound

   c. Holding

   d. Pickup

26. What is the highest level of importance that can be set using the importance property in CDONTS?

   a. cdoHigh

   b. cdoVeryHigh

   c. cdoNormal

   d. cdoLow

27. You cannot attach files to an e-mail message using CDONTS. True or False?

28. To install a third-party component you must have administrative rights and access to the server. True or False?

29. Which program is run from the Command Prompt to register COM objects on the server?

   a. RegeditSvr32.exe

   b. Regt32.exe

   c. Regedit.exe

   d. Regsvr32.exe

10

HANDS-ON PROJECTS

Project 10-1

In this project, you will use the Browser Capabilities Detection File to identify the browsers that are supported by the Browser Capabilities component. You will also compare the Browser Capabilities component with the third-party browser component named BrowserHawk.

1. Using Notepad, create a new Web page. Add the basic HTML tags.

```
<html><head><title>Browser Detection</title></head>
<body>
<h2>Browser Detection</h2>
```

2. Using a separate instance of Notepad or your text editor, open the Browser Capabilities Detection File. On a Windows 98 computer, the file is located at `c:\windows\system\inetserv\Browscap.ini`, while on a Windows NT or Windows 2000 computer the file is located at `c:\winnt\system32\inetsrv \browscap.ini`.

3. What is the date that the Browser Capabilities Detection File was last updated? Where are the default browser settings located in the Browser Capabilities Detection File? Write the answers in the body of the Web page.

```
The date of my Browscap.ini file is _____.<br><br>
The default browser settings are located in <br>
the Browser Capabilities Detection File at the <br>
_____.<br><br>
```

4. Create the following table using information from the Browser Capabilities Detection File. Specify "T" if the feature is supported, "F" if the feature is not supported. Specify which browser version you are reviewing. You can format the table using different colors, fonts, and cell properties. Save your Web page as **bcini.asp** in your data directory, but do not close the file. You will be adding more content to the page in Step 6.

Feature	Default Browser	Netscape	IE
FRAMES			
TABLES			
COOKIES			
BACKGROUNDSOUNDS			
VBSCRIPT			
JAVASCRIPT			
JAVA APPLETS			
ACTIVEX CONTROLS			

5. Go to the Internet to retrieve a more up-to-date Browser Capabilities Detection File at *http://www.cyscape.com/browscap/*. Follow the online instructions for downloading the file. You will have to unzip the file using file compression software such as WinZip. If you do not have any file compression software, you can go to a Tucows mirror site (*www.tucows.com*) to download freeware file compression software. Open the file in WordPad or another word processor. (The current version is too large to be opened in Notepad.)

6. When was the browscap.ini file last updated? What is the most recent version of Netscape that is supported? What is the most recent version of Internet Explorer that is supported? Write the answers in the body of the Web page. (*Hint:* You can read the information in the heading of the page to locate this information.)

```
<br><br>
<h2>Recent Versions of the
Browser Component Detection File</h2>
The most recent version of the <br>
Browscap.ini file was updated on: <br>
_____ <br><br>
Version _____ contains information about: <br>
Netscape _____ and <br>
MSIE _____ <br><br>
```

7. List at least 13 features that are supported by the BrowserHawk component but not by the Browser Capabilities component. (*Hint:* A summary of features is listed at *http://www.browscap.com/products/bhawk/compare.asp*.) Create a bulleted list that contains the features. (*Hint:* There should be 13 list item tags.) You can format the list using line breaks if needed.

```
<h2>Features of BrowserHawk</h2>
Here are some of the features that BrowserHawk <br>
supports that are not supported by the <br>
Browser Capabilities component. <br><br>
<ol>
<li>_____</li>
</ol>
```

8. Close the Browser Capabilities Detection File. Do not save changes to the Browser Capabilities Detection File.

9. Save the changes to **bcini.asp** in your data directory. View your Web page in a browser. Print your Web page.

Project 10-2

In this project, you will use the Browser Capabilities component to detect which features a browser supports.

1. Using Notepad, create a Web page. Add the basic HTML tags. Add the title and a heading 2 that says **Left Frame**.

```
<html><head><title>Left Frame</title></head>
<body>
<h2>Left Frame</h2>
</body></html>
```

2. Save the Web page as **left.asp** in your data directory.

3. Save the left.asp page as **right.asp** in your data directory. Change the title and heading to **Right Frame**.

4. Save the right.asp page as **noframes.asp** in your data directory. Change the title and heading to **No Frames**.

5. Create a Web page that contains two frames, right.asp and left.asp. Save the page as **frames.asp** in your data directory. Use the sample code below to create your Web page.

```
<html><head><title>Frames</title></head>
<frameset cols="150,*">
  <frame name="contents" target="main" src="left.asp">
  <frame name="main" src="right.asp" target="main">
</frameset>
</html>
```

6. Create a new ASP page named **bcframes.asp**, using Notepad or your ASP-compatible tool. Because no HTML will be displayed by this page, you do not need to add the basic HTML tags.

7. At the top of the page, declare a variable named **bc** to hold the Browser Capabilities component. Create the browser object using the createobject method of the server object.

```
<% response.buffer = "true"
Set bc = server.createobject("MSWC.BrowserType")
```

8. Create a script that detects whether the browser supports frames. If the browser supports frames, then redirect the user to a page that contains multiple frames (Frames.asp); otherwise, redirect the user to a page that does not contain frames (noFrames.asp). (*Hint:* You can use server-side redirection with the redirect method of the response object, as shown below, or client-side redirection with the HREF method of the location object. You can also use the meta tag Refresh command to redirect the visitor to a new page.)

```
if bc.frames = TRUE then
     response.redirect "frames.asp"
else
     response.redirect "noframes.asp"
end if
%>
```

9. Modify the appearance of all of the Web pages with your favorite fonts, colors, and images.

10. Save the changes as **bcframes.asp** to your data directory.

11. View the bcframes.asp Web page. If your browser supports frames, you will be redirected to the frames.asp page. Print your source code for each Web page.

Project 10-3

In this project, you will create a Web page that displays a rotating banner advertisement.

1. Create four graphics files of the same size for your banner ads. (Name them ad1.gif...ad4.gif.) You can create them in your graphics program or use the banner generator form at Coder.com (*http://www.coder.com/creations/banner/banner-form.pl.cgi*).

2. Create the Schedule File, and call it **adschedule2.txt**. Specify a height, width, and border appropriate for your image files.

3. Specify the parameters for each banner ad. The first image should redirect the user to the Microsoft MSDN Web site at *http://msdn.microsoft.com*. The alternate text is **MSDN Home**. The ad should be displayed **10** % of the time. The second image should redirect the user to the Microsoft Scripting Library site at *http://msdn.microsoft.com/scripting*. The alternate text is **Scripting Library**. The ad should be displayed **20** % of the time. The third image should redirect the user to the Microsoft IIS Web site at *http://www.microsoft.com/iis*. The alternate text is **Internet**

Information Server. The ad should be displayed **30** % of the time. The fourth image should redirect the user to the Microsoft MSDN Web site at *http://msdn.microsoft.com/vstudio.* The alternate text is **Visual Studio.** The ad should be displayed **40** % of the time.

4. Create the Redirect Asp page, and call it **changepage.asp.** Add the code to redirect the user to the link that was passed from the Web page.

5. Create a Web page named **adpage2.asp.**

6. Write the code to create the AdRotator component and display the banner ad. (*Hint:* Declare two variables named objAd and varAd. Use the createobject method of the server object to create a new instance of the AdRotator component. Assign objAd to the new instance of the AdRotator component. The name of the AdRotator component is MSWC.AdRotator. Use the GetAdvertisement method to generate the HTML to create the ad. The parameter for the GetAdvertisement method is AdSchedule2.txt. Assign the result from the GetAdvertisement method to the varAd variable. Use the write method to write the value of varAd to the Web page.)

```
<% Dim objAd, varAd
Set objAd = Server.CreateObject("MSWC.AdRotator")
varAd = objAd.GetAdvertisement("AdSchedule2.txt")
response.write varAd
%>
```

10

7. Modify the Web page appearance with your favorite fonts, colors, and images.

8. Save the pages to your data directory. View the AdPage2.asp page.

9. Print your source code for your ASP page, the AdRedirect page and the Rotator Schedule File.

Project 10-4

In this project, you will create a Web page that sends e-mail using a form. You will only be able to complete this activity if you are running NT Server with SMTP Mail Server, Windows 2000 Professional with IIS, or Windows 2000 Server.

1. Create a Web page. Add the basic HTML tags. The title of the page should be **Create E-mail Message.** Add a heading formatted as heading 2 and centered that says **Create an e-mail message.**

2. Add a form that uses the **post** method and that points to the **sendmail.asp** Web page.

3. Create a form with three fields. The first field, called **txtEmail**, should be a text box that is a maximum of **25** characters long, which will contain the recipient's e-mail address. The other text field should be named **txtSubject** and be **25** characters in length. The last form field is a text box that is named **txtComments** and is **25** characters in length. Add a Submit button that says **Send.**

4. Modify the Web page appearance with your favorite fonts, colors, and images. You can use line breaks, tables, and other HTML tags to format the layout of the page. Save the page in your data directory as **createmail.asp.**

5. Create a second page named **sendmail.asp**. Set the buffer property of the response object to true. Add the basic HTML tags. The title of the page should be **Send E-mail**. Add a heading 2 that says **Send E-mail**.

6. Create a new instance of the CDONTS object and assign it to a variable named **objMail**.

7. Assign your e-mail address to the **From** property.

8. Retrieve the values from the form using the forms collection of the request object. Assign the txtEmail form field value to the **To** Property of the objMail object. Assign the txtSubject form field value to the **Subject** property of the objMail object. Assign the txtComments form field value to the **Body** property of the objMail object.

9. Send the mail using the **Send** method of the objMail object. Set the objMail to nothing, to free the variable.

10. Add the closing HTML tags. (*Hint*: Add the closing body and closing HTML tag.)

11. Save the sendmail.asp page to your data directory.

12. View the Web page, complete the form, and submit the form.

13. Print your page and the source code for both pages.

CASE PROJECTS

Monroe Markets—Detecting the Browser Version

You have been hired in the Marketing Department of Monroe Markets to assist them in developing their Web site. Your manager is concerned because Netscape Navigator does not support the current layout and design of the Web pages. Your job is to create a script that detects the browser version, and then redirects the user to a page that supports that browser version. Note that without the most up-to-date version of the Browser Detection File, the newest Netscape browser will be detected as a generic browser. If the Netscape browser is detected, redirect the user to a page named monroe1.asp. If the Internet Explorer browser is detected, redirect the user to a page named monroe2.asp. If a browser version is not detected, send the user to a page named monroe3.asp. Create the three Web pages: monroe1.asp, monroe2.asp, and monroe3.asp. Modify each Web page appearance with your favorite fonts, colors, and images. Create an ASP page named monroe.asp that contains the Browser Capabilities component and server-side redirection script. You can use line breaks, tables, and other HTML tags to format the layout of each page. Save your pages in your data directory. View the Web page in different browser versions. Print out the pages and the source code.

Monroe Markets—Browser Components

The Marketing Department asks you to develop a proposal to use a third-party component to detect the browser version, instead of using the Browser Capabilities component. Visit the CyScape Web site at *http://www.cyscape.com*. Create a short proposal discussing the reasons why a company might wish to use a third-party component such as BrowserHawk 2000. Compare the features, installation, software requirements, documentation, technical support, and cost. Provide a recommendation to use or not to use the third-party software. Provide reasons for your selection. Create a Web page named bcproposal.asp that displays your proposal. Modify the appearance of the Web page. Save the Web page to your data directory. View the Web page in a browser. Print out the Web page.

Monroe Markets—Customer Feedback Form

You are hired by Monroe Markets to alter their customer support Web site. You discover that the site's feedback form is being sent using the mailto: protocol. You recommend that the form be modified to send the results using ASP. After learning that the server has SMTP installed, you recommend using CDONTS to send the form results from the Web page. Create a new form on a Web page named monroecreate.asp. The form should include the return address of the user along with the user's comments. The form should not allow the user to alter the destination address or the subject, and it should use the post method and the action monroesend.asp. Create the monroesend.asp page, which will be used to send the results through the SMTP server. Retrieve the values from the form and assign them to variables. After creating the SendMail object from the CDONTS component, use the variables to change the properties of the SendMail object. Modify the To property to your own e-mail address. Modify the Subject property to say Customer Support Feedback Form. Modify the appearance of the monroecreate.asp page. Save both Web pages to your data directory. View the monroecreate.asp page in a browser. Print out each Web page and the source code. Send an e-mail message using the form. View the e-mail message using your e-mail program. Print the e-mail message.

Hunter Books—Counting Banner Ad Clicks Using Application Variables

You are hired by Hunter Books to create a Web page that rotates banner ads. The marketing manager asks you to create a Web page that displays at least three banner ads. The marketing manager would like to receive payment for displaying the banner ads. Your first task is to use your graphic image creation software or banner ad generator to create three graphics named hunt1.gif, hunt2.gif, and hunt3.gif. Your second task is to create three application variables named hunt1, hunt2, and hunt3 in the global.asa file which will be used to track the hits to the ads. Your third task is to create an ASP page named hunt.asp that displays the rotating banner ads. The parameter for the GetAdvertisement method should be huntschedule.txt. Modify the appearance of the hunt.asp page using graphics, fonts, and text. Save the hunt.asp page to your data directory. Your fourth task is to create the Rotator Schedule File named huntschedule.txt. You can select the image parameters to include in the Rotator Schedule File. Direct them to three bookstores that distribute Hunter books—Amazon at *www.amazon.com*, Borders Books and Music at *www.borders.com*, and Barnes and Noble at *www.barnesandnoble.com*. Each ad is displayed an equal amount of time. Your fifth task is to create the Redirection File named huntredirect.asp and include a script, which will count the number of times that each ad was displayed to a specific user. It does not matter if the visitor has seen the ad before, or has visited the page previously. When the user clicks on the image, the image and URL parameters

10

are passed in the querystring. Retrieve the querystring values. Determine which image was clicked. If the hunt1 image was selected, lock the hunt1 application variable and increment it by one. If the hunt2 image was selected, lock the hunt2 application variable and increment it by one. Otherwise, increment the hunt3 application variable by one. Your last task is to create a page named huntuser.asp that informs the visitor of the number of times that each ad was clicked, by displaying the application variable. Show the total hits for each ad and the grand total. The grand total is the sum of all three application variables. Save all of the ASP pages to your data directory. View each page in a browser. Print out the Web page and the source code for all of your Web pages, including the Global Application File.

Hunter Books—File Upload Components

You are hired as part of the Hunter Books Web consulting team. The team is building a business-to-business Web site for the company. The manager must be able to upload files from their network to their business partner's network. They decide that they would like to use a Web browser to interface with their network. Your job is to recommend methods that would allow the user to upload a file from one network to another network, using a browser. Visit Web sites to assess their third-party upload components. Software Artisans (*www.softwareartisans.com*) produces SA-FileUp *http://www.softwareartisans.com/saf.html*. Microsoft provides a file upload component called the Posting Acceptor for free, from Site Server Express. Site Server Express is available on the NT Option Pack CD-ROM. Read the support documentation on the Posting Acceptor at *http://msdn.microsoft.com/workshop/server/asp/server052499.asp*. Additional documentation on the Posting Acceptor component is available at:

◻ *http://support.microsoft.com/support/kb/articles/Q217/4/25.ASP*

◻ *http://support.microsoft.com/support/kb/articles/Q184/3/52.ASP*

◻ *http://support.microsoft.com/support/kb/articles/Q189/6/51.ASP*

◻ *http://support.microsoft.com/support/kb/articles/Q222/6/18.ASP*

Visit e-mail groups that support ASP to determine whether other ASP upload components or upload solutions are available. Some e-mail groups that support ASP include ASP (*www.egroups.com/list/asp*) and ASP-Beginner (*www.egroups.com/group/asp-beginer*) at eGroups (*www.egroups.com*). Create a Web page named upload.asp that compares all the file upload solutions. Modify the appearance of the upload.asp page using graphics, fonts, and text. Save the upload.asp page to your data directory. Print out the Web page.

11

THE SCRIPTING LIBRARY OBJECTS

In this chapter you will:

♦ Learn how scripting library objects are accessed from an ASP page
♦ Store and retrieve data using the dictionary object
♦ Manage files on the server using the FileSystemObject
♦ Store and retrieve data from a file on the server using the textstream object
♦ Use the err object to handle errors and error messages

In previous chapters you learned how to use third-party objects to perform activities such as displaying a rotating banner ad, or sending e-mail from a Web page. In this chapter, you will learn how to use the scripting library objects to perform file system activities such as creating a text file, displaying the directory contents, and reading the contents of a file. You will also learn how to use the error object to obtain information about the type of error that has occurred.

THE SCRIPTING LIBRARY

As you learned in previous chapters of this book, third-party objects are simply components that are installed on the server. These components are compiled programs that are executable (.exe) files or dynamic-link libraries (.dll). DLL files are also known as libraries. When IIS is installed, a DLL called the **Microsoft Scripting Runtime** (also known as the **Microsoft Scripting Library**) is installed. This file is located by default in C:\winnt\system32\ scrrun.dll. The Scripting Library contains three objects: the FileSystemObject, the dictionary object, and the err object. The FileSystemObject contains several objects and methods that allow your Web application to interact with the server's file system. The dictionary object allows you to store two-dimensional data in a collection. More information on the objects found in the Scripting Library can be found in the Microsoft Windows Script Technologies Web site at *http://msdn.microsoft.com/scripting/default.htm?/scripting/vbscript/default.htm*.

THE DICTIONARY OBJECT

The dictionary object is used to store **two-dimensional** data. Two-dimensional data consists of two pieces of data, the key and the item. The key and the item are stored together. You can retrieve the value of the item by specifying the name of the related key. The dictionary object can be used to store many types of data, such as a list of HTML tags and their meanings, article names and their summaries, user preferences and their values, user information and its values, and form field names and their values. To create a dictionary object, use the server object's CreateObject method .

```
Dim objDictPreferences
Set objDictPreferences = Server.CreateObject("Scripting.Dictionary")
```

The dictionary object contains methods such as add and remove, which allow you to add or remove a key/item pair from the dictionary object. You can use the RemoveAll method to delete all of the key/item pairs. The keys method will return a single-dimension array of all of the keys within the dictionary object, while the items method returns an array of all the items. To avoid error messages, you should detect whether the key exists before you retrieve the item or key, or add or remove a key/item pair. The exists method is used to determine whether a specific key exists. A list of the methods and properties available to the dictionary object is given in Table 11-1.

Table 11-1   Properties and Methods of the ObjName Dictionary Object

Properties and Methods	Description	Example
ObjName.Add key, item	Adds a key/item pair	`ObjDAddress.Add "State", "IL"`
ObjName.Remove("Key")	Removes a key/item pair	`ObjDAddress.Remove ("State")`
ObjName.RemoveAll	Removes all the key/item pairs	`ObjDAddress.RemoveAll`
ObjName.Count	Returns the number of key/item pairs	`Num =ObjDAddress.Count`
ObjName.Exists("Key")	Checks if a key exists	`ObjDAddress.Exists ("State")`
ObjName.Items	Returns all the items in an array	`ObjDAddress.Items`
ObjName.Keys	Returns all the keys in an array	`ObjDAddress.Keys`
ObjName.Item("Key")	Can be used to set or return the value of an item	`ObjDAddress.Item("State")`
ObjName.Key("Key")	Can be used to set or return the value of a key	`ObjDAddress.Key("State")`

The following example illustrates how to create an ASP application that can store the values from a form in the dictionary object. To use the dictionary object to store the values from a form:

1. Create a new ASP page using Notepad or your ASP editor.

2. Create the member registration form using the following code:

```
<html><head><title>Registration Form</title></head>
<body>
<h2 align="center">Member Registration Form</h2>
<form method="POST" action="dictFormProcess.asp">
<table border="0" align="center">
<tr><td>Member ID</td>
<td>
<input type="text" name="memberid" size="20">
</td></tr>
<tr><td>First Name</td>
<td>
<input type="text" name="fname" size="20">
</td></tr>
<tr><td>Last Name</td>
<td>
<input type="text" name="lname" size="20">
```

```
</td></tr>
<tr><td>Address</td>
<td>
<input type="text" name="address" size="20">
</td></tr>
<tr><td>City</td>
<td>
<input type="text" name="city" size="20">
</td></tr>
<tr><td>State</td>
<td><input type="text" name="state" size="4">
</td></tr>
<tr><td>Zip Code</td>
<td><input type="text" name="zipcode" size="10">
</td></tr>
<tr><td>Country</td>
<td><input type="text" name="country" size="4">
</td></tr>
<tr><td>Dues Paid</td>
<td>
<input type="radio" value="Yes" checked name="paidDues">Yes
<input type="radio" name="paidDues" value="No">No
</td></tr>
<tr><td>Amount Paid</td>
<td><input type="text" name="AmountPaid" size="10">
</td></tr>
<tr><td><p>Committee</td>
<td><p>
<input type="checkbox" name="general" value="General">
General Member <br>
<input type="checkbox" name="board" value="Board">
Board Member<br>
</td></tr></table>
<div align = "center"><br>
<input type="submit" value="Submit" name="btnSubmit">
</div></form></body></html>
```

3. Save this page to your data directory as **dictionaryForm.asp**.

4. Create a Web page using Notepad that will process the form. Add the basic HTML tags.

```
<html><head><title>Process Form</title></head>
<body>
<h2 align="center">Process Form</h2>
```

5. Retrieve the form field values from the form collection. Because the method used was post, the form collection is used to retrieve the values from the form. Assign the values retrieved from the form fields to variables.

```
<%
memberid = Request.Form("memberid")
fname = Request.Form("fname")
lname = Request.Form("lname")
address = Request.Form("address")
city = Request.Form("city")
state = Request.Form("state")
zipcode = Request.Form("zipcode")
country = Request.Form("country")
paiddues = Request.Form("paiddues")
amountpaid = Request.Form("amountpaid")
general = Request.Form("general")
board = Request.Form("board")
%>
```

6. Create the dictionary object using the CreateObject method. The dictionary object will be used to store the values from the form collection.

```
<% Dim objDMember
Set objDMember =
Server.CreateObject("Scripting.Dictionary")
%>
```

11

7. Then use the add method to set variables that hold the form field values to the dictionary key names. Use the add method to add the name of the form field as the name of the keys.

```
<%
objDMember.Add "memberid", memberid
objDMember.Add "fname", fname
objDMember.Add "lname", lname
objDMember.Add "address", address
objDMember.Add "city", city
objDMember.Add "state", state
objDMember.Add "zipcode", zipcode
objDMember.Add "country", country
objDMember.Add "paiddues", paiddues
objDMember.Add "amountpaid", amountpaid
```

8. If the user checks one of the membership boxes (general or board) on the form, then add those values to the dictionary object. This will prevent you from adding an empty value in the dictionary object.

```
if general <> "" then
     objDMember.Add "general", general
else
end if
```

```
if board <> "" then
     objDMember.Add "board", board
else
end if
%>
```

9. Display the total number of entries in the dictionary object, using the count property.

```
<h4>Thank you for your registration.</h4>
<font face="Trebuchet MS">
You have entered <% = objDMember.count %> fields
<br><br>
Your membership entry will show the following information:
<br><br>
```

10. Retrieve the values of the dictionary object keys, using the item property and the write method.

```
Member ID -- <% = objDMember.Item("memberid") %><br>
First Name -- <% = objDMember.Item("fname") %><br>
Last Name -- <% = objDMember.Item("lname") %><br>
Address -- <% = objDMember.Item("address") %><br>
City -- <% = objDMember.Item("city") %><br>
State -- <% = objDMember.Item("state") %><br>
Zip Code -- <% = objDMember.Item("zipcode") %><br>
Country -- <% = objDMember.Item("country") %><br>
Dues Paid -- <% = objDMember.Item("paiddues") %><br>
Amount Paid -- <% = objDMember.Item("amountpaid") %>
<br><br>
```

11. Because the member fields can be checked or unchecked, the entry in the item may be empty. You can detect if the item does not exist by using the exists property.

```
<%  if objDMember.Exists("general")  then
     response.write "You are a general member"
else
     response.write "You are not a general member"
end if %>
<br><br>
<% if objDMember.Exists("board")  then
     response.write "You are a board member"
else
     response.write "You are not a board member"
end if %>
</font></body></html>
```

12. Modify the Web page appearance by changing the background, font, and colors, and adding content.

13. Save the page as **dictFormProcess.asp** in your data directory.

14. View the dictionaryForm.asp Web page in the browser. Complete and submit the form.

15. View the source code for each page. Print out the Web page and the source code for each page.

THE FILESYSTEMOBJECT OBJECT

The FileSystemObject is one of the three scripting objects in the Scripting Library. The FileSystemObject provides methods, objects, and collections that can interact with the file system on the server. For example, using the FileSystemObject, you can retrieve information about the drives, create text files on the server, copy files from one directory to another directory, and delete files on the server. The FileSystemObject contains several other objects, such as the drive object, the folder object, the file object, and the textstream object.

To create an instance of the FileSystemObject, declare a variable to hold the object. It is useful to prefix this variable with objFSO, to indicate that it is holding a FileSystemObject. Then, use the CreateObject method of the server object to create the FileSystemObject. This FileSystemObject can be used to retrieve the drive object, the folder object, and the file object.

```
Dim objFSO, objDrives
Set objFSO = Server.CreateObject("Scripting.FileSystemObject")
```

The FileSystemObject contains several methods that you can use to manipulate drives, folders, and files. Table 11-2 lists the FileSystemObject objects and methods. The FileSystemObject methods listed in Table 11-2 are used in combination with the methods and properties of the drive, folder, and file objects. The paths, filenames, and folders that are passed as parameters to the methods of the FileSystemObject can be passed as a string, an expression, or a variable. Note that the methods of the FileSystemObject can only manipulate drives, folders, and files on the server. The FileSystemObject cannot manipulate drives, folders, and files on the client. When calling the FileSystemObject, it is optional to include the name of the FileSystemObject. If the object or path passed does not exist, an error may occur. It is useful to verify whether an object exists, using the FolderExists or FileExists property, before manipulating it.

```
Dim objFSO
Set objFSO = server.createobject("Scripting.FileSystemObject")
Set objDrives = objFSP. MethodName(parameters)
```

11

Table 11-2   FileSystemObject Methods

Target Object	Method Name	Purpose	Example
Drive	GetDrive	Returns a drive object from the drives collection; can be a drive letter C or C:, or a network share such as \\servername\sharename	`objFSO.GetDrive("a:")` `objFSO.GetDrive("a:")` `objFSO.GetDrive ("\\server1\marketing")`
Drive	GetDriveName	Returns the name of the drive	`objFSO.GetDrive ("c:\test\")`
Folder	GetFolder	Returns a folder object from the folder collection	`objFSO.GetFolder ("c:\test\")`
Folder	GetSpecialFolder	Returns the folder object for three special folders; uses a constant or number to represent the special folder. The Windows folder is WindowsFolder or 0. The System folder is SystemFolder or 1. The Temp folder is Temporary Folder or 2.	`objFSO.GetSpecialFolder (0)` `objFSO.GetSpecialFolder (WindowsFolder)`
Folder	GetFolder ParentName	Returns the Parent Name for the folder	`objFSO. GetFolderParentName ("c:\test\test2\file. txt")`
Folder	FolderExists	Determines whether a folder exists; returns true or false.	`objFSO.FolderExists ("c:\file.txt")`
Folder	CreateFolder	Creates a folder	`objFSO.CreateFolder "c:\test"`
Folder	CopyFolder	Copies a folder from one location to another. A Boolean value is used to indicate whether the destination file should be overwritten if it exists.	`objFSO.CopyFile "c:\source\", "c:\target", true`
Folder	MoveFolder	Copies a folder from one location to another and deletes the source folder	`objFSO.MoveFolder "c:\source", "c:\target"`
Folder	DeleteFolder	Deletes a folder	`objFSO.DeleteFolder "c:\test"`

Table 11-2   FileSystemObject Methods (continued)

Target Object	Method Name	Purpose	Example
File	GetFile	Returns a file object from the files collection	`objFSO.GetFile ("c:\test\file.txt")`
File	FileExists	Determines whether a file exits; returns true or false	`objFSO.FileExists ("c:\test\file.txt")`
File	CreateTextFile	Creates a file and returns a TextStream object that is used to read from or write to a text file	`objFSO.CreateTextFile ("c:\test\file.txt")`
File	CopyFile	Copies a file from one location to another. A Boolean value is used to indicate whether the destination file should be overwritten if it exists.	`objFSO.CopyFile "c:\test\source.txt", "c:\test\target.txt", true`
File	MoveFile	Copies a file from one location to another. You can delete the file using the DeleteFile method	`objFSO.MoveFile "c:\test\source.txt", "c:\test\target.txt", true`
File	DeleteFile	Deletes a file	`objFSO.DeleteFile "c:\test\file.txt"`
File	OpenTextFile	Opens an existing file and returns a TextStream object that is used to read from or write to a text file. Parameters are used to indicate whether you are reading, writing, or appending to a file, and the type of file.	`objFSO.OpenTextFile ("c:\test.txt", forappending, false)`
File	GetFileName	Returns the name of the file. For (c:\test\file.txt) it would return 'file.txt'.	`objFSO.GetFileName ("c:\test\file.txt")`
File	GetExtension Name	Returns the extension name for the last item in the path. (For file.txt it would return 'txt'.)	`objFSO.GetExtensionName ("c:\test\file.txt")`
File	GetbaseName	Returns the file name up to the extension. (For file.txt it would return 'file'.)	`objFSO.GetbaseName ("c:\test\file.txt")`

11

Table 11-2 FileSystemObject Methods (continued)

Target Object	Method Name	Purpose	Example
File	GetTempName	Returns a randomly generated name for the file or folder, which is used when working with temporary files	`objFSO.GetTempName()`
Path	BuildPath	Appends a file or folder name to the current path. Inserts a backslash (\) to separate the current path and the name. Pass the path and the name to append.	`objFSO.BuildPath ("c:\test, ProjectFolder")`
Path	GetAbsolute PathName	Returns the full path for the current file or folder	`objFSO. GetAbsolutePathName ("c:\test\file.txt")`

It is important to note that the GetDrive method requires both the object and the drive parameter in order to return a drive object from the drives collection.

You can pass the path parameter as a string, for example `C:\test\F1`. You can also store the path in a variable, and then use the variable as the parameter.

Using the FileSystemObject

You can use the methods of the FileSystemObject to manage files and folders. To create, copy, move, and delete folders and files using the methods of the FileSystemObject:

1. Create a folder in your data directory named **FolderTest**. This folder will hold all of the files and folders that will be created in this exercise.

2. Create an ASP page, using Notepad or another ASP-compatible editor.

3. Add the basic HTML tags.

```
<html><head><title>FSO Folder and File Methods
</title></head>
<body>
<h3 align = "center">Manipulating Folders</h3>
```

4. Create a variable that will hold the path to your folders and files. Replace the value of fp with the path to your FolderTest directory, which you created in Step 1.

```
<%
dim fp
fp = "c:\chapter11\FolderTest"
```

5. Create the variables that will hold the folder names. Assign the variables the folder names, as shown below. The fp variable is used to store the path to the folder. The path is concatenated with the folder name.

```
folderCreate = fp & "\F1"
folderCopy1 = fp & "\F2"
folderCopy2 = fp & "\F3"
folderSrc = fp & "\F4"
folderDest = fp & "\F5"
folderDel = fp & "\F6"
```

6. Add the script to create the FileSystemObject named objFSO.

```
Dim objFSO
Set objFSO = CreateObject("Scripting.FileSystemObject")
```

7. Create four of the folders using the CreateFolder method of the FileSystemObject.

```
objFSO.CreateFolder folderCreate
objFSO.CreateFolder folderCopy1
objFSO.CreateFolder folderSrc
objFSO.CreateFolder folderDel
```

8. Use the CopyFolder method of the FileSystemObject to copy folderCopy1 to folderCopy2. Pass an additional parameter, "True", to indicate that the existing folder should be overwritten if it is present.

```
objFSO.CopyFolder folderCopy1, folderCopy2, True
```

9. Use the MoveFolder method to move the folderSrc folder to the folderDest folder. The move method will delete the original folderSrc folder after the folderDest folder is created.

```
objFSO.MoveFolder folderSrc, folderDest
```

10. Use the delete method of the FileSystemObject to delete the folderDel folder.

```
objFSO.DeleteFolder folderDel
```

11. Close the script and add the word "Done" along with a heading for the next piece of code, which will manipulate files instead of folders.

```
%>
Done
<h3>Manipulating Files</h3>
```

11

12. Create variables to hold the filenames. Use the filenames below. You should replace the studentFolderPath with the complete absolute path to your data directory.

```
<%
fileCreate = fp & "\F1.txt"
fileCopy1 = fp & "\F2.txt"
fileCopy2 = fp & "\F3.txt"
fileSrc = fp & "\F4.txt"
fileDest = fp & "\F5.txt"
fileDel = fp & "\F6.txt"
```

13. Create the following four files, using the CreateTextFile method of the FileSystemObject. Because the FileSystemObject was already instantiated in the above script, you do not have to create it again.

```
objFSO.CreateTextFile fileCreate
objFSO.CreateTextFile fileCopy1
objFSO.CreateTextFile fileSrc
objFSO.CreateTextFile fileDel
```

14. Use the CopyFile method to copy fileCopy1 to fileCopy2. Pass the value "True" as a parameter to overwrite the fileCopy2 file if it already exists.

```
objFSO.CopyFile fileCopy1, fileCopy2, True
```

15. Use the MoveFile method to move the fileSrc file to the fileDest file. The original fileSrc file will be deleted after the fileDest file has been created.

```
objFSO.MoveFile fileSrc, fileDest
```

16. Delete the fileDel file, using the DeleteFile method of the FileSystemObject.

```
objFSO.DeleteFile fileDel
```

17. Close the script and add the closing HTML tags

```
%>
</body></html>
```

18. Modify the Web page appearance by changing the background, font, and colors, and adding content.

19. Save the page as **fsoMethods.asp** to your data directory.

20. View your Web page in the browser.

21. View the files in your data directory. You should have folders named F1, F2, F3, and F5 in your data directory. You should also have files named F1.txt, F2.txt, F3.txt, and F5.txt.

22. Print out the Web page and source code to your Web page. If you view the page again, you need to first delete the files in the chapter11 directory. Otherwise, the script detects that a file is being overwritten and will produce an error message that says the file already exists.

The Drive Object

As you know, computers store information on devices called disk drives. The drive object contains a collection of all of the disk drives attached to the server. The drive object is the drives collection within the FileSystemObject that allows you to retrieve information about the drives that are accessible on the server. The drive object allows you to retrieve information about the drives on the server, and to access the properties of the individual disk drives. To access the drive object's properties, you use the FileSystemObject object. For example, the DriveLetter and the DriveType properties return the letter assigned to the drive, and the type of disk drive. Because the drive object is a collection within the FileSystemObject, you do not create a drive object. The drive object contains an array of the disk drive objects. You can retrieve properties of a specific disk drive device or all the drive devices.

```
Dim objFSO, objDrive
Set objFSO = server.createobject("Scripting.FileSystemObject")
Set objDrive = objFSP.Drives
ObjDrive.Property
```

Properties of the Drive Object

The drive object contains many read-only properties that can be accessed from your scripts. Table 11-3 lists the properties of the drive object. Before accessing the properties of a drive object, you should test to see if the drive is accessible, using the IsReady property. The IsReady property returns a value of "True" if the disk drive is accessible. Listed below are the drive object's properties.

- AvailableSpace
- Count
- DriveLetter
- DriveType
- FileSystem
- FreeSpace
- IsReady

- Path
- RootFolder
- SerialNumber
- ShareName
- TotalSize
- VolumeName

11

Table 11-3   Properties of the Drive Object and Drive Collection

Name	Description	Example	Returned Value
Count	Returns the number of drives in the drives collection	`objDrives.count`	5
IsReady	Returns "True" if the device is ready or "False" if it is not ready	`keyDrv.IsReady(c)`	True
DriveType	Returns a number indicating the storage format: O Unknown 1 Removable 2 Fixed 3 Network 4 CD-ROM 5 RAM Disk	`keyDrv.DriveLetter`	2
FreeSpace	Returns the total free disk space of the current drive in bytes	`keyDrv.FreeSpace`	191627264
TotalSize	Returns the total size of the current drive in bytes	`keyDrv.TotalSize`	2146467840
AvailableSpace	Returns the total available disk space of the current drive in bytes	`keyDrv.Available Space`	191627264
FileSystem	Returns the file system installed on the drive.	`keyDrv.FileSystem`	FAT
DriveLetter	Returns the drive letter	`keyDrv.DriveLetter`	C
Path	Returns the path for the drive	`keyDrv.Path`	C
RootFolder	Returns the root directory for the drive	`keyDrv.RootFolder`	C:\
SerialNumber	Returns the serial number of the disk drive	`keyDrv.SerialNumber`	542314471
ShareName	Returns the share name if the drive is a network drive	`keyDrv.ShareName`	Server1
VolumeName	Returns the volume name if one was assigned when the drive was installed	`keyDrv.VolumeName`	Blackcat

The drive object has a property called DriveType that returns a number representing the type of drive being accessed. There are many types of disk drive devices. Floppy disk drives are used to store small amounts of data on removable disks. Other removable disk drives include Zip drives, Jaz drives, and hard disk removable drives. The DriveType property returns the number "1" for removable disk drives. Hard disk drives store large amounts of data. Because most hard disk drives are not removed from the system, they are called fixed hard drives. The DriveType property for fixed drives is "2". CD-ROMS and DVD devices are generally used to store large amounts of data in a read-only format. The DriveType property for CD-ROMS is "4".

The amount of data that a disk drive can store is measured in bytes. The FreeSpace property returns the amount of free space on the disk drive measured in bytes, while the TotalSize property returns the drive's total space. The AvailableSpace property returns the number of bytes that could be used on the disk drive. Often the FreeSpace property returns the same value as the AvailableSpace property.

The numbers returned for the FreeSpace, TotalSize, and AvailableSpace properties are measured in bytes. There are about 1,048,576 bytes in one megabyte. A floppy drive typically stores about one megabyte of data. There are about 1,073,741,824 bytes in one gigabyte. Hard drive disks can typically store from one to twenty gigabytes of data. You can convert the value returned from the disk drive properties to megabytes by dividing the number returned by 1,048,576.

The numbers returned for the FreeSpace, TotalSize, and AvailableSpace properties are formatted as plain numbers, such as 1073741824. To make the number more readable, you can format the number with commas, for example 1,073,741,824. The formatNumber method can be used to format a number. The FormatNumber method is passed an expression that evaluates to a number. You can specify the number of digits to display after the decimal. For example, if the number was 3459.33124, and the DecimalDigits parameter was 2, the number returned by the formatNumber method would be 3459.33. If you want a leading digit to be used, then specify the LeadingDigit parameter as "-1". The NegParenthesis parameter formats the number within parentheses if it is negative. The GroupDigits parameter is often used to indicate whether to group the numbers. If the GroupDigits parameter is 0, the number will be formatted with the group delimiter specified in the server's settings in the server's control panel. The number returned from the AvailableSpace property can be formatted using the formatNumber method.

FormatNumber(Expression [,DecimalDigits [,LeadingDigit [,NegParenthesis [,GroupDigits]]]])

Use the following code to convert the AvailableSpace property of the keyDrv drive object from bytes to megabytes.

```
formatNumber((keyDrv.AvailableSpace/1048576),0)
```

11

Other Drive Object Properties

Operating systems will store the information on the disk drive using different file system methods. The FileSystem property of the drive object will return the format method used for the disk drive device. Windows 95 and 98 frequently use the FAT or FAT32 method to store data. Windows NT frequently uses the FAT or NTFS method to store data. The NTFS method allows the system administrator to protect individual files and folders on the disk drive by assigning user permissions to the files and folders. Some file systems only support filenames that are eight characters long, with a three-character file extension.

 If the server is running Microsoft Internet Information Server, the FileSystem property will return FAT, NTFS, or CDFS. You cannot run an NT Server using the FAT32 file format.

The operating system assigns a letter to each disk drive device. Typically, the floppy disk drive is assigned the letter A, and the hard disk is assigned the letter C. Some computer systems have additional disk drives. The drive letters assigned to these disk drives will vary with the system. The DriveLetter property of the drive object will return the letter that represents the disk drive device. For example, the DriveLetter property might return "C" for the hard disk drive.

Like the folders in a file cabinet, folders are used to organize the files on the disk drive. The path for the drive represented by the drive letter "C" is "C:". Notice that a colon is appended after the drive letter in the path. The path property returns the path for the drive. The root folder of a drive contains all of the files and folders on the disk drive. The RootFolder property for the drive represented by the drive letter "C" would return "C:\".

Each hard disk drive is provided with a serial number during the manufacturing process. When the hard disk drive is installed, it can be assigned a volume name. When the hard disk drive is shared with other computers over a network, the hard disk drive is also assigned a share name so that other computers will be able to locate it. The SerialNumber, the ShareName, and the VolumeName properties return the serial number, share name, and volume name for the disk drive.

Figure 11-1 below shows how you can use the disk drive object to retrieve and display the disk drive properties. The sample below shows the code that was used to display the properties of the disk drives. Once you retrieve the properties, you can easily store the information in a variable, write the information in a file, or store the information in a database.

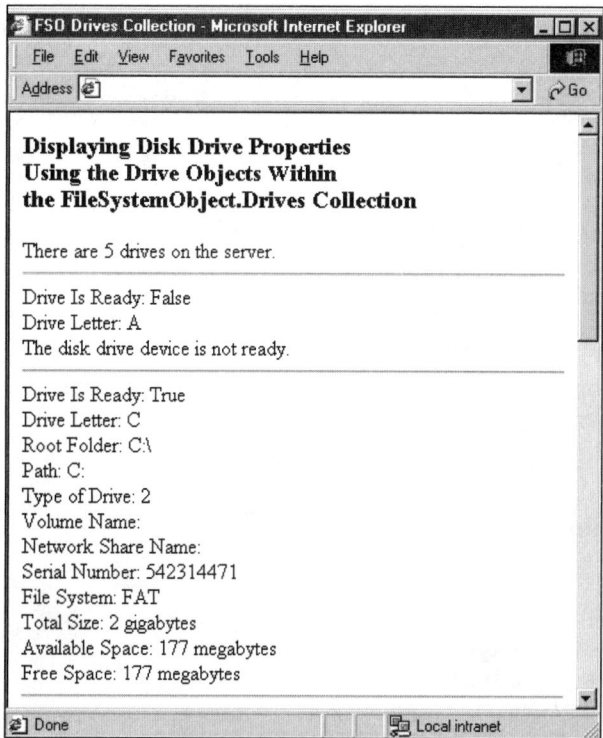

Figure 11-1   Displaying the properties of the disk drive object using the drives collection of the FileSystemObject

To display the properties of the disk drives using the drives collection of the FileSystemObject:

1. Create an ASP page using Notepad or another ASP-compatible editor.

2. Add the basic HTML tags and the heading as indicated below.

```
<html><head><title>FSO Drives Collection</title></head>
<body>
<h3>Displaying Disk Drive Properties <br>
Using the Drive Objects Within <br>
the FileSystemObject.Drives Collection</h3>
```

3. Add the script to create the FileSystemObject named objFSO.

```
<% Dim objFSO, objDrives, keyDrv
Set objFSO= CreateObject("Scripting.FileSystemObject")
```

4. Add the script to store the drives collection in a drive object named objDrives.

```
Set objDrives = objFSO.Drives %>
```

5. Use the count property of the drives collection to display the number of drives in the drives collection. The count property applies to the drives collection, not to an individual drive object.

```
There are
<% = objDrives.count %> drives on the server.
<HR>
```

6. Each drive is a member of the drives collection. Therefore you can loop through each drive using the For Each statement. Then, you can access all the properties of that drive.

```
<% For Each keyDrv in objDrives
```

7. Use the IsReady property to determine if the drive is available. If the drive is available, then you will display the properties of the drive object; otherwise, display a message that the drive is unavailable. The properties for the drive object are not available if the drive is inaccessible.

```
If keyDrv.IsReady = True Then %>
```

8. Display the properties for the drive object.

```
Drive Is Ready: <% = keyDrv.isReady  %><BR>
Drive Letter: <% = keyDrv.DriveLetter  %><BR>
Root Folder: <% = keyDrv.RootFolder %><BR>
Path: <% = keyDrv.Path %><BR>
Type of Drive: <% = keyDrv.DriveType %><BR>
Volume Name: <% = keyDrv.VolumeName %><BR>
Network Share Name: <% = keyDrv.ShareName %><BR>
Serial Number: <% = keyDrv.SerialNumber %><BR>
File System: <% = keyDrv.FileSystem %><BR>
```

9. Display the properties related to the size of the disk drive. The size properties retrieve the size in bytes. Make sure to convert the numbers returned from the AvailableSpace and FreeSpace properties to megabytes, and the number returned from the TotalSize property to gigabytes. Add a horizontal rule to separate the entries for each disk drive.

```
Total Size:
<% = (formatNumber(keyDrv.TotalSize/1073741824 ,0)) %>
gigabytes<BR>
Available Space:
<% =(formatNumber(keyDrv.AvailableSpace/1048576,0)) %>
megabytes<BR>
Free Space:
<% = (formatNumber(keyDrv.FreeSpace/1048576,0)) %>
megabytes<BR>
<hr>
```

10. If the drive is not ready, you can only access the DriveLetter and isReady properties.

```
<% Else %>
Drive Is Ready: <% = keyDrv.isReady  %><BR>
Drive Letter: <% = keyDrv.DriveLetter  %><BR>
The disk drive device is not ready. <BR>
<hr>
```

11. Close the If Then statement. Then get the next drive object, and repeat the For Each loop.

```
<% End if %>
<% Next %>
</body></html>
```

12. Modify the Web page appearance by changing the background, font, and colors, and adding content.

13. Save the **fsoDisplayDrives.asp** Web page to your data directory.

14. View your Web page in the browser.

15. Print out the Web page and the source code.

16. If you are viewing the page using your Personal Web Server or IIS, you will have access to the disk drives on your local system. If there is no disk in the A drive, your page will say that the disk drive device is not ready. If you have a disk in the A drive, your page will display the properties for that disk. This will only work when Personal Web Server is installed as your local Web server. If you are saving your Web pages on a remote server, you will not have access to the server, and therefore cannot put a disk in the A drive.

The Folder Object

The FileSystemObject contains a folders collection, which provides access to specific folder objects. Folder objects are used to access the properties and methods of a folder. The folder object contains two collections: the files collection, which contains the files in the folder, and the folders collection, which contains the subfolders within the folder.

To access the folder from the folders collection, you must create a FileSystemObject first. Then you can use the GetFolder method of the FileSystemObject to retrieve a specific folder. The path to a file or folder is the combination of the disk drive letter, the folders and subfolders, and the filename. Folders can be nested within other folders. Folders that contain other folders are called parent folders. You can pass the folder path using a string or an expression. In the following sample of code, the GetFolder method is retrieving the folder located at C:\test\. The folder location can be passed as an expression or as a variable. Folders have many properties that can be accessed using the folder object. Once you have retrieved the folder object, you can access all of the properties of that folder.

ObjFolder.Property

For example, the size property of the folder object allows you to access the size of the folder. To retrieve the size property, you must first create the FileSystemObject. Then, you must use the GetFolder method of the FileSystemObject to retrieve a folder from the folder collection. In the following section of code, the folder path is at C:\test\. Once the folder object is returned, you can retrieve the size property, using the name of the folder object followed by the size property.

```
Dim objFSO, objFolder
Set objFSO= CreateObject("Scripting.FileSystemObject")
Set objFolder = objFSO.GetFolder("c:\test\")
Response.write(objFolder.size)
```

Folder Properties

The folder object contains many read-only properties that can be retrieved by your Web application. Some of the properties provide information about where the folder is located on the disk drive. The drive property displays the letter of the drive on which the folder is stored. For example, the path property returns the path to the specific folder. Also, the IsRootFolder property is a Boolean property that returns true if the folder is the root folder. If the folder is stored in the root folder, the property is true; otherwise, the property is false. Lastly, the ParentFolder property returns the folder object for the parent of that specific folder. Table 11-4 lists some of these properties.

Folders can be assigned attributes to help you manage the file. The attributes property of the folder object will return the numbers that correspond to the attributes assigned to that folder. The read-only attribute means that a user cannot alter the contents or delete the folder. The attributes property will return a value of 1 if the folder has been assigned the read-only attribute. The hidden attribute means that the folder is not viewable by default. The attributes property will return a value of " for folders that are hidden. Additional attributes are available, depending upon the operating system installed on the server.

Table 11-4   Properties of the Folder Object

Property	Description	Example
Datecreated	Returns the date the folder was created	`objFolder.Datecreated`
Datelastaccessed	Returns the date the folder was last accessed	`objFolder.Datelastaccessed`
Datelastmodified	Returns the date the folder was last modified	`objFolder.Datelastmodified`
Size	Returns the size of the folder	`objFolder.Size`
Drive	Returns the letter of the drive that the folder resides on	`objFolder.Drive`
Path	Returns the path to the folder	`objFolder.Path`

Table 11-4   Properties of the Folder Object (continued)

Property	Description	Example
ShortPath	Returns the path to the folder, using the 8.3 naming convention.	`objFolder.ShortPath`
Name	Returns the name of the folder	`objFolder.Name`
ShortName	Returns the name of the folder, using the 8.3 naming convention	`objFolder.ShortName`
IsRootFolder	Returns "True" if the folder is the root folder, False if it is not	`objFolder.IsRootFolder`
ParentFolder	Returns the name of the parent folder	`objFolder.ParentFolder`
Attributes	Returns the attributes for the folder	`objFolder.Attributes`
Subfolders	Returns the SubFolder collection	`Set subFolder = objFolder.Subfolders`

 Recall that the DOS 8.3 naming convention limits the number of characters of a filename to eight, with an additional three characters for the file extension.

In order to access the properties of the folder, you need to create a FileSystemObject. You can use the GetFolder method of the FileSystemObject to retrieve a specific folder object from the folder collection. You can specify the path using a string, expression, or variable. Then you can use the folder object to retrieve any of the folder properties by specifying the name of the property.

Dim objFSO, objFolder
Set objFSO = server.createobject("Scripting.FileSystemObject")
Set objFolder = objFSP.GetFolder("pathToFolder")
objFolder.Property

Date-related Properties of the Folder Object

The DateCreated, DateLastAccessed, and DateLastModified properties return the date and time on which the folder was created, last accessed, and last modified, respectively.

```
Dim VarDC, VarLA, VarLM
VarDC = ObjFolder.dateCreated
VarLA = ObjFolder.dateLastAccessed
VarLM = ObjFolder.dateLastModified
```

You can use the DateDiff VBScript function to determine the interval between two dates by passing two dates and a time interval. The two dates are two valid date objects. You can pass the date using a string such as "January, 1, 2000", or you can use the date returned from a function such as Now() or Date(). You can also use the date returned from the DateCreated, DateLastModified, and DateLastAcessed functions.

The time interval parameter specifies what measurement should be used to compare the two dates. The interval parameter can have many values, including year (yyyy), month (m), day (d), hour (h), or minute (n). Additional parameters can be passed to the DateDiff function to specify the first day of the week and the first week of the year.

DateDiff(interval, date1, date2)

The following example writes out the difference measure in days between January 1, 2000 and the current date, and illustrates how the DateLastModified property can be used as one of the date parameters in the DateDiff function. This example also returns the difference between the date created and today's date, measured in minutes.

```
<% = DateDiff("d","January,1,2000",now) %>
<% varDM = objFolder.datelastmodified %>
Difference between date created and today's date:
<% = DateDiff("n",varDM ,now) %>minutes <br>
```

 You can convert a date that is a string to a date object, using the DateValue function. The string "January,1, 2000" can be passed to the DateValue function and converted to a date object. All the properties and methods for the date object would be accessible. You could repeat this process with the file object to retrieve information on when a file was last modified.

Retrieving the SubFolders Collection

The SubFolders property returns the subfolders as a folder. To retrieve the SubFolders collection, you must first create the FileSystemObject. The FileSystemObject is used to retrieve a specific folder from the folders collection. You can then use the SubFolders collection of the folder object to retrieve the collection of folder objects. Then, you can access the properties of the subfolders. You can use a For Each loop to retrieve the name property for each of the subfolders. The following code illustrates how you can retrieve the names of all of the subfolders.

```
<% Dim objFSO,  objFolder, subFolder, keyFolder
Set objFSO= CreateObject("Scripting.FileSystemObject")
Set objFolder = objFSO.GetFolder("c:\test\") %>
<% Set subFolder = objFolder.Subfolders
For each keyFolder in subFolder %>
    Name:<% =  keyFolder.Name %><br>
<% Next %>
```

Figure 11-2 shows some of the properties that can be retrieved using the folder object. The folder object was created by accessing the FileSystemObject, and then retrieving the folder collection. Subfolders are often referred to as child folders, and the folder that they are contained within is referred to as the parent folder.

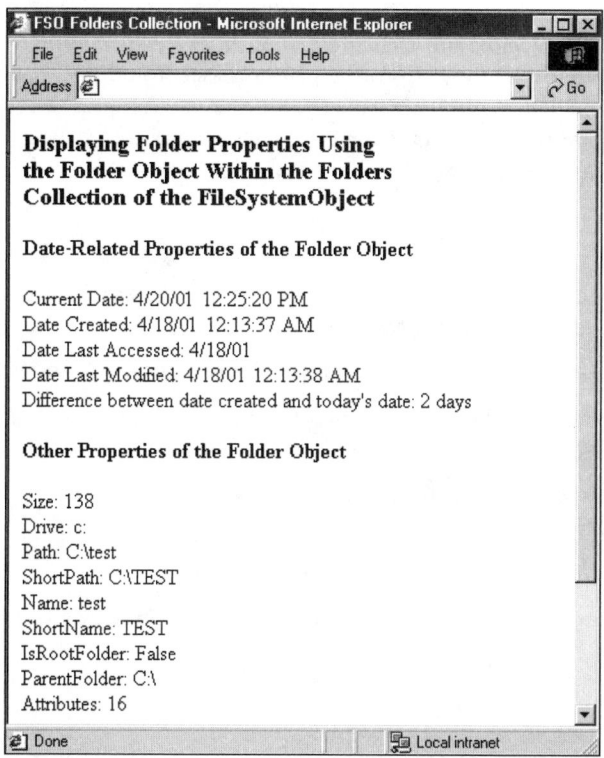

Figure 11-2 Displaying the properties of the folder using the FileSystemObject

To display the properties of the parent folder and the child subfolders, using the folder collection of the FileSystemObject:

1. Create a folder named **SubFolderTest** in the root directory of your data directory, and then create a subfolder within the SubFolder Test directory called **SubTest**.

2. Create a Web page, using Notepad or your ASP-compatible program.

3. Add the basic HTML tags and headings, as shown below.

```
<html><head><title>FSO Folders Collection</title></head>
<body>
<h3>Displaying Folder Properties Using <br>
the Folder Object Within the Folders <br>
Collection of the FileSystemObject</h3>
```

4. Declare your variables.

```
<% Dim fp, objFSO, objFolder, subFolder, keyFolder
```

5. Assign the absolute path to your data directory to the fp variable. The path to your data directory may vary.

```
fp = "c:\chapter11\SubFolderTest\"
```

6. Assign the filespec variable to the path to the parent folder stored in the variable named fp. Replace the path with the complete absolute path to your data directory. (*Note*: You can also pass the path parameter as a string such as c:\test\. However, by using variables to store the path, you can repeat the exercise using other paths.)

```
filespec = fp & "SubTest\"
```

7. Add the code to declare your variables and create the FileSystemObject, using the CreateObject method of the server object.

```
Set objFSO= CreateObject("Scripting.FileSystemObject")
```

8. Use the GetFolder method of the FileSystemObject to retrieve a folder. Pass the GetFolder method the filespec variable that contains the path to the parent folder.

```
Set objFolder = objFSO.GetFolder(fp) %>
```

9. Display the date-related properties for the folder object. Display the dates on which the folder was created, last accessed, and last modified.

```
<h4>Date-Related Properties of the Folder Object</H4>
Current Date:
<% = Now %><br>
Date Created:
<% = objFolder.datecreated %><br>
Date Last Accessed:
<% = objFolder.datelastaccessed %><br>
Date Last Modified:
<% = objFolder.datelastmodified %><br>
```

10. Display the number of days that have passed between the date the folder was created and the current date. You can use the DateDiff function to calculate the difference between the two dates.

```
Difference between date created and today's date:
<% = DateDiff("d",objFolder.datecreated, now) %>
days <br>
```

11. Display the other properties of the folder.

```
<h4> Other Properties of the Folder Object</H4>
Size: <% = objFolder.Size%><br>
Drive: <% = objFolder.Drive%><br>
Path: <% = objFolder.Path%><br>
ShortPath: <% = objFolder.ShortPath%><br>
```

```
Name: <% = objFolder.Name%><br>
ShortName: <% = objFolder.ShortName%><br>
IsRootFolder: <% = objFolder.IsRootFolder%><br>
ParentFolder: <% = objFolder.ParentFolder%><br>
Attributes: <% = objFolder.Attributes%><br>
```

12. Retrieve the subfolders collection from the folder object.

```
<h4> The Subfolders Collection of the Folder Object</H4>
<% Set subFolder = objFolder.Subfolders
```

13. Retrieve the subfolders collection from the folder object, using the subfolders property. The member folders of the subfolders collection are represented by the variable keyFolder. Use a For Each loop to move through each member folder in the subfolders collection. Display the name, path, and parent folder for each member folder.

```
For each keyFolder in subFolder %>
    Name:<% =  keyFolder.Name %><br>
    Path: <% = keyFolder.Path%><br>
    ParentFolder: <% = keyFolder.ParentFolder%><br>
<% Next %>
```

14. Add the closing tags to the Web page.

```
</body></html>
```

15. Modify the Web page appearance by changing the background, font, and colors, and by adding content.

16. Save the page as **fsoDisplayFolders.asp** to your data directory.

17. View your Web page in the browser. (*Note*: The page will display properties of the parent folder and the child subfolder.)

18. Print out the Web page and the source code.

Creating, Copying, Moving, and Deleting Folders

Recall that the FileSystemObject has methods called CreateFolder, CopyFolder, MoveFolder, and DeleteFolder to create, copy, move, and delete folders. The folder object has similar methods that can be used to create, copy, move, and delete folders—namely, the add, copy, move, and delete methods. As you can see, there is more than one method that can be used to create, copy, move, and delete folders.

The File Object

The file object allows you to retrieve the properties of a specific file. Some of these file object properties are similar to properties that belong to a folder object, such as the attribute properties. Table 11-5 lists the properties of the file object.

You can use the Server.MapPath method to determine the path to a file. If you pass a relative path to MapPath from Request.ServerVariables("PATH_INFO"), the absolute path to the file will be returned. This code might look like: `fp = server.mappath(Request.ServerVariables("PATH_INFO"))`.

Table 11-5   Properties of the File Object

Property	Description	Sample
Datecreated	Returns the date the file was created	`objFile.datecreated`
Datelastaccessed	Returns the date the file was last accessed	`objFile.datelastaccessed`
Datelastmodified	Returns the date the file was last modified	`objFile.datelastmodified`
Size	Returns the size of the file	`objFile.Size`
Drive	Returns the letter of the drive that the file resides on	`objFile.Drive`
Path	Returns the path to the file	`objFile.Path`
ShortPath	Returns the path to the file, using the 8.3 naming convention	`objFile.ShortPath`
Name	Returns the name of the file	`objFile.Name`
ShortName	Returns the name of the file, using the 8.3 naming convention	`objFile.ShortName`
Type	Returns the file type	`objFile.Type`
ParentFolder	Returns the name of the parent folder	`objFile.ParentFolder`
Attributes	Returns the attributes for the file	`objFile.Attributes`

Figure 11-3 shows how you can display the properties of the file object. You must first create the file object, using the FileSystemObject. In order to do this, you need to know the path to the file. The example below shows how to create a page that will display the properties of a particular file.

Figure 11-3   Displaying the properties of the file object using the FileSystemObject

To display the properties of the file using the file object of the FileSystemObject:

1. Create a folder named **FileTest** in your data directory.

2. Create a file called **Test.txt**, using Notepad or your other Web processing editor. The file should be saved in the FileTest directory.

3. Create a Web page, using Notepad or your ASP-compatible program.

4. Add the basic HTML tags and headings.

```
<html><head><title>File Object</title></head>
<body>
<h3>Displaying File Properties <br>
Using the File Object </h3>
```

5. Declare your variables.

```
<% Dim fp, filespec, objFSO, objFile
```

6. Assign the fp variable to the absolute path of your data directory. You should replace the path with the complete absolute path to your data directory.

```
fp = "c:\chapter11\"
```

7. Assign the filespec variable to the path to the file. (Note that you can also pass the path parameter as a string such as c:\test\test.txt.)

```
filespec = fp & "FileTest\Test.txt"
```

8. Add the code to declare your variables and create the FileSystemObject, using the CreateObject method of the server object.

```
Set objFSO = CreateObject("Scripting.FileSystemObject")
```

9. Use the GetFile method of the FileSystemObject to retrieve a file. Pass the GetFile method the filespec variable that contains the path to the file.

```
Set objFile = objFSO.GetFile(filespec) %>
```

10. Display the date-related properties for the file object. Display the dates on which the file was created, last accessed, and last modified.

```
<h4>Date-Related Properties of the File Object</H4>
Current Date: <% = Now %><br>
Date Created: <% = objFile.datecreated %><br>
Date Last Accessed:
<% = objFile.datelastaccessed %><br>
Date Last Modified:
<% = objFile.datelastmodified %><br>
```

11. Display the other file properties.

```
<h4> Other Properties of the File Object</H4>
Size: <% = objFile.Size%><br>
Drive: <% = objFile.Drive%><br>
Path: <% = objFile.Path%><br>
ShortPath: <% = objFile.ShortPath%><br>
Name: <% = objFile.Name%><br>
ShortName: <% = objFile.ShortName%><br>
Type: <% = objFile.Type%><br>
ParentFolder: <% = objFile.ParentFolder%><br>
Attributes: <% = objFile.Attributes%><br>
```

12. Add the closing tags to the Web page.

```
</body></html>
```

13. Modify the Web page appearance by changing the background, font, and colors, and by adding content.

14. Save the page as **fsoDisplayFile.asp** to your data directory.

15. View your Web page in the browser.

16. Print out the Web page and the source code.

The copy, move, and delete methods of the file object can be used to copy, move, and delete files. The OpenAsTextStream method will return a TextStream object. The TextStream object is used to read, write to, and append to a file. In order to access the properties of the file, you need to create a FileSystemObject. You can use the GetFile method of the FileSystemObject to retrieve a specific file object from the file collection. You can specify the path using a string, an expression, or a variable. Then you can use the file object to retrieve any of the folder properties by specifying the name of the property. The sample below shows how you could delete a file.

```
Dim objFSO, objFile, source
source = "c:\chapter11\testfile.txt"
Set objFSO =
server.createobject("Scripting.FileSystemObject")
Set objFile = objFSO.GetFile("pathToFile")
objFile.Delete source
```

Notice that the source was stored in a variable. You could retrieve the source information from a form, database, cookie, or another file. Once it is retrieved, you simply assign that value to the source property. The sample below shows how you might select the source from a form. The form field txtsource is passed to the source variable, which is then used as the parameter for the source file for the delete method.

```
Dim objFSO, objFile, source
source = Request.form("txtsource")
Set objFSO =
server.createobject("Scripting.FileSystemObject")
Set objFile = objFSO.GetFile("pathToFile")
objFile.Delete source
```

Table 11-6 shows the methods that can be applied to the file object. When you use the copy method, you must specify the destination. If you do not identify the path separator (\), the file will be copied to the file specified in the source parameter. Therefore, it is recommended that you specify the path using the path separator. You can also append a filename to the source parameter. You can append the same filename as the source filename. If you append a filename different from the source filename, the file is copied to another location with the new filename. In the sample below, the source file is explicitly stated. You must also pass a parameter to identify whether you want the file to be overwritten if the file already exists. If the value is true, the file will be overwritten if it exists.

```
Dim objFSO, objFile
Set objFSO= CreateObject("Scripting.FileSystemObject")
Set objFile = objFSO.GetFile(source)
    objFile.Copy  "c:\chapter11\copytest.txt" , true
```

If you want, you can specify a source name explicitly, or use a variable. The destination filename and directory can then be retrieved from a form, database, cookie, or other file. Below is a sample that shows how you could use the copy method using a form. First, retrieve the

11

values from the form and assign them to variables. Then, use those variables as the parameters in the copy method statement. Notice that the overwrite parameter, filename, and path are all retrieved from the form.

```
overwrite = request.form("overwrite")
    ' this form field passed the values true
    ' or false to indicate if the file is to be
    ' overwritten if the file already exists
filelist = request.form("filelist")
    ' this form field contains the original file name
currentDir = request.form("currentpath")
    ' this form field contains the original file
    ' path without the path separator (\)
source = currentDir & "\" &  filelist
    ' this variable contains the path to the source file
filename = request.form("filename")
    ' this form field has the new file name
copytargetDir = request.form("copydirectory")
    ' this form field has the new path name
if filename <> "" then
    copytarget = copytargetDir & "\" &  filename
else
    copytarget = copytargetDir & "\" &  filelist
end if
    ' the above If Then statement determines if
    ' the copy method should use the original
    ' filename, or a different filename
Dim objFSO, objFile
Set objFSO= CreateObject("Scripting.FileSystemObject")
    ' create the FileSystemObject
Set objFile = objFSO.GetFile(source)
    ' Create the File Object
objFile.Copy  copytarget, overwrite
    ' Call the copy method of the File Object and
    ' pass the variables as the parameters to the method
```

When you move the file, you can use the move method. Again, if you do not identify the path separator (\), the file will be copied to the file specified in the source parameter. Therefore, it is recommended that you specify the path, using the path separator. You can also append a filename to the source parameter. You can append the same filename as the source filename. If you append a filename different from the source filename, the file is copied to another location with the new filename. The difference between the move and copy methods is that the move method will delete the original file. The destination parameter identifies where the file will be moved. If the file already exists, an error will occur.

```
filelist = request.form("filelist")
currentDir = request.form("currentpath")
source = currentDir & "\" &  filelist
    ' the variables above retrieve the source file
```

```
movetargetDir = request.form("movedirectory")
movetarget = movetargetDir & "\"
    ' the variables above define the destination file
Set objFSO= CreateObject("Scripting.FileSystemObject")
Set objFile = objFSO.GetFile(source)
    ' the source file object is created
objFile.Move movetarget
```

The delete method will delete the file specified. You can force the delete method to delete files that are marked read-only by using the force parameter. The force parameter is false by default. The possible values for the force parameter are true or false.

The two other file object methods, CreateTextFile and OpenAsTextStream, can be used to create files and to read, write to, or append to a file. However, these methods are also available with the FileSystemObject. Therefore these methods are covered in more depth in the next section.

Table 11-6   Methods of the File Object

Method	Description	Example

Copy Method	Copies a file from a source destination to a target destination. You can specify to overwrite the destination file if it exists.	`objFile.copy "c:\source.txt",`
		`"c:\target.txt",`
		`true`

Move Method	Moves the file specified to the new location	`objFile.move "c:\source.txt",` `"c:\target.txt"`
Delete Method	Deletes the file specified. You You can specify to delete a file that is read-only.	`objFile.delete` `"c:\source.txt", false`
CreateTextFile	Creates a file. You can create files of types other than text, such as Word docs.	`objFile.CreateTextFile` `"c:\target.txt"`
OpenAsTextStream	Opens a file and returns the file as a TextStream object. The TextStream objects are used to read, write to, and append to files.	`objFile.OpenAsTextStream` `"c:\target.txt"`

Using the TextStream Object

There are several ways to read, write to, and append to files. The CreateTextFile and OpenTextFile methods of the FileSystemObject return a TextStream object that can be used for reading from, writing to, and appending to files. The OpenAsTextStream method is used by the file object to return a TextStream object that can also be used for reading from, writing to, and appending to files. The TextStream object has several methods and properties, which are listed in Table 11-7.

Table 11-7   Methods and Properties of the TextStream Object

Method or Property	Description	Example
Write Method	Writes the contents of a string, expression, or variable to a file	`txtfile.Write("Office Supply Store")`
WriteLine Method	Writes the contents to a file, and writes a newline character	`txtfile.WriteLine ("Product Inventory List")`
WriteBlankLines Method	Writes a specified number of blank lines	`txtfile.WriteBlankLines(2)`
Read Method	Reads a specified number of characters	`txtfile.Read(2)`
ReadLine Method	Returns the next line as a string	`txtfile.ReadLine [txtfile.ReadLine]`
ReadAll Method	Reads the entire file and returns it as a string variable; not useful for large files	`txtfile.ReadAll [txtfile.ReadAll]`
Skip Method	Skips over a specified number of characters	`txtfile.Skip`
SkipLine Method	Skips over the next line	`txtfile.SkipLine`
Close Method	Closes the file	`txtfile.Close`
AtEndOfStream Property	Returns a Boolean value that indicates True if you are at the end of the file	`txtfile.AtEndOfStream`
AtEndOfLine Property	Returns a Boolean value that indicates True if you are at the end of a line	`txtfile.AtEndOfLine`
Column Property	Returns the number of the current column	`txtfile.Column`
Line Property	Returns the number of the current line	`txtfile.Line`

Creating and Writing to a File

The CreateTextFile method of the FileSystemObject returns a TextStream object. The CreateTextFile parameters include the name of the file, a Boolean value to indicate whether the file should be overwritten, and a Boolean value to indicate whether the file should be created as Unicode ("True") or ASCII ("False"). The TextStream object has four methods that are used to write to a file. The write method writes a string to the file. The WriteLine method writes a string and a newline character. The WriteBlankLines method adds a blank line to the file. You can pass a number to the WriteBlankLines method to indicate the number of blank lines to add. The close method is used to close the TextStream object.

You can use a form to collect the information needed to create the form. You can assign the name of the file, or have the user enter the filename and location. You can collect the information from form fields. You can use the textarea form field to collect a large amount of free text. If you use the textarea form field, and the user presses the Return button, the contents wrap to the next line. This hard return will also appear within the document created. It is useful to store information in a file if you do not have access to a database.

To write to a file using the CreateTextFile method of the FileSystemObject:

1. Create an ASP page, using Notepad or your ASP-compatible editor.

2. Add the basic HTML tags and heading.

```
<html>
<head><title>Writing to a File</title></head>
<body>
<h3>Writing to a File</h3>
```

3. Declare a variable to hold the FileSystemObject and the TextFile.

```
<% Dim fp, fileSys, txtFile, filePath
```

4. Assign the absolute path to your data directory to the fp variable. The path to your data directory may vary.

```
fp = "c:\chapter11\"
```

5. Create a variable to hold the path to your new file, which will be named **NewFile.txt**. Replace The fp variable holds the path to your data directory. (Note that you can also pass the path parameter as a string such as c:\test\test.txt.)

```
filePath = fp & "NewFile.txt"
```

6. Create the FileSystemObject.

```
Set fileSys = CreateObject("Scripting.FileSystemObject")
```

7. Create the text file using the CreateTextFile method. The object returned is a TextStream object. In this example, txtfile is the TextStream object. The filePath parameter indicates the path and filename to use when creating the file. The true parameter indicates that the file is an ASCII type file. The TextStream object returned is assigned to the txtfile variable.

```
Set txtFile = fileSys.CreateTextFile(filePath, true)
```

8. Use the write, WriteLine, and WriteBlankLines methods to write content to the file.

```
txtFile.Write("Office Supply Store")
txtFile.WriteLine("Product Inventory List")
txtFile.WriteBlankLines(2)
txtFile.WriteLine("Pens")
txtFile.WriteLine("Pencils")
txtFile.WriteLine("Paper")
```

11

9. Close the file using the close method of the TextStream object.

```
txtFile.Close
%>
```

10. Add the closing HTML tags.

```
<h2>The file has been written</h2>
</body></html>
```

11. Modify the Web page appearance by changing the background, font, and colors, and by adding content.

12. Save this page as **fsoCreateFile.asp** to your data directory.

13. View your Web page in the browser. Check to see if the file was created. Open the file to see if the text was written to the file.

14. Print out the Web page and the source code.

 You can create files other than text files using this method. To create a Word document, specify the name of the file and the file extension .doc. You can then use programming techniques such as Visual Basic for Applications (VBA) to manipulate the Word document. You will be able to automate tasks in Word such as Mail Merge. With VBA, you can also integrate your Web application with Excel spreadsheet files and Access databases. If you are interested in learning more about VBA, you can read *Visual Basic for Applications* by Diane Zak (*http://www.course.com/at/viewtitle.cfm?isbn=0-619-00020-1*).

Appending Content to a File

In order to append content to a file, you must first open it. You can open a file using the OpenTextFile method. The OpenTextFile method returns a TextStream object, which allows you to write or append to a file. You must pass the name of the file to the OpenTextFile method. You can indicate whether the file is being opened for reading, writing, or appending. Writing to a file means that the contents of the file will be overwritten. Appending to a file means that the new content will appear below the existing content. The parameter that indicates if you are reading, writing to, or appending to a file is known as the **iomode** argument. The iomode argument indicates the input and output mode. An iomode value of 1 means that you are going to be reading the file, but cannot write to the file. An iomode value of 2 means that the file can be written to, but you can't read from the file. An iomode of 8 means that you can append content to the end of the file. A Boolean parameter can be used to indicate whether the file should be overwritten if a file with the same name exists. A value of "True" indicates that a new file should be created even if the file currently exists. The default format parameter is ASCII. However, you can change the parameter to open the file using the system default format, Unicode, or ASCII format.

Note that the iomode and format arguments are the same for the CreateTextFile and OpenTextFile methods.

ObjFSO.OpenTextFile(filename, iomode, overwrite, format)

To open a file using the OpenTextFile method of the FileSystemObject and append content to the file:

1. In your data directory, create a new file named **AppendFile.txt**, using Notepad.

2. Create an ASP page, using Notepad or your ASP-compatible editor.

3. Add the basic HTML tags and heading.

```
<html>
<head><title>Appending to a File</title></head>
<body>
<H3>Appending to a File</H3>
```

4. Declare a variable to hold the path to your data directory, FileSystemObject, and the TextFile.

```
<% Dim fp, filePath, objFSO, txtFile
```

5. Assign the absolute path to your data directory to the fp variable. The path to your data directory may vary.

```
fp = "c:\chapter11\"
```

6. Create a variable to hold the path to your new file. Replace fp with the path to your data directory.

```
filePath = fp & "AppendFile.txt"
```

7. Create the FileSystemObject.

```
Set objFSO = CreateObject("Scripting.FileSystemObject")
```

8. Create the text file using the CreateTextFile method. Add the number 8 parameter to indicate that the file is to be opened in the Appending iomode. Add the False parameter to indicate that the file is an ASCII type file. The TextStream object returned is assigned to the txtfile variable.

```
Set txtFile = objFSO.OpenTextFile(filePath, 8,  False)
```

9. Use the WriteLine method to append content to the file.

```
txtFile.WriteLine("Glue")
txtFile.WriteLine("Scissors")
txtFile.WriteLine("Tape")
```

10. Close the file using the close method.

```
txtFile.Close
%>
```

11

11. Add the closing HTML tags.

```
<h2>The file has been appended</h2>
</body></html>
```

12. Modify the Web page appearance by changing the background, font, and colors, and by adding content.

13. Save this page as **fsoAppendFile.asp** to your data directory.

14. View your Web page in the browser. Open the file to see if the text was written to the file.

15. Go back and view the Web page in the browser. Open the file to see if the text was written to the file. You should see that the list of supplies was written twice to the browser because the second time the page was viewed, the school supply list was appended to the first supply list.

16. Print out the Web page, the source code, and the contents of the text file.

Note that in the above exercise the filename was fixed as AppendFile.txt. You could easily change the file extension from .txt to .doc. Also, you could easily have changed the filename from AppendFile to a variable. Then, the name of the file could come from a form, a cookie, or a database. The following sample code shows how you could retrieve the filename from a form.

```
Dim fp, filePath, filename
fileName = Request.form("txtFileName")
fp = Request.form("txtFilePath")
filePath = fp & filename & ".txt"
```

Opening and Reading a File

You can open a file to be read using the OpenAsTextStream method of the FileSystemObject. The OpenAsTextStream method returns a TextStream object. The following example uses the OpenTextFile and reads the contents line by line, using the ReadLine method of the TextStream object. The example uses a Do While loop to detect whether the current line is at the end of the file. If the AtEndOfStream property is true, then the line is at the end of the file and the loop will end. If not, the loop will continue, read the next line, then write the line to the Web page.

To read a file using the OpenTextFile method of the TextStream object:

1. Using Notepad, create a file named **ReadFile.txt** in your data directory.

2. Open the file and enter the text below.

```
You have opened the ReadFile.txt file.
This was opened using the OpenTextFile method
of the TextStream object.
```

3. Save the changes and close the file.

4. Create an ASP page, using Notepad or your ASP editor.

5. Add the basic HTML tags and headings.

```
<html><head><title>Reading from a File</title></head>
<body>
<h3> Reading a File Using the OpenTextFile <br>
Method of the TextStream Object</h3>
```

6. Declare the variables used in the script.

```
<% Dim fp, filePath, fileSys, txtFile, line
```

7. Assign the absolute path to your data directory to the fp variable. The path to your data directory may vary.

```
fp = "c:\chapter11\"
```

8. Assign the filePath variable to the path to your file. Replace the path with the path to your data directory.

```
filePath = fp & "ReadFile.txt"
```

9. Create the FileSystemObject.

```
Set objFSO = CreateObject("Scripting.FileSystemObject")
```

10. Use the OpenTextFile method to open the filePath file for reading. Indicate that the file will be opened as an ASCII file for reading by passing the parameters 1, 0. The TextStream object returned is assigned to the txtFile variable.

```
Set txtFile = objFSO.OpenTextFile(filePath, 1, 0)
```

11

11. Create the Do Until loop. When the loop reaches the end of the file, the AtEndOfStream property will be true, and the loop will be closed. If the loop has not reached the end of the file, then assign the line variable to the results returned from the ReadLine method. The ReadLine method will read one line of text. Then use the Response.Write method to write out the line and a line break tag. The layout for each line will be the same as in the text file.

```
Do Until txtFile.AtEndOfStream
    line = txtFile.ReadLine
    Response.Write line & "<br>"
Loop
```

12. Close the TextStream object and add the closing HTML tags.

```
txtFile.Close
%>
</body></html>
```

13. Modify the Web page appearance by changing the background, font, and colors, and by adding content.

14. Save the file as **fsoReadFile.asp** in your data directory.

15. View your Web page in the browser.

16. Print out the Web page and the source code.

THE ERR OBJECT

You should always try to anticipate where errors might occur within your code. When an error occurs, you can "handle" the error by skipping over it and continuing your code, using the On Error statement. If you do not include this error-handling statement, when an error occurs, the script will stop executing and an error message will be generated. In combination with the On Error statement, you can use the built-in err object to provide more information about the error. The err object has several properties and methods that can display the error number and a description of the error. Table 11-8 lists some of the properties and methods of the err object. You can also create functions within your script to detect and handle errors.

On Error Resume Next

Table 11-8   Properties and Methods of the Err Object

Properties and Methods	Description	Example
Number Property	Returns an integer that uniquely identifies the error that occurred	`Err.Number`
Description Property	Returns a description of the error	`Err.Description`
Source Property	Returns the name of the object or method that caused the error	`Err.Source()`
HelpFile Property	Returns the path and filename to a help file. You can also set this property. If the user clicks Help or F1, the error dialog box appears for that file.	`Err.HelpFile (pathToHelpFile)`
HelpContext Property	Sets or returns the ID for the Help topic. Used to display the Help topic when an error occurs.	`Err.HelpContext`
Clear Method	Clears out all the properties of the err object	`Err.Clear`
Raise Method	Generates an error for testing. You can pass any of the properties of the err object as parameters.	`Err.Raise`

The following sample code illustrates how to use the err object and on Error statement. The sample declares a variable to hold the results of a function and write the variable to the Web page. The variable is the amount of money owed per month. The function uses the On Error statement to allow the program to continue if an error occurs. The function defines a variable that divides a number by zero, which would normally cause an error message to occur. Because the On Error statement is present, the error message will not appear. Instead, the function traps the error and displays the error number and description, and then the script executes the next statement. If there is no error, the function displays the results.

1. Create an ASP page, using Notepad or your ASP-compatible editor.

2. Add the basic HTML tags and headings.

```
<html><head>
<title>Err Object and On Error Statement</title></head>
<body>
<h1>Handling Errors with the <br>
Err Object and On Error Statement</h1>
```

3. Declare a variable to hold the amount that is owed per month.

```
<% Dim AmtPerMonth, Total, NumMonths, Result
```

4. Assign values to the Total and NumMonth variables. The 1000 value is the amount owed, and the 0 value is the months that it will take to pay off the loan.

```
Total = 1000
```

```
NumMonths = 0
```

5. Call the AmountPerMonth function. Pass the variables to the AmountPerMonth function. The value passed back from the function is assigned to the Result variable.

```
Result = AmountPerMonth(Total, NumMonths)
```

6. Write the value of the amount to the Web page.

```
Response.Write Result
```

7. Create the function named AmountPerMonth. The two parameters passed are the amount of money owed and the number of months to pay off the loan. Notice that the names of the parameters do not have to be the same as the names of the variables that were used to pass the values as parameters.

```
Function AmountPerMonth(Amount, Months)
```

8. Call the On Error statement to handle errors that may occur.

```
On Error Resume Next
```

9. Declare a local variable in the function that will store the amount owed per month. Then, calculate this value from the amount and months parameters that were passed to the function.

```
Dim MonthlyAmount
MonthlyAmount = Amount / Months
```

10. Add the code that displays the error message.

```
If Err.Number <> 0 Then
      AmountPerMonth = _
      "Sorry, an error occurred. Enter your numbers again."
Else
      AmountPerMonth = MonthlyAmount
End If
End Function
%>
```

11. Add the closing HTML tags.

```
</body></html>
```

12. Save the page as **DisplayError.asp** in your data directory.

13. View the page in the browser.

14. Print the page and your code.

CHAPTER SUMMARY

Scripting Library

❑ The Microsoft Scripting Library is the Microsoft Scripting Runtime program that contains the dictionary, FileSystemObject, and err objects. The Scripting Library is used to access the files and folders on the server.

The Dictionary Object

❑ The dictionary object stores two-dimensional data as a key and item pair. You can retrieve the item value by specifying the name of the key.

The FileSystemObject

❑ The FileSystemObject provides access to several objects, methods, and collections. The FileSystemObject contains the drives and folders collections. The drives collection is used to access the drive objects. The folders collection provides access to the folder objects. The FileSystemObject contains methods that can retrieve a specific drive object, folder object, or file object. The FileSystemObject methods can be used to create, copy, move, or delete files and folders. The CreateTextFile and OpenTextFile methods return a TextStream object that can be used to write to, append to, and read from files. The file object has an OpenAsTextStream method that can also return a TextStream object.

Err Object

❑ The On Error statement prevents scripts from terminating when an error occurs. The err object can be used to provide information about the type of error that occurred.

To create an instance of the dictionary object

```
Set objDMember = Server.CreateObject("Scripting.Dictionary")
```

To add a key/item pair to the dictionary object

```
objDMember.Add "memberid", memberid
```

To retrieve the value for the item in a dictionary object

```
objDMember.Item("memberid")
```

To retrieve the number of key/item pairs of data in a dictionary object

```
objDMember.count
```

To create a FileSystemObject

```
Set objFSO =
Server.CreateObject("Scripting.FileSystemObject")
```

To create a folder using the CreateFolder method of the FileSystemObject

```
objFSO.CreateFolder "c:\test\"
```

To copy a folder using the CopyFolder method of the FileSystemObject

```
objFSO.CopyFolder "c:\test\", "c:\testCopy\", True
```

To move a folder using the MoveFolder method of the FileSystemObject

```
objFSO.MoveFolder "c:\test3\", "c:\test4\"
```

To delete a folder using the DeleteFolder method of the FileSystemObject

```
objFSO.DeleteFolder "c:\test5\"
```

To create a file using the CreateFile method of the FileSystemObject

```
objFSO.CreateTextFile "c:\test\sample.txt"
```

To copy a file using the CopyFile method of the FileSystemObject

```
objFSO.CopyFile "c:\test\s1.txt", "c:\test\s2.txt", True
```

11

To delete a file using the DeleteFile method of the FileSystemObject

```
objFSO.DeleteFile "c:\test\testfile.txt"
```

To retrieve the drives collection

```
Set objDrives = objFSO.Drives
```

To retrieve the drive type with the DriveType property of the drive object

```
keyDrv.DriveType
```

To retrieve the total size of the disk drive in gigabytes using the TotalSize property

```
formatNumber(keyDrv.TotalSize/1073741824 ,0)
```

To retrieve the available space of the disk drive in megabytes using the AvailableSpace property

```
formatNumber(keyDrv.AvailableSpace/1048576,0)
```

To retrieve a specific folder object

```
Set objFolder = objFSO.GetFolder("c:\test\")
```

To retrieve the date on which the folder was created

```
ObjFolder.dateCreated
```

To retrieve the date on which the folder was last modified

```
ObjFolder.dateLastModified
```

To find the number of days between the dates the folder was created and last modified

```
DateDiff("d",objFolder.datecreated,
objFolder.datelastmodified)
```

To retrieve the path property for a folder object

```
objFolder.Path
```

To retrieve the SubFolders collection of the folder object, using the SubFolders property

```
Set subFolder = objFolder.Subfolders
```

To retrieve a file object using the GetFile method of the FileSystemObject

```
Set objFile = objFSO.GetFile("c:\test\test.txt")
```

To display the size of a file, using the size property of the file object

```
objFile.Size
```

To create a TextStream object using the CreateTextFile object

```
Set txtfile = filesys.CreateTextFile(FilePath, true)
```

To write to a file using the TextStream object

```
txtfile.Write("Office Supply Store ")

txtfile.WriteLine("Product Inventory List")

txtfile.WriteBlankLines(2)
```

To append to a file using the TextStream object

```
Set txtfile = objFSO.OpenTextFile(FilePath, 8,  False)
```

To open a file for reading using the TextStream object

```
Set txtfile = objFSO.OpenTextFile(filePath, 1, 0)
```

To read a line of text from a file, using the TextStream object

```
txtfile.ReadLine
```

To enable error handling

```
On Error Resume Next
```

To display the error number using the err object

```
Err.Number
```

11

Review Questions

1. The scripting objects are made available through which dynamic-link library?

    a. ssp.dll

    b. scrrun.dll

    c. win.dll

    d. iis.dll

2. What type of information can be stored in the dictionary object?

    a. a single variable

    b. a two-dimensional array

    c. a three-dimensional array

    d. a multidimensional array

3. You created a dictionary object named objDAddress, with a key of "State" and an item value of "IL". Which statement would correctly retrieve the value of the item?

    a. objDAddress.Add "IL"

    b. objDAddress.Get "State"

    c. objDAddress.Key "State"

    d. objDAddress.Key "IL"

4. Which property will return the number of key/item pairs in the objDAddress dictionary object?

    a. objDAddress.Get

    b. objDAddress.Count

    c. objDAddress.Total

    d. objDAddress.Number

5. Network drives can be accessed using the drive object within the drives collection. True or False?

6. Which FileSystemObject method is used to retrieve a specific folder object?

    a. objFSO.SpecialFolder

    b. objFSO.GetDrive

    c. objFSO.Folder

    d. objFSO.GetFolder

7. Which is not one of the three special folders of the FileSystemObject?

    a. Temp

    b. Windows

    c. Programs

    d. System

8. Which method of the FileSystemObject is used to move a folder?

    a. objFSO.CopyFolder

    b. objFSO.Move

    c. objFSO.MoveObject

    d. objFSO.MoveFolder

9. Which method of the FileSystemObject will return the file extension for a file?

    a. objFSO.GetFileName

    b. objFSO.GetName

    c. objFSO.GetExtensionName

    d. objFSO.GetShortName

10. Which drive letter is usually reserved for the first hard disk drive?

    a. A

    b. B

    c. C

    d. D

11. Which property will return the size of the hard drive?

    a. objDrive.Size

    b. objDrive.TotalSize

    c. objDrive.AvailableSpace

    d. objDrive.FreeSpace

12. Which file type is not compatible with a drive that is running Microsoft NT Server?

    a. FAT

    b. FAT32

    c. NTFS

    d. CDFS

13. Which value is returned by the path property?

    a. C

    b. C:

    c. C:\

    d. C:\\

14. Which property will return the name of the parent folder for a folder object?

    a. objFolder.Parent

    b. objFolder.ParentFolder

    c. objFolder.SubFolder

    d. objFolder.RootFolder

11

15. Which method is used to calculate the difference between two dates?

    a. date

    b. DateDiff

    c. diff

    d. DiffDate

16. Which property is available with the file object but not the folder object?

    a. dateCreated

    b. path

    c. ShortPath

    d. type

17. Which method is used to write a string and a newline character?

    a. write

    b. WriteLn

    c. WriteLine

    d. WriteBlankLines

18. Which method is used to read a file line-by-line?

    a. ReadAll

    b. ReadLN

    c. ReadLine

    d. line

19. Which object contains the methods for writing to, appending to, and reading from files?

    a. FileSystemObject

    b. dictionary object

    c. file object

    d. TextStream object

HANDS-ON PROJECTS

Project 11-1

In this project, you will locate additional resources on the FileSystemObject at the Microsoft Windows Script Technologies Web site. The Microsoft Windows Script Technologies Web site is located at *http://www.microsoft.com/scripting*. You will locate and read the FileSystemObject topics within the Microsoft Windows Script Technologies Web site.

1. Visit the Microsoft Windows Script Technologies Web site at
   http://msdn.microsoft.com/scripting/default.htm?/scripting/vbscript/default.htm.

2. On the left menu are several selections such as VBScript and JScript. Click the **VBScript** selection. A submenu will appear that contains additional selections.

3. Click **Documentation**. A submenu will appear that contains additional selections.

4. Click **FileSystemObject User's Guide**. Read through each of the topics listed on the right. The topics contain information and code samples.

5. Create a Web page named **fsoTutorial.asp**.

6. On the Web page, describe three topics that were discussed in the Web pages.

7. Display the sample code in the browser with your description.

8. Modify the appearance of the Web page. Save the page to your data directory.

9. View the Web page in your browser. Print the Web page.

Project 11-2

In this project, you will locate additional resources on the FileSystemObject at the Microsoft Windows Script Technologies Web site.

1. Visit the Microsoft Windows Script Technologies Web site at *http://msdn.microsoft.com/scripting/default.htm?/scripting/vbscript/default.htm*.

2. On the left menu are several selections such as VBScript and JScript. Click the **VBScript** selection. A submenu will appear that contains additional selections.

3. Click **Documentation**. A submenu will appear that contains additional selections.

4. Click **Scripting RunTime Reference**.

5. Click the **Objects** link in the main body of the Web page. The main body of the Web page is the page that is loaded into the right frame. A list of objects built into the Scripting Library will appear in the main body of the Web page.

6. Read through the documentation on four of the objects listed.

7. Create a Web page named **fsoDocumentation.asp**.

8. Describe what you learned about the four objects.

9. Display the sample code in the browser with your description.

10. Modify the appearance of the Web page. Save the page to your data directory.

11. View the Web page in your browser. Print the Web page.

Project 11-3

In this project, you will create a Web page that detects the amount of available space on a disk drive.

1. Create an ASP page, using Notepad or your ASP-compatible editor. This page will detect if any of the disk drives have more than 90% used space. Add the basic HTML tags and heading.

11

```
<html><head><title>FSO Drives Collection</title></head>
<body>
<h3 align = "center">DISK WARNING </h3>
<div align = "center">
<hr size = 1 width="250">
```

2. Create the disk drive objects. The objFSO will contain the FileSystemObject, and the objDrives will contain the drive collection.

```
<% Dim objFSO, objDrives, keyDrv
Set objFSO= CreateObject("Scripting.FileSystemObject")
Set objDrives = objFSO.Drives %>
```

3. Use a For Each statement to loop through each drive object in the drive collection. If the drive is ready, then you can retrieve the information about the drive.

```
<% For Each keyDrv in objDrives
If keyDrv.IsReady = True Then %>
```

4. Retrieve the properties of the drive object. Then, calculate the total space and the free space available, using the TotalSize and FreeSpace properties. The percentOpen is calculated from the properties. The percentUsed is calculated on the basis of the percent open. (*Hint:* When you calculate a percentage from 20/100, the percentage is .2 and therefore less than 1. If you subtract .2 from 1, you will have .8 as the percent used.)

```
<% total = (formatNumber(keyDrv.TotalSize/1048576,0))%>
<% available =
(formatNumber(keyDrv.AvailableSpace/1048576,0))%>
<% freespace = (formatNumber(keyDrv.FreeSpace/1048576,0))%>
<% percentOpen = keyDrv.FreeSpace/keyDrv.TotalSize%>
<% percentUsed = (1 - percentOpen)  %>
```

5. Write the drive letter to the Web page.

```
Drive Letter: <% = keyDrv.DriveLetter  %><BR>
```

6. If the percent used is less than 90%, then write out the percentage used. You can use the formatpercent method to format the output to two decimal places with the percent sign attached.

```
<% If percentUsed < .90 then %>
  You have used <% = formatpercent(percentUsed) %>
  <br> of disk space on this drive.
  <hr size = 1 width="250">
```

7. Otherwise, if the percent used is greater than 90%, then write out a warning statement and the percentage that is used.

```
<% else %>
    <b>---- WARNING ----- </b><br>
    You have used more than
    <% = formatpercent(percentUsed) %> <br>
    of disk space on this drive.
    <hr size = 1 width="250">
<% end if %>
```

8. Close the scripts and the Web page.

```
<% Else %>
<% End if %>
<% Next %>
</div></body></html>
```

9. Modify the appearance of the Web page.

10. Save the page as **fsoDiskWarning.asp** to your data directory.

11. View the Web page in your browser. Print the Web page.

Project 11-4

In this project, you will create a file using values from a form field. This is an excellent way to create files on the server if you do not have a file upload component.

1. Create a folder called **CreatedFiles** in your data directory to store the files that will be created by this form.

2. Using Notepad or your Web page editor, create a Web page that contains a form. One form field should be for the name of the file that you will create on the server. Another field should display a drop-down list and should be used for the file extension (.asp, .txt, .htm, and .doc). The other fields will be stored in the file on the server. Use the sample code below to create your form.

```
<html><head><title>Creating a File</title></head>
<body>
<h2 align = "center">Creating a File From a Form</h2>
<form method="POST" action="fsoProcessForm.asp">
  <table align = "center" border="0"
    width="72%" cellspacing="0" cellpadding="3">
    <tr><td width="19%">File Name</td>
      <td width="81%">
      <input type="text" name="filename" size="25"></td>
    </tr>
    <tr><td width="19%">File Type</td>
      <td width="81%">
     <select size="1" name="ext">
          <option value=".txt">Text File</option>
          <option value=".htm">Web Page</option>
          <option value=".doc">Word Document</option>
          <option value=".asp">Active Server Page</option>
        </select></td>
    </tr>
    <tr><td width="19%">Title</td>
      <td width="81%">
      <input type="text" name="title" size="70"></td>
    </tr>
    <tr><td width="19%">Author</td>
      <td width="81%">
      <input type="text" name="author" size="70"></td>
```

11

```
          </tr>
          <tr><td width="19%">Comments</td>
            <td width="81%">
            <textarea rows="7" name="comments" cols="60">
            </textarea></td>
          </tr>
          <tr><td width="19%"></td>
            <td width="81%">
            <input type="submit" value="Submit" name="B1">
           <input type="reset" value="Reset" name="B2"></td>
          </tr>
        </table>
      </form></body></html>
```

3. Save the page as **fsoCreateForm.asp** in your data directory.

4. Create a Web page, using Notepad or an ASP editor, that retrieves the values from the form fields and creates the new file. First add the basic HTML tags and a heading, using the code below.

```
<html><head><title>Creating a File</title></head>
<body>
<h2 align = "center">Your file has been created.</h2>
```

5. Retrieve the form field values and assign the form fields to variables.

```
<% dim fileName, fileExt, title, author, comments, fp, fn
fileName = request.form("filename")
fileExt = request.form("ext")
title = request.form("title")
author = request.form("author")
comments = request.form("comments")
```

6. Concatenate the file path, filename, and fileExt and store the results in the fn variable. The fn variable holds the absolute path to the new file that will be created by the script.

```
fp = "c:\chapter11\"
fn = fp & fileName & fileExt
```

7. Create the FileSystemObject.

```
Dim fileSys, txtFile
Set fileSys = CreateObject("Scripting.FileSystemObject")
```

8. Use the CreateTextFile method of the FileSystemObject to create a TextStream object.

```
Set txtFile = fileSys.CreateTextFile(fn, true)
```

9. Use the variables to create the file, and write the contents to the file. (*Hint:* You can use the WriteLine method to write the names and values of the form fields on separate lines. Use the write, WriteLine, and WriteBlankLines methods to write content to the file.)

```
txtFile.WriteLine(Title)
txtFile.WriteLine(Author)
txtFile.WriteBlankLines(1)
txtFile.WriteLine(Comments)
txtFile.Close
%>
```

10. Add a heading that tells the user where the file was created, and close the file.

```
<h3 align = "center">The file has been created at
<br><br>
<% = fn %>
</h3>
</body></html>
```

11. Modify the appearance of the Web page.

12. Save the page as **fsoProcessForm.asp** in your data directory.

13. View the Web page in your browser. Create a page using the form. Select the Text File format in the drop-down list.

14. View the page that was created. Print the newly created page, the Web page, and the source code.

15. You can view the Web page again, and recreate the page, using the other file formats in the drop-down list. Note that although the file can be saved as a Web page or an ASP page, unless you enter HTML tags, the content is rendered as plain text on the page. If you save the page as a Word document, the text will appear in the Word document, but it will be unformatted text.

CASE PROJECTS

Jim's Golf Magazine—Renewal Form

You are hired in the Distribution Department at *Jim's Golf Magazine* to assist them in developing their department's Web site. The department head wants to enable visitors to the Web site to fill out a form. Create the form below and save your Web page as GolfForm.asp in your data directory.

```
<html><head><title>Registration Form</title></head>
<body bgcolor="#99FF99" text="#008000">
<h2 align="center">Member Subscription Renewal Form</h2>
<form method="POST" action="GolfFormProcess.asp">
<table border="0" align="center">
<tr><td>Member ID</td>
<td><input type="text" name="memberid" size="20">
</td></tr><tr><td>First Name</td>
<td><input type="text" name="fname" size="20">
</td></tr><tr><td>Last Name</td>
<td><input type="text" name="lname" size="20">
</td></tr><tr><td>Address</td>
<td><input type="text" name="address" size="20">
</td></tr><tr><td>City</td>
<td><input type="text" name="city" size="20">
</td></tr><tr><td>State</td>
<td><input type="text" name="state" size="4">
</td></tr><tr><td>Zip Code</td>
```

11

```
<td><input type="text" name="zipcode" size="10">
</td></tr><tr><td>Country</td>
<td><input type="text" name="country" size="4">
</td></tr><tr><td>Renew Subscription</td>
<td>
<input type="radio" value="Yes" checked name="renew">Yes
<input type="radio" name="renew" value="No">No
</td></tr><tr><td><p>Tips</td>
<td><p>
<input type="checkbox" name="putt"
     value="Great Putting Tips">
Great Putting Tips <br>
<input type="checkbox" name="green"
     value="Green Acres">
Green Acres<br>
<input type="checkbox" name="sand"
     value="Sand &amp; Water Tips">
Sand &amp; Water Tips<br>
<input type="checkbox" name="tee" value="Tee Shots">
Tee Shots<br>
<input type="checkbox" name="clubs" value="Selecting Clubs">
Selecting Clubs
</td></tr></table>
<div align = "center"><br>
<input type="submit" value="Renew" name="btnSubmit">
</div></form></body></html>
```

Create an ASP page named GolfFormProcess.asp that retrieves each of the form fields. (*Hint*: You can retrieve each form field individually, for example `memberid = Request.Form("memberid")` or use a generic form handler.) If the visitor does not renew the order, display a message that says "You can renew your subscription later". If the visitor wants to renew the subscription, place the names of the fields as the keys, and the values of the fields as the items in the dictionary object. (*Hint*: The following code would add the ID of the member to the dictionary object: `objDMember.Add "memberid", memberid`.) Then, write a message that says "You will receive our extra Tips magazines list:". Use a definitions list to format the list of Tips magazines that the subscriber will receive. Modify the format of the page using break line tags or table tags. Modify the appearance of the page by adding images, text, and colors. Save both pages to your data directory. View the form in a browser and submit the form. Print both pages, and the source code for both pages.

Jim's Golf Magazine—Online Articles

You are temporarily transferred to the Editorial Department to help them develop online articles. The editor is concerned because they can't keep track of when files were created. Your job is to create a server-side include file named "lm.inc" that contains a generic script that will display the date the page was created. (*Hint*: You can retrieve the absolute path to the file using the following code: `fp = server.mappath(Request.Server Variables("PATH_INFO"))`. If you assign it to the variable fp, then you just need to pass the fp variable to the GetFile method. Don't forget to create the FileObject first, using the FileSystemObject. Calculate the number of minutes and the number of days that have elapsed since the file was created. (*Hint*: The code `DC = objFile.dateCreated` assigns the DC variable the dateCreated property of the file object. The code to display the number of minutes since the file was created would be `<% = DateDiff("n", DC, now) %>` `minutes <br><br>`. You can alter the code to also display the number in days, or calculate the number of days since the file was created.) Create a generic page called "lm.asp" and include the "lm.inc" file in the footer of the Web page. You can demonstrate this page to the editor before the script is included within the rest of the Web site. In the script, determine if the page is older than 100 days. Add a horizontal rule and display the current date and the dates the file was created, last accessed, and last modified. If the file is older than 100 days, add a hyperlink to a page called "lmOld.asp". Create the lmOld.asp page. Include a message on the page indicating that the file is older than 100 days. (*Hint*: Use the DateDiff method to calculate the number of days that has elapsed between the two dates.) Modify the appearance of the Web page by adding content, graphics, horizontal rules, and colors. Save the pages to your data directory and view them in a browser. Change the system date on your computer to 101 days from today. You can double-click on the time on the desktop to bring up the system Date/Time properties. You can change the system date here, using the calendar. View the page to see the hyperlink. Print all of the pages and the source code. Change your system date back to the current date.

Jim's Golf Magazine—Department File & Folder Index

You are transferred to the Customer Support Department at *Jim's Golf Magazine*. You discover that because they have a default index page, they have no way to view the directory information from the Internet site in a browser. Your job is to create a generic script that will display a list of the subfolders and their properties. First, declare your variables named fp, objFSO, objFolder, subFolder, keyFolder, and objFile. Next, you decide to retrieve the file path by applying the MapPath method to the PATH_INFO server variable. You place this value in a variable. (*Hint*: you can use `fp = server.mappath(Request.ServerVariables ("PATH_INFO"))`. Then, when you create the FileObject, using GetFile, you can pass the variable as the path parameter.

```
Set objFSO= CreateObject("Scripting.FileSystemObject")
Set objFile = objFSO.GetFile(fp)
```

To retrieve the current folder path information, you decide to use the ParentFolder property of the file object and store that in a variable. Then, you can pass the variable to the GetFolder method to create a folder object for the current folder.

```
folderspec = objFile.ParentFolder
Set objFolder = objFSO.GetFolder(folderspec)%>
```

From there you can display the name and path of the current folder because they are properties of the current folder object. (*Hint*: Try using `<% = objFolder.Path%>` to retrieve the path property.) Add a heading that says "The Subfolders collection of the Current Folder Object". To display the list of subfolders, you will need to retrieve the subfolders collection from the folder object and store the collection in a variable. Then, you can use a For Each loop to display the name of each folder by using the name property. You modify the displayed name by adding the anchor tag, which will change the text into a hyperlink. (*Hint*: Use the sample code below to retrieve the folder names as hyperlinks.)

```
<% Set subFolder = objFolder.Subfolders
For each keyFolder in subFolder %>
    <a href="<% = keyFolder.Name %>">
        <% = keyFolder.Name %>
    </a><br>
<% Next %>
```

The script will also display a list of the files within the directory and their properties. Add a heading that says "The Files collection of the Current Folder Object". (*Hint*: Use the sample code below to retrieve the filenames as hyperlinks.)

```
<%
For each objFile in objFolder.Files %>
    <a href="<% = objFile.Name %>">
        <% = objFile.Name %>
    </a><br>
<% Next %>
```

Modify the appearance of the page by adding images, text, and colors. Save the page as GolfFolder.asp to your data directory. View the page to test the generic script. Print your Web page and the source code.

Jim's Golf Magazine—Managing Server Files

The Webmaster would like to be able to manage the files on the server from a browser. Create a Web page named GolfCopy.asp. Create a script that will retrieve the names of the files in the folder and the path to the current folder. Then, place the names of the files in a drop-down list box in the Web page. Place the path to the folder in a text box. Add a drop-down list box, which will contain the commands for copying, moving, or deleting the file. Add additional drop-down list boxes, which will contain the parameters for copying and moving files. (*Hint*: You might want to use the methods that are available to the file object or the FileSystemObject.) Create a second page named GolfCopyProcess.asp, which will retrieve the form fields and perform the action identified by the form. (*Hint*: You might want to retrieve the form field values and place them into variables. Then, you can refer to the variables in the script. The following sample code will generate a drop-down list box populated with the filenames in the directory. You still need to create the FileSystemObject and FolderObject first.)

```
<select size = "1" name = "filelist">
    <option value = "" selected>Select a file</option>
    <% For each objFile in objFolder.Files %>
        <option value ="<% = objFile.Name %>">
            <% = objFile.Name %>
        </option>
    <% Next %>
</select>
```

At the bottom of GolfCopyProcess.asp, put a hyperlink to the GolfCopy.asp page. Modify the appearance of the pages. Save your Web pages to your data directory. Create a test page in Notepad named golf1.txt. View the GolfCopy.asp Web page in a browser. Use the GolfCopy.asp page to copy the golf1.txt page to the same directory. The new filename should be golf2.txt. Print out each Web page and the source code.

11

12

INTEGRATING DATABASES WITH ASP PAGES

In this chapter you will:

♦ Create a database with a table in Microsoft Access

♦ Learn how database models allow you to connect Active Server Pages to a database

♦ Create a Data Source Name (DSN) to a Microsoft Access database

♦ Create a connection string to a Microsoft Access database

♦ Create a Web page that displays data from a database table, using the recordset object

♦ Identify Internet resources on connecting Web applications to a data source

---

In previous chapters you learned how to use built-in and third-party objects, properties, and methods to enhance your Web applications. In this chapter, you will learn how to enable your Web application to access data from a variety of data sources. Database access via the Web is vital to many of today's business applications. In e-commerce, databases store the product catalog, shipping, tax, and customer information. These databases facilitate ordering and fulfillment, and also allow the management team to review sales trends and customer profiles that can be used to develop marketing campaigns. Databases are also used to store company data that employees need access to. For example, the Finance Department might want to have access to the current sales so that sales employees who travel can remotely access and update their sales data. Businesses also want to share information with customers and other partners. For example, an advertising company might want to allow its customers to view how often visitors to its Web site view the banner ads. You can build a portal to your Web site for customers who can view only data that is related to them. You can also allow them to retrieve that data and update their own database with your data.

You can use ASP with other database technologies to develop database-driven Web sites. There are many resources available for learning how to connect databases to Web pages. In this chapter, you will learn how to locate Internet resources that provide information on databases, SQL, and the ADO model.

CREATING A DATABASE-DRIVEN WEB APPLICATION

Creating a database-driven Web application involves several technologies, tools, and a variety of programming methods. In general, you can follow the process described in this chapter to develop Web pages that access a database. In the following chapter, you will learn how to modify the Web program to perform additional activities such as inserting new records, modifying records, and deleting records. As you learn the basic steps, you can see how easy it is to expand upon them. For example, once you learn how to build advanced SQL statements, you can easily build more interactivity into the Web application. You would retrieve the values to build the SQL statements from the user from a form. However, unless you understand the basic steps, you can easily become "lost" in code. If you understand the basic steps, you can always start from the basics, and build complexity into your code step by step. Below is a list of the tasks that are used to develop a Web page that displays data from a database. Each step of this process will be thoroughly explained within this chapter.

1. Create the database (Access 2000 will be used here, but any ODBC or OLEDB database will work).

2. Create a database connection (either DSN or connection string).

3. Create an ASP page (again, using Notepad or your ASP-compatible editor).

4. Create a recordset object. (The ADO model provides objects to access the database. The recordset object will contain the records.)

5. Open the recordset object and retrieve the records. (You can retrieve the entire table or a subset, using SQL commands.)

6. Retrieve and display the field information for each record. (Individual fields can be retrieved.)

7. Close the recordset object.

As indicated, there is more than one way to retrieve a recordset. The recordset object will allow you to retrieve the records. But you can explicitly open a connection to the database with a connection object, and then use the recordset object to retrieve the records via that connection.

The choice of method depends upon the performance and level of control. Using a connection object allows you to explicitly open and close the connections to the database.

Below is a list of the steps taken to modify the process to include the connection object. Each step of this process will be thoroughly explained within this chapter.

1. Create the database.

2. Create a database connection.

3. Create an ASP page.

4. Create a connection object.

5. Open the connection to the database, using the connection object.

6. Create the recordset object.

7. Open a recordset, using the connection provided by the connection object.

8. Retrieve and display the field information for each record.

9. Close the recordset object.

10. Close the connection object.

CREATING A DATABASE USING ACCESS 2000

Database management systems (DBMS) are applications that store and manage data. Databases store data differently. **Relational databases** store data in one or more tables. Each table consists of records. Each row in a table corresponds to a single record. Records are made up of fields, and each field contains a single item of data. A group of records is known as a **recordset**. A collection of the same field across multiple records is called a column. Therefore, each table is made up of columns and rows.

12

Databases can be created using many different database programs, such as Access 2000, FoxPro, SQL Server, and Oracle. When you create a database table, you must identify the field name and data type for each field. The data type defines how the table will store the data. In Access, the view that defines the table structure is called **Design view**. The description of how the data is stored is called the data structure. After creating the table structure, you can enter data into the table. Databases have different user interfaces for creating the database structure and for entering data. However, the basic principles behind creating tables are the same across relational database programs. Some programs, such as Access 2000, also offer graphical wizards that help you build your tables using templates. The following example illustrates how to create a basic database and a table, using Access 2000.

To create a database and a table using Access 2000:

1. Open Access 2000. By default, the shortcut to the Access 2000 program can be executed by clicking **Start**, then **Programs**, then **Microsoft Access**.

2. A dialog box appears (see Figure 12-1) that is used to indicate whether you are creating a new blank database, creating a new database from a wizard, or opening an

existing database. Select the radio button that says **Blank Access database** to create a new database file, and click **OK**. The File New Database dialog box will open.

Figure 12-1   Opening a database in Microsoft Access

3. In the filename text box, enter **customer** for the name of the database. You do not need to type the file extension. Access will add the .mdb file extension automatically. Click the **Save in** list arrow to locate your data directory (see Figure 12–2). Click the **Create** button to save the database to your data directory.

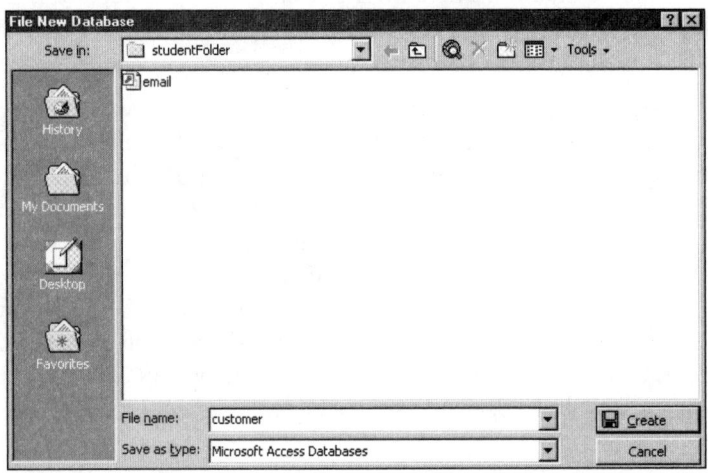

Figure 12-2   Saving your new database in your data directory

4. The customer database will open. On the left are the objects available from within Access. These objects include tables, queries, forms, reports, pages, macros, and modules. By default, the database opened inside the Table tab. There are three

options listed on the right. The "Create table in Design view" option is selected by default. Double-click the **Create table in Design view** option to open a new table in Design view. There are two views, or ways, to look at your table. Design view allows you to create and modify the structure of the database.

5. In the first Field Name box, type in the field name **id**, which will represent the customer ID. Field names can be up to 64 characters long. It is recommended that you not use spaces in the field name, although some databases allow you to do so.

6. Click the **Tab** key to move to the Data Type drop-down list. Select the **text** data type from the drop-down list. In the Description box, type **Customer ID**. The description is optional, but is useful to document information about the field.

7. At the bottom of the table window is the General tab, which contains several field properties that you can set for the field. The default field size is 50 characters; change the field size property to **10**.

8. In the Required field property text box, change the **Required** property from No to **Yes**. This means that when a new record is created, a value must be placed in this field (see Figure 12-3). Enter the rest of the names of the fields and the data types according to the list in Table 12-1, located below.

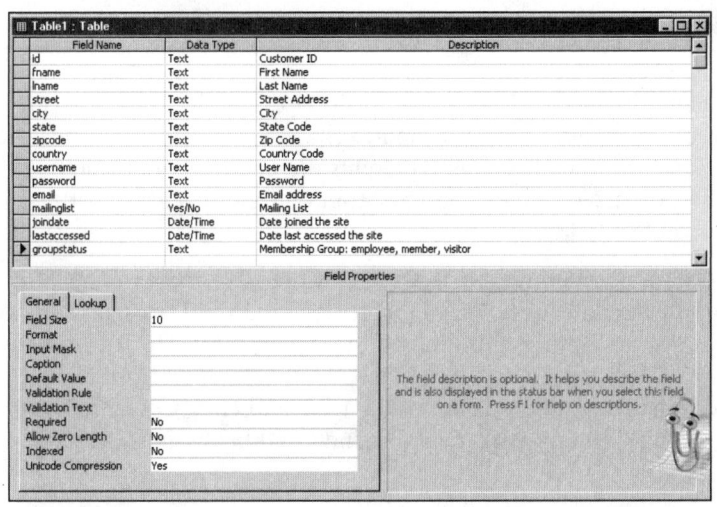

12

Figure 12-3   Creating the customer database structure in Access 2000

Table 12-1   Creating the Structure for the Customer Database

Field Name	Data Type	Description	Field Properties
id	Text	Customer ID	Field size 10; Required Yes
fname	Text	First Name	Field size 25
lname	Text	Last Name	Field size 25
street	Text	Street Address	Field size 20
city	Text	City	Field size 20
state	Text	State	Field size 2
zipcode	Text	Zip Code	Field size 10
country	Text	Country Code	Field size 2
username	Text	User Name	Field size 10
password	Text	Password	Field size 10
keyword	Text	Keyword	Field size 10
email	Text	E-mail address	Field size 50
mailinglist	Yes/No	Mailing List	
joindate	Date/Time	Date joined the site	
lastaccessed	Date/Time	Date last visited the site	
groupstatus	Text	Membership Group: employee, member, visitor	Field size 10

Click the left box next to the id field to select the id field row. A triangle will appear in the box, indicating that the id field is selected. On the table toolbar, click the **key** icon. The key icon represents the primary key. By setting the id field as the primary key field, you have configured the field so that no duplicates can appear in this field.

9. Click the **view** icon on far left-hand side of the table toolbar. The view icon allows you to toggle between the Design view and the Datasheet view. An Access dialog box appears stating, "You must first save the table. Do you want to save the table now?" Click **Yes**. The Save As dialog box will appear. In the Save As dialog box, enter **customer** as the name of the table and click **OK**. The Datasheet view opens. Enter the data for each record as indicated below in Table 12-2.

Table 12-2   Data for the Customer Table

Field Name	Record1	Record2	Record3
id	1	2	3
fname	John	John	Jane
lname	Garcia	Barnes	Monroe
street	555 Main Street	412 State Street	312 Lake Street
city	Greenbay	Wilmette	West Lafayette
state	WI	IL	IN

Table 12-2   Data for the Customer Table (continued)

Field Name	Record1	Record2	Record3
zipcode	73432	98773	49872
country	US	US	US
username	jgarcia	jbarnes	jmonroe
password	mickey	flamingo	ghost
keyword	objection	turbo	java
email	jgarcia@oakton.net	jbarnes@webedit.net	jmonroe@kalata.com
mailinglist	Yes (check the box)	Yes (check the box)	No (leave the box cleared)
joindate	7/10/2001	6/25/2001	7/16/2001
lastaccessed	7/16/2001	7/25/2001	7/28/2001
groupstatus	employee	member	visitor

10. Click the **save** icon on the table toolbar, which will save the table (see Figure 12-4).

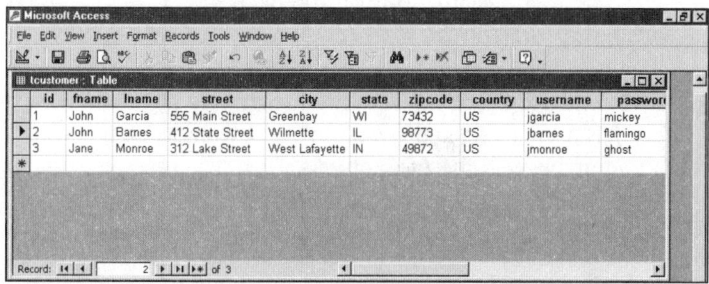

Figure 12-4   Save the customer table

11. Click **File** on the menu bar, and then click **Close** to close the table. The database window will show the new customer table.

12. Click **File** on the menu bar, and then click **Close** to close the database.

13. Click **File** on the menu bar, and then click **Exit** to exit Access.

DATABASE MODELS

In the past, database management systems were proprietary; stored data could only be accessed via the program that was used to create the database. Programs could not share data unless there was an interface built between the database applications. Today, business needs demand database management systems that are more flexible. This flexibility has been achieved by means of the **Universal Data Access (UDA)** model. The Universal Data Access model provides a method whereby data can be shared across different applications and platforms. The UDA is implemented by standards called open database connectivity (ODBC) and OLEDB, and the ActiveX Data Object model (ADO) and ADO+.

One of the best resources for understanding how the UDA is implemented is the Microsoft UDA Web site at *http://www.microsoft.com/data/default.htm*.

How all this works is not straightforward, because there are many ways to connect your Web application using this UDA model. First you should build your database tables and determine what information you want to retrieve from your database. Then, you will decide if you need to use the ODBC drivers or OLEDB providers to connect to your database. Next, you will create either a Data Source Name (DSN) or connection string. The DSN or connection string identifies the location of the database (the data source) and the connection method (an ODBC driver or an OLEDB driver), along with any other connection settings such as username or password. Then, you can create a Web page that will connect to the database. You can use the built-in objects within ADO to connect to the database, execute commands, and return a recordset from the database. From there you can display the data, write the information in a cookie, or perform calculations on the data.

Because there are differences between ODBC and OLEDB, and because of the differences between the ADO objects, this process may vary slightly with each Web application. It is recommended that you first work with Access and ODBC until you feel comfortable with the ADO objects. Then, you can convert your Access application to SQL Server and use OLEDB.

ODBC and OLEDB

In 1992, a standard known as **open database connectivity** (ODBC) was created to provide a common interface for relational database systems. ODBC drivers are used to provide access to an ODBC-compliant database. Using ODBC drivers, an application can access a database without an application- or database-specific interface. You do not need to know how the database application is storing the data in order to access the data. The ODBC drivers provide the low-level interface to the database applications. ODBC drivers are available for most DBMSs, including Access, SQL Server, and Oracle. Figure 12-5 illustrates how ODBC drivers are used with the ADO model to access ODBC-compliant databases.

E-mail programs, such as Exchange Server, store data in a different format than relational database applications. The UDA model provides a method for accessing relational database stores and these nonrelational data stores, which is called **OLEDB** (OLEDB stands for object linking and embedding database). Using OLEDB allows your application to access a database without an application- or database-specific interface. You do not need to know how the database application is storing the data in order to access the data. OLEDB providers are available for most common data stores, including Access, SQL Server, and Exchange Server. Microsoft provides an OLEDB provider that will interface with the ODBC driver in order to support legacy database applications. For example, if your database application does not have an OLEDB provider, but does have the ODBC driver, you can use the OLEDB provider for ODBC to access the database. Figure 12-5 illustrates how the OLEDB providers are used with the ADO Model to access OLE-DB-compliant databases. The Web application interacts with objects built within the ADO model. Then ADO interfaces through the ODBC and OLEDB to the database.

 Microsoft provides an excellent presentation on why they developed OLEDB at *http://www.microsoft.com/data/oledb/olap/presentations/muda/sld01.htm.*

The ODBC drivers and OLEDB providers enable the low-level interface to the database. However, there must be a method to send requests to and receive responses from ODBC and OLEDB. Microsoft provides Microsoft Data Access Components (MDAC), which includes not only the OLEDB provider and ODBC driver, but also the components that would be used to interface to ODBC and OLEDB. This collection of components is known as ADO (ActiveX Data Objects).

MDAC contains ODBC drivers for text files, Access, FoxPro, Paradox, dBase, Excel, SQL Server, and Oracle. MDAC also provides additional files, including the ODBC Driver Manager. In Windows 98, the ODBC Driver Manager is located in C:\Windows\system\odbc32.dll. In Windows 2000, the ODBC Driver Manager is located in C:\Windows\system32\odbcad32. You can access the ODBC Driver Manager through the Control Panel. The ODBC Driver Manager is used to create DSNs. DSNs contain the connection information required to connect to an ODBC or OLEDB data source. Later in this chapter you will learn to create a DSN. In Windows 2000, the ODBC Driver Manager is accessed using the Microsoft Management Console (MMC). The most common way to connect a Web application to a database is to use ActiveX Data Objects (ADO), which come as part of the Windows MDAC, or Microsoft Data Access Components.

Older computers may not have MDAC installed. MDAC can be downloaded from the Microsoft Web site at *http://www.microsoft.com/data/download.htm.* MDAC is also installed when you install programs such as Visual InterDev, Personal Web Server, Internet Information Server, Visual Basic, and Visual Studio. There are different versions of ASP, MDAC, and ADO. When you install Personal Web Server or Internet Information Server, you are also installing support for ASP version 2.0 as well as MDAC version 1.5 and ADO version 1.5. If you install any of the Visual Studio 6.0 programs, you are installing MDAC version 2.0 and ADO version 2.0. MDAC and ADO version 2.1 are available from Internet Explorer version 5.0 and with Office 2000 applications. Although MDAC and ADO version 2.5 come with Windows 2000, you can also download MDAC version 2.5 directly from Microsoft. Support for ADO+ will be available from Microsoft during mid-2001.

12

ADO+ will be available as part of the second release of Windows 2000. Below is the sample code that will identify which version of ADO is installed on the server.

```
<%
set oC = server.createobject("ADODB.connection")
Response.write oC.Version
%>
```

The ADO model, ODBC drivers, and OLEDB providers reside on the server, not the client. In future versions of ASP+ and ADO+, you will be able to use disconnected recordsets, which are recordsets downloaded from the database to the client. Disconnected recordsets are used locally. Then, after changes are made, the recordsets are synchronized with the database on the server.

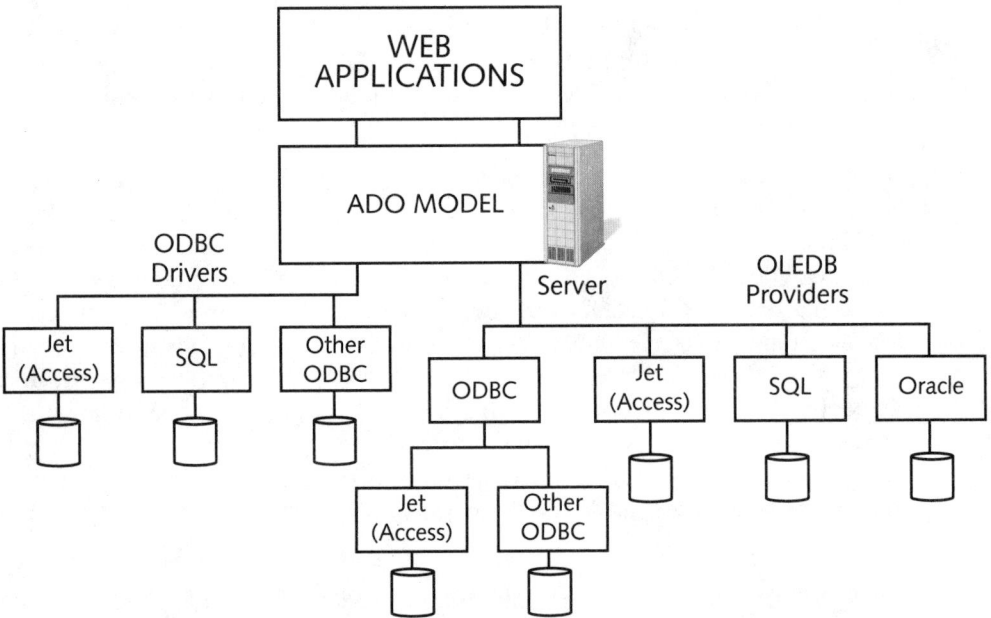

Figure 12-5   How the ADO model uses the ODBC drivers and OLEDB providers to connect Web applications to a variety of databases

Database Connections

In order to connect your Web application to a data source, you need to know the location and type of the data, and what parameters to send with the connection request. This information can be stored within a Data Source Name (DSN) or connection string. The DSN stores the connection data in the Registry on the computer where the DSN was created. To create a DSN, you must have local access to the computer, and in general Web developers do not have local access to the server. Your Web server might be in Hong Kong, and you might live in Chicago. It would be more economical to have the connection information stored in an external file that you could upload to the Web server. The connection information can be placed in a connection string and stored in an external file.

A connection string contains the connection data in a string within the application. In a Web application, the connection string may be stored in the Web page that is accessing the database, or in a separate server-side include file. The benefit of using the connection string is that you do not have to have local access to the server. You can FTP the file that contains the connection string to the server. You can also use the publishing feature within FrontPage, InterDev, Visual Studio 7, or Dreamweaver to send the file that contains the connection string to the server. Whether you use a DSN or connection string, you must identify the same information required to make the connection to the data source.

DSNs

The three types of DSNs are file DSNs, user DSNs, and system DSNs. A **file DSN** contains the data connection information in a file that has a .udl extension. A file DSN can be shared among all users if they have the same drivers installed, and need not be present on the local system.

User DSNs and **system DSNs** are also called machine DSNs because they only exist on the local system. If you create a user or system DSN on one system, and later move the database application to another system, you will need to recreate the DSN on the new system. Both the user and system DSNs store the data connection information in the system Registry. The user DSN stores the data connection information in the HKEY_CURRENT_USER Registry subtree, while the system DSN stores the data information in the HKEY_LOCAL_MACHINE Registry subtree. While the system or any authenticated user can use a system DSN, a user DSN can only be used by the current user.

For Internet-based applications such as Web applications, you will want to use a system DSN to store your database connection information.

Creating a System DSN   You can use the ODBC Driver Manager in the Control Panel to create DSNs. Note that the ODBC Administrator is called ODBC Data Sources (32-bit) on a Windows 95 or 98 system, and ODBC on a Windows NT system. On Windows 2000, the ODBC Administrator is labeled Data Sources (ODBC) and is located in the Windows Control Panel under Administrative Tools. You can also open it directly through the ODBC plug-in in the Microsoft Management Console (MMC).

The procedure for creating a DSN will vary with the type of DSN, the data source, and the version of the Microsoft Data Access Components (MDAC) that are installed on the server.

To create a system DSN to an Access database in Windows 98:

1. Click **Start**, then point to **Settings**, then click **Control Panel**.

2. Double-click the icon labeled **32-bit ODBC** to open the ODBC Administrator.

3. Click the **System DSN** tab to open the ODBC Data Source Administrator dialog box (see Figure 12-6). Notice that there is currently only one system data source defined on this system. You may have no DSNs defined or several, depending on what software you currently have installed. Your system may say system DSN or System on the tab.

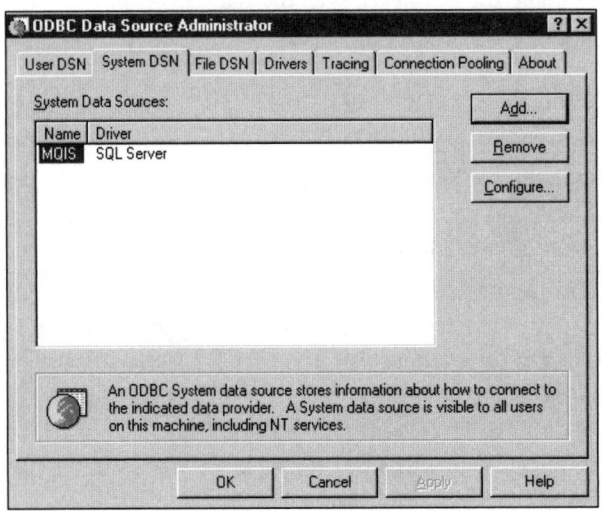

Figure 12-6   Creating a system DSN in the ODBC Data Source Administrator

4. Click the **Add** button to add a new system DSN. A list of the installed drivers will appear in the Create New Data Source dialog box.

5. Because the list is alphabetical, the Microsoft Access Driver is usually the first driver, and is therefore selected by default. If it isn't, click **Microsoft Access Driver (*.mdb)** to select it. In Windows 2000, you may see additional drivers in this list (see Figure 12-7).

6. Click **Finish** to accept the Access driver. The "ODBC Microsoft Access Setup" dialog box appears.

7. In the Data Source Name text box, type in the name of the system DSN, **dsnEmail**. This name will be used within your Web page to reference the DSN. (*Hint:* You are not required to enter any text in the Description text box. The DSN in this example is dsnEmail. The DSN does not have to be the same name as the database name or the table name.)

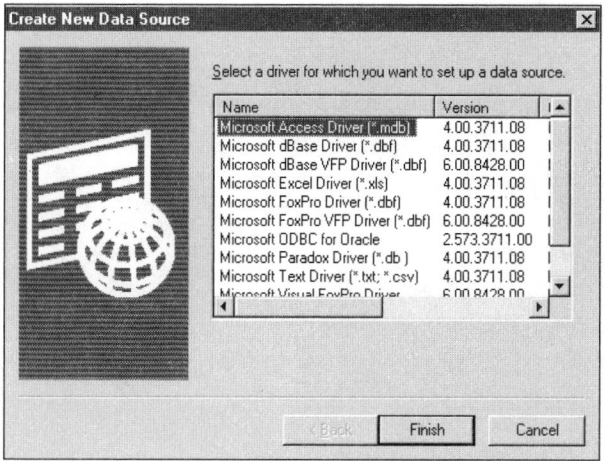

Figure 12-7   Drivers and providers available in the ODBC Data Source Administrator

In a classroom, you might be instructed to name your system DSN according to a naming convention such as dsn_UserID_databaseName, UserID_databaseName, or UserID_dsnName. You cannot have more than one system DSN with the same name on the same computer.

8. Click the **Select** button to open the Select Database dialog box. On the right, locate your data directory using the Drives and Directories list arrows.

9. In the Database Name text box on the left-hand side of the dialog box, click on the name of the database you created in the previous activity, **customer.mdb**.

You can create a database within the ODBC Driver Manager. You must create the database before you can finish creating a DSN, because the DSN needs to know the location of the database. This method creates an Access database file that is compatible with Access version 7.0 or greater, but does not contain any tables or data.

10. Click **OK**. A dialog box will appear, indicating that the database was successfully created. You will be returned to the ODBC Microsoft Access Setup dialog box (Figure 12-8). Notice that the location of the database is now listed directly above the Select button.

12

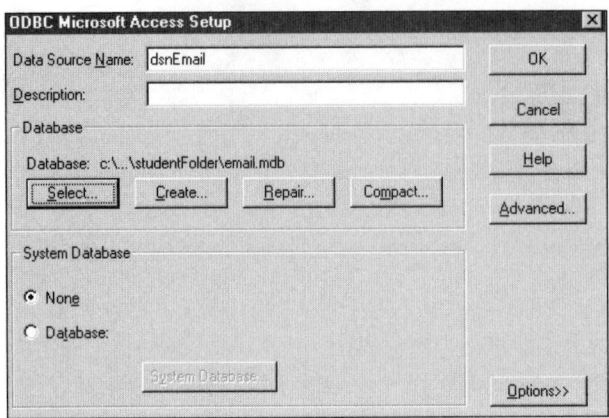

Figure 12-8   The ODBC Microsoft Access Setup dialog box

 Clicking the Advanced button opens a Set Advanced Options dialog box where you can set the login name and password to secure the database. It is easier to create and test your Web application first, before adding the security layer.

11. Click **OK**. The DSN that you just created should be in the system data sources list. Click **OK** to close the ODBC Data Source Administrator dialog box.

Using the System DSN   Once you have created the system DSN, you can refer to it in your ASP page. The following sample code shows how to open a connection using the connection object and a system DSN named dsnProducts. You can explicitly identify the DSN using the keyword DSN and an equal sign, or you can simply specify the name of the DSN.

```
Dim oC
set oC = server.createobject("ADODB.connection")
oC.open "dsn=dsnProducts"
```

When you create a DSN that has a username and password associated with the database, you must pass these parameters when you request to open the connection to the database using the DSN. In this sample code, the DSN is for an ODBC connection to an Access database.

```
Dim oC
set oC = server.createobject("ADODB.connection")
oC.open "dsn=dsnProducts; uid=admin; pwd=pass;"
```

Connection Strings

If you do not have access to the local computer where the data source is stored, you can use a connection string to store the data connection information. The connection string contains the same connection information that is stored within the system DSN. The most basic connection string, which is used to connect to an Access database, consists of three parts. The first part is the variable, which will hold the connection string. The second part is the name of the driver. The third part is the physical location of the Access database. Below is a sample connection string to an Access database named customer.

```
CS = "DRIVER={Microsoft Access Driver (*.mdb)};
      DBQ= c:\chapter12\customer.mdb;"
```

The connection string must appear on one line because it is a string. Because of the limited number of characters that can fit on one line in this book, the string appears split. You cannot split a string across two lines. However, it is possible to split the connection string into smaller, more manageable strings.

There is a space between the second r in Driver and the opening parenthesis, "(".

Because connection strings are case sensitive and because the driver name must match exactly the name of the driver installed on the server, it is recommended that you split the connection string into two variables, and then concatenate the two variables into a single variable. This way, you do not have to retype the name of the driver each time you want to reuse the connection string. The following sample code illustrates how you can use variables to separate the connection string into smaller strings. The DR variable stores the Access ODBC driver. The DBQ stores the location to the Access database. Then, the strDriver and strDBQ variables are concatenated and the results stored in the CS variable.

```
<% dim DRV, DBQ, CS
DRV = "DRIVER={Microsoft Access Driver (*.mdb)}; "
DBQ = "DBQ= c:\chapter12\customer.mdb;"
CS = DRV & DBQ
```

12

Connection strings can be created within the Web page that displays the recordset, or they can reside in a server-side include file. If you are going to use the database with other Web pages, then it is easier to maintain the connection string in an SSI file that you can include in each Web page that accesses the database. In this way, if the name or location of the database changes, you only have to change the information in one central location. You can also keep connection strings to other databases within the same Web page.

When you are working with an Access database, you can use an ODBC driver or an OLEDB provider to connect to the database. Below is the sample code for the OLEDB driver that can be used to connect to an Access database. Notice that the keyword provider is used instead of driver. Also, notice that the keyword DBQ has been replaced with Data Source. A newer version of the OLEDB provider is available and is named "Microsoft.Jet.OLEDB.4.0".

```
CS = "Provider=Microsoft.Jet.OLEDB.3.51;
      Data Source= c:\chapter12\customer.mdb;"
```

To create a connection string to an Access database:

1. Using Notepad or your Web page editor, create a new file named **conxsample.inc**.

2. Declare your variables. The CS variable will hold the connection string. The DRV variable will hold the driver name, and the DBQ variable will hold the file location.

```
<% dim DRV, DBQ, CS
```

Because the connection string is used to access a database on the server, you must use server script tags, not client-side script tags.

3. Set the DRV variable to the Microsoft Access ODBC driver.

```
DRV = "DRIVER={Microsoft Access Driver (*.mdb)}; "
```

It is imperative that the name of the driver be spelled correctly and that the driver keyword, file extension, parentheses, semicolon, and curly braces all appear as indicated. Any typographical error in the driver name will result in a connection error.

4. Set the DBQ variable to the physical location of the database. Replace "c:\chapter12\customer.mdb" with the location and name of your database. You must include the correct path, database name, and file extension, and the DBQ keyword exactly as indicated. Any typographical error in the file location will result in a connection error.

```
DBQ = "DBQ= c:\chapter12\customer.mdb;"
```

5. Concatenate the two variables and assign the results to the CS variable.

```
CS = DRV & DBQ
%>
```

6. Save the file as **conxsample.inc** in your data directory. If you are working in Notepad, you should save the filename enclosed in quotes. Other editors may also require you to save the filename in quotes. Now the connection string will be available to any of your Web pages!

In some cases you might not know the location of your database. Hosting providers do not always allow developers access to their file systems through Telnet. Therefore, you might not know the absolute path to your database. If you know the relative path to the directory, you can modify the connection string to use the MapPath method of the server object. Using the MapPath method instead of a static path provides greater flexibility. When you move the Web application, you should not have to change the connection string. The sample below shows how you could pass the path information to the MapPath method. The MapPath method translates the relative path into an absolute address.

```
<% dim DR, DBQ, CS
DRV = "DRIVER={Microsoft Access Driver (*.mdb)}; "
DBQ = "DBQ ="
& "Server.MapPath(/chapter12/customer.mdb) & ";"
CS = DR & DBQ
%>
```

Recall that in HTTP 1.1 there is a server environmental variable named PATH_TRANSLATED that will provide the absolute path to the current file. You can retrieve this path using
`Request.ServerVariables("PATH_TRANSLATED")`.

Another method is to create a file that displays the path information for you. If you place the information in the same directory as the database, both the relative and absolute paths will be displayed. Below is a sample page called displayPath.asp that will display the relative and absolute path. The code retrieves a server variable called PATH_INFO that provides the relative address for the current page. After viewing the page, you can copy the absolute path displayed into your connection string. You must remove the name of the current page (displayPath.asp) from the string, and add the name of your database. This method is often used to debug errors in the connection string.

```
<html><head><title>PATH_INFO</title></head>
<body>
<% dim PI, PP
PI = Request.ServerVariables("PATH_INFO")
PP = Server.MapPath(PI) %>
<h3>The Web - Relative path to this file is:
<br><br><% = PI %>
<hr>
The Physical path to this file is:
<br><br> <% = PP %>
</h3></body></html>
```

Connection Strings for SQL Server   Connection strings for SQL Server are similar to connection strings for an Access database. You need to provide the name of the provider, the user ID and password associated with the database, the name of the SQL server, and the name of the data source. Below is a sample of an ODBC connection string to a SQL Server database. Notice that the name of the driver used is SQL Server, and this is a driver, not provider. The entire connection string should be placed on one line.

```
<%
CS = "Driver={SQL Server}; SERVER=Windamere;
      UID=sa; PWD=; DATABASE=customer"
%>
```

The sample code below shows how to use an OLEDB connection to a SQL Server database. Notice that the keyword used is provider, not driver. The name of the database is identified as the initial catalog. The name of the server is identified as the data source. Below is a sample of an OLEDB connection string to a SQL Server database. This string should also be placed on one line.

```
<%
CS = "Provider=SQLOLEDB.1; Data Source=Windamere;
      User ID=sa; PASSWORD=; Initial Catalog=customer;"
%>
```

THE ACTIVEX DATA OBJECT MODEL (ADO)

Once you have created your database and your connection information, the next step is to create the Web pages that will interact with the database. The **ActiveX Data Object Model (ADO)** provides a method for accessing databases from your Web pages. The primary objects in the ADO model are the connection object, the recordset object, and the command object. The field object is accessed from a recordset object. The parameter object is a parameter of the command object. The err object is created when a connection error occurs. Figure 12-9 illustrates the objects defined within the ADO model.

 The main benefits of the ADO model include low memory overhead and high speed, which are ideal for Web-based applications.

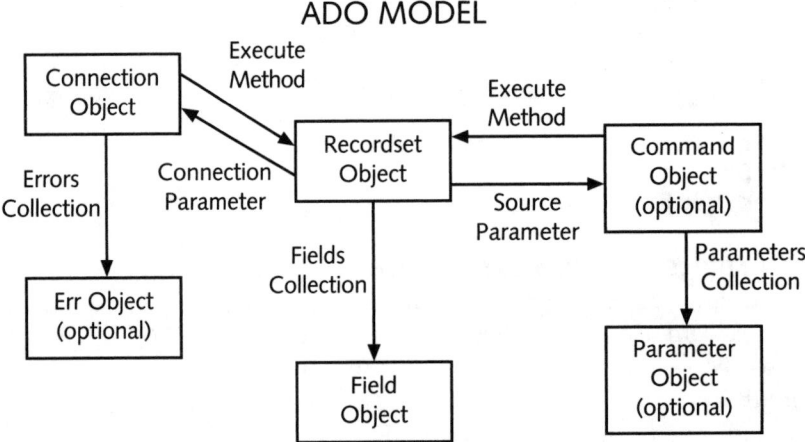

Figure 12-9   The main objects within the ADO model

The ADO model isn't an autocratic hierarchy. In other words, you don't have to create the second tier of objects (such as the recordset or command objects) under a single connection object. For example, you could create a recordset object that is separate from a previously defined connection object. The recordset object that you define will exist under a newly created connection object. The recordset object will create the connection object for you, without having to explicitly create the connection object. Although you aren't confined to a strict hierarchy, you will typically use the structured nature of the ADO model to provide organization for your objects and code.

More information on the ADO and UDA models can be found in the Microsoft ADO Web site at *http://www.microsoft.com/data/ado/*.

The Connection Object

The connection object is the central object in the model. Every other object in the model is related to the connection object. This hierarchy makes sense, because the other objects can't exist without a connection to the database. The connection object is most often used to establish a connection between a Web page and a database.

You can create a connection object using the CreateObject method of the server object. The connection object can open a connection to a database using the open method. The open method is passed at least one parameter, the connection parameter. The connection parameter can be a Data Source Name (DSN) or **connection string**. Both the DSN and connection string identify the path and name of the database. The DSN and connection string also identify the ODBC driver or OLEDB provider used to connect to the database.

You can use the open method of the connection object to open a connection to a database. You must pass the DSN or connection string to the open method. In the following sample, the connection object, called oC, opens a connection to a database using a DSN named dsnProducts.

```
Dim oC
set oC = server.createobject("ADODB.connection")
oC.open "dsnProducts"
```

You should always close your connections to a database, using the close method, when you are finished using it. Set the variable to "nothing" to release the memory that was used to store the object. You must close the connection before you can assign "nothing" to the variable. By closing the connection, and releasing the variable, you will conserve resources on the server.

```
oC.Close
set oC = nothing
```

You should close a connection immediately after using it. When the Web server is handling several requests at once, it may be a while before it closes the connection if you put it at the end of a Web page. You should also set the value "nothing" to the variable to release the memory that was used to store the object. You can close connections and release the objects in an include file.

The connection object can also be used to execute commands. You can pass a command to the open method of the connection object. The command object will execute the command. These commands are often requests for tables or SQL statements. The SQL "select" statement is used to retrieve records from a database. When the connection object executes a "select" statement, a group of zero or more records is returned as a recordset object. The group of zero or more records is referred to as a **recordset**. The recordset object that is returned is configured with the default properties, such as read-only. The following sample code illustrates how the connection object can execute a SQL "select" statement to return a recordset.

```
Dim oC
set oC = server.createobject("ADODB.connection")
oC.open "SELECT * FROM products", "dsnProducts"
```

You can also use the connection object to execute other SQL statements. The following sample code illustrates how the connection object can execute a SQL "insert" statement to insert a new record. You will learn how to build a SQL insert, delete, and update statements in the next chapter.

```
Dim oC
set oC = server.createobject("ADODB.connection")
oC.open "INSERT INTO Products(name, price, data, number)
    VALUES('chair',153.00,#12/1/2000#,NULL)", "dsnProducts"
```

 If you are inserting a new record, you must identify values for all fields in sequential order, or you must identify the field names. If there is no value, you can pass the keyword NULL instead of a value.

The connection object contains several properties. The CommandTimeout property indicates how long to wait, in seconds, before it stops executing the command. The default CommandTimeout is 30 seconds. You can change this property. The ConnectionTimeout property indicates the length of time to wait, in seconds, before it aborts the connection attempt. The default ConnectionTimeout is 15 seconds. The version property provides the version of ADO.

```
CMT = oC.CommandTimeout
Response.write CMT
CNT = oC.ConnectionTimeout
Response.write CNT
Response.write oC.Version
```

You can set the ConnectionTimeout and CommandTimeout properties. However, you cannot change the ConnectionTimeout or CommandTimeout properties if the connection object is open.

```
oC.CommandTimeout = 60
oC.ConnectionTimeout = 60
```

The Recordset Object

The recordset object can be used in combination with the connection object to open the connection and to retrieve a recordset. In the following sample code, the recordset object uses a connection opened by the connection object. The recordset object then retrieves a table named products.

```
Dim oC
set oC = server.createobject("ADODB.connection")
oC.open "dsnProducts"
Dim oRS
set oRS = server.createobject("ADODB.recordset")
oRS.open "products", oC
```

You should close the recordset object using the close method. You should also set the value "nothing" to the recordset variable to release the memory that was used to store the recordset object. You must close the recordset before you can assign "nothing" to the variable. By closing the recordset, and releasing the variable, you will conserve resources on the server. Note that you must close the recordset object before closing the connection object. The following sample code illustrates how to close the recordset object before the connection object.

You must close the recordset object before you can close the connection object, or an error message will occur. You can write the code to close your recordset and connection objects at the bottom of the Web page. However, you can also write this code in a separate file, such as "close.inc", and include this file at the bottom of the page, using a server-side include statement.

```
oRS.Close
set oRS = nothing
oC.Close
set oC = nothing
```

The recordset object also contains methods that can open the connection without explicitly creating a connection object. If this method is used, the connection may not close immediately after the records are retrieved. If you want control over the connection, then you should explicitly define and open the connection, using the connection object. As you can see, although each of the ADO objects has a primary purpose, they can also perform additional methods, and can be used in combination with each other. In the following sample code, the recordset object uses the open method to open a connection and retrieve a table named products.

```
Dim oRS
set oRS = server.createobject("ADODB.recordset")
oRS.open "products", "dsnProducts"
```

12

You can execute SQL statements from the recordset object. In the following sample code, the recordset object uses the open method to open a connection. It then executes the SQL "select" statement and retrieves a recordset.

```
Dim oRS
set oRS = server.createobject("ADODB.recordset")
oRS.open "SELECT * FROM products", "dsnProducts"
```

A recordset object is an object, with properties and methods. A recordset is a set of database records.

The Field Object

The field object is available through the recordset object. Once you have retrieved a record-set, you can access all of the records and fields within the recordset. You can access the names of the fields and the values. You can retrieve the value of a field by specifying the name of the field. In the following sample code, the recordset represented by oRS contains records from the products table. Then, it uses a loop to display the name and price for each product in the table. Note how the formatCurrency method can be applied to the value passed from the price field. Once you retrieve a value from a field, you can apply methods to it, use it in a calculation, write it to a cookie, file, or database, or store it in a local, session, or application variable.

```
Dim oC
set oC = server.createobject("ADODB.connection")
oC.open "dsnProducts"
Dim oRS
set oRS = server.createobject("ADODB.recordset")
oRS.open "products", oC
do until oRS.EOF
     response.write "Product name: "
     response.write oRS("name")
     response.write "Product price: "
     response.write formatCurrency(oRS("price"))
End If
oRS.movenext
loop
```

The Command Object

The command object enables you to specify a specific command that you are going to exe-cute on a database. This command is often a request for a table or a SQL statement such as select, insert, update, or delete. However, the command object cannot independently use the select query to retrieve a recordset without using other ADO objects. The sample code below demonstrates how the command object executes a SQL statement. First, the connection object is created and opens the connection, using the open method. Then, the command object is created. The ActiveConnection property of the command object is set to the current connection object. A SQL "select" statement is assigned to the CommandText property. The CommandText property tells the command object what command to execute. The adCmdText constant is assigned to the CommandType property. This constant tells the command object that the command is a SQL statement, and not a table or other type of command.

```
Dim oC
set oC = server.createobject("ADODB.connection")
oC.open "dsnProducts"
Dim oCM
set oCM = server.createobject("ADODB.command")
SQL = "Delete FROM Products WHERE ProductName='chair'"
oC.open CS
oCM.ActiveConnection = oC
oCM.CommandText = SQL
oCM.CommandType = adCmdText
oCM.Execute
```

It is useful to store the SQL statement in a variable, and then assign the variable to the CommandText property. Then, if an error occurs, it is easy to use the response.write method to determine what the SQL statement is. It is also useful to use the constant adCmdText instead of a numeric value. In order to use a constant, you will have to include the file that contains the database constants, called ADOVBS.inc. This file is available from Microsoft for free. When you installed support for ADO, two include files containing constants were installed. The ADOVBS.inc file is intended for server-side scripting with VBScript, and is located in c:\Program Files\Common Files\System\ado\. The ADCVBS.inc file is intended for client-side scripting with VBScript, and is located in c:\Program Files\Common Files\System\msadc\.

You can modify the SQL commands to retrieve a select group of records. In the previous sample you retrieved the listing of products with the product name "chair". The following sample shows how you could retrieve the information using a variable, which could be retrieved from a form field, database, or text file. Notice that the single quotes are used because the form field is passing a string. If the value passed is a number, you do not need the single quotes. This method to retrieve subsets of records can be used with the command object, the recordset object, or the connection object.

```
fldName = Request.Form("txtProductName")
SQL = "Delete FROM Products WHERE ProductName='" & fldName
& "'"
oCM.CommandText = SQL
```

When you open a recordset with the open method of the recordset object, you specify a SQL statement; this identifies which recordset to retrieve from the database. What this means is that the recordset object is implicitly using a command object as the source parameter, just as the recordset object used the connection object implicitly as the connection parameter.

12

The command object is often used to execute stored procedures. **Stored procedures** are programming statements that can be reused. They can contain SQL commands and can be as simple as a select statement. You can also pass values as parameters to the stored procedures. In Access, a stored procedure is called a **parameter query**. For example, you can develop a SQL statement that selects all records where the state field contains a value that matches a variable called strState. This SQL statement can be saved as a stored procedure and executed at a later time. When the stored procedure is called, you can then pass the value of the state, such as "IL," to the state variable strState. Not all databases support the concept of stored procedures. The command object will be discussed in more detail in the next chapter.

RETRIEVING AND DISPLAYING RECORDSETS

The ADO model allows you to retrieve a recordset using the recordset object, the connection object, or the command object. If you create a recordset object, you use the open method to retrieve a recordset. If you create a connection object, you can use the open method of the connection object to open a connection, and then execute a command that returns a recordset object. If you plan to use multiple recordsets within the same Web page, then you should explicitly create a single connection object. This is more efficient because only one connection would be required. Both of these methods will be presented in this chapter. In the next chapter, you will learn how to use the command object to retrieve a recordset and execute commands.

Using the Recordset Object to Open a Recordset

The recordset object can be used to retrieve recordsets from the database. First, you must create a recordset object using the Create Method of the server object. In the following sample code, the recordset object is assigned to the variable oRS.

```
set oRS = server.createobject("ADODB.recordset")
```

After creating the recordset object, you can retrieve the recordset. The open method of the recordset object is used to open a connection to the database and retrieve the recordset. The open method takes several parameters. The first required parameter is the **source** parameter. Usually, the source parameter is a SQL statement, the name of a table, or a command object. SQL is the Structured Query Language, which is the standard language for querying databases. After the source parameter, you must pass the connection parameter, which contains the connection information. The connection parameter can be a DSN or a connection string. Recall that both the DSN and the connection string contain the location of the database and the name of the driver or provider.

Additional parameters can be passed to the open method to indicate the type of recordset to return. The recordset uses a cursor to maintain information that is used to navigate through records within the recordset. The **cursorType** parameter is used to identify what methods can be used to navigate between records within the recordset object. The **lockType** parameter indicates whether the recordsets within the record object can be modified, or are read-only. The **options** parameter is used to indicate how to interpret the source parameter if the source parameter is not a command object. If none of these additional parameters is passed to the open command, then the default recordset is returned.

 The only way you can specify a cursorType and lockType is by explicitly creating a recordset object. You cannot configure this with the command or connection objects.

recordsetName.Open source, connection, cursorType, lockType, Options

The default recordset is set as read-only. Therefore, the default recordset can only be used to display recordsets. You cannot create new records, modify records, or delete records using the default recordset. The default recordset only allows you to move forward through the recordset using the movenext method. You cannot move backward or move to a specific record with the default recordset. The count property, which identifies the number of records in a recordset, is not available in the default recordset. Although there are limitations to the default recordset, the default recordset can be easily implemented to display the records.

In the following sample code, the recordset is opened using the recordset object's open method. The table can also be used as the source parameter, which is passed to the open method. The following example retrieves the table named customer. The DSN named dsnEmail is used as the connection parameter, which is used to locate the connection information. Because no additional parameters are listed, the default recordset is returned.

```
<% oRS.Open "customer", "DSN=dsnEmail" %>
```

The SQL statement can be used as the source parameter to indicate which records to retrieve from the database. The select command is a SQL command that is used to retrieve records from the database. You must pass the names of the fields that you want to retrieve to the select command, or use an asterisk to retrieve all of the fields. You must also use the keyword "from" along with the name of the table, to indicate which table the fields are located in, even if you specify the field names, since it is possible for field names to be duplicated across tables.

In the sample code below, the recordset object is opened using the open method. However, instead of the table name, a SQL statement is used to retrieve all of the fields from a table named customer. The connection parameter uses the connection string stored in the variable CS to locate the connection information. Because no additional parameters are listed, the default recordset is returned. The following sample code shows how to open a recordset object using a connection string that is stored in a variable named CS.

```
<% dim CS, Drv, DBQ, oRS
DRV = "Driver={Microsoft Access Driver (*.mdb)}; "
DBQ = "DBQ= D:\chapter12\customer.mdb;"
CS = DRV & DBQ
oRS.Open "SELECT * FROM customer", CS
%>
```

12

In SQL, keywords are usually placed in all caps, although this is not required.

Retrieving the Field Values

The fields collection contains the field objects returned from the recordset object. You can retrieve the value of a particular field by passing the name of the field to the recordset object. The value of the field can then be displayed in the page, assigned to a variable, or used in an expression.

RecordsetName("FieldName")

You can explicitly request to retrieve the value of a field using the field name property. You can also request the name of the field by specifying the value property.

```
oRS("field1").Value
oRS("field1").Name
```

You can loop through the entire fields collection. The individual fields are only available as part of the fields collection of the field object. Therefore, you can use a For Each loop to view the name of each field in the collection.

```
<% For each fld in oRS.Fields
       Response.write fld.Name
       Response.write "<br>"
Next %>
```

Populating Drop-Down List Boxes   You could easily format the output from the fields in a comma-separated list, table, or drop-down list box. The following sample code shows how you would format the output of a fields list as a drop-down list box. Notice that the value for each option does not have to be the same as what is displayed in the list. Note how the HTML tags can be mixed within the server-side script.

```
<select name="customernames" size="1">
<% do while not oRS.EOF %>
    <option value="<% = oRS("email") %>">
        <% = oRS("name") %>
    </option>
<% oRS.movenext
loop %>
</select>
```

Formatting the Output in a Table   The table opening and closing tags are outside of the loop that displays the recordset. If you have a header row with names, you should put the row outside of the loop. For each loop, a pair of table row tags is used to indicate the beginning of a new row. The individual fields are displayed within table cell tags. You can list multiple fields in cells. The following sample code will list all of the field names in a table.

```
<table border="0" width="400">
<tr><td>E-mail Address</td><td>Name</td></tr>
 <% do while not oRS.EOF %>
     <tr>
          <td><% = oRS("email") %></td>
          <td><% = oRS("name") %></td>
     </tr>
<% oRS.movenext
loop %>
</table>
```

Creating Hyperlinks and Mailto Links with Values from the Database   You can easily modify the same code to create a hyperlink or a mailto link. The sample code below shows how you can iterate through the fields collection and create a mailto link. Note how the code is split between server script and HTML tags.

```
<% do while not oRS.EOF %>
     <a href = mailto:"<% = oRS("email") %>">
          <% = oRS("name") %>
     </a><br>
<% oRS.movenext
loop %>
```

There may be times when you want to create a hyperlink from a URL stored in a database. If you store the URL without the http:// protocol, it is easier to maintain the database. Then, you can append the protocol when you create the anchor tag. If you have a page that you want to direct the user to, you can specify this in the HREF property of the anchor tag.

```
<% do while not oRS.EOF %>
     <a href = http://"<% = oRS("url") %>">
          <% = oRS("companyName") %>
     </a>
<% oRS.movenext
loop %>
```

Passing Values Using the QueryString   It's really just a jump away to creating a page that can pass information from one page to another. In the sample below, the first code displays the product list from the database. Notice that the page name that the user will be redirected to, the question mark, the name property, and the equal sign are hard-coded into the anchor tag.

```
<% do while not oRS.EOF %>
<a href="product.asp?productid=<% = oRS("productid")%>">
     <% = oRS("productname")%>
</a>
<br><br>
<% oRS.movenext
loop %>
```

12

In the next page, you would just need to retrieve the value from the querystring. Then, you can use that parameter in your SQL statement, and retrieve a specific record based on the value that was passed from the previous page. If your productid is a primary key, and no other record matches this value, then you do not have to use the Do While looping statement to loop through the recordset, because there is only one record. This is one of the common methods used to build shopping carts and online catalogs.

```
<% productid = request.querystring("productid")
set oRS = server.createobject("ADODB.recordset")
sql = "SELECT * FROM products where productid = '" &
productid & "'"
oRS.Open sql, CS %>
<% = oRS("productid") %> <br>
<% = oRS("productname") %> <br>
<% = oRS("description") %> <br>
<% = oRS("cost") %>
```

There might come a time when you want to populate a form with the data from the database. Again, after retrieving the data, you can mix HTML tags and the server-side tags. Simply specify the value of the form field as the value from the database. The following sample code would display four text boxes. The values would be data retrieved from the database.

```
<% productid = request.querystring("productid")
set oRS = server.createobject("ADODB.recordset")
sql = "SELECT * FROM products where productid = '" &
productid & "'"
oRS.Open sql, CS %>
<form action="somepage.asp" method="post">
Product ID:
<input type="text" size="25"
    value="<% = oRS("productid") %>">
<br>Product Name:
<input type="text" size="25"
    value="<% = oRS("productname") %>">
<br>Product Description:
<input type="text" size="25"
    value="<% = oRS("description") %>">
<br>Product Description:
<input type="text" size="25"
    value="<% = oRS("cost") %>">
<input type="submit" value="Buy Me!">
</form>
```

Note that while text boxes are easy to define using the value property, with check boxes and radio buttons, the value property identifies what value is sent when the form is submitted. The checked property identifies whether the element is checked or not. Therefore, you will have to add additional code to determine if the value is checked. If it is, then you set the property to checked. If not, then you do not add the checked property. In addition, if you store the data within an Access database as a Yes/No field, the field actually stores the data as −1 or 0. True is represented by −1 and false by 0.

Using the Recordset Object

To retrieve a recordset using the recordset object:

1. Create an ASP page, using Notepad or your ASP-compliant editor. Add the basic HTML tags as follows:

```
<html><head><title>Customer Email List</title></head>
<body bgcolor="#FFCC99" text="#800000">
<h2 align="center">Current Customer Email List</h2>
<hr><h3 align="center">
```

2. Create the connection string to the database. Make sure to change the path to where your file is located on your server.

```
<% dim CS, DRV, DBQ, oRS
DRV = "Driver={Microsoft Access Driver (*.mdb)}; "
DBQ = "DBQ= D:\chapter12\customer.mdb;"
CS = DRV & DBQ
```

3. Create the recordset object using the CreateObject method of the server object.

```
set oRS = server.createobject("ADODB.recordset")
```

4. Open the recordset object using the open method. Pass a SQL statement and the connection string to the open method. In the SQL statement, use the asterisk to select all of the fields from the customer table. Because the SQL statement is a string, it is enclosed within quotes.

```
oRS.Open "select * from customer", CS
```

5. Use a "Do While" loop to display all of the records within the recordset. The recordset will be returned with the recordset open on the first record. You can use the end of the file property (RS.EOF) of the recordset to determine if you are on the last record.

```
do while not oRS.EOF
```

6. Use the field object to return the value of each field. Pass the recordset object the name of the field to display. The name of the field is passed within quotes, inside

parentheses. You can use the write method of the response object to write out the value of the fields to the Web page.

```
Response.write oRS("fname")
Response.write " "
Response.write oRS("lname")
Response.write ", "
Response.write oRS("email")
Response.write "<br>"
```

Programming Tip

You can retrieve the value of the field by explicitly retrieving the value property of the field object. To retrieve the value of the field lname, you would use the code "oRS("lname").value".

7. Use the movenext method of the recordset object to move the cursor to the next record. The default recordset can only move forward. Use the loop command to loop to the beginning of the "Do While" loop statement.

```
oRS.movenext
loop
```

8. Close the recordset object and release the variable by setting it to the nothing keyword.

```
oRS.Close
set oRS = nothing
%>
```

9. Close the HTML heading and page tags.

```
</h3>
</body></html>
```

10. Modify the Web page appearance by changing the background, font, and colors, and adding content. Save this page as **recordset.asp** in your data directory.

11. View the recordset.asp Web page in the browser. View the source code for the page. Print out the Web page and the source code for each page.

Using a Connection Object to Retrieve a Recordset

You can use the connection object along with the recordset object to retrieve the records from the database. The connection object can be used to create and open a connection to the database. The recordset object will use the connection object as the connection parameter passed to the open method. In this example, you will retrieve a subset of records from the table. Only one record will match the criteria and be returned in the recordset. In the next chapter, you will learn to create more complex select queries and action queries that allow you to insert, delete, and modify records.

To retrieve a recordset using the connection object and the recordset object:

1. Create an ASP page using Notepad or your ASP–compliant Web development tool. Add the basic HTML tags, as follows:

```
<html><head><title> Customer Email List</title></head>
<body bgcolor="#FFCC99" text="#800000">
<h2 align="center">Customer Email List</h2>
<hr><h3 align="center">
```

2. Create the connection string to the database. Make sure to change the path to the location where your file is located on your server.

```
<% dim CS, DRV, DBQ, oRS, oC, sql
DRV = "Driver={Microsoft Access Driver (*.mdb)}; "
DBQ = "DBQ= D:\chapter12\customer.mdb;"
CS = DRV & DBQ
```

3. Create the connection object, using the CreateObject method of the server object.

```
set oC = server.createobject("ADODB.connection")
```

4. Open the connection object, using the connection object's open method. You must pass the name of the DSN connection string to the open method so that it can locate the database and the driver.

```
oC.Open CS
```

If you use a DSN, you only need to pass the name of the DSN in quotes. You do not have to indicate that you are passing a DSN. For example, you could use `oC.open "dsnEmail"`.

5. Create the recordset object, using the CreateObject method of the server object.

```
set oRS = server.createobject("ADODB.recordset")
```

6. In the SQL statement, select the fields from the customer table. Use the asterisk to select all of the fields from the table. In the following code, the sql variable will hold the entire string. In this sample, the where clause is used to specify a subset of records that is to be conditionally retrieved. In this case, the open method will retrieve the record only if the state field matches the criteria string "IL". The string must be in quotes, but since the entire SQL statement is within quotes, you can avoid confusion by using double quotes to enclose the entire SQL statement, and single quotes to enclose the criteria string.

```
sql = "SELECT lname, fname, email FROM customer "
sql = sql & "WHERE state = 'IL'"
```

Because the SQL statement is a string, it is enclosed within quotes. If the SQL statement becomes so long that it wraps to the next line, you must split the string into smaller strings. Then, you will have to concatenate the variable to the string on the next line. This is convenient because SQL statements can become very long.

12

7. Open the recordset object, using the open method. Pass a SQL statement and the connection string to the open method. After the SQL statement, you must also pass the name of the connection object, which contains the connection information. In this example, the name of the connection object is oC.

```
oRS.Open sql, oC
```

8. Use a "Do While" loop to display all of the records within the recordset. The recordset will be returned with the recordset open to the first record. You can use the recordset's end of the file property to determine whether you are on the last record.

```
do while not oRS.EOF
```

9. Use the field object to return the value of each field. Pass the name of the field to the recordset object. The field name is passed within quotes, enclosed in parentheses. You can use the write method of the response object to write out the value of the field to the Web page.

```
Response.write oRS("fname")
Response.write " "
Response.write oRS("lname")
Response.write ", "
Response.write oRS("email")
Response.write "<br>"
```

10. Use the movenext method of the recordset object to move the cursor to the next record. The default recordset can only move forward. Use the loop command to loop to the beginning of the Do While loop statement.

```
oRS.movenext

loop
```

11. Close the recordset object and release the variable by setting it to the nothing keyword.

```
oRS.Close
set oRS= nothing
%>
```

12. Close the HTML heading and page tags.

```
</h3>
</body></html>
```

13. Modify the Web page appearance by changing the background, font, and colors, and adding content. Save this page as **connection.asp** in your data directory. View the page in a browser. View the source code and print out the page and the source code for each page.

INTERNET RESOURCES

A variety of Internet resources contain information about ADO, UDA, SQL, ODBC, OLEDB, databases, and data-driven Web applications. While Microsoft supports this technology, other vendors may not support it. For example, Java provides an alternate solution that involves using JDBC, the Java Database Connection. These technologies are not used only for Internet applications, but also for client/server applications and local database applications. Unlike other professions, this field publishes most of the latest information on the Internet, not in journals. You should try to review these Web sites frequently to keep current with the latest database technologies.

- Microsoft ADO—*http://www.microsoft.com/data/ado/*
- Microsoft UDA—*http://www.microsoft.com/data/default.htm*
- Microsoft OLE DB—*http://www.microsoft.com/data/oledb/default.htm*
- Microsoft ODBC—*http://www.microsoft.com/data/odbc/default.htm*
- MSDN Online Library—*http://www.msdn.microsoft.com/library*/default.asp
- Internet Database Connectivity and ASP with FrontPage—*http://support.microsoft.com/support/FrontPage/fp98/internet.asp*
- SQL Server at Microsoft—*http://www.microsoft.com/sql*
- Yahoo SQL Link—*http://dir.yahoo.com/Computers_and_Internet/Programming_Languages/SQL/*
- SQL Reference Page—*http://www.contrib.andrew.cmu.edu/~shadow/sql.html*
- SQL & Web sites—*http://www.sqlweb.com/*
- ANSI—*http://www.ansi.org/*
- JCC SQL standards links—*http://www.jcc.com/SQLPages/jccs_sql.htm*
- SQL tutorial by James Hoffman—*http://w3.one.net/~jhoffman/sqltut.htm*
- Oracle—*http://www.oracle.com/*
- Sybase—*http://www.sybase.com/*
- Informix—*http://www.informix.com/*
- SQL FAQ Berkeley—*http://epoch.cs.berkeley.edu:8000/sequoia/dba/montage/FAQ/SQL_TOC.html*
- Tutorials from MuppetLabs—*http://www.muppetlabs.com/library/tech/tutorials/*
- Programming Tutorials on the Web—*http://www.eng.uc.edu/~jtilley/tutorial.html*
- SQL Reference and Examples—*http://users.neca.com/ltruett/sql.html*
- Access on the Web, Princeton—*http://www.princeton.edu/~hannahk/WebPubl.htm*

12

- MySQL—*http://www.mysql.com*
- SQL from Cramsession—*http://www.cramsession.com/*
- Database Jump Site—*http://www.pcslink.com/~ej/dbweb.html*
- Lee's SQL Tutorial—*http://sql.terrashare.com/*
- SQL Interpreter and Tutorial—*http://www.sqlcourse.com/*
- Learn SQL Jim Hoffman (new)—*http://www.willcam.com/sql/*
- SQL Topics—*http://www.sqlschool.org/*
- Ask the SQL Server Pro—*http://www.inquiry.com/techtips/thesqlpro/*
- SQL for Web Nerds—sample course—*http://photo.net/sql/*
- Fatbrain.com—*http://www.1computerliteracy.com/003/dc_001*
- SQL Server Magazine—*http://www.sqlmag.com/Update*
- SQL tutorial—*http://www.geocities.com/SiliconValley/Vista/2207/sql1.html*
- More SQL Sites—*http://www.sql-zone.com/sites.asp*
- Links to Developer Support—*http://www.borland.com/devsupport/sqllinks/*
- A Gentle Introduction to SQL—*http://www.dcs.napier.ac.uk/~andrew/gisq/what.htm*

CHAPTER SUMMARY

Active Data Object Model

- The Active Data Object (ADO) model provides a means by which you can access a database from within your Web applications, using built-in objects, properties, and methods.

- Facilitating access to different types of source data from different clients is one of the goals of Universal Data Access (UDA).

Database Connections

- DSNs contain connection information that is stored in the Registry on the server. In general, you must have local access to the server in order to create a system DSN on the server.

- The connection string also contains connection information. However, the connection string is created and used within the Web application. You do not need local access to the server to create a connection string.

- Both DSNs and connection strings contain connection information, which consists of the location of the database, and the driver or provider to be used to make the connection.

- Some databases may require additional parameters such as username, password, and server name to be passed in the connection string.

Displaying Recordsets

❏ A set of database records is referred to as a recordset. A recordset can be retrieved using the connection, recordset, or command object.

❏ The command object is used in conjunction with the connection object to execute commands. However, the command object cannot independently retrieve a recordset.

❏ The connection object will always retrieve the default recordset. The recordset object can be used to retrieve the fields collection. The fields collection is the collection of field objects that are in the recordset.

❏ You can display the contents of a field by passing the name of the field to the recordset object.

To create a connection object

```
set oC = server.createobject("ADODB.connection")
```

To open a connection object using a system DSN

```
oC.open "dsnEmail"
```

To close a connection object

```
oC.Close
set oC = nothing
```

To create a recordset object

```
set oRS = server.createobject("ADODB.recordset")
```

To open a recordset object using a connection object

```
oRS.open "customer", oC
```

To close a recordset object

```
oRS.Close
set oRS = nothing
```

To create a connection string to an Access database

```
DRV = "DRIVER={Microsoft Access Driver (*.mdb)}; "
DBQ = "DBQ= c:\chapter12\customer.mdb;"
CS = DRV & DBQ
```

To open a recordset with a system DSN

```
oRS.Open "customer", "DSN=dsnEmail"
```

12

To open a recordset with a variable that contains a connection string

```
oRS.Open "select * from customer", CS
```

To retrieve the value of a field

```
oRS("fname")
```

To create a SQL query statement that selects all fields from a table and all records

```
sql = "select * from customer "
```

To create a SQL query statement that selects several fields from a table and all records

```
sql = "select lname, fname from customer"
```

To create a SQL query statement that selects a subset of records based on some criteria

```
sql = "select * from customer where state = 'IL'"
```

To create a SQL query statement that selects a subset of records based on some criteria using a value passed from a form

```
strState = request.form("state")
sql = "select * from customer "
sql = sql & "where state = '" & strState & "'"
```

REVIEW QUESTIONS

1. A row in a table in a database is known as a _____.

   a. database

   b. table

   c. field

   d. record

2. When OLEDB providers become available, you will not be able to use the ODBC driver interface. True or False?

3. Which version of ADO ships with Windows 2000?

   a. 2.1

   b. 2.3

   c. 2.5

   d. 3.1

4. Can you add a new record to the default recordset object?

   a. no

   b. yes

   c. sometimes

   d. if there are fewer then 10 records

5. What method of the server object is used to create a connection object?

   a. createmethod

   b. createobject

   c. servercreate

   d. createconnection

6. Where is the system DSN stored?

   a. on the client's computer

   b. in the windows directory on the server

   c. in the cookies directory

   d. in the server's system Registry

7. Which statement should be executed last?

   a. set oRS = nothing

   b. set oC = nothing

   c. oC.Close

   d. oRS.Close

8. Which type of DSN will allow any user account to access the database?

   a. file

   b. user

   c. system

   d. session

9. Where is the ODBC Data Source Program located in Windows 95, 98, or NT?

   a. in My Computer

   b. under Programs

   c. in the Control Panel

   d. in the Windows folder

10. Which statement contains the correct name for the ODBC Microsoft Access Driver?

    a. "Driver={Microsoft Access Driver (*.mdb)};"

    b. "Driver={Microsoft Access Driver};"

    c. "Microsoft Access Driver;"

    d. "Driver={(*.mdb)};"

12

11. Which property is set to true when the cursor is after the last record in a recordset?

    a. BOF

    b. EOF

    c. ODBC

    d. DSN

12. Which statement writes the value of a field named fname to the Web page?

    a. Response.write oRS()

    b. Response.write("fname")

    c. oRS("fname")

    d. Response.write oRS("fname")

13. Which method is used by the default recordset to move forward?

    a. moveforward

    b. moveone

    c. moveup

    d. movenext

14. Which method explicitly closes the connection to the database?

    a. oRS.Close

    b. oC.Close

    c. set oRS = nothing

    d. set oC = nothing

15. Which method releases the connection variable from memory?

    a. oRS.Close

    b. oC.Close

    c. set oRS = nothing

    d. set oC = nothing

16. Which object(s) in the ADO model can be used independently to return a recordset?

    a. recordset

    b. connection

    c. command

    d. both a and b

17. Most of the documentation on ADO is not available through the Internet. True or False?

18. What is the standard language used to query databases?

   a. Java

   b. Visual Basic

   c. VBScript

   d. SQL

19. Which type of recordset does the connection object return?

   a. default

   b. null

   c. read & write

   d. no recordset can be returned

20. Which property is used to determine how the cursor will navigate through the recordset?

   a. LockType parameter

   b. CursorType parameter

   c. options parameter

   d. source parameter

21. Which property of the recordset object is used to specify whether a recordset should be writeable or read-only?

   a. LockType parameter

   b. CursorType parameter

   c. options parameter

   d. source parameter

12

HANDS-ON PROJECTS

Project 12-1

In this project, you will create a connection string, using values from a form. You will also retrieve the field names from the form. You will display the database fields, using the field names retrieved from the form.

1. Create a Web page, using Notepad or your ASP-compatible program.

2. Add the basic HTML tags to the Web page.

```
<html><head><title>Connection String</title></head>
<body bgcolor="#FFCC99" text="#800000">
<h2 align="center">Connection String Form</h2>
```

3. Add a form on the page. The method should be post. The action should be **connresults.asp**.

```
<form action="connresults.asp" method="post">
```

4. Add a text box named **txtDBQ** that will store the location to the database file. The size should be **50**. The label should read **Absolute path to the database**.

```
Absolute path to the database <br>
<input type="text" name="txtDBQ" size="50">
```

5. Add a drop-down list object to store the driver name and value. The label should be **Select a driver**. Display a common name such as Access ODBC, but give the value the full name for the driver. For now, only enter the Access driver in the drop down list.

```
<br><br>Select a driver<br>
<select size="1" name="txtDriver">
<option
     value="Driver={Microsoft Access Driver (*.mdb)}; ">
     Access ODBC Driver
</option></select>
```

6. Add a text box named **tblName** with the label **Table Name**, which will be used to hold the name of the table. The size should be **20**.

```
<br><br>Table Name<br>
<input type="text" name="tblName" size="20">
<br><br>
```

7. Using the input tag, create four text boxes named ff1, ff2, ff3, and ff4. Add the labels **Field 1**, **Field 2**, **Field 3**, and **Field 4**. These text boxes will be used to retrieve the field names to display.

```
<input type="text" name="ff1" size="20"> Field 1<br>
<input type="text" name="ff2" size="20"> Field 2<br>
<input type="text" name="ff3" size="20"> Field 3<br>
<input type="text" name="ff4" size="20"> Field 4<br>
```

8. Add a Submit button named **btnSubmit**.

```
<br>
<input type="submit" value="Submit" name="btnSubmit">
</form></body></html>
```

9. Modify the Web page using text, headings, and images. Save the Web page as **connform.asp** in your data directory.

10. Create a new page that will be used to process the form, using Notepad or your ASP-compatible editor.

11. Add the basic HTML tags.

```
<html><head><title>Connection String</title></head>
<body bgcolor="#FFCC99" text="#800000">
<h2 align="center">Results</h2>
```

12. Add code to retrieve the values from the form fields that will be used to build the connection string. Because the driver name was passed with the key "Driver = ", it

does not need to be added here. However, because the "DBQ= " was not passed with the form field, it does need to be concatenated with the form field results.

```
<% dim CS, oRS, DRV, DBQ, F1, F2, F3, F4, TN
DRV = request.form("txtDriver")
DBQ = "DBQ= " & request.form("txtDBQ")
```

13. Use the driver and database location variables to create the connection string.

```
CS = DRV & DBQ
```

14. Add code to retrieve the values from the form fields that will be used to build the SQL statement.

```
TN = request.form("tblName")
F1 = request.form("ff1")
F2 = request.form("ff2")
F3 = request.form("ff3")
F4 = request.form("ff4")
```

15. Use the table name and field names to create the sql variable.

```
sql = "SELECT "
sql = sql & F1 & ", " & F2 & ", " & F3 & ", " & F4
sql = sql & " FROM " & TN
```

16. Create the recordset object.

```
set oRS = server.createobject("ADODB.recordset")
```

17. Open the recordset object, using the sql and oC variables.

```
oRS.Open sql, CS
```

12

18. Display the field values, using the field object. Pass the variable, which contains the field name, to the recordset object to retrieve the field.

```
do while not oRS.EOF
        Response.write oRS(F1)
        Response.write ", "
        Response.write oRS(F2)
        Response.write ", "
        Response.write oRS(F3)
        Response.write ", "
        Response.write oRS(F4)
        Response.write "<br>"
oRS.movenext
loop
```

19. Close the recordset object and release the variable.

```
oRS.Close
set oRS = nothing
%>
</body></html>
```

20. Save your Web page as **connresults.asp** in your data directory.

21. View the connform.asp Web page in your browser. Submit the form using four field names from the customer database. You can select the four fields from the list below. Make sure to specify the absolute path to your database.

❏ id	❏ zipcode	❏ mailinglist
❏ fname	❏ country	❏ joindate
❏ lname	❏ username	❏ lastaccessed
❏ street	❏ password	❏ groupstatus
❏ city	❏ keyword	
❏ state	❏ email	

22. The results should be displayed in a comma-delimited list. Each record will be on its own line.

23. Print the connform.asp and connresults.asp pages.

Project 12-2

In this project, you will locate information in the Help files within ODBC Administrator using Windows 98 or Windows NT Workstation.

1. Click **Start**, then point to **Settings**, and then click **Control Panel**.

2. Double-click the **ODBC icon** to open the ODBC Data Source Administrator.

3. Click the **System DSN** tab.

4. Select your DSN.

5. Click the **Configure** button to open the ODBC Microsoft Access Setup dialog box.

6. Click the **Help** button to open the ODBC Microsoft Desktop Database Drivers Help program.

7. Click the **Contents** button on the button bar to open the Help Topics window.

8. Double-click the **User's Reference**. Double-click **Data Types (advanced users)**.

9. Double-click **Microsoft Access**.

10. Read the information about Data Types, and answer the following questions.

    a. What is the datetime delimiter?

    b. How is the date "March 5, 1996" represented in programming?

    c. How many characters can appear in a char (text) field?

    d. Suppose your text field contains a string such as "O'Hara". If you need to develop a SQL query to an Access database, what can you use to represent the (single quotation mark)?

11. Read one more Help page within the Help Topics. Write a paragraph summarizing what you have read.

12. Click the **Cancel** button. Then close each dialog box. Click the **Close** button, then the **OK** button twice.

13. Create a Web page named **odbchelp.asp**, using Notepad or your ASP-compatible editor. Save the page to your data directory.

14. Write the answers to the above questions on the Web page.

15. Modify the appearance of the Web page. Save the page to your data directory.

16. View the Web page in your browser. Print the Web page.

> To access the ODBC Data Source Administrator in Windows 2000, click Start, then point to Programs, then Administrative Tools, and then click Data Sources (ODBC). Click the System DSN tab. Click the Help button to open the ODBC Help dialog box.

Project 12-3

In this project, you will create an ASP page that uses a connection string from a server-side include file. You will output your information in a table. This project requires you to have already created the customer database as described in the chapter.

1. Using Notepad, create a new page. Save the page as **conxcustomer.inc** in your data directory. You should place quotes around the file when you save it.

2. Add the following code to create the connection string. Replace the path below with the path to your database.

```
<% dim CS, DRV, DBQ, oRS
Drv = "Driver={Microsoft Access Driver (*.mdb)}; "
DBQ = "DBQ= D:\chapter12\customer.mdb;"
CS = DRV & DBQ
```

3. Create the recordset object, using the CreateObject method of the server object. Notice that this is being created within the server-side include file. It therefore does not have to be created in the ASP page.

```
set oRS = server.createobject("ADODB.recordset")
%>
```

4. Save this page as **conxcustomer.inc** to your data directory.

5. Using Notepad or your ASP-compatible editor, create a new ASP page.

6. Add the include command to include the file that contains the connection string.

```
<!--#include file="conxcustomer.inc"-->
```

7. Add the basic HTML tags.

```
<html><head><title>Customer Address List</title></head>
<body bgcolor="#FFCC99" text="#800000">
<h2 align="center">Current Customer Address List</h2>
<hr><h3 align="center">
```

12

8. Open the recordset object, using the open method. Pass a SQL statement and the connection string to the open method. In the SQL statement, use the asterisk to select all of the fields from the customer table. Because the SQL statement is a string, it is enclosed within quotes.

```
<%
oRS.Open "select * from customer", CS
```

9. Add a table tag which will be used to format the records.

```
Response.write "<table border=1 width=500 "
Response.write " cellspacing=0 cellpadding=4>"
```

10. Use a "Do While" loop to display all of the records within the recordset.

```
do while not oRS.EOF
```

11. Use the field object to return the value of each field, and then write the value to the Web page. Add table row tags for each record, and cell tags for each field.

```
Response.write "<tr><td>"
Response.write oRS("fname")
Response.write "</td><td>"
Response.write oRS("lname")
Response.write "</td><td>"
Response.write oRS("street")
Response.write "</td><td>"
Response.write oRS("city")
Response.write "</td><td>"
Response.write oRS("state")
Response.write "</td><td>"
Response.write oRS("zipcode")
Response.write "</td><td>"
Response.write oRS("country")
Response.write "</td></tr>"
```

12. Use the movenext method of the recordset object to move the cursor to the next record.

```
oRS.movenext
loop
```

13. Close the recordset object, release the variable, and close the table and HTML tags.

```
oRS.Close
set oRS = nothing %>
</table></h3>
</body></html>
```

14. Modify the Web page appearance by changing the background, font, and colors, and adding content.

15. Save the page as **conxCustomer.asp** in your data directory.

16. View your conxCustomer.asp Web page in the browser.

17. View the source code for the page. Print out the Web page and the source code for each page.

Project 12-4

In this project, you will create a form that will retrieve a user's password based on the e-mail address and keyword that the user enters in the form. This project requires you to have already created the customer database as described in the chapter.

1. Create a new page, using Notepad or your ASP-compatible editor.

2. Add the basic HTML tags.

```
<html><head><title>Customer Passwords</title></head>
<body bgcolor="#FFCC99" text="#800000">
<h2 align="center">Password Retrieval</h2>
<hr>
```

3. Create a form, using the post method, and set the action to **displayrecord.asp**.

```
<form action="displayrecord.asp" method="post">
```

4. Add a text box named **email** with a size of **50**. Add a label that says **E-mail Address**. Add a text box named **keyword** with a size of **10**. Add a label that says **My Keyword**. Add a Submit button named btnSubmit that says **Submit**.

```
Email Address<br><br>
<input type="text" name="email" size="50">
<br><br>My keyword<br><br>
<input type="text" name="keyword" size="10"><br><br>
<input type="submit" value="Submit" name="btnSubmit">
```

5. Add the closing form and HTML tags.

```
</form></body></html>
```

6. Modify the Web page appearance. Save the page as **displayrecordform.asp** in your data directory.

7. Create a new page, using Notepad or your ASP-compatible editor.

8. Add the following code to create the connection string. Replace the path with the path to your database.

```
<% response.buffer = "true" %>
<% dim CS, DRV, DBQ, oRS
DRV = "Driver={Microsoft Access Driver (*.mdb)}; "
DBQ = "DBQ= D:\chapter12\customer.mdb;"
CS = DRV & DBQ
```

9. Create the recordset object, using the CreateObject method of the server object.

```
set oRS = server.createobject("ADODB.recordset")
```

10. Retrieve the values from the form and assign them to variables.

```
email = request.form("email")
keyword = request.form("keyword")
%>
```

12

11. Add the basic HTML tags.

```
<html><head><title>Customer Passwords</title></head>
<body bgcolor="#FFCC99" text="#800000">
<h2 align="center">Password Retrieval</h2>
<hr>
```

12. Create the SQL query string and assign it to a variable. Use the where clause to search for a record that matches the e-mail address in the recordset with the e-mail address from the form.

```
<%
sql =  "SELECT * FROM customer WHERE email='" & email & "'"
```

13. Open the recordset object, using the open method. Pass the SQL statement and the connection string.

```
oRS.Open sql, CS
```

14. Use an If Then statement to detect whether a record was found. If no record was found, then redirect the user to the displayrecordform.asp page.

```
If oRS.EOF = TRUE Then
    Response.Redirect("displayrecordform.asp")
Else
End If
```

15. If a record is found, you can use another "If Then" to detect if the keyword from the form matches the keyword in the database. Notice that the value is explicitly requested. If no match is found, then redirect the user to the displayrecordform.asp page.

```
If keyword <> oRS("keyword").Value Then
    Response.Redirect("displayrecordform.asp")
Else
End If
```

16. If the user does have a valid e-mail address, and the keyword does match, display the user's password in the browser.

```
Response.write("Your password was: ")
Response.write("<br><br> ")
Response.write oRS("password")
```

17. Close the recordset object, release the variable, and close the HTML tags.

```
oRS.Close
set oRS = nothing %>
</body></html>
```

18. Modify the Web page appearance by changing the background, font, and colors, and adding content.

19. Save the page as **displayrecord.asp** in your data directory.

20. View your displayrecordform.asp Web page in the browser. Print the Web page.

21. Test the form using the values you entered in the database (jgarcia@oakton.net, objection). The password should be written to the browser. Print the results Web page. Print out the source code for each page.

Project 12-5

In this project, you will create a Web page that populates a form based on values in the database. This project requires you to have already created the customer database as described in the chapter.

1. Create a new Web page, using Notepad or your ASP-compatible editor.

2. Add the following code to create the connection string. Replace the path with the path to your database.

```
<% dim CS, DRV, DBQ, oRS
DRV = "Driver={Microsoft Access Driver (*.mdb)}; "
DBQ = "DBQ= D:\chapter12\customer.mdb;"
CS = DRV & DBQ %>
```

3. Add the basic HTML tags.

```
<html><head><title>Customer E-mail Addresses</title></head>
<body bgcolor="#FFCC99" text="#800000">
<h2 align="center">Customer E-mail Addresses</h2>
<hr><h3 align="center">
```

4. Add a form, using the method post and the action retrieveCustomer.asp.

```
<form action="retrieveCustomer.asp" method="post">
```

5. Add the HTML select tag to create a drop-down list. You can add the default option that is selected before you retrieve the e-mail names from the database.

```
<select size="1" name="email">
<option value="------" selected>
    Select an e-mail address
</option>
```

6. Create the SQL querystring and assign it to a variable. Open the recordset object, using the open method. Pass the SQL statement and the connection string.

```
<% sql = "select" * from customer"
set oC = server.createobject ("ADODB.connection")
oC.Open CS
set oRS = server.createobject ("ADODB.recordset")
oRS.open sql, oC
```

7. Retrieve the values of the fields and place them as parameters of the select tag. Notice that the text displayed is the first name concatenated with a blank space, followed by the last name. However, the e-mail address is the value that is passed to the next page.

12

```
    do while not oRS.EOF %>
        <option value="<% = oRS("email")%>">
            <% = oRS("fname") & " " &  oRS("lname") %>
        </option>
<% oRS.movenext
loop %>
</select>
```

8. Add a submit button and close the form. Then, close the recordset object, release the variable, and close the HTML tags.

```
<input type="submit" value="Submit" name="btnSubmit">
</form>
<% oRS.Close
set oRS = nothing
oC.close
set oC = nothing
%>
</body></html>
```

9. Modify the appearance of the Web page. Save the page as **displayfield.asp** in your data directory.

10. Use Notepad to create another ASP page that will be used to retrieve the password.

11. Add the code that contains the connection string. Modify the path statement to reflect the absolute path to your customer database.

```
<% dim CS, DRV, DBQ, oRS
DRV = "Driver={Microsoft Access Driver (*.mdb)}; "
DBQ = "DBQ= D:\chapter12\customer.mdb;"
CS = DRV & DBQ
%>
```

12. Add the basic HTML tags.

```
<html><head><title>Customer Passwords</title></head>
<body bgcolor="#FFCC99" text="#800000">
<h2 align="center">Password Retrieval</h2>
<hr>
```

13. Retrieve the value from the form and assign it to a variable named email. Create the SQL statement that will retrieve all the records in which the e-mail address passed from the form matches the e-mail address within the database. Because each e-mail address is unique, only one record should be returned.

```
<% email = request.form("email") %>
<% sql = "select * from customer where email = '" & email
& "'"
```

14. Create the connection and recordset objects. Open the recordset object. Use the "On Error Resume Next" statement to handle errors that may occur with the connection.

```
set oC = server.createobject("ADODB.connection")
oC.Open CS
set oRS = server.createobject("ADODB.recordset")
oRS.open sql, oC
on error resume next
```

15. Retrieve the password from the database and display it in the browser.

```
do while not oRS.EOF
    response.write "<p align=center>Your password is "
    response.write oRS("password")  & "</p>"
oRS.movenext
loop %>
```

16. Close your connections to the objects, and add the closing HTML tags.

```
<% oRS.Close
set oRS = nothing
oC.close
set oC = nothing
%>
</body></html>
```

17. Save the page as **retrieveCustomer.asp**.

18. View the displayfield.asp Web page in your browser. Select one of the addresses and click **Submit**. Print both Web pages and the source code.

Project 12-6

In this project you will locate Internet resources on ADO, SQL, and database-driven Web sites.

1. Visit at least five Web sites listed in this chapter.

2. Read through documentation on each site.

3. Create a Web page named **dbInternet.asp**.

4. Write a short summary of what you have learned about connecting your database to the Web.

5. Modify the appearance of the Web page. Save the page to your data directory.

6. View the Web page in your browser. Print the Web page.

CASE PROJECTS

Odds and Ends—Displaying an Online Catalog

You are hired in the Marketing Department at Odds and Ends to help set up an online product catalog. Your task is to create the basic online product catalog. The catalog should contain at least 10 products. Create a database, using Access or your database management tool, that contains the name of each product, the product ID number, the cost, a short description, the manufacturer, and the name of the graphics image. The graphic image should be stored in your data directory, not in the database. You can visit Life Beyond Yahoo to search for graphics for your products (*http://www.lifebeyondyahoo.com/life/graphics.asp*). You can create a connection file that contains the connection string to the database, or place the information within the ASP page. Create a Web page that will display a list of all 10 products (see Figure 12-10). Create a hyperlink for each product name. The hyperlink will direct you to a second page. (*Hint*: Use an anchor tag <a> and use the HREF property to specify the URL. The URL is the path concatenated with the product ID from the database. You can display the product ID between the two anchor tags. You can use the following sample code as a guide: `<a href = "oeproduct.asp?productid=<% = oRS("productid")%>"><% = oRS("productname") %></a>`. Create the second page named oeproduct.asp. On this page, display the name of the product, the product ID number, the cost, a short description, the manufacturer, and the actual graphic image. (*Hint*: You can format the currency using the formatCurrency method, for example `<% = formatCurrency(oRS("cost")) %>`. You can use an image tag <img> and specify the source of the image from the name in the database, for example `<img src="<% = oRS("imagename")%>">`.) Modify the appearance of the page by adding images, text, and colors. Save the page as oeonlinecat.asp to your data directory. View the oeonlinecat.asp page in your browser. Print both pages and the source code.

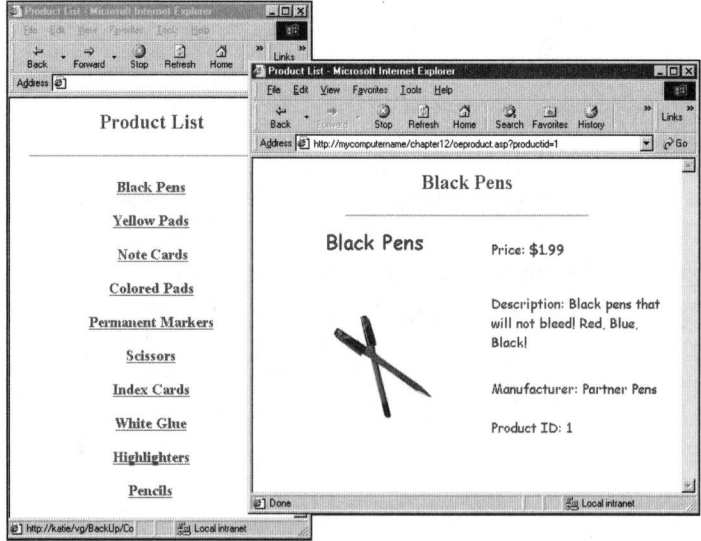

Figure 12-10   Displaying records from a database

Odds and Ends—Upsizing your Access Database to a SQL Server Database

At Odds and Ends they have used an Access database to store their product catalog data. You have discovered by reading the log files that there are many users trying to connect to the database at the same time. To handle more concurrent users, you propose using a SQL Server database instead of Access. The database administrator (DBA) has purchased a license for SQL Server for the Web site. The DBA has told you that you can use the SQL Server to store your database. Instead of recreating the database in SQL Server, you decide to use the Upsize Wizard to convert the Access database to SQL Server. Read the Help files in Access 2000 to learn how to "upsize" your database to a SQL Server database. You can also visit the Microsoft Web sites listed in this chapter. Create a Web page, using Notepad or your Web page editor. Identify reasons why you would want to upsize to SQL Server. Indicate what activities should be performed before attempting to upsize the database. Identify the steps in the procedure to upsize the database from Access to SQL Server. You will have to upgrade your connection string. Write a sample connection string to your SQL Server database. The name of the new server is Goldman, and the data source is oeproducts. The username is Franklin, and the password is bear. Write your responses on your Web page. Modify the appearance of the page by adding images, text, and colors. Save the page as convertAccess.asp to your data directory. View the convertAccess.asp page. Print the page.

Odds and Ends—Creating a Login Form

Odds and Ends has decided to create a membership area on its Web site. Your boss has concerns that members may routinely forget their passwords and call the company to find them out. Your boss wants you to plan a registration system that will also provide users with their passwords, if they should happen to forget them. Create a new database named oe, using Access or your other database management program. Then, create a new table named members. If you already have created a database named oe, just create a new table named members within that database. The members table contains each member's e-mail address, first and last name, username, password, question, and answer. Enter at least five recordsets of data. Next week you will create the page that will allow users to register into the database. For right now, you are just going to test the system with five records. There are six pages that you will need to create. (See Figure 12-11 for the four pages that provide the password reminder feature.) First, you will create an ASP page named oeloginform.asp that will contain the login form. There should be a text box for the username and the e-mail address, and a Submit button. The form will point to oelogin.asp. Place a hyperlink on the oeloginform.asp page that will point to a page named oeemail.asp. Create the page oelogin.asp, which will retrieve the member's username and password from the login form, then retrieve the member's record, and verify the member's password. If the username does not exist, return the user to the oeloginform.asp page. If the password does not match, return the user to the oeloginform.asp page. If the password does match, first store the user's name in a session variable. You can concatenate the first name with a space, then the last name. Then, store this value in the session variable. Then, redirect the user to a page called oemember.asp. Create the oemember.asp page. This page will welcome the member by name. You can retrieve the user's name from the session variable that you just created. Create another page named oeemail.asp. The page should have a form with one field, the e-mail address, and a Submit button. When users submit an e-mail address, they are taken to a page named oequestion.asp. Create the oequestion.asp page. This page retrieves the e-mail address from the oeemail.asp page. Then, it retrieves that member's record. You will have to create a SQL statement that retrieves the member's record. If no member matches that e-mail address, then redirect the user to the oeemail.asp page. You can use the "On Error Resume Next" statement to catch any connection errors. Otherwise, display the question that the user selected when registering. This question is stored in the question field in the database. Add a form to the oequestion.asp page that contains a text field for the member's answer. You should also pass the member's e-mail address as a hidden field, and add a Submit button. This form points to oeanswer.asp. Create the oeanswer.asp page. Retrieve the member's record by using the e-mail address passed from the form. Then, compare the answer the member provided in the form to the answer in the database answer field. If they match, then display the e-mail address, username, and password. If there is not a match, redirect the user to the oeemail.asp page to try again. Modify the appearance of the pages by adding images, text, and colors. Save the pages to your data directory and view them in a browser. Print the pages and the source code of each page.

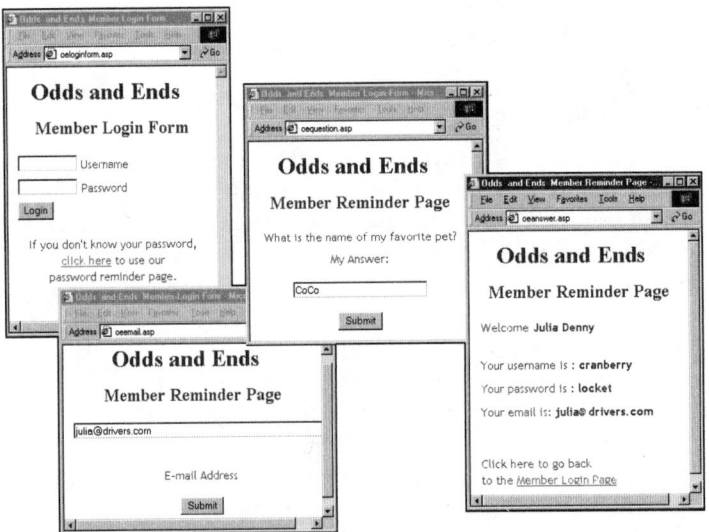

Figure 12-11   Displaying data across multiple Web pages

Odds and Ends—Displaying a Recordset Using a Table

At Odds and Ends you are upgrading the online catalog. The store clerk would like to have an inventory list of each item in the online catalog. (*Hint*: If you have not created the database named oe.mdb and the products table in the first case project, then you will have to create the database, using Access or your database management tool. Then, you will have to create a table named products that contains the name of the product, the product ID number, the cost, a short description, the manufacturer, and the name of the graphics image. Then, enter at least 10 products.) Create an ASP page that retrieves the values from the database table and displays them in a Web page, using a table. You can create a connection file that contains the connection string to the database, or place the information within the ASP page. Use the properties of the table tag, the table cell tags, and the table rows to format the layout of the table. Modify the appearance of the page by adding images, text, and colors. Save the page as oeinventory.asp to your data directory. View the page in your browser. Print your Web page and the source code.

12

13

ADVANCED WEB DATABASE INTEGRATION

In this chapter you will:
- Build advanced queries using Access and SQL
- Update a database using SQL and ASP
- Update a database using ADO and ASP

E-commerce and e-business applications are becoming more common on the Internet. These businesses offer product information on their Web sites, and allow customers to make online purchases. To facilitate these purchases, you can integrate the data from the shopping cart with a credit card authorization component or a shipping component. These components are available from third-party developers, or you can build your own, using Visual Basic or another programming language. But these online tools are more than just a method of informing and selling to customers. You can build database connectivity into your Web applications, so that the data from a variety of sources can be easily integrated. This allows companies to use Web data for a variety of purposes, for example to facilitate inventory control, create targeted marketing plans, and develop advertising schemes. To build these robust database-driven Web applications, you must have a strong understanding of database technologies, connection methods, ADO, and SQL. In this chapter you will use Access and its sample Northwind database to learn about and practice advanced Web database integration.

THE NORTHWIND DATABASE SAMPLE APPLICATION

Access 2000 comes with a sample database called Northwind. The Northwind database contains eight tables, already populated with sample data. Northwind also contains sample queries, forms, reports, and other database objects. The default location for the Northwind database is c:\Program Files\Microsoft Office\Office\Samples. If the database has not been installed, you can download it from the Microsoft Web site at *http://officeupdate.microsoft.com/2000/downloadDetails/Nwind2K.htm*.

 Microsoft provides information to assist you in understanding the Northwind database objects at *http://support.microsoft.com/support/access/content/nwind/default.asp*. This Web site provides information on Northwind for Access 97. However, the explanations about database objects and tasks also apply to Access 2000.

To download and open the Northwind database:

1. Connect to the Internet, and using your Web browser visit the Northwind Traders Sample Database for Microsoft Access 2000 Web site at *http://officeupdate.microsoft.com/2000/downloadDetails/Nwind2K.htm*.

2. Click the **Download Now!** hyperlink to start the download process.

3. Click the **Save this program to disk** radio button, and click **OK** to continue.

4. Browse your network to locate your data directory. Type **nwind** in the file name text box and click **Save**. The Download Complete dialog box will open when the file has finished downloading.

5. Click **Open Folder** to open your data directory with the downloaded file.

6. Double-click the nwind program icon in your data directory.

7. Click the **Yes** button to install the sample database. The license agreement will open. Read the agreement and click the **Yes** button.

8. Click the **Browse** button to locate your data directory and place the path in the location text box. The location text box indicates where the sample database will be installed. Click **OK** to continue. An "Installation successful" message will appear. Click **OK** to continue. The nwind.mdb database is now listed in your student folder.

9. Double-click the Nwind.mdb program icon to open the database. A dialog box will appear, which allows you to convert the database to Access 2000. Select the **Convert Database** radio button and click **OK** to continue. A dialog box will appear, asking you to indicate the name for the new file and the location. Enter the name **nwind2000** for the name of the database, then click **Save** to save the converted database to your data directory. The Northwind Traders dialog box opens. Click **OK** to continue. The Northwind database main window opens in the table view. There are eight tables listed in the table view.

What's in the Northwind Database

The Northwind database comes with eight tables and fifteen predefined queries. You can use these queries to view, change, and analyze data. The following is a list of the eight tables in the Northwind database, and a description of their contents.

- *Categories*—Contains a categoryID, name, description, and picture
- *Customers*—Contains the customerID and customer contact information
- *Employees*—Contains the employeeID, position information, and employee contact information
- *Order Details*—Contains the orderID and productID, the order quantity, and price information
- *Orders*—Contains the orderID, customerID, employeeID, shipping method, and delivery information
- *Products*—Contains the productID, name, category, price, and inventory information
- *Shippers*—Contains the shippingID and the shipping company information
- *Suppliers*—Contains the ID of the supplier, company name, and company contact information

Access allows you to define relationships between tables. Figure 13-1 illustrates the relationships among the tables in the Northwind database. For example, the customer table identifies information about the customer, such as address and customerID. The customerID field is a primary key field. No two customers may have the same customerID. Each order is listed in the orders table. The order contains the orderID, which uniquely identifies the order. The orderID is a primary key field, and therefore no two orders may have the same order ID. The orders table keeps track of which customerID made the order. A single customer may place many orders. Therefore, there is a many-to-one relationship between the orders table and the customers table.

13

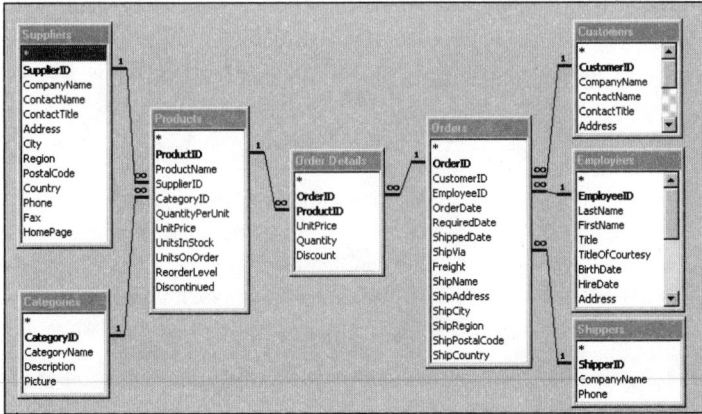

Figure 13-1   Table relationships within the Northwind database

BUILDING THE CONNECTION SERVER-SIDE INCLUDE PAGE

In this section you will create a server-side include file, which will be used to hold the connection string, and to create the connection and recordset objects. This connection server-side include page can be reused for all of the queries that you will be creating in this chapter.

To create the connection server-side include page:

1. Create a file named **nwconx.inc**, using Notepad, and save it to your data directory.

2. Add the following code to declare the variables, create the connection string, and create the connection, recordset, and command objects. Change the path to the absolute path where the Northwind database is installed.

You need to put the HTML tags on the same line. Do not split HTML statements across lines in Notepad or your HTML editor.

```
% dim DRV, DBQ, CS, oC, oRS
DRV = "Driver={Microsoft Access Driver (*.mdb)}; "
DBQ = "DBQ= c:\yourfolder\nwind2000.mdb;"
CS = DRV & DBQ
set oC = server.createobject("ADODB.connection")
set oRS = server.createobject("ADODB.recordset")
set oCM = server.createobject("ADODB.command")
%>
```

3. Save the page to your data directory.

BUILDING QUERIES USING ACCESS

In the previous chapter, you created a select query using basic SQL commands to retrieve data from the database. You identified the table as the source of the data, using the keyword FROM. You can also use the graphical user interface available within Access to create SQL statements. To build a query in Access you will identify which table to use as the data source. You can test your queries in Access before you cut and paste the SQL statements into your database Web application.

The SQL generated within Access is fully compatible with Access databases, but there are some slight variations in SQL syntax across database management systems. It is important to always test your SQL queries with data to verify that the results expected match the results returned. For example, if you plan to use your SQL queries built with Access in SQL Server, you will have to change all of the double quotes to single quotes.

To create a query in Access:

1. Start Access if it is not already open. Maximize the window by clicking the **Maximize** button on the Access database window.

2. Open the Northwind database in Access if it is not already open. The Northwind database lists the database objects on the left side of the Northwind database window. Maximize the Northwind database window by clicking the **Maximize** button.

3. Click the **Queries** tab to open the list of predefined queries.

4. Click the **New** button to open the New Query dialog box. Design View is already selected by default. Click **OK** to open the Show Table dialog box. This dialog box is used to identify which tables the query should be based on. In other words, you identify one or more tables that contain the data that you are trying to retrieve.

5. Click **Products**, and then click **Add**. The products table will be added to the query designer. Click **Close** to close the dialog box. If you cannot see the entire list of fields from the products table, you can resize the field list box. Notice that the query design window is split into two windows. The top window contains the tables that are used to build the queries. The lower window contains the design grid used to build the queries.

6. Drag and drop the **ProductID** field from the Product table list to the Field box in the first column in the design grid. The field name and the name of the table appear in the column.

7. Repeat Step 6 with the following fields, placing each field in its own column: **ProductName, CategoryID, UnitPrice, UnitsInStock**, and **Discontinued**. Notice that the field names and the table name appear in each column.

8. Below the File menu is the View list arrow (the icon looks like a table). There are three views: Design View, Datasheet View, and SQL View. Design View allows you to create the structure of the query using the graphical design tools. Datasheet View shows you the results of the query after the query has been run. SQL View shows you the SQL statements that were built from the information that was provided in the Design View. The View list arrow allows you to switch between the three views. Click the **View** list arrow, and click **DataSheet View**. You can preview the results from the query in Datasheet View. All of the records are displayed. The number of records, 77, appears at the bottom of the window.

9. Click the **View** list arrow and then click **SQL View** to preview the SQL statements generated from the query. The SQL statement displayed is "SELECT Products.ProductID, Products.ProductName, Products.CategoryID, Products.UnitPrice, Products.UnitsInStock, Products.Discontinued FROM Products;". Notice that the SQL statement is a select query. The field names are fully identified, which means that the name of the field is preceded by the name of the table. A period (.) separates the table name and the name of the field. Although it's not necessary to fully qualify field names, it is a good idea, since

13

there can be duplicate field names across tables. By default, Access will always fully qualify field names. Notice that the SQL statement includes the keyword "FROM" to identify the table Products.

You can create the SQL statements manually. However, using a graphical tool will help you decrease errors and improve efficiency.

10. Click the **View** list arrow, and then click **Design View**.

11. In the Sort row under the UnitPrice field column, click the list arrow, and then click **Descending**, which will show the most expensive products first. You can sort the results from the query in ascending or descending order based on one or more fields.

12. In the Criteria box under the CategoryID, type **=8**. There are eight possible categories of products. In the products table, instead of referring to the category ID, which may be difficult to remember, the database can look up the category ID based on the category name that is selected from the list. In the category table, a relationship between the category name and category ID is defined. This type of field is called a lookup or combo box.

13. In the CategoryID column, click the **Show** check box to deselect it under the CategoryID field. Notice in Figure 13-2 that when you dragged the names to the design grid, the Show check box was checked by default. You do not have to show the field, even though the field is used in the query. In this example, you are not going to display the category ID because the category ID for all of the products is Seafood.

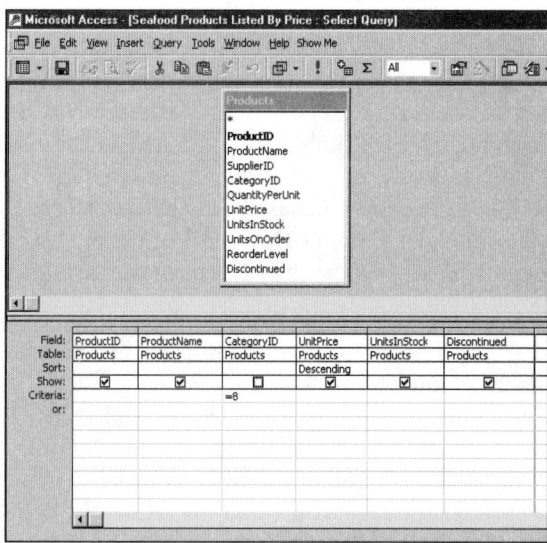

Figure 13-2   Modifying the query in Access

14. Click the **View** list arrow, and then click **SQL View**. The SQL statement displayed is "SELECT Products.ProductID, Products.ProductName, Products.UnitPrice, Products.UnitsInStock, Products.Discontinued FROM Products WHERE (((Products.CategoryID)=8)) ORDER BY Products.UnitPrice DESC;". Notice that the "WHERE" clause is used to identify the criteria you placed in the criteria box. The "ORDER BY" clause is used to identify the field to sort on, and the sort order.

15. Click the **View** list arrow, and then click **DataSheet View** to preview your results. There are 12 products listed. Notice in Figure 13-3 that the category ID field is not shown, and that the list is sorted in descending order on the UnitPrice field.

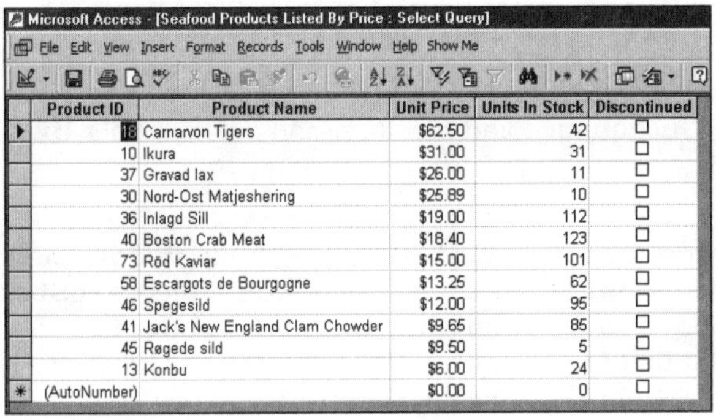

Product ID	Product Name	Unit Price	Units In Stock	Discontinued
18	Carnarvon Tigers	$62.50	42	☐
10	Ikura	$31.00	31	☐
37	Gravad lax	$26.00	11	☐
30	Nord-Ost Matjeshering	$25.89	10	☐
36	Inlagd Sill	$19.00	112	☐
40	Boston Crab Meat	$18.40	123	☐
73	Röd Kaviar	$15.00	101	☐
58	Escargots de Bourgogne	$13.25	62	☐
46	Spegesild	$12.00	95	☐
41	Jack's New England Clam Chowder	$9.65	85	☐
45	Røgede sild	$9.50	5	☐
13	Konbu	$6.00	24	☐
(AutoNumber)		$0.00	0	☐

Figure 13-3 Northwind database query results

16. Click **File** on the menu bar, and then click **Save** to save the query. Type the name **Seafood Products Listed By Price** in the Query Name text box in the Save As dialog box. Click **OK** to continue.

Using an Access Query in ASP Pages

You can copy and paste the query you built in Access into your ASP pages. First you must create the ASP page and add the connection information. Then, copy and paste the SQL generated by the Access query to the ASP page. When you view the page, the same recordsets are returned. However, when you are using a Web page to display the records, you must also display the recordset by adding code to read through each record and display the results. The same results should be displayed whether you ran the query from within Access or from within an ASP page.

To create an ASP page that uses a query created in Access 2000:

1. Create a file named **nwproductsseafood.asp** in your data directory, using Notepad.

2. Add the following code to include the connection string include file, which contains the connection string and the connection and recordset objects. Add the basic HTML tags and headings.

```
<!--#include file="nwconx.inc"-->
<html><head>
<title>Seafood Products</title>
</head>
<body>
<h1>Seafood Products</h1>
```

3. Select the entire SQL string from the Access database and paste it into the page. Assign the string to the SQL variable. Because the SQL string crosses over several lines, you will have to concatenate the string, or place the entire string onto one line of text. Because SQL statements often exceed one line, it is useful to know how to concatenate the SQL string. The following code illustrates how to concatenate the SQL statement over a series of lines. Notice that there is a blank space after the words Discontinued and Products, and before Order By.

```
<%
dim SQL
SQL = "SELECT Products.ProductID, Products.ProductName, "
SQL = SQL & "Products.UnitPrice, Products.UnitsInStock, "
SQL = SQL & "Products.Discontinued FROM Products "
SQL = SQL & "WHERE (((Products.CategoryID)=8)) "
SQL = SQL & "ORDER BY Products.UnitPrice DESC; "
```

4. Open the recordset, using the connection defined in the CS connection string, and using the SQL command.

```
oRS.Open SQL, CS %
```

5. Add an HTML table tag to start the table. The table tag must be outside the loop.

```
<table border=1 cellspacing=0 cellpadding=5>
```

6. Create a loop that will rotate through the recordset, and display the results within table cells. Create the loop as you did in the last chapter, using a Do Until statement that ends at the end of the recordset. Use the table row and table cell variables to write out the table row and table cell tags. Format the unit price and units in stock cells using the align right table cell tag. Use the movenext method to rotate to the next record, and the loop command to start the loop over.

```
<% do until oRS.EOF %>
<% = "<tr><td>" %>
<% = oRS("ProductID") & "</td><td align=left>" %>
<% = oRS("ProductName") & "</td><td align=right>" %>
<% = formatcurrency(oRS("UnitPrice")) &
"</td><td align=left> %>"
<% = oRS("UnitsInStock") & "</td><td align=left>" %>
<% = oRS("Discontinued") & "</td></tr>" %>
<% oRS.movenext
loop
```

7. Add the code to close the recordset object. Add the closing tags for the table and the page.

```
oRS.close
set oRS=nothing
%>
</table>
</body></html>
```

8. Modify the Web page appearance by changing the background, font, colors, and images, and by adding content.

9. Save the Web page to your data directory.

10. View the nwproductsseafood.asp Web page in a browser, as shown in Figure 13-4.

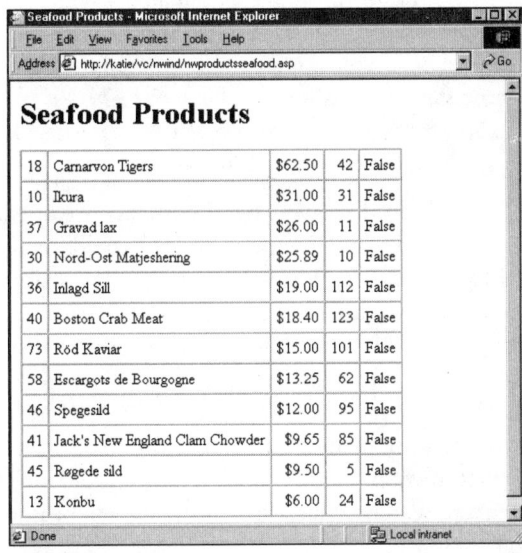

Figure 13-4 nwproductsseafood.asp viewed in a browser

11. View the source code for the page. Print out the Web page and the source code. You can also use variables to format the recordset in a table. Use the variables to create a beginning row tag and ending row tag. You can modify the format of the cells without altering the basic content of the table. Separating the content and presentation of data will make it easier for you to maintain your code. The following sample code shows how you could have altered the ASP page to separate the content from presentation.

```
<% dim tr, etdr, etdl, etr
tr = "<tr><td>"
etdr = "</td><td align=right>"
etdl = "</td><td align=left>"
etr = "</td></tr>"
```

```
%>
<% do until oRS.EOF %>
<% = tr %>
<% = oRS("ProductID") & etdl %>
<% = oRS("ProductName") & etdr %>
<% = formatcurrency(oRS("UnitPrice")) & etdl %>
<% = oRS("UnitsInStock") & etdl %>
<% = oRS("Discontinued") & etr %>
<% oRS.movenext
loop
%>
```

Building Advanced Queries Using SQL

A search condition evaluates to true or false. Until now, we have evaluated a single search condition within a single statement. For example, a search condition "WHERE username='John'" would evaluate to true or false. In Access and SQL you can create more complex queries using multiple search conditions within the same statement. When the keyword AND is used to separate conditions, both search conditions must be resolved to true. If the keyword OR is used to separate conditions, only one of the search conditions needs to be resolved to true.

The search condition consists of an expression, followed by a comparison operator, and another expression. An expression can be simple, such as the name of a field, or it can be a string, number, or value passed from a form. If the expression is a string, the string must be entered using quotation marks. Strings are case sensitive when used as expressions. So, "products" and "PRODUCT" are not evaluated as equal expressions. An expression that contains a date must append the pound sign (#) before and after the date. The keyword NULL can be used to search for empty fields. An empty string is not the same as a NULL field. NULL fields do not contain any data. The word NULL would be used as the expression. A comparison operator is used to evaluate the expression. Valid comparison operators include +, <, >, <>, IS, and ISNOT. The syntax to create search criteria in a SQL statement is as follows:

WHERE [expression1][comparisonoperator][expression2]

The following are sample valid expressions that use multiple search criteria. Notice how the strings are enclosed with quotes, the dates with pound signs. Numbers, variables, and constants do not use quotes.

```
WHERE user="katie" AND pwd="pass"
WHERE state="IL" OR state="IN" AND people>=10000
WHERE lastVisit>#11/12/2000# OR member="new"
WHERE member="staff" AND salary>35000
WHERE birth=IS NULL OR email=IS NULL
```

By using the keywords AND and OR you can combine multiple search criteria within the same SQL statement. For example, you can create a query that would list the product names for any product where the number of items is less than five. You could give this to the person in charge of ordering new supplies. However, you don't need to order discontinued products. Therefore, you would also want to make sure that none of the items was discontinued. By using combination queries, you can combine all of these search criteria into one SQL statement. The following sample SQL statement would display a list of product names where the units in stock were equal to zero, or the reorder level is less than the number of units in stock plus units on order.

```
SELECT ProductName, UnitsInStock, UnitsOnOrder, ReorderLevel
FROM Products
WHERE (UnitsInStock=0) OR
(ReorderLevel>(UnitsInStock+UnitsOnOrder))
ORDER BY UnitsInStock;
```

SQL allows you to perform arithmetic operations on a group of records. You can perform these calculations as part of your SQL query. You know that the default recordset does not allow you to use the count property. In the following example, you need to retrieve information about the salaries in your department for employees with salaries greater than $35,000. You can retrieve the count, average, minimum, maximum, and total for a field called salary.

```
SELECT COUNT(salary) AS CountSal;
AVG(salary) AS AvgSal; SUM(salary) AS SumSal;
MIN(salary) AS MinSal; MAX(salary) AS MaxSal;
FROM employees
WHERE salary > 35000
```

Using Access to Build Multiple Conditional Expressions

You can use Access to help you build multiple search criteria statements. In Access, in the Criteria box, you can enter the criteria across multiple column fields to create an AND condition. If you want to create a conditional expression that will pick up either condition, then enter the condition on the next line that says OR. In the following example, you will create a query using a conditional expression. The query searches for products where the sum of the units in stock and the units on order is less than the reorder level, or for products where the number of units in stock is equal to zero.

To create a multiple search condition SQL statement in Access:

1. Start Access and open the Northwind database if it is not open.

2. Click the **New** button on the top of the Northwind database window to open the New Query dialog box. Design View is already selected by default. Click **OK** to open the Show Table dialog box.

3. Click **Products**, and then click **Add**. Click **Close** to close the dialog box.

4. Drag and drop the following fields onto the design grid: **ProductName, UnitsInStock, UnitsOnOrder**, and **ReorderLevel**.

5. Select **Ascending** from the drop-down list in the sort box for the UnitsInStock field.

13

6. Under the Criteria box for the UnitsInStock, enter **=0** to show any product that has no inventory.

7. Right-click the **or** box under the ReorderLevel field column to open a shortcut menu. Click **Build** to open the Expression Builder dialog box. The top box contains the expression that will be used (see Figure 13-5). The three boxes below list the available objects and methods.

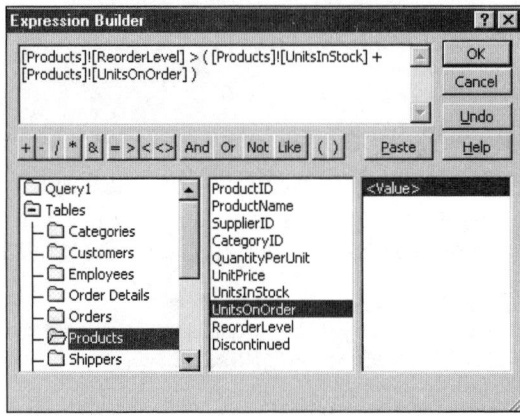

Figure 13-5   Using the Access Expression Builder

8. Double-click **Tables** in the lower left-hand box to bring up a list of available tables, then click **Products** to bring up the Products table field list.

9. Double-click **ReorderLevel** in the field list to enter it in the expression box.

10. Click on the ">" button to enter the greater than sign into the expression box.

11. Click on the "(" to enter the beginning parentheses into the expression box. Parentheses are required when you combine multiple conditional criteria in the same statement.

12. Double click the **UnitsInStock** field to enter it in the expression box.

13. Click the "**+**" button to place the plus sign into the expression box.

14. Double-click the **UnitsOnOrder** field to enter it into the expression box.

15. Click the closing parenthesis sign ")".

16. Click **OK** to close the Expression Builder. The expression that was in the expression box is now in the or box in the design grid.

17. Click **File** on the menu bar, and then click **Save**. Save the Query as **ReorderProducts**.

18. Click the **View** list arrow, and then click **DataSheet View** to preview your results. There are seven products listed.

19. Click the **View** list arrow, and then click **SQL View**. Notice that Access lists the fields using their fully qualified names. Also, the conditional expressions use parentheses to identify the order in which the conditions are evaluated.

20. Click **File**, and then click **Close** to close the query.

UPDATING A DATABASE USING SQL AND ASP

Updating a database can consist of creating a new record, modifying an existing record, or deleting a record. You can accomplish this by using SQL commands, or by using the recordset object built into ADO. In the examples below, you will use the command object and SQL commands to insert a new record, update an existing record, or delete an existing record. The command object has its own set of properties and methods that can be configured.

Creating a New Record Using SQL and the Command Object

In SQL, inserting a new record requires creating an INSERT query. Insert queries can only be performed on one table at a time, and only one record at a time can be inserted. Furthermore, you must specify a value for every field. If no value is available, you can substitute the word NULL for the value. You must enter strings using quotation marks. If you enter the fields without specifying the field names, you must enter them in the order that the fields appear in the database structure. The syntax for inserting a new record using SQL is as follows.

INSERT INTO tablename

VALUES (value1, value2, value3/....valueN)

For example:

```
INSERT INTO Products
VALUES ("chair", 153.00, #12/1/2000#, NULL, "furniture")
```

You can specify the field names in parentheses after the table if you plan to enter only values for a subset of fields. The following sample code demonstrates how to enter only the product name and price.

```
INSERT INTO Products (productName, price)
VALUES ("chair",153.00)
```

The Shippers table in the Northwind database only contains three fields: the ShipperID, CompanyName, and phone. Currently there are only three records in the table. The ShipperID is an autonumber, which is assigned when the shipper record is entered into the database. The steps below show how to use SQL in a Web page to create a new record. Because the insert command is used, you need to use the command object. The command object can be used with the connection object or the recordset object. Table 13-1 lists a subset of the methods and properties of the command object.

13

Table 13-1   The Command Object Properties and Methods

Method	Description	Example
Execute method	Executes a SQL statement or stored procedure identified by the CommandText property	`oCM.Execute`
Cancel method	Cancels the current command	`oCM.Cancel`
ActiveConnection property	Assigns the connection object (oC) or connection string (CS)	`oCM.ActiveConnection = CS` `oCM.ActiveConnection = oC`
CommandText	Specifies the SQL statement (SQL) or stored procedure	`oCM.CommandText = SQL`
CommandType	Describes the CommandText	`oCM.CommandType = adCmdText` `oCM.CommandType = adCmdStoredProc`

You must specify the ActiveConnection, CommandText, and CommandType property before calling the execute method. The value of the ActiveConnection is the name of the connection object, the connection string, or the name of the variable that stores the connection string. If the command is a SQL query, then the CommandType value would be &H0001. So that you don't have to remember all of the possible values and their meanings, Microsoft has provided a text file that contains a list of constants that represents values used in conjunction with ADO. The name of the file is adovbs.inc, and it was installed when you installed support for Microsoft Data Access Components. Because it is a text file, it can easily be opened in Notepad. The values that are available for the CommandType property are referred to as CommandTypeEnum. The four constants and their values are listed below. In your ASP page, after including the adovbs.inc file, instead of referring to the value, you can use the constant. You can refer to Chapter 7 for samples and directions for including a text file within an ASP page. The next example will include the adovbs.inc file, and refer to constants declared within the adovbs.inc file.

- Const adCmdUnknown = &H0008
- Const adCmdText = &H0001
- Const adCmdTable = &H0002
- Const adCmdStoredProc = &H0004

The adovbs.inc is installed in the c:\Program Files\Common Files\System\ado\ folder by default. The client version of adovbs.inc can be used to access these same constants using client-side scripting. The client version of adovbs.inc is installed in the c:\Program Files\Common Files\System\msadc\ folder by default.

To create a new record in the Shippers table using SQL and the command object:

1. Create a new page called **shipnewsql.asp**, using Notepad.

2. Add the server-side includes, basic HTML, and headings.

```
<!--#include file="nwconx.inc"-->
<!--#include file="adovbs.inc"-->
<html><head>
<title>New Shipping Record</title>
</head>
<body>
<h1>New Shipping Record</h1>
```

3. Create the SQL statement, using the insert command, and assign the string to the SQL variable.

```
<%
SQL = "INSERT INTO Shippers "
SQL = SQL & "(ShipperID, CompanyName, Phone) "
SQL = SQL & "VALUES (42,'FedNight','(555) 800-8888')"
```

4. Open a connection, using the connection object, and pass the connection object the connection string variable.

```
oC.open CS
```

5. Set the properties of the connection object. You can set the property to the connection string or the connection object. Assign the CommandText property to the SQL string. Assign the CommandType property to adCmdText. The CommandType is usually adCmdText for SQL command statements, or adCmdStoredProc for stored procedures. Then, call the execute method to execute the command, using the command object.

```
oCM.ActiveConnection = oC
oCM.CommandText = SQL
oCM.CommandType = adCmdText
oCM.Execute
```

6. Write out the SQL statement to the browser and close the HTML tags.

```
response.write SQL
%>
</body></html>
```

7. Modify the page using your favorite fonts, colors, images, and content.

8. Save the page to your data directory folder.

9. View the Web page in a browser. The SQL statement displayed in the ASP page should read "INSERT INTO Shippers (ShipperID, CompanyName, Phone) VALUES (42,'FedNight','(555) 800-8888')".

10. Print the Web page and the source code.

11. View the Shippers table in Access to verify that the record was added.

13

Modifying a Record Using SQL and the Command Object

You can also use SQL and the command object to modify an existing record, as demonstrated in the next example. The SQL statement uses the update command instead of the select or insert commands. The update command needs to know which table to update, and which fields and values. The keyword set is used to assign the values to the field names. The execute method is called to perform the update. You can use the WHERE clause to update a single record or a group of records. If you do not specify a search condition using the WHERE clause, the value will be updated for all records within the database. In the following example you will create a Web page that will change the phone number that you entered in the previous example.

To update a record in the Shippers table using SQL and the command object:

1. Create a new page called **shipupdatesql.asp**, using Notepad.

2. Add the server-side includes, basic HTML, and headings.

```
<!--#include file="nwconx.inc"-->
<!--#include file="adovbs.inc"-->
<html><head>
<title>Update Shipping Record</title>
</head>
<body>
<h1>Update Shipping Record</h1>
```

3. Create the SQL statement, using the UPDATE command, and assign the string to the SQL variable. Notice that the criterion is for the shipperID that equals 42. This shipperID matches the shipperID that you created in the previous exercise.

```
<%
SQL = "Update Shippers "
SQL = SQL & "Set CompanyName='ExpMail',"
SQL = SQL & "Phone='(222) 800-8888' "
SQL = SQL & "WHERE ShipperID=42"
```

4. Open a connection, using the connection object, and pass the connection string variable to the connection object.

```
oC.open CS
```

5. Set the properties of the connection object. Then, call the execute method.

```
oCM.ActiveConnection = oC
oCM.CommandText = SQL
oCM.CommandType = adCmdText
oCM.Execute
```

6. Write out the SQL statement to the browser and add the closing HTML tags.

```
response.write SQL
%>
</body></html>
```

7. Modify the page using your favorite fonts, colors, images, and content.

8. Save the page to your data directory.

9. View the Web page in a browser. The SQL statement displayed should say "Update Shippers Set CompanyName='ExpMail',Phone='(222) 800-8888' WHERE ShipperID=42". Print the Web page and the source code.

10. View the Shippers table in Access to verify that the record was updated.

 Although in a production environment you will not usually write out the SQL statement to the browser, it is useful to do this the first time you run the script, in order to view the SQL statement. Most of the errors that occur are related to the syntax of the SQL statement. You can verify the SQL statement by writing the results to the Web page. If you are using this method to debug a Web page, you can use the response.end statement to stop processing the page after displaying the SQL statement.

Deleting a Record Using SQL and the Command Object

You can also use SQL and the command object to delete a record. The delete command needs to know which table to delete. The execute method of the command object is called to perform the deletion. You can specify a single record to delete, using the WHERE clause. If you do not specify a specific record or set of records using the WHERE clause, the entire recordset will be deleted. This example will delete the record you created in the previous exercise.

To delete a record in the Shippers table using SQL and the command object:

1. Create a new page called **shipdeletesql.asp** in Notepad.

2. Add the server-side includes, basic HTML, and headings.

```
<!--#include file="nwconx.inc"-->
<!--#include file="adovbs.inc"-->
<html><head>
<title>Delete Shipping Record</title>
</head>
<body>
<h1>Delete Shipping Record</h1>
```

3. Create the SQL statement, using the DELETE command, and assign the string to the SQL variable. Notice that the criterion is for the shipperID that equals 42. This shipperID matches only the shipperID that you created in the previous exercise. Therefore, only one record will be deleted.

```
<%
SQL = "Delete FROM Shippers "
SQL = SQL & "WHERE ShipperID=42"
```

13

4. Open a connection, using the connection object, and pass the connection string variable to the connection object.

```
oC.open CS
```

5. Set the properties of the connection object. Then, call the execute method.

```
oCM.ActiveConnection = oC
oCM.CommandText = SQL
oCM.CommandType = adCmdText
oCM.Execute
```

6. Write out the SQL statement to the browser and add the closing HTML tags.

```
response.write SQL
%>
</body></html>
```

7. Modify the page using your favorite fonts, colors, images, and content.

8. Save the page to your data directory.

9. View the Web page in a browser. The SQL displayed should say "Delete FROM Shippers WHERE ShipperID=42".

10. Print the Web page and the source code.

11. View the Shippers table in Access to verify that the record was deleted.

UPDATING A DATABASE USING ADO AND ASP

Although you can use SQL to create new records, or to update or delete existing records, the ADO Model also contains methods to perform these common functions. These methods do not require the command object. The records are not modified in the database until the update method is called.

You can learn more about the objects within the ActiveX Data Objects 2.1 at *http://msdn.microsoft.com/library/techart/ado_objm.htm*.

Creating a New Record Using ADO and ASP

You can create a new record by using the AddNew method of the recordset object. In the example below, you will add a new record to the Shippers table. Notice that the SELECT SQL query is used to select all the records or a subset of records. You can apply a filter to determine whether a record already exists. If the record exists, then do not create a new record. Otherwise, create a new record, get the values for the fields, and then update the database. The record is not added to the database until the update method is called. When you are finished, you can remove the filter, which returns the recordset to the complete set of records. You can release the filter by setting the property to the adFilterNone constant in the adovbs.inc file, or by setting it to an empty string. Filters are useful because they can be reapplied to the same recordset within the same ASP page without having to return to the database to retrieve a new recordset. You should always verify that the primary field was not used before creating a new record.

To add a record in the Shippers table using the ADO commands:

1. Create a new page called **shipaddado.asp** in Notepad.

2. Add the server-side includes, basic HTML, and headings.

```
<!--#include file="nwconx.inc"-->
<!--#include file="adovbs.inc"-->
<html><head>
<title>Add Shipping Record</title>
</head>
<body>
<h1>Add Shipping Record</h1>
```

3. Open a connection, using the connection object and the connection string variable.

```
<%
oC.open CS
```

4. Create the SQL statement, using the SELECT command, and assign the string to the SQL variable.

```
SQL = "SELECT * FROM Shippers"
```

5. Open the recordset object, using the SQL query and the connection object. Parameters are passed to indicate the CursorType, LockType, and CommandType. The CommandType is adCmdText, which indicates that the command passed is a SQL statement.

```
oRS.Open SQL,oC,adOpenDynamic,adLockOptimistic,adCmdText
```

6. Use the filter method of the recordset object to search for a specific record. Notice that the filter criterion is for the CompanyName that equals OverNight.

```
oRS.Filter = "CompanyName = 'OverNight'"
```

 You can pass the value for the filter from a form or a variable.

7. If there is no record that matches, then the cursor moves to the end of the file, and you use the AddNew method to add a new record. Set the values for the fields. You don't need to set the ShipperID; it will be set by the database because the field is formatted as autonumber. Call the update method, which will write the record to the database. Finally, release the filter by assigning it to adFilterNone.

```
If oRS.EOF Then
    oRS.AddNew
```

13

```
        oRS("CompanyName") = "OverNight"
        oRS("Phone") = "(222) 555-1234"
        oRS.Update
    End If
    oRS.Filter = adFilterNone
```

8. Write out the SQL statement to the browser and add the closing HTML tags.

```
response.write SQL
%>
</body></html>
```

9. Modify the page using your favorite fonts, colors, images, and content.

10. Save the page to your data directory.

11. View the Web page in a browser. Notice that the SQL statement should say "SELECT * FROM Shippers".

12. Verify that the record was added to the Shippers table. The ADO AddNew method added the new record.

13. Print the Web page and the source code.

Modifying a Record Using ADO and ASP

ADO can also be used to modify one or more existing records. In the following example, the SELECT SQL query is used to select all the records or a subset of records. Then, you can apply a filter to determine if a record exists. The filter can be used to retrieve a single record or a group of records. If the record exists, then modify the fields with the new values and update the database. Notice that the code to modify the record is similar to the code that used the AddNew method. The record is not updated in the database until the update method is called.

To modify a record in the Shippers table using SQL and the command object:

1. Create a new page called **shipmodifyado.asp** in Notepad.

2. Add the server-side includes, basic HTML, and headings.

```
<!--#include file="nwconx.inc"-->
<!--#include file="adovbs.inc"-->
<html><head>
<title>Modify Shipping Record</title>
</head>
<body>
<h1>Modify Shipping Record</h1>
```

3. Open a connection, using the connection object and the connection string variable.

```
<%
oC.open CS
```

4. Create the SQL statement, using the SELECT command, and assign the string to the SQL variable.

```
SQL = "SELECT * FROM Shippers"
```

5. Open the recordset object, using the SQL query and the connection object. Parameters are passed to indicate the CursorType, LockType, and CommandType. The CommandType is adCmdText, which indicates that the command passed is a SQL statement.

```
oRS.Open SQL,oC,adOpenDynamic,adLockOptimistic,adCmdText
```

6. Use the filter method of the recordset object to search for a specific record. Notice that the filter criterion is for the company name that equals OverNight. The record must exist in order for you to be able to modify the record.

```
oRS.Filter = "CompanyName = 'OverNight'"
```

7. If the end of the file is not reached, then there is a match, and a recordset will be returned. Because only one record matches, there is only one record in the recordset. Set the values for the fields and call the update method, which will rewrite the field values to the database.

```
If not oRS.EOF Then
    oRS("CompanyName") = "OverNight"
    oRS("Phone") = "(444) 555-1234"
    oRS.Update
End If
oRS.Filter = adFilterNone
```

8. Write out the SQL statement to the browser and add the closing HTML tags.

```
response.write SQL
%>
</body></html>
```

9. Modify the page using your favorite fonts, colors, images, and content.

10. Save the page to your data directory.

11. View the Web page in a browser. The SQL statement should say "SELECT * FROM Shippers". Print the Web page and the source code.

12. View the Shippers table in Access to verify that the record was modified.

Deleting a Record Using ADO and ASP

You can delete a record from a database using the ADO delete method of the recordset object. In the following example, a record is deleted from the Shippers table. Notice that the SELECT SQL query is used to select all the records or a subset of records. Then, you can perform a filter to determine whether a record exists. If the record exists, then delete the record and update the database. Notice that after you call the delete method, you must call the update method. The record is not deleted from the database until the update method is called.

To delete a record in the Shippers table using the ADO delete method

1. Create a new page called **shipdeleteado.asp** in Notepad.

2. Add the server-side includes, basic HTML, and headings.

```
<!--#include file="nwconx.inc"-->
<!--#include file="adovbs.inc"-->
<html><head>
<title>Delete Shipping Record</title>
</head>
<body>
<h1>Delete Shipping Record</h1>
```

3. Open a connection, using the connection object and the connection string variable.

```
<%
oC.open CS
```

4. Create the SQL statement, using the SELECT command, and assign the string to the SQL variable.

```
SQL = "SELECT * FROM Shippers"
```

5. Open the recordset object, using the SQL query and the connection object. Parameters are passed to indicate the CursorType, LockType, and CommandType. The CommandType is adCmdText, which indicates that the command passed is a SQL statement.

```
oRS.Open SQL,oC,adOpenDynamic,adLockOptimistic,adCmdText
```

6. Use the filter method of the recordset object to search for a specific record. Notice that the filter criterion is for the shipperID that equals 52.

```
oRS.Filter = "CompanyName = 'OverNight'"
```

 You can pass the value for the filter from a form or a variable.

7. If there is a match, delete the record with the delete method, and then call the update method.

```
If not oRS.EOF Then
      oRS.Delete
      oRS.Update
End If
oRS.Filter = adFilterNone
```

8. Write out the SQL statement to the browser and add the closing HTML tags.

```
response.write SQL
%>
</body></html>
```

9. Modify the page using your favorite fonts, colors, images, and content.

10. Save the page to your data directory.

11. View the Web page in a browser. The SQL statement displayed says "SELECT *
    FROM Shippers".

12. Print the Web page and the source code.

13. View the Shippers table in Access to verify that the record was deleted.

Updating Batch Records Using ADO

There are other methods and properties built into ADO. For example, UpdateBatch can be
used to update several records at one time. However, because you can modify records, you
should lock the recordset so that other users do not try to modify the record at the same
time. The adLockBatchOptimistic property locks the recordset until the UpdateBatch
method is used. The adOpenKeySet cursor property of the recordset object will allow the
cursor to move forward and backward through the recordset. An example of code that uses
the UpdateBatch method is as follows:

```
oRS.open adOpenKeySet, adLockBatchOptimistic
oRS("fieldname")=value1
oRS.MoveNext
oRS("fieldname")=value2
oRS.MoveNext
oRS("fieldname")=value3
oRS.UpdateBatch
```

Only some providers allow you to update records in batches. You can learn
more about the providers available with ADO, and the properties and methods
available, at *http://msdn.microsoft.com/library/psdk/dasdk/mdap99m7.htm*.

13

Moving Through Recordsets Using ADO

As you learned in the previous chapter, the database cursor is a location in memory where
the records from the recordset are stored. The recordset is similar to a Rolodex, from which
you can access each individual address card. You can access records row by row within the
recordset object, using the cursor. The CursorType, which is specified when you retrieve the
recordset, indicates which methods and properties apply to the recordset. The types of cur-
sors that are supported include the Forward Only, Static, Keyset, and Dynamic.

The default recordset cursor, Forward Only, is identified by the parameter
adOpenForwardOnly, and allows you to move forward in the database, record by record. This
type of recordset can only be used with the SELECT query. This type of recordset is read-only.
The cursor can use the MoveFirst and MoveNext methods to navigate through the recordset.

The Static recordset, configured with the adStatic parameter, is also only used with the SELECT
query. However, the Static recordset locks the records. When the data in the recordset is updated,

the changes are not reflected in the current recordset. The Static recordset provides more flexible methods for navigating the recordset. For example, it allows you to use bookmarks to maintain the location of the cursor within the database. The default bookmarks include adBookmarkCurrent, adBookmarkFirst, and adBookmarkLast. ADO also allows you to create your own bookmarks. Navigational methods of the Static recordset include MoveFirst, MoveNext, MoveLast, and MovePrevious, as well as a Move method that allows you to move to a specific record using a relative address. The Move method takes two parameters, the number of records to move through, and the starting position. Negative numbers allow you to move backwards in the recordset. The following is the syntax for the Move method.

ORS.MOVE(#recordsToMove, startPosition#)

For example, to move to the fourth record, using the move property in a static recordset:

```
ORS.MOVE(3, 1)
```

The adOpenKeySet cursor parameter defines the Keyset recordset. The Keyset recordset supports bookmarks and moving around within the recordset, and in addition it allows you to update the records if you specify the LockType parameter when the recordset is created. Therefore, you can see updates that are made to the existing records.

You specify the Dynamic recordset by using the adOpenDynamic parameter when the recordset is defined. This recordset is the most flexible for navigating within the recordset, and also makes immediately visible all changes made by other users—but it also carries the most overhead in terms of server resources, because it must maintain additional information to allow you to freely navigate within the recordset.

CHAPTER SUMMARY

Building Queries in Access

❐ Connection objects, connection strings, and related ADO objects are often created in a separate file, which can be included in the ASP page. Using server-side includes helps to keep the connection information centralized. In order to use the ADO constants, you must include the adovbs.inc file in the ASP page.

❐ Access provides a graphical user interface to create queries. There are three views that you can toggle between in the Query tab. The Design view lets you configure the query graphically, using a design grid. The SQL view lets you see or edit the raw SQL code. The DataSheet view lets you preview the results from your query.

❐ Access adds additional parentheses and fully qualifies all of the fields and tables within the query. Fully qualifying the field means identifying the name of the table and the name of the field, separated by a dot (.).

❐ Microsoft provides the Northwind database as a training tool for learning Access.

❐ You can use Access to create queries that sort data and combine multiple search conditions. The SQL created by Access can be used within the Web page. You can split the SQL across multiple lines by concatenating the SQL variable.

Advanced Queries in Access, SQL, and ADO

❑ When you combine multiple search conditions with the AND operator, both conditions must be true for the record to be retrieved. If you use the OR operator, only one of the conditions must be true for the record to be retrieved. You must use parentheses when you combine multiple conditions into a single SQL statement. Access has a built-in Expression Builder that can be used to build complex queries graphically.

❑ SQL can be used with ASP to create advanced queries, such as inserting new records, updating records, and deleting records. You must use the command object to execute the SQL commands.

❑ ADO can also be used with ASP to create advanced queries, such as inserting new records, updating records, and deleting records. You cannot use the default recordset to perform these advanced queries.

❑ You can use a filter to search the recordset for a subset of records. The filter can be removed, which returns the original recordset. Filters can be reused within the same page.

❑ The CursorType parameter of the recordset object identifies what navigational methods are available within the recordset. You can only move forward with the adOpenForwardOnly recordset using the MoveNext and MoveFirst methods.

To create a command object

```
set oCM = server.createobject("ADODB.command")
```

To include the adovbs.inc file and the connection file

```
<!--#include file="adovbs.inc"-->
<!--#include file="conx.inc"-->
```

To execute a SQL statement with a command object

```
oCM.ActiveConnection = oC
oCM.CommandText = SQL
oCM.CommandType = adCmdText
oCM.Execute
```

To create a new record using SQL

```
SQL = "INSERT INTO Shippers "
SQL = SQL & "(SID, Cname, NDate) "
SQL = SQL & "VALUES (42,'BD',#8/1/2000#)"
```

To update an existing record using SQL

```
SQL = "Update Shippers "
SQL = SQL & "Set CName='EL' "
SQL = SQL & "WHERE SID=42"
```

13

To delete a record using SQL

```
SQL = "Delete FROM Shippers "
SQL = SQL & "WHERE SID=42"
```

To apply a filter on a recordset object

```
oRS.Filter = "SID = 999"
```

To open a recordset for writing

```
oRS.Open SQL,oC,adOpenDynamic,adLockOptimistic,adCmdText
```

To create a new record using the ADO recordset object

```
oRS.AddNew
oRS("CName") = "O.N.T."
oRS.Update
```

To update an existing record using the ADO recordset object

```
oRS.Filter = "SID = 52"
oRS("CName") = "AAA Movers"
oRS.Update
```

To delete an existing record using the ADO recordset object

```
oRS.Filter = "SID = 52"
oRS.Delete
oRS.Update
```

To remove a filter on a recordset object

```
oRS.Filter = adFilterNone
oRS.Filter = ""
```

To update a group of records using the recordset object

```
oRS.open adOpenKeySet, adLockBatchOptimistic
oRS("Price")=21.50
oRS.MoveNext
oRS("Price")=32.50
oRS.UpdateBatch
```

To move to a specific record with a static recordset

```
ORS.MOVE(3, 1)
```

REVIEW QUESTIONS

1. Which view in Access allows you to modify the query using a design grid?

    a. Datasheet view

    b. Design view

    c. SQL view

    d. Expression Builder

2. Which value will be displayed first if a field is sorted in descending order?

    a. 25

    b. 23

    c. 2

    d. 1.5

3. To create a search condition where the price is equal to eight dollars, what should you type in the criteria box under the price column?

    a. "8"

    b. = 8

    c. = "8"

    d. = "8.00"

4. If the Show box is checked under the price field, the field can be used to sort the results. True or False?

5. If the Show box is checked under the price field, then the field will be displayed. True or False?

6. To create a search condition where the lastVisited date is equal to September 1, 2000, what should you type in the criteria box under the lastVisited column?

    a. = "9/1/2000"

    b. = #9/1/2000#

    c. = 9/1/2000

    d. "9/1/2000"

7. To create a search condition where a field named phone is empty, what should you type in the criteria box under the phone column?

    a. = " "

    b. = NULL

    c. = "NULL"

    d. <> NULL

13

8. Which function will return the average of a field named Price?

    a. Average(Price)

    b. AVG(Price)

    c. COUNT(Price)

    d. SUM(Price)

9. Which SQL command will insert a new record into a recordset?

    a. Update

    b. AddNew

    c. Add

    d. Insert

10. When you are using SQL to add a new record into a recordset, which statement will correctly identify the customer table as the target table?

    a. FROM customer

    b. INTO customer

    c. Customer VALUES

    d. INSERT customer

11. If a value for a field that contains price information is not available, what is the best thing to do?

    a. Insert " " to place an empty string in the field.

    b. Insert NULL to act as a place holder for the field.

    c. Insert a "3.00" to act as a place holder for the field.

    d. Don't add the value in the value string.

12. Which statement would assign the active connection property of a command object named oCM to a connection object named oConn?

    a. oConn.ActiveConnection = oCM

    b. oCM.ActiveConnection = oC

    c. oCM.ActiveConnection = oConn

    d. oCM.ActiveConnection = CS

13. Which value is assigned to the CommandType parameter to indicate that the command is a SQL statement?

    a. adCmdText

    b. adCmdStoredProc

    c. adCmdSQL

    d. adCmdTable

14. Which SQL command will remove a record from the database?

    a. ORS.Delete

    b. Update

    c. Remove

    d. Delete

15. Which method executes the SQL statement identified in the command object?

    a. OCM.update

    b. oCM.run

    c. oCM.execute

    d. commandExecute

16. Which method is used by the Static recordset to move to a specific record?

    a. Move

    b. MoveOne

    c. MoveUp

    d. MoveNext

17. Which method removes the filter from the recordset object named oRS?

    a. oRS.adFilterNone

    b. oRS.adFilter = None

    c. set oRS.Filter = nothing

    d. oRS.Filter = adFilterNone

18. Which ADO method allows you to insert a new record into the recordset?

    a. oRS.Insert

    b. oRS.New

    c. oRS.Add

    d. oRS.AddNew

19. Which ADO recordset parameter allows you to write to the record?

    a. adCommandText

    b. adLockOptimistic

    c. adOpenForwardOnly

    d. adOpenKeyset

20. What is the purpose of a bookmark?

    a. to maintain the location of the cursor

    b. to maintain the location of the field in a recordset

    c. to change the type of recordset cursor used

    d. to dynamically change the commandtype parameter used

13

HANDS-ON PROJECTS

Project 13-1

In this project, you will create a customer registration database and a server-side include file that can contain connection information to the customer registration database.

1. Open Access. Create a new database called **cemail.mdb**. Save the database in your data directory.

2. Double-click **Create table in Design view** to create a new table named customer. Add the fields listed in the table below to the table structure. Define the e-mail field as the primary key field. Save the table as **customer**.

Field Name	Data Type	Description
email	Text	E-mail Address
sessID	Text	SessionID
signup	Text	Signup Date
fname	Text	First Name
lname	Text	Last Name
pwd	Text	Password
keyword	Text	Keyword

3. Enter the following data into the table using the Datasheet view. You can add additional records, but enter this record as the first record. Remember that the e-mail field is the primary key field, and therefore cannot contain duplicate values.

Field Name	Values
email	Julie@VisualInterdev.org
sessID	1069168305
signup	8/1/2001
fname	Julie
lname	Murphy
pwd	hurricane
keyword	snoopy

4. Save the customer table. Close the cemail database, then exit Access.

5. Create a server-side include page named **emailconx.inc**, using Notepad to connect to the cemail database. Add the following code to declare the variables, create the connection string, and create the connection, recordset, and command objects. Change the path to the absolute path where the cemail database is located.

```
<% dim DRV, DBQ, CS
DRV = "Driver={Microsoft Access Driver (*.mdb)}; "
DBQ = "DBQ= c:\yourfolder\cemail.mdb;"
CS = DRV & DBQ
%>
```

6. Save the page to your data directory. Print the source code of the emailconx.inc page.

Project 13-2

In this project, you will pass values from a form to the ASP page; these values are used to create a new record. (*Note:* This project requires that you first complete Project 13-1.)

1. Using Notepad, create a new page named **CEmailADORegister.asp**, which will contain the registration form. Save the page to your data directory.

2. Create a form using the fields listed in the table below. The form method should be post, and the action should be **CEmailADOAdd.asp**. Notice that the signup and sessID are not listed. Those values will be retrieved from the server, not the user. You can modify the field properties, except the name, form field HTML tag, and type property. You can modify the page using your favorite fonts, colors, text, and images. Save the page to your data directory.

Form Field Name	Form Field HTML Tag and Type Property
email	Input type=text
fname	Input type=text
lname	Input type=text
pwd	Input type=password
keyword	Input type=password

3. Using Notepad, create a page called **CEmailADOAdd.asp**, which will be used to retrieve the form values and add the values into a new record. Save the page to your data directory.

4. Add the following basic HTML tags and headings to your CEmailADOAdd.asp page.

```
<!--#include file="emailconx.inc"-->
<!--#include file="adovbs.inc"-->
<html><head>
<title>Add Customer</title>
</head>
<body>
<h1>Add Customer</h1>
```

5. Add the code to retrieve the values from the form and assign them to variables. Notice that the signup variable is assigned to the current date, not a value from the form. The sessID is the sessionID from the session object on the server, not a value from the form.

13

```
<%
email = Request.Form("email")
fname = Request.Form("fname")
lname = Request.Form("lname")
pwd = Request.Form("pwd")
keyword = Request.Form("keyword")
sessID = Session.SessionID
signup = Date()
```

6. Add the code to open the connection and recordset objects. Use a SELECT SQL statement to retrieve the records from the customer table.

```
set oC = server.createobject("ADODB.connection")
set oRS = server.createobject("ADODB.recordset")
oC.open CS
SQL = "SELECT * FROM customer"
oRS.Open SQL,oC,adOpenDynamic,adLockOptimistic,adCmdText
```

7. Apply a filter to the recordset. The filter will look for a matching record, using the e-mail address entered in the form.

```
oRS.Filter = "email ='" & email & "'"
```

8. Write a conditional statement such that if there is a matching record, then a new record is not created. If you are at the end of the file, and no match has been found, add a new record using the AddNew method of the recordset object. Assign the values to the fields, using the variables that contain the values that were passed from the form. Use the update method to update the database.

```
If oRS.EOF Then
  oRS.AddNew
  oRS("email") = email
  oRS("sessID") = sessID
  oRS("fname") = fname
  oRS("lname") = lname
  oRS("pwd") = pwd
  oRS("keyword") = keyword
  oRS("signup") = signup
  oRS.Update
End If
oRS.Filter = adFilterNone
```

9. Close your recordset and connection objects, and HTML tags. Add a link to the CEmailADODisplay.asp page that will be used to display the recordset.

```
oRS.close
set oRS = nothing
oC.close
set oC = nothing
%>
<a href = "CEmailADODisplay.asp">
Display the customer list </a>
</body></html>
```

10. Save the changes to the CEmailADOAdd.asp page.

11. Create a Web page named **CEmailADODisplay.asp** that will verify that the record was added in the database by displaying the records in the customer table.

12. Add the server-side includes and the basic HTML tags.

```
<!--#include file="emailconx.inc"-->
<!--#include file="adovbs.inc"-->
<html><head>
<title>Display Customers</title>
</head>
<body>
<h1>Display Customers </h1>
```

13. Open the connection and retrieve the basic recordset. Since you are only viewing the records, the default recordset can be used.

```
<%
SQL = "SELECT * FROM customer"
set oC = server.createobject("ADODB.connection")
oC.open CS
set oRS = server.createobject("ADODB.recordset")
oRS.Open SQL, oC
%>
```

14. Add the table HTML tag to create the table.

```
<table border=1 cellspacing=0 cellpadding=5>
```

15. Create a Do While statement to loop through each record in the recordset until it reaches the end of the file. For each record, write out the values of the fields in the cell.

```
<% do while not oRS.EOF
  response.write "<tr><td>"
  response.write oRS("email") & "</td><td>"
  response.write oRS("sessID") & "</td><td>"
  response.write oRS("fname") & "</td><td>"
  response.write oRS("lname") & "</td><td>"
  response.write oRS("pwd") & "</td><td>"
  response.write oRS("keyword") & "</td><td>"
  response.write oRS("signup") & "</td></tr>"
oRS.movenext
loop
oRS.close
set oRS = nothing
oC.close
set oC = nothing
%>
```

16. Add the closing table and closing HTML tags.

```
</table></body></html>
```

13

17. Modify the Web page appearance by changing the background, font, and colors, and adding content.

18. Save the Web pages to your data directory. View the CEmailADORegister.asp page. Add the following information into the form:

Form Field Name	Value
email	rshea@academia.org
fname	Robert
lname	Shea
pwd	Irish
keyword	Ireland

19. Click on the hyperlink to display the recordset. Print the Web page and the source code for each page.

Hands-on Project

Project 13-3

In this project, you will pass values from a form to the ASP page; these values are used to delete a record. (*Note:* This project requires that you first complete Projects 13-1 and 13-2.)

1. Using Notepad, create a new page named **CEmailADODeleteForm.asp**, which will contain the customer deletion form. This form will be used to select the user to delete. Save the page to your data directory.

2. Create a form with one input field named email. The form method should be post, and the action should be **CEmailADODelete.asp**. You can modify the field properties, except the name, form field HTML tag, and type property. You can modify the page using your favorite fonts, colors, text, and images. Save the page to your data directory.

3. Using Notepad, create a page called **CEmailADODelete.asp**, which will be used to retrieve the form values and delete the record. Save the page to your data directory.

4. Add the following basic HTML tags and headings to your CEmailADODelete.asp page.

```
<!--#include file="emailconx.inc"-->
<!--#include file="adovbs.inc"-->
<html><head>
<title>Delete Customer</title>
</head>
<body>
<h1>Delete Customer</h1>
```

5. Add the code to retrieve the values from the CEmail form field and assign them to the CEmail variable.

```
<%
email = Request.Form("email")
```

6. Add the code to open the connection and recordset objects. Use a SELECT SQL statement to retrieve the records from the customer table. Because you are deleting a record, you need to specify the cursorType and lockType parameters.

```
set oC = server.createobject("ADODB.connection")
set oRS = server.createobject("ADODB.recordset")
oC.open CS
SQL = "SELECT * FROM Customer"
oRS.Open SQL,oC,adOpenDynamic,adLockOptimistic,adCmdText
```

7. Apply a filter to the recordset. The filter will look for a matching record, using the e-mail address entered in the form.

```
oRS.Filter = "email ='" & email & "'"
```

8. If there is a match, then display the name, e-mail address, and sessionID. Then delete the record and update the database. Remove the filter applied to the recordset.

```
If not oRS.EOF Then
  Response.Write "Customer name: "
  Response.Write oRS("fname") & " " & oRS("lname") & "<br>"
  Response.Write "E-mail address: "
  Response.Write oRS("email") & "<br>"
  Response.Write "Customer ID: "
  Response.Write oRS("sessID") & "<br>"
  oRS.Delete
  oRS.Update
End If
oRS.Filter = adFilterNone
```

9. Close your recordset and connection objects, and add the closing HTML tags. You can add a hyperlink on the CEmailADODelete.asp page that points to the CEmailADODisplay.asp page.

```
oRS.close
set oRS = nothing
oC.close
set oC = nothing
%>
<a href = "CEmailADODisplay.asp">
Display the customer list </a>
</body></html>
```

10. View the CEmailADODeleteForm.asp page in your browser, and enter an e-mail address that you know exists in the database.

11. View the CEmailADODisplay.asp page to verify that the record was deleted in the database, by displaying the records in the customer table.

12. Modify the Web page appearance on each page by changing the background, font, and colors, and adding content.

13. Save the Web pages to your data directory.

14. Print the Web pages and the source code for each page.

Project 13-4

In this project, you will pass values from a form to the ASP page; these values are used to modify values in a record. (*Note:* This project requires that you first complete Projects 13-1, 13-2, and 13-3.) The first page, CEmailADOUpdateForm.asp, is used to retrieve the e-mail address of the customer from a form. The second page, CEmailADOUpdateDisplay.asp, shows the values of the record retrieved from the database. The values are assigned to a new form. The user can modify the form values and submit the changes. The CEmailADOUpdate.asp page will modify the record and update the database.

1. Using Notepad, create a new page named **CEmailADOUpdateForm.asp**, which will contain the customer update form. This form will be used to select which user to update. Save the page to your data directory.

2. On the CEmailADOUpdateForm.asp page, create a form named email which has one input field named email and a Submit button. The form method should be post, and the action should be **CEmailADOUpdateDisplay.asp**. You can modify the field properties, except the name, form field HTML tag, and type property. You can modify the page using your favorite fonts, colors, text, and images. Save the page to your data directory.

```
<html><head>
<title>Modify Customer</title>
</head>
<body>
<h1>Modify Customer</h1>
<form method="post" action="CEmailADOUpdateDisplay.asp">
<input type="text" name="email" size="30">
<input type="submit" value="Submit">
</form>
</body></html>
```

3. Using Notepad, create a page named **CEmailADOUpdateDisplay.asp**, which will be used to retrieve the form values. Save the page to your data directory.

4. Add the following basic HTML tags and headings to your CEmailADOUpdateDisplay.asp page.

```
<!--#include file="emailconx.inc"-->
<!--#include file="adovbs.inc"-->
<html><head>
<title>Modify Customer</title>
</head>
<body>
<h1>Modify Customer</h1>
```

5. Add the code to retrieve the values from the email form field and assign the values to the email variable. Add the code to open the connection and recordset objects. Use a SELECT SQL statement to retrieve the records from the customer table. Because you are reading a record, you do not need to specify the CursorType and LockType parameters. Apply a filter to the recordset. The filter will look for a matching record, using the e-mail address entered in the form.

```
<%
email = Request.Form("email")
set oC = server.createobject("ADODB.connection")
set oRS = server.createobject("ADODB.recordset")
oC.open CS
SQL = "SELECT * FROM customer"
oRS.Open SQL, oC
oRS.Filter = "email ='" & email & "'"
```

6. Add code so that if there is a match, then the values and the form are displayed. Display the email, sessID, and signup outside of the form. You do not want the user to be able to change these values. The form method is assigned post, and the action should be assigned to **CEmailADOUpdate.asp**. Retrieve the values and assign the value to the value property in the form field tags. Because you want to use the e-mail address in the next page, you need to pass the e-mail address as a hidden value in the form. You will still need to use quotation marks outside of the server code, to satisfy browsers that require quotation marks. Then delete the record and update the database. Remove the filter applied to the recordset.

 You need to put the HTML tags on the same line. Do not split HTML statements across lines in Notepad or your HTML editor.

```
If not oRS.EOF Then %>
E-mail address: <% = oRS("email")%><br>
Date Joined: <% = oRS("signup")%><br>
Customer ID: <% = oRS("sessID")%><br><br>
<form method="post" action="CEmailADOUpdate.asp">
<input type="hidden" name="email">
 value="<% =oRS("email")%>">
<input type="text" name="fname" size="20">
 value="<% =oRS("fname")%>">
First name <br>
<input type="text" name="lname" size="20">
 value="<% =oRS("lname")%>">
Last name <br>
<input type="text" name="pwd" size="20">
 value="<% =oRS("pwd")%>">
Password <br>
<input type="text" name="keyword" size="20">
 value="<% =oRS("keyword")%>">
Keyword <br><br>
<input type="submit" value="Submit" name="btnSubmit">
</form>
```

7. Close your recordset and connection objects. Add the closing HTML tags.

```
<%
else
```

13

```
        end If
        oRS.Filter = adFilterNone
        oRS.close
        set oRS = nothing
        oC.close
        set oC = nothing
        %>
        </body></html>
```

8. Create the **CEmailADOUpdate.asp** page that will retrieve the form field values and update the user information. The code for this page is very similar to the code used to add a customer.

9. Add the server-side include files and the basic HTML tags.

```
        <!--#include file="emailconx.inc"-->
        <!--#include file="adovbs.inc"-->
        <html><head>
        <title>Modify Customer</title>
        </head>
        <body>
        <h1>Modify Customer</h1>
```

10. Retrieve the values from the form and assign them to variables.

Notice that you can retrieve the value from the hidden form field just as you do with other form fields.

```
        <%
        email = Request.Form("email")
        fname = Request.Form("fname")
        lname = Request.Form("lname")
        pwd = Request.Form("pwd")
        keyword = Request.Form("keyword")
```

11. Open the connection and recordset objects. Because you are modifying the recordset, you need to pass the CursorType and LockType parameters. Use a filter to locate the recordset for the user based on the user's e-mail address.

```
        set oC = server.createobject("ADODB.connection")
        set oRS = server.createobject("ADODB.recordset")
        oC.open CS
        SQL = "SELECT * FROM customer"
        oRS.Open SQL,oC,adOpenDynamic,adLockOptimistic,adCmdText
        oRS.Filter = "email ='" & email & "'"
```

12. If you are not at the end of the recordset, then you have a match, so assign the value from the variable to the fields of the recordset object.

```
        If not oRS.EOF Then
          oRS("fname") = fname
```

```
oRS("lname") = lname
oRS("pwd") = pwd
oRS("keyword") = keyword
oRS.Update
End If
```

13. Remove the filter, close the recordset and connections, and add the closing HTML tag. Add a link to CEmailADODisplay.asp, which displays the customer records.

```
oRS.Filter = adFilterNone
oRS.close
set oRS = nothing
oC.close
set oC = nothing
%>
<a href="CEmailADODisplay.asp">
Display the customer list </a>
</body></html>
```

14. View the CEmailADOUpdateForm.asp in your browser, and enter an e-mail address that you know is in the database. Modify the data using the form on the CEmailADOUpdateDisplay.asp page.

15. View the CEmailADODisplay.asp page to verify that the record was modified in the database, by displaying the records in the customer table.

16. Modify the appearance of each page by changing the background, font, and colors, and adding content.

17. Save the Web pages to your data directory.

18. Print the Web pages and the source code for each page.

Project 13-5

In this project, you will create a page that displays a quiz that is graded and stored in a database.

1. Create a database named **quiz.mdb** in Access. Create a table called **student** that contains the fields listed in the table below.

Field Name	Data Type	Description
email	Text	E-mail address
sessID	Text	Session ID
d	Text	Date
Q1	Text	Student answer 1
Q2	Text	Student answer 2
score	Text	Student score

13

2. Enter a sample record using the values in the table below.

Field Name	Values
email	teacher@visualinterdev.org
sessID	1069168303
d	8/1/2000
Q1	a
Q2	a
score	100

3. Create the **quizform.asp** page that contains the quiz. Add the basic HTML tags.

```
<html><head><title>QUIZ</title>
</head>
<body>
<h1>HTML Quiz</h1>
```

4. Create the form using the post method, and set the action to **quiz.asp**. Add fields to retrieve the e-mail address.

```
<form method="post" action="quiz.asp">
Enter your e-mail:
<input type="text" name="email" size="25" maxlength="25">
<br><br>
```

5. Add the code for the first question.

```
1. Which tag creates a table cell?<br><br>
a. <input type="radio" name="Q1" value="a" checked>TD<br>
b. <input type="radio" name="Q1" value="b">TR<br>
c. <input type="radio" name="Q1" value="c">TH<br>
d. <input type="radio" name="Q1" value="d">TABLE<br><br>
```

6. Add the code to create the second question.

```
2. Which tag is used to create a line break?<br><br>
<select name="Q2" size="1">
<option selected value="a">BR
<option value="b">BL
<option value="c">LB
<option value="d">HR
</select><br><br>
```

7. Add the Submit button and the closing HTML tags. Save the page to your data directory.

```
<input type="submit" value="Submit Form">
</form></body></html>
```

8. Create a page named **quiz.asp** to process the quiz. Add the code for the server-side include files and the basic HTML tags.

```
<!--#include file="adovbs.inc"-->
<html><head><title>Quiz Score</title></head>
```

```
<body>
<h1>Quiz Score</h1>
```

9. Get the values from the form and assign them to variables.

```
<%
dim email, sessID, d, Q1, Q2, score
email = Request.Form("email")
sessID = Session.SessionID
d = Date()
Q1 = Request.Form("Q1")
Q2 = Request.Form("Q2")
score = 0
```

10. Correct the questions and write out the answers and the final score.

```
response.write "Your answers:<br><br>"
response.write "1. " & Q1 & " "
  if Q1 = "a" then
  score = 50
  response.write "Correct"
else
  response.write "Wrong"
end if
response.write "<br><br>"
response.write "2. " & Q2 & " "
if Q2 = "a" then
  score = score + 50
  response.write "Correct"
else
  response.write "Wrong"
end if
response.write "<br><br>"
response.write "Your score is: " & score
response.write "<br><br>"
```

13

11. Open the connection and recordset. Change the path to the absolute path where the quiz database is located.

```
dim DR, DBQ, CS, oC, oRS
DR = "Driver={Microsoft Access Driver (*.mdb)}; "
DBQ = "DBQ= C:\yourfolder\quiz.mdb;"
CS = DR & DBQ
set oC = server.createobject("ADODB.connection")
set oRS = server.createobject("ADODB.recordset")
oC.open CS
SQL = "SELECT * FROM student"
oRS.Open SQL,oC,adOpenDynamic,adLockOptimistic,AdCmdText
```

12. Use a filter to see whether the student has taken the quiz; if not, then write the values to the database.

```
oRS.Filter = "email ='" & email & "'"
If oRS.EOF Then
  oRS.AddNew
  oRS("email") = email
  oRS("sessID") = sessID
  oRS("d") = d
  oRS("Q1") = Q1
  oRS("Q2") = Q2
  oRS("score") = score
  oRS.Update
```

13. If the user has taken the exam, then display a message that he or she has taken the exam, and show the previous score.

```
Else
  response.write "<br><br>"
  response.write "You have already taken this exam on "
  response.write oRS("d") & "<br>"
  response.write "Your previous score was: "
  response.write oRS("Score")
End If
```

14. Add the closing tags. Save the page to your data directory.

```
oRS.Filter = adFilterNone
oRS.close
set oRS = nothing
oC.close
set oC = nothing
%>
</body></html>
```

15. Modify the appearance of the Web page. Save the page to your data directory.

16. View the Web page in your browser. Print the Web page.

CASE PROJECTS

Tumbleweed University—Building an Online Quiz-Grading System

You are hired in the Education Department of Tumbleweed University to help them set up an online course. They want you to develop an online quiz. You will create the database and four Web pages to administer the quiz. The first page, named tquizform.asp, contains a quiz with at least five questions. Create a database named tquiz.mdb to store the students login information and answers. Create a database table named student that will be used to store the students e-mail address, SessionID, date of the exam, and the student's answer for each question. For each question, add a corresponding field that displays if the user is correct or incorrect. Add a field to store the student's score. Create a second Web page named tsignin.asp where users login to take the quiz. The login form will be processed by a page named tcheck.asp. The tcheck.asp page will determine whether the user has taken the quiz or not. If the user has taken the quiz, display the previous grade and answers, but does not let the user take the quiz. If the user has not taken the quiz, then redirect the user to the tquizform.asp page that displays the quiz. You must modify the tquizform.asp page to verify that the visitor has been referred to the page by tcheck.asp by validating that the e-mail address has been passed from the login form. Otherwise, the visitor would be able to type in the name of the quiz, and take the quiz. When the user submits their quiz, the tquiz.asp page will grade the answers, store the answers in the database, and show the user the answers. Indicate which answers are wrong and the user's total score. Modify the appearance of the page by adding images, text, and colors. Save each page and the database to your data directory. View the quiz and take the quiz. Print the page, and the source code for each page.

Monroe Health Club—Creating a New Member Form

13

Create a membership database called monroe.mdb in Access. Create a table called members. The table should contain the username and e-mail address for each member. The e-mail address should be the primary key for the table. Create a page called mdisplay.asp that displays all the members. Format the e-mail address as a "mailto:" hyperlink using the anchor tag. Create a page called mform.asp that you can use to sign up a list of five members into the membership database. On the mform.asp page, create a form that allows you to enter the names and e-mail addresses of five members. The form should point to madd.asp. The madd.asp page will process the new members, using the AddNew command. Modify the appearance of the pages by adding images, text, and colors. Save the pages to your data directory and view them in a browser. Print the pages and the source code.

Northwind Traders—Using Filters to Display Multiple Sets of Records

Use the Northwind database that you used in the chapter. Create a Web page that will retrieve all of the records in the Products table. Don't forget to add the connection information or a server-side include file that contains the connection information. After retrieving all of the records, use a filter to display the records that match category 1, the beverages category. Then, remove the filter. Reapply the filter, but this time display the records that match category 8, the seafood category. Display the product name and price. Format the price as currency. Create a heading for each category displayed, describing the name of the category. Modify the appearance of the page by adding a table, images, text, headings, and colors. Save the page to your data directory as nwfilterproducts.asp. View the page to test the generic script. Print your Web page and the source code.

Northwind Traders—Displaying Multiple Recordsets

You are developing a marketing plan for Northwind Traders. You are to send out the price list to customers who are likely to purchase your seafood products. Use the Northwind database that you used in the chapter. View the Products and the Customers table. Create a Web page that will retrieve all of the records in the Products table. Create a heading for the seafood products section. Use a filter to list the product name and price for any seafood product. Format the price as currency. Remember that you must use the number that represents the seafood category in the filter statement. Remove the filter. Close the recordset object, but do not set the recordset or connection object to nothing. Open a new recordset to retrieve the fields in the Customers table. Display only the customers in the United Kingdom (UK). You can use a filter, or use the SQL statement to generate the recordset. List the CustomerID, CompanyName, and City. Close the recordset and connections, and set the objects to nothing. Save the page as nwmarketing.asp to your data directory. Modify the appearance of the page by adding images, text, and colors. Save the page to your data directory. View the page. Print your Web page and the source code.

Index